# MISCELLANEA

# GENEALOGICA ET HERALDICA

### EDITED BY

### JOSEPH JACKSON HOWARD

*SECOND SERIES*

*Volume 3*

Elibron Classics
www.elibron.com

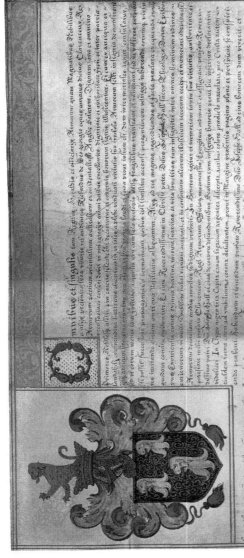

GRANT OF ARMS TO JOSEPH HALL, D.D., BISHOP OF EXETER.

*Dated 12th May, 1631.*

# Miscellanea

# Genealogica et Heraldica.

EDITED BY

JOSEPH JACKSON HOWARD, LL.D., F.S.A.

VOLUME III.

SECOND SERIES.

LONDON:

MITCHELL AND HUGHES, 140 WARDOUR STREET, W.

1890.

# PREFATORY NOTE.

ANOTHER Volume has now been completed, and the Editor trusts that it will be found not inferior in interest to any of its predecessors.

The coloured facsimiles of Grants of Arms, etc., have attracted considerable attention, and with an extended Subscription List the number of these illustrations would be increased. The Editor trusts therefore that subscribers will commend the Magazine to the notice of their friends and to all interested in family history.

*July*, 1890.

# CONTENTS.

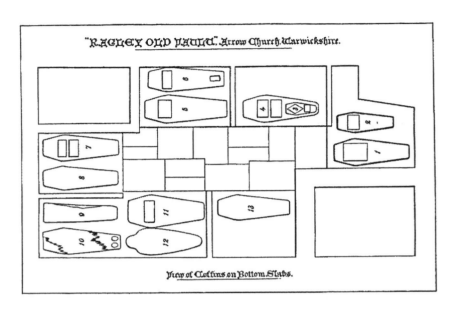

"RAGLEY OLD VAULT." Arrow Church. Warwickshire.

View of Coffins on Bottom Slabs.

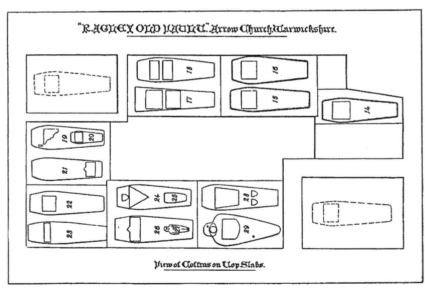

"RAGLEY OLD VAULT." Arrow Church. Warwickshire.

View of Coffins on Top Slabs.

# Miscellanea Genealogica et Heraldica.

## INSCRIPTIONS ON COFFINS IN "RAGLEY OLD VAULT," ARROW CHURCH, WARWICKSHIRE.*

### Bottom Slabs.

#### 1.

Coffin entire, with arms and inscription on brass plate.

(Arms.)

Lady Anne Horatia Seymour
Wife of Lord Hugh Seymour
Daughter of
James Earl of Waldegrave
Born Nov^r 8^th 1762.   Died July 12^th 1801.

*Burial Register.*—1801.   *July* 22.   *Lady Horatia Seymour.*

#### 2.

Coffin entire, with inscription on brass plate.

William Chatham Richard
Seymour
fourth son of the Right Honorable
Vice Admiral
Lord Hugh Seymour
Died 31^st July 1801.
Aged 8 Years.

*Burial Register.*—1801.   *Nov.* 22.   *Wm. Seymour.*

#### 3.

Lead coffin, in very good state, with two inscriptions upon it, one in the lead, and one upon a loose brass plate.

Miss
Eloisha Anne
Conway Daughter
of y^e Right Hon^ble
Lord Vicount Beauchamp
Died 26 Aug^st 1771
Aged 7 weeks
& 2 days.

*Burial Register.*—1771.   *Aug.* 31.   *Hon. Alicia Anne Conway Daughter of Francis Lord & Lady Alice Elisabeth Beauchamp.*

* Communicated by Mr. RICHARD SAVAGE of Stratford-on-Avon, and printed by permission of the Most Honourable MARQUIS OF HERTFORD. These inscriptions were copied in January 1871.

4.

Lead coffin, in good state, with two inscriptions, one in the lead, and one (with arms) upon a loose brass plate.

(Arms.)

The Right Hon^ble
Alice Elizabeth Lady
Vicountess Beauchamp
Born May 10th 1749
Died Feb^ry 11th 1772
Aged 22 Years & 9 months.

*Burial Register.*—1772. *Feb.* 20. *Right honourable Alice Elizabeth Lady Beauchamp.*

_____

5.

Lead coffin, in a very good state, with an inscription in the lead only.

The Right Hon^ble
Henry Seymour Conway
Field Marshal of his Majesties
Forces
Colonel of the Royal Regiment
of Horse Guards Blue
Governor of the Island of Jersey
& one of the Lords of his
Majesty's most Hon^ble
Privy Council
Obiit 9 July 1795
Ætatis Suæ 75.

*Burial Register.*—1795. 20th *July. The Honble. Field Marshal Henry Seymour Conway.*

_____

6.

Lead coffin, with a portion of the top fallen in at the foot about 1 foot long by 5 inches wide. An inscription in the lead only.

The Hon^ble
& Rev^d
Edw^d S. Conway
Died 29th August
1785
Aged 28 Years.

*Burial Register.*—*The Honb^le & Rev^d Semour Conaway of the Parish of Arrow was buried 18th September 1785.*

_____

7.

Lead coffin, with two inscriptions, one in the lead, and one upon a loose brass plate.

The Hon^ble
Jane Conway
Died May 5th 1749
Aged 33 Years.

*Burial Register.*—1749. *May* 13. *Was Buried the Hon^{ble} M^{rs} Jane Conway, Daughter of y^e late, & Sister of y^e Present R^t Hon^{ble} L^d Conway. She was Daughter of the late L^d by His second Lady Jane.*

*May* 13. *The forfeiture was paid for Her not having been Buried in woollen.*

---

8.

Lead coffin, in a very good state, but has no inscription whatever.

---

9.

Lead coffin, very much fallen in on the left-hand side, but still entire. It has no inscription upon it.

---

10.

Lead coffin, in a very good state, but has no inscription. A portion of the wood still remains upon the top, and upon the foot lie two skulls.

---

11.

Lead coffin, in very good condition. The only inscription upon it is cut in a loose piece of lead.

Popham Seymour
1699.

*Burial Register.*—1699. *Jun.* 23. *Was Buried the Hono^{ble} Popham Conway al's Seymour Esq.*

*Memorand. that information was made June* 30 *of y^e Hono^{ble} Popham Conway being buried contrary to y^e Act & y^t y^e* 5^1 *forfeiture was paid & distributed according to y^e Act directs viz.* 2^1 10^s *to y^e poor & the rest to the informer.*

---

12.

Lead coffin, in very good state, but has no inscription upon it.

---

13.

Lead coffin, in excellent condition. Upon the top of this coffin (as if done by a nail) are scratched the words :

Quaker Lady.

If any reliance may be placed upon this simple inscription, this coffin undoubtedly contains the remains of Anne, Viscountess Conway, wife of Edward, Viscount Conway, who died 11 Aug. 1683 (see No. 26), and mother of Heneage Conway, who was buried 23 Oct. 1660 (see No. 27). Her Ladyship died at Ragley 23 Feb. 1678, and was buried at Arrow 17 April 1679.

At the time of her death, Lord Conway being in Ireland, the famous Baron Francis Mercury Van Helmont preserved her in her coffin above ground, in spirits of wine, having a glass over her face, in order that her husband might see her before her interment.

Lady Conway having, through many years of most severe bodily pain, sought relief in intense mystical devotion, she was led to admire the patient quietude of the Quakers ; and with the opinions of this sect (at that time flushed with all the fervour attendant on novelty, persecution, and success) she was eventually induced to comply.

*Burial Register.*—1679. *Apr.* 17 *was buried Anne Vicountess Conway.*

*Affidavit for Anne Vicountess Conway was brought Apr.* 23.

14

Coffin entire, excepting handles, which were taken when vault was broken into in 1861. Arms and inscription on brass plate :

(Arms.)

The Most Noble
Francis Charles Seymour Conway
Marquis of Hertford
Earl of Hertford & Yarmouth
Vicount Beauchamp
Baron Conway
& Baron Conway of Killultagh in Ireland
Knight of the Most Noble
Order of the Garter
and Lord High Warden
of the Stannaries
Born 11th March 1777
Obiit 1st March 1842.

*Burial Register.*

1842.  *Name: Francis Charles Seymour Conway, Marquis of Hertford, Knight of the Garter, &c., &c.*
*Abode : Dorchester House, London.*
*When Buried : March 19.*
*Age : Years 64.*
*By whom the ceremony was performed : H. C. Carleton, Rector.*

---

15.

Coffin entire, excepting handles.  Arms and inscription on brass plate.  Prior to the robbery there was a coronet upon this and No. 16 coffins.

(Arms.)

The Most Noble
Francis Ingram
Marquis of Hertford
Earl of Hertford & Yarmouth
Vicount Beauchamp
Baron Conway & Baron Conway of
Killultagh in Ireland
Knight of the Most Noble Order of the Garter
Lord Lieutenant of the County of Warwick
&c.        &c.        &c.
Obiit 17th June 1822.
Ætat. 79.

*Burial Register.*

1822.  *Name: The Most Noble Francis Ingram Seymour Conway, Marquis of Hertford, &c., Knight of the Garter, Ld Lieut. of this County.*
*Abode : London & Ragley, died in London.*
*When Buried : Died June 17, Buried June 28.*
*Age : Years 79.*
*By whom the ceremony was performed : H. C. Carleton, Rector.*

The beautiful cenotaph (by Chantrey) in Alcester Church was erected " To the memory of her justly and deeply lamented husband Francis Ingram Seymour Conway, Marquis of Hertford, Earl of Yarmouth, Viscount Beauchamp, Baron Conway of Ragley and Killultagh, Knight of the Most Noble Order of the Garter, and Lord Lieutenant of the County of Warwick, Isabella Anne Ingram, Marchioness of Hertford, has dedicated this Monument.  He was born February 1743, and died June 1822."

*(To be continued.)*

# Key Pedigree of Browne Genealogy.*

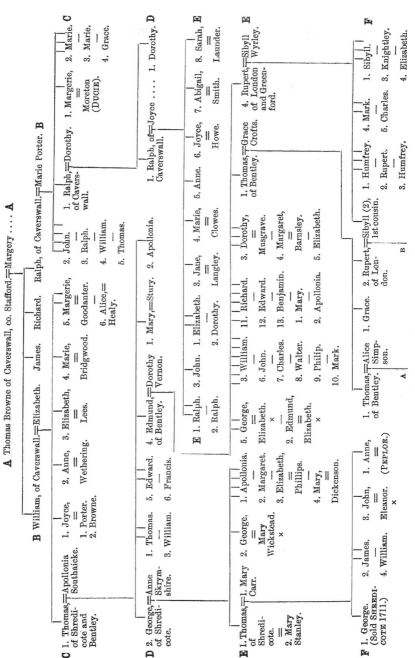

* Communicated by MORGAN BLACKER, Esq.

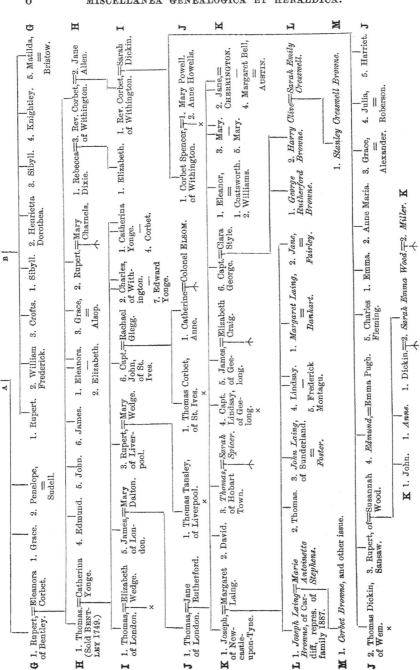

(Names printed in italics denote those who are now living.)

*⁎* The alphabetical letters at sides of pedigree refer to the generation in the detailed genealogy.

# Genealogy of Browne

## OF CAVERSWALL AND SHREDICOTE, CO. STAFFORD; AND OF BENTLEY HALL, HUNGRY-BENTLEY, CO. DERBY.

**A. Thomas Browne** of Caverswall, co. Stafford (bur. [in Caverswall Church, M.I.] 7 Feb. 1562-3), mar. Margery. . . . (bur. [in Caverswall Church, M.I.] 31 Jan. 1559-60). Issue :—

**B.** 1. William Browne. (*Vide infra.*)
    2. James Browne (d. . . . .), legatee under his brother William's will 1602, who bequeathed him "yf he survive or overlyve me xl*s*. in money."
    3. Richard Browne (dead 1602), mentioned in his brother William's will 1602 as having bequeathed legacies to his niece Joyce Browne.
    4. Ralph Browne of Caverswall* (bur. [in Caverswall Church, M.I.] 9 May 1598), mar. ([at Caverswall] 10 Feb. 1562-3) Marie Porter† (bur. [in Caverswall Church, M.I.] 7 April 1615). Issue :—

**C.** 1. Ralph Browne of the Meere, parish of Caverswall‡ (bapt. there 1 Jan. 1562-3; bur. there, M.I., 26 April 1642). Held a "knight's fee" in Caverswall. Compounded for refusing knighthood, and paid a fine of £10, *temp.* Chas. I. Ex'or under his uncle William Browne's will 1602, mar. Dorothy . . . . (bur. [in Caverswall Church, M.I.] 17 Aug. 1618). Issue :—

**D.** 1. Ralph Browne of the Meere and Cookshill,§ parish of Caverswall (bapt. there 14 July 1598 ; bur. there, M.I., 14 April 1670. Will dated 9 Oct. 1669 ; codicil 7 April 1670 ; pr. [at Lichfield] by nephew John Clowes, sole ex'or, 13 May 1670. Bequeathed xxx*s*. yearly for ever to the poor of Caverswall, and a "present" of x*s*. yearly for ever to the Vicar of Caverswall, in addition to legacies bequeathed by his son John Browne). Mentioned in William Browne's will 1602 as "godson Rauffe Browne my cozen‖ Rauffe Browne's little boye," who bequeathed him "one ewe and a lambe." Mar. Joyce . . . . (bur. [in Caverswall Church, M.I.] 5 Feb. 1632-3). Issue :—

**E.** 1. Ralph Browne (bapt. [at Caverswall] 21 Feb. 1623 ; bur. there, M.I., 29 March 1625).
    2. Ralph Browne (bapt. [at Caverswall] 8 April 1625 ; dead 1665 ; bur. there, M.I.), mar. . . . . Issue :—

---

* Neither will nor letters of administration are recorded at Lichfield or Somerset House.

† A note (*in MS.*) at the foot of p. 79, vol. i., of a copy of Shaw's 'Staffordshire,' in the British Museum, gives the following pedigree of Ralph Browne's wife, but which I have been unable to corroborate:

"William Whitehall⊤Mary, d. and coh. of John Hardwick
  of Bloxwich.      of Lindley (d. 1565).

1st, Robert Porter of Stallington.=Mary Whitehall.⊤2nd, Radulphus Browne of Caverswall.

William Browne de Shredicote."

‡ No wills at Lichfield for 1642-3.

§ "*Ralph Browne*" was a tenant of certain lands in Dilhorne, near Caverswall, belonging to Richard Egerton, which were confiscated by the Commonwealth for "treason" 4 May 1654.— 'Royalist Composition Papers' (1st Series, vol. xxiii., p. 673).

‖ As now designated, the relationship between William Browne and "Rauffe" Browne would be nephew, not cousin. See also will of Apollonia Browne, in which she calls her brother's child her *cousin*, instead of *nephew*. Shakespeare, in 'Romeo and Juliet,' makes Lady Capulet, on seeing the corpse of Tybalt, exclaim :—

"Tybalt, *my cousin* ! oh ! *my brother's child* !"

**F.** 1. Ralph Browne (under the age of 21 in 1669), legatee under his uncle John Browne's will 1665, who bequeathed him £50; and legatee under his grandfather's will 1669, who bequeathed him "one silver watch, one silver boule, one silver gilded salt, six silver spoones, one clocke, one jacke."

3. John Browne of Cookshill, parish of Caverswall (bapt. there 11 May 1626; d. unm.; bur. in Church there, M.I., 13 Dec. 1665, æt. 39. Will dated 24 Nov. 1665; pr. [at Lichfield] 31 May 1666 by his father and Alexander How the ex'ors). Bequeathed £3 to the poor of Caverswall yearly for ever, and xls. yearly to the vicar for preaching two sermons, one upon the anniversary of his burial (13 Dec.), and one upon St. John the Baptist's Day.

**E.** 1. Elizabeth (bapt. [at Caverswall] 27 Sept. 1618; dead 1665 ?).

2. Dorothy (bapt. [at Caverswall] 29 June 1619; d. . . . .).

3. Jane (bapt. [at Caverswall] 29 July 1621; living 1669), legatee under her father's will 1669, who bequeathed her £60, mar. (ante 1669) the Rev. William Langley, Clerk in Holy Orders, of Hartwell, co. Stafford; legatee under Ralph Browne's will 1669, who bequeathed him vs.

4. Marie (bapt. [at Caverswall] 9 Dec. 1622; living 1669), mar. (ante 1669) . . . . Clowes* (dead 1669). Legatee under her father's will 1669, who bequeathed her *one shilling*. Issue :—

**F.** 1. John Clowes (living 1670), legatee and sole ex'or under his grandfather Ralph Browne's will 1669, which he pr. in 1670, who bequeathed him the residue of personal estate, and "that he take care that the severall sumes of money and legacies given by my deceased sonne John Browne, which are secured to bee paid by a lease made to me for one thousand yeares of Hartwell Farme . . . . be truly paid."

2. Marie Clowes (living 1669), legatee under her grandfather Ralph Browne's will 1669, who bequeathed her £30.

3. Sarah Clowes (living 1669), legatee under her grandfather Ralph Browne's will 1669, who bequeathed her £30.

5. Anne (bapt. [at Caverswall] 14 May 1627; dead 1669 ?).

6. Joyce (bapt. [at Caverswall] 15 June 1628; dead 1665 ?), mar. Alexander Howe† (dead 1669), ex'or under John Browne's will 1665. Issue :—

**F.** 1. Alexander Howe, ⎫ legatees under their grandfather
2. Joyce Howe,     ⎪ Ralph Browne's will 1669, who be-
3. Ellin Howe,     ⎬ queathed £20 to be equally divided
4. Sarah Howe,     ⎭ between them.

7. Abigail (bapt. [at Caverswall] 18 Oct. 1629; living 1665), legatee under her brother John Browne's will 1665, who bequeathed her an annuity of £5 for life, and the sum of £100; legatee under her father's will 1669, who bequeathed her £10, mar. (ante 1669) Henry Smith,

---

* The present owner of Bentley Hall is S. W. Clowes, Esq.
† Probably a son of the Rev. Alexander Howe, B.A., who was Vicar of Caverswall in 1620.

legatee under Ralph Browne's will 1669, who bequeathed him vs.

8. Sarah (bapt. [at Caverswall] ....? ; living 1669), legatee under her father's will 1669, who bequeathed her £60, mar. (*ante* 1669) Thomas Launder, legatee under Ralph Browne's will 1669, who bequeathed him vs.

**D.**  1. Dorothy (bapt. [at Caverswall] 10 Sept. 1599 ; d. . . . .).
**C.**  2. John Browne (bapt. [at Caverswall] 8 Oct. 1565 ; d. . . . .).
   3. Ralph Browne (bapt. [at Caverswall] 17 Nov. 1566 ; d. . . . .).
   4. William Browne* (bapt. [at Caverswall] 5 May 1574 ; d. . . . .).
   5. Thomas Browne (bapt. [at Caverswall] 14 Sept. 1576 ; d. . . . .).
   1. Margerie (bapt. [at Caverswall] 22 June 1563 ; d. 1633), mar. ([in Caverswall Church] 15 June 1584) Edward Moreton, Esq., of Ingleton, co. Stafford (b. 1552 ; d. 1630), son of Matthew Moreton (*vide* Visitations of Staffordshire, 1582 and 1614, College of Arms), from whom the present Right. Hon. Henry John Moreton, third Earl of Ducie, is directly descended. Arms : *Quarterly*—1, *Argent, a chevron gules between three square buckles tongues downwards sable* (for MORETON) ; 2, *Quarterly,* i. *and* iv., *Ermine ;* ii. *and* iii., *Paly of six or and gules within a border azure, a crescent for difference* (for KNIGHTLEY) ; 3, *Azure, a buck's head cabossed or* (for COLOVER) ; 4, *Argent, on a saltire sable five swans of the field* (for BURGH.)
   2. Marie (bapt. [at Caverswall] 15 March 1568-9 ; bur. there between 25 and 31 March 1569-70).
   3. Marie (bapt. [at Caverswall] 5 March 1569-70 ; d. . . . .).
   4. Grace (bapt. [at Caverswall] 8 April 1570, bur. there 30 July 1570).

(*To be continued.*)

# Bacon Wills.†

FROM IPSWICH REGISTRY.

T. Willi'mi Baco' de Winston.    In the name of god, Amen. The xij[th] daye of October in the xvj yere of the reigne of o[r] Souereigne Ladie Quene Elizabethe that nowe is ꝑ in the yere of o[r] Lorde god m ccccc lxxiiij. I Will'm Bacon of Winston in the countie of Suff. and dioc's of Norwiche singleman calling to remembraunce the uncertentye of this transitory life whiche I haue here in this worlde and thinkinge that the tyme of my deathe dothe nowe approche beinge Trobled with greate sicknes doe by these p'sents Revoke Renounce and Repeale all and singuler former willes devises and Testamentes heretofore by me made and doe only ordeine and make this my p'sente last will and Testamente as well touchinge the disposic'on of all and singuler my landes and Ten'ts whiche by god's sufferaunce and ꝑvidence I haue authoritye to dispose as also all and singuler my goodes and moveables nowe in my goverment ꝑ possessio' in manner and forme folowinge first I bequeathe my soule into thandes of almightie god my Savioure and redemer trustinge that uppo' my repentaunce of my sinnes heretofore by me committed and done to have forgivenes of them at his mercifull handes and that by the meritts of his most blessed passion after my departure out of this vaine liffe I shall entre possesse and enioye the lyfe euerlasting ꝑpared for his servauntes and electe people And my bodie I will to be buried in the church yarde of Winston aforesaide where myne executors shall thinke meate.   Item I giue and bequeathe unto Michaell Bakon my brother

---

* Probably identical with the William Browne who married, at Caverswall 14 Oct. 1594, Marie " Bobyn." His wife was probably the same " Mary " who was buried there 21 Jan. 1600.
† Continued from Vol. II., p. 378.

all that my close of lands or Pasture called Medowplott seituate lyinge and beinge
in Ashe Bockinge whiche I had of the gifte and bequeaste of John Bacon my father
late of Helmingh'm deceased as by his Testamente and last will dothe appeare To
haue and to holde the seide close of lande or Pasture with all and singuler
thappurtenaunces unto the seide Michaell Bacon his heyeres and assignes for eu'.
It'm I will and my full intente and meaninge is that the seide Michaell his executors
administrators or assignes (in considerac'on of my seide gifte before to him given
and bequeathed) shall paye or cause to be payde emongest the residue of my brethers
and sister the full som'e of thirtie eyght poundes of good and lawfull money of
Englonde in manner and forme ffolowinge (that is to saye) unto Thomas Bacon my
brether tenne poundes within Twoe monethes nexte after my depture And to
Will'm Bacon my brother the somme of eyght poundes of good and like lawfull
money within one hole yere nexte after the first paye.   And to Rose Bacon my
sister the somme of tenne poundes within twoe yeres nexte after the seide first paye.
And to Richarde Bacon my Brother the somme of tenne poundes to be payde unto
him at the ffeaste of Saynte Michaell Tharchaungell whiche shalbe in the yeare of oʳ
Lorde god m ccccc lxxix And if it happe' any of my seide brothers or Sister to depte
this p'sente lyfe before the tyme of the receypte of his or her pte before by me
giuen and bequeathed Then I will that his her or theire pte so departinge shalbe
equallye devided amongest my brethers and Sister then lyvinge of which pte or ptes
of him her or them so departinge I will the seide Michaell shall haue his porcio' as
it shall amounte unto.   It'm I giue unto the poore people of Winston aforesayde
Three shillinges ℮ fower pence to be distributed unto them by myne executors at
the daye of my buriall.   It'm I giue unto Elizabethe Payne servaunte with my
seide Brother Michaell the somme of five shillinges to be payde unto her by myne
executors within Twoe dayes nexte after my departure.   It'm I giue unto the
widowe Woodd my Keper ijˢ vjᵈ.   All the residue of my goodes and moveables
unbequeathed (my detts beinge payde and my funerall expenses deducted) I will
shalbe at the discretion of myne executors whome I doe ordeine and make the seide
Michaell ℮ Will'm my Bretherne myne executors givinge them authoritie to take
uppo' them the pbate and execuc'on of this my p'sente last will and Testamente.
In witnese wherof to this my p'sente laste will ℮ Testamente I haue put to my
hande in the p'sence of Bartelmewe Wilkin ℮ Simon Jafferye al's Sponer wᵗʰ others ℮ᶜ.
       Proved at Ipswich 6 December 1575.

| | |
|---|---|
| Testame'tu'<br>Agnet's Bacon<br>de Helmingh'm. | In the name of God, Amen.   The fifte daie of September in the<br>yeare of oʳ Lorde God A Thowsande five hundred seaventie five and<br>in the xvijᵗʰ yeare of the reigne of Oʳ Souereigne ladie Elizabethe by |

the grace of God of Englonde ffraunce and Irelonde Quene Defender of the faithe
℮ᶜ I Agnes Bacon of Helmingh'm in the countie of Suff. wedowe being in good and
perfight remembraunce thanks be given to God doe ordaine and make this my
present testament and last will in manner and forme followinge that is to saie ffirst
and principallie I commyt my sowle to Almightie God my maker and redemer by
whome onelie I beleve stedfastlie to be saved and my body to be buried in the
churchyarde of Helmingh'm aforesaid.   Item I give to the poore people of
Helmingh'm thre shillinges fower pence to be distributed and paied by my
executors within one moneth after my decease wheare they shall thinke most mete.
Item I give to Richarde Bacon my sonne my horse mill as it nowe standeth in the
howse.   Item I give to the saied Richarde my sonne twoe milche kine.   Item I give
to Thomas Bacon my sonne twoe milche kine.   Item I give to Elizabeth Bacon my
daughter fower milche kine and A heckforde my best fetherbedd with the bolster
coveringe blankets and twoe pillowes with the bedsted as it now standeth.   Item I
give to Johane Wade my daughter a heckforde and my twoe best gownes a red
petcoate and a flockbedd a paier of shetes and a paier of blanketts.   Item I give to
Elizabeth my daughter my cupborde standinge in the hall.   Item I give to Robte
Wade my godson'e a chiste made of borde. Item I give to Thomas Bacon my sonne
fortie shillings.   Item I give to Elizabeth my daughter fortie shillings.   Item I

give to Lionell Hardicke son'e of Thomas Hardicke five Powndes of good and lawfull money of Englonde to be paied at the age of xxj yeares of the saied Lionell and if it shall happen that the saied Lionell doe dye before he come to thage of xxj yeares then I will that the saied five powndes to be equallie deuided amongst my children's children All which saied som'es of money I will it shalbe paied by my executors owte of my goodes unbequeathed And the rest of my goodes after my deathe I will that it shalbe equallie deuided betwe'n Richarde Thomas and Elizabeth my thre children Of this my laste will I make and ordaine Richarde Bacon and Thomas Bacon my sonnes my executors.  In Witnes unto this my last will I call to Remembraunce Nicholas ffakes Peter . . . . John . . . . with others.

Proved at Ipswich 18 January 1579.

T.<br>Johan'is Bacon<br>de Holleslye.

In the name of God, Amen.  The xvij[th] of Januarye m ccccc lxxvj I John Bacon of Holleslye within the Dioces of Norw[ch] beinge holl of mynd but sicke in bodie Do make this my last will and Testament in maner and forme followinge ffirste I bequeth my sowle to Allmightie God my redemer And my bodie to be buried in the parishe churche or churche yarde where (*sic*) it shall please God to call me.  Item I gyve to Johan Bacon my Wief all my howses and landes lyenge in Glemham or ells where for the space of xxiiij yeres and then I will that John my son'e shall enter it beinge of that age if he dothe lyve. Item I gyve my Wief all my moveable goods towarde the bringinge up of my childe and paienge of my debts.  Item I will that the Legacies due to my sisters shalbe paid out of my land to the fulfillinge of my fathers will.  Item I will that my Wief shall paye to my uncle John Wythe of Tunstall the som'e of fiftie shillings that I doe owe hym and ix combes Rye and seaven busshells of Wheate.  And I make and orde'n my true and lovinge executors John Weythe of Tunstall and Harrye Hayle of Wickh'm for the fulfillinge of this my laste will.  In Witnes wherof I sette my marke in the p'sence of Richard Evans clarke pson of Holleslye Will'm Gowltie Thomas Browne Robert Copland with others.

Proved at Beccles 28 January 1576.

T.<br>Johane Bacon<br>de Holleslye.

In the name of God, Amen.  The xxiij daye of Januarie in the yere of o[r] Lorde God m ccccc lxxvj Johan Bacon of Holleslye in the countie of Suff. wedowe holl of mynde and pfyght of remembrance did make and declare her last will and Testament nuncupatyve in maner and forme followinge ffirste she bequethed her sowle to the Infinite mercie of Allmightie God And her bodie to be buried in the church yard of Holleslye.  Item she did gyve and bequeth to John Bacon her son'e all her Goods and Cattalls whatsoeuer w[ch] latelye were gyven unto her by the laste will and testament of John Bacon her husbond.  Item she did com'itte the governaunce and bringinge up of her seid son'e unto her uncle John Weyth of Tunstall he to bringe up her seyde childe with the same goods and to delyuer unto her seid childe when he come to lawfull age all suche of her seid goods and Cattalls whatsoeuer w[ch] shall remayne (the bringinge up of the seid childe allowed).  Item she did orde'n and make the seid John Wythe her sole Executo[r] These beinge Witnesses Richard Evans clerke Will'm Goltie Thomas Browne and Henrie Hayle.

Proved at Beccles 27 January 1576.

(To be continued.)

---

PEVEREL ('Mis. Gen.,' Vol. II., Second Series, p. 379).—The younger daughter (or sister?) of Andrew Peverel, Knt., 49 Edw. III., married a Brocas, not Browne. Brocas is the name given in the 3rd edition of Hutchins' ' Dorsetshire,' and in the ' Rotulorum Originalium Abbreviatis,' vol. ii., p. 335, where mention is made of security to be taken from " Edwardo Fitzherberd militi filio Reginaldi filio Lucie unius sororum Andree Peverel, militis, defuncti, et Johanni Brocas filio Margarete, filie Alesie alterius sororum eiusdem Andree."

*Rockbeare Manor, Exeter.*                                F. B. J.

# Pedigree of Darwin.*

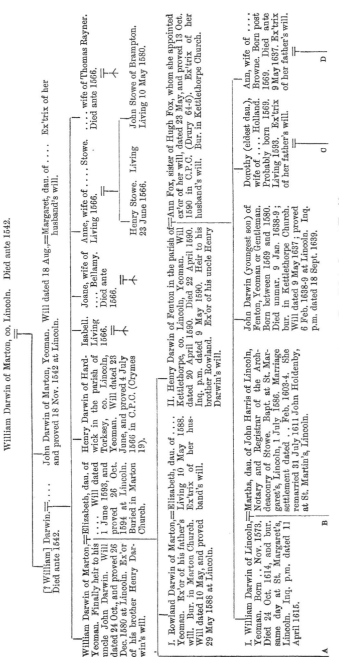

William Darwin of Marton, co. Lincoln. Died ante 1542.

John Darwin of Marton, Yeoman. Will dated 18 Aug., and proved 18 Nov. 1542 at Lincoln. = Margaret, dau. of .... Ex'trix of her husband's will.

[? William] Darwin. Died ante 1542. = ....

William Darwin of Marton, Yeoman. Finally heir to his uncle John Darwin. Will dated 24 Oct., and proved 26 Dec. 1580 at Lincoln. Ex'or of his brother Henry Darwin's will. = Elizabeth, dau. of .... Will dated 1 June 1593, and proved 26 Oct. 1594 at Lincoln. Buried in Marton Church.

Henry Darwin of Hardwick in the parish of Torksey, co. Lincoln, Yeoman. Will dated 23 June, and proved 4 July 1566 in C.P.C. (Crymes 19).

Isabell. Living 1566.

Joane, wife of .... Bellamy. Died ante 1566.

Anne, wife of .... Bellamy. Living 1566.

.... Stowe.

.... wife of Thomas Rayner. Died ante 1566.

Henry Stowe. Living 23 June 1566.

John Stowe of Brampton. Living 10 May 1580.

I. Rowland Darwin of Marton, Yeoman. Ex'or of his father's will. Bur. in Marton Church. Will dated 10 May, and proved 29 May 1588 at Lincoln. = Elizabeth, dau. of .... Living 10 May 1588. Ex'trix of her husband's will.

II. Henry Darwin of Fenton in the parish of Kettlethorpe, co. Lincoln, Yeoman. Will dated 20 April 1690. Died 22 April 1690. Inq. p.m. dated 9 May 1690. Heir to his brother Rowland Darwin's will. = Ann Fox, sister of Hugh Fox, whom she appointed ex'or of her will, dated 28 May, and proved 13 Oct. 1590 in C.P.C. (Drury 64-5). Ex'trix of her husband's will. Bur. in Kettlethorpe Church.

I. William Darwin of Lincoln, Yeoman. Born .. Nov. 1573. Died 24 Oct. 1614, and bur. same day at St. Margaret's, Lincoln. Inq. p.m. dated 11 April 1615. = Martha, dau. of John Harris of Lincoln, Notary and Registrar of the Archdeaconry of Stowe. Bapt. at St. Margaret's, Lincoln, 1 July 1586. Marriage settlement dated .. Feb. 1603-4. She remarried 31 July 1611 John Holdenby, at St. Martin's, Lincoln.

John Darwin (youngest son) of Fenton, Yeoman or Gentleman. Born between 1669 and 1580. Died unmar. 9 Jan. 1638-9; bur. in Kettlethorpe Church. Will dated 9 May 1637; proved 6 Feb. 1638-9 at Lincoln. Inq. p.m. dated 18 Sept. 1639.

Dorothy (eldest dau.), wife of .... Holland. Probably born 1569. Living 1593. Ex'trix of her father's will.

Ann, wife of .... Browne. Born post 1569. Died ante 9 May 1637. Ex'trix of her father's will.

A        B        C        D

* Compiled by H. Farnham Burke, Esq., F.S.A., Somerset Herald.

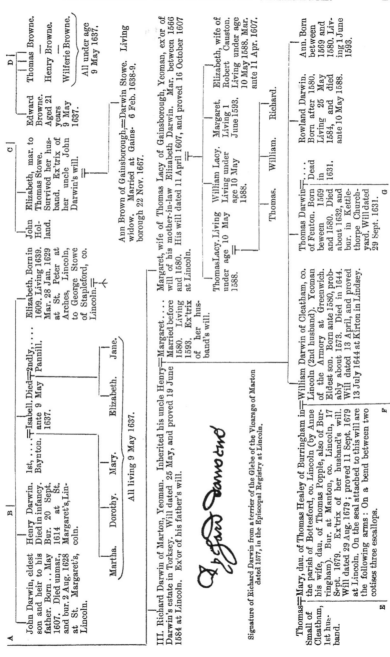

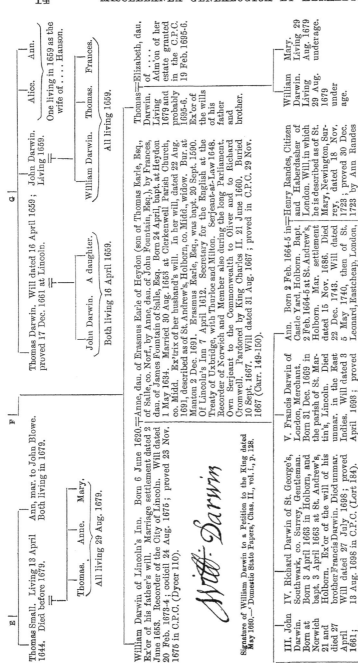

E |

Thomas Small. Living 13 April 1644. Died before 1679.

Anne. Thomas. All living 29 Aug. 1679.

Ann, mar. to John Blowe. Both living in 1679.

Anne. Mary.

F |

Thomas Darwin. Will dated 16 April 1659. proved 17 Dec. 1661 at Lincoln.

Alice. One living in 1659 as the wife of .... Hanson. Ann.

John Darwin. Living 1659.

A daughter.

John Darwin. Both living 16 April 1659.

Thomas. Frances. All living 1659.

William Darwin.

G |

Thomas=Elizabeth, dau, Darwin. of .... Living Adm'on of her 1679 and estate granted probably in the C.P.C. 1695-6. 19 Feb. 1695-6. Ex'or of the wills of his father and brother.

William Darwin. Living 29 Aug. 1679 under age.

Mary. Living 29 Aug. 1679 underage.

William Darwin of Lincoln's Inn. Born 6 June 1620.=Anne, dau. of Erasmus Earle of Heydon (son of Thomas Earle, Esq., Ex'or of his father's will. Marriage settlement dated 2 of Salle, co. Norf., by Anne, dau. of John Fountain, Esq.,), by Frances, June 1653. Recorder of the City of Lincoln. Will dated dau. of James Fountain of Salle, Esq. Born 24 April, bapt. at Heydon 20 Feb. 1673-4; codicil 24 Aug. 1675; proved 23 Nov. 1 May 1634. Married 30 Aug. 1653 at Clerkenwell Parish Church, 1675 in C.P.C. (Dyer 110). co. Midd. Ex'trix of her husband's will. In her will, dated 22 Aug. 1691, described as of St. Andrew's, Holborn, co. Midd, widow. Bur. at Manton 2 Dec. 1691. Erasmus Earle, Esq., was bapt. 20 Sept. 1590. Of Lincoln's Inn 7 April 1612. Secretary for the English at the Treaty of Uxbridge, with Thurloe and Milton. Serjeant-at-Law 1648. Recorder of Norwich and Member also during the long Parliament. Own Serjeant to the Commonwealth to Oliver and to Richard Cromwell. Pardoned by King Charles II. 21 June 1660. Buried 10 Sept. 1667. Will dated 31 Aug. 1667; proved in C.P.C. 29 Nov. 1667 (Carr. 149-150).

Signature of William Darwin to a Petition to the King dated May 1660.—'Domestic State Papers,' Chas. II., vol. i., p. 128.

III. John Darwin. Born at Norwich 21 and died 27 April 1661; bur. at Heydon.

IV. Richard Darwin of St. George's, Southwark, co. Surrey, Gentleman. Born 3 April 1663 in Holborn, and bapt. 3 April 1663 at St. Andrew's, Holborn. Ex'or of the will of his brother Francis Darwin. Died unmar. Will dated 27 July 1698; proved 13 Aug. 1698 in C.P.C. (Lort 184).

V. Francis Darwin of London, Merchant. Born 31 Dec. 1669 in the parish of St. Martin's, Lincoln. Died unmar. in the East Indies. Will dated 3 April 1698; proved 27 May 1696 in C.P.C. (Bond 64).

Ann. Born 2 Feb. 1664-5 in=Henry Randes, Citizen Castle Yard, Holborn. Bapt. and Haberdasher of 2 Feb. 1664-5 at St. Andrew's, London. Will, in which Holborn. Mar. settlement he is described as of St. dated 15 Nov. 1686. Died Mary, Newington, Sur- 22 Dec. 1743. Will dated rey, dated 18 Nov. 5 May 1740, then of St. 1723; proved 30 Dec. Leonard, Eastcheap, London, 1723 by Ann Randes widow; proved 22 Dec. 1743 the relict. by Henry Little, sole ex'or.

William=....=Ann.=2nd husb, Carew Darwin. Little. Weekes or Wickes. Living 29 Aug. 1679 under age.

Richard Randes, late Master of the Merchant Ship the Pindar Galley, bachelor. Died unmarried. Adm'on 23 June 1715 to his father Henry Randes.

Erasmus Randes of Newington Butts, Surrey. Died in=Hanna. the Merchant Ship "Northampton." Adm'on 17 Sept. 1723 to Hanna Cheney, widow, principal creditor, the relict, Hanna Randes, renouncing.

1st husb.,=Ann.=2nd husb, Carew .... Little. Weekes or Wickes.

Henry Little of St. Leonard's, Eastcheap, pewterer. Proved his grandmother's will 22 Dec. 1743.

A daughter.

H |

H

I. William Darwin. Born 27 July 1655 at Southampton Buildings in the parish of St. Andrew's, Holborn, co. Middx., and bapt. there 5 Aug. following. Died 28 and bur. 29 Aug. 1682 at Elston. M.I. = Anne, only dau. and heir of Robert Waring of Wilford, co. Notts (who was buried at Wilford 12 Feb. 1662), by Anne his wife, who mar. secondly George Lascelles of Elston. Became possessed of Elston Hall, co. Notts. Bapt. at Wilford 16 Jan. 1662. Mar. at Heydon 9 Sept. 1680. Died at Elston 23 May 1722, aged 58 years. Will dated 18 May 1722. Bur. 26 May following in chancel of Elston Church. M.I.

II. Erasmus Darwin of Hull, co. York, Alderman. Born 8 July 1659 in Castle Yard, Holborn. Ex'or of the wills of his mother and brother Richard Darwin. Died 8 Jan. 1736 in Holborn; bur. 10 Jan. following at Hull, aged 77 years. = Elizabeth, dau. of Hugh Mason of Hull. Living 27 July 1698.

Elizabeth, mar. to her cousin William Darwin.

Signature of Anne Darwin to a note dated 16 May 1716, addressed to her son William.

*Anne Darwin* [signature]

Robert Darwin of Elston, co. Notts, and of Lincoln's Inn, Barrister-at-Law. Aug. 1682. Died 20 Nov. 1754 at Elston, aged 72 ; bur. at Elston. M.I. = Born 12 — Elizabeth, dau. of John Hill of Sleaford, co. Lincoln. Born 18 Dec. 1702. Mar. 1 Jan. 1723-4 at Balderton, co. Notts. Died 26 April 1797, aged 94 ; bur. at Elston. M.I.

*Eliz Darwin* [signature]

Signature of Elizabeth Darwin to letter dated 14 Nov. 1767.

I

*Robt Darwin* [signature]

Signature of Robert Darwin to a deed, dated 23 April 1713, granting an annuity of £50 to his mother Anne Darwin out of lands at Elston.

1st wife, Elizabeth, dau. of Erasmus Darwin of Hull. Born 1688. Mar. 15 Aug. 1706 at St. Mary's, Hull. Died 9 June 1713 at Newark, aged 25 years ; buried at Elston 12 June 1713. M.I. = William Darwin of Cleatham, which, it is said, he afterwards sold. Born 21 June 1681; bapt. 4 July following. Died 24 Sept. 1760, aged 79 ; bur. at Elston. M.I. = 2nd wife, Mary, dau. of Edward Secker of Grantham, Gent. Born at Grantham 4 Aug.; bapt. 22 Aug. 1683. Mar. 2 Feb. 1715-16 at Thorpe. Died at Newark 14 May 1747, aged 63 ; bur. the day following at Elston. M.I. = 3rd wife, Mary Hurst of Grantham. Born 18 Dec. 1705. Mar. 26 Oct. 1749 at Thorpe. Died 1 Jan. 1766 ; bur. at Grantham.

*Wm Darwin 1713* [signature]

Signature of William Darwin from old Family Bible.

*Elizth Darwin* [signature]

Signature of Elizabeth Darwin from an old Family Bible in the possession of Francis Darwin, Esq., of Creskeld.

J

K

K

Waring Darwin. Born 5 May 1725. Died 17 Nov. 1725 at Newark. Bur. 19 Nov. following at Elston.

Mary. Born at Newark 5 Nov. 1716. Bapt. 7 Dec. following. Died 19 April 1720 at Newark. Bur. at Elston. M.I.

Anna Maria. Born at Newark 13 July 1719. Bapt. 1 Sept. following. Died 28 Nov. 1754 at Bath, aged 35. Buried at Elston. M.I.

Eleanor. Born at Newark 27 Dec. 1721. Bapt. 2 Feb. following. Died 30 March 1722 at Newark. Bur. at Elston. M.I.

Arabella. Born 13 Nov. 1723. Married to John Broadhurst of Newark. Died 13 Nov. 1778, and bur. at Elston. S.p.

Erasmus Darwin. Born 12 Aug. 1707 at Elston. Bapt. 4 Sept. 1707. Died 15 Dec. 1707 at Newark. Bur. 17 Dec. following at Elston. M.I.

William Morgan Darwin of Jesus College, Cambridge, and of Gainsborough, M.D. Born 17 Oct. 1710 at Newark. Bapt. 27 Oct. 1710, the sureties being Richard Newdigate, William Hugh Mason, and Mrs. Ann Morgan. Died 20 July 1762 at Gainsborough, and bur. there.

= Elizabeth, dau. of Thomas Hutton of Gate Burton, Gent. Mar. at Gainsborough 18 Aug. 1741. Marriage settlement dated 14 May 1740. Died 24 Sept. 1751, and bur. at Gainsborough.

Anne. Born 25 April 1709 at Newark. Bapt. 12 May following. Died 24 Aug. 1714 at Beverley. Bur. at Hull 26 Aug. following.

Elizabeth. Born 7 Feb. 1712-13 at Newark. Bapt. 26 Feb. following. Died unmarried 13 June 1736. Bur. at Elston.

Elizabeth. Born 5 April 1743 at Gainsborough. Mar. . . Sept. 1762, in Scotland, to Brian Cook, an Attorney at Doncaster, co. York, grandson of Sir George Cooke of Wheatley, Bart.

Mary. Born 23 Sept. 1745. Died 7 March 1756 at Gainsborough. Bur. there.

Charlotte. Born 22 Jan. 1746. Mar. to Henry Cook of Newark, Esq. (brother of the aforesaid Brian Cook), who died 8 May 1779 at Newark; a Lieut. in Gen. Burgoyne's Regt. of Dragoons. Marriage settlement dated in 1768.

Ann. Born . . Aug. 1748. Mar. in 1772, at Lincoln, to Col. John Bromhead.

Benjamin Bromhead. Bapt. at St. Margaret's, Lincoln, 23 Jan. 1773.

John Bromhead. Bapt. at St. Margaret's, Lincoln, 13 July 1774 ; bur. there 26 March 1775.

John Bromhead. Bapt. at St. Margaret's, Lincoln, 19 July 1776.

James Bromhead, Bapt. at St. Margaret's, Lincoln, 9 July 1778.

Robert Waring Darwin of Elston. Born 17 Oct. 1724. Died 4 Nov. 1816, aged 92 ; Will proved in C.P.C. 16 April 1817, and bur. at Elston.

Rev. John Darwin, Rector of Elston. Born 28 Sept. 1730, and was educated at Cambridge. Died at Carlton Scroop 24 May 1805 ; bur. at Elston. Will proved 26 Aug. 1805 in C.P.C.

Signature of Robert Waring Darwin to letter, dated "Elston 23 ffeb. 1772," addressed to "Doctor Darwin, Lichfield, Staffordshire."

Signature of Robert Waring Darwin to a letter, dated "Elston, 19 May 1802," addressed to "Doctr. Darwin, Shrewsbury, Shropshire."

Signature of John Darwin as a witness to deed of release dated 19 Oct. 1757.

K

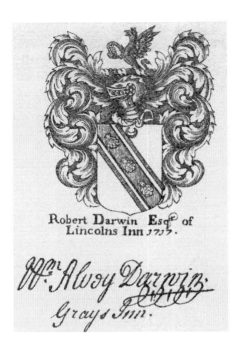

Robert Darwin Esq.^r of
Lincolns Inn 1727.

W.^m Alvey Darwin.
Grays Inn.

E CONCHIS OMNIA.
ERASMUS DARWIN M.D.F.R.S.
LICHFIELD 1771.

DARWIN BOOKPLATES.

**Pedigree of Darwin—continued.**

K

William Alvey Darwin of Elston, and of Gray's Inn. Born 3 Oct. 1726. Educated at Cambridge. Died 7 Oct. 1783 at Sleaford, co. Lincoln; bur. at Elston. M.I. Will proved 31 Dec. 1783 in C.P.C.

= Jane Brown of Swineshead, co. Lincoln, dau. of Joseph Brown of Swineshead, co. Lincoln, and afterwards of Balderton, co. Notts. Born 29 Sept. 1746. Mar. 28 Oct. 1772 at Elston. Died 7 Jan. 1835 at Osmaston, near Derby, aged 89; bur. at Elston. Portraits of William Alvey Darwin and his wife are at Creskeld.

See Pedigree A, post.

Signature of Jane Darwin to a deed, dated 1 Nov. 1776, relating to property at Swineshead.

Signature of William Alvey Darwin to a deed of release dated 19 Oct. 1757.

L

1st wife, Mary, dau. of Charles Howard (by Penelope, dau. of Paul Foley of Prestwood, Esq.) of Lichfield. Born 12 Feb. 1740. Mar. there 30 Dec. 1757. Died 30 June 1770. Bur. in the Close of Lichfield Cathedral.

= Erasmus Darwin, M.D., F.R.S. of Lichfield, co. Derby, and afterwards of Breadsall Priory, and sometime of St. John's College, Cambridge. Born 12 Dec. 1731. Died 18 April 1802. Bur. at Breadsall, near Derby. The well-known Poet and Philosopher. Author of 'The Botanic Garden,' 'The Loves of the Plants,' etc. M.I. in Lichfield Cathedral.

= 2nd wife, Elizabeth, dau. of . . . , Collier, and widow of Colonel Edward Sacheverel Chandos-Pole (who died 27 Nov. 1780) of Radborne, near Derby. Born in 1747. Mar. 6 March 1781. Died 5 Feb. 1832.

Signature of Elizabeth Darwin to a statement of account dated 24 April 1802.

See Pedigree B, post.

Signature of Charles Howard to a letter dated "Lichfd. 22d July 1761."

Signature of Mary Darwin to a letter, dated Lichfield, 14 Jan. 1767, to her son Charles.

Signature of Erasmus Darwin to a letter, dated 18 July 1783, addressed to "Josiah Wedgwood, Esq., Etruria, Newcastle, Staffordshire."

K

C

K

L

Rev. Thomas Hall, A.M., Rector of Westborough, co. Lincoln. Died there 19 July 1776, aged 58; bur. there 22 July. M.I.
Arms: Argent, on a chevron between three talbots' heads erased sable a mullet or; impaling DARWIN.

*Tho: Hall*

Signature of Thomas Hall to deeds of lease and release, dated 13 and 14 Sept. 1771, between Mrs. Elizabeth Darwin, widow, and others, and Robert Waring Darwin and Rev. John Darwin.

= Elizabeth. Born 15 Sept. 1725. Mar. 3 Oct. 1751 at Elston. Died 8 April 1800 at Newark. Bur. at Westborough.

Ann. Born 12 Nov. 1727. Died 3 Aug. 1813 at Sleaford. Bur. at Elston. Will proved 12 Aug. following at Lincoln.

*Ann Darwin*

Signature of Ann Darwin to a letter, dated "Sleaford, 1st April 1809," addressed to "Dr. Darwin, Shrewsbury, Shropshire."

Susanna. Born 10 April 1729. Died 29 April 1789 at Sleaford. Buried at Elston. M.I. Will proved 24 July 1789 at Lincoln.

*J. Darwin*

Signature of Susanna Darwin to a letter, dated "Sleaford, 21 Dec. 1788," addressed to "Mr. Darwin, Derby."

Rev. Thomas Hall, Rector of Westborough. Born 22 April 1753 at Stubton, co. Lincoln; bapt. there. Died 11 Jan. 1801, aged 47, and buried at Westborough. M.I.
= Catharine Litchford of Grantham. Mar. there 21 Sept. 1778. Died 4 Aug. 1841, æt. 87. Bur. at Westborough. M.I.

William Hall. Born 29 Nov. 1759 at Westborough, and bapt. there 1 Dec. 1759. Died 1790.
= Elizabeth Middlemoor of Grantham. Mar. 3 Sept. 1781 at St. Nicholas Church, Nottingham.

Elizabeth. Born 15 June 1754 at Elston, and bapt. there 20 July following. Mar. 17 Sept. 1777, at Westborough, to Roger Vaughton of Hamstead Park, near Birmingham, who was then about 31 years of age.
= Simon Harris Vaughton. Born in 1782.

Gertrude. Bapt. 17 Dec. 1756. Died in 1757. Buried at Westborough 8 April 1757.

Robert Hall. Bapt. 28 May 1758 at Westborough. Died in June following; bur. June 9.

George Hall. Bur. 14 April 1787 at Westborough.

Erasmus Hall. Bur. 10 Jan. 1790 at Westborough.

... Born 2 July 1783 at Grantham.

Mary. Born 2 Aug. 1779.

Johannah. Born 10 Oct. 1780.

Robert Hall. Born 1 June 1782 at Grantham.

Thomas Hall. Buried at Westborough 3 Nov. 1785.

Robert Hall. Bapt. 26 Dec.1784. Bur.at Westborough 7 June 1861.

Charles Hall. Bapt.1786. Bur.at Westborough 2 Nov. 1852.

John Hall. Bapt. 16 March 1790.

Elizabeth Ann. Born 8 July 1778. Died 1 Nov. 1780.

William Hall. Bapt. 19 Dec. 1787.

Elizabeth Mary. Bapt. 29 Aug. 1779 at Westborough.

Ann. Bapt. 26 Nov. 1781 at Westborough. Died 21 Sept. 1846, aged 64. Buried at Westborough. M.I.

Catherine. Bapt. 3 Dec. 1782 at Westborough.

Susanna. Bapt. 16 Dec. 1792. Died 9 Dec. 1801, aged 8. Bur. at Westborough. M.I.

Thomas Hall. Bapt. 21 Oct. 1780 at Westborough. Died 22 Jan. and bur. 23 Jan. 1781.

Thomas Hall. Bapt. 18 Dec. 1783 at Westborough. Died 9 Feb.1802, aged 18. Bur. at Westborough. M.I.

L

Charles Darwin of Christ Church, Oxford. Born 3 Sept. 1758 at Lichfield. Died 15 May 1778 at Edinburgh. Bur. there at St. Cuthbert's. M.I.

Signature of Charles Darwin to a letter, dated "Edinburgh, Dec. 12" (no year stated), and addressed to his brother "R. W. Darwin, Lichfield."

Erasmus Darwin, Solicitor. Born 11 Oct. 1759 at Lichfield. Died 29 Dec. 1799 at Derby. Bur. at Breadsall, near Derby. M.I.

Signature of Erasmus Darwin, Junior, as witness to a deed, dated 1 Nov. 1778, relating to property at Swineshead.

William Alvey Darwin. Born 27 July 1767 at Lichfield. Died 15 Aug. 1767; bur. in Lichfield Cathedral 18 Aug.

Elizabeth. Born 19 Nov. 1763. Bapt. at Lichfield Cathedral 23 Dec. 1763. Died 29 March 1764; bur. 1 April following in Lichfield Cathedral.

Robert Waring Darwin, M.D., F.R.S., of Shrewsbury, co. Salop. Born 30 May 1766 at Lichfield. Died 13 Nov. 1848.

Signature of Robert Waring Darwin to a settlement of account dated 24 April 1802.

=Susannah, dau. of Josiah Wedgwood of Etruria, co. Stafford, the celebrated Potter. Born 3 Jan. 1765. Married 18 April 1796 at St. Marylebone, London. Died 15 July 1817.

Signature of Josiah Wedgwood to a letter, addressed to Dr. Darwin, dated "Etruria, 27 Dec. 1788."

Erasmus Alvey Darwin of Queen Anne Street, London, and sometime of Christ's Coll., Cambridge. Born 29 Dec. 1804. Died 26 Aug. 1881, aged 77, at Queen Anne Street, London; bur. at Down, co. Kent.

Charles Robert Darwin, M.A., F.R.S., of Down, co. Kent. In the Commission of the Peace. Born 12 Feb. 1809. Died 19 April, and buried 26 April 1882 in Westminster Abbey.

Signature of Charles Robert Darwin to a letter dated "Down, Beckenham, Kent, Jan. 21, 1882."

=Emma, youngest dau. of Josiah Wedgwood of Maer Hall, Stafford, afterwards of The Grove, Beckenham. The well-known Cambridge. Born 2 May 1808. Mar. 29 Jan. 1839.

Signature of Emma Darwin.

Marianne, Born 7 April 1798 at The Crescent, Shrewsbury. Mar. 9 Nov. 1824 to Henry Parker, M.D., of Overton, co. Flintshire (descended from the Newdigate Family), who died June 1866. She died 18 July 1858.

Caroline Sarah.=Josiah Wedgwood Born 14 Sept. 1800. Married 1 Aug. 1837. Died at Leith Hill Place, Dorking, 5 Jan. 1887, aged 87.

Josiah Wedgwood of Leith Hill Place, Dorking. Born 12 Jan. 1795. Died 11 March 1880 at Leith Hill.

Susan Elizabeth, of The Mount, Shrewsbury. Born 3 Aug. 1803. Died 3 Oct. 1866 at Shrewsbury.

Rev. Charles Langton,=2nd wife. son of George Langton of Langton. Died at Frankfort 26 Aug. 1886. Bur. at Bournemouth, Hants. Married 1st, Charlotte, sister of the before-mentioned Emma Wedgwood.=

2nd wife. Emily,=3rd w., Catherine. Born 10 May 1810. Married .. Oct. 1863. Died 2 Feb. 1866, s.p., and buried at Shrewsbury.

3rd w., Emma Augusta Juliana. 2nd dau. of Col. Henry Dawkins of Over Norton, co. Oxford. Mar. about 1883.

---

Margaret Susan.=Rev. Arthur Charles Born 29 Sept. 1843; bapt. at Shrewsbury. Married at Coldharbour, near Dorking, 22 Feb. 1868.

Rev. Arthur Charles Vaughan Williams, of Down Ampney, co. Gloucester, 3d son of Sir Edward Vaughan Williams, Justice of Common Pleas. Born .. Nov. 1835. Died 9 Feb. 1875.

Lucy Caroline.=Matthew James Harrison, R.N., Born 17 Nov. 1846 at Shrewsbury; bapt. there. Mar. 29 April 1874 at Coldharbour, near Dorking.

Matthew James Harrison, R.N., son of James P. Harrison of Ewhurst, Surrey. Born 22 July 1846 at Montague Place, London. Bapt. 1 Sept. 1846 at Holmwood, near Dorking. Arms : Or, on a cross azure five pheons of the field.

Edmund=Emily Caroline Langton, elder Langton of Bournemouth, Hants. Died 28 Nov. 1875.

Emily Caroline Langton, elder dau. of Charles Langton Massingberd, and niece and coheir of Algernon Langton Massingberd of Gunby Park aforesaid. Mar. 2 March 1867. By Royal Licence, 20 May 1887, she assumed the surname and arms of Massingberd.

---

Sophy Marianne. Born 13 Dec. 1838. Died 31 Jan. 1889.

Katherine Elizabeth. Born 17 Feb. 1842.

Hervey Wedgwood Williams. Born 14 April 1869. Bapt. at Coldharbour Church.

Margaret. Born 13 Dec. 1870. Bapt. 29 Jan. 1871 at Down Ampney Church.

Ralph Williams. Born 12 Oct. 1872. Bapt. 1 Dec. 1872 at Down Ampney Church.

Geoffrey Richard Harrison. Born 15 Feb. 1876 at Ipswich. Died 7 Dec. 1882 at Sheerness.

Anne Dorothea. Born 30 July 1877 at Sydenham; bapt. there.

Thomas Edmund Harrison. Born 16 April 1879 at Sheerness. Bapt. at Coldharbour, near Dorking.

George Basil Harrison. Born 26 Oct. 1882 at Sheerness; bapt. there.

Lucy Ursula. Born 17 June 1884 at Horsham; bapt. there.

---

Robert Parker. Born 8 Sept. 1825, Sometime Surgeon E.I.C.S.

Henry Parker, Fellow of Oriel College, Oxon. Born 29 Aug. 1827.

Francis Parker of Chester,=Cecile, dau. of the Rev. Solicitor. Born 7 Feb. 1829. Died .. Jan. 1871.

Cecile, dau. of the Rev. J. Longueville of Eccleston, co. Chester. Mar. 18 May 1860.

Rev. Charles Parker. Born 11 Dec. 1831. Of Quarry Place, Shrewsbury.

Mary Susan. Born 31 Jan. 1836. Mar. in April 1866, at St. George's Church, Frankwell, Shrewsbury, to Major Edward Mostyn Owen (of the Owens of Woodhouse). son of the Rev. Edward Mostyn Owen of Cound, co. Salop.

---

Darwin Harry Parker.

Frank Cecil Parker.

Erasmus Darwin Parker.

Henry Owen. Born 1 Aug. 1868. Bapt. 11 Sept. 1868 at Astley.

Ralph Owen. Born 7 Aug. 1871. Bapt. 12 Oct. 1871 at Astley.

Richard Owen. Born 19 June 1874. Bapt. 22 Oct. 1874 at Baschurch, near Shrewsbury.

Henrietta Susan. Born 9 July 1867. Bapt. 22 Aug. 1867 at Astley, near Shrewsbury.

Maud. Born 3 Dec. 1869. Bapt. at Astley. Died 11 Aug. 1887 at Yeaton, near Shrewsbury.

M

William Erasmus Darwin, Christ's Coll., Cambridge.=Sara Price Ashburner, Of Southampton, Hants, Banker. Born 27 Dec. dau. of Theodore Sedg-1839.　wick, Counsellor-at-Law, of Stockbridge, Mass., and New York, U.S.A. Born 8 Nov. 1839. Married 29 Nov. 1877.

George Howard Darwin, F.R.S., Fellow of Trinity=Martha Haskins (Maud), Coll., Cambridge. Barrister-at-Law and Plumian 2nd dau. of Charles Mere-Professor of Astronomy in the University of dith Du Puy of Phila-Cambridge. Born 9 July 1845.　delphia, U.S.A. Born 26 July 1861 at Chicago. Mar. 22 July 1884 at Erie, Pennsylvania.

Charles Galton Darwin. Born 19 Dec. 1887 at Cambridge.

Gwendolen Mary. Born 26 Aug; 1885 at Newnham Grange, Cambridge. Bapt. 7 Oct. following at Hayes, co. Kent.

Francis Darwin, M.A. Trinity College, Cambridge. F.R.S.=1st wife, Amy Richenda, 2nd dau, of Lawrence Ruck=2nd wife, Ellen Wordsworth, 2nd dau. Of Wychfield, Cambridge. Born 16 Aug. 1848.　of Pantiludw, Machynlleth, and of Cranbrook Manor of John Crofts of Leeds, co. York. House, Newington, Kent. Born 9 Feb. 1848. Mar. Born 13 Jan. 1856. Married 13 Sept. 23 July 1874. Died 11 Sept. 1876; buried at Corris 1883 at Headington, Oxford. in Wales.

Bernard Richard Meirion Darwin. Born at Down, co. Kent, 7 Sept. 1876.

Frances Crofts. Born 30 March 1886 at Cambridge.

Charles Waring Darwin. Born 6 Dec. 1856. Died 28 June 1858 ; buried at Down aforesaid.

Anne Elizabeth. Born 2 March 1841. Died 22 April 1851 at Malvern, co. Worcester. Bur. at Malvern Priory Church.

Mary Eleanor. Born 23 Sept. 1842. Died 16 Oct. 1842.

Henrietta Emma. Born 25 Sept. 1843. Mar. 31 Aug, 1871 to Richard Buckley Litchfield, M.A. Trin. Coll., Camb.; of the Ecclesiastical Commission ; Barrister-at-Law ; who was born 6 Jan. 1832 (son of Captain Richard Litchfield of Cheltenham, co. Gloucester, R.A.).

Elizabeth. Born 8 July 1847.

Leonard Darwin, Captain in the Royal=Elizabeth Frances, Engineers. Born 15 Jan. 1850.　dau. of George Robbins Fraser of London, Barrister-at-Law. Born 15 Dec. 1846 at Kings-town in Ireland. Mar. 11 July 1882 at St. Mary's, Wimbledon, co. Surrey.

Horace Darwin of The Orchard, Cambridge. M.A. Trinity College,=Emma Cecilia, only dau. Cambridge. Assoc. Memb. Inst. C.E. Born 13 May 1851.　of Sir Thomas Henry Farrer of Abinger Hall, co. Surrey, Bart., some-time Permanent Secretary of Board of Trade. Born 7 Nov. 1854. Mar. 3 Jan. 1880 at St. Mary's, Bryanston Square, London.

Erasmus Darwin. Born 7 Dec. 1881 at Cambridge.

Ruth Frances. Born 1883 at Cambridge.

Emma Nora. Born 20 Aug. 1885 at Cambridge.

Emma Nora. Born 22 Dec. 1885 at Cambridge.

# Bacon Wills.*

T.
Thome Bacon
de Rushmere.

In the name of God, Amen. The x^th daie of februarie in the xxij^th yeare of the reigne of o^r Souereigne Ladye Elizabeth by the grace of God of Englonde ffraunce and Irelonde Quene Defender of the feith e̅c I Thomas Bacon of Rushemere in the countye of Suff. husbondman being sick in bodie but of holl and pfecte memorie (thankes be given to God) doe make this my last will and testament in manner and forme following ffirst I commende my sowle to thandes of Almightie God my Savio^r and onlye redemer and my bodie to be buried in the churche yarde of Rushemere aforesaied. And as concerning the disposic'on of my worldlie goodes ffirst I give and bequeathe to Elizabeth my wief for and during her naturall lief my howse whearein I nowe dwell with all the edifice and londes therto belonging And after her decease I will and gyve my saied howse Edifice and landes with there app'tenaunces to my sonne Robte Bacon and his heieres Provided alwaies that my saied wief shall meynteyne upholde and kepe the saied howse and Edifice in good and sufficient reparac'on from tyme to tyme and at all tymes nedefull during the saied naturall lief And alsoe prouided that my daughter Alyce Bacon shall haue her dwellinge in my sayed dwelling howse frank and frelye with A convenient Rome to set her bedd in by and duringe the tyme she shall kepe her selfe sole and unmaried. Item I give and bequeathe to my daughter Susan Bacon fyve powndes of currant money of Englonde to be payde her by my executors at the daie of her mariage. Item I geve and bequeathe to my saied daughter Alyce Bacon five powndes of lawfull English money to be paied her likewise by my executors at the daie of her mariage. Item I give and bequeathe to my saied daughter Alyce the bedd bedstedd and the furniture belonging therto wherein she nowe liethe And if it shall fortune that anie of my saied twoe daughters depte this present worlde before they shalbe married That then I will and bequeathe the saied legacies of fyve powndes a pece given them and they or anie of them soe deceassed shalbe equallie deuided betwixt my saied wyff and thre of my sonnes namelie Thomas Bacon John Bacon and Edwarde Bacon. Item I give and bequeathe to Anthonye Bacon my grandchilde twentye shillinges to buye him twoe sylver spones to be payed him by my executors. Item I will and bequeathe that the saied son'e Robte Bacon shall paye owte of my saied howse and landes to my son'e Thomas Bacon five powndes to my son'e John Bacon five powndes and to my son'e Edwarde Bacon five powndes of currant money of Englonde to be paied them within one yeare nexte after the decease of my saied wyff And yf it shall fortune that if anie of my saied thre sonnes depte this world before the tyme that they be to receyue there saied legacies of fyve Powndes a pece that then I will his or there pte soe deceassed shalbe equallie deuided amongste my sonnes which shalbe then lyving. Item I will that my saied sonne Robte shall paie to my granchilde Robte Brame when he shall accomplishe his full age of twentie one yeares twentye shillinges And to Margerie Brame to Margaret Brame to Elizabeth Brame and to Anne Brame my granchildren xxv^s a pece of currant money of Englonde as they and euerie of them shall accomplishe there full age of xxj^tie yeares. Item I will to Thomas Dawson, John Dawson and Henrie Dawson my grandchildren xxxiij^s iiij^d a pece of currant money of Englonde to be likewise paied them by my saied sonne Robte as they shall come to their full ages of xxj^tie yeares. Item I geve and bequeathe to my saied wyff fyve powndes of currant money of Englonde. Item I gyve to my saied sonne Robte Bacon fyve powndes of lawfull Englishe money and the use of my barne stable and Cartehowse with fre ingresse egresse and regresse to and from the same and euerie of them till suche tyme as he shall haue a barne stable and Cartehowse of his owne. Item I give to my saied sonne Robte my harrowes and my Carte wheles And the reste of my goodes bothe moueable and Inmoueable (my debts legacies and funerall charges paied) I give and bequeathe to my saied wief whome I make and appointe

* Continued from p. 11.

"CONWAY" ARMS.

FROM SOUTH WINDOW, ARROW CHURCH, WARWICKSHIRE.

and my saied sonne Robte Bacon together my executors of this my laste will and testament. Witnesses of this my will beinge openlie redd and published Will'm Medowe and Will'm Kinge.

Proved at Ipswich 24 October 1580.

Test'm' Will'i  In the name of God, Amen. About the Second daye of ffebruarye
Bacon de     An'o D'ni 1586 William Bacon late of Humerffield deceased made his
Homersfeilde. last Will and Testament nuncupative in manner and forme following.
Imprimis he gave and bequeathed his soule to Almightie God and his bodie to the yearthe. Item he gaue to Anne Bacon his daughter a weaning calfe and a Coult of the same age. Item he gaue to the Childe that his wife was with at that p'sent likewise a Calfe and a Coult. And further willed that yf eyther of them did die the other surviving should have his pte. The residewe of his goods he gave to his wieff Isabell whome he made his Executrix. These beinge witnessis John ffreman John Toft and John Cogswell with others.

Proved at Homersfield 8 December 1590.

*(To be continued.)*

---

INSCRIPTIONS ON COFFINS IN "RAGLEY OLD VAULT," ARROW CHURCH, WARWICKSHIRE.*

16.

Coffin entire, excepting handles.  Arms and inscription on brass plate.  Coronet gone.

(Arms.)

The most Noble
Isabella Anne Ingram
Dowager
Marchioness of Hertford
Relict of
Francis the second Marquess
and Daughter of
Charles Ingram
Vicount Irwin
Died 12th April 1834
Aged 74 Years.

*Burial Register.*

1834. *Name : Isabella Anne Ingram, Marchioness Dowager of Hertford.*
*Abode : Died in Manchester Sq., London.*
*When Buried : Buried Apl. 26.*
*Age : Years 64.*
*By whom the ceremony was performed : H. C. Carleton, Rector.*

---

17.

Lead coffin, in very good state, with two inscriptions upon it, one in the lead and one upon a loose brass plate.

*Inscription in the lead.*

The Most Noble
Francis Seymour Conway
Marquis of Hertford
Died 14 June
1794
Aged 76 Years.

* Continued from p. 4.

*Inscription on loose brass plate.*

The Most Noble
Francis Seymour Conway
Marquis & Earl of Hertford
Vicount Beauchamp
Lord Conway, Baron of Ragley
& Baron Conway of Killultagh in Ireland
Knight of the Most Noble Order of the Garter
& Custos Rotulorum of the County of Warwick
Died 14th June 1794
Aged 76 Years.

*Burial Register.*—1794.   23 *June.   Marquis of Hertford.*

---

TOP SLABS.

18.

Lead coffin, in very good state, bearing two inscriptions, one in the lead and one (with arms) upon a loose brass plate.

(Arms.)

The Right Honble
Isabella Conway
Countess of Hertford
Died 10th November
1782
Aged 56 Years.

*Burial Register.*—1782.   20 *Nov.   Isabella, Countess of Hertford.*

---

19.

Lead coffin, in very good state, excepting there being a small hole in the top on the right-hand side of the head.   Upon this coffin lies a broken piece of brass plate which undoubtedly belongs to the small coffin (No. 20) lying upon the foot, as it bears the following words, which agree with those in the lead of that coffin:

Miss Charlott
Daughter of the
Francis

This coffin, I conclude, contains the remains of Charlotte, the third wife of the Right Honourable Francis Seymour Conway.   Her burial register is as follows :

1733.   ffebr. 23 *was Buried Charlotte Relict of the late Rt Honoble ffrancis Seymour Conway, Baron Conway of Ragley.*
  Mar. 1.   *ffifty Shillings was paid upon account of ye late Rt Honoble Lady Conway's being Buried contrary to the Act &c. and distributed soon after among the poor of Arrow by James Round, Overseer.*
*Richard Jennings, Rector.*

---

20.

Lead coffin, in very good state, bearing an inscription in the lead only.

Miss Charlott
Daughter of the Rt
Honble Francis Ld
Conway by his
Third Wife died
Augt ye 12th 1717
age 3 weeks.

*Burial Register.*

1717. *Aug.* 17. *was Buried Charlotte the Daughter of the R$^t$ Hono$^{ble}$ ffrancis L$^d$ Conway Baron of Ragley & Charlotte his Lady.*

*Memorand. y$^e$ 50$^s$ was paid for the use of the poor being the forfeiture for Charlotte Conways being Bur$^d$ not according to the Act for Bur. in Woollen, & that was distributed accordingly p. Henry Roberts overseer.*

---

21.

Lead coffin, in very good state, with loose brass plate upon it, bearing the following inscription:

(Arms.)

The Hon$^{ble}$ Catherine
Conway : Died
June y$^e$ 14$^{th}$ 1737
Aged 28 Years.

*Burial Register.*

1737. *Jun.* 19. *Was Buried the Hono$^{ble}$ M$^{rs}$ Catharine Conway.   50$^s$ paid & distributed to the poor of y$^e$ p'ish Jun. 27.*

---

22.

Lead coffin, in very good state, with the following inscription in the lead only :

M   C
Died
Jan the 25
1708
Aged
30.

*Burial Register.*

1708. *ffebr.* 4. *was Buried the Right Hono$^{ble}$ the Lady Mary, wife of the Right Hono$^{ble}$ ffrancis Lord Conway Baron of Ragley & Daughter of the Right Hono$^{ble}$ Lawrence Earl of Rochester & affidavit for the Lady Mary Conway that shee was not buryed in woolin was made before Mr. Fra : Sheldon one of her Ma$^{ties}$ Justices of the pease feb : th 10. & the 50$^s$ forfeiture paid & distributed to the poor Sep. 16.*

---

23.

Lead coffin, in a very good state, bearing a loose piece of lead with the following perforated in it :

Lord Conway
1732.

There is no entry of the burial of this nobleman in Arrow Parish Church Registers.

---

24.

Lead coffin in excellent state, with arms and inscription raised in the lead. The whole of the inscription is composed of Roman capitals and figures as used at that period upon monumental brasses, etc., but without the usual stop between the words.

(Arms.)

Elizabeth second Wife
of Edward Earl of Con
way, Daughter of Ge
orge Lord Delamer
by the Lady Eliza
beth his wife, died
in child-bed of
her first child
July the 4
Anno Dom
ini 1681.

*Burial Register.*

1681. *July* 21 *was Buried the Right Honourable Elizabeth Countess of Conway,
the wife of the Right Honourable Edward Earl of Conway.  And
her still-born son was then also buried, but he without the use of
the Burial-Office.*

*Memorandum : Nov.* 3. *ffive pounds were paid for the Right Hon. Elizab.
Countess of Conway's burial contrary to the Act: whereof fifty shillings was given to
Mr ffr. Parsons ·the Informer, and fifty shillings distributed among the poor by
Richard Standly overseer.*

(*To be continued.*)

# Genealogy of Browne

## OF CAVERSWALL AND SHREDICOTE, CO. STAFFORD ; BENTLEY HALL, CO. DERBY ; AND GREENFORD, CO. MIDDLESEX.*

B.   **William Browne** of Cookshill, parish of Caverswall, "yeoman," son of
Thomas Browne of Caverswall (bur. there 30 May 1603.   Will dated 30 Dec.
1602 ; inventory 10 June; pr. [at Lichfield] 18 July 1603 by son-in-law
John Bridgwood and cousin Ralph Browne), mar. Elizabeth . . . . (bur. [at
Caverswall] 9 April 1591).   Issue :—

C.   1. Thomas Browne, ancestor of the Brownes of Shredicote and Bentley
Hall, etc.   (*Vide infra.*)

1. Joyce (bapt. [at Caverswall] 25 April 1563 ; d. . . . .), legatee and
sole executrix of her second husband's will 1631, who bequeathed her a
messuage, etc., in Marston, co. Derby, and personal estate for life ;
legatee under her brother Thomas Browne's will 1630, who bequeathed
her and her children xls. apiece.   Mar., first, . . . .† Porter (d. *ante*
1602).   Issue :—

D.   1. William Porter (d. . . . .), legatee under his stepfather's will 1630,
who bequeathed him an annuity of £12 for life, land, etc., at
Woodhouses, near Marston, and a "bedstead and fether bedd,
boulster, and other necessary furniture thereto belonging, which
he now lies on."

1. Margery Porter (d. . . . .), legatee under her father . . . . Porter's
will, who bequeathed her 100 marks as a marriage portion, as
mentioned in her stepfather's will 1630.

2. Elizabeth Porter (d. . . . .), legatee under her stepfather's will 1630,
who bequeathed her xs., two silver spoons, and "all goods, house-

---

* Continued from p. 9.
† Probably "*Robert*" or "*William.*"

bold ymplements, and wainscote in the house she dwelleth in."
Mar. . . . . Alcocke (d. . . . .).

3. Izabell (d. . . . .), legatee under her stepfather's will, who bequeathed
   her x*s.* and two silver spoons. Mar. . . . . Parkes (d. . . . .).

**C.**  Mar. secondly William Browne of Marston, co. Derby, Attorney-at-
Law (?) (d. . . . . Will dated 12 Jan. 1630 ; pr. [at Lichfield] 31 March
1631 by Joyce his wife and sole executrix. His brothers James and
Thurstan, together with his wife, to have debts owing to him for
"law causes," and desires that "Thurstan who must have the managing
of those bisnessess deale not rigorously with any whoe can bringe p'bable
p'o'ses [promises] of the paym$^t$ of such debts eyther to me or any that
were my clarkes"), son of Henry Browne of Marston-Montgomery,
co. Derby,* who d. 1606. Legatee under his father-in-law William
Browne's will 1602, who bequeathed him "x*l*s. for and in full payment
and satisfac'on of all such legacies w$^{ch}$ he might have or clayme from
me w$^{ch}$ weare given unto his wife by my brother Richard Browne."
Issue :—

**D.**  1. Anne (d. . . . .), legatee under her father's will 1630, who bequeathed
   her "the second ffether bedd, bolster, blanketts, and sheets to
   furnishe it, and the orange tawney Rugge after my death, and
   best silver salt after wife's death, but would have her have the
   lesser deepe silver goblett to be delivered her p$^r$sently." Mar.
   Francis Fitzherbert, Esq., of Somersal-Herbert, co. Derby (bapt.
   [at Somersal] 27 Feb. 1631 ; d. intestate June 1643. Adm'on
   granted by P.C.C. 11 Feb. 1645). Legatee under his father-in-
   law's will 1630, who bequeathed him the close called Hollyhurst
   with timber, etc., and all lands at Woodhouses after his wife Joyce
   Browne's death, on condition that he forego a balance of £200
   remaining unpaid of his dau. Anne's marriage portion of £500 as
   covenanted with his father, and pay the £100 owing to Margery
   Pater, etc. Arms (*Vide* Coll. of Arms, MS. C 34, fo. 47):
   *Quarterly—1 and 4, Gules, three lions rampant or ; 2, Argent, in
   chief a fess vair or and gules, over all a bend sable ; 3, Or, on a
   bend sable three butterflies argent.* Issue three sons and four dau's.

**C.**  2. Anne (bapt. [at Caverswall] 4 Feb. 1564-5 ; d. . . . .), legatee under
   her father's will 1602, who bequeathed her x*l*. ; legatee under her
   brother Thomas Browne's will 1630, who bequeathed her x*l*s. Mar.,
   first, ([in Caverswall Church] 4 June 1588) Edmunde Wethering ;
   dead 1630. Issue :—

**D.**  1. Joyce Wethering (living 1602–1630), legatee under her grandfather's
      will 1602, and under her uncle Thomas Browne's will 1630, who
      bequeathed her x*l*s.
   2. Mary Wethering (living 1602–1630), legatee under her grandfather's
      will 1602, and under her uncle Thomas Browne's will 1630, who
      bequeathed her x*l*s.
   Mar. secondly (*ante* 1629) Thomas Beech (d. . . . .). Issue :—
   1. "Their child" (bapt. [at Caverswall] 11 March 1629).

**C.**  3. Elizabeth (bapt. [at Caverswall] 26 Jan. 1567-8 ; dead 1602 ?), mar.
   ([in Caverswall Church] 4 Aug. 1588) William Lees (d. . . . .).
   Mentioned in William Browne's will 1602, who bequeathed his two
   dau's xij$^d$ apiece. Daughters also legatees with their cousins (dau's of
   George Healey "being four in all") under Thomas Browne's will 1630,
   who bequeathed them x*l*s. apiece.
   4. Marie (bapt. [at Caverswall] 5 March 1569-70 ; living 1630), legatee
   under her brother Thomas Browne's will 1630, who bequeathed her x*l*s. ;

---

* See summary of will.

mar. ([in Caverswall Church] 20 Nov. 1594) John Bridgwood, ex'or
of William Browne's will 1602. Issue :—

D. 1. Thomas Bridgwood (bapt. [at Caverswall] 17 Nov., bur. there
17 Dec. 1598).

2. John Bridgwood (bapt. [at Caverswall] 11 March 1599 ; bur. there
17 April 1626).

3. George Bridgwood (bapt. [at Caverswall] 28 Oct., bur. there 29 Nov.
1602).

1. Marie Bridgwood (bapt. [at Caverswall] 28 Oct. 1597 ; d. . . . .);
mar. ([in Caverswall Church] 1 Feb. 1619-20 ?) John Reade
(d. . . . .).

C. 5. Margerie (bapt. [at Caverswall] 26 Jan. 1571-2 ; d. . . . .), legatee under
her father's will 1602, who bequeathed her ijs. vjd. ; legatee under her
brother's will 1630, who bequeathed her and each of her children xls. ;
mar. Thomas Goodanter of Caverswall, witnessed the codicil of his
brother-in-law Thomas Browne's will in 1632. Issue :—

D. 1. Henry Goodanter (bapt. [at Caverswall] 17 Oct. 1605 ; d. . . . .).
Witness to codicil of his uncle Thomas Browne's will 1630.

1. Dorothie Goodanter (bapt. [at Caverswall] 22 May 1603 ; d. . . . .).

2. Anna Goodanter (bapt. [at Caverswall] 10 Aug. 1604 ; d. . . . .).

3. Maria Goodanter (bapt. [at Caverswall] 1 July 1607 ; d. . . . .).

C. 6. Alice (bapt. [at Caverswall] 1 Jan. 1573-4 ; dead 1602 ?), mar. Thomas
Healy (or Hely), legatee with two children under his father-in-law's
will 1602, and two children legatees under their uncle Thomas Browne's
will 1630, who bequeathed them xls. apiece.

(*To be continued.*)

## Dalison Notes.*

Lincoln'. Rex Vicecomiti Lincoln' salutem. Scias quod Galfridus de Nevill
et Ricardus de Alencun finem facerunt nobiscum pro habenda custodia terre et
heredis Alexandri de Nevill per centum libras nobis reddendas quas predictus
Alexander nobis debuit de relevio suo et per centum libras . . . . quas heres predicti
Alexandri nobis debet de relevio suo, et ut respondeant nobis ad Scaccarium nostrum
de debitis que predictus Alexander nobis debuit de debitis Judeorum. Ita tamen
quod predictus Ricardus de Alencun habetit saisinam predicte custodie, et reddet
nobis per annum ad Scaccarium nostrum xx marcas de predictis releviis et debitis
donec predicte ducente libre et debita Judorum nobis omnino persolvantur. Si vero
de ipso Ricardo humanitus contingat antequam heres predicti Alexandri plene etatis
fuerit, predictus Galfridus de Nevill saisinam predicte custodie habebit usque ad
etatem heredis per eundem finem. Et ideo tibi precipimus quod accepta securitate
a predicto Ricardo de predictis releviis et debitis nobis reddendis sicut predictum
est, plenam ei saisinam de predicta custodia, cum pertinentiis, habere facias. Scire
autem facias per literas tuas Vicecomitibus Ebor' et Cumberland' quando securitatem
illam a predicto Ricardo ceperis. T. H., etc., apud Westmonasterium xiij die Junii.

Fine Roll, 6 Hen. 3, m. 5, 13 June A.D. 1222.

Pro Ricardo de Alencun.

Mandatum est Vicecomiti Lincoln quod deferat Ricardo de Alencun in quantum
poterit de sectis Comitatus et wapentaciorum et treingorum quandiu fuerit in
servicio Domini Regis per preceptum suum in castro de Scardeburg. Teste H., etc.,
apud Westmonasterium iij die Novembris, etc.

Close Roll, 7 Hen. 3, m. 29, part 1, 3 Nov. A.D. 1222.

* Communicated by W. BOYD, Esq.

Rex Vicecomiti Lincoln, salutem.

Precipimus tibi quod subscriptis servientibus nostris moram facientibus in castro nostro Lincoln per preceptum nostrum, videlicet, Rogero de Haye, Elia de Alencin, etc., habere facias undecim libras de liberacionibus suis, etc. Teste H., etc., apud Westmonasterium xix die Maii anno eodem.

Close Roll, 7 Hen. 3, m. 10, 19 May A.D. 1223.

Rex Vicecomiti Lincoln salutem.

Precipimus tibi quod subscriptis servientibus et balistariis nostris moram facientibus in castro nostro Lincoln per preceptum nostrum, videlicet Rogero de Haya, Elye de Alencun, etc., quorum quilibet habet per diem septem denarios et obolum, habere facias x libras et xv solidos de liberacionibus suis, etc. Teste ut supra (vj die Julii).

Close Roll, 7 Hen. 3, m. 7, 6 July A.D. 1223.

Rex E. Thesaurario F. et W. Camerariis. Liberate de thesauro nostro balistariis nostris subscriptis, videlicet, . . . . Elye de Alencun, etc., quadraginta et quinque libras de prestito, scilicet, cuilibet illorum triginta solidos . . . . Teste ut supra (iiij die Augusti).

Close Roll, 7 Hen. 3, m. 5, 4 Aug. A.D. 1223.

Rex E. Thesaurario et F. et W. Camerariis, salutem. Liberata de thesauro nostro quinque servientibus et uni balistario ad unum equum, scilicet, Ranulpho Brusemuster Heine Pe de chevaler, Waltero Asmeins, Elye de Alenchun, etc., centum et xij solidos et vj denarios . . . . Teste H., etc., xxvij die Augusti, anno regni nostri, vij.

Close Roll, 7 Hen. 3, m. 3, 27 Aug. A.D. 1223.

Rex. E. Thesaurario et F. et W. Camerariis, salutem. Liberata de thesauro nostro balistariis et servientibus nostris subscriptis, scilicet Britoni Balistario . . . . Thiello de Alena, etc., quinquaginta et octo libras et x. solidos, etc. Teste H. apud Westmonasterium xxvij die Augusti anno regni nostri vij.

Close Roll, 7 Hen. 3, m. 3, 27 Aug. A.D. 1223.

Rex Vicecomiti Ebor salutem. Scias quod commisimus Briano de Insula ad voluntatem nostram quamdiu nobis placuerit manerium de Laghton, cum pertinentiis, quod ipse prius tenuit de baillio Domini J[ohannis] R[egis] patris nostri, etc.

Close Roll, 8 Hen. 3, part 1, m. 6, A.D. 1223-1224.

Rex. E. Thesaurario et F. et W. Camerariis, salutem. Liberate de thesauro nostro . . . . Thyel de Alency, etc., xv. libras, etc. Teste me ipso apud Westmonasterium xxiii die Januarii, anno regni nostri viij.

Close Roll, 8 Hen. 3, m. 13, 23 Jan. A.D. 1224.

Rex E. Thesaurario et F. et W. Camerariis salutem. Liberate de thesauro nostro Thome de Haia ad opus balistariorum et servientium nostrorum subscriptorum, videlicet, Britonis et Ferrandi Balistariorum . . . . Thielli de Alencun, Petri de Mirebel—liij libras et xviij solidos, etc. Teste Rege apud Westmonasterium ij die Maii anno regni nostri, viij.

Close Roll, 8 Hen. 3, m. 6, 3 May A.D. 1224.

Rex E. Thesaurario et F. et W. Camerariis, salutem.
Liberate de thesaurario nostro Thome de Haia ad opus balistariorum et servientium nostrorum subscriptorum, videlicet [inter alios].
    Thielli de Alencun liij libras et xviij solidos de liberacionibus suis per xlix dies,
etc. Teste Rege iij. die Maii, anno regni nostri, viij., etc.
                                    Close Roll, 8 Hen. 3, m. 6, 3 May A.D. 1224.

———

Rex E. Thesaurario et Camerariis salutem.
Liberate de thesauro nostro . . . . Thiello de Alencun, etc., balistariis existenti-
bus in castro nostro de Windlessor . . . . septem libras pro liberacionibus suis de xx
diebus. Etc.
                                    Close Roll, 9 Hen. 3, part 1, m. 17, A.D. 1224-1225.

———

Rex tali Vicecomiti salutem.
Scias quod constituimus te Justiciarium nostrum una cum dilectis et fidelibus
nostris talibus ad assisas nove disseisine capiendas et gaiolam deliberandam in
Comitatu tali, etc.
Norfolk et Suffolk.
    Predicti Simon et Ricardus, Willielmus filius Rocetini,* Willielmus de Fran-
chevill', Herbertus de Alencun, Bartholomeus de Glainvill.*
    In Crastino Sancti Jacobi apud Gipeswicum de Comitatu Suffolk, et in Octabis
Sancti Jacobi apud Norwicum de Comitatu Norfolk.
    [Teste Rege . . . . xiiij die Junii.]
                                    Close Roll, 9 Hen. 3, part 2, m. 11 d, 14 June A.D. 1225.

———

Suffolk.    Mandatum est Vicecomiti Suffolk quod recognitores magne assise inter
Herebertum de Alencun, petentem, et Godefridum de Waure tenentem de manerio
de Dinnineton, cum pertinentiis, unde idem Godefridus posuit se in magnam
assisam Domini Regis et petiit rectum fieri uter eorum majus jus habeat in manerio
illo, et quam Dominus Rex postea venire precepit coram Justiciariis assignatis ad
assisas nove disseisine capiendas, etc., apud Gipewicum in itinere suo et ab eis
nondum capta est, venire faciat coram Justiciariis apud Westmonasterium a die
Sancti Michaelis in xv. dies. Et habeat ibi hoc breve. Teste Rege apud Waling-
ford vj die Septembris.
                                    Close Roll, 9 Hen. 3, part 2, m. 9 d, 6 Sept. A.D. 1225.

———

Rex Vicecomiti Ebor salutem.
Precipimus tibi quod de ducentis libris quas Galfridus de Nevill, camerarius
noster, percipit per annum ad Scaccarium nostrum pro custodia castri nostri de
Scardeburg habere facias Ricardo de Alencun ad opus ipsius Galfridi C. libras ad
terminum Pasche anno regni nostri decimo, et computabitur tibi ad Scaccarium.
Teste ut supra [viij die Decembris] anno, etc., xº.
                                    Close Roll, 10 Hen. 3, m. 28, 8 December A.D. 1225.

———

Mandatum est Hereberto de Alencun quod inquirat, etc., quantum bladi
Henricus filius Aucheri posuit in terris de Framelingham de dominico seminandis
per preceptum Domini Regis post mortem W.    Comitis Sarrum et secundum
inquisitionem quam inde fecerit bladum illud ei reddi faciat de bladis crescentibus
in manerio predicto.
Teste Rege ut supra (viii die Julii).
                                    Close Roll, 10 Hen. 3, m. 10, 8 July A.D. 1226.

                        * Erased in original.

# Upton.*

## ABSTRACTS OF WILLS AND RECORDS OF ADMINISTRATION.

60. Robert Upton, who died beyond seas. Adm'on 12 June 1666 to Robert Terry, attorney deputed, etc.

61. Nathaniel Upton† of St. Giles, Cripplegate, London. Dated 12 May 1666. To Nathaniel‡ my son £300, and to him and his wife each £6 for mourning; to John Sutton my son £20, and to him and his wife each £6 for mourning; to his daughter Anne Sutton £10; to my mother, my sister Penrose, and my brother and sister Stuckey each £6 for mourning; to Mrs. Goddard 20s. for a ring; to poor of St. Giles, Cripplegate, £10; appoint my wife Dorothy§ executrix. Witness, John Stuckey. Proved 15 June 1666 by exec'x. (106 Mico.)

62. John Upton [in Calendar "Pts"]. Dated 11 Dec. 1666. To my wife Elizabeth and my brother Mr. Robert Hubbard and my sister his wife each a diamond cutt; to my wife 36 cornelian rings, etc.; to my mother Elizabeth Upton, widow, and my sister Emlin each a piece of Taffety; the £197 2s. 6d. which remains in the hands of Mr. Henry Hamlin in partnership of goods bought at Suratt, which I consigned to my brother Mr. Robert Hubbard, merchant in London, for use of my wife Elizabeth, to be given to her, and also my wages due from the H.E.I. Co. Adm'on 7 Aug. 1667 to the relict Elizabeth. (111 Carr.)

63. Dorothy Upton‖ of Saltram in parish Plymouth, Devon, widow. Dated 20 July 1668. To poor of Newton Ferris [Newton Ferrers, Devon] 10s.; whereas I promised to my son-in-law Mr. Anthony Ingram, as a marriage portion with my daughter Dorothy, £400, I will the same to be paid and they to resign all claim to the barton of Pustnich [Puslinch, Devon]; to my son William Upton, Esq., a gold ring; residue to my son Mark Upton, and appoint him executor. Proved 20 Nov. 1668 by ex'or. (148 Hene.)

64. Anthony Upton [translated out of Spanish], Englishman, at present residing in the City of Sivill, son of John and Dorothy Upton, dec'd, late of Oton near Dartmouth in the kingdom of England, where I was born. Dated 9 May 1663. To my brothers Hugh¶ and Thomas¶ Upton, dwelling in the City of London, viz., to Hugh 1000 reals and to Thomas 500 reals; to Christopher Boone of London 500 reals for a jewel for my friendship for him; to my partner Benjamin Bathurst** and my book-keeper Joseph Gilbert each 500 reals, and they are to be my trustees and executors, with my brother Gilbert Upton,†† now dwelling in London. Codicil, dated in Sevill 18 July 1669, confirming the will: I now appoint executors my brothers Mr. Gilbert Upton and Mr. Thomas Upton and my nephew Mr. William Champneys; the surplus of my estate to go to my nephews and nieces. Proved 25 Jan. 1669-70 by said Gilbert and Thomas Upton. (11 Penn.)

65. Anne Upton of St. James, Duke's Place, London, spinster. Adm'on 18 April 1670 to her father Hugh Upton.‡‡

66. Richard Upton of Limehouse, parish Stepney, Midd^x, mariner. Dated 23 Nov. 1668. Outward bound in ship "John and Martha" of London, John Goffe commander, for a voyage to the East Indies. All estate to my friend and landlord

---

* Continued from Vol. II., p. 351.

† The testator was called "Chirurgeon, Master of the Pest House," and was buried May 29, 1666. His son Benjamin was baptized 7 Oct. 1647, and buried 7 June 1659. I think he was son of William Upton, No 57, *ante*.

‡ The son Nathaniel made will No. 89.

§ The widow Dorothy Upton made will No. 81.

‖ The testatrix was daughter of Robert Lane, and widow of Mark Upton of Puslinch, Devon, Esq.

¶ Of these brothers, Hugh is No. 77, and Thomas No. 75, *post*.

** Afterwards Sir Benjamin Bathurst, Governor of the East India Company, and father of the first Earl Bathurst.

†† The brother Gilbert Upton made will No. 83.

‡‡ The father Hugh Upton is No. 77, *post*.

Rowland Gittings of Limehouse aforesaid, cooke, and Prudence his wife, and appoint them executors. Proved 4 Aug. 1670 by Prudence Gander *alias* Gittings, surviving ex'or. (105 Penn.)

67. William Upton, late of ship "Chesthunt Pinck," who died in the East Indies, a widower. Adm'on 8 May 1671 to Christian Stevens, widow, principal creditor.

68. John Upton, late of the Isle of Wight, but died in the ship "Anne," a bachelor. Adm'on 20 Dec. 1673 to Elianor Upton his sister and next of kin.

69. Henry Upton,* the elder, of Burlescombe, Devon, gent. Dated 17 Nov. 1674. To be buried by my father in Burlescombe Churchyard. To William† my son my mess. and tenement in Stawleigh, Somerset ; to Henry my son two tenements, etc., in Burlescombe ; to my daughter Sarah Upton the messuage, etc., in which I dwell ; to my grandchildren James, Mary, and Elizabeth Cadbury each 20s. when 15 ; residue to daughter Sarah, and appoint her executrix. Proved 7 July 1675 by exec'x. (79 Dycer.)

70. Arthur Upton of Falmouth, Cornwall, gent. Dated 3 Dec. 1675. To my children Anthony, Thomas, and Elizabeth Upton each £100 ; to my daughter-in-law Priscilla Blackman 1s. besides the £100 I gave her a bond for ; to poor of Falmouth £3 ; to Mr. Peter Hill of Falmouth 40s. to assist my executrix ; to Benjamin Cood of Penryn, gent., £5 for his pains in looking after me in my sickness ; to Mr. Francis Bedford of Falmouth, Clerk, 40s. to preach my funeral sermon ; residue to my wife Anne, and appoint her executrix. Proved 16 Feb. 1675-6 by exec'x. (25 Bence.)

71. Nicholas Upton‡ late of Stoke Newington, Midd[x], bachelor, died on or about 26 June 1678 in his father's house in Stoke Newington, and on Sunday the 23rd of said month made his will nuncupative thus : to my brother Anthony§ Upton £50 and to my brother Arthur‖ Upton £100, in presence of his father John Upton, Esq., his mother-in-law Joane Upton,¶ and Francis Bray. Adm'on 11 July 1678 to his father John Upton, Esq. (C.P.C., 79 Reeve.)

72. John Upton of Andover, co. South[ton], feltmaker. Dated 10 Sept. 1678. To poor there £5 ; to kinsman Nathaniel Brise of Andover, maultster, and his heirs a messuage, etc., in Andover, paying my sister Susan Younge 50s. per annum for life, and each of her children £30 ; to each of my sister Rebecca's children £30 ; to my son Popincig's children Joseph, Anny, Ellin, Sarah, and Martha each £5 ; residue to said Nathaniel Brice, and appoint him executor. Proved 16 Sept. 1680 by ex'or. (123 Bath.)

73. George Upton of Dorking, Surrey. Adm'on 27 Sept. 1682 to the relict Unica.

74. Nathaniel Upton** of St. Olave, Southwark, Surrey, brewer. Dated 15 March 1679-80. My wife Anne to enjoy my messuage, etc., in Shad Thames in said parish for life, she maintaining Nathaniel†† my son till 21; to John Upton my brother 12d.; appoint wife Anne executrix. Proved 29 Dec. 1682 by exec'x. (151 Cottle.)

75. Thomas Upton,‡‡ Clerk, Rector of East Lockings, Berks. Dated 30 May 1684. To poor there £5; all real and personal estate to wife Dorothy, and appoint her executrix. (John Upton a witness.) Proved 4 Nov. 1684 by exec'x. (155 Hare.)

(*To be continued.*)

* The testator was son of Henry Upton, No. 32, *ante*.
† The son William made will No. 76.
‡ Testator was son of John Upton who made will No. 79, and he was buried at Stoke Newington June 28, 1678.
§ The brother Anthony Upton made will No. 108.
‖ I think the brother Arthur is No. 78, *post*.
¶ The mother-in-law (*i.e.* step-mother), Joane Upton, *née* Stow, made will No. 104, *post*.
** The testator was a brewer and yeoman, and died in Dec. 1682. He had three wives, viz., (1st) Jone, buried Sept. 16, 1665 ; (2nd) Susan Vadney, married Aug. 8, 1666, died in June 1671 ; (3rd) Anne Thomas, his executrix, married Oct. 22, 1671. The widow Anne made will No. 91.
†† The son Nathaniel Upton was bapt. Jan 30, 1667-8, being son of the wife Susan, and was living in 1702.
‡‡ Rev. Thomas Upton was son of John and Dorothy (Rouse) Upton, and brother of Nos. 64, 77, 79, and 83.

# Darwin Pedigree—PEDIGREE A. (*Vide* p. 17.)

William Alvey Darwin.=Jane Brown.

William Brown Darwin of Elston. Born 12 Feb. 1774 at No. 47 Hatton Street, Holborn, London. Bapt. 21 March following in the parish of St. Andrew, Holborn. Of St. John's Coll., Camb. Died 10 June 1841 at Elston, and bur. there. = Elizabeth de St. Croix, dau. of Nicholas de St. Croix of Homerton. Born 1790 at Ivy House, Homerton. Mar. 22 May 1817 at St. John's Church, Hackney. Died 31 Oct. 1868 at Clanna, Lydney, co. Gloucester. Bur. at Elston.

John Hill Darwin. Born 23 July 1780 at Sleaford, co. Lincoln. Bapt. there 6 Sept. following. Died 8 April 1781 at Elston, and buried there 12 April following.

John Alvey Darwin. Born 29 April 1784. Died same year, and was bur. at Elston.

*Signature of William Brown Darwin to a letter dated "Thurlston Grange, 4th Dec. 1816."*

*W. B. Darwin* (signature)

A son, still-born 10 April 1819 at Thurlston Grange, Elvaston, near Derby. Bur. 12 of same month at Elston.

William Waring Darwin. Born 6 April 1823 at Thurlston Grange. Bapt. 14 April at Elvaston. Died 6 Nov. 1835 at Bath. Bur. 15 Nov. at Elston, aged 13 years.

Robert Alvey Darwin of Elston Hall, Newark. Born 17 April 1826 at Thurlston Grange. Bapt. at Elvaston 19 April. Of Exeter Coll., Oxford. Died at Madeira 7 Dec. 1847, unmar. Bur. at Madeira.

*R. A. Darwin.* (signature)

Elizabeth. Born 3 May 1820 at Thurlston Grange. Bapt. at Elvaston 8 May. Died 6 May 1835 at Bath. Buried at Elston 13 May following, aged 15.

Jane Eleanor. Born 18 April 1824 at Thurlston Grange. Bapt. 24 April at Elvaston. Died 26 Dec. 1838 at Elston, and bur. 31 Dec. following at Elston, aged 14 years.

Charlotte Maria Cooper. Born 4 May 1827 at Thurlston Grange. Bapt. 19 May at Elvaston. Mar. 25 July 1849 at St. George, Hanover Square. Died 22 June 1885 at Creskeld Hall, Poole, co. York. Bur. at Bramhope. = Francis Rhodes, afterwards Darwin, of Creskeld Hall, Poole, co. York, and of Elston Hall, co. Notts. 4th son of William Rhodes, Esq., of Bramhope Hall, Capt. 19th Light Dragoons. Of Christ's Coll., Camb. M.A. Born 12 June 1825 at Bramhope. Assumed the surname and arms of Darwin 1 Jan. 1850 (? 21 Feb. 1850) under the will of his brother-in-law Robert Alvey Darwin.

*Francis Darwin.* (signature)

*C. M. C. Darwin.* (signature)

Sarah Gay Forbes. Born 13 Feb. 1830 at Thurlston Grange. Bapt. 15 Feb. following at Elvaston. Mar. 24 Aug. 1848 at Elston. = Edward Andrew Noel of Elston Hall, Notts, eldest son of Honble. and Rev. Francis Charles James Noel, brother of 1st Earl of Gainsborough. Late Capt. 31st Regt. and one of the Gentlemen at Arms. Born 2 Jan. 1825 at Teston Rectory, co. Kent.

*P. A. Noel.* (signature)

A    B    C

B |                                                                                                          | C

1st wife, Josephine = William Frederick = 2nd wife, Elizabeth,
Annie, da. of Joseph | Noel, Capt. Royal | eldest da. of Rev.
Watts Halliwell of | Engineers. Born | Joseph Christopher
Stratford Park, co. | 8 Aug, 1849. | Bradney, M.A. Mar.
Gloucester, Mar. 4 |              | 1885 at St. George's,
Feb. 1879. |                       | Hanover Square.

Edward William Middleton.   Gerald Frederick   A da.,
Born 18 March 1880.         Cecil. Born 1881.  Born 1886.

Cecil Edward Berkeley Noel, Born 23 Dec. 1860. Died 18 Jan. 1869.

Francis Charles Methuen Noel, Lieutenant R.N., Born 5 June 1852. Mar. 27 Oct. 1886, at Exeter, Wilmot Juliana, da. of T. Maitland Snow, Esq., of Cleve House, Exeter.

Robert Gambier Lascelles Noel, R.N. Born 27 June 1855. Mar. 25 March 1887, at Surbiton, Letitia Louisa Carmela, da. of Rev. D. S. Koelle of Richmond House, Middx.

James Wriottesley Noel. Born 3 Oct. 1861.

Anne Noel. Born 31 Oct. 1853. Mar. 5 Aug. 1873, at Alvington, co. Gloucester, to Thomas Hamilton Forsyth. Died 10 Dec. 1887.

Matilda Catherine, Born 5 Oct. 1857.

Eleanor Agnes. Born 9 Nov. 1859.

Edith Mary, dau. of William Andrew = Francis Alvey Rhodes Darwin, M.A., Barrister-at-
Fairbairn of Heppington, Canterbury. | Law. Born 19 Aug. 1861 at Markington, co. York.
Born 26 July 1853 in Manchester. | Bapt. 21 Sept. following at Markington. Of
Mar. 2 Dec. 1886 at St. Mary's, Huck- | Trin. Coll. Camb. Clerk of the Peace for West
ington, near Canterbury. | Riding of the County of York.

Gerard Lascelles Darwin. Born 25 Nov. 1852 at Creskeld Hall. Bapt. 10 March 1853 at Bramhope.

William Waring Darwin. Born 30 May 1854 at Ventnor. Died 1 June 1854. Bur. 2 June at Ventnor.

Charles Waring Darwin. Born 28 Aug, 1855 at Nursted House, Hants. Bapt. 3 Sept. at Buriton, Hants. Major 68th Light Infantry. In the Army.

Arthur William Darwin. Born 30 Oct. 1864 at Creskeld Hall. Bapt. 2 Dec. at Arthington.

Robert Henry Darwin. Born 19 June 1875 at Creskeld Hall. Bapt. 19 July at Arthington.

Charlotte Elizabeth Anne. Born 27 May 1850 at Elston. Bapt. there 23 June following. Died Sept. 1868 at Creskeld Hall, aged 18. Bur. at Elston.

Mary Eleanor = John Charles Griffith of Priors Mesne, Lydney, co. Gloucester. Born 14 Feb. 1862 at Ripon. Bapt. 9 July 1852 at Ripon Cathedral.
Born 7 Sept. 1857 at Nursted House, co. Hants. Bapt. 1 Nov. following at Buriton. Mar. 23 June 1880 at Arthington, co. York.

Caroline Edith. Born 17 March 1861 at Madeira. Bapt. there.

*Francis Alvey Darwin*

*Gerald Darwin*

Signature to a letter.

*Charles Darwin*

A

Elizabeth Hill. Born 3 Oct. 1775 in Hatton Street, London. Bapt. 28 Oct. following in the parish of St. Andrew, Holborn. Died 30 Jan. 1776 in Hatton Street, and bur. at Elston, M.I.

2nd wife, Ann, in Hatton Garden, London. Bapt. 28 Aug. following in parish of St. Andrew, Holborn. Mar. 7 March 1799 at St. Paul's, Covent Garden. Died 7 April 1859 ; bur. at Whitchurch, near Edgware.

Samuel Fox of Thurlston Grange, near Derby. Born 1777 == 1st, Martha, dau. of Jedediah Strutt, Esq., of Derby (grandfather of Edward Strutt, 1st Lord Belper). Died 20 March 1851 at Rendalls, co. Herts. March 1765.

Elizabeth Hill. Born 16 July 1782 at Sleaford. Bapt. 10 Oct. following. Died 31 Aug. 1804 at Scarborough. Buried at Elston. Will proved 24 Jan. 1805.

*Sam'l Fox* (signature)
*Anna Fox* (signature)

(Dau.) Died in infancy.

Samuel Fox. Born .. Jan. 1793. Died unmar. 1859 ; bur. at Derby.

Julia, Born 10 May 1809,

Eliza. Born 14 Oct. 1801. Died 10 Nov. 1886. Bur. at Sandown, Isle of Wight.

Emma. Born 21 Sept. 1803. Died 31 March 1885. Bur. at Whitchurch.

Frances Jane. Born == Rev. John Hughes, Vicar of Penally, 11 Nov. 1806. Mar. near Tenby, South Wales; Preben- 28 Oct. 1862 at Al- dary of St. David's. Born 17 Jan. denham, co. Herts. 1794. Died at Penally Vicarage 9 May ; bur. 17 May 1873 in Penally Churchyard, Pembrokeshire.

1st, Harriet, 2nd dau. of Sir Richard Fletcher, Bart., R.E. Born 15 Feb. 1799. Mar. at Ryde 11 March 1834. Died 19 March 1842 ; buried 28 March 1842 at Dela- mere, co. Chester.

Rev. William Darwin Fox == of Delamere Rectory, co. Chester, and afterwards of the Isle of Wight. Born 23 April 1805. Died 8 April 1880 ; bur. at San- down, Isle of Wight.

2ndly, Ellen Sophia, dau, of Basil George Woodd, Esq., of Hillfield, Hampstead, co. Middx. Born 3 Jan. 1820. Died Mar. 20 May 1846. 1 Oct. at Broadlands, San- down, Isle of Wight ; bur. 5 Oct. 1887 at Sandown.

1st wife, Mary Ann, Born 4 Feb. 1800. Mar. 11 Dec. 1821 at Osmaston, near Derby. Died 19 April 1829 at Clif- ton, and bur. there.

Samuel Ellis Bristowe == 2ndly, Lady Alicia Mary of Beesthorpe, co. Notts, Needham, dau. of Francis and Twyford, co. Derby, Jack, 1st Earl of Kil- J.P. and D.L. Born 10 morey. Born 5 Sept. March 1800 in United 1798. Mar. 6 July 1836. States of America. Died Died 31 Jan. 1886 ; bur. 15 June 1855; bur. at at Datchet, co. Bucks. Caunton, co. Notts.

F    G

Eliza Ann. Born 10 Jan. 1836 at Binstead, near Ryde. Died 4 Nov. 1874, and was buried at Skidby, near Hull.

Rev. Henry == Martyn Sanders, Vicar of Skidby, Hull.

Harriet == Samuel Emma. Charles- Born 24 worth April Overton. 1837 at Ryde.

Agnes Jane. Born 7 April 1839 at Os- maston Hall; bapt. at St. Michael's, Derby.

Julia Mary Anne. Born == Samuel Everard 26 April 1840 at Osmas- Woods. ton Hall ; bapt. at St. Michael's, Derby. Mar. 26 April 1883 at Kens- ington.

Rev. Samuel William == Euphemia Rebecca Darwin Fox, Vicar of Bonar, eldest dau. St. Paul's, Maidstone, of Andrew Bonar, Born at Osmaston Esq., of Edinburgh. Hall 3 July 1841 ; Mar. 10 Feb. 1876 bapt. 2 Jan. 1843 at at Torquay. Delamere.

D    E

F  G

D  E

Frederick Arnold Overton.

Annie Maud.

Charles Ernest Overton.

Agnes Frances.

William Darwin Overton. Deceased 1883.

Henry Bernard Overton.

Ellen Margaret.

Charles Henry Martin Sanders.

Agnes Marian.

Laura Katherine.

John Fox Sanders.

Edgar Christian Sanders.

Gerard Arthur Fletcher Sanders.

Harriet Monica.

Rhoda.

Eliza.

Charles Wood Fox. Born 23 Feb. 1847. Of Broadlands, Sandown, Isle of Wight.

Frances Maria. Born 28 Feb. 1848. Mar. 17 Sept. 1878, at Sandown, Isle of Wight, Alexander Pearce, and has issue Nathaniel, born 20 June 1879; and Margery, born 16 Jan. 1881.

Robert Gerard Fox. Born 1 Oct. 1849. Mar. 7 Oct. 1880, at Sandown, Emily Mary, da. of William Chance of Edgbaston, born 8 June 1854.

Louisa Mary. Born 28 Dec. 1850. Died 29 Aug. 1853. Buried at Delamere, Cheshire.

Ellen Elizabeth. Born 26 Feb. 1852. Bapt. 2 June 1852. Mar. 26 Aug. 1875, at Dibden, Baron Dickinson Webster, Esq,

Theodora. Born 16 June 1863. Died 5 July 1878. Bur. at Sandown.

Gertrude Mary. Born 27 Sept. 1854. Married at Dibden Frederick Charles Tindal Bosanquet, son of Thomas Bosanquet of Enfield.

Frederick William Fox. Born 8 Dec. 1855.

Erasmus Pullein Fox. Born 30 Dec. 1858.

Reginald Henry Fox. Born 28 Oct. 1860.

Edith Darwin. Born 13 Feb. 1857.

Gilbert Basil Fox. Born 16 Dec. 1864.

Theodora. Born 4 Oct. 1880.

Victor William Darwin Fox. Born 8 May 1883.

Gerard Fox. Born 30 May 1885.

A daughter. Born 16 Dec. 1887.

Samuel Boteler Bristowe of Beesthorpe Hall, co. Notts, Q.C. M.P. for Newark-on-Trent from 1870 to 1880. Judge of Nottingham County Court and a Bencher of the Inner Temple. Born 5 Oct. 1822. Bapt. at Caunton, co. Notts.

Albertine, dau. of Jean Jacques Lavit of Paris. Born 3 Sept. 1835. Mar. 1 July 1856 at St Mary's, Bryanston Square, London.

Albert William Bristowe. Born 27 May 1858 at 11 Chester Square, London. Bapt. at St. Michael's, Chester Square, 23 June 1858.

Charles John Bristowe. Born 29 July 1862 at 11 Chester Square. Bapt. at St. Michael's, Chester Square, 24 Aug. 1862. Of Trinity Hall, Cambridge. Rowed stroke of the Cambridge Boat in the University Boat Race 1887.

Frederick Edward Bristowe. Born 3 Aug. 1866 at 3 Hertford Street, Mayfair. Bapt. at St. Michael's, Chester Square, 1 Sept. 1866.

Isabella. Bapt. at St. Michael's, Chester Square, 21 May 1857. Died 8 Jan. 1858; buried at Brompton Cemetery, London.

Edith Caroline. Born 18 Sept. 1859 at 11 Chester Square. Bapt. at St. Michael's, Chester Square, 11 Nov. 1859.

Amilia Mary. Born 16 Jan. 1868 at 4 Charles Street, Lowndes Sq. Bapt. at St. Michael's, Chester Square, 2 March 1868.

Arms of Baron Dickinson Webster, Esq.

G

Sir Henry Fox Bristowe, Q.C., Vice-Chancellor of the County Palatine Lancaster. A Bencher of the Middle Temple. Born 8 May 1824. Bapt. at Caunton, co. Notts. Knighted 5 Aug. 1887.=Selina, only dau. of the Hon. Orlando Henry Bridgeman, 3rd son of Orlando, 2nd Earl of Bradford, and the Lady Selina, dau. of Francis Jack, 12th Viscount and 1st Earl of Kilmorey. Born 15 Feb. 1825. Married 2 April 1850. Died 15 May 1886; buried at Datchet, co. Bucks.

Henry Orlando Bristowe. Born 7 April 1851. Bapt. at St. Peter's, Eaton Square, London, 10 May, 1851.

Leonard Hugh Bristowe. Born 11 June 1859 in London. Bapt. at St. Stephen's Church, Westminster, 8 July 1859.

Alice Mary. Born 9 Sept. 1855 in London. Bapt. at St. Stephen's, Westminster, 6 Oct. 1855,

Georgiana Emily. Born 6 Feb. 1858 in London. Bapt. at St. Stephen's, Westminster, 10 March 1858.

2nd wife, Anna Maria. Born 16 June 1826. Bapt. at Caunton. Mar. 20 Jan. 1850 at Aldenham, co. Herts. Died 24 Sept. 1862 at Oversfield, Torquay. Bur. at Warmley.=Baron Dickinson Webster, Esq., of Penns, co. Warwick, J.P. and D.L.; Capt. Staffordshire Yeomanry. Born Jan. 1818 at Penns. Died there 4 Aug. 1860. Bur. at Warmley, co. Warwick.=1st, Anna Maria, 2nd dau. of Stanley Pipe Wolferstan, Esq., of Statfold, co. Stafford, J.P. and D.L. Mar. 4 May 1844 at Tamworth. Died 26 July 1848 at Ilfracombe. Bur. at Warmley.

Baron Dickinson Webster, Esq., of Newland Court, Great Malvern. Born 7 Nov. 1850 at Penns. Bapt. 8 Dec. following at Penns.=Ellen Elizabeth, 7th dau. of the Rev. William Darwin Fox, Rector of Delamere, Cheshire. Born 26 Feb. 1852 at Delamere. Bapt. 2 June 1852 at St. Peter's, Delamere. Mar. 26 Aug. 1875 at Dibden, co. Hants.

Godfrey Fox Webster of Bramley Grange, Guildford, late Captain 20th Regiment. Born 28 April 1852 at Penns, and bapt. there.=Amy Laura, youngest dau. of Henry Booth, Esq., and niece of Sir Charles Booth, Bart. Married 24 July 1878 at St. Mary's, Datchet.

Baron Dickenson Webster. Born 10 June 1876 at Newland. Bapt. at Newland 14 July 1876.

Charles Payne Webster. Born 8 Dec, 1845 at Penns. Died 14 May 1862 at Statfold, Buried at Warmley.

Amy Rose Webster. Born 5 June 1879 at Stoke, near Plymouth.

Gladys Nina. Born 10 Nov. 1883 at Torquay.

Frances Sharpe. Born 25 July 1847 at Penns. Mar. 21 April 1870 at St. Matthias Church, Malvern Link.=Stanley Edward Hicks, Esq., eldest son of Edward Hicks, Esq., of Wilbraham Temple, co. Cambridge, by Grace, eldest dau. of Stanley Pipe Wolferstan, Esq., of Statfold.

Baron Webster. Born 31 Jan. 1845 at Ashfurlong. Died 21 March 1846.

Reginald Hicks. Born 22 Nov. 1871.

## Haines.

William Haines the elder, Citizen and Merchant Taylor⊤Alice Haines, living
of London. Will dated 5 Sep. 1590. Adm'on 23 Sep. │ 1610-11, and also
1590 to his relict Alice.  Lands and tenements in │ in 1612.
Allhallows, Barking, London, etc.

Amye, bur. at Hackney=1. Benedict Haynes, eldest son.  (Held the=. . . .
2 Oct. 1604.        Wyck lands in Hackney 1600–1607.)  He was
                    bur. at Hackney 2 Jan. 1609-10.

Henry Haynes⊤. . . .  Elizabeth, bap.  Edward, bap.  Robert, bap. 15 Oct.
of Hackney,         21 Sept. 1600.   24 Oct. 1606.  1609.  Bur. 19 Oct.
died before his     —                —              —
son was of age.     Susan, bap. 13   Ales, bap. 13  Benedict Haynes, bap.
                    July 1605.       May 1608. .    27 Dec. 1619.

Hackney Parish Register.

Thomas Haynes of Hackney, gent.  Will dated     Thomas Baynham.=Mary.
8 Sep. 1641 (then a prisoner in the King's Bench);
proved 8 Jan. 1651-2 by his sister and her husband.

2. William Haines of Chesington, co.⊤Anne, survived her hus-     Elizabeth
Surrey,Esq.; bur. there.  Died 14 Feb. │ band, and made her will   Sander,
9 James I.  Inquis. 16 April 9 Jac. I. │ 4 May 1612 ; proved      "my daur."
Will dated 26 Jan. 1610 ; proved 22 April │ 14 May 1612 ; to be bur.
1611 (30 Wood).                         │ near her husband.

William Haines, died a    Matthew Haines, died a minor.   Robert=Alice, aged
minor.  Inq. p.m. 11      Inq. p.m. 15 Jac. I.  Aged 12   Hatton,  23,15 Jac.I.
Jac. I.  Aged 13 years,   years, 10 months, and 20 days,  Esq., 15
9 months, and 28 days     9 James I.  Died 24 July 14     Jac. I.
on 14 Feb. 9 James I.     James I.

Jane Haynes,    Anne Haynes,   Thomasine Haynes, aged 13⊤Sir John Evelyn
aged 18,        aged 15,       years and 7 months, 24 July │ of Godstone.  Mar.
15 Jac. I.      15 Jac. I.     15 Jac. I.  Mar. when only │ in 1618.
                               about 14 years of age.     ↟

EXTRACTS FROM COURT ROLLS, MANOR OF KINGSHOLD, HACKNEY.

1585  May 26  Henry Offley, Esq., has lic. to demise to Nichs Haynes, gent.
1598  June 6  Alice Haynes, widow, surrenders to herself for life, remainder to
              Benedict Haynes, gent., her son and heir.
1607  May 18  Elizabeth and Benedict Haynes occupy the Wyck Farm, Hackney.
1645  April 29  Mary, wife of Thomas Baynham, is found to be grandda. and next
              heir of Benedict Haynes.
1645  Dec. 23  Thomas Baynham and Mary his wife surrender to Wm Taylor,
              cit. and haberdasher of London.

## INQUISITIONS.

RECORD OFFICE, CHANCERY INQ. P.M., 9 JAC. I., PART 2, No. 175.

Inquisition taken at Southwark, 10 Aug. 8 Jac. I., after the death of John
Cockes al's Hayne of Wotton, co. Surrey, yeoman, who died seised of a capital mess.
and lands called Hale lands, sometime of Edwᵈ at Hale, and situate in Wotton,
and lands called Tuttyes Croft, etc., also in Wotton. The sᵈ John Cockes al's
Hayne and Agnes his wife were also jointly seised of lands called ffrenches in
Wotton. He held also lands called Hitchcockes al's Wolfins land in Rugewycke,
Sussex, and lands, etc., called Hytchcockes al's Haymondys in Wotton afsᵈ. By
Ind're 3 Feb. 34 Eliz. the sᵈ lands called Hitchcockes al's Wolfins and Hytchcockes
al's Haymondys were confirmed to Richᵈ Cockes al's Hayne (now decᵈ), son of the
afsᵈ John. The sᵈ John Cockes al's Hayne was also seised of lands called Sampsons,
Brodemeade, etc., in Ewhurst, Surrey, lands called Pollyngfold in par. of Abynger
al's Abyngworth, and lands at Ockley, co. Surrey. The sᵈ John Cockes al's Hayne,
with his sons John and Edward, were seised of lands at Rugewicke and Wisborough
Greene, Sussex, and the sᵈ John Cockes al's Hayne with his son William were seised
of lands called Knights and Burchetts in Rugewick.

The lands called Hale lands, Hytchecockes al's Haymondes, etc., etc., in Wotton,
were held of Johanna Evelyn, widow, as of her manor of Wotton. The lands at
Rugewicke, etc., Sussex, were held of Walter Bartellot, gent., as of the manor of
Denn in Warnham. The lands called Sampsons, etc., were held of Richᵈ Evelyn,
gent., as of his manor of Westland. Lands called Haymans and Brodemeades were
held of Edwᵈ Braye, gent., as of the manor of Somshall Towerhill. The lands
called Pollyngfold were held of Edward, lord Abergavenny, and the lands in Ockley
were held of Sir Edwᵈ Culpepper, Knᵗ, as of his manor of Ockley, etc., etc.

The sᵈ John Cockes al's Hayne died at Wotton afsᵈ 19 April last past, and
William Cockes al's Hayne is his son and next heir and was aged 22 and upwards at
the time of his father's death.

RECORD OFFICE, CHANCERY INQ. P.M., 11 JAC., PART 1, No. 55.

Inquisition taken at Southwark, 7 May 11 Jac., after death of William Haines
[son and h. of Wᵐ Haines, esq., decᵈ], a minor.

Quotes an Inquisition taken 16 April 9 Jac. on death of the afsᵈ Wᵐ Haines,
esq. (the father), who was seised of the manor of ffreren al's ffrearne, the manor or
farm of Chesingdon al's Chesington apud Hooke, lands and woods called Lynell
Coppice, ffurres Grove Coppice, Betrice hill Coppice, Barnett's Grove, Goldsborough
hill Grove in the par. of Chesingdon al's Cesington, Long Ditton and Kingston,
Surrey.

The sᵈ Wᵐ Haines of Chesingdon by Ind're (24 Jan. 8 Jac.) between him the sᵈ
Wᵐ Haines of 1 pᵗ and Wᵐ Campion of Layton, Essex, and Abraham Campion of
London, Brewer, of the other part, makes provision for the jointure of his wife
Anne Haynes. And by another Ind're (6 Jan. 40 Eliz.) between him and Benedict
Haynes, gent., and Robᵗ Goodwyn, he grants certain tenemᵗˢ in Allhallows, Barking,
for a term of years to Alice Haines of Chisleton, mother of the sᵈ Wᵐ Haines, esq.
The sᵈ Wᵐ Haines, esq., died 14 Feb. 9 Jac. at Chesington, and William Haines was
his son and next heir, and of the age of 13 years, 9 months, and 28 days. The
abovesᵈ Anne Haines the wife and Alice Haines, widow, the mother of the sᵈ defunct
appear to survive.

The abovesᵈ William Haines (the son), a minor, and in ward to the King, died
12 Jan. (10 and 11 Jac.) last past at Chesington, and Mathew Haines is brother
and next heir, and of the age of 12 years, 10 months, and 20 days.

Anne Haines, wid. of Wᵐ Haines (the father), appears to decease 11 Jan.
10 and 11 K. James.

In the Inq. p.m., Wards and Liveries, 11 Jac. I., bundle 16, No. 119, an Inq.
of the date as above (7 May 11 Jac.) occurs to the same effect as the above.

RECORD OFFICE, INQ. P.M., 15 JAC. I., WARDS AND LIVERIES, BUNDLE 25, No. 30.

Inquis. taken at Southwark, 17 Oct. 15 Jac. I., on death of Matthew Haynes (son of William Haynes, dec^d), late a ward to the King, and seised of the manor of ffreren al's frearne, the manor or farme of Chesingdon al's Chesington apud Hooke, and other lands, etc., in Chesington, Long Ditton, Kingston, Surrey [see Inq. p.m., W^m Haines, 16 April 9 Jac. I.], and tenem^ts in Allhallows, Barking, London, now in the possession or tenure of Benedict Haynes, gent., and Rob^t Goodwin, or their assigns [see the afs^d Inq. of W^m Haines]. The s^d Matthew Haynes died 24 July last past (under age) seised of the abovenamed lands, etc., and Alice, now wife of Robert Hatton, esq., Jane Haynes, Anne Haynes, and Thomasine Haynes are his sisters and next heirs. The s^d Alice aged 23 and upw^ds, Jane aged 18 and upw^ds, Anne aged 15 and upw^ds, and Thomasine, aged 13 years and 7 months.

The afores^d lands appear to have been held of the King as of his Manor of Est Greenwich.

---

## INSCRIPTIONS ON COFFINS IN "RAGLEY OLD VAULT," ARROW CHURCH, WARWICKSHIRE.*

### 25.

Lead coffin, in very good state, with inscription in raised capitals, etc., as No. 24 covering the whole top of the coffin.

The son of
Edward Ea
rl of Conw
ay by the
lady Eli
zabeth
his sec
ond wi
fe was
still
born J
uly t
he 3 a
no Do
1681.

For Burial Register see No. 24, p. 26.

---

### 26.

Lead coffin, in a very good state, with a beautiful loose brass plate upon its centre, and upon the foot a small lead shell, shaped to the body and features of a child. When in the vault, 11 Jan. 1871, I found the brass plate lying between the coffin and the wall, entirely out of sight, and why I should have been led to look for anything there has ever since seemed somewhat mysterious to me.

Heare . lyeth . the .
body . of . the .

Right Hon^ble
Edward Earle of Conway, Vicount Conway and of
Killulta in the Kingdome of Ireland Baron Ragley Lord
Lieu^t of the County of Warwick. Lieutenant Generall of the
Horse in the Kingdome of Ireland and one of his
Ma^ties most Hon^ble Privy Councill w^ch died the 11
of August 1683 & in hope of a Blessed resurrecti^on.

* Continued from p. 26.

*Burial Register.*

1683. *Aug.* 25 *was buried the Right Honourable Earl of Conway.*

*Mem. Sept.* 13 *ffifty shillings were then distributed to the poor, and fifty more given to $M^r$ Constantine Magenis, being the forfeiture for the Earl of Conway's burying contrary to the Act.*

---

27.

Body and feature-shaped lead shell (in good condition) which (I believe) undoubtedly contains the remains of Heneage, son of Edward Viscount Conway (No. 26) and Anne his wife (No. 13), whose baptismal and burial registers are as follow :

*Baptism.* 1658. *Henneag Son of Edward Viscount Conway & Killultah was Baptized ffeb : the* 17 $An^o$ 1658. *Dan : Whitbee vid Register Westmonastery.*

*Burial. Henneg Conway the sonn of the Right hono^ble Lord Conway was buried October* 23, 1660.

---

28.

A very fine lead coffin, in excellent preservation, with inscription in Roman capitals of the period, stops between each word, also two shields of arms, all raised in the lead.

> Heare : lyeth : the : body :
> of : the : right : honorable :
> the : Lady : Dowager : Fran
> ces : Vicountese : Conway :
> Daughter : of : Sir : Fran-
> cis : Popham : she : dyed :
> the : Seaventh : day :
> of : May : 1671 :
> being : the : 74 :
> yeare : of :
> her : age :

*Burial Register.*

1671. *The Right Hono^ble Frances Viscountess Dowager of Conway departed this life may $7^{th}$ and was buried June $16^{th}$ 1671.*

---

29.

Lead coffin, in a very good state, excepting there being two small holes in the lead on the top, one on the left side of the head, and one towards the foot on the right side. An inscription appears to have existed and been torn off. Upon the head lies a helmet in a somewhat rusty state.

(*To be continued.*)

---

# Dalison Notes.*

Liberate pro nunciis.

Rex E. Thesaurario et Camerariis suis salutem. Liberate de thesauro nostro . . . . Rogero Passavant eunti ad Vicecomites Essex et Hertford, London, Norfolk et Suffolk, Middlesex, et ad Herebertum de Alencun et ballivos nundinarum de Jernem'. Teste me ipso . . . . primo die Octobris, anno regni nostri, $x^o$.

Close Roll, 10 Hen. 3, m. 4, 1 Oct. A.D. 1226.

* Continued from p. 30.

Johannes de Chaviny et Petronilla uxor ejus capti et detenti apud Leicester pro morte Rogeri la Weyte, et Willielmus Haunselin' captus et detentus pro eadem morte habent litteras quod tradantur in ballium usque ad adventum Justiciariorum responsuri Elene que fuit uxor ipsius Rogeri de predicta morte unde eos appellat. Teste Rege apud Wudestok' xv die Augusti.

Close Roll, 11 Hen. 3, m. 5, 15 August A.D. 1227.

Pro Ricardo de Alencun.

Eodem modo scribitur eisdem Justiciariis pro Ricardo de Alencun de novem marcis quas Johannes de Nevill filius et heres Alexandri de Nevill qui est in custodia sua debet Roesie que fuit uxor Cocky Judee, et de ix marcis quas debet Benedicto de Oxon' Judeo pro Alexandro de Nevill patre suo allocandis predictis Roesie et Benedicto in debito quod Regi debent, etc. Teste Rege ut supra (vi die Februarii).

Fine Roll, 14 Hen. 3, m. 8, A.D. 1230.

Hec est finalis Concordia facta in Curia Domini Regis apud Lincoln in Octabis Sancti Dionisii Anno regni Regis Henrici filii Regis Johannis decimo octavo, etc. Inter Margeriam que fuit uxor Simonis de Bekering, petentem, et Ricardum de Alencun tenentem de tercia parte triginta acrarum terre, cum pertinentiis, in Fulnedeby. Quam terciam partem predicta Margeria clamabat esse de rationabili dote sua de libero tenemento quod fuit predicti Simonis quondam viri sui in eadem villa. Et unde, etc., scilicet quod predicta Margeria remisit et quiete clamavit de se eidem Ricardo, etc., totum jus, etc., quod habuit in tota predicta tercia parte, etc.

Feet of Fines, Lincoln, 18 Henry 3, No. 166, (76), [19 March A.D. 1234].

Hec est finalis concordia facta, etc., die Veneris proxima post Festum Sancti Nicholai, anno regni Regis Henrici filii Regis Johannis, nonodecimo, etc. Inter Eadmundum de Alencun, petentem, et Petrum Abbatem de Leyston, quem Juliana de Brahan vocavit ad warrantum et qui ei warantizavit, de viginti et quatuor acris terre in Tedberton. Predictus Eadmundus remisit et quietum clamavit predicto Abbati totum jus, etc., in predicta terra imperpetuum. Idem Abbas dedit Centum solidos.

Feet of Fines, Suffolk, 19 Hen. 3, No. 171, 8 Dec. A.D. 1234.

Hec est finalis concordia facta, etc., in Octabis Sancti Martini anno regni regis Henrici filii Regis Johannis, vicesimo quarto, etc. Inter Tristanum de Rindham querentem, et Herebertum de Alencun deforciantem de advocacione ecclesie de Rindham. Predictus Tristanus recognovit advocacionem esse jus ipsius Hereberti.

Feet of Fines, Suffolk, 24 Hen. 3, No. 34, A.D. 1239.

Rex M[auricio] Filio Geroldi Justiciario Hybernie salutem, etc. Et cum ad nos veneritis adducatis vobiscum in Anglia filiam Gilberti de Lassy heredem Walteri de Lascy que est in custodia Galfridi de Alecon cui mandamus una cum Margereta de Lasey que ei inde litteras suas mittit patentes quod ipsam vobis liberet, etc.

Teste Rege apud Glouc' 16 die Junii, [A.D. 1241].

Et mandatum est Galfrido de Alecon quod predictam filiam liberet predicto Justiciario ducendam ad Regem in Anglia.

Patent Roll, 25 Hen. 3, m. 4 d.

Rogerus Buzun ponit loco suo Willielmum de Alenzun versus Willielmum de Wylegheby de placito Custodie, etc.

Assize Roll, Lincoln, M-8-13 1 m. 2 d., [29 Hen. 3, A.D. 1244-5].

Rogerus Buzun et Ricardus de Alenzun summoniti fuerunt ad respondendum Willielmo de Wyuelesby de placito quod reddant ei Laurettam filiam et unam heredum Alani de Cotes, cujus custodia ad ipsum pertinet, eo quod predictus Alanus de eo tenuit per servicium militare, etc.

Et Rogerus Buzun per attornatum suum venit et vocavit inde ad warantum predictum Ricardum de Alenzun, etc. Judicium attachiantur quod sint in Octabis Apostolorum.

Assize Roll, Lincoln, M-3-13 1, m. 31, [29 Hen. 3, A.D. 1244-5].

Omnibus Christi fidelibus, etc. R[ogerus] Bygot Comes Norfolch et Marescallus Anglie salutem, etc. Noveritis nos concessisse, etc. Deo et Hospitali Sancti Egidii de Norwico, Magistro et fratribus ejusdem Hospitalis ad sustentacionem pauperum totam terram quam venerabilis pater Walterus Norwicensis Episcopus de nobis tenuit in villa Hethill, etc. Hiis testibus ; Dominis Radalpho Bygot ; Herberto de Alezun, etc., Militibus, etc.

Add. Ch. 7207, Brit. Mus., Undated, [A.D. 1253-1270].

Hec est finalis concordia facta, etc., a die Sancti Johannis Baptiste in quindecim dies anno regni Regis Henrici filii Regis Johannis tricesimo nono, etc. Inter Herbertum de Alenzun querentem & Willielmum le Blunt de hoc quod idem Willielmus acquietaret predictum Herbertum de servicio quod Ricardus Comes Cornubie exigebat ab eo de libero tenemento suo quod de predicto Willielmo tenet in Westleton, Snapes, etc., scilicet de feodo trium militum, etc.

Feet of Fines, 39 Hen. 3, No. 215, Suffolk, A.D. 1255.

## THE MONUMENTAL INSCRIPTIONS OF RUSHALL, CO. WILTS.*

*South wall of Chancel.*

In a vault | under the Communion table in this chancel | lie interred the remains of Mʳ Francis Giffard | of Uphaven in this County, | who died April 9ᵗʰ 1802, aged 80 years. | Also of Jane his wife, | who died October 17ᵗʰ 1794, aged 56 years.

Beneath | are deposited the | Remains | of Mʳˢ Sarah Peck, | Widow & Relict of Kenrick Peck | of Cornish in the County of Denbigh Esqʳ, | who died July 20ᵗʰ 1802, Aged 70. | Also the Remains | of Beatrice Peck | their Daughter ; | who died Janʳʸ 12ᵗʰ 1807, | aged 42.

Anne | Daughter to Alex. Reading Esq., | The wife of Wᵐ Baxter B.D., | Rector of this Church, | Dyed in childe-bed of the 9ᵗʰ childe, | (Leaving 5 sons & 3 Davghters surviving,) | Iune 8ᵗʰ Anᵒ Ætat. 38 D'niq. 1670.

*North wall of Chancel.*

In memory of | the Revᵈ Kenrick Peck M.A. | of Notton Lodge in this county | formerly curate of this parish ; | who died Febʳʸ 17ᵗʰ 1837 aged 69. | And of four children of | the Revᵈ Kenrick Peck, | and Mary his wife & relict ; | Kenrick, the eldest son aged 17, | (buried at Clyst St. Mary Devon,) | Jasper William, an infant, | Samuel Richardson, aged 13, | William the youngest aged 16.

Near this Place | lyes Interr'd the Body | of the Revᵈ Mʳ | Thomas Giffard, | Rector of this Church, | Who Died | the 15ᵗʰ Day of August | 1746 | aged 64 years.

*South wall of Nave.*

Vnder | this tombe lyeth | ye Body of Mʳ | Roger Pinckney | who Departed | This Life ye 13ᵗʰ | day of January | Annᵒ Domini | 1706 | Aged 75 years.

* Communicated by ARTHUR SCHOMBERG, Esq.

*A piece of sculpture consisting of two panels let into the wall, in one,* W. P., *in the other,* a fess lozengy.

ARMS : Or, a fess lozengy.    CREST : Out of a coronet a griffin's head.

Sacred | to the Memory of | George Henry Pinckney Esq[r] | of Tawstock Court, | Barnstaple, | and Middlesex House, | Batheaston, | Died January 12th 1883 | aged 71 years.

*On the floor of Nave.*

Here lyeth the Body | of Elizabeth the | Daughter of Stephen | and Mary Rutt . . . .

Barbarah Webb Died March 2 A.D. 1723 | Ætatis 54.    (M.I.)*

Here Lyeth the Body of Lucie, the Wife of | John Chandler, Yeoman, who Departed this life February | the 15 | A.D. 1705.   (M.I.)

Frances Sadleir . . . .

*North wall of Nave.*

Beneath rest the Remains of | David Edmonds, Gent. ; | who died Oct[r] 14th 1812, Aged 76 years, | 40 of which he resided in | the Parish of St. Mary le Strand | in the City of Westminster, | and Justly obtained the character | of an Upright and honest man.

Beneath are deposited the remains of | Richard, son of | Richard and Ann Stratton, | who died Nov[r] 25th 1810 | aged 18 months. | Also of Mary their beloved Daughter | who died August 5th 1828, | aged 21 Years. | Also of James their Son | who died January 2nd 1835 | Aged 12 Years. | Also of Ann, the beloved wife of | Richard Stratton, | who died June 3rd 1849, Aged 71 Years.

Sacred to the memory of | John Hayward | of this parish | who departed this life | November 19th 1869 | aged 45 years.

*North Chapel.*

ARMS : Argent, a fess azure between three mullets gules ; impaling, Argent, three wolfs' heads erased in pale proper, METHUEN.
CREST : A cubit arm erect, vested sable, charged with two mullets in fess or, slashed argent, cuffed ermine, grasping in the hand an arrow proper.

In a vault beneath are deposited the remains of | Edward Poore Esq[r] | Lord of the manors of Rushall and Charlton ; | He was the eldest son of Abraham Poore Esq[r] of Longstreet | and married Barbara | daughter of Paul Methuen, Esq[r] of Bradford in this county | and by her he had issue four sons, of whom two died in their infancy, | the other two Edward and John Methuen survived him. | He died Ap. 10, 1788, aged 73.†

* M.I. signifies that those Inscriptions to which these initials are attached are now destroyed, illegible, or lost, and have, therefore, been supplied from the rare 'Monumental Inscriptions of Wiltshire, 1821,' of which only six copies were printed.
† On the north wall of nave is a hatchment of POORE, with badge of Ulster, and motto, *Honor fidei merces ;* and over the outside window of the north chapel are the arms and crest of this family carved in stone.

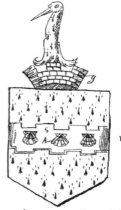

Browne of Hungry=Bentley.

K 9·75

.Respite taken for proofe of these
Armes; but no proofe made.

But vide M·2· f°3· in Coll. Arms·

Thomas Browne = Apolina dau: to George
of Shreddicote in | Southwike merchant of
the parish of Brad- | London widow of Wil-
ley in com: Staff: | liam Fairfax a Gold-
gent: died a° 1633. | smith in London.

| 5 | 4 | | 3 | 2 | 1 | 1 | 2 |
|---|---|---|---|---|---|---|---|
| Edward Browne of Waldley in com:Derb· | Edmund Brown of Hungry Bentley in co: Derb: gent: æt:51 an: 11·Aug: 1662. | =Dorothy 1ᵈ dau: to Sʳ Edward Vernon of Sudbury in co: Derb. kᵗ | William Browne an Utter Barri- ster of Grays Temple æt:57. ann: 1662. | George Browne of Shredi- cote died A° 1652. | Thomas died un- married. | Mary wife of Carew Sterry of Rossall in Com: Salop: | Apolina died un- married. |

1. Thomas
2. Edmund
3. William
4. Rupert
5. George } all now
6. John   living·
7. Charles
8. Walter
9. Philip
10. Marke.

Edward,
Benjamin (de-
Richard } ceased.

1. Mary
2. Apolonia
3. Dorothy
4. Margaret-
5. Elizabeth

Certified by William Browne
and Edmund Browne.

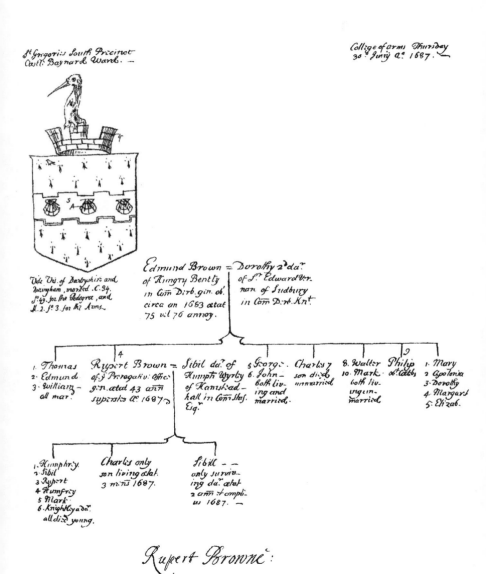

St Grigoriis South Precinct
Castl: Baynard Ward. —

Collige of Arms Thursday
30° Junij a°. 1687.

Vide Vis: of Darbyshire and
Nottingham, marked .C.34.
fo.49. for the Pedigree, and
H. 2. fo.3. for the Arms.

Edmund Brown = Dorothy 2°da.
of Hungry Bently
in Com Dirb. gin. ob.
circa an 1683 ætat
75 vel 76 annoy.

of Sr. Edward Ver-
nan of Sudbury
in Com D.rb. Knt.

1. Thomas
2. Edmund
3. William —
all mar.

4
Rupert Brown =
of ŷ Prerogativ: Offic:
g:n. ætad 43 aññ
superstes a°. 1687.

Sibil da. of
Humph Wyrly
of Hanstead —
hall in Com Sts.
Esqr.

5 George.
6. John —
both liv-
ing and
married.

Charls 7
son died
unnarried

8. Walter
10. Mark.
both liv-
ing un-
married

Philip
ob. Cælb,

1. Mary
2 Apolonia
3. Dorothy
4. Margaret
5. Elizab.

1. Humphry.
2 Sibil
3 Rupert
4 Humfrey
5 Mark
6. Knight & ya da.
all did young.

Charles only
son living ætat.
3 m:ñs 1687.

Sibill —
only surviv-
ing da. ætat
2 aññ & compli-
us 1687. —

Rupert Browne:

# Genealogy of Browne.*

**C.** **Thomas Browne** of Shredicote, parish of Bradeley, co. Stafford, only son of William Browne of Caverswall (bapt. [at Caverswall] 22 May 1561; d. 5 April, bur. [in Bradeley Church, M.I.] 8 April 1633. Will dated 27 Oct. 1631 ; codicil 14 Feb. 1632; pr. P.C.C. by Apollonia his wife and sole executrix 28 May 1633), a Proctor-General† of the Arches Court of Canterbury, and co-Governor of the Hospital of King James I. in Charter-house, London, nominated by the Founder, Thomas Sutton. Owned the manor of Shredicote, co. Stafford, freehold lands in Marston and Scropton, co. Derby, Upper Tame, co. Stafford, etc. The Manor of Hungry-Bentley, co. Derby (purchased from Thomas, sixth Baron Windsor, K.G., by deed, dated 20 April 1613, for £2600), lands in Alkmonton and Middleton Park, co. Derby (purchased from "Lord Stanhoppe" by deed, dated 1 July 1621). Legatee under the will of his father-in-law George Southaicke 1604, who bequeathed him "one ringe of golde of the valewe of fortie shillings and tenne pounds in money for a gentle remembrance and a token of the loue and good will which I have ever borne vnto him having received the like good will and kindness in his loue and paines taken ever for me much more then I am able to requite for lacke of abilitie." Arms, etc.—Crest : *Out of a mural coronet gules a stork's head issuing erased ermines, beaked azure.* Arms : *Ermine, on a fess embattled counter-embattled sable three escallops argent,* for BROWNE (confirmed to Thomas Browne by Sir William Camden, Clarencieux, in May 1614); *impaling* (as emblazoned on shield in Bradeley Church), *Argent, on a fess dancettée gules an annulet or, from the sinister chief an arm issuing from clouds proper, vested gules, touching in the chief point a heart of the last between two spear-heads sable pointing inwards,* for SOUTHAICKE. Mar. Apollonia, dau. of George Southaicke, citizen and grocer of London (member of the Grocers' Company, and a Governor of the Hospital of Bridewell), and relict of William ffayrefax, citizen and goldsmith of London. Legatee under her father's will 1604, who bequeathed her £20 ; legatee and sole executrix under her first husband's will, dated 2 Dec. 1595, which she pr. P.C.C. 8 Dec. 1595, who bequeathed her £500 and half of residue of real and personal estate ; legatee and sole executrix under her second husband's will 1633, who bequeathed her freehold lands in Upper Tame, co. Stafford, the rents, etc., of Hungry-Bentley estate for seven years, and of all other estates for her life (bur. with her second husband [in Bradeley Church, M.I.] 25 May 1653. Will dated 1 April 1653; pr. P.C.C. by her dau. Apollonia, sole executrix, 24 Aug. 1653). Issue :—

**D.** 1. Thomas Browne (living 1604; dead 1631), presented with a "greate gilte spoone"‡ at his christening which his mother bequeathed in 1653 to her grandson Thomas Browne. Legatee under the will of George Southaicke 1604, who bequeathed him a "ringe with a deathes head in gold."

   2. George Browne of Shredicote, co. Stafford. (*Vide infra, Genealogy of Browne of Shredicote.*)

* Continued from p. 28.
† A Proctor was one who undertook another man's business in any Court of Civil or Ecclesiastical Law. Previous to 1858 he practised in the Prerogative Court of Canterbury, the Diocesan Courts of the Bishops, the High Court of Admiralty, the Faculty Court, and the Arches Court of Canterbury. It is only since 1858 that these Courts have been thrown open to the Bar, whereas, previously, they had to instruct a Proctor to act for them, as only Doctors in Civil Law who were styled "Advocates" could plead in such courts. (See Sir R. Phillimore's 'Ecclesiastical Law.')
‡ Probably an "Apostle's spoon," silver gilt.

3. William Browne of Gray's Inn,* London (b. 1605 ? ; æt. 57 at Visitation of Derbyshire by Sir William Dugdale 11 Aug. 1662, and co-signee of pedigree entered; d. . . . . .), Barrister-at-Law. Legatee under his father's will 1630, who bequeathed him an annuity of £50 out of Hungry-Bentley estate, and entailed upon him the manor, etc., of Hungry-Bentley in default of issue of his brother Edmund, and other estates in default of issue of his brothers George and Edward. Living at Shredicote and legatee under his mother's will 1653, who bequeathed him her "roane mare" and "the bed hee usually lyeth upon, boulster, pillow, bed cloathes, one paire of sheetes, one pillow beere, and table cloth, and one dozzen of flaxen napkins." Legatee under the will of his sister Apollonia 1659, who bequeathed him £20 and the "mare called by the name of Starr Mare, and the curteyns and valense belonginge to y^e bed called the Blewbed, one chest w^th Drawyers, one chayre, and two stooles suitable therevnto in the Dyneing Room."

4. Edmund Browne of Hungry-Bentley or Bentley Hall, co. Derby. (*Vide infra.*)

5. Edward Browne (bapt. [at Bradeley, co. Stafford] 20 July 1614; d. intestate and unmar. at Bentley Hall. Letters of Administration granted by Consistory Court of Lichfield to his brother Edmund 15 Jan. 1678-9) of Waldley, co. Derby, in pedigree 1662. Legatee under his father's will, who bequeathed him an annuity of £50 out of the Hungry-Bentley Estate, entailed upon him the manor, etc., of Hungry-Bentley in default of issue of his brothers Edmund and William, and other estates in default of issue of his brother George. Living at Shredicote and legatee under his mother's will 1653, who bequeathed him her "browne bay mare, the feather bedd, boulster, pillow usually lynge upon a truckle bedstead in the parlour chamber, one yellow rugge, a paire blanketts, one paire of sheetes, one pillow beere, and one dozzen of flaxen napkins." Legatee under his sister Apollonia's will 1659, who bequeathed him £20 and "a colt and one chest w^th Drawyers in the kitchen chamber and the feather bed w^ch my sister Leuinge hath of mine and ye greene curtyns belonginge to the same in which I vsed to lye and one mare called by the name of Button."

6. Francis Browne (bapt. [at Bradeley] 17 Nov. 1616; dead 1630?).

1. Mary (d. . . . .), legatee under her father's will 1630, who bequeathed her £10 ; legatee under her mother's will 1653, who bequeathed her the "bedtoppe and vallence she desired of mee, one duzzen of napkins layd worke marked with the letter 'A,' and one paire of Aundirons with brasse tops;" legatee under her sister Apollonia's will 1659, who bequeathed her "one twenty shilling peece of gold and the pin pillow w^ch her Daughter wrought w^th the Effigies of the King and Queene thereon." Mar. (*ante* 1623) Carew Stury, Esq., of Rosshall, parish of St. Chad, Shrewsbury (b. 1601 ? ; æt. 22 at Visitation of Salop 1623† [Harl. MS. 1396, fos. 370–1], dead 1653 ?), son of Walter Stury, Esq., of Rosshall (living 1623), by his wife Lowry, dau. of John Griffith of the Grange, co. Stafford. Legatee under his father-in-law's will 1630, who bequeathed him £5. Arms: *Argent, a lion rampant double-queued purpure* (for Stury) ; *impaling* Browne. Issue :—

E.   1. Elizabeth Stury (bapt. [at St. Chad's, Shrewsbury] 1 May 1623 ; d. . . . .), legatee under her grandfather's will 1630, who bequeathed her £10, and under her grandmother's will, which she witnessed in 1653, who bequeathed her xxs. to buy a ring.

---

* There is no record of his admission in the registers of Gray's Inn. He is so denominated in the Visitation pedigree, 1666.

For Pedigree of Stury see Harl. MSS. 1982, fo. 85^b, and 615, fo. 263.

2. Apollonia Stury (bapt. [at St. Chad's, Shrewsbury] 11 Nov. 1624 ; d. . . . .), legatee under her grandfather's will 1630, who bequeathed her £40.

3. Rachell Stury (b. after 1630 ?), legatee under her grandmother's will 1630, who bequeathed her xxs. to buy a ring.

2. Apollonia of "the Rule," parish of Bradeley, co. Stafford (d. unmar. [at London] ; bur. in the Gunter vault [St. Michael's, Cornhill, London] 9 March 1658-9. Will dated 2 March 1658-9 ; pr. P.C.C. by her brother Edmund, sole ex'or, 18 April 1659), legatee under her father's will 1630, who bequeathed her " £500 to be paid at day of marriage and if she marry with the consent of her mother and brother to be made up to £800," and "my ringe sett with five litle diamonds." Legatee and sole executrix under her mother's will 1653, who bequeathed her the residue of personal estate.

(*To be continued.*)

---

# Upton.*

## ABSTRACTS OF WILLS AND RECORDS OF ADMINISTRATION.

76. William Upton† of London, factor. Dated 24 June 1685. To James Cadbury son of my brother James Cadbury by his former wife Elizabeth‡ £50 at 21, but if he die before, then same to his sister Elizabeth Cadbury at 18 or marriage ; to my niece Elizabeth Upton, daughter of my late brother Henry Upton, late of Burlescombe, dec'd, £100 at 18 or marriage ; to poor of Burlescombe £12 ; to Mrs. Paris Sloughter and George Gresham each 20s. for a ring ; all my lands, etc., and residue of personalty to my sister Sarah Upton, and appoint her executrix. Proved 8 Oct. 1685 by exec'x. (127 Cann.)

77. Hugh Upton,§ of Trinity Minories, London. Adm'on 31 Oct. 1688 to the relict Anne.

78. Arthur Upton,‖ who died at Surinam beyond seas, a bachelor. Adm'on 8 March 1688-9 to his father John Upton. Adm'on *de bon. non* 17 June 1689 to his brother John Upton, jr., the father John Upton, Esq., to whom former letters, renouncing.

79. John Upton¶ of the City of London, Esq. Dated 22 July 1689. To be buried at the discretion of Joane** my wife. Whereas by Articles of Agreement before marriage with my said wife dated 5 Aug. 1673 I agreed to leave her £3000 or the thirds of my personal estate, and gave my bond thereto to Mr. Charles Gibbs†† and Mr. Benjamin Agar, now if she resign her claim to said £3000 and resort to her thirds, I direct that, after the payment of £3000 to my son John Upton,‡‡ according to covenant with my brother William Warren,§§ she shall have

---

* Continued from p. 32.
† The testator was son of Henry Upton who made will No. 69.
‡ Testator's sister Elizabeth Upton married James Cadbury.
§ This Hugh Upton was son of John and Dorothy (Rouse) Upton, and brother of Nos. 64, 75, 79, and 83. His daughter is No. 65.
‖ This Arthur Upton was son of John Upton who made will No. 79. His brother John is No. 97, *post.*
¶ The testator was son of John and Dorothy (Rouse) Upton, and brother of Nos. 64, 75, 77, and 83.
** Joane Upton, *née* Stow, widow, successively, of Mr. Agar, Rev. James Meggs, and John Upton, Esq., was the testator's third wife. She made will No. 104.
†† Rev. Charles Gibbes. D.D., sixth son of Sir Ralph Gibbes of Honington, Warwickshire, Kt., married Ann Stow, sister of testator's wife Joane.
‡‡ The son John Upton is No. 97, *post.*
§§ This William Warren was father of Mary, wife of the testator's son John Upton.

one-third of my personalty, etc. ; to said wife sundry plate, jewels, furniture, etc.,
and £500 E. India Stock of hers for which I gave a receipt to Roger James, Esq.
Whereas it hath pleased God to bless me with five* children, viz., John and
Anthony,† Elizabeth Farrington,‡ Mary Sayer,§ and Jeane Uvidall,‖ and I have
given them already sufficient portions, etc.  Whereas my son Anthony Upton by
writing dated 23 Feb. 1683-4 covenanted to pay me £60 per annum for life, I will
that the arrears be divided between my sister Mary Upton, relict of my brother
Ambrose Upton,¶ and my sister Ann Upton, relict of my brother Hugh Upton.**
To my son Anthony £300; to my brother Daniel Farrington, Esq.,†† and my two
executors £600 to be laid out in lands for use of my daughter Elizabeth Farrington
for life, remainder to my grandson Daniel Farrington at 21, remainder to my granddaughter Elizabeth Farrington at 21 ; to my daughters Mary Sayer and Jeane
Uvidall each £300 ; to my niece Elizabeth, daughter of my brother Gilbert Upton,‡‡
£400 at 21 or marriage, with remainder to her two sisters Ann and Rebecca at 21
or marriage ; to my brother Gilbert Upton £50 for mourning for himself and
daughter Elizabeth ; to my brother Daniel Farrington, my brother Giles Aytcoe
[? Lytcott§§], my sister Thurler,‖‖ my sister Ursula Upton,¶¶ my brother William
Warren and wife, my sister Mary Upton,*** Ann Upton,††† sister Ann Gibbs,‡‡‡
my sisters Champnyes,§§§ Horne, Thomas,‖‖‖‖ and Stockbridge each £10 for
mourning ; to the poor of Stoke Newington £5 ; if a certain £3500 lent on mortgage be recovered, then to wife Joane £500 more ; to my niece Rebecca, daughter of
my late brother Hugh Upton, and my niece Arabella, daughter of my late
brother Ambrose Upton, each £100 at 21 or marriage ; residue of personalty
to brother Wm. Warren and son Anthony Upton in trust to purchase lands to be
settled on my son John Upton for life, remainder to my grandson William Upton,
remainder to grandson John Upton, remainder to grandson Anthony Upton,
remainder to other son or sons of said John Upton in succession, remainder to my
son Anthony and his sons in succession, remainder to my right heirs ; appoint my
sons John and Anthony executors.  Codicil,¶¶¶¶ without date, revokes disposition
of residue, and gives it to son John Upton ; to my four daughters Elizabeth
Farrington, Mary Sayer, Jane Uvidale, and Mary Upton**** each ten guineas more.
Proved 24 Jan. 1689-90 by son John, power reserved to Anthony.  (C.P.C.,
13 Dyke.)

*(To be continued.)*

* The testator had eight children, but three of them were dead at this time, viz., Anne, who
died unmarried before 1687 ; Nicholas, No. 71, *ante;* and Arthur, No. 78, *ante.*
   † The son Anthony made will No. 108.
   ‡ Elizabeth Upton married Soloman Farrington in 1672.
   § Mary Upton married (1st) John Sayer, (2nd) Richard Knightley.
   ‖ Jeane Upton married Thomas Uvedall, Uvidall, or Uvedale in 1680.
   ¶ The brother Ambrose Upton married Mary Charleton.
   ** The brother Hugh Upton is No. 77, *ante.*
   †† I think Daniel Farrington was not brother-in-law of the testator, but father of the Soloman
Farrington who married testator's daughter.
   ‡‡ The brother Gilbert Upton made will No. 83.
   §§ Testator's second wife was Jane Lytcott.
   ‖‖ Sister " Thurler " was Anne, *née* Lytcott, wife of Mr. Secretary John Thurloe, and sister
of the testator's second wife.
   ¶¶ Sister "Ursula Upton " was sister of Jane and Anne Lytcott mentioned above, and widow
of testator's nephew John Upton of Lupton.  She made will No. 100, *post.*
   *** Mary Upton was widow of testator's brother Ambrose.
   ††† Ann Upton was widow of testator's brother Hugh.
   ‡‡‡ Ann Gibbs, as noted above, was sister of testator's third wife.
   §§§ Testator's sister Ann married John Champneis in 1642.
   ‖‖‖‖ Testator's sister Phillippa married Samuel Thomas in 1653.
   ¶¶¶¶ Upon the death of Sir John H. G. Upton *alias* Smyth, Bart., in 1873, some, as yet unknown,
descendant of the testator John Upton became heir male and head of this ancient family.  But
for this unfortunate codicil, a great landed estate would have been created, much to the
advantage of the present head of the family, and of all persons who would fain trace the obscure
line of the testator's descendants.
   **** Mary Upton was not daughter of the testator, but wife of his son John.

# Grant of Arms to Robert Iason of Enfield, 1588.

To all and Singvler Nobles and Gentles of what estate dignitie or degree bearing Armes To whom theise presents shall come, I William Dethick Garter principall
King of Armes send my due salutations & greetings. Knowe yee that by the
authority and Custome of my Office from the Queens most excellent Ma^tie & her
highnes most noble and princely progenitors I am to take generall notice & to
make testimony and records for all matters & causes of Armes Honor & Chiualry,
& for all Pedigrees and descents of Nobles & Gent' throughout all her Ma^ties
Kingdoms Dominions, Principalities, Isles & Prouinces To thende that auntient
names & Familes & descents may haue and enioy their due Ensignes of their
Armes. So it is that Robert Iason now of Enfielde in the Countie of Middlesex
Esquire being descended of auntient name and Family in the North, but now
setled his Estate in theis parts of this Realme in right Worshipfull degree and
calling, brought unto mee this his Armes depicted in an old parchment booke of
their Pedigrees left unto him by his Auncessors, required me the said Garter
according to the authority of my Office to take notice & to make generall testimony
of record for him the said Robert Iason of the sheilde of his Armes & Creast Lawfull
to be enioyed and borne by himselfe his children Issue & posteritie for euer as of
due right belonging vnto their Auntient name & famile In regarde wherof I haue
blazd & exemplified the same by theise presents Viz: he beareth Azure a golden
Fleece within a double Tressure counterflore of the same, and for his Crest a
Pegasus d'or bearing in his mouth a Burr proper mounted on a Shapeau vpon the
Helme With mantles Azure doubled Or, together as I haue thought good with the
Sheilde of Armes of Susan his wife (daughter of Iohn Lyon Esquire of the parts
beyond the Seas in Holland naturalized of England in the tyme of King Henry the
8^th) viz. y^e feild gules a Lyon passant gardant d'argent with a Canton of the Red-
cross ; for that their sole Childe Robert Iason the younger is likewise heir vnto the
house of the said Lyon & is for euer to haue and to beare theise two seuerall
Coates of Armes quartred as his true auntient and Lawfull Ensignes of Armes and
Creast also to be borne and vsed by their Children seede and posteritie to their
proper vse and behoofe for euer with theire due differences in all vertuous Warlike
facts & ciuill vse or exercise according to the Lawes of Armes & Customes that to
all gent' belongeth, In Witnes & perpetuall remembrance Wherof I haue registred

in the Office of Armes (for a true testimony of recorde) theise pre'nte; And hereunto subscribed my name & fastened the Seale of my Office endorsed with the Signet of my Armes, Geuen at y^e office of Armes London y^e 10^th of March & in the 30^th yeare of y^e Raigne of o^r Soueraigne Lady Elizabeth Queene of England France & Ireland defendor of the Faith &c. Anno Domini 1588.

## Genealogy of Browne.*

D.   **Edmund Browne** (fourth son) of Hungry-Bentley,† parish of Alkmonton, co. Derby (b. 1611 ? [æt. 51 in 1662]; d. 27 June, bur. [in the chancel of Longford Church, co. Derby, M.I. evident in 1819] 29 June 1684, æt. 73), legatee under his father's will 1630, who entailed upon him the manor, etc., of Hungry-Bentley, also the reversion of lands, etc., in Shredicote, Bradeley, and Barton, in default of issue of his brothers George, Edward, and William; legatee under his mother's will 1653, who bequeathed him her black mare; legatee and sole ex'or under his sister Apollonia's will, which he proved 1659, who bequeathed him " one feather bed whereon I vsed to lye and two payre of sheets ; co-signee of pedigree entered at the Visitation of Derbyshire by Sir William Dugdale 10 Aug. 1662 ; administered his brother Edward's estate 1679.   Arms : BROWNE, *impaling*, Argent, a fret sable (for VERNON). Mar. Dorothy, second dau. of Sir Edward Vernon, Knight, of Houndhill, parish of Marchington, co. Stafford, and of Sudbury Hall, co. Derby (bapt. [at Marchington, co. Stafford‡] 29 Sept. 1613 ; bur. [at Longford, co. Derby] 16 Jan. 1659-60), legatee under Apollonia Browne's will 1653, who bequeathed her xxs. to buy a ring.   Issue :—

E.     1. Thomas Browne (eldest son and heir).   (*Vide infra*.)
       2. Edmund Browne of the parish of St. Stephen's, co. Hertford (bapt. [at Longford] 14 June 1638 ; d. s.p. 27 July 1716 ; bur. with his wife in the chancel of St. Stephen's Church, co. Hertford, M.I.   Will [unsigned] dated 20 Aug. 1712.   Attestatory affidavit made 5 Sept., pr. P.C.C. 6 Sept. 1716 by his sister Dorothy Musgrave, niece Sibyll Browne, and nephew Thomas Townley).   Arms (as on tombstone): BROWNE, *impaling*, . . . . a fess between three talbots' heads erased . . . . (for . . . .?). Mar. Elizabeth, dau. of . . . .   Mr. Jarman Burton mentioned in her husband's will as her kinsman (d. s.p. 20 May 1711 ; bur. in the chancel of St. Stephen's Church, M.I.).
       3. William Browne (bapt. [at Longford] 24 Oct. 1639 ; living unmar. 1662 ; mar. 1687; dead 1712 ?), legatee under his aunt Apollonia's will 1659, who bequeathed him £40.   Mar. . . . .
       4. Rupert Browne of Lyon's Inn 1667, of the parish of St. Gregory-by-St. Paul's, London, and of Greenford Magna,§ co. Middlesex (bapt.

---

   * Continued from p. 47.

   † Extract from the ' Mercurius Politicus,' a news sheet of January 1654: " Last week a new conspiracy was detected against his Highness [Oliver Cromwell] and the present Government. Five chests and two trunks of arms were discovered in one place in London which were to be conveyed into the country.   Divers persons are apprehended and in custody in the Tower. . . . . Divers arms were conveyed out of London into Derbyshire to the house of one Mr. Edward Vernon, second son of Sir Edward Vernon, who is brought up and committed also, and with him was brought up his uncle Mr. Vernon of Stockley Park, and one Mr. Brown of Hungry-Bentley in the county of Derby."   Until recent years Hungry-Bentley or Bentley Hall was in the parish of Longford, co. Derby.

   ‡ "1613.   Dorothia Vernon filia Edwardi Vernon bapt. fuit xxix d. Sept^s."—Register of Marchington.

   § " The other part [of the parish of Greenford Magna], containing 447 acres, was leased, a° 1640, to Sir Charles Gerrard, Bart.   The lease came afterwards successively to Rupert Browne and John Bridger ; the latter made it over to Mr. Way, who conveyed it to Richard Lateward, Esq. ; John Lateward, Esq., is the present lessee."—' Environs of London,' Rev. Daniel Lyssons, Lond., 1795, pp. 438–9.   This property is now (1885) in the possession of Thomas Dix Parker, Esq., of Greenford Green, Harrow.

[at Longford] 16 July 1644 [father's name incorrectly entered in Longford Register as "Edward"]; æt. 43 in 1687 ; d. intestate* 29 May 1711 ; bur. [with his wife at the right of the communion table in Greenford Magna Church, M.I.], and affidavit made as to burial in woollen† 6 June 1711. Letters of administration granted by P.C.C. to his dau. Sibyll, wife of his nephew Rupert Browne, 13 June 1711), Barrister-at-Law and Clerk in the Prerogative Court, London. Entered his pedigree at the Visitation of London by Sir Henry St. George, Clarencieux King of Arms, 30 June 1687, and signee of pedigree entered. Arms : BROWNE, *with a martlet for difference; impaling, Argent, three bugle-horns sable stringed vert* (for WYRLEY). Mar.‡ (Marriage Allegation filed at Vicar-General's Office 20 Jan. 1667) Sibyll, eldest dau. of Humfrey Wyrley of Hamstead Hall, parish of Handsworth, co. Stafford (of St. Clement Danes, London, at time of marriage), a Prothonotary of the Court of Common Pleas, by Sibyll his wife, dau. of Christopher Masters, Esq., of Westminster and Kent (d. 21 Dec., bur. [at the right of the communion table, Greenford Magna Church, M.I.] 26 Dec., affidavit made as to burial in woollen 30 Dec. 1710). Issue :—

**F.** 1. Humfrey Browne (dead 1687).
2. Rupert Browne (bur. [at St. Gregory-by-St. Paul's] 28 Oct. 1678).
3. Humfrey Browne (bapt. [at St. Gregory's] 31 July 1675 ; bur. there 2 June 1679).
4. Mark Browne (bapt. [at St. Gregory's] 5 Jan. 1677 ; bur. there 4 June 1681).
5. Charles Browne (b. 27 March, bapt. [at St. Gregory's] 30 March 1687 ; living 30 June 1687 ; dead 1711).
1. Sibyll (bur. [at St. Gregory's] 18 July 1674).
2. Sibyll (b. 30 May, bapt. [at St. Gregory's] 31 May 1685 ; desires to be buried at Perrivale [*alias* Little Greenford], co. Middlesex, in her unattested will, dated 5 July, attested codicil 9 Dec. 1752 ; affidavit as to attestation of will 9 Sept. 1767; pr. P.C.C. by Sibyll, eldest dau. and sole executrix), mar. her first-cousin Rupert Browne, Esq. **E.** (*Vide infra.*)
3. Knightley (b. 30 Nov., bapt. [at St. Gregory's] 5 Dec. 1680 ; bur. there 19 Dec. 1683).
4. Elizabeth (bur. [at St. Gregory's] 21 March 1679).

**E.** 5. George Browne of London (bapt. [at Longford] 2 Oct. 1645; living 1712), mar. Elizabeth .... (d. .....). Both legatees under his brother Edmund's will 1712, who bequeathed them £10. Issue :—

**F.** 1. Dorothy (bapt. [at St. Gregory's] 23 Aug. 1674; d. ....), legatee under her uncle Edmund Browne's will 1712, who bequeathed her £10 and a "silver tea or coffee pot."
2. Anne (bapt. [at St. Gregory's] 18 Aug. 1680; d. ....).
3. Elizabeth (d. ....), legatee under her uncle Edmund Browne's will 1712, who bequeathed her £50.
6. John Browne (living 1662 ; d. ....), mar. (before 1687) Mary .... Both legatees under his brother Edmund's will 1712, who bequeathed them £10 apiece.

* "Rupert Browne, gent., one of the Clerks of the Prerogative Office, died May 29, 1711 ; buried June 2 at Gaynsford [*sic*] in Middlesex."—'Le Neve's Obituary,' 1711 (p. 213).
† For particulars of this custom see Water's 'History of Parish Registers,' etc.
‡ In Shaw's 'Hist. of Staffordshire,' vol. ii., p. 116, a large engraving is given of the picturesque old home of the Wyrleys, called "Hamstead Hall ;" also a very long and accurate pedigree of the family. " 1667, 20 Jan. Rupert Browne of Lyon's Inn, Gent., Bach[r], about 23, and M[rs] Sybell Wyrley of S[t] Clement Danes, Sp[r], ab[t] 17 ; her father's consent; at S[t] Bartholomew the Great or Less."—Harl. Soc., vol. xxiii., 144.

7. Charles Browne (living 1659 ; dead unmar. 1687), legatee under his aunt Apollonia's will 1659, who bequeathed him £10.
8. Walter Browne (living 1659 ; bur. [at Longford] 19 April 1723), legatee under his aunt Apollonia's will 1659, who bequeathed him £10 ; legatee under his brother Thomas's will 1708, who bequeathed him an annuity of £10 out of the Hungry-Bentley estate ; legatee under his brother Edmund's will 1712, who bequeathed him £10.
9. Philip Browne (bapt. [at Longford] 27 May 1652 ; living 1662 ; dead 1687), legatee under his aunt Apollonia's will 1659, who bequeathed him £30.
10. Mark Browne (living unmar. 1662-87 ; dead 1712 ?).
11. Richard Browne (bapt. [at Longford] 12 May, bur. there 7 Sept. 1656).
12. Edward Browne (dead 1662).
13. Benjamin Browne (dead 1662).
1. Mary (bapt. [at Longford] 23 May 1637 ; living 1687), residing at Shredicote and legatee under Apollonia Browne's will 1653, who bequeathed her " the bedd shee usually lyeth upon with the boulster, pillow, the bed cloathes thereunto belonginge, one pair of course sheetes and pillow beere, and one duzzen of course napkins." Legatee under her aunt Apollonia's will 1659, who bequeathed her " one bed and blankets in her chamber, and one payre of flaxen sheets, two pillow beers, twelve napkyne, and all my best wearing clothes w^ch I have here in London," £2 and a life annuity of £6.
2. Apollonia (bapt. [at Longford] 19 Nov. 1640 ; living 1687).
3. Dorothy (bapt. [at Longford] 23 Dec. 1641 ; d. . . . .), legatee under her aunt Apollonia's will 1659, who bequeathed her £10 ; legatee and executrix under her uncle Edmund Browne's will 1712, who bequeathed her £30. Mar. (by licence [in St. Gregory-by-St. Paul's, London] 24 May 1664) George Musgrave,* Esq., of . . . . (d. . . . .).
4. Margaret (living 1652-1715), legatee under her aunt Apollonia's will 1659, who bequeathed her £10, and legatee under her brother Edmund Browne's will 1712, who bequeathed her £20 ; sole executrix of and proved her son Rupert Barnsley's will 1715. Mar. Peter Barnsley, Esq., of London and Alkmonton, parish of Longford, co. Derby (living 1715), third son of Charles Barnsley of Alkmonton (Captain of a troop of horse *temp.* Chas. I. Certified pedigree at Visitation of Derbyshire, 5 Aug. 1662), by his second wife Anne, dau. of William Langford, Esq., of Longford, co. Derby (*vide* also College of Arms, Vincent MS., C 34, fo. 5ᵃ ; Harl. MSS., 1596, fo. 172, 1147, fo. 170, and 6104, fo. 6ᵇ). Arms : *Sable, a cross between four roses barbed vert and seeded or, with mullet for difference,* BARNSLEY ; *impaling* BROWNE. Issue :—

F. 1. Rupert Barnsley of London, a Proctor of the Arches Court of Canterbury (bur. [at St. Gregory-by-St. Paul's] 19 April 1715. Unattested will dated 10 Dec. 1711 ; affidavit made as to attestation in P.C.C. by James Pinfold and William White ; pr. by his mother Margaret Browne [uxoris Petri Barnsley], sole executrix, 22 April 1718). Bequeathed £5 to William Knight, and £5 to Mr. John Windham and his wife " where I now lodge " in recognition of kindness received. Legatee under Edmund Browne's will 1712, who bequeathed him £10.

---

\* Extract from the Index to Wills, etc., at Somerset House :
  " 1662. Letters of Administration of—

      Musgrove  }
      oth'w'se  } George Middlesex."
      Musgrave  }
All further records of administration for that year are missing.

1. Isabell Barnsley (d. . . . .), legatee under Edmund Browne's will 1712, who bequeathed her £20.
2. Sarah Barnsley (bapt. [at Longford] 21 Dec. 1678 ; dead 1712 ?).

**E.** 5. Elizabeth (living 1659–1712), legatee under her aunt Apollonia's will 1659, who bequeathed her £10 ; legatee under her brother Thomas Browne's will 1708, who bequeathed her a farm, etc., in Alkmonton, co. Derby, for life ; and legatee under her brother Edmund Browne's will 1712, who bequeathed her £10.

**E. 𝕿𝖍𝖔𝖒𝖆𝖘 𝕭𝖗𝖔𝖜𝖓𝖊** (eldest son) of Hungry-Bentley, co. Derby (bur. [at Longford] 17 July 1708. Will dated 22 May 1708 ; pr. . . . . ?).* Entered as a student at Gray's Inn,† London, 23 May 1653. Legatee under his grandmother Apollonia Browne's will 1653, who bequeathed him "my great cheste in his father's custody and one greate gilte spoone that was given my sonne Thomas Browne deceased at his Christeninge ; " legatee under his aunt Apollonia's will 1659, who bequeathed him £20. Mar. ([in Brampton Church, co. Derby] 20 Oct. 1663) Grace, dau. and coh. of Anthony Crofts, Esq. (by his wife Eliza, who was bur. at Longford 19 April 1673), of Brampton, near Chesterfield, co. Derby (bur. [at Longford] 6 July 1690).

**F.** 1. Thomas Browne, eldest son. (*Vide infra.*)
2. Rupert Browne of the parish of St. Gregory-by-St. Paul's, London, and of Greenford Magna, co. Middlesex (bapt. [at Longford] 9 Jan. 1671 ; bur. [at Greenford Magna] 24 Jan. 1739-40. Will dated‡ 30 May 1711 ; pr. P.C.C. 20 March 1739-40 by Sibyll his wife, only person named and sole executrix). J.P. co. Middlesex 1716. Legatee under his father's will 1708, who entailed upon him the estate of Brampton, co. Derby, on payment of £500 to the ex'ors ; legatee under his uncle Edmund Browne's will 1712, who bequeathed him £20. Arms: BROWNE, and upon a shield of pretence, BROWNE, *with a martlet for difference.* Mar. Sibyll (first-cousin) only surviving dau. and heir of his uncle Rupert Browne, Esq., Barrister-at-Law, of St. Gregory-by-St. Paul's, and of Greenford Magna, co. Middlesex (b. 30 May, bapt. [at St. Gregory's] 31 May 1685 ; died 1767 ? Desired to be buried at Perrivale§ [*alias* Little Greenford], co. Middlesex, in her unattested will. Will dated 2 July 1751 ; attested codicil 9 Dec. 1752 ; attestatory affidavit made 9 Sept. 1767 ; pr. P.C.C. by Sibyll, eldest dau. and sole executrix). Administered her father's estate in 1711. Legatee and co-executrix under her uncle Edmund Browne's will 1712, who bequeathed her £120 ; sole executrix under her husband's will, which she proved 1740, and afterwards resided in the parish of St. Marylebone, London. Issue :—

**G.** 1. Rupert Browne (bapt. [at Greenford Magna] 18 March 1713 ;‖ dead 1751 ?).
2. William Frederick Browne (bapt. [at Greenford Magna] 20 May 1715 ; dead 1751 ?).
3. Crofts Browne (bapt. [at Greenford Magna] 25 May 1722 ; d. . . . .), eldest surviving son and legatee under his mother's will 1751, who bequeathed him £20. Arms : *Quarterly :* 1 *and* 4, BROWNE ; 2 *and* 3, BROWNE, *with a martlet for difference.*
1. Sibyll (bapt. [at Greenford Magna] 21 March 1711 ; bur. there 30 April, and affidavit made as to burial in woollen 6 May 1713), legatee under Edmund Browne's will 1712, who bequeathed her £100.

* A copy of this will was discovered with the title-deeds of the Bentley estate. It does not appear, after careful search, to have been proved at either Lichfield or London.
† "Thomas Browne, eldest son of Edmund B. of Hungry-Bentley, co. Derby, gen., 23 May 1653."—Register of Gray's Inn (fol. 1083).
‡ This will, made about the time of his marriage, contains only a few lines.
§ This register has been carefully searched, but no record of her burial occurs.
‖ A daughter, "Henrietta Dorothea," bapt. same month.

2. Henrietta Dorothea (bapt. [at Greenford Magna] 27 March 1713;
    bur. there 4 June, and affidavit made as to burial in woollen
    10 June 1713).
3. Sibyll (d. . . . .), legatee and sole executrix under her mother's will,
    which she pr. P.C.C. 1767, who bequeathed her the residue of
    personal estate.
4. Knightley (bapt. [at Greenford Magna] 28 Jan. 1720 ; d. . . . .),
    legatee under her mother's will 1751, who bequeathed her £20.
5. Matilda (d. . . . .), legatee under her mother's will 1751, who
    bequeathed her £20. Mar. . . . . Bristow (dead 1752 ?). Issue:—
  H.  1. Henry Bristow (d. . . . .), legatee under Sibyll Browne's will
        1751, who bequeathed him £20.
  F.  1. Grace (bur. [at Longford] 15 April 1684).

(*To be continued.*)

## Haines Wills.

RICHARD HAYNES of Waregrove, Berks, yeoman. Will dated 11 March 1566;
proved 14 Dec. 1566 by Wᵐ Grove, proctor for Anne the relict. (33 Crymes.)
To be burᵈ in Wargrove Church at my pews end. Poor of Wargrave 10s., of
Shepelake 10s., and of Sᵗ Giles, Reading, 10s. My house in Henton to my brother
Thomas Haynes for life, and after to Richᵈ Heyne, son of my brother Nicholas
Hayne. My sister Annys wife of my sᵈ brother Thomas. My brother John. My
brother Christofer. My brother Nicholas H. and his children. My brother Wᵐ
Haynes. Residue to my wife Anne, sole ex'trix. Wᵐ Grove and Wᵐ Millett,
overseers. My sister Christian Gunnell and her husb. and childⁿ. Wit., Alice
Alldworth, Wᵐ Castell, Bartellmew Benwell, etc.

CHRISTOPHER HAYNES of Arundell, Sussex, gent. Will dated 26 Nov. 1586;
proved 28 Nov. 1586 by Wᵐ Babham, proctor for Wⁿ Haynes the ex'or.
(60 Windsor.) My brother John Haynes, Esq., a nest of silver bowls, etc.
Bequests to John Vincent, John Clerk, Wᵐ Clerk, etc. Jasper Booker my wife's
kinsman. My cousin Moyses. My brother Nicholas Haynes, his dau. Alice
Haynes, and his son Richᵈ Haynes. To the wife of my brother Wᵐ Haynes a nest
of silver tonne cups, parcel gilt. To my wife Elizabeth a house in Arrundell. My
lands and ten'ts in Arundell to my brother William Haynes for life, remʳ to Richᵈ
Haynes, son of my brother Nicholas Haynes. Residue to my sᵈ brother Wᵐ Haynes,
sole ex'or. My friends William Lussher, gent., and Thoˢ Taylor the elder of
Arundell. Wit., Paul Hawkins, Wᵐ Woodward, Nicholas Hawes, Robert Banck-
worthe.

WILLIAM HAINES the elder, citizen and merchant taylor of London. Will
dated 5 Sept. 1590 ; adm'on 23 Sept. 1590 to his relict *Alice Haynes*. (60 Drury.)
To be burᵈ in the Church of the place where I die. All my goods, lands, and tent's
to my wife Alice for life. To the poor of Sᵗ Dunstan's in the East and *Allhallows
Barking, London*, to each parish £5 yearly for ever out of the tenement of which I
am the right owner, over against Sᵗ Dunstan's Church. After death of my wife
Alice my lands and tenemᵗˢ in Mark Lane and Seething Lane to be equally divided
between *my eldest son Benedict Haynes and my 2ᵈ son Wᵐ Haynes*. My da.
Elizabeth Sander £100. Elizᵗʰ Bybye 40s. for a gown. Wit., James Barckley,
Richard Jeffreys.

BENEDICT HAINES* of Hackney, co. Midd., gent. Will dated 28 Dec. 1609;
proved 8 Feb. 1609-10 by his son Henry Haynes. (Commissary Court of London,
1607-11, fo. 223.) My son Henry Haynes, sole ex'or. To my wife Christian

* Parish Register of Hackney, co. Midd.: " 1609-10, Jan. 2, Benedict Haynes, gent., burᵈ."

Haynes an annuity of £50. My son Edward Haines, and my dau'rs Elizabeth Haynes and Alice Haines the younger £150 each. My son-in-law Benedict Car £30. To my dau. Alice Barbor a ring of 40s. Humfrie Smith and Nicholas Leoman, overseers. Wit., Francis Columbell, scr., Humfrie Smith, Nicholas Leoman.

WILLIAM HEYNES of Chesington, co. Surrey, Esq. Will dated 26 Jan. 1610; proved 22 April 1611 by the ex'or. (30 Wood.) To be bur. in Chesington Church, and to the poor there 40s. I am a freeman of the City of London. By an Ind're of the 24th of this present January between me of the one part and Wm Campion of Layton, Essex, Esq., and Abraham Campion of London, Brewer, of the other part, I have assured to my wife in recompence of her jointure, all my manors, lands, and tent's in Chesington, Long Ditton, and Kingston, Surrey, for her life. To my da. Alice £500 at age of 21 or marriage. To my wife Anne all her jewels and apparel. To my mother Mris Alice Heynes 30 ounces of silver gilt plate. My friends Mr Arthur Bromfeild of Titchfeilde, co. Southamp., Esq., and Mr Henry Timberlake of London, Mercht, to be ex'ors, and to each £100. My friend Adryan Stoughton of the Inner Temple, Esq., and the aforesd Abraham Compion, overseers. My friend Mr Edwd Quinby of Titchfeld, esq., 53s. 4d. for a ring. Chidley Merricke my Clerk £6 13s. 4d. My apprentice Thos Cutts £10. Mary Robinson, wid., and her sister Elizth 40s. each. Mudwyn, wife of Wm Coxe, 40s. for a ring. Residue amongst my six childn, viz., my 2 sons Wm and Mathewe Heynes and my 4 dau'rs Alice Heynes, Jane Heynes, Anne Heynes, and Thomasine Heynes, at ages of 21, my wife to be Guardian. I desire that the Earl of Salisbury, Master of the Court of Wards, will allow my ex'ors to have the wardship of my son and heir, and that my friend the Earl of Southampton will assist in obtaining that permission, and I give to the sd Earl of Southampton my standing gilt cup made like a bunch of grapes. Wit., Ly. Wright, Tho. Watson, Edmond Baily, Will'm Styant.

ANNE HEYNES, late wife of William Heynes of Chissington, co. Surrey, Esq., decd. Will dated 4 May 1612; proved 14 May 1612 by Henry Tymberlake. (47 Fenner.) To be burd in Chissington Church, near my decd husband. To my eld. son Wm Heynes, who is well provided for, my best diamond ring, etc. To my son Mathew Heynes a gilt bason and ewer at age of 21 or marriage. To my eld. da. Allce Heynes so much as (with her father's legacy) will make up £1000 at age of 21 or marriage. My sister Barbary Lucus, widow, £20, etc. My sister Baker, widow, £20. Bequests to servants. To my mother Alice Heynes 10 ounces of plate. Residue between my son Mathew Heynes and my dau'rs Jane, Agnes (sic), and Thomasine Heynes, equally, at ages of 21 or marriage. My friend Henry Tymberlake of London, gent., sole ex'or. Wit., Henry Smith, Margett Tymberlake.

HENRY HEYNES of Hackney, co. Midd., gent. Will dated 26 Dec. 1627; adm'on 16 Feb. 1628 to his sister Elizabeth Haynes, the ex'ors renouncing. (19 Ridley.) To my dau. Eliz. Heynes £300, my eld. son Thos Heynes £200, to my 3 younger sons and my 3 younger dau'rs, Henry, Benedick, and Wm Heynes, and Amy, Mary, and Anne Heynes, £100 each, the sd legacies to be paid to my sd children at ages of 21, etc. My friends Thos Deering and Richd Hotchkins 50s. each, and to my servt Robt Cowley 40s. My capital mess. or mansion house commonly called the Wick in par. of Hackney, my mess., ten't, and lands called Coome in par. of Croydon, Surrey, and all other lands in the parishes of Hackney and Stebunheth al's Stepney, Midd., to be sold by my ex'ors, and with the proceeds to pay my debts, legacies, etc., and the residue to be divided equally amongst my aforesd children. My cousin Tobye Wood, esq., and my friend Geo. Robyns, cit. and vintner of London, ex'ors. My friends Sir Geo. Reynell, Knt., and Thos Dudson, gent., overseers, and to each 40s. for rings. Wit., Raphe Cardsey, Robt Jewell, Robt Cowley, John Godson, Thos Deeringe, Richd Hotchkins.

THOMAS HAYNES of Hackney, gent., now a prisoner in the King's Bench. Will dated 8 Sept. 1641; proved 8 Jan. 1651-2 by the ex'ors. (8 Bowyer.) Lands of great value were left to me by my grandfather Benedict Haines and my father Henry Haines, who died before I became 21. My wardship was procured by John Baylie, esq., whose lands adjoined mine at Hackney, and I have been kept in prison by the s$^d$ Baylie, who wishes to deprive me of my estate, I having sealed a conveyance of my s$^d$ lands under threats.   My sister Mary and her husband Tho$^s$ Baynham to be ex'ors, and to recover by lawful means from the s$^d$ Baylie my said lands called Wick lands, of which I never made any conveyance but what was forced from me being in durance.   Samuel Brasey and his wife.   Wit., George Lyon, Lawr. Horspoole, Edward Gyll.

# Dering Bookplates.

Facsimile of the Bookplate of Sir Edward Dering of Surrenden Dering copied from an original impression belonging to Dr. Haslewood, Vicar of Chislet, Kent. A copy of this plate is to be found among the Harleian MSS. Brit. Mus. 1432, fo. 279, and another belongs to the Rev. Francis Haslewood of St. Matthew's, Ipswich. This plate is even of greater rarity than the Dering Bookplate, a facsimile of which was given in Vol. I., p. 285 (Second Series).

The Bookplate of Deborah Lady Dering is perhaps even more scarce than the foregoing.   It is reproduced from the fine impression belonging to Dr. Haslewood of Chislet.

Lady Deborah Dering was the only daughter of John Winchester of Nethersole, co. Kent, and married 1 Jan. 1765, at Womenswold, Sir Edward Dering, M.P. for New Romney.   She died 20 and was buried 27 March 1818, aged 73, at Pluckley. Her will, dated 1 Nov. 1817, was proved 8 April 1818 (168 Cresswell).

The arms of Winchester are, Argent, a vine growing out of the base leaved and fructed, between two popinjays endorsed feeding upon a cluster of grapes, all proper.

Charlotte, daughter of Sir Edward Dering by Lady Deborah his wife, married at Lambeth Palace, 13 Dec. 1803, Rev. Phillips Monypenny, Vicar of Hadlow, Kent (see his Bookplate).   He died 4 Jan. 1841, aged 78, and she, 12 Nov. 1836, æt. 64, both being buried in Rolvenden Church.

FRANCIS HASLEWOOD, F.S.A.

# INSCRIPTIONS ON COFFINS IN "RAGLEY OLD VAULT," ARROW CHURCH, WARWICKSHIRE.*

ENCLOSED VAULT AT S.E. CORNER OF "RAGLEY OLD VAULT."

There is a brass plate upon the west wall of this vault with the following inscription upon it:

Here Lies
That Excellent Man
Lord Hugh Seymour
Vice Admiral of the Blue
Who having died
in the West Indies
of the Yellow fever
Posterity is cautioned
at no future period
of time
however distant
to bring into activity
So baneful a disease
By
Disturbing what is here enclosed
12$^{th}$ September 1801.

*Burial Register.*—1801.   *Nov.* 22.   *Lord Hugh Seymour.*

* Continued from p. 41.

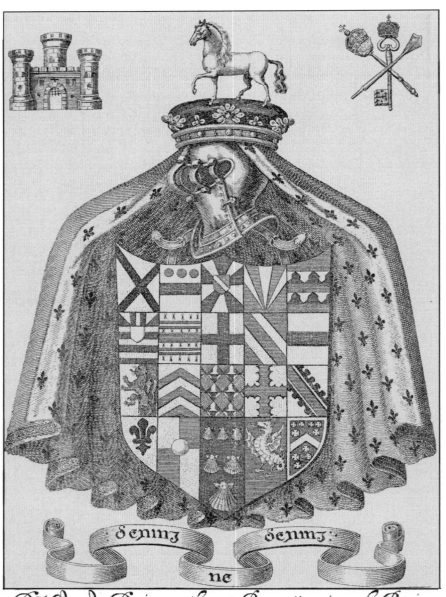

Dñs Edoardus Dering miles et Baronettus, in aula Regia
Priuatis Cameris adiuratus Locum-tenens in officio
Conestabularia Castri Douor, Vice-Custos Pro-Cancel=
iarius atq3 Hygo-Thalaßiarcha Quinq3 Portuum. etc.
1630.

*D. Dering*

TEMPERAT ÆQUOR.

*Rev. Phillips Monypenny.*

ENCLOSED VAULT AT N.W. CORNER OF "RAGLEY OLD VAULT."

Up to the present time I have been unable to learn definitely whose remains lie within this vault, but from information obtained I am inclined to believe they are those of the Honourable Harriet Conway, whose burial register runs thus :

1771. May 14. Hon. Harriet Conway (from Chichester).

REGISTERS OF BURIAL OF MEMBERS OF THE RAGLEY FAMILY WHO WERE BURIED AT ARROW, BUT WHOSE RESTING-PLACES CANNOT BE IDENTIFIED.

1588. November 6. The Lady Elinor Conway wife unto the right worshipfull S$^r$ John Conway K.
1603. December 1. The right worshipfull S$^r$ John Conway Knight.
1604. Jan. 30. Dennis Conway gent.
1609. Octob$^r$ 20. m$^r$ John Conway gent.
1612. March 5$^{th}$. The Ladye Dorothy Conway wife to the Right worshipfull S$^r$ Edward Conwaye.
1630. February the 12$^{th}$. Edward Lord Viscount Conway.
1630. March the 18$^{th}$. Alice Conway.
1715. ffebr : 26 was Buried the R$^t$ Hono$^{ble}$ Jane Lady Conway second wife to the R$^t$ Hono$^{ble}$ ffrancis L$^d$ Conway Baron of Ragley.
The fifty shillings forfeiture paid March y$^e$ 9$^{th}$ & distributed according to y$^e$ Act amongst the Poor of the p'ish p. John Green Overseer.
1716. Apr. 8 was Buried Edward the Son of the R$^t$ Hono$^{ble}$ ffrancis L$^d$ Conway Baron of Ragley & Jane his Lady.
Apr. 23 was paid the fifty shillings forfeiture for Edward the son of the R$^t$ Hono$^{ble}$ ffrancis L$^d$ Conway, being Buried not according to the Act for Burying in Woollen to be distributed among y$^e$ poor p. by John Smyth Overseer.

*Burial.* June 16, 1655. The Lord Viscount Conway at Lyons in ffrance.

Within the vault are deposited the remains of the Rev. Gavin Millar, to whose memory the tablet in the church was erected, bearing the following inscription :

To the Memory of
the Rev$^d$ Gavin Millar
late Rector of Binton in this Neighbourhood
this Monument is erected as the only mark of Gratitude
I now am enabled to shew for his uniform Friendship &
unremitted attention in the Education of my Son.
The Remains of this valuable Man
are deposited in the Vault, which is destined
hereafter to receive my own
HERTFORD.
26$^{th}$ November 1794.

A COPY OF ENTRIES IN ARROW PARISH CHURCH REGISTERS RELATING TO RAGLEY'S NOBLE FAMILIES.

*Christeninge.*

1593. Feb. 15$^{th}$ John Conway the sonne of the right worshipfull Edward Conway gent.
1594. Aug. 10$^{th}$ Edward Conway the sonne of the right worshipfull Edward Conway gent.

# 58     MISCELLANEA GENEALOGICA ET HERALDICA.

1622. Novemb$^r$ y$^e$ 15$^{th}$ John the sonne of S$^r$ Edward Conway Knight borne
Octob$^r$ y$^e$ 18$^{th}$ and baptized Novemb$^r$ the 15$^{th}$ at Littlecot 1622.
1707. March 8 was baptized Katharine the Daughter of the R$^t$ Hono$^{ble}$ ffrancis
Lord Conway and the Lady Mary his Consort.
vid Register de Blockley in Comtu. Wigorn.
1714. Nov. 2 was baptized Jane the Daughter of the R$^t$ Hon$^{ble}$ ffrancis L$^d$ Conway
& Jane his Lady.
1715. ffebr. 23 was Baptized at Sandiwell in the p'ish Dowdeswell in the County
of Gloucester Edward the Son of the R$^t$ Hono$^{ble}$ ffrancis L$^d$ Conway
& Jane his Lady.
vid Regist de Dowdeswell
p. me B. E. GABFIELD minister
de Charleton-Abbots.
1718. July 5 was Born and Aug. 2 was Baptized at Chelsea neer London ffrancis
the Son of the Right Hono$^{ble}$ ffrancis L$^d$ Conway Baron of Ragley &
Charlotte his Lady. vid Registr. *Ibid.*
1719. Aug$^t$ 12 was baptized at Ragley Henry the son of the R$^t$ Hon$^{ble}$ Francis
Lord Conway and Charlotte His Lady.

*Weddinge.*

1613. August 4$^{th}$ Willia$^m$ Wellam Esquire to m$^{ris}$ ffrancis Conway daughter of S$^r$
Edward Conway.
Anno Domini 1654. Septem. the 4. George Rawdon of Rawdon in the parrish of
Guisley and County of Yorke Esquier And m$^{tris}$ Dorothy Conway daughter
to the Right hono$^{ble}$ Lord Viscount Conway and Cilultar of Ragly in the
parrish of Arrow and Countie of Warwicke were married by me
MATH: BRIDGES.

---

EXTRACT FROM 'THE STRATFORD-ON-AVON HERALD' FOR FRIDAY, 29 NOV. 1861.

"SACRILEGE AT ARROW.—On Sunday morning, the 17th inst., when Mr. Ingram, parish
clerk of Arrow, was about to enter the church previous to the morning service, he discovered
that the burial vault of the ancient family of Conway, now represented by the Most Noble the
Marquis of Hertford, had been sacrilegiously entered by burglars, and the coffins of the noble
dead despoiled of a portion of their ornaments, and otherwise injured and defaced. The family
vault of the Conways is of considerable extent, and is situated at the east end of the church,
immediately under the chancel and communion table. The legitimate entrance to this receptacle
of the dead is within the church, which, however, is closed up by masonry, and is only opened for
the purpose of its receiving a fresh occupant ; but on the outside of the east wall of the church
is an aperture of an oval shape, which, however, is secured by transverse iron bars, within which
is a latticework of strong wire, in addition to which, projecting from the wall of the church, is
a massive semi-circular iron railing of above five feet in height, the top of which is again secured
by horizontal bars of iron of considerable thickness. Notwithstanding all these impediments,
the marauders managed to effect an entrance. Two bars of the outside railing were, by the
exertion of considerable force, so bent as to enable a man to pass through, thus giving them
access to the aperture in the wall of the church. Across this opening, in a horizontal direction,
was a strong bar of iron, the two ends of which were let into and firmly fixed in the wall ; across
this were three iron bars placed perpendicularly, and the depredators contrived to break off and
force out the upper part of the central perpendicular bar above mentioned, and by that means
obtained an entrance to the vault. To do this, very great force must have been used. The stone-
work on the left side, though a foot in thickness, has been actually split, apparently by a crow-
bar being placed against it in forcing out the iron bar in the centre of the opening, which is but
small, and only sufficient to admit a man of moderate dimensions. The thieves were probably
incited to these sacrilegious proceedings by the expectation that the coronets placed upon the
coffins, together with the handles and other ornaments, were of the precious metals. The coffins
and coronets were distinctly visible in the daytime from the churchyard ; and when the sun was
shining upon them, presented a remarkably glittering appearance. The rascals appear to have
tested the coffin plates and handles, and finding that 'all that glitters is not gold,' and that they
were for the most part only plated, did not think them worth carrying away. It was at first
supposed that only some of the coronets were missing, but the vault being again examined, it was
found that not only five coronets but two coffin plates have been carried away."

## SOME UNINDEXED WILLS AT LINCOLN.

The following Wills have recently been found in the Bishop's Registry at
Lincoln, amongst a collection of Marriage and Administration Bonds, and as they
almost all relate to a period for which Lincoln is comparatively destitute of records,
(those in actual use at the time of Cromwell's visit having apparently been destroyed,)
this list will no doubt be of interest, especially as most of these Wills are not found
in the Indexes of the Probate Registry.

4 *Minster Yard, Lincoln.*                                                    A. G.

Abell, Richard, Woolstrop, 1638.
Andrew, Michael, 1638.
Appleby, Robert, N. Somercotes, 1638.
Ayre, Thomas, Wiberton, 1640.
Backe, Thomas, Deeping, 1640.
Baines, William, Skellingthorpe, 1638.
Baker, Robert, Weston, 1638.
Baldrick, James, Gayton, 1640.
Banbery, Richard, 1640.
Barnes, John, St. Botulph, 1638.
Beech, James, Stallingbro', 1640.
Beetson, John, Swineshead, 1638.
Bell, Henry, Lincoln, 1640.
Blankes, John, Gedney Hill, 1638.
Blythe, John, Deeping St. James, 1640.
Bonfray, John, Burgh le Marsh, 1638.
Booth, Henry, Bourne, 1640.
Boston, Robert, Welburne, 1640 ?
Boulton, Thomas, Stickford, 1638.
Bouthe, Robert, Quadring, 1638.
Brittaine, Tho⁸, Donington, 1638.
Brookes, Martyn, Wrangle, 1640.
Broughton, Ann, Kirton Holland, 1639.
Browne, Robert, Boston, 1638.
„      John, Long Bennington, 1638.
„      Richard, Whaplode Drove, 1639.
Cammack, Richard, Grantham, 1638.
Carter, Lionel, Donington, 1638.
Cassell, John, Billingay, 1640.
Cawdrey, Thomas, M.D., 1640.
Cheales, Robert, 1638.
Cherie, George, Stickney, 1638.
Chissell, John, Hatton, 1638.
Clapton, Roger, Uffington, 1638.
Clarke, Rich⁴, Hagworthingham, 1638.
Clesby, Valentine, Steeping, 1640.
Colborne, Lawrence, Stickford, 1638.
Coles, Daniel, Hougham, 1638.
Conte, John (proved at Grantham), 1639.
Cooper, Ann, Croyland, 1640.
Cowper, William, Butterwick, 1640.
Coxall, William, 1638.
Coy, Richard, 1638.
Cressey, Frances, Stickford, 1638.
Crowder, John, Holbeach, 1640.
Dale, Wᵐ, rector of Hagworthingham, 1638.
Dales, Henry, Sutterton, 1640.
Day, Michael, Long Bennington, 1595.
Dickenson, Wᵐ, Donington, 1639.
Dobbs, Elizabeth, Welby, 1638.
Dowdeswell, Tho⁸, Gᵗ Limber, 1638.
Drewry, William, Ulceby, 1638.
Eldred, . . . ., Stamford, 1638.
„      George, Thurlby, 1640.
Farrowe, John, Nettleton, 1638.
Faunt, William, E. Barkwith, 1638.
Fellowes, James, Mᵏᵗ Deeping, 1638.
Fisher, Ann, Boston, 1636.

Fossit, Geo., Mᵏᵗ Deeping, 1638.
Foster, Ann, Horsington, 1640.
Fridle, Elizᵗʰ, N. Thoresby, 1640.
Funtance (?), Richard, 1640.
Gardiner, Solomon, Gᵗ Grimsby, 1639.
Gibson, Christʳ, S. Ferriby, 1638.
„      Robert, Greatford, 1638.
Gilbert, Anne, Claypole, 1638.
Gladell, Frances, Fulstow, 1652.
Gleges, Margery, Kirton, 1639.
Goodson, Anne, Grantham, 1638.
Gresswell, Tho⁸, Leasingham, 1640.
Guterson, Geo., Friskney, 1640.
Guy, Ralph, Boston, 1639.
Gyles, Mary, Swineshead, 1638.
Hall, Edmund, Boston, 1640.
Hanson, John, N. Stoke, 1638.
Hardwick, Robert, 1640.
Harle, Richard, Benniworth, 1640.
Harrison, Thomas, 1638.
Hastings, John, Hannay, 1638.
Haynton, John, Lincoln, 1639.
Hoggerston, Tho⁸, Osbornby, 1640.
Hogsum, Richard, Sibsey, 1638.
Horby, Richard, clerk, Wiberton, 1638.
Horneby, Christopher, 1640.
Hornewould, John, 1638.
Houghton, Samuel, Lincoln, 1632.
Hoult, Edee, Barrowby, 1638.
Hudson, George, Winthorpe, 1640.
„      Zachariah, Deeping, 1640.
Hutchinson, Edward, Fenton, 1638.
„      Henry, Wainfleet, 1639.
Jessup, Ellen, N. Willingham, 1638.
Keightley, Ellen, 1640.
Kelsey, William, Frieston, 1638.
Kidder, Hugh, Lissington, 1638.
Kighley, Anne, Marsh Chapel, 1640.
King, Richard, Stickney, 1638.
„      William, senʳ, Wootton, 1640.
Knight, Elizᵗʰ, Bassingham, 1640.
Laine, Francis, Brandon, 1640.
Lampson, William, Bardney, 1638.
Langham, . . . ., 1638.
Laurington, Rob., Cawthorpe, 1638.
Laxton, William, Barholme, 1638.
Longcaster, Robert Mumby, 1638.
Love, Robert, Pinchbeck, 1639.
Niccolls, Thomas, Swinstead, 1640.
Normanton, John, Baston, 1638.
Osbourne, William, 1638.
Pallmer, John, Quadring, 1638.
Pany, Edward, Deeping Sᵗ James, 1640.
Pateman, Christʳ, Boothby Paynell (?), 1638.
Patman, Richard, Bennington, 1638.
Pearson, Edward, Aunsby, 1638.
„      John, Burwell, 1638.
„      Nicholas, Tealby, 1640.

Pennell, Jane, Thornton, 1640.
Phillips, Anthony, 1638.
Plummer, Nichˢ, Hagworthingham, 1640.
Portwood, William, Sutterton, 1640.
Priste, Robert, Welby, 1591.
Procter, Elizᵗʰ, Springthorpe, 1588.
Pryor, Thomas, Swinstead, 1638.
Randes, John, Fleete, 1640.
Rankine, John, Lower Toynton, 1640.
Raven, Thomas, Edenham, 1640.
Rayneton, Thoˢ, Washingbro', 1638.
Read, Humphrey, Fleet, 1639.
Repingale, James, 1638.
Richardson, Nathaniel, Gretford, 1639.
Robin, James, 1638.
Robson, Christʳ, Ruskington, 1638.
Sanderson, Robert, Stallingbro', 1640.
Sapcote, Eleanor, 1638.
Saunders, Zachary, Bourne, 1640.
Sawell, Matthew, Welby, 1638.
Sawer, Hugh, Barton on Humber, 1638.
Seshens, Isabell, Foston, 1638.
Sharpe, Thomas, Swineshead, 1639.
Sharpley, Robert, Langtoft, 1638.
Sharprey, John, Gretford, 1638.
Shepley, Thomas, Frisby, 1638.
Shepperd, Robert, Quadring, 1640.
Sicker, Geo., Brant Broughton, 1640.
Simkin, Jane, Croyland, 1640.
Skelton, Thomas, 1640.
Smeeting, Edward, Boston, 1640.
Smith, Christʳ, Audby, gent., 1636.
„   Clement, Skinnand, widow, 1640.
„   Edward, vicar of Saxelby, 1580.
„   Henry, Boston, 1638.

Smith, Joseph, Kirton Holland, 1638.
„   Robert, Bennington, 1640.
Smithson, William, Nettleton, 1638.
Somerby, Richard, Bytham, 1640.
Starke, Robert, Fotherby, 1638.
Stevens, William, 1638.
Stevenson, Hector, Killingholme, 1695.
Stockins, Robert, Steeping, 1638.
Sutton, William, Spalding, 1640.
Swanne, Barbara, Benniworth, 1638.
Symson, William, Wainfleet, 1560.
Taylor, William, Gᵗ Coates, 1638.
Thewe, Edward, Ashby Puerorum, 1652.
Thurlan, Richard, W. Keale, 1639.
Tomson, Hugh, Itterby in Clee, 1640.
Topliche, John, Donington, 1588.
Waring, William, Spalding, 1638.
Waterfall, Robert, Thurlby, 1640.
Watson, Eustace, Eagle, 1638.
„   Matthew, 1638.
Welberrie, George, Burgh, 1638.
Whytt, William, Little Hale, 1638.
Wildman, William, Edenham, 1640.
Wilkinson, John, Marton, 1640.
Williams, William, clᵏ, Aswarby, 1638.
Willson, Thomas, Leverton, 1638.
Wilson, Jacob, S. Somercotes, 1640.
Winge, Anthony, Braceby, 1640.
Winsloe, Thoˢ, Stapleford, co. Leic., 1638.
Wright, Edmund, Metheringham, 1640.
„   Edward, Sibsey, 1638.
„   John, Wiberton, 1639.
„   Richard, Stickney, 1638.
„   William, Stallingbro', 1638.
Write, John, Surfleet, 1640.

---

# Dalison Notes.*

Placita coram Domino Rege a die Sancti Michaelis anno xliv° incipiente xlv°. Suffolk.

Anglia que fuit uxor Georgii de Badingham appellat Willielmum de Alenzun de morte ipsius Georgii viri sui, etc. Et Willielmus venit et dicit quod Clericus est quod non vult hic inde respondere, etc. Et dictum est ei quod in foro ecclesiastico secundum libertatem ecclesie plenam et celerem justiciam ei exhibeat.

Coram Rege Roll, Mich. 44, 45 Hen. 3, Roll 3, A.D. 1260.

---

[Placita de Juratis et Assisis 56 Hen. 3, A.D. 1271-2.]

Assisa venit recognitura si Willielmus Sakespee, pater Alani Sakespee, fuit seisitus in dominico suo ut de feodo de uno tofto, cum pertinenciis, in Olypseby, die quo, etc. Et si, etc., quod Johannes de Alazun et Matillis uxor ejus tenent. Et ipsi non venerunt. Et resummoniti, etc. Ideo capiatur assisa versus eos per defaltam.

Juratores dicunt super sacramentum suum quod predictus Willielmus, etc., obiit seisitus de predicto tenemento in dominico suo ut de feodo, etc. Et quod predictus Alanus propinquior heres ejus est. Et ideo consideratum est quod predictus Alanus recuperet seisinam suam, etc. Et Johannes et Matillis in misericordia. Et quia juratores testantur quod predicti Johannes et Matillis sunt capitales domini feodi illius. Ideo satisfacient ei de dampnis suis, etc.

Assize Roll, Lincoln, M-3-13 2, m. 24,

* Continued from p. 43.

Adhuc de Juratis et Assisis [56 Hen. 3, A.D. 1271-2].

Johannes filius Ricardi de Alenzun summonitus fuit ad respondendum Petro de Alenzun de placito quod teneat ei convencionem de quatuor bovatis terre et quatuor acris prati, cum pertinentiis, in Fulneteby, etc.
Et Johannes venit et concordati sunt, etc.

Assize Roll, Lincoln, M-3-13 2, m. 31.

Suffolk.
Nichola que fuit uxor Willielmi de Alezun dat dimidiam marcam pro uno brevi ad terminum habendo. Et mandatum est Vicecomiti Suffolk.

Fine Roll, 56 Hen. 3, m. 4 [alias 3], A.D. 1271-1272.

Wapentacium de Walescrofte.
Item dicunt quod Ricardus de Houton tenet in Houton unam carucatam terre de Johanne de Alacon et uxore sua et est illa terra de hereditate uxoris predicte, per servicium militare et valet per annum—xxxs. ; et dictus Johannes et uxor ejus tenuerunt illam de Comite Cornubye per medium, et Comes de R[ege] in capite, quo servicio et a quo tempore et quo waranto dicunt quod nessciunt.

Hundred Roll, Lincoln, p. 360.

Wapentachium de Aslachon in Lindesey.
[Juratores] dicunt quod Simon West appellatus per Willielmum Dalazun probatorem dedit, etc., Vicecomiti—xls., etc.

Hundred Roll, Lincoln, Vol. I., p. 379.

Wapent' de Wraghou.
Ricardus de Alencun tenet in eadem et Belethorp feodum dimidii militis de Willielmo de Ros et idem Willielmus ut supra [de Domino Rege in capite].

Testa de Nevill, p. 331.

Lincoln.
Feoda Episcopi Lincoln'.
Ricardus Alencun et Alicia de Nevill tenent iiij^{tam} partem unius feodi militis in Refam.

Testa de Nevill, p. 304.

Lincoln.
Jollanus de Nevill et Willielmus De Baill', collectores, reddunt compotum de eodem auxilio [Domino Regi ad maritandum sororem suam Romano Imperatori] assiso in Comitatu Lincoln in Lindesey.
Iidem reddunt compotum de xvj li. receptis per manus Ricardi de Alecon de feodo Cecilie de Cruequer que heres Alexander de Nevill tenet, etc.

Testa de Nevill, p. 351 (578).

Suffolk.
De auxilio ad sororem Regis maritandam.
Herebertus de Alenzun, Johannes filius Roberti et Ricardus de Braham, collectores in hoc Comitatu non reddiderunt compotum. Ideo, etc., ut supra.

Testa de Nevill, p. 413 (862).

Lincoln.
Feoda Willielmi de Roys.
Ricardus de Alencuy, Willielmus Burde't tenent dimidium feodum in Fulnethby et Ellethorp.

Testa de Nevill, p. 310 (409).

# Darwin Pedigree—PEDIGREE B. (*Vide* p. 17.)

Erasmus Darwin.=Elizabeth Collier.

Edward Darwin of Mackworth. In the 3rd Dragoons. Born 31 Jan. 1782. Died 30 July 1829. Bur. at Breadsall, near Derby; unmarried.

Sir Francis Sacheverel Darwin, Knight, of Breadsall Priory, co. Derby, and sometime of Enmmanuel College, Cambridge. In the Commission of the Peace, and Deputy Lieutenant, Born 17 June 1786. Died 6 Nov. 1869. Bur. at Breadsall, near Derby.

=Jane Harriett, youngest dau. of John Ryle of Park House, Macclesfield (descended from the Ryles or Royles of Royle, co. Lancaster). Born 11 Dec.1794. Mar. 16 Dec. 1815 at St. George, Hanover Square. Died . . April 1866. Bur. at Breadsall, near Derby.

Rev. John Darwin, Rector of Elston aforesaid. Born 5 Sept. 1787. Died 13 Nov. 1818. Bur. at Elston; unmarried.

Henry Darwin. Born 10 April 1789. Died 25 April 1790. Buried at Radbourne, co. Derby.

Signature of Francis S. Darwin to a letter, dated "Mackworth, 30th July 1829," addressed to "Dr. Darwin, Shrewsbury."

Reginald Darwin of Fern, near Buxton, co. Derby. In the Commission of the Peace. Born 4 April 1818.

=Mary Anne, dau. of Charles Rogers Sanders of Exeter, co. Devon, Banker. Mar. 10 May 1843.

Edward=Harriet, dau. Levett of Francis Darwin of Jessopp of Buxton, Derby. Mar. co. Derby. 11 April Born 1850. 12 April 1821.

John Robert Darwin. Born 29 March 1835.

Mary Jane.=Charles Carill Born 12 Feb. Worsley of 1817. Mar. Platt Hall, co. 14 Jan. 1840. Lanc., and Died in 1872. Winster, co. Derby, Esq. Bapt. at Platt Chapel 12 May 1800. Died at Platt 14 Aug. 1864.

Elizabeth.=Nicolas, eldest son of Born 13 Feb. Acton Tindal of the 1857. Mar. Manor House, Ayles-24 May 1875. bury, who assumed names and arms of Carill Worsley by Royal Licence in 1878.

Signature of Reginald Darwin, Esq.

Sacheverel Charles Darwin, Captain R.N. Born 5 March 1844.

Mary Clementia. Born 3 Nov. 1845. Died 2 June 1848.

A son. Born 1847. Died in 1849.

Charles Nicolas Carill Worsley. Born 20 Aug. 1876. Died 21 July 1877.

John Acton Carill Worsley. Born 20 July 1877. 1877.

Acton Carill Worsley. Born 9 Sept. 1878.

Ralph Carill Worsley. Born 27 Dec. 1881.

Clementia. Born 27 May 1884.

B

A

B

Georgiana Elizabeth. = Rev. B. Swift of Southport, co. Lancaster.
Born 12 Aug. 1823.

Violetta Harriot. Born 5 March 1826. Died 9 Jan. 1880.

Ann Eliza Thomasine. Born 2 June 1828.

Millicent Susan. = Rev. H. Oldershaw of Lichfield, co. Stafford. Born 26 March 1833.

Francis Darwin Swift. Born at Southport, Sept. 1864; bapt. at St. James's, Southport.

Benjamin Swift. Born at Southport Oct. 1866; bapt. at St. James's, Southport.

Millicent Evelyn. Born 4 Feb. 1862.

Henrietta Constance. Born 29 Dec. 1863.

Frances Amy. Born 6 Aug. 1866.

All born at Lichfield, and bapt. at St. Mary's, Lichfield.

1st, Augusta Matilda, only dau. of Charles Champion, Esq., of Beaumont Chase. Mar. 3 Feb. 1831. = Edward Woollett Wilmot, J.P., of Chaddesden, co. Derby (sixth son of Sir Robert Wilmot, Bart., of Chaddesden). Born 1808. Died 25 June 1864. Bur. at Burbage, near Buxton. = 2ndly, Emma Elizabeth. Born 27 Feb. 1820. Mar. 13 Jan. 1842 at Darley Dale, Derbyshire.

1st, Rev. Gustavus Barton of Congleton, co. Chester, Mar. 23 Jan. 1845. Died 2 June 1846; buried at Exeter. = Frances Sarah. Born 19 July 1822. Died 23 Oct. 1881. Bur. Oct. 1881 at Breadsall, Derbyshire. = 2ndly, Marcus Huish of Castle Donington, co. Leicester. Born 9 July 1815. Mar. 15 Sept. 1849. Bur. 26 1849. Died 9 Feb. 1868. Bur. 15 Feb. 1868 at Breadsall.

Emma Maria. = Godfrey Franceys Meynell, Esq., of Meynell Langley, co. Derby. Born 1843. Mar. 11 Oct. 1866 at Chaddesden.

Frances Jane.

Reginald Mead Wilmot. Born 15 May 1862.

Lucy Augusta. Born 11 Dec. 1831. Married April 1861 C. P. Sculsby, Esq., Ob. s.p. of Buxton. Ob. s.p. 1854.

Robert Charles Wilmot. Born 11 Jan. 1834. Mar. Elizabeth, da. of Dr. Robertson of Buxton. Ob. s.p. May 1866.

Edmund Wilmot. Born 11 June 1836.

Rev. Darwin Wilmot. Born 14 Oct. 1845 at Worksop. M.A. Magdalen College, Oxford. Head Master Macclesfield Grammar School. Chaplain 5th C.R.V. = Louisa Lilla, dau. of Rev. Charles Bickmore, D.D., Mar. 3 Oct. 1876 at Leamington.

Woollett Wilmot, Lieut. R.M. Born 10 April 1847. Died 31 July 1879. Bur. at Malta.

Cicely. Born 21 Dec. 1879. Bapt. 1 Feb. 1880 at St. Michael's, Macclesfield.

Dorothy. Born 16 March 1878. Baptized 24 April 1878 at St. Michael's, Macclesfield.

Sacheverel Darwin Wilmot. Born 22 Feb. 1885. Bapt. 8 April 1885 at St. Michael's, Macclesfield.

Caroline Eliza. = Archibald William, son of William Macfarlane, Esq. Born 14 Sept. 1855; bapt. at Castle Donington. Married 18 Feb. 1886.

Frances Violetta Darwin. Born 14 April 1858; bapt. at Castle Donington.

Edward Darwin Wilmot. Born 19 March 1882. Bapt. 23 April 1882 at St. Michael's, Macclesfield.

Florence. Born 5 Oct. 1853; bapt. at Castle Donington. Married Jan. 1880 at Smalley, co. Derby. = William Wavell, Esq., son of Major-General Wavell, F.R.S., of London.

Frances Darwin Huish. Born 19 June 1850; bapt. at Castle Donington, Leicestershire.

Frances Gwendoline. Born 30 Dec. 1881.

A

A

Samuel Tertius Galton=Frances Anne Violetta. of Duddeston House, co. Warwick. Born 23 March 1783 in Birmingham. Bapt. at Radbourne, co. Derby. J.P. and D.L. for co. Warwick. Died 23 Oct. 1844 at St. Leonard's. Bur. 30 Oct. following in Claverdon Churchyard, co. Warwick. M.I.

Frances Anne Violetta. Born at Radbourne, co. Derby, 23 April 1783. Bapt. at Radbourne. Mar. 30 March 1807 at Breadsall. Died 12 Feb. 1874 at Bertie Terrace, Leamington. Buried 18 Feb. following at Claverdon, co. Warwick. M.I.

Signature of Mrs. F. A. V. Galton.

Emma Georgiana Elizabeth. Born 24 Aug. 1784. Died 6 March 1818. Bur. at Breadsall, near Derby; unmarried.

Signature of Emma Darwin to a letter, dated "The Priory, Dec. 23d 1804," addressed to Dr. Darwin, Shrewsbury.

Harriot. Born 5 July 1790. Mar. . . Dec. 1811 to Admiral Thomas James Maling (who died . . Jan. 1849). Died 5 Aug. 1825 at Valparaiso in South America. Buried at Breadsall, near Derby,

Signature of Harriot Maling to a letter, dated "The Priory, April 7th," addressed to "Doctor Darwin, Shrewsbury."

Darwin Galton of Claverdon Leys, co. Warwick. Born 18 March 1814 at Ladywood, co. Warwick. Bapt. April following at St. Martin's, Birmingham.

=2ndly, Frances Jane, 3rd dau. of Peter Arkwright, Esq., of Willersley, co. Derby. Mar. 21 Jan. 1873 at Matlock Old Church, co. Derby.

1st, Mary, dau. of John Phillips of Edstone, co Warwick. Born 18 March 1822. Mar. 22 Sept. 1840 at Wootten Wawen, co. Warwick. Died 26 Nov. 1869 at Claverdon, co. Warwick. Bur. at Wootten Wawen.

Erasmus Galton of Loxton Manor, co. Somerset, J.P. and D.L. Born 31 May 1815 at Ladywood, co. Warwick. Bapt. 30 June following at St. Martin's, Birmingham.

Francis Galton, F.R.S.=Louisa Jane, dau. of Rev. George Butler, D.D., Dean of Peterborough, and sister of the Rev. H. Montagu Butler, Head Master of Harrow School, and afterwards Master of Trinity College, Cambridge. Mar. 1 Aug. 1853 at Peterborough Cathedral. The well-known traveller and scientific writer. Born 16 Feb. 1822 at Birmingham. Bapt. 20 March 1823 at St. Martin's, Birmingham.

John Samuel Phillips Galton. Born 23 Nov. 1841 at Leamington. Died 20 Aug. 1842 at Edstone, co. Warwick. Bur. at Wootten Wawen, co. Warwick.

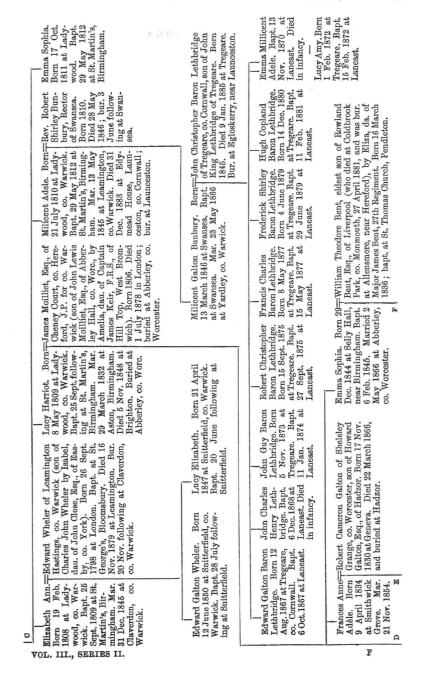

F

B

D

Ewen Cameron Galton, Born 22 Oct. 1856 at Hadzor House, co. Worc. Bapt. at Hadzor Church. B.A. Clare Coll., Camb., and of the Inner Temple, Barrister-at-Law.

Lucy Ethel, Born 6 Oct. 1855 at The Elms, Abberley; bapt. at Hadzor Church.

Amy Caroline.=Rev. Herbert Johnson, Born 23 April eldest son of the late 1858 at Hadzor Dean of Wells. Of House; bapt. Exeter Coll., Oxford, at Hadzor M.A. Vicar of Crock-Church. Mar. ham, Edenbridge, 22 June 1882 Kent, in London.

Adèle Vera Harcourt,=Rev. Frederick Bennett, eldest son Born 11 Aug. 1859 of Rev. F. H. Bennett, Vicar of at Kilchberg, Lake of Freeland, Oxon, by Anne, da, of Zurich; bapt. at Had-Rev. G. D. Renaud. M.A. Merton zor Church. Married Coll., Oxford. Rector of Farleigh, 5 May 1886 at Shels-Surrey. Born and bapt. at St. ley, co. Worcester. John's Vicarage, Worcester, May 1844.

Violet Darwin. Born 12 Aug. 1862 at Hadzor; bapt. at Hadzor Church.

William Lionel Galton Bennett. Born 4 March 1887 at Worthing.

Rowland Theodore Bent. Born 5 April 1868. Bapt. 10 June 1868 at St. John's Church, Fairfield, Liverpool.

William Ernest Bent. Born 21 Nov. 1874. Bapt. 26 Jan. 1875 at All Saints Church, Childwall.

Harold Edward Furnival Bent. Born 1 Oct.1878. Bapt. 24 Oct. 1878 at St. Mary Abbott's, Kensington.

Edith Lucy. Born 14 Feb. 1867. Bapt. 31 March 1867 at Hanley, near Tenbury.

Elizabeth Eva. Born 1 June 1869. Bapt. 27 July 1869 at Bishop's Frome, near Bromyard.

Louisa Constance. Born 11 Oct. 1870. Bapt. 29 Nov. 1870 at All Saints Church, Childwall.

Frances Maud. Born 25 March 1872. Bapt. 26 June 1872 at All Saints, Childwall.

Sophy Elsee. Born 27 Jan. 1876. Bapt. 28 Feb. 1876 at All Saints Church, Childwall.

Sophy Flora. Born 14 July 1873. Died 26 July 1874.

Kathleen Mabel. Born 6 May 1877. Bapt. 12 July 1877 at All Saints Church, Childwall.

James Keir Moilliet=Sophia Harriet, dau. of Rev. John of Cheyney Court. Finlay, late Vicar of Aveley, Essex; Born 27 July 1836 at sometime Chaplain to the Earl of Smithwick, co. Staff., Gainsborough. Granddau. of Thomas and baptized there. Mainwaring, Esq., of Whitmore, co. Twin with John Stafford. Mar. 20 Aug. 1874 at St. Lewis. Giles, Camberwell.

John Lewis Moilliet. Born 27 July 1836 at Smithwick. Bapt. at Smithwick. Twin with James Keir. M.A. Trinity Coll., Camb. Rector of Abberley, Stourport.

Tertius Galton Moilliet.=Grace, dau. of Rev. Robert Shuckburgh of Born 5 Sept. 1843 at Selly Alborough, Norfolk (who died 3 April 1860, Hall, near Birmingham. having mar. Elizabeth, dau. of Giles King Bapt. 13 Oct. following. Lyford, Esq., of Winchester, born and bapt. at Alborough, died 13 May 1876). Mar. 14 July 1870 at Aylsham, co. Norfolk.

G

H

D

Bernard Rambold Keir Moilliet. Born 14 Nov. 1876 at Abberley, and bapt. there 26 Dec. 1876.

Hubert Mainwaring Keir Moilliet. Born 11 Oct. 1877 in London. Bapt. 14 Nov. following at St. Augustine's, London.

Alexander Keir Moilliet. Born 16 Feb. 1880 in London. Privately bapt. 19 Feb. following.

John Lewis Moilliet. Born 20 March 1882 in London. Bapt. 30 May following at Abberley.

Theodore Albert Moilliet. Born 11 May 1883 in London. Bapt. 25 July 1883 at Abberley.

Constance Madeline Keir. Born 10 March 1885 in London. Privately bapt. 19 March following.

Amy Elizabeth Lucy. Born 15 May 1871 at Leamington. Bapt. at Bishop's Frome. Died 22 Jan. 1878 at Leamington.

Evelyn Shuckburgh Galton Moilliet. Born 7 March 1877 at Leamington. Bapt. 2 April following. Died 4 Feb. 1882 at Leamington.

Lucy Amelia. Born 3 May 1833 at Smithwick Grove.=Rev. George Hesketh Biggs (son of Rev. George Biggs, Rector of Upton Warren, co. Worcester). Born 7 Oct. 1823 at Upton Warren. Mar. 9 Aug. 1854 at Abberley, co. Worcester. Died 14 Aug. 1867 at Paris; buried 22 Aug. following at Ettington, co. Warwick. — Bapt. at Upton Warren. M.A. Worcester College, Oxford. Vicar of Ettington, Stratford-on-Avon, 1866.

Rev. Walter Bree Hesketh Biggs, Curate of Leamington 1884. Born 7 Nov. 1856, and bapt. at Hawling, co. Gloucester. Of St. John's Coll., Camb. B.A. in 1880.

Harcourt Galton Biggs. Born 19 April 1863. Bapt. at Upton Warren.

Amy Mary Constance. Born 15 May 1855, and bapt. at Hawling. Mar. 20 Dec. 1884 at Ettington.=Thomas Henry Gibbons Pearson (son of Rev. John Pearson of Suckley, co. Worcester). Born 11 Dec. 1853 at Suckley. Bapt. at Suckley. Of St. John's Coll., Camb.

Sophy Adèle. Born 14 Feb. 1858. Bapt. at Hawling.

Lucy Evelyne. Born 16 Dec. 1864. Bapt. at Upton Warren.

John Hesketh Pearson. Born 20 Feb. 1886 at Hawford, co. Worcester. Bapt. 6 April following at Ombersley, co. Worcester.

Edward Hesketh Gibbons Pearson. Born 20 Feb. 1887 at Hawford. Bapt. 16 April following at Ombersley.

## Genealogy of Browne.*

F.  **Thomas Browne** (eldest son) of Hungry-Bentley, co. Derby (d. 18 Sept.,
bur. [at Longford] 21 Sept. 1717. Will dated 12 Sept. 1717 and mislaid ;
affidavit made as to execution thereof ; pr. at Lichfield and copy filed
28 March 1718).  Legatee under his father's will 1708, who bequeathed
him £250, and entailed upon him the manor of Bentley and lands in
Rocester, Middleton Park, Marston-Montgomery, etc.  Mar. Alice, dau. of
Richard Simpson, Esq., of Barton Hall, co. Derby (by Elizabeth his wife,
sister and coh. of John Merry, Esq., of Barton).  Legatee and sole executrix
under her husband's will 1717, who bequeathed her an annuity of £60 out
of lands devised to dau's ; household goods, furniture, plate, jewels, and
coach with four mares and harness, etc. (bur. [at Longford] 24 Jan. 1731-2).
Issue :—

    G.   1. Rupert Browne, eldest son and heir.  (*Vide infra.*)
         2. Grace (bapt. [at Longford] 15 March 1695; d. . . . .), legatee under her
grandfather's will 1708, who bequeathed her £1000, and under her
father's will 1717, who bequeathed her lands, etc.
         2. Penelope (bapt. [at Longford] 9 June 1701; d. . . . .), legatee under
her grandfather's will 1708, who bequeathed her £1000, and under
her father's will 1717.  Mar. Charles Sudell, Esq., of Lichfield
(d. . . . .).

G.  **Rupert Browne** (eldest son) of Bentley Hall,† co. Derby (bapt. [at Long-
ford] 5 Dec. 1698; bur. there 29 May 1733.  Will dated 3 April 1733 ;
pr. at Lichfield 20 Oct. 1742 by Richard Fitzherbert, co-ex'or).  Legatee
and sole ex'or under his grandfather's will 1708, who entailed upon him the
manor of Bentley, etc.  Arms : BROWNE ; *impaling, Or, two ravens proper
within a bordure of the field,* for CORBET.  Mar. Eleanora, dau. of Roger
Corbet, Esq., of Leigh, Shrewsbury, and sister of Andrew Corbet, Esq., of
Sundorne Castle, co. Salop (bapt. [at Battlefield, co. Salop] 30 Aug. 1705 ;
bur. [at Longford] 2 Sept. 1766.  Will dated 25 June 1766; pr. [at Lichfield]
by her son Rev. Corbet Browne, M.A., sole ex'or, 24 Oct. 1766).  Legatee
under her husband's will 1733, who bequeathed her an annuity of £100 out
of tenement "known by the name of Bentley Old Hall ;" mentioned in her
son Thomas Browne's will 1764, who bequeathed £2000 on trust to secure
the payment of an annuity of £90.  Issue :—

    H.   1. Thomas Browne, eldest son.  (*Vide infra.*)
         2. Rupert Browne (b. 1727? ; d. 10 May 1785), mar. Mary, dau. of
Thomas Charnels, Esq., of Little Eaton, co. Derby (d. 7 July 1787).
Ancestor of the Brownes of Chesterfield, co. Derby, now represented
by the Rev. Rupert Montagu Browne, Rector of Rushock, co.
Worcester, who has issue.
         3. Corbet Browne of Withington, co. Salop (b. 1728 ? ; bur. [in Withing-
ton Church, M.I.] 6 Nov. 1807, æt. 80.  Will dated 23 Jan. 1806 ;
pr. [at Lichfield] by Jane Browne his wife and sole executrix 28 April
1808).  Entered as a sizar of Queen's College, Cambridge, 9 April
1747 (tutor Mr. Morris); graduated in Arts—B.A. 12 Jan. 1751-2,
and M.A. 2 July 1754 ; admitted to Holy Orders ; instituted to the
Rectory of Upton Magna *cum* Withington, co. Salop, 29 Sept. 1752,
which he held until his death.  Estate of Bentley, etc., entailed upon
him in default of issue of his elder brothers Thomas and Rupert ;

---

* Continued from p. 54.
† According to a letter written by Thomas Browne of Chesterfield in 1828, this Rupert
Browne restored Bentley Hall and added the later portion.  From this period it is described as
"Bentley Hall" or "Bentley Old Hall."

co-ex'or under his eldest brother's will, which he proved in 1764; sole ex'or and proved his mother's will 1766. Mar., first, Rebecca, dau. of the Rev. J . . . . Dixie, in Holy Orders, of . . . . (bur. [at Withington, M.I.] 3 March 1769). Issue :—

**I.** 1. Elizabeth (b. 1769 ? ; bur. [at Withington, M.I.] 14 Jan. 1788, æt. 19).

Mar., secondly, by licence [in Upton Magna Church] 6 Nov. 1773, Jane, dau. of . . . . Gregory, and relict of . . . . Allen of Withington (b. 1733 ? ; d. 13 Oct., bur. [at Withington, M.I.] 18 Oct. 1822, æt. 89. Will dated 4 July 1821; pr. [at Lichfield] 24 April 1823 by her sons, Rev. Corbet Browne, B.A., and John Allen the ex'ors). Issue :—

**I.** 1. Corbet Browne (only son and heir) of Withington (b. 1777 ? ;* d. 17 April, bur. [in Withington Church, M.I.] 22 April 1854, æt. 77. Will dated 16 Oct. 1849 ; pr. [at Lichfield] 26 April 1855 by son Thomas Dickin Browne, sole ex'or). Entered St. John's College, Cambridge, 16 May 1794 (previously educated at Shrewsbury School); graduated in Arts—B.A. 19 Jan. 1798 ; admitted to Holy Orders. Succeeded his father in the Rectory of Upton Magna *cum* Withington, and instituted thereto 28 April 1808, which he held until his death. Legatee and co-ex'or under his mother's will 1823, who bequeathed him £400. Mar. ([at Wem, co. Salop] 29 July 1799) Sarah, eldest dau. of Thomas Dickin, Esq., of Loppington House, Wem, co. Salop, High Sheriff of Salop 1799 (bapt. [at Wem] 19 Aug. 1777 ; d. 9 Oct. 1831; bur. [in Withington Church, M.I.], æt. 53). Issue :—

**J.** 1. Corbet Spencer Browne of Withington (bapt. [at Uffington, co. Salop] 15 Nov. 1800 ; received into Withington Church 15 April 1803 ; d. s.p. 1 March, bur. [at Withington, M.I.] 5 March 1869). Legatee under his mother's will 1831, who bequeathed him £100. Mar., first (at Barrow?), Mary Powell of Charlton, Barrow (d. s.p. . . . .), and, secondly, Anne, dau. of John Howells, Esq., of the Marsh Farm, Barrow, co. Salop (b. 1797 ? ; d. s.p. 2 Oct., bur. [at Withington, M.I.] 6 Oct. 1874, æt. 77).

2. Thomas Dickin Browne† of Wem, co. Salop, (bapt. [at Uffington] 30 Sept. 1802 ; received into Withington Church 15 April 1803 ; d. unmar. and bur. [at Wem] 30 Jan. 1871, æt. 70). Attorney-at-Law and Lieut. in North Shropshire Yeomanry.

3. Rupert Browne of Sansaw Heath, co. Salop (bapt. [at Withington] 17 Feb. 1805; died 15 June, bur. [at Withington, M.I.] 17 June 1869). Mar. ([at St. Chad's, Shrewsbury] 2 Feb. 1836) Susannah, dau. of John Wood, Esq., of Onslow, parish of St. Chad's, Shrewsbury (b. 1804 ? ; d. and bur. [at Withington, M.I.] 27 Jan. 1854, æt. 50). Issue :—

**K.** 1. John Browne (bur. [at Withington, M.I.] 3 Jan. 1837, æt. 2 months).

1. Anne (living unmar. 1886).

* The earlier register of Withington has been mislaid, and, at the time of my visit to Withington in 1885, was not forthcoming.

† Upon the bookplate of Thomas Dickin Browne his arms are erroneously displayed as follows : *Ermine, on a fess embattled* (should be *counter-embattled*) *three escallops argent ;* and upon a shield of pretence, *Vair-en-point argent and gules, on a pale or three trefoils slipped vert* (for TURNER of Swanwick). Mr. Browne lived and died a bachelor, while displaying to the present and future generations of the (heraldic) world his marriage with an heiress upon his bookplate ! This mistake arose from copying the coat of arms given in Glover's 'History of Derbyshire,' which recorded the marriage of Thomas Browne of Chesterfield with an heiress of the Turner family. A copy of this curious bookplate is in the possession of Mrs. Miller of Hamilton Square, Birkenhead.

**K.** 2. Sarah Emma Wood (living 1886), mar., first ([at Oxon Church in parish St. Chad, co. Salop], 1 Nov. 1860) William Atcherley Dickin, Esq. (b. 3 June 1834; d. 9 Aug. 1867; bur. at Farnworth, Lanc.), fourth son of Roger Spencer Dickin, Esq., of The Hall, Wem. Issue:—

**L.** 1. Sarah Annie Jane Dickin (b. 4 May, bapt. [at The Birches, parish of Wem] 9 May 1865; living 1886). Mar. secondly ([at Loppington, co. Salop] 28 Feb. 1879) Hugh Miller, Esq., M.D., of Hamilton Square, Birkenhead (b. 23 Sept. 1846; living 1886). Issue :—

**L.** 1. Mary Grace Miller (b. 13 Aug. 1880; d. 14 July 1883; bapt. at St. Mary's, Birkenhead); bur. at cemetery there.

2. Dorothy Beatrice Miller (b. 28 June 1882; d. 28 Dec. 1883; bapt. at St. Mary's, Birkenhead); bur. at cemetery there.

**J.** 4. Edmund Browne of Withington (b. 1811; living 1886), mar. (at Upton Magna) Emma, dau. of . . . . Pugh and relict of John Humphreys, Esq., of Upton Magna (d. s.p., bur. [at Upton Magna] 1862 ?).

5. Charles Flemyng Browne (bapt. [at Withington] 14 Oct. 1815; d. unmar. [at Shrewsbury] 1 Oct., bur. [at Withington, M.I.] 6 Oct. 1860).

1. Emma (d. unmar. March (?) 1860, bur. at Kensal Green Cemetery).

2. Jane Maria (bapt. [at Withington] 14 June 1812 ; d. unmar. Sept. 1872 ; bur. in Lichfield Cathedral).

3. Grace (bapt. [at Withington] 23 Feb. 1814; d. s.p., bur. [at St. John's, Windsor] 1873 ?). Mar. Richard Alexander, Esq., of Windsor (d. s.p., bur. [at St. John's, Windsor] 1870 ?).

4. Julia (bapt. [at Withington] 8 May 1818; d. s.p., bur. there 2 Feb. 1870). Mar. ([at Withington] 7 Jan. 1850) the Rev. Sidney Philip Roberson, B.A. (his second wife), of Castle Terrace, Shrewsbury (d. 1876), Vicar of Rowton, co. Salop. Entered Worcester College, Oxford ; graduated in Arts—B.A. 1836 ; admitted to Holy Orders 1839. Resigned the living of Rowton in 1876.

5. Harriet (bapt. [at Withington] 24 July 1819 ; d. unmar. Jan. 1871 ; bur. at St. John's, Windsor).

**H.** 4. Edmund Browne (bapt. [at Longford] 7 Oct. 1729 ; living 1733; d. . . . .).

5. John Browne (bapt. [at Longford] 7 Feb. 1730; dead 1733 ?).

6. James Browne (bapt. [at Longford] 11 May 1733 ; bur. there 30 Sept. 1737).

1. Eleanora (bapt. [at Longford] 23 Feb. 1724 ; d. . . . .).

2. Elizabeth (bapt. [at Longford] 9 March 1731 ; d. . . . .).

3. Grace (d. . . . .), mar., first, William Alsop, Esq., of Ashbourne, co. Derby, Barrister-at-Law ; and, second, the Rev. . . . . Tench, in Holy Orders, of Kate's Cabin, Hunts (d. . . . .). Both legatees under her mother's will 1766. Issue :—

1. Eleanora Tench, } living 1766.
2. Mary Tench,

(*To be continued.*)

# Annotations to the Heraldic Visitation of London, 1633.

## Gore.*

### WILLS.

Thomas Gore, Citizen and Merch$^t$ Taylor of London. Will dat. 7 Aug. 1585 ; pr. 3 Jan. 1585-6 by Richard Gore and Gerrard Gore, with Rich$^d$ Windor, notary pub., proctor for Suzan the relict. To be buried where my ex'ors think fit. To my wife Suzan one third of my goods, etc., and £100, and to my da. Helene Gore and any other children living at my decease one third of my goods. Gold rings of an ounce, each with a death's head engraven, to my father Gerrard Gore and my mother his wife, my brother-in-law Reginald Williams, gent., and my sister Margaret his wife, my brother Rich$^d$ Gore and Mary his wife, my brethren John Gore, Gerrarde Gore, W$^m$ Gore, Rob$^t$ Gore, Raphe Gore, and Powell Gore, and also to my uncle Thomas Gore, grocer, and my cousin Margarett his dau$^r$, and to my wife Susan, and my son-in-law Nicholas Toolye. To my friend Tho$^s$ God a ring of 40s. To my wife's sister Anne Lankard £10 at marriage. My godson Richard Williams, son of my s$^d$ sister Margarett, £10 at age of 21. Poor of Christ's Hospital, prisons, etc. Black gowns to 20 poor men attending my funeral. To my brothers Rich$^d$ and Gerrard Gore £20 each for their pains as ex'ors. If I leave any other children besides my daughter Helen (after deducting £200 more to my wife) to be divided amongst them. My s$^d$ dau. Helene is under age and my wife Suzan to be her guardian. I stand bound to Rob$^t$ Brandon, Chamberlain of London, for £679 7s. 8½d., being the moiety of the part and portion of Nicholas Tooley, son of my predecessor William Tooley, Leatherseller, dec$^d$, my brothers Richard and Gerrarde Gore to have the custody of the money till such time as the same shall be due to the said Nicholas Tooley. My wife Suzan and my s$^d$ brethren Richard and Gerrarde Gore, ex'ors. My brethren John Gore and Rob$^t$ Gore, overseers. Wit., Symon Wrenche, scr. Codicil 13 Dec. 1585. To John Davenaunte, Merch$^t$ taylor, and Judith his wife, to Ascanius de Remaline and Eliz. his wife, to Helene, wife of John Whitebye, and to Jone, wife of Gyles Fayrecloughe, rings of 40s. each. (4 *Windsor*.)

Thomas Gore of London, Grocer. Will dat. 11 June 39 Eliz., and then in his 71$^{st}$ year ; pr. 30 June 1597 by Tho$^s$ Lovell, notary pub., proctor for the da. Margaret Bonde *al's* Gore. "My funeralls be decentlie performed but without superfluous or vaine pompe and not omittinge that threescore and eleauen poore men be clothed therefore." My only child Margarett now wife of W$^m$ Bond of London, haberdasher, sole ex'trix. Legacies to my grandchildren, etc., as under. To Gore son of my da. Margaret Bond £40 for a chain, and to her dau'rs Anne (eldest), Elizabeth (2$^{nd}$), and Margaret the 3$^{rd}$, £400 each. My friend and cousin M$^r$ W$^m$ Lambard and my antient servant Tho$^s$ Dodde, overseers, and to the said M$^r$ W$^m$ Lambard £40, and to his wife 5 marks for a jewel. To the s$^d$ Tho$^s$ Dodde my tenem$^t$ in S$^t$ Stephen's, Walbrooke, adjoining to my now dwelling house, and also 5 marks for a ring. Bequests to servants, hospitals, prisons, etc. The 71 poor persons to be clothed as abovement$^d$ to be chosen out of Walbrooke Ward, S$^t$ Sepulchres, London, and Lewisham, co. Kent. To my brother M$^r$ Gerard Gore a ring of 5 marks, and to his sons rings of 40s. each, and they and their wives to have mourning. To the Grocers' Company £20 for a dinner. Rings, etc., to M$^r$ Morris, apothecary, Rich$^d$ Milles, grocer, and my cousin Tho$^s$ Laughton. M$^r$ Justice Owen a ring of £3 6s. 8d. My son Bonde's servants mourning, etc. Wit., Ric. Dikenson, John Maie, Whettendall Tilghman. (50 *Cobham*.)

Hugh Gore of Heston, co. Midd., gent. Will dat. 19 May 1651 ; pr. 13 Aug. 1651 by Anne Gore the relict. To be buried in Heston Churchy$^d$ and to the poor

* Continued from Vol. II., p. 350.

there 40s.  My house and lands purchased of Ralph Porter and also the lands of
John Geere to my wife Anne for life, remainder to my dau'r Ann Gore.  My household goods, a lease of Pury Place, and £100 to my wife.  To my da. Anne Gore a
silver tankard and salt, and all my cattle, corn, etc.  My s⁴ wife and dau'r ex'trices.
To my father Thoˢ Gore and my 3 sisters Joane, Elizabeth, and Mary 5s. each, and
to my cousin's 3 children 2s. 6d. each.  My mother-in-law Anne Cole, my two
sisters Susan and Mary, and my brother John Brent 20s. each.  My father-in-law
Wᵐ Cole and my uncle Robᵗ Cole, both of Heston, overseers.  Wit., Anne Cole,
Susan Brent.  (159 *Grey*.)

Richard Gore of Sᵗ Mary Aldermary, London, deputy of the Company of Merchᵗ
Adventurers at Hamborough in Germany.  Nuncupative will at Hamborough in the
month of October 1622.  Adm'on 15 Jan. 1622 (1622-3) to Mary Gore the relict,
she having renounced probate.  Gave all his estate to his wife Mary Gore, sole
ex'trix, she to have a motherly care of his and her children.  Wit., Nicholas Basse,
Thoˢ Younge, Minister, and others.  (4 *Swan*.)

John Gore of Sᵗ Benett Sherhog, London, Clothdrawer.  Will dat. 30 July
1657; pr. 2 Oct. 1657 by Larie Gore the relict.  My lands of inheritance and also
one third of my goods, etc., to my dau'r, and if she dies before coming to full age
then the s⁴ lands to go to my wife.  Residue to my wife Larie, sole ex'trix.  Wit.,
Alice Marter, James Read, scr.  (371 *Ruthen*.)

## GRANT OF ARMS TO GEORGE TOLLET, COMMISSIONER OF THE NAVY, 1708.

To all and singular to whom these Presents shall come Sʳ Henry Sᵗ George
Knt. Garter Principal King of Armes & John Vanbrugh Esqʳ Clarenceux King of
Armes send greeting Whereas the Right Honᵇˡᵉ Henry Earl of Bindon &c., one of
the Lords of her Majestys most Honᵇˡᵉ Privy Council and Deputy (wᵗʰ her
Majesties approbation) to his Grace Thomas Duke of Norfolk Earl Marshal &
Hereditary Marshal of England, hath by Warrant or Order under his hand & Seal
bearing Date the 26 day of August last past Signified unto us that George Tollet
Esqʳ one of the Commissioners of the Navy hath by his Petition humbly prayed
that such Coat and Crest may be granted & assigned unto him as he and his heirs,
and the other Descendents of his Body lawfully begotten and to be begotten may
bear & use, and whereas the said Earl of Bindon being satisfied by a Certificate
annext to the said Petition that the said George Tollet is a person of good Repu-
tation, Loyalty & affection to the Government, and of estate sufficient to support
the state of Gentility, & likewise that he being possessed of a considerable real
Estate & designing to settle the same on the Issue of his Body begotten & to be
begotten, and for want of such Issue, on the Issue male of his deceased brother
John Tollet late of Dublin in Ireland, and for want of such Issue male, in the Issue
male of his second Brother Thomas Tollet deceased late of Sᵗ Margarets Westminster,
and for want of such Issue on his youngest Brother, Charles Tollet of Wandsworth
in the County of Surrey & on the Issue male of his Body, did by his said Warrant
Order & Direct us to devise and (after his Loᵖˢ consent & approbation) Grant &
Assign to the said George Tollet such Arms and Crest as he & the Heirs & other
Descendents of his Body lawfully begotten & to be begotten may bear & use & for
want of such Issue to such of the Issue male of his said Brothers deceased, & for
want of such Issue to his said Brother Charles Tollet & his Issue male respectively
as shall enjoy the real Estate of the said George Tollet after his Decease.  Know ye
therefore that we the said Garter and Clarenceux in pursuance of the Consent of
the said Earl of Bindon & by vertue of the Letters Patent of Our Offices to Each
of us respectively Granted under the Great Seal of England have devised (& with
his Loᵖˢ approbation) do Grant & Assign unto the said George Tollet the Arms &
Crest hereafter mentioned, viz : Chequy Argent & Azure, on a Chevron Ingrailed or

PRUDENTIA IN ADVERSIS

George Tollet Esqr.

MISCELLANEA GENEALOGICA ET HERALDICA.

three Anchors sable, on a Chief Gules a Lion passant of the first, & for his Crest on a wreath Argent and Azure a Pyramid erected on a Pedestal of one Degree silver enwrapped about the top with a serpent descending proper respecting on an Escrole with these words PRUDENTIA IN ADVERSIS as the same is in the margin hereof more plainly depicted. To be borne & used by him the said George Tollet & the heirs and other descendents of his Body lawfully Begotten & to be Begotten & for want of such Issue then by the Issue male of his Brother John Tollet aforesaid deceased & for want of such Issue then by the Issue male of his Second Brother Thomas Tollet aforesaid deceased & in default of the Issue male of the Body of the said Thomas Tollet the said Arms & Crest to be born by his said Brother Charles Tollet & his Issue Male respectively as shall have & enjoy the real Estate of the said George Tollet after his decease & not otherwise with their due differences according to the Law of Armes without the Lett or Interruption of any Person or Persons whatsoever. In Witness whereof We the said Garter & Clarenceux Kings of Arms have to these Presents subscribed our names & affixed the Seals of Our respective offices this third day of December in the seventh year of the Reign of Our Sovereign Lady Anne by the Grace of God Queen of Great Britain France & Ireland Defender of the Faith &c. Annoq. D'ni 1708.

HEN. S<sup>t</sup> GEORGE      JOHN VANBRUGH,
Garter principal King of Arms.      Clarenceux King of Arms.

---

## HAWKER FAMILY.

The following notes relating to this family are extracted from a Bible and Prayer Book bound together, the latter being in black letter, and printed at London by Robt. Barker 1604, the former 1606.

This Boock was New Bownd in 1722 and giuen to mee John Hawker by my Father Jonathan Hawker Jan<sup>y</sup> y<sup>e</sup> 1 day.

Jan. 1, 1681 John Hawker was born and baptised.
Oct. 18, 1675 Mary Hawker was born and baptised.
Dec. 1, 1705 John and Mary Hawker was marred.
Aug. 10, 1715 Joseph Hawker was born and baptised.
June 1, 1717 Marrgreat Hawker was born and baptised.
July 22, 1739 Joseph and Elizabeth Hawker was marred.

---

Ant Eals Knowls dyed Apriel 25 in 1725.
My grandmother Hawker dyed Jan. 3, 1730-1 aigged 82 years.
My grandfather Hawker dyed Apriel 16 aged 79, 1734.
Mary Hawker har Book Oct. 6, 1723.
Mary Perkins her Book. My mother died April 9, 1802 aged 84. (These two
    entries are in the same hand.)
April 9, 1802 died my mother Margaret Dunk aged 85 years.
Jonathan Hawker, Calfe (*sic*), Joseph Hawker his book 1723.
Joseph Hawker had the smallpox in nouember aigged 6 years in 1721.
Margreat Hawker had the smallpox in nouember aigged 4 yeares in 1721.
April 1754 John Hawker had the smallpox aged 5 years 6 months.
May 1754 Joseph Hawker had the smallpox aged 5 years 6 months.

L. L. D.

# Petley.

### *Marriages.*

| | | | |
|---|---|---|---|
| 1611 | July | 15 | Thomas Petley & Ann Redage. |
| 1619 | Nov. | 16 | John Petly & Elizabeth Burbidge. |
| 1653 | Sept. | 26 | James Pettley & Jane Seaman. |
| 1672 | July | 2 | James Petly & Susanna Everist. |

### *Baptisms.*

| | | | |
|---|---|---|---|
| 1594 | April | 22 | Child of James Petley. |
| 1597 | April | 12 | George son of James Petley. |
| 160½ | Mar. | 5 | Child of James Petley. |
| 1603 | Nov. | 27 | Alice da. of James Petlie. |
| 1604 | Dec. | 9 | James son of James Petlye. |
| 1607 | April | 11 | Edward son of James Pettly. |
| 1609 | June | 11 | Joane da. of James Petley. |
| 1614 | April | 10 | Anne da. of James Petley. |

### *Burials.*

| | | | |
|---|---|---|---|
| 1580 | June | 27 | John Petlye. |
| 1603 | Dec. | 5 | Alice da. of James Petlie. |
| 1617 | Oct. | 30 | James Petley. |
| 1623 | Mar. | 27 | Ursula Petley. |
| 1624 | Sept. | 5 | John Petley. |
| 1627 | June | 8 | Thomas Petly. |
| 1642 | Oct. | 22 | Elizabeth da. of James Pettly. |
| 1650 | Jan. | 7 | William Petley. |
| 1650 | Feb. | 19 | James Petley. |
| 1662 | Aug. | 29 | Ann da. of George Petley. |
| 1670 | Dec. | 24 | George Petley of the Town of Bromley. |
| 1673 | Sept. | 9 | Thomas Petly of yᵉ Common. |
| 169¾ | Feb. | 23 | John Petley.. |

### *Baptisms.*

| | | | |
|---|---|---|---|
| 1658 | May | 27 | Sarah da. of Roger Pettley. |
| 166½ | Jan. | 8 | Elizabeth da. of Rodger Pettley; born 21 December. |
| 1663 | Nov. | 4 | John son of Roger Pettley; born 21 October. |

---

## WALDO NOTE.

The following entries may be of value to those interested in this family. They were discovered accidentally during a search made for other purposes, and occur in the Registers of Daventry, Northants.

### *Marriage.*

1640.   Mʳ Lawrence Waldoe and Mary Bechino July 1.

### *Burials.*

1660.   Mʳ Lawrence Waldo Decemb : 8.
1669.   Mary Waldoe Aprill 23.

No Waldo baptisms were found during the corresponding period.

E. H. H.

# Langley Pedigree—Pedigree B. (*Vide* Vol. II, p. 274.)

## LANGLEYS OF LANCASHIRE AND AFTERWARDS OF IRELAND.

Roger de Langley of Agecroft Hall, co. Lancaster. Ob. 21 Oct. 1393.⊤Margaret,* fil. .... Bothe of Barton.

Henry Langley, Clerk, occ. 1404.

Peter de Langley, Rector of Prestwich, co. Lanc., 1409-1445.

Robert de Langley of Prest-Hall. Nat. 1378.⊤Katherine, fil. Sir William Atherton, Kt. Nup. ante 1393.

Ralph Langley, Rector of Prestwich 1445-1493. Will dated 29 May 1493; probate 22 Oct. 1493.

Thomas de Langley⊤Margaret, fil. Sir John Assheton of Agecroft Hall. of Ashton-under-Lyme.

Ralph Langley, Rector of Prestwich 1493-1498. Mentioned in his uncle Ralph Langley's will.

.... fil. .... relict .... Osbaldestone.⊤John de Langley of Agecroft Hall. Ob. 11 Hen. VII.⊤.... fil. Ralph Radclyffe.

.... filia Thomas=James Hopwood de Langley. of Hopwood.

Nicholas Langley.

Ralph [? John] de Catherall=Katherine Langley.

1. Robert de Langley of Agecroft Hall. Nat. 1462. Ob. 1512.⊤Eleanor, fil. William Radclyffe of Ordsall.

Margaret=Geoffrey, de Lang-ley. fil. Peter Shakerley of Shakerley.

Agnes=Ralph [? Anne] Holt of Langley. Gristle-hurst.

3. Ralph Langley, a Priest.

4. James Langley.

5. Richard Langley.

2. Thomas de Langley, Rector of Prestwich 1498-1525. Mentioned in his great-uncle Ralph Langley's will.

A

* Called Katherine on page 274, vol. ii, in error.

▲

....fil.=Anne Langley. John Grembury of Cramdills.

Ralph Prestwich of Holme.=Agnes Langley.

2. William Langley, Rector of Prestwich. 1525-1552. Ob. 1552.

1. Thomas de Langley. Ob. vitâ pat.=Cecil, fil. William Davenport of Bromhall.

3. Osmond Langley.

4. Lawrence Langley. Ob. ante 1560.=Katherine, fil.....

Thomas Holland of Denton.=Ellen Langley.

Robert Holt.=Joan Langley.

Ralph Langley. Ob. s.p.

Thomas Langley, B.D., Secretary to Cranmer.

William Langley, nat. 1512. Rector of Prestwich 1552-1569.

Sir Robert Langley, Knight, nat. 1492. Knighted 22 Feb. 1547. Ob. 1561.=Cecily, fil. Sir Edmund Trafford of Trafford, Kt., by Elizabeth his wife, fil. Sir Ralph Langford, Kt.=Edmond Holland of Denton. Mar. 2.

Dorothy Langley, fil. et coh. Ux. James Assheton of Chadderton.

Katherine Langley, fil. et coh. Ux. Thomas Leigh of Lyme.

Margaret Langley, fil. et coh. Mar. 1, Richard Holland. Mar. 2, John Redish of Redish.

Anne Langley, fil. et coh. Nupta 1561. Ux. Wm. Dauntsey.

3. William Langley, M.A., Rector of Prestwich. 1569-1611. Sep. 14 Oct. 1613 at Prestwich.=Anne, fil. ....

1. Robert Langley, nat. 1534. July 1606. Sep. 2=Mabel, fil. Thomas Tildesley of Wardley.

2. Isabel Langley. Mar. 1, Edmᵈ Chadderton. Mar. 2, Wm. Radclyffe.

Thomas Langley of Brazenose Coll., Oxon, 1579.

Two sons and two daughters.

Mary Langley.=Symond Harward, Rector of Warrington. Nup. 25 Sept. 1582.

William Langley, M.A., Rector of Cheadle, co. Staff.=Katherine, fil. James Assheton of Chadderton.

B

B

1. Deodatus Langley, Sep. at Prestwich 16 Jan. 1628-4. = Maria, fil. .... Edge. Nup. 16 Nov. 1612 at Prestwich.

2. John Langley, Rector of Prestwich 1611–1632. = .... fil. .....

3. Matthias Langley. = Mary, fil. .... Moore of Bank Hall, co. Lanc.

4. William Langley.

5. James Langley.

Elizabeth Langley, ux. John Glover. Nup. 23 July 1604 at Manchester.

Ellinor Langley, ux. William Edge. Nup. 27 Jan. 1606-7 at Prestwich.

Anna Langley, bap. at Prestwich 4 Oct. 1612. Sep. at Prestwich 6 Sept. 1623.

William Langley, bap. at Prestwich 18 Oct. 1615.

1. William Langley, Vicar of Wellington, co. Salop. Nat. 1618. = Jane, fil. Browne of Meere, co. Staff.

2. John Langley.

Ralph Langley.

Joan Langley, bap. 17 April 1617.

Ellen Langley, bap. 26 Aug. 1621. Sep. 13 Sept. 1621.

Anne Langley.

*Willm Langley* [signature]

William Langley, nat. 1648. Matriculated Christ Church, Oxon, 16 Oct. 1665. B.A. Oxon 1 July 1669.

William Langley, bap. 18 Oct. 1615. Of Whittle, co. Lanc. Living Overseer 1666. of his brother Henry's will.

Matthias Langley, nat. 1650. Matriculated Christ Church, Oxon, 30 March 1666. B.A. 26 Oct. 1669.

Henry Langley, bap. 23 Aug. 1618 at Prestwich. Served at the Siege of Clonmel in 1649. Will dated 2 Feb. 1666. at Clonmel.

Went to Ireland. Ob. 1666. = Anne, fil. Sep. .... Mentioned in her husband's will.

Ralph Langley.

Joy Langley.

Jane Langley.

Jane Langley, bap. 21 Jan. 1616-17.

Dorothea Langley, bap. 6 Jan. 1620-1 at Prestwich. Living at Bury, co. Lanc, in 1666. Mentioned in her brother Henry's will.

Edmund Langley, bap. 5 May 1622 at Prestwich.

Thomas Langley. Sep. 27 June 1615 at Prestwich.

From an Award dated 15 March 1657.

c

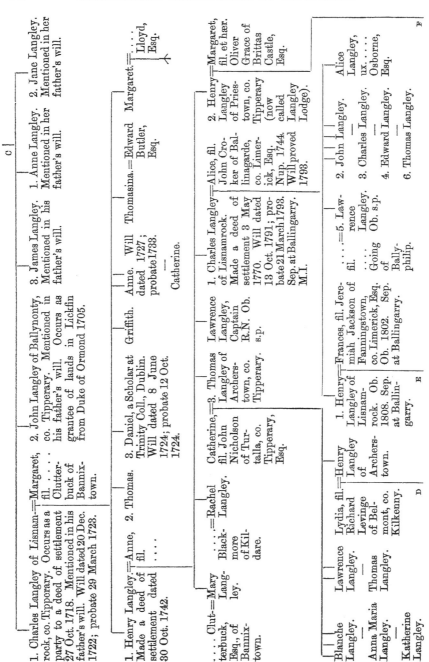

c |

1. Charles Langley of Lisnamrock, co. Tipperary. Occurs as a party to a deed of settlement 27 Oct. 1718. Mentioned in his father's will. Will dated 20 Dec. 1722; probate 29 March 1723. = Margaret, fil. .... Clutterbuck of Bannixtown.

2. John Langley of Ballynonty, co. Tipperary. Mentioned in his father's will. Occurs as grantee of lands in Lickfin from Duke of Ormond 1705.

3. James Langley. Mentioned in his father's will.

1. Anne Langley. Mentioned in her father's will.

2. Jane Langley. Mentioned in her father's will.

1. Henry Langley = Anne, fil. .... Made a deed of settlement dated 30 Oct. 1742.

2. Thomas.

3. Daniel, a Scholar at Trinity Coll., Dublin. Will dated 8 June 1724; probate 12 Oct. 1724.

Griffith.

Anne. Will dated 1727; probate 1733.

Thomasina. = Edward Butler, Esq.

Catherine.

Margaret = .... Lloyd, Esq.

1. Charles Langley of Lisnamrock. Made a deed of settlement 3 May 1770. Will dated 13 Oct. 1791; probate 21 March 1798. Sep. at Ballingarry. M.I. = Alice, fil. John Croker of Ballinagarde, co. Limerick, Esq. Nup. 1744. Will proved 1798.

Lawrence Langley, Captain R.N. Ob. s.p.

2. Henry Langley of Priestown, co. Tipperary (now called Langley Lodge). = Margaret, fil. et hær. Oliver Grace of Brittas Castle, Esq.

2. John Langley.
3. Charles Langley.
4. Edward Langley.
6. Thomas Langley.

Alice Langley, ux. .... Osborne, Esq.

5. Lawrence Langley. Ob. s.p. = ...., fil. .... Going of Ballyphilip.

.... Clutterbuck, Esq., of Bannixtown. = Mary Langley.

.... Black-Langley. = Rachel Blackmore of Kildare.

Catherine, fil. John Nicholson of Turtalla, co. Tipperary, Esq. = 3. Thomas Langley of Archerstown, co. Tipperary.

1. Henry Langley of Lisnamrock. Ob. 1808. Sep. at Ballingarry. = Frances, fil. Jeremiah Jackson of Fanningstown, co. Limerick, Esq. Ob. 1802. Sep. at Ballingarry.

Lydia, fil. Richard Levinge of Belmont, co. Kilkenny. = Henry Langley of Archerstown.

Lawrence Langley.
Thomas Langley.

Blanche Langley.
Anna Maria Langley.
Katherine Langley.

F   E   D   B

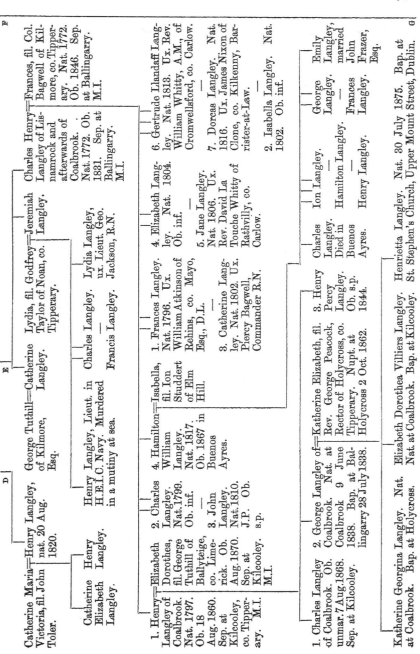

G

2. Oliver Langley. Ob. Nov. 1825.=Elizabeth Butler. Nup. 1783.

Mary, fil. John Bagwell, of Marlfield, co. Tipperary, M.P. for co. Tipperary. Ux. 2.=1. Henry Langley of Brittas Castle. Ob. s.p.

Grace=Sophia, fil. ... Tenison, Esq. Ux. 1.

Susanna, fil. Taylor of Noan, co. Tipperary, Esq. Ob. s.p. Ux. 2.=3. Godfrey Langley.

3. Lawrence=Grace Langley.

Anne, fil. Richard Moore of Barne, co. Tipperary, Esq., High Sheriff in 1744. Ux. 1.

Henry Augustus Langley of Brittas Castle and Langley Lodge. Captain 6th Dragoons. Ob. s.p.

Margaret Langley, ux. Richd Phillips, Esq.

Mary Langley, ux. John Hurst, Esq.

Elizabeth Maria Langley, ux. Col. Henry Penton, her cousin.

Catherine Langley.

Fanny Langley, ux. Percy Gough, Esq., nephew of Hugh, Viscount Gough.

Marion Langley.

Florence Langley.

Grace Langley.

Constance Laura Mary Langley.

Isabel Augusta Kitty Langley.

Henry Langley of Brittas Castle. Major in the Army.=Maria, fil. Henry Penton of Pentonville, co. Middlesex, M.P. for Winchester. Nup. 1845.

Richard Langley. Lieut. in the Army.

Oliver Langley. In Holy Orders.

Lawrence Langley.

John Langley of Parkstown, co. Tipperary.=Mary, fil. Nathaniel Taylor of Sommerville, co. Tipperary.

Adelaide Langley.

Helena Langley.

Susanna Langley.

Mary Langley.

Henry Langley (formerly of Brittas Castle) of Queen's Gate Terrace, London. Nat. 19 Sept. 1820. Living 1887.=Harriet, fil. James Bradshaw, Esq., M.P. for Canterbury. Nup. 1845.

Oliver Langley. Col. 16th Regiment.=Marie, fil. J. E. Wilkinson.

Grace Langley.

Isabella Langley, ux. Edward Bagwell Purefoy of Greenfields, co. Tipperary, D.L.

Mary Langley, ux. William Perry of Woodroff, co. Tipperary, D.L.

Sophia Langley.

Algernon Arthur Langley. Born at Queen's Gate Terrace 25 March 1863.

Claude Spencer Langley. Born at Queen's Gate Terrace 25 Sept. 1867.

1. Henry Fitzroy James Langley. Nat. at 28 South Street, London, 8 Dec. 1846. Died at Buenos Ayres 31 Nov. 1884 (in Diplomatic Service).

2. Gerald Charles Langley. Nat. at 28 South Street, London, 13 Oct. 1848. Commander in R.N. Living 1887.

Hubert Boyle Langley. Nat. at Coblentz 1852. Died in Australia 13 Jan. 1873.

Walter Louis Frederick Goltz Langley. Born at Coblentz 22 Feb. 1855.

# Notes on the Visitation of Lincolnshire, 1634.

## Clipsham.

Arms : Argent, two chevrons between three cinquefoils or, CLIPSHAM ; impaling, Gules, a crescent between three mullets argent, HANSARD.

Michaell Clipsham of Thorpe in the co. of Rutland.=

Edmond Clipsham of Otby=Dorothy da. of Rich^d Bridges of
in co. Linc. | Combe in Gloucestersh. Esq^r.

| Michaell Clipsham of Otby marr^d Ann da. of George Ellis gent. | Richard Clipsham=Mary d. and sole of Cadby in co. heire of S^r W^m Lincoln gent. Hansard of Gayton K^t. | Edmond 3. — Nicholas 4. | Margaret. — Elizabeth. |

Edmond 2 sonn. | Richard. 3 sonne. | William Clipsham sonne and heire apparent. | Michaell. | Anne.

Otby is a hamlet in the parish of Walesby, near Market Rasen.   " Cadby " is Cadeby-cum-Wyham, near Louth.

### WILLS AT LINCOLN.

Will of Richard Clipsham of Manthorpe, gent. (apparently father of the first Michael in the pedigree) ; proved at Lincoln 1618.   To son Lyon the lands which I bought of M^r Bartlemew, Esq^r, and S^r William Armine his son ; sons Henry, Michaell, and Edmund ; daughters Frances and Bridget; father-in-law George Lyon, dec^d ; wife Dorothy executrix.

Will of Henry Clipsham of Manthorpe, gent. ; proved at Lincoln 1626.   To wife Elisabeth my lease in Londonthorpe and lands in Gonerby, and I authorize her to sue the Chenzes, Gannocke, and Skepper.

Will of Edmond Clipsham of Fishtoft, gent. ; proved at Lincoln 1631.   To be buried in Fishtoft Church ; to dau. Elisabeth a silver boule and 6 silver spoons formerly her grandmother Dorothy Clipsham's ; wife Anne executrix.

Will of Anne Clipsham of Fishtoft, wid. ; proved at Lincoln 1632.   Daughter Elisabeth ; Edmond, son of my brother-in-law Michael Clipsham.

Will of Anne Hansard, relict of Sir W^m Hansard, Knight, late of Gayton, dec^d ; proved at Lincoln 1644.   Mentions dau. Mary Clipsham, and son-in-law M^r Richard Clipsham.

Will of Richard Clipsham of Gayton le wold, gent. ; dated 19 Dec. 1645 ; proved at Lincoln 1646.   Recites deed of 7 June 1641, whereby testator and Mary his wife agreed to levy a fine on lands in Cadeby to raise money to pay debts, etc. ; George Ellis of Wyham, Esq., and Michael Clipsham of Otby, gent., being parties to the same.   Brother-in-law Joseph Bilcliffe of Normanby super Montem, gent., and Margaret his wife; mother M^rs Dorothy Clipsham, widow ; my three brethren Michael, Edmund, and Nicholas Clipsham, gentlemen ; son Edward to be educated at an University.

Will of Ellinor Clipsham of Grantham, wid. ; proved at Lincoln 1646.   Sons Edward and George Clipsham.

Will of Dorothy Clipsham of Walesby, wid.; proved at Lincoln 1646.   To be buried in Walesby Church.   Son-in-law M^r Joseph Bilcliffe; late son Richard

Clipsham ; sons Michael and Nicholas Clipsham ; son Edmund's dau. Dorothy
Clipsham ; dau. Sergeant ; dau. Clipsham of Gayton.
Will of Margaret Clipsham of Lincoln, dated 1669 ; proved at Lincoln 25 Oct.
1671.   To Mʳⁱˢ Elizabeth Scortrith "my virginalls."

## WALESBY PARISH REGISTER.

1610   Michaell sonne of John Bridges, gentlema', bapt. the iiijᵗʰ of October.
1612   Edmond sonne of Edmond Clypsham bapt. yᵉ vᵗʰ of Octob.
161¾  Dorothy daughter of John Clypsham bapt. the ixᵗʰ of Jan.
1616   Katheren daughtʳ of John Clypsha' bapt. the xvjᵗʰ of Nove'ber.
1618   Richard sonne of John Clypsha' was baptized yᵉ last of May.
1620   John Hansarde and Anne Clypsham were maried yᵉ xxiijᵗʰ of November.
1631   John Sergeant and Elizᵗʰ Clipsham married Sept. j by Lycence.
1633   Edmond Clipsham was buried May 23ᵗʰ.
163⁴  Alice Clipsham daughter of Michaell Clipsham and Ann his wife was bapt.
         Jan. xiijᵗʰ.
1638   Michaell sonn of Michaell Clipsham and Ann his wife was bapt. June vijᵗʰ.
1639   Ann dau. of ditto bapt. Oct. xxviijᵗʰ.
16³⁹⁄₄₀  Ditto buried.
1643 (?)   Wᵐ son of ditto bapt. and buried.
         Michaell Clipsham was buried Aug. 19ᵗʰ.
1644   Edmond son of Edmond Clipsham was buried July 24ᵗʰ.
         An dau. of Michaell Clipsham and An his wife was baptized November 2 ;
         Burᵈ Dec. 3.
164⁴  Richard son of Edmond Clipsham and Susan his wife was bapt. Feb. 4ᵗʰ.
164⁵  Ellis son of Michaell Clipsham and An his wife was bapt. Feb. xiijᵗʰ.
1648   Richard son of Michaell Clipsham and Ann his wife wās bapt. Aprill 27ᵗʰ.
1651   Edmond son of Edmond Clipsham was buried Aug. 15.
1655   Margarett Clipsham was buried May 1ˢᵗ.
         Jhon and Joseph sons of Edmond Clipsham and Susanna his wife bapt.
1657   Joseph Clipsham was buried Sep. 21.
         John Clipsham was buried Dec. 11ᵗʰ.
1659   Nicholas son of Edmond Clipsham and Susanna his wife was bapt. May 4ᵗʰ.
1663   Edmund Clipsham was buried Oct. the 6ᵗʰ.
1666   Susanna the dau. of Susanna Clipsham was buried Oct. 1ˢᵗ.
1669   Richard Clipsham, Churchwarden.
1682   Susanna dau. of Richᵈ Clipsham and Eliz. his wife bapt. Sept. 13.
1683   Richard Clipsham, Churchwarden.
1693   Mʳ Richᵈ Clipsam and Widdow Joyes of this parrish were married abroad at
         the Collegiate Church at Tattershall by Mʳ Mick. Taylour, Curate,
         Aug. 27 or 28.
1710   Sept. 5ᵗʰ  William Clipsham of Gaton and Margarett Bilcliff of Walesby
         were marry'd by a License.
1715   November 18ᵗʰ  Mʳ Nicholas Clipsham was Bury'd ; affidᵗ made Novᵇᵉʳ 20.
1716   May 27ᵗʰ  Elisabeth yᵉ wife of Mʳ Richard Clipsham Bury'd ; affidavit made
         June 1ˢᵗ.
         July 24ᵗʰ  Eleanor Clipsham widow was Bury'd ; Affidavit made 29ᵗʰ.
         [Her will is at Lincoln.]
1721   Sept. 7ᵗʰ  Mʳ Richᵈ Clipsham was Buried; affidavit made Septᵇᵉʳ 11ᵗʰ. [His
         will is at Lincoln.]

## MISCELLANEOUS NOTES.

1625   Lion Clipsham of Manthorpe compounded for not taking up his knighthood
         at the Coronation of Charles I.
1637   Nov. 2  Marriage Licence.  Edmond Clipsham, of Cateby, gent., and
         Susanne West, of Raithby, spʳ.  Application by Edw. Parker, of
         Maultby.  To be solemnized at Legburne or Raithby.

1638 Archdeacon's Visitation. M<sup>r</sup> Michaell Clipsham presented for sittinge in a seate of an excessive height in the parish church of Walesby.

Nicholas Clipsham presented for y<sup>t</sup> hee did not receave y<sup>e</sup> holy Sacrem<sup>t</sup> at this feast of Easter.

Edmund Clipsham and his sonne Michaell for plowing their lands in Otby northwards and plowing up y<sup>e</sup> markett wayes, so that the parson cannot distinguish his glebe as set forth in the Terrier of 1579. Also y<sup>t</sup> the parson is constreined to pay £7 to Michaell Clipsham for grounds allotted to the Rectory in 1626, but he says it was to stopp the mouthes of the Lord B'pp and Chancello<sup>r</sup> but never ment the Church should have the land.

4 *Minster Yard, Lincoln.* A. G.

## Bacon Wills.*

### FROM IPSWICH REGISTRY.

T. Johan'is Bakon de fframlingh'm.    In the name of God, Amen. The xix daye of June in the ffortith yere of the Raigne of o<sup>r</sup> Soueraigne Ladye Elizabethe nowe Queene of England &c. I John Bacon of fframlingh'm at the Castle in the Cowntye of Suff. Husbandman beinge in good and p'fecte minde and memorye though sicke in Bodye doe constitute and make this my last will and Testament in mano<sup>r</sup> and fforme followeinge Revoking hereby all former wills by me at any tyme made eyther by worde or wrightinge ffirste and principallye I Com'end and Com'itte my soule into the handes of Allmightie god and my body to be buried in Xpian buriall where it shall please God to call me And as concerninge my worldly goodes I geve and bequeathe them in man'er and forme followeinge; ffirste I will that my executor in this my wyll hereafter ordeined shall have my howses and landes in fframlingh'm aforesaide untill the feaste of S<sup>t</sup> Michaell the Archangell w<sup>ch</sup> shalbe in the yere of o<sup>r</sup> Lord God 1599 And then at the same feaste I geve and bequeath the same landes & tenements howses and buildings w<sup>th</sup> all & singuler thapp'tenc's (except herinafter excepted) unto John my sonne and to the heires of his bodye lawefully begotten And for default of such heires to Will'm my sonne and to the heires of his bodye lawefully begotten and for defaulte of such heires to Ursula my daughter and to her heires for euer. Item I geve unto Nicholas Bakon my Eldest sonne all my lease landes in fframlingh'm aforesaide for and duringe the Continuance of the same lease in force to him and his assignes and also one little medowe in fframlingham aforesaid w<sup>ch</sup> I latelye boughte of Richard Darneforth beinge holden by Coppie of Court Role untill the Decease of Grace my wiefe And Imediately after the decease of the saide Grace I geve and bequeathe the same little medowe to Will'm Bacon my sonne and to his heires for eu' w<sup>th</sup> the Stodes and Cottes notw<sup>th</sup>standinge uppon the same w<sup>ch</sup> Stoodes and Cotes I will my sonne Nicholas shall mainteine and keepe in as good Reparac'ons duringe all the tearme geven him by this my will in the same medowe as they nowe be or shalbe at the tyme of his entringe into the same. Item I geve and bequeath unto Nicholas my sonne all those my landes and tenements howsinges and buildings w<sup>th</sup> all and singuler there app'tenc's whatsoeu' scittuat and beinge in Willish'm in the Cownty of Suff. aforesaide or in any other Towne thereunto adioyning aswell thoese that I have in posession as thoese in Reu'sion to have holde and enioye the same to him and to his heires for eu'. Item I geve and bequeath unto Nicholas my sonne all my moueable goodes Corne and Cattell and ymplements of howsholde whatsoeu' except hereafter in this my will otherwise bequeathed And nowe as concerninge such p'te of my worldly goodes as my mynde and will is that Grace my wiefe shall have for and towards her maintenance w<sup>ch</sup> is the som'e yerely of fower powndes of

* Continued from p. 23.

lawefull English monye I will the same to be paid her yererely and euerye yere duringe her naturall liefe in this man'er viz<sup>t</sup> at the ffeaste of S<sup>t</sup> Michaell the Archangell xx<sup>s</sup> And at the feaste of the Nativitye of o<sup>r</sup> Lord xx<sup>s</sup> And at the feaste of Thanuncac'on of the Virgen Marye xx<sup>s</sup> and at the feaste of S<sup>t</sup> John Baptiste xx<sup>s</sup> And so q'terly at eu'ye of the saide feaste xx<sup>s</sup> successively as they shoulde come one after another duringe her liefe to begine at the feaste of any of the foresaide feastes w<sup>ch</sup> shall next followe after my decease ; Prouided alweis that yf the saide Grace my saide wiefe shall happen againe to be married to any man duringe her liefe then I will and my meaninge ys that she shall have but xl<sup>s</sup> yerely to be paide her at the foresaide feasts duringe her naturall liefe proportionablye as the foresaide fower powndes shoulde have bene paide yf she had kepte her sellfe sole and unmaried w<sup>ch</sup> foresaide yerely som'e of fowre powndes to be well and truely paid unto her out of my goodes and landes afore in this my will geven and bequeathed I geve and bequeath the same unto her for and in Considerac'on of her thirdes or dower in all my landes and Tenements whatsoeu' And I will the same shalbe paide unto her in man'er and forme aforesaid by my sonnes Nicholas Bacon and John Bacon there heires Executors or assignes in this manner (that is to saie) Nicholas my sonne so longe as he shall have my howses and landes whoely in fframlingh'm aforesaid by force of this my will I will that he his Executors or assigns shall paie her the whoele fower powndes yerelye in man'er and forme aforesaide or yf she marrye then but the said fourty shillings and after his tyme expired w<sup>ch</sup> shalbe at the feaste of S<sup>t</sup> Michael th'archangell 1599 as is before in this my will Remembred Then I will that the said Nicholas my sonne his Executors or assigns shall paie her yerely six and forty shillings & eight pence duringe her liefe quarterlye by euen portions at the feasts aforesaide p'cell of the foresaide yerelye som'e of fowre powndes And my sonne John his heyres or assignes or the owners thereof shall paye her out of thoese my landes before geven unto him yerelye the som'e of xxxiij<sup>s</sup> iiij<sup>d</sup> duringe her liefe quarterlye by euen portions at the aforesaide feastes beinge the Reste of the foresaide som'e or yerelye Rent of fowre powndes w<sup>ch</sup> saide seueral paiments I will shalbe made in the south Church porch of fframlingh'm aforesaid And yf it shall happen my said wief to marry againe then I will that my sonne Nicholas his execut' or assignes shall paye her yerelye duringe her liefe naturall the forsaid som'e of forty shillings in man'er aforesaide And after her marriage so had or doene my sonne John to be clerely accquited of his paiements unto her for euer aftere. And for the more p'fecte and suer paiments aforesaid to be made in man'er and forme aforesaide I will that my sonne Nicholas shall enter bond and seale and deliu' the same good and effectuall in lawe unto my superviso<sup>r</sup> in this my will appointed for himselfe his heires executors and adm'strators in the som'e of Twenty Powndes of lawefull English monye w<sup>th</sup> Condic'ons thereunto Indorsed or sub-scribed for the true paiments of such som'es of monye as ar limitted and appointed him to paye unto my saide wiefe by this my last will and Testament accordinge to my very true entente & meaninge w<sup>th</sup>in one moneth nexte after my decease And yf he cannot speake w<sup>th</sup> my saide sup'viso<sup>r</sup> w<sup>th</sup>in the saide moneth then to leave the saide bonde sealed and deliu'ed to his use at his dwellinge howse in Kettle-borough whole sownde & p'fecte and to goode effecte in Lawe And as for thoese paiments limitted and assigned by this my will to be made to Grace my wiefe by my sayde sonne John his heires or assignes out of thoese lands geven unto him I will and my true intente ys that yf he his heires or assignes or the owners of thoese landes shall make any defaulte in any of thoese paiments That then Imediatelye after such defalte made It shalbe lawefull for my saide wiefe or her assignes to enter into all thoese landes and tenements w<sup>th</sup>in and by this my will and testament I have geven him And the same to have occupye and enioy w<sup>th</sup> all and singuler the p'fittes and com'odities thereof unto her owne use untill she be fully and whoelye satisfied so much as was due unto her from my saide sonne John his heires or assignes out of the landes afore geven unto him for her yerelye Rent before herein specified before here entre made. Item I will that my sonne Nicholas his heires or assignes shall paye or cause to be payde out of thoese my landes and tenements in

Willish'm aforesaide before in this my will geven unto him the som'e of Thirty pownds of good and lawefull English monye in man'er and forme followinge viz$^t$ unto Ursula my daughter the somme of five powndes thereof uppon the feaste daye of S$^t$ Michaell th'archangell next and Imediatelye followeinge after the decease of the longest lives of Emme Bacon my mother & Grace my saide wiefe And other five powndes of the same monye unto John my son'e at and uppon the feaste daye of S$^t$ Michaell th'archangell successively followeinge the former paiment And unto Will'm my son'e other five powndes p'cell of the saide xxx$^{li}$ at and uppon the feaste daye of S$^t$ Michaell the Archangell next followeinge the foresaide Seconde paiment due unto Ursala my saide daughter other five powndes to be paide her at the feaste of S$^t$ Michaell th'archangell next followeinge after the aforesaide Third paiment made The other five powndes p'cell of the aforesaide xxx$^{li}$ to be paide unto William my son'e at and uppon the feaste daye of S$^t$ Michaell th'archangell next ensuinge the aforesaide forthe paiment made And the other ffive powndes being the whole & p'te of the saide xxx$^{li}$ to be paide unto Ursela my daughter and Will'm my sonne euenlye betwene them at & uppon the feaste of S$^t$ Michaell th'archangell nexte followeinge the foresaide fifte paiment. And yf anye of my foresaide Children dep'te this lief before the tyme limitted them to Receive there foresaide paiments or any p'te or p'cell thereof Then I will and my meaninge ys that his her or ther p'te so deceased shalbe equally devided amongste the Reste of my Children then livinge to be payde unto them at Such daies as he or she or they so deceased shoulde have Received the same yf they had lived. Prouided alwaies my mynde is that yf my landes in fframlingh'm shall (by force of th'entaile of them made before in this my will) decend or Come unto Ursula my daughter before her p'te of the aforesaide xxx$^{li}$ be paid to her that the same paiment to her geven shall cease and Remaine & be to my sonne Nicholas his executors & assignes And yf the same landes shall happen to decend unto my daughter by force of the foresaide Intaile after she have Received the saide paiments or any of them then I will she her heires executors or assignes shall paie the somme or sommes w$^{ch}$ she Received unto my saide sonne Nicholas his executors or assignes w$^{ch}$ yf she or they shall not truely doe w$^{th}$in three moneths after the same landes are soe decended unto her I will my saide sonne Nicolas his executors or assignes shall enter into the saide landes & take the whoele p'fittes thereof unto his or there owne use or uses untill he or they be fullye satisfied and paid the sommes as she Received before the same landes soe decended unto her. And all and eu'ye of the aforesaide seuerall paiments of the foresaide xxx$^{li}$ to be paide out of the saide Landes by my saide sonne Nicholas as aforesaide. And I will that he the saide Nicholas his heires or assignes shall make paiment thereof at eu'ye of the aforesaide feaste dayes in or at the south porch of the p'ish Church of Willish'm aforesaid. And yf he the saide Nicholas my sonne his heires or assignes shall make defaulte in any of the aforesaide paiments at the dayes and place aforesaide Contrarye to my true Intent and meaninge Then I will that he or she of my Children w$^{ch}$ shall want of there paiments shall enter into all thoese my landes and tenements in Willish'm aforesaide untill he or she be fully satisfied and paid so much (as was due unto him or her before his or her entrie made) And take the whoele p'fittes thereof to his or her owne use duringe the Tyme. Prouided alwaies if Twoe or all Three of my saide Children shalbe unpaide by the Slacknes of my saide sonne Nicholas Any of there portions of the foresaide xxx$^{li}$ all at one tyme, then I will that they all or so manye of them as shalbe unpaide shall Joyntelye entre into all the foresaide landes in Willish'm aforesaide and take the p'fittes Joyntelye amongste or betwixte them untill eu'ye of them be fully satisfied so much as was due unto them or any of them before there entrie made. Item I will that whereas I have geven unto Nicholas my sonne all my moveable goodes except in this my will otherwise bequeathed In Considerac'on of that gift geven unto him I will and my whoele Intent and meaninge is that the saide Nicholas my sonne his executors or assignes shall uppon that daye twelve monethes nexte after the buriall daye of Emme Bacon his grandmother paie unto Ursula his sister John his brother & Will'm his brother unto eu'ye of them the som'e of five powndes six shillings &

eight pence of lawefull English monye in or at the south porch of the p'ish Church
of fframlingh'm aforesaide. And if any of his brothers or sister dep'te this lief
before the saide daie of paiment I will the suruiu' or suruiuours shall euenly deuide
the p'te and portion of him or her so deceased amongste them by euen devision
thereof to be made by my executo$^r$. Item I geve and bequeath unto Grace my
wiefe the use of the chamber wherin I nowe lye sicke untill the feaste of S$^t$
Michaell th'archangell nexte after my decease w$^{th}$ free ingresse and Regresse And
more I geve unto her to be deliu'ed her Imediately after my decease by my Executo$^r$
hall the Corne that nowe is in my howses of what kinde soeu' the same be of and
halfe the olde hempe And three Kettles the biggest one of the middle ones & the
lessest and a Spit a frienge panne & a dripping pan a fier pan & a paier of tonges
a pashell & a Towe Combe All my owne pewter one bed wheron I nowe lye sicke
w$^{th}$ all the furniture belonginge to yt as yt nowe standeth and all the Linnen whatsoeu' and Twoe Cofers in the Chamber where I nowe lye beinge the Twoe
lesseste there And all her wollen belonginge to her wearinge A skillet possenett and
a Restiron. Item I ordeine & make Nicholas my sonne my sole executo$^r$ of this my
last will & testament w$^{ch}$ I havinge heard deliberatelye Redde doe p'nounce the same
to be my laste will & Testament charginge him to p'forme y$^e$ same Trulye accordinge
to my true meaninge & y$^e$ Trust that I Repose in him as he will answere the Contrarye at the daye of Judgement And I will him to paye my debtes & take my
debtes and se me honestlye buried. And I ordeine & heartilye Require Will'm
Worlich of Kettleborough aforesaide the son'e of Will'm Worlich late deceased to be
my sup'viso$^r$ of this my will & to be aidinge and assistinge unto my executo$^r$ what
he may w$^{th}$ his good advise & dyscretion And for his paynes I geve unto him five
shillings of Lawefull English monye to be payde him by my saide executo$^r$. Witnesses to this my will Will'm Worlich Robert Atherton the wrighter and Robte
Chem'inge.                                        JOHN BACON his marke.
    Proved at Framlingham 10 August 1598.

# Dalison Notes.*

ADDITIONAL MANUSCRIPT 12269, BRITISH MUSEUM.

Lincoln.
    Alexander de Neovilla filius et heres Alexandri de Neovilla questus fuit Domino
Regi quod cum fecisset ei homagium suum de terris quas predictus Alexander pater
suus tenuit de eo in capite et unde vicecomes preceptum habuit quod de omnibus terris
predictis de quibus predictus Alexander pater ejus fuit seisitus die quo obiit seisinam ei
facere idem vicecomes seisinam ei facere noluit de manerio de Haketorpe, cum pertinentiis, occasione donacionis quam Ricardus de Alenzan qui habuit custodiam predic-
tarum terrarum dicit factam fuisse a predicto Alexandro Clemencie filie predicti
Alexandri quam Willielmus frater ipsius Ricardi duxit in uxorem et unde preceptum est
vicecomiti quod venire faceret xij legales homines itam milites, etc., de visneto de
Haketorpe ad recognoscendum, etc., utrum predictus Alexander dictum manerium
dedit prefate Clemencie et utrum ipsa Clemencia in vita prefati Alexandri inde fuit in
seisina, et per quantum tempus ante mortem ipsius Alexandri et quod venire faceret
coram predictis liberos homines de predicto manerio libere tenentes ad recognoscendum
utrum post mortem prefati Alexandri homagium fecerunt predicto Alexandro filio
suo dum fuit in custodia ipsius Ricardi. Et Randulfus de Hamewella et alii
juratores, etc., dicunt quod predictus Alexander pater ipsius Alexandri tercio die
ante mortem suam habuit in animo promovendi dictam Clemenciam dedit ei terram
illam et misit ibi duos servientes cum predicta Clemencia et fecit ei seisinam et
statim reversa est illa Clemencia ad patrem suum, et ipse Alexander tercio die obiit,
et mortuo eo statim cepit Dominus [Rex] manerium illud in manum suam simul

cum aliis terris que fuerunt ipsius Alexandri, et illud simul cum aliis terris commisit in custodia predicto Ricardo simul cum filio primogenito et herede ipsius Alexandri, quem quidem heredem idem Ricardus maritavit cuidam sorori sue, et mortuo eodem herede primogenito assignavit idem Ricardus dotem sorori sue de eadem terra, et eciam fecit ipsum Alexandrum filium ipsius Alexandri post mortem fratris sui primogeniti capere homagia liberorum hominum libere tenencium de eodem manerio sicut ipsi liberi homines presentes hoc testantur.

Et dicunt quod, jam duobus annis elapsis, venit [Ricardus] ad hundredum et wapentachium et ostendit cartam factam eidem Clemencie de feofemento, set illa nullam aliam habuit inde seisinam nisi secundum quod predictum est.

[Judicium.] Et ideo consideratum est quod Alexander recuperavit seisinam et Ricardus custodiatur. Et vicecomes per sacramentum proborum hominum diligenter inquirat que dampna idem Alexander habuit postquam seisinam habuit de aliis terris et tenementis que fuerunt predicti Alexandri patris sui, et facta inquisicione illa habere faciat predicto Alexandro de catallis ipsius Ricardi. Postea fecit finem, etc.

[Coram Rege Roll, 21 Henry 3, A.D. 1236-7.]*

Adhuc de Quindena Sancte Trinitatis, [2 Edw. 1].
Lincoln.
Jacobus de Lissington, essoniator Hawisie de Brynkel, optulit se quarto die versus Desideratam Dalyzun de placito duorum mesuagiorum, etc., in Hakethorn que clamat ut jus suum, etc. Et ipsa non venit, etc. Et ipsi summonentur quod sint in Octabis Sancti Michaelis quia alium diem, etc.
De Banco Roll, Edw. 1, No. 6, m. 23 d., A.D. 1274.

Wapentakium de Haselachou in Lindeseye anno regni Edwardi, tercio.
Dicunt quod Simon West, appellatus per Willielmum de Alatum, probatorem, dedit Thome de Bolton vicecomiti tres marcas cum habuit plevinam sufficientem usque ad liberacionem. . . . Rad' de Ingham tunc ballivo xs. Waltero Greek Constabulario castelli Lincoln dimidiam marcam.
Hundred Roll, Lincoln, 3 Edw. 1, m. 2, p. 114 and 379, [A.D. 1275-6].

Placita apud Westmonasterium in Octabis Sancti Hillarii . . . . anno Regis Edwardi, primo.
Nichola que fuit uxor Willielmi Alenzun optulit se quarto die versus Willielmum de Alenzun de placito tercie partis unius mesuagii, novies viginti acras terre, etc., in Cranesford. . . . . Et versus Isoldam filiam Willielmi Alenzun de placito tercie partis trium acrarum terre cum pertinentiis in eadem villa quas clamat in dotem versus eos, etc.
Nichola que fuit uxor Willielmi de Alanson ponit loco suo Johannem Bacan vel Robertum filium Willielmi versus Willielmum filium Willielmi de Alanson et alios, etc.
De Banco Roll, 1 Edw. 1, No. 1, m. 1 d., 10, Suffolk, A.D. 1273.

Adhuc de Quindena et tercia septimana Sancti Hillarii, [2 Edw. 1].
Lincoln.
Juliana que fuit uxor Philippi de Merk per attornatum suum petit versus Petrum Dalezun terciam partem duorum toftorum et duarum bovatarum terre cum pertinentiis in Suthlend, etc. Et Petrus et omnes alii venerunt, etc. Et predictus Petrus de tercia parte versus eum petita dicit quod non potest ei inde respondere sine quadam Alicia uxore sua que conjunctim feoffata est cum ipso de predicto tenemento. Et predicta Juliana non potest hoc dedicere. Et petit licenciam recedendi de brevi suo et habet, etc.
De Banco Roll, Edw. 1, No. 7, m. 31, A.D. 1274.

* No Roll extant. This MS. is in "Bracton's Note Book."

Wappentakium de Tykehull.

Dicunt quod Magister Raymund et Petrus le Parker ballivi de Tykehull ceperunt de Willielmo Alezun felono capto pro morte hominis decem marcas et permiserunt ipsum evaderi.

Hundred Roll, York, 4 Edw. 1, m. 4, p. 364, [A.D. 1275-6].

Lincoln.

Elias de Bekingham et Johannes de Metingham consignantur ad assisam nove disseisine capiendam quam Johannes de Alazun et Matillis uxor ejus arrainiaverunt versus Rogerum de Arcy et alios de tenementis in Nettleton.

Patent Roll, 4 Edw. 1, m. 33 d., A.D. 1275-1276.

Lincoln.

Iidem consignantur ad assisam capiendam quam Petrus Dalazoun arrainiavit versus Stephanum Burdette de quodam forssato (sic) levato in Heleghethorp.

Iidem consignantur ad assisam nove disseisine capiendam quam Petrus Dalazoun arrainiavit versus Willielmum Dalazoun de tenementis in Fulnethby.

Patent Roll, 7 Edw. 1, m. 16 d., A.D. 1278-1279.

(To be continued.)

# GRANT OF SUPPORTERS TO SIR ROBERT MURRAY KEITH, K.C.B., 1772.*

To all and singular to whom these Presents shall come Stephen Martin Leake Esquire Garter Principal King of Arms sendeth greeting Whereas the Kings Most Excellent Majesty in Consideration of the great Merit Virtue and Loyalty of Sir Robert Murray Keith his Majesty's Minister at the Court of the King of Denmark, hath been graciously pleased to create him a Knight Companion of the Most honorable Military Order of the Bath, And Whereas by a Statute of the said Order it is decreed that the Knights Companions for their greater Distinction and Honor shall upon all Occasions whatever bear and use Supporters to their Arms and that Garter Principal King of Arms for the Time being shall grant Supporters to such Companions as shall not be entitled thereto by Virtue of their Peerage. Now Know Ye that I the said Garter pursuant to the said Decree do by these Presents grant unto the said Sir Robert Murray Keith Knight Companion of the Most Honorable Military Order of the Bath the Supporters following that is to say, On each Side A Roebuck proper attired and unguled Or both collared the dexter collar Gules charged with three Pallets of the second, the sinister Azure charged with three Stars of six points Chains affixed thereto Gold as the same are in the Margin hereof more plainly depicted to be borne and used by Him the said Sir Robert Murray Keith according to the Tenor of the aforesaid Statute And I do hereby Certify that in pursuance of the Direction of the right Honorable Richard Earl of Scarbrough Deputy with the Royal approbation to the Most Noble Edward Duke of Norfolk Earl Marshal and hereditary Marshal of England I have caused this Grant to be registered in the College of Arms. In Witness whereof I the said Garter have to these Presents subscribed my Name and affixed the Seal of my Office this second day of June in Twelfth Year of the Reign of Our Sovereign Lord George the Third by the Grace of God King of Great Britain France and Ireland Defender of the Faith &c. and in the Year of Our Lord God one Thousand seven hundred and seventy two.

S. MARTIN LEAKE, Garter Principal King of Arms.

* The original grant is in the possession of A. F. C. LANGLEY, Esq., of Peterston-super-Ely.

*Robert Keith Esq.ʳ*

SIR ROBERT MURRAY KEITH K.B.

## MONUMENTAL INSCRIPTIONS OF HOLY TRINITY, BRADFORD-ON-AVON, CO. WILTS.*

### NORTH WALL OF CHANCEL.

*A large monument with life-size statue in costume of William III.*†

Arms : Or, a fess checky argent and azure, a bordure ermine; impaling, Sable, a lion passant-guardant or between three esquire's helmets argent garnished of the second.
Crest : A royal crown proper.

Triste Monumentum intuere, Lector ! et postquam Epitaphium tacitè | perlegisti, nigrum sub pedibus aspice marmor. Tunc si possis, | supprime luctus. | Ab annosâ prosapiâ ac honestis parentibus ortus, nunc fato correptus | Carolus Steward | multorum lachrymis inibi sepelitur | Dum superstes mirâ integritate innocuus, dulcique indole comis et affabilis, | Bonis moribus ornatus, ac virtutibus tam eximie decoratus ut æquando | haud parem reperies. | Proh Dolor. | quamplurima vita pensum absolvunt, et supremum inducunt diem. | Hic casu infausto ex equo labente delapsus, mox graviter pectore contusus, | Tandem apostemate intumuit, languit et occubuit xi Julii An'o D'ni | MDCXCVIII. | Amice valeto, | Summum nec metuas diem, nec optes. | Justa hæc piæ memoriæ chari mariti uxor lugubris | Maria Steward dicavit, et marmora parentavit | MDCCI.

---

Daniel Clutterbuck | of this Place, Gent. | died the 16ᵗʰ of April, 1786, | Aged 56 years.

Arms : Azure, a lion rampant argent langued gules, in chief three escallop-shells of the second.

---

Beneath this Monument among his Ancestors | is deposited the body of Francis Yerbury, | of Belcomb Brook in this Parish Esquire, | who closed this scene of mortal life | on the 28ᵗʰ of April, 1778, | in the 72ⁿᵈ year of his age. | Also of Mary his Wife | who died September the 18ᵗʰ, 1775, Aged 59. | And of Francis, their eldest Son, | who was drowned by attempting to swim, | on the 8ᵗʰ of October, 1752-3, | in the 14ᵗʰ year of his age. | Also of Richard, their second Son, | who died February 12ᵗʰ, 1772, Aged 31. | And of John William, their youngest Son, | who departed this life | on the 8ᵗʰ of October, 1824 | in the 74ᵗʰ year of his age. | Also of Hester, the much lamented and beloved Wife | of the above named John William Yerbury Esqʳᵉ, | who departed this life on the 18ᵗʰ of Novʳ, 1842, Aged 82.

Arms : A lion rampant; impaling, On a fess engrailed three fleurs-de-lys between as many nag's heads erased, BAYLEY.
Crest : A lion's head erased.

---

Arms : Quarterly—1 and 4, CLUTTERBUCK; 2 and 3, Or, a cross quarterly counterchanged gules and sable, in the dexter chief an eagle displayed of the third, WEBB ; impaling, Per bend ermine and erminois, a lion rampant or, EDWARDS.
Crest : A buck sejant.

Sacred to the memory | of Daniel Clutterbuck Esqʳᵉ, | of Bradford-Leigh in this parish | who died the 17ᵗʰ of June, 1821, | aged 77 years. | Also to the memory | of Elizabeth Clutterbuck, Relict | of Daniel Clutterbuck Esqʳᵉ, | who died April 28, 1826, | in her 79ᵗʰ year.

---

Near this Place | in the Family Vault | are interred the Remains of | Mʳ Mawbey Tugwell, | youngest Son of the late | Mʳ William Tugwell ; | He married Penelope, | fourth Daughter of | Daniel Clutterbuck Esqʳ | of Bradford Leigh, | and departed

---

* Communicated by ARTHUR SCHOMBERG, Esq.
† Vid. 'Herald and Genealogist,' vol. ii., part vii. Compton of Hartpury bears : *Argent, a fess nebuly gules, on a chief of the second a helmet between two lion's heads erased or.* The Arms on the monument are those of the Marquess of Northampton's family. The Crest of the Stewards is : *A stag proper gorged checky argent and azure.*

this Life | 13<sup>th</sup> of May, 1815, aged 41 Years ; | Leaving Issue by her | 5 Infant Children ; | She died at Brighton | 26<sup>th</sup> of Nov<sup>r</sup>, 1861, aged 80, | and was buried at Hove.

Arms : Azure, three garbs or, on a chief argent a boar's head couped sable langued and tusked proper ; impaling, CLUTTERBUCK.
Crest : A hart's head erased.

———

To the Memory of | M<sup>r</sup> Humphry Tugwell; | In Religion He was Zealous and Sincere ; | He was Generous, Just and Benevolent ; | A warm and steady Friend, | An indulgent Husband, A fond Parent ; | A kind and humane Master | He carried on an extensive Manufactory | in this Town, upwards of fifty Years | with unblemish'd Integrity, | And departed this Life the 22<sup>d</sup> day of August, 1775, | Aged 71 Years. | He had Issue by Elizabeth his Wife, |

FitzDaniel Tugwell who died Dec<sup>r</sup> 3<sup>rd</sup>, 1747, Aged 10 Years.
Thomas Tugwell . . . . . May 24<sup>th</sup>, 1769, Aged 24 Years.
William Tugwell . . . . . Dec<sup>r</sup> 25<sup>th</sup>, 1774, Aged 32 Years.

Also three other Children | who died in their Infancy. | Also to the Memory of the above | M<sup>rs</sup> Elizabeth Tugwell | who was exemplary in the | performance of every religious | and parental duty | and died on the 7<sup>th</sup> of June, 1801, | Aged 90 Years.

Arms : TUGWELL ; impaling, Per fess sable and argent, in chief a royal crown or, in base a lion passant of the first, JONES.

———

Sacred to the memory of | Elizabeth Tugwell, | second daughter of the late | Mawbey Tugwell Esq<sup>r</sup> ; | she died at Widcombe Crescent, Bath, | the 9<sup>th</sup> day of November, 1822. | Also of Thomas Tugwell Esq<sup>r</sup>, | the only son of the said Mawbey Tugwell, | who died at College Street, Westminster, | the 25<sup>th</sup> of December, 1840, | aged 27 years, | and was buried at S<sup>t</sup> John's church, | Westminster.

Arms : Quarterly—1 and 4, TUGWELL ; 2 and 3, Argent, on a pale sable three crescents of the field, HAYWARD ; impaling, Quarterly, 1 and 4, CLUTTERBUCK ; 2 and 3, WEBB.
Crest : A hart's head erased.

In a vault beneath are interred the remains | of George Hayward Tugwell Esq<sup>r</sup>, | of Crowe Hall, near Bath, | who died beloved and respected | January 14 : 1839, aged 71 years. | Also of Sarah, his wife, | daughter of Daniel Clutterbuck Esq<sup>r</sup>, | of Bradford Leigh, who died May 31 : 1853, | aged 76 years.

———

SOUTH WALL OF CHANCEL.

*A painted window:* At Rest W. J. April 5<sup>th</sup> 1855. *On brass plate underneath:* An Offering by William | Henry Jones, Vicar of this Parish, | in Memory of a loved and loving Father.

———

*A large white marble monument with grey marble sarcophagus.*

Arms : I. Argent, three wolf's heads erased proper ; on a shield of pretence, Argent, two bars engrailed azure between nine martlets gules, MOORE.*
  II. METHUEN quartering MOORE; impaling, Quarterly, 1 and 4, Ermine, three chevrouels gules, SELFE ; 2 and 3, Argent, a fess between six annulets gules, LUCAS. (M.I.)†

Ad Ædis hujusce latus boreale | viri præstantissimi | Antonij Methuen, Arm'. | Conduntur Exuviæ, | Pauli Methuen, de Bradford, Arm', | Filij natu secundi, | antiquissimo | stemmate de Methuen, in Regno Scotiæ, | oriundi ; et Gertrudæ, | Conjugis Pientissimæ, | Thomæ Moore, de Spargrove, in com. Somerset. Arm'. | (Ex Elizabetha Uxore, | Filia primogenita D'ni Johannis Bampfylde, | de Poltimore, in Agro Devon. | Baronetti) | Filiæ et Cohæredis. | Obierunt | Ille, Maij 10, 1717,

———

* ' Wilts. Arch. Mag.,' v., 238.
† (M.I.) signifies that the Arms or Monuments to which these letters are attached are destroyed or illegible, and therefore are supplied from the rare printed ' Monumental Inscriptions of Wiltshire, 1821.'

Annos Natus 67. | Illa, Jul. 20, 1699, Annos Nata 40. | Juxta Proavorum Cineres, | Thomæ Methuen, Arm' : | Antonij et Gertrudæ, | Filij Unici, | Requiescit Depositum : | Qui nihil non æquum et liberale, | Et fecit semper et cogitavit, | Tranquillus, patiens, clemens, benignus, | Ingenio minime vulgari, | Singulari prorsus humanitate ; | Et Annæ Uxoris, | Filiæ Isaaci Selfe, Arm'. | De Beanacre, in Agro Wiltonensi | (Ex Uxore Penelope, | Præhonorabilis Caroli Lucas, Baronis de Shenfield, in Com. Essex, | Filia et Cohærede) | Cujus Formam inter Primas venustam, | Et commendabant et superabant, | Ineffabilis morum Suavitas, | Animiq' cunctis virtutibus ornati | Potentiores Illiciæ. | Obierunt ¦ Ille, Jan. 2, 1737, Ætat. 53. | Illa, Maij 15, 1733, Ætat. 37. | Parentibus bene meritis, | Paulus Methuen, Arm' : Heres et Filius Unicus. | P.

*A brass plate.*

Arms : Gules, three stirrups leathered in pale or.

Roger Deverell of ffranckelen near Bradford in the | County of Wilts. was buried in this Churchyard 1546. | Isabell widow of the above Roger Deverell. | John son of the above Roger Deverell of ffranckelyn. | Richard Deverell of ffranklyn was buried here 28th January 1627. | Widow Deverell of ffranklyn was buried here 1st March 1629. | John Deverell of ffrankly born 1680 was buried here 15th ffeby 1726. | Elizabeth widow of the above John Deverell of ffrankly.

*(To be continued.)*

## Genealogy of Browne.*

H. **Thomas Browne** of Bentley Hall, co. Derby† (bapt. [at Longford] 16 Dec. 1723; bur. [at Battlefield, co. Salop] 1 July 1764. Will dated 5 June 1764; pr. P.C.C. 9 Aug. 1764 by his wife Catherina, his brother Rev. Corbet Browne, and Roger Kynaston, Esq., the ex'ors). Inherited Bentley Estate under his father's will 1733. Sold the whole of the estates by deed dated 21 Feb. 1749 for £12,000 to Edward Wilmot, Esq., M.D., of London. Afterwards resided in the parish of St. Julian Friars, Shrewsbury. Mar. ([in St. Julian's Church] 9 Feb. 1748; pre-nuptial settlement dated 15 Jan. 1748) Catherina, dau. of Charles Yonge of St. Julian's, Merchant, and Lowry his wife (bapt. [at St. Julian's] 23 April 1721 ; bur. [at Battlefield, co. Salop] 13 Aug. 1766). Legatee and executrix under her husband's will 1764. Issue :—

I. 1. Thomas Browne of Gate Street, Lincoln's Inn Fields, London (bapt. [at St. Julian's] 2 Oct. 1750 ; died s.p. ; bur. at St. Giles in the Fields).

---

* Continued from p. 70.

† Miniature in possession of Dr. Elsom, in brooch, about 2 by 1½ inches, representing Thomas Browne in a white toupee dress-wig with side curls, scarlet coat and waistcoat laced with gold, lace neckerchief, very refined looking face, fair complexion, and hazel eyes.

Legatee under his father's will 1764, and under his brother Charles's will 1797. Mar. ([at St. Clement Danes, Strand ?] . . . .) Elizabeth Wedge, who survived him, and bur. at St. Giles in the Fields.

2. Charles Browne (bapt. [at St. Julian's] 13 April 1752 ; d. unmar. [at Withington Rectory] ; bur. there 6 April 1797. Will dated 7 Jan. 1797; pr. P.C.C. 12 July 1797 by his brother John Browne). Legatee under his father's will 1764.

3. Rupert Browne of H.M. Customs, Liverpool (bapt. [at St. Julian's] 9 Nov. 1753 ; bur. [at St. John's, Liverpool] 1 Nov. 1815). Legatee under his brother Charles's will 1797. Mar. ([in St. Saviour's Church, Southwark] 3 Feb. 1795) Mary Wedge (? sister of Elizabeth Wedge, who mar. his eldest brother) of the parish of St. Saviour's, Southwark, who survived him (d. . . . .). Issue :—

**J.** 1. Thomas Tansley Browne (bapt. [at St. Peter's, Liverpool] 10 Oct. 1813 ; d. unmar. . . . . ?).

4. Corbet Browne (bapt. [at St. Julian's], 22 Nov. 1755; bur. there 27 May 1763).

5. James Browne (of whom again).

6. John Browne* (bapt. [at St. Julian's] 30 June 1758; d. [at Allscott, co. Salop] 4 April, bur. [at Withington] 8 April 1826. Will dated 16 March 1811 ; pr. P.C.C. 10 May 1826 by his son Thomas Corbet Browne). Lieutenant in Huntingdon Militia at time of marriage. Mar. ([in St. Ives Church, Hunts], 11 May 1783) Rachael, dau. of John Glegg, Esq., of Langum, co. Pembroke (by his wife Ann, dau. of Cæsar Mathias, Esq., of Hook, Langum, co. Pembroke), (bapt. [at Langum] 14 Aug. 1753 ; bur. [at St. Giles in the Fields, London] 19 Dec. 1805). Issue :—

**J.** 1. Thomas Corbet Browne† of Shrewsbury (b. 10 April, bapt. [at St. Ives, Hunts] 16 April 1788 ; d. unmar. 1854. Will dated 18 Nov. 1854 ; pr. P.C.C. 4 Dec. 1854 by his niece Frances Lovie Elsom). Lieutenant in Huntingdon Militia by Commission dated 3 March 1808. Legatee under his uncle Charles's will 1797.

1. Catherine Anne‡ (b. 12 Jan., bapt. [at Twickenham, co. Middlesex], 23 Jan. 1786 ; d. 22 Feb. 1851). Legatee under her uncle Charles's will 1797. Mar. ([at St. Leonard's, Shoreditch], 9 Oct. 1806) Colonel George Elsom§ of Holloway, London (b. 5 March 1789 ; d. and bur. at Angostura, S. America, 13 Sept. 1819. M.I. Highgate Cemetery). Commissary General to the Columbian Army under Bolivar. Issue :—

---

\* Two miniatures of John Browne in possession of Dr. Elsom, one, on ivory, size 3 by 2 inches, in scarlet uniform of the Hunts Militia, high black stock, epaulettes, white shoulder belt ; hair cut very short probably for wig ; handsome face, fair complexion, hazel eyes, and brown hair. The other miniature, in a ring, ¾ inch by ½ inch, by Cipriani, in toupée or tie wig, white lace neckerchief, dull red coat, lavender embroidered waistcoat.

† Miniature in possession of Dr. Elsom, size 3 by 2 inches, in scarlet uniform of Hunts Militia, high black stock, epaulettes, white shoulder belt ; fair complexion, hazel eyes, brown hair arranged in curls at sides of forehead. In the possession of R. S. Boddington, Esq., are two letters from John Browne to Mrs. Isaac Hawkins Browne of Badger, dated 1 and 29 July 1818, and one from Thomas Corbet Browne, dated 30 July 1818, all relating to the legacy, £50 apiece, bequeathed to them by Isaac Hawkins Browne, and written from Godmanchester.

"In the year 1808 I had the offer of a Lieutenancy in the 7th Fusiliers without purchase, which would have been as good to me (had I accepted it) as five hundred and fifty pounds . . . . I had another of a Commission in the 14th Reg^t . . . . after that I had the offer of a Lieutenancy in the 5th Reg^t . . . ."—Thomas Corbet Browne's letter, 1818.

‡ Two miniatures in possession of Dr. Elsom, one, at an early age, by Sir W. Beechey, on ivory, size 2½ by 1½ inches : fair complexion, dark blue eyes, light brown hair with fringe cut straight over forehead ; low-bodied dress of pale blue and red ceinture. The other, also on ivory, size 3 by 2 inches, taken about 22 years of age : dark hair dressed high and disposed in light curls, shading a very good-looking face ; blue eyes ; dressed in a round evening full-bosomed gown plaited at the breast.

**K.**　1.　George Elsom (b. 1 Aug. 1808 ; d. 15 Jan. 1861 ; bur. Tower Hamlets Cemetery). Mar. ([at St. John's, Hoxton] 22 Aug. 1836) Rebecca Lydia, dau. of John Grace, Esq., of Prince's Risborough, Bucks (d. 2 Nov. 1885; bur. at Lower Norwood Cemetery). Issue :—

**L.**　1.　George Frederick Elsom of Boston, Massachusetts, U.S.A. (b. 15 Sept. 1837 ; living unmar. 1887).
　　2.　Henry Claudius Elsom of Sundorne House, Pinner (b. 30 Dec. 1838 ; living 1887). Mar. ([at St. Bride's, Fleet Street, London] 22 May 1869) Caroline Harriet, eldest dau. of Thomas James Williams of Milton next Gravesend, Kent (living 1887). Issue :—

**M.**　1.　Corbet Elsom (b. 22 June 1871),
　　2.　Thomas Elsom (b. 21 Nov. 1874),
　　3.　Harry Williams Elsom (b. 25 Feb. 1877),
　　1.　Carrie Claudine (b. 19 Feb. 1870),
　　2.　Lilian (b. 3 Dec. 1872),
　　3.　Grace Williams (b. 22 Nov. 1878),
　　4.　Elsie Williams (b. 15 Dec. 1881),
　　5.　Dorothy Williams (b. 15 Oct. 1884),

}living 1887.

**L.**　3.　Albert Leander Elsom (b. 30 Sept. 1842 ; d. 30 April 1845 ; bur. at St. Paul's, Shadwell).
　　4.　Alfred Howard Elsom (b. 18 Nov. 1847 ; living 1887) of Garfield, Sydenham, Kent.
　　1.　Adelaide Rebecca, } living unmar. 1887.
　　2.　Alice Elizabeth,

**K.**　2.　Henry Elsom of London (b. 3 March 1810 ; d. unmar. 22 July 1850).
　　3.　Frederick Joseph Elsom of Limehouse, London (b. 10 July 1812; d. 16 March 1880; bur. at Tower Hamlets), M.R.C.S.E. Mar. (4 April 1842) Mary, dau. of Richard and Mary Livett, and relict of John Lander, F.R.G.S. (an African Explorer and Discoverer, to whom is public monument in Truro, Cornwall), (b. 2 Sept. 1812 ; living 1887). Issue :—
　　1.　Frederic Joseph Elsom of Whitwell, Chesterfield (b. 13 June 1845 ; living unmar. 1887), Physician and Surgeon.
　　2.　George Nicholas Elsom of London (b. 21 Jan. 1850 ; living 1887).
　　3.　Alfred Elsom of Stretford, Essex (b. 10 May 1855 ; living 1887), mar. Martha Spiers.
　　1.　Josephine (b. 4 Nov. 1843 ; living 1887), mar. J. J. Udale, Esq., Physician and Surgeon.
　　2.　Catherine Isabella (b. 12 Feb. 1847 ; d. 31 Dec. 1877).
　　1.　Frances Lovie (b. 25 Dec. 1814 ; d. unmar. 16 Aug. 1883).

**I.**　7.　Edward Yonge Browne (bapt. [at St. Julian's] 17 Aug. 1759 ; bur. there 31 Dec. 1775).
　　1.　Catherina Yonge (bapt. [at St. Julian's] 10 Aug. 1749 ; bur. there 20 May 1752).

**I.**　**James Browne,** fifth son of Thomas Browne of Bentley (bapt. [at St. Julian's] 27 April 1757. To Jamaica and died on board the "Hero" of Liverpool 1791). Mentioned as deceased in his brother Charles's will 1797, and as having left a son Thomas Browne, then under age. Mar. ([by licence dated 17 Dec. 1778 at St. Peter's, Cornhill, London] 19 Dec. 1778) Mary, dau. of Thomas Dalton, Esq., of London. Left England for Jamaica with two children and never returned. (Her sister Sarah Dalton mar., first,

. . . . Waters of London, and, secondly, Rev. Dr. James Lindsay of Grovehall, Stratford-le-Bow, whose will, dated 25 April 1820, with codicil 6 Feb. 1821, was pr. P.C.C. 30 May 1821.)   Issue :—

**J.**  1. Thomas Browne.

(*To be continued.*)

# Upton.*

## ABSTRACTS OF WILLS AND RECORDS OF ADMINISTRATION.

80. George Upton† of Fitzhead, Somerset, gent.  Dated 15 Oct. 1689.  To be buried in Fitzhead churchyard; to my daughter Joane Spireing £10; to my grandchildren John, Anstice, Elizabeth, Katherine, Elianor, Joane, and Anne Spireing each £5 at 21 ; to Elizabeth Rich my daughter £10, and my grandchildren Charles, Nicholas, Ann, Elianor, and Sarah Rich each £5 at 21 ; to my grandchildren Anne and Catherine Upton each £5 ; to poor of Milverton 20s., and of Fitzhead 20s.; to Nathaniel‡ my son my lands in Huish-Chamflewer,§ Chattworthy, Brompton Ralph, Over Stowey, Stogursey, and Spraxton, Somerset, and to his heirs for ever; to Priscilla Collins my daughter £15 per annum for life to be paid to her use ; to my kinsman John Harrison of Fitzhead, gent., and my son-in-law John Spireing of Halse, Somerset, gent. ; all residue to Nathaniel my son, and appoint him executor. Proved 1 Feb. 1689-90 by ex'or.  Adm'on *de bon. non* 9 May 1702 to Anne Upton, relict and adm˟ of said Nathaniel Upton the ex'or, now also deceased.  Further adm'on 5 Nov. 1738 to Anne ux. William Brewford and Catherine ux. Henry Manning, daughters of said Nathaniel Upton the ex'or.  (133 Dyke.)

81. Dorothy Upton‖ of St. Giles, Cripplegate, Midd˟, widow.  Dated 18 Aug. 1691.  Old and weak.  Whereas I have £400 in the Chamber of London, I give to Nathaniel Upton my son £220, and to his son Nathaniel £20 ; to my son John Sutton £100, and to his son and two daughters, viz., Thomas Sutton, Anne ux. Richard Skinner, and Jane Sutton, each £20 ; to my sister Alice Stuckey £5 ; to Mrs. Goddard £4 ; to my sister Mary Penrose 20s. ; to Mr. Beckley and wife each 20s. for a ring ; to Nathaniel and William Kinner [*sic*, Skinner ?] each £5 ; residue to said Nathaniel Upton¶ my son, and appoint him executor.  Proved 1 March 1691-2 by ex'or.  (47 Fane.)

82. Robert Upton of Stepney, Midd˟, mariner.  Dated 19 Feb. 1691-2.  All my goods, etc., to my honoured mother Mary Rigg ; appoint executors William Roach of Stepney, victualler, and Anne his wife.  Proved 1 June 1692 by Wm. Roach, power reserved to Anne Roach.  (121 Fane.)

83. Gilbert Upton** of London, merchant.  Dated 11 Dec. 1693.  To be buried at St. Catherine's Church near the Tower near my late wife.  To my eldest daughter Dionitia Upton, besides the £50 given her by my father Smith,†† and the £447 7s. 10d. assigned her out of the overplus of the estate of my late brother Anthony Upton,‡‡ £502 12s. 2d. to make up £1000 to be paid to her at marriage.  Whereas I have paid my son Gilbert Upton sundry sums and been at great expense for his education in Spain, I now give him £500 more ; to my two daughters Ann Upton

---

* Continued from p. 48.
† The testator's parents made wills Nos. 42 and 59.  He had a son Roger, matriculated at Balliol College, Oxford, in 1675, and daughters Katherine and Ann, who are not named in his will.
‡ The son Nathaniel is No. 84, *post*.
§ The manor of Huish-Chamflower was purchased by John Norman in 1548.  A descendant, Rev. John Norman, married Eliza Blake, who *may* have been related to this George Upton (see will of his father), for she was *not*, as has been claimed, sister of Admiral Blake.  Sarah Upton, *née* Norman, who made will No. 123, was of this family and probably sister of said Rev. John.
‖ Testatrix was widow of Nathaniel Upton who made will No. 61.
¶ Her son Nathaniel Upton made will No. 89.
** Testator was son of John and Dorothy (Rouse) Upton, and brother of Nos. 64, 75, 77, and 79, *ante*.
†† Testator's wife was Dorcas Smith.           ‡‡ See will No. 64, *ante*.

and Rebecca Upton and my son Arthur Upton each £100 ; to my 6th daughter Ann two messuages, etc., in Chelmondistone and Hackested, Suffolk ; to my 7th daughter Rebecca another messuage in Chelmondistone and my messuages, etc., in Rushell and Needham, Norfolk, remainder to my youngest son Arthur Upton ; to said Arthur £200 at 21 ; appoint executors my brother Daniel Farrington, Esq., and my four sons-in-law Mr. John Wilsher, Richard Malcher, Peter St. Hill, and John Wade ; to Dionysia my daughter the silver bason given her by her grandmother Smith ; to my daughter Wade a necklace ; to my daughter St. Hill my wife's diamond ring ; to my daughter Malcher £50 ; to my grandchildren John Wilsher, Ann Wilsher, Gilbert Malcher, and Gilbert St. Hill each £25 at 21 or marriage. Codicil, 23 Jan. 1693-4 : As to said two messuages to daughter Ann, remainder to her issue, remainder to her present husband Edward Kecke for life. Proved 28 Feb. 1693-4 by Richard Malcher, Peter St. Hill, and John Wade, power reserved to John Wilshire and Daniel Farrington. (C.P.C., 205 Box.)

84. Nathaniel Upton* of Fitzhead, Somerset. Adm'on 17 March 1693-4 to the relict Anne.

85. William Upton of St. Andrew's, Holborn, Midd[x]. Adm'on 31 Aug. 1694 to the relict Catherine.

86. Dame Mary Upton, late of Castle Norton,[†] co. Antrim, Ireland. Adm'on (C.P.C.) 31 May 1695 to her husband Clotworthy Upton, Esq.

87. Nathaniel Upton, who died in King's Ship "Essex," a widower. Adm'on 14 Jan. 1695-6 to his sister Mary Kinnard *alias* Upton, ux. John Kinnard.[‡]

88. Dorothy Goodlad *alias* Upton of Mile End, Midd[x], widow. Adm'on 22 April 1696 to Thomazine Goodlad, exec'x named in will of Richard Goodlad, while he lived husband of deceased.

89. Nathaniel Upton§ of the City Pest House, St. Giles, Cripplegate, Midd[x], of Physick Professor. Dated 26 May 1696. Whereas I have a vault or burying place in the burying ground next the Artillery Ground in said parish where my wife and several children deceased lie interred, I desire to be buried there and a marble stone to be erected there costing about £30 ; my funeral charges not to exceed £40. To my brother John Sutton £5 for mourning ; to Anne Pawling my housekeeper £5 for mourning, and for her faithful services for several years past £10 per annum for life out of my three messuages in Tokenhouse Yard, London ; to Gartrude Stobbard 40s. for mourning ; said messuages and residue of personalty to Nathaniel Upton my son, and appoint him executor. Proved 6 June 1696 by ex'or. (104 Bond.)

90. John Upton,|| sen[r], of y[e] town of Redding in the county of Middlesex in the Province of Massachusetts Bay in New England, husbandman. Dated 16 Nov. 1697. Being very weak in body. Soul to God, body to Earth, nothing doubting but at the Generall Resurrection I shall receive the same. To my son John¶ y[e] Lott of upland that I purchast of Thomas Hodgman joining the land he now dwells on, that I did give him by deed of gift, and also a parcel of land y[t] I bought of Capt. John Browne, that was Serg[t] Thomas Kendalls, etc., and other lands, including a lott gave me by the town and lands bought of Thomas Burt, Samuel Dix, and Capt. Brown ; the latter piece formerly was Robert Burnap's, jun[r] ; also medow joining his own at Martings Pond ; son John's son Joseph to have said lands at John's decease. If said Joseph doth not out live his father, then his next son shall have it. To my two sonnes James** and Joseph my homestead and land bought of Capt. Browne and Isaac Hart, to be equally divided, excepting that room I leave my wife for her

* He left daughters Anne and Catherine, who administered the estate of his father, No. 80, *ante*.
† Now Castle Upton. She is identical with No. 96, *post*.
‡ John Kinnard of All Hallows, Barking, London, widower, barber chirurgeon, aged about 29, there married Jan. 28, 1671-2, Mary Upton of St. Leonard's, Eastcheap, virgin, aged about 20, by licence, her mother consenting.
§ Testator's parents made wills Nos. 61 and 81, *ante*.
|| The testator John Upton was ancestor of most of the Uptons of the United States.
¶ The son John made will No. 114, *post*.
** The son James made will No. 92.

life; to my two sonnes William* and Samuel that ffarme lying in Salem bounds known as wood hill, also land bought of Scolly and Roose,† also my negro,‡ they to pay my daughter Mary £20 within two years after my decease; to my son Ezekiel land bought of Lieut. John Pearson and fifty acres more, bought of Capt. Browne and Isaac Hart, joining my homestead; to my five sonnes James, William, Samuel, Ezekiel, and Joseph aforesaid other lands to be equally divided among them; but if James die without issue, this land to be divided between the other four that are partners with him, and the homestead to go to my son Joseph; to son James certain furniture, two oxen and a cow; to my dearly beloved wife Elenor the west lower room in my now dwelling house, the Garrett over it, an interest in yᵉ cellar, two cows, one horse, and a third of the homested; my sonnes William, Samuel, Ezekiel, and Joseph shall " tend theire § mothers thirds of land," etc., and my five sons John, William, Samuel, Ezekiel, and Joseph shall pay to "my wife Elenor" £5 a year, viz., 20s. a peice, so long as she lives my widow;§ to my daughter Ann ffraile‖ £5 within one year; to my granddaughter Elizabeth ffraile £5 at 18; my will is yᵗ the lands above given shall remain to true heireship to their severall children from generation to generation for ever, so that my sonnes nor theire children shall not dispose of the same without it be to and among them; to my daughter Mary Upton £20 more within two years; to my daughter Abigail wife to my son Joseph my Long Joyntable; mentions medow bought of Thomas Nickolls for sons William and Samuell with their money; give all residue to wife Elenor, and appoint her and my two sons William and Samuel Upton executors. (Sealed with a *fleur-de-lis*.) Witnessed by Shuball Stearns, John Phelps, and Joseph Burnap. Proved 31 July 1699. (Middlesex, [Mass.,] Probate Records, ix., 531.)

91. Anne Upton¶ of St. Olave, Southwark, Surrey, widow. Dated 19 April 1699. To my sister Elizabeth 5s.; to kinswoman Sarah Penstone, widow, and her sister Anne Penstone each 50s.; to Anne Arnott daughter of Joseph Arnott of St. Olave 10s. for a ring; residue to Nathaniel Upton my son-in-law, and appoint him executor. Proved 3 July 1702 by ex'or. (123 Hern.)

92. James Upton** of North Reading, Mass., N.E. Dated 1 May 1702. Mosᵗ of his property to his brother Joseph Upton and the latter's children. Mentioɪ neither wife nor child. (Middlesex Probate Records.)

93. Ambrose Upton, belonging to the " Speedwell," Capt. Arthur Smith, comᵈʳ. Dated 4 Sept. 1702. All my wages and other estate to Thomasine my wife, of St. George's, Southwark, and appoint her executrix. Proved 31 March 1704 by exec'x. (75 Ash.)

(*To be continued.*)

---

Any information of the family, birthplace, etc., of Nathaniel Souther (Sowther), who was Secretary of Plymouth Colony 1636 to 1646, or of Joseph Souther (Souter), who was of Boston, Mass., in 1657, will be thankfully received.

*Springfield, Ill., U.S.A.*                                  GEORGE H. SOUTHER.

PARMELIN, PARMELEE.—Is the name of Parmelin, Parmelee, Parmelié, Palmerly, with any similar form of spelling, or with any prefix of De, Van, Von, etc., known in England? If so, where? Has it ever been an English name?—Replies requested to be sent to Mrs. EDWARD ELBRIDGE SALISBURY, New Haven, Connecticut, U.S.A.

---

* The son William made will No. 125.
† John Scollay and John Ross of Malden, Mass.
‡ The slave, Thomas, was liberated by William and Samuel Upton in Dec. 1717, "he having faithfully served our father."
§ I suspect testator's son John was by a former marriage; and, though the testator was at this time aged over seventy, his wife Eleanor was sufficiently young to make him fear she might re-marry.
‖ Testator's daughter Ann Upton married Samuel Fraile in 1684.
¶ The testatrix was third wife of Nathaniel Upton who made will No. 74. Her "son-in-law" Nathaniel Upton was her step-son.
** Testator was son of John Upton who made will No. 90.

# Genealogy of Browne.*

**J.  Thomas Browne,** as above, only surviving son of James Browne (b. 6 July, bapt. [at Aldgate] 29 July 1781; died 15 April, bur. [at Guernsey, St. Peter's Port] 19 April 1850).  Legatee under his uncle Charles Browne's (of Withington) will 1797.  Educated by his maternal uncle the Rev. James Lindsay, D.D.  Mar. ([at St. Mary's Woolnoth, Lombard Street, London] 25 March 1804) Jean, dau. of the Rev. James Rutherford (Presbyterian Church) of Hounam, Kelso, N.B. (b. 23 Nov., bapt. [at Hounam] 7 Dec. 1780; d. [at Guernsey]; bur. there May 1850).  Issue:—

**K.**  1. Joseph Browne (eldest son).
   2. David Browne (b. 5 Dec. 1813; bapt. [at Stepney] 8 Feb. 1824; abroad 1830; d. . . . . ?).
   3. Thomas Browne, C.E. (b. 10 March 1816; bapt. [at Stepney] 8 Feb. 1824; d. [at Hobart Town, Tasmania] 23 Dec. 1870), City Surveyor of Hobart Town.  Mar. [at Launceston, Van Diemen's Land] Sarah, dau. of . . . . Spicer, and sister of Mrs. Shepard Ransom of Ipswich (living 1884).  Issue (twelve children, names, etc., unknown).
   4. Lindsay Browne (b. 8 Jan. 1818; bapt. [at Stepney] 8 Feb. 1824; d. unmar. [at Geelong] 1849?), Captain in the Merchant Service.
   5. James Browne (b. 26 May 1821; bapt. [at Stepney] 8 Feb. 1824; d. [at Gisborne, N.Z.] 1885).  To Geelong, Australia.  Editor of "Standard," "Herald," etc., there.  Mar., first, Elizabeth Craig of Geelong (b. 8 Feb. 1824; d. [at Auckland] 3 July 1873).  Issue:—

**L.**  1. Montague Browne.
   2. Marshall Browne.
   3. James Browne.
   4. Thomas Browne.
   5. George Browne.
   6. Harry Browne.
   1. Eleanora.
   2. Mary.
   3. Jane.

   6. George Browne (b. 16 May 1823; bapt. [at Stepney] 8 Feb. 1824; d. 31 May 1872; bur. at Epping), Captain P. and O.'s "Haddington."  Mar. ([at St. Botolph's, Aldgate] 9 March 1848) Clara, dau. of Thomas Style, Esq., of Houndsditch (b. 8 Dec. 1828; d. 21 Oct. 1882; bur. at Southampton).  Issue:—

**L.**  1. George Rutherford Browne (b. 8 Oct. 1852; bapt. [at St. Philip's, Sydney] 6 July 1853; abroad; living 1887?).
   2. Harry Clive Browne (b. 3 Sept. 1854; bapt. [at All Souls, Marylebone] . . . .), mar. ([at Parish Church, Marylebone] 22 July 1882) Sarah Emily, dau. of Charles Christopher Cresswell, Esq., of Epping (living 1887).  Issue:—

**M.**  1. Stanley Cresswell Browne (b. 11 May 1883; bapt. [at St. Luke's, Southampton] 28 Sept. 1883; living 1887).
   1. Eleanor (b. 3 April 1805; privately bapt. June 1805; d. 15 June, bur. [at Highgate Cemetery] June 1884), mar., first ([in All Souls Church, Marylebone] 19 June 1834), Henry Coatsworth, Esq., of St. Ives, Hunts (b. Aug. 1812; d. 22 June 1838, aged 26).  Issue:—

**L.**  1. Henry Coatsworth (b. 4 Feb. 1836; bapt. [at All Souls, Marylebone] . . . .; d. 22 June 1838).
   2. Eleanor (b. 4 Sept. 1837; bapt. [at All Souls] . . . .; d. May 1838).  Mar., secondly ([in St. James's Church, Westminster] 25 April 1840), Evan Williams, Esq., of Pentre-felyn, co. Carnarvon (bapt. [at Ynyscyuhaiarn, co. Carnarvon] 16 July 1803; d. 13 Dec. 1867).

* Continued from p. 94

2. Jane (b. 4 Nov. 1806 ; privately bapt. 9 April 1807 ; d. s.p. 8 Oct. 1855),
mar. ([at Islington] 28 Dec. 1831) Charles Cherrington, Esq. (d.
25 July 1842). Issue:—(with others)
   **L.**   1. Jane Cherrington (living 1887).
3. Mary (b. 5 Feb., privately bapt. 19 April 1810 ; d. 23 Jan. 1816).
4. Margaret Bell (b. 9 Jan. 1812 ; d. 14 Feb. 1853), mar. (18 Oct. 1830)
John William Austin, Esq., of Bank of England (d. 1849). Issue (six
children).
5. Mary (b. 17 Sept. ; d. 23 Oct. 1819).

**K.**  **Joseph Browne,** eldest son of Thomas Browne (b. 14 March 1808 ; d.
16 Dec. 1847 ; bur. at Jesmond Old Cemetery, Newcastle-on-Tyne).
Mar. ([at Tynemouth] 5 July 1838) Margaret, dau. of John Laing, Esq.,
of Preston, North Shields (b. 30 Oct. 1808 ; d. 13 May 1886 ; bur. at Jesmond
Old Cemetery). Issue:—
   **L.**   1. Joseph Laing Browne (eldest son).
      2. Thomas Browne (b. 31 May 1841 ; bapt. [St. Andrew's, Newcastle-on-
Tyne] . . . . ; d. [at Gateshead] 16 April 1884 ; bur. at Jesmond Old
Cemetery). Mar. ([Christ Church, Byculla, Bombay] 24 Feb. 1869)
Sarah Brown, dau. of Francis Clough, Esq., of Bombay (b. [at Bombay]
2 Nov. 1852 ; living 1888). Issue:—
      **M.**   1. Percival Lindsay Lewis Browne (b. 20 April 1871 ; living 1888).
         2. Thomas Montagu Browne (b. 16 Aug. 1875 ; d. 21 July 1876).
         3. Thomas Frederick Montagu Browne (b. 18 July 1877 ; living 1888).
         4. Albert Joseph Laing Browne (b. 9 Dec. 1878 ; living 1888).
         5. Joseph Browne (b. 3 Oct. 1882 ; d. 31 Jan. 1883).
         1. Ethel Margaret,
         2. Florence Maud Bankart,
         3. Celinda Sarah Clough,     } living 1888.
         4. Mary Adrene,
         5. Margaret Browne [*sic*],
         6. Amy,
      3. John Laing Browne of Sunderland (b. 26 Sept. 1842 ; bapt. at St.
Andrew's, Newcastle-upon-Tyne ; living 1888). Mar. ([Bishopwear-
mouth Church] 13 March 1873) Elizabeth, second dau. of Joseph
Foster, Esq., of Sunderland, and Elizabeth Taylor his wife, dau. of
Emmanuel Taylor, Esq., of N. Shields (b. 15 Nov. 1846 ; living 1888).
Issue :—
      **M.**   1. Harold Montagu Browne (b. 15 Sept. 1877),
         2. Arthur Laing Browne (b. 9 July 1881),
         3. Lindsay Foster Browne (b. 29 May 1883),
         4. John Corbet Browne (b. 17 Feb. 1885),    } living 1888.
         5. Leonard Southaicke Browne (b. 22 May 1887),
         1. Lucy Foster,
         2. Jessie Foster,
      4. Lindsay Browne (b. 24 Oct. 1845 ; d. unmar. 1 May 1858).
      5. Frederick Montagu Browne (b. 21 June ; d. 8 Oct. 1848).
      1. Margaret Laing (living 1887), mar. ([St. Thomas Church, Sunderland]
8 July 1869) Hubert Bankart, Esq., of King's Langley, co. Herts
(b. 23 March 1835 ; living 1887). Issue:—
      **M.**   1. Hubert Stanley Montague Bankart (b. 26 Nov. 1872 ; living 1888).
         1. Margaret Evelyn Elizabeth Mary [Eva] (b. 26 March 1871 ; living
1888).
      2. Jane (living 1888), mar. ([in Trinity Church, St. Marylebone, London]
4 Sept. 1866) William Clark Fairley, Esq., of Sunderland, co. Durham
(b. 20 Aug. 1832 ; living 1888). Issue:—
      **M.**   1. William Fairley (b. 22 Feb. 1875 ; living 1888).

    1. Margaret Edith (b. 11 July 1867 ; living 1888).
    2. Gertrude Eleanor (b. 4 Sept. 1868 ; d. unmar. 28 Dec. 1885).
    3. Constance Bankart (b. 15 Feb. 1870; living 1888).

L. **Joseph Laing Browne** of Cardiff (living 1888), mar. ([at Christ Church, N. Shields] 3 Feb. 1863) Mary Antoinette, dau. of Charles Rutherford Stephens and his wife Antoinette Ardenghi (living 1888), and has issue :—
    1. Corbet Browne (b. 15 Jan. 1869),
    2. Lindsay Charles Browne (b. 1 Oct. 1870),
    3. Anthony Browne (b. 26 June 1875),
    4. Daniel Edward Stephens Browne (b. 17 March 1877),
    5. Joseph Browne (b. 22 March 1879),          living 1888.
    1. Marie Josephine,
    2. Anna Elizabeth,
    3. Margaret Mabel,
    4. Eleanor Gladys,

(To be continued.)

---

# Bacon Wills.*

## FROM IPSWICH REGISTRY.

T. Thome
Bacon de
Lowestofte.
    In the name of God, Amen. The fourth day of Aprill An'o D'ni 1600 and in the xlij[th] yere of the Raigne of o[r] Sou'aigne Ladye Elizabethe by the grace of God of Englande ffraunce and Irelande Quene defend[r] of the faith &c I Thomas Bacon of Lowestofte in the County of Suff. Carpent[r] beinge of p'fecte remembrance though sicke in bodye the Lord be praised therefore doe ordeine and make this my laste will and testament in man'er and forme followeinge that ys to saye ffirste I bequeath my soule to Allmightye God my maker hopinge through the merits & passion of Jesus Christe my redem[r] to be saved and my bodye I comitt to the earth when and where it shall please God. Item I geve and bequeath to my sonne George Bacon the house wherin I nowe dwell to him and to his heires for eu'. Item I geve to my saide sonne George all the timber that I have in the yarde and about the house. Item I geve my saide son George five pounds of good English mony to be paid him at his age of xx[tie] yeres. Item I geve to my saide sonne George my great Cheste. Item I geve to my sonne Robert Bacon five pounds to be paide him at his age of xx[tie] yeres. Item I geve to my saide sonne Robert one little Coffer. Item I geve to him more a hachet, a parcer and halfe my wimbles. Item I geve to Anne my daughter five pounds of mony and a Cofer the mony to be paide at her age of xx[tie] yeres. Item I geve more to Anne my daughter a Kettle. Item I give Elizabeth my daughter five pounds of mony to be paide unto her at her age of xx[tie] yeres. Item I geve to each of my daughters a ham'er. Item I give Elizabeth my daughter a Kettle and a ferken. Item I ordeine and make George my sonne to be my sole executo[r] of this my testam[t] & laste will. Item I geve to Anne my daughter a fetherbed a bolster and blancket. Item I geve to Elizabeth my daughter a fetherbed a bolster and a Coueringe. I will that my kinsman Thomas Bacon of Bungay be my Sup'viso[r] & he to put out my mony to the beste use for my Children untill they come to ther seu'all age of xx[tie] yeres. These witnesses Adrian Tim'ons & George Rugge.
Sign'    THOME BACON.

Proved at Beccles 26 April 1600.

W. Bacon of
Walton in Norfolk,
Yeoman.
    This is the last will nuncupative of William Bacon late of Walton in the Countie of Norff. Yeoman who deceased the xviij[th] day of November and in the eight yeare of the Reigne of James the King's Ma[tie] that now is of England &c[r] in the Countie Goale in Ipiswich

---

* Continued from p. 86.

Anno Domini 1610.   Lyinge uppon his death bed he reposed a faithfull trust unto one John Chandler a prisoner there and deliuered into his hands one Indenture of Covenants formerlie made betweene Charles Suckleinge of Wooton in the Countie of Norff. gent. of one p'te and the said William Bacon now deceased of that other p'te being dated the fifte day of June in the yeare of the Raigne of James the Kings Ma[tie] that nowe is of England and of Scottland the fortie By w[ch] Indenture it appeareth that the said Charles Suckleine is To paie unto the said Willia' Beacon to his heires executors or assignes two hundred pounds of lawfull money of England at a certeyne Day heareafter to come as by the said Indenture it doth more playnlie appeare w[ch] Indenture remayneth in the handes and Custodie of the said John Chandler Which said som'e of cc[li] his will and mynd was that the said John Chandler or his assignes should receive and uppon the receipte hee did will and bequeath unto Cordwell Bacon his daughter the sum'e of Thirtie Pounds p'cell of the twoe hundred pounds to be paid unto the said Cordwell Bacon the daughter of the said William Bacon by the said John Chandler immediatelye after the receite of the said cc[li] or of the receite of soe much of the twoe hundred pounds as will amounte unto xxx[li] without fraude.   Allsoe hee did will and bequeath unto George Denne thelder his kinde frinde the sum'e of ten poundes of lawfull money of England to be paid by the said John Chandler immediatelie after the receite of the said cc[li] aforesaid.   Alsoe hee did will and bequeath unto George Denne the yonger sonne of the said George Denne thelder the summe of five pounds to be likewise paid by the said John Chandler his executo[rs] or assignes uppon the receite of the cc[li] aforesaid. In like manner hee did give and bequeath unto John Stodder his fellow prisoner for his paynes taken with him in the tyme of his Sicknesse ffortie shillings of lawfull money of England to be paid by John Chandler aforesaid in manner and forme aforesaid.   And that this was his last will and Testament we whose names be underwriten will alwaies Justifie and mayntayne by oath.   Dated the xxvj[th] day of December in the eight yeare of the Reigne of James the Kings Ma[tie] that nowe is of England &c[r] and of Scottland the fortie and foure Annoq' Domini 1610. John Coo John Hovell and John Stodder.

Proved at Ipswich 12 February 1610-11.

(*To be continued.*)

## MONUMENTAL INSCRIPTIONS OF HOLY TRINITY, BRADFORD-ON-AVON, CO. WILTS.*

### ON FLOOR OF CHANCEL.

Arms : STEWARD impaling COMPTON.
Crest : A royal crown proper.

Plurimis summa probitate notus | Omnibus in vita Charus | Cunctis in morte Flendus | Hic jacet | Carolus Steward | Armiger | de Cummerwell Parochiæ hujus Appendice | Fragili valedicens Mundo xi Iulij | Anno MDCLXXXXVIII | Mœstissimam relinquens conjugem | (Mariam) ex Antiqua Comptonorum | Familia in Agro Gloucestrensi. | Æterna pace Quiescat.

Arms : COMPTON, without lion ; a crescent for difference.

Here Lyeth ye Body of | Dennis Compton Iun[r] Son of | Walter Compton E[qre] of Hartpury | who Departed this Life ye 16 of May 1714 | he was Dame Mary Stuard Brother.

Arms : THRESHER ; impaling, Crusily,† a lion rampant between two flaunches, LONG.
Crest : A demi-hart rampant between two boughs slipt.

Here lyeth the Body | of Iohn Thresher Esq. | who died 17 of August 1741 |

---

* Continued from p. 91.

† The flaunches are here not ermine, but crusily.   The crosses on the plate of the shield of Long of Whaddon on p. 326, vol. ii., Second Series, of the 'Miscellanea,' seem to be not patty, but cross-crosslets.

Aged 52 years. | Also the Body of Ellin Wife of | the said John Thresher Esq. | who died April the 17, 1753 | Aged 42 Years.

*A brass with figure of a woman.**

Arms : Sable, a lion passant argent, on a chief of the second three cross-crosslets of the field.

Here lyeth bvryed the body of Anne lately sole | davghter and heire of Iohn Yewe of Bradforde | in the Covnty of Wilts Gent. and wife of Gyf | ford Longe Gent. who had Issve by her Anne and | Catheryn their davghters. She dyed the xxvi[th] of | March 1601. Whose knowne good lyfe sheweth | that God hath taken her sowle to His mercy.

Arms : THRESHER impaling LONG.†
Crest *ut supra.*

Here lieth the Body | of Dionysia Thresher | wife of Edward Thresher | of this Parish Esq. | who Departed this life Nov. 10th | 1692 Aged 32 Years. | Also the Body of the said | Edward Thresher | who died the 18th (?) of Feb. 1725 | Aged 65.

*A brass plate :* D. Clutterbuck. | 1769.

*A brass plate :* To | the memory | of | Lieu[t] General Henry Shrapnel, | Colonel Commandant | 6th Battalion of Artillery, | Obiit | 13th March, 1842, | Ætat. 80 years.

Here lieth interred the Body of | Quærina Curll, the wife of Iohn Curll | of this parish, Clothiere. She depa | rted this life the 28 day of Aprill an° Dom. 1678, | aged 34 yeares. | Also here lieth the Body of Wal | ter Curll, the son of Iohn Curll | and Quærina his wife, hee depar | ted this life the 30th day of Aprill, | A° Dom. 1667, | aged one year and 7 Monthes.

Rev. Rob[t] Taunton L.L.D. July 17th, 1797, Aged 54 years. Frances Taunton, May 24th, 1803, Aged 16 years. Elizabeth Weeks Taunton, March 11th, 1815, Aged 33 years. Frances Taunton, Nov. 25th, 1819, Aged 67 years. (M.I.)‡

Here Lyeth the Body of John Peirce, Gent., who Departed this life the 20 day of November, Anno Dom. 1697, Aged 24 years.

* Vid. Kite's ' Monumental Brasses of Wiltshire,' p. 77.
† See note † on p. 100.
‡ (M.I.) signifies that the Arms or Monuments to which these letters are attached are destroyed or illegible, and therefore are supplied from the rare printed ' Monumental Inscriptions of Wiltshire, 1821.'

Underneath | is Interred Elizabeth | Daughter of George | and Sarah Bethell, | who died January the 2ᵈ 1770, | Aged nine months. | Also Sarah, the Wife of George Bethell, who died | January the 7ᵗʰ 1777, Aged 54 years. | George Bethell, Esq. | died March the 26ᵗʰ, 1795, | Aged 65 years. (M.I.)

(*To be continued.*)

## Dalison Notes.*

Placita Corone in Octabis Sancte Trinitatis [9 Edward 1].
Radulphus Alizon de Gunwardbey, etc., appellaverunt Thomam filium Willielmi de Adelington, etc., de plagis verbatura et pace Domini Regis fracta, etc., ideo omnes in misericordia.
Juratores, Lindeseye, Willielmus Dalyzun.
Assize Roll, Lincoln, M-3-15 2, m. 7 d., m. 50, A.D. 1281.

Lincoln.
Prior de Bolinton ponit loco suo Rogerum Alacon vel Rogerum de Ormesby versus Osbertum filium Willielmi Motekan de placito amens' accionis Paske.
De Banco Roll, Hill., 12 Edw. 1, m. 69 d., A.D. 1284.

Lincoln scilicet.
Iidem consignantur ad assisam mortis antecessoris capiendam, quam Robertus filius Willielmi Russel de Hakethorn arrainiavit versus Desideratam de Alazcon de Hakethorn et Radulphum Stagge, de octo acris terre et medietate unius acre prati cum pertinentiis in Hakethorn.
Patent Roll, 14 Edw. 1, m. 25 d., A.D. 1285-1286.

Essonia de malo veniendi capta . . . . apud Lincoln die Lune proxima post Festum Exaltacionis Sancte Crucis, anno regni Regis Edwardi, quartodecimo.
Desiderata de Alenzon de Hakethorn versus Robertum filium Willielmi Russell de Hakethorn, de placito assise mortis antecessoris per Rogerum de Alenzon.
Assize Roll, Lincoln, M-3-19 2, m. 39, 16 Sept. A.D. 1286.

Essonia de malo veniendo capta apud Lincoln, die Lune proxima post Festum Exaltacionis Sancte Crucis, anno regni Regis Edwardi, xiiij°.
Desiderata de Alenzon de Hakethorn versus Robertum filium Willielmi Russell de Hakethorn de placito assise mortis antecessoris, per Rogerum de Alenzon. Ad prefatum terminum.
Assize Roll, Lincoln, M-3-19 2, m. 39, 16 Sept. A.D. 1286.

Lincoln scilicet.
Ricardus de Cornubia per attornatum suum optulit se iiijᵗᵒ die versus Radulphum de Karum, Johannem the Parsoneserjant de Lacton, Johannem Dalazon, Rogerum filium Hugonis, Johannem filium Hugonis, Hugonem filium Gerardi, Adam filium Gerardi, Rogerum Bleuet, Ingeranum de Schalleby, Rogerum Blanchard, etc., de placito quod predictus Radulphus faciet ei consuetudines et recta servicia que ei facere debet de libero tenemento suo quod de eo tenet in Lachton, etc.
Judicium ; attachiantur quod sint hic a die Pasche in xv dies, etc.
De Banco Roll, Edw. 1, No. 66, Mich., 14-15 Edw. 1, m. 98 d., [A.D. 1286].

[Mich., 15-16 Edw. 1, A.D. 1287.]
Ricardus de Cornubia qui tulit breve de consuetudine, etc., versus Radulphum de Karum . . . . Johannem Alacoun de tenemento in Laghton, petit licenciam recedendi de brevi suo. Et habet.
De Banco Roll, Edw. 1, No. 71, m. 49 d.

* Continued from p. 88.

Lincoln scilicet.

Martinus filius Henrici de Northerynton summonitus fuit ad respondendum Johanni De Launzoun de placito quod reddat ei custodiam terre et heredis Willielmi Dalazoun, etc. Unde queritur quod cum predictus Willielmus pater predicti heredis tenuit de eo unam carucatam terre, cum pertinenciis, in Foulnetteby per servicium unius oboli per annum, et ad scutagium quadraginta solidos, cum acciderit, quatuor solidos et ad plus plus et ad minus minus, de quibus idem Johannes seisitus fuit per manus predicti Willielmi et ea ratione custodia, etc., ad ipsum pertineat. Prefatus Martinus injuste ei detinet predictam custodiam, etc.

Et Martinus . . . . dicit quod ipse nichil tenet de eo. Et de hoc ponit se super patriam, etc.

De Banco Roll, Edw. 1, No. 77, m. 157 d., Mich., 16-17 Edw. 1, [A.D. 1288].

---

Adhuc de essoniis captis apud Lincoln in Crastino Sancti Jacobi Apostoli, anno xvj$^{mo}$ [Edw. 1].

Agnes uxor Rogeri de Alenson versus eundem de eodem per Robertum Rape, etc.

Assize Roll, Lincoln, M-3-19 2, m. 43 d., 26 July A.D. 1288.

---

De assisis, etc., die Lune proxima ante Festum Sancti Michaelis, anno Regis Edwardi, xvj$^{o}$.

Rogerus filius Willielmi de Alenzon qui tulit assisam mortis antecessoris versus Robertum filium Johannis de Northkelesey et Matillidem uxorem ejus, de tribus toftis, octo bovatis et quatuor acris terre et dimidia, cum pertinentiis, in Hakethorn et Hanewrth, non est prosecutus. Ideo ipse et plegii sui de prosequendo in misericordia, scilicet, Gilbertus de Kyrketon, Clericus, et Radulphus Stagge de Hakethorn, etc.

Assize Roll, Lincoln, M-3-19 2, m. 25, [4 October A.D. 1288].

---

De assisis captis apud Lincoln die Lune proxima ante Festum Sancti Michaelis anno Regis Edwardi, xvj$^{o}$.

Assisa venit recognitura si Willielmus Russel pater Roberti filii Willielmi Russel fuit seisitus in dominico suo ut de feodo de octo acris terre et medietate unius acre prati, cum pertinentiis, in Hakethorn die quo, etc. Et si, etc., unde Desiderata de Alenzon septem acras terre et dimidiam et medietatem unius acre prati, et Radulphus Stagge medietatem unius acre terre inde tenent, etc.

Et Desiderata venit, et de tenementis versus eam petitis vocavit ad warantum Rogerum filium Willielmi de Alenzon; habeat eum apud Graham, die Lune proxima post Festum Sancti Hillarii per auxilium Curie . . . . Et predictus Radulphus . . . . modo non venit. Ideo capiatur assisa versus eum per defectum. Set ponitur in respectum usque ad prefatum terminum apud Graham, etc.

Assize Roll, Lincoln, 14-17, Edw. 1, P.R.O., M-3-19 1, m. 25, [4 October, A.D. 1288].

---

Adhuc de assisis captis apud Lincoln, die Lune proxima post Festum Sancti Michaelis, anno Regis Edwardi, xvj$^{o}$.

Rogerus filius Willielmi de Alenzon qui tulit assisam mortis antecessoris versus Robertum filium Johannis de Northkelesey et Matillidem uxorem ejus de tribus toftis, octo bovatis et quatuor acris terre et dimidia, cum pertinentiis, in Hakethorn et Hanewurth non est prosecutus. Ideo ipse et plegii sui de prosequendo in misericordia, etc.

Assize Roll, Lincoln, M-3-19 2, m. 25, [4 October A.D. 1288].

*(To be continued.)*

# Caldwell of Rolleston.

VISITATION OF STAFFORD, 1663.

*Offlow Hundred.*                    *Lichfeild, 31 Mart.* 1663.

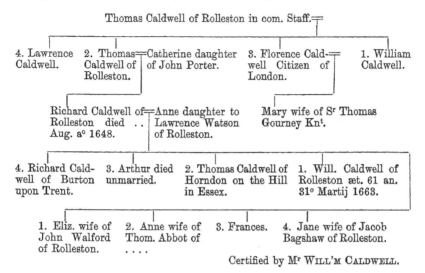

Thomas Caldwell of Rolleston in com. Staff.⸗

4. Lawrence Caldwell.

2. Thomas⸗Catherine daughter Caldwell of of John Porter. Rolleston.

3. Florence Cald-⸗ well Citizen of London.

1. William Caldwell.

Richard Caldwell of⸗Anne daughter to Rolleston died .. Lawrence Watson Aug. aº 1648. of Rolleston.

Mary wife of Sʳ Thomas Gourney Knᵗ.

4. Richard Cald-well of Burton upon Trent.

3. Arthur died unmarried.

2. Thomas Caldwell of Horndon on the Hill in Essex.

1. Will. Caldwell of Rolleston æt. 61 an. 31º Martij 1663.

1. Eliz. wife of John Walford of Rolleston.

2. Anne wife of Thom. Abbot of . . . .

3. Frances.

4. Jane wife of Jacob Bagshaw of Rolleston.

Certified by Mʳ WILL'M CALDWELL.

## Funeral Certificate.

DANIEL CALDWELL OF HORNDON.

Daniell Caldwell of Horneden in the county of Essex 4ᵗʰ sonne of Lawrence Caldwell of Batersey in the county of Surrey Gent. died at his house at Horneden aforesaid and lyeth interred in the Chauncell of the same church. He had byn the husband of 3 wives the first was Elizabeth one of the daughters of — Toldervey of Kent Gent. by whom he had dyuers children yᵗ died all young, his 2ᵈ wife was Mary one of the daughters of Georg Duncombe of Cliffords Inne Gent. by whom he had yssue one da. Mary now about the age of 9 or 10 yeares. His 3ᵈ wife was Alice one of the daughters of James Mayne of Bovingdon in the county of Hertford Esqʳ by whom he had 3 daughters Mary the first by the 3ᵈ venter of the age of 7 yeares at the tyme of her fathers decease Elizabeth the 2ᵈ 5 yeares old and Anne 4 yeares old. He made his coheires yᵉ aforesaid Mary his da. by his 2ᵈ wife the da. of George Duncomb and his other 3 daughters vizᵗ Mary Elizabeth and Anne which he had by his last wife Alice the da. of James Mayne and also he made his last wife Alice his sole executrix of his will and testament who gaue relacon for yᵉ drawing of this Certificate which was taken by me William Penson Lancaster herauld and the truth thereof testified by the said Alice the defuncts widow by subscripcon of her name.

ALICE CALDWELL.

MONUMENT IN THE CHURCH OF HORNDON ON THE HILL, ESSEX,
NORTH WALL OF CHANCEL,
COMMEMORATING
DANIEL CALDWALL, 1634.

## REGISTERS.

### St. Michael, Cornhill, London.

*Baptisms.*

| | | | |
|---|---|---|---|
| 1586 | Mar. | 3 | Edward Caldwell son of Lawrence. |
| 1593 | Sep. | 9 | Danyell Caldwell son of Lawrence. |
| 1583 | Feb. | 16 | Florence Caldwell son of Lawrence. |
| 1579 | Aug. | 16 | Susanna Caldwell da. of Francis [*Lawrence*]. |
| 1580 | Aug. | 21 | Syndony Caldwell da. of Francis [*Lawrence*]. |
| 1581 | Oct. | 1 | William Cawldwell (*Tattersall*) son of James. |
| 1577 | Feb. | 16 | Marye Caldwell da. of Lawrence. |
| 1582 | Jan. | 13 | Rycharde Cawldwell son of Lawrence. |
| 1585 | Jan. | 23 | Marye Caldwell da. of Lawrence. |
| 1588 | Oct. | 27 | Richard Caldwell son of Lawrence. |
| 1591 | July | 25 | Margaret Caldwell da. of Lawrence. |
| 1595 | June | 15 | Sara Cawldwell da. of Lawrence. |
| 1604 | Oct. | 21 | Lawrence Cawdwell son of W^m Cawdwell. |

*Marriages.*

| | | | |
|---|---|---|---|
| 1591 | Feb. | 6 | Florence Caldwell & Sibell Brokebank, widow. |
| 1597 | June | 18 | John Wall & Martha Cawdwell, widow. |
| 1597 | Sep. | 15 | W^m Cawdwall & Margett Bryce; p' lic. |
| 1583 | Jan. | 26 | Will'm Page & Elizabeth Cadwell. |

*Burials.*

| | | | |
|---|---|---|---|
| 1584 | July | 27 | Richarde Cawldwell son of Lawrence. |
| 1625 | Nov. | 28 | M^r Lawrence Cawldwell, free of the Vintners. |
| 1577 | Mar. | 5 | Marye Caldwell, a crysomer. |
| 1621 | Nov. | 13 | M^rs Mary Caudwell. |
| 1576 | Jan. | 8 | Raphe Caldwell. |
| 1604 | Dec. | 9 | Willia' Cawdwell serv^t to M^r Parsemouth, of a consumption. |

---

## WILLS.

Sibell Cauldwell of S^t Martin, Ludgate, London, widow. Will dated 1 Sept. 1615; proved 5 Dec. 1615 by Cassandra Greene. (114 Rudd.) To be bur^d in S^t Martin, Ludgate. Mourning gowns to poor women of S^t Martin, Ludgate, S^t Michael's, Cornhill, and S^t Botolph, Aldgate. To my cousin Cassandra Greene and her sister Sibell Greene £50 each. To my son in law Sir Tho^s Gourney "my skincke pott of silver " and a brass clock, and to the lady his wife a nest of bowls and a snake ring of gold which belonged to her father M^r fflorence Cauldwell. My sister Eme Pasmore silver pots. My sister Agnes Pryor £6 13s. 4d. Welmett Wilson wife of Rob^t Wilson. Poor of Charleton, co. Staff., where I was born, £5, and to poor of S^t Martin, Ludgate, £10. My sister Mary wearing apparel. Residue to my cousin Cassandra Greene, sole ex'trix. My brothers M^r Laurence Cauldwell and M^r John Pasmore overseers, and to each a silver bowl. Wit., John Ashenden, sc^r, John Bourde.

Lawrence Caldwall of Battersey, Surrey, Cit. and Vintner of London. Will dated 12 Feb. 1624; proved 4 May 1626 by W^m Caldwall, power reserved. (68 Hele.) To be bur^d in S^t Michael's, Cornhill, London, to which church I give a tenem^t in Three Tuns Alley, S^t Botolph, Bishopsgate, and three sermons preached yearly on Christmas Day, Easter Day, and Whitsunday. To the parson and churchwardens of Rowleston, co. Staff., where I was born, £5 yearly out of my moiety of messuages in Fleet Street, towards the salary of a schoolmaster at a Grammar school in Rowleston. To my son in law W^m A'Court, Cit. and Haberdasher of London, who marr^d Susan, one of my da^s, £10, and to my grandson and godson Lawrence

A'Court £50, and to every child of my s<sup>d</sup> da. Susan £10, as the gift of my late wife Mary Caldwall, their grandmother, at their ages of 21 or marriage. To my son in law John Withers, Cit. and Draper of London, who m<sup>d</sup> Mary, ano<sup>r</sup> of my da<sup>s</sup>, £10, and to each of the children of my s<sup>d</sup> da. Mary £10, as the gift of my late wife, their grandmother. To my son Edw<sup>d</sup> Caldwall £10. To each of the child<sup>n</sup> of my da. Margaret Duncombe £10, as the gift of my s<sup>d</sup> late wife, their grandmother. My godson Lawrence Duncombe £50 at age of 21. To the children of Sindeney my dau., late wife of Edward Clarke, Cit. and Grocer of London, £10 each, as the gift of my s<sup>d</sup> late wife. As touching the children of my afs<sup>d</sup> da. Sindenie Clarke, I have given them as follows, viz. : to Lawrence Clarke my godson, to Marie Clarke my wife's godda., and to Alice Clarke £200 each, and to Thomas Clarke, Sara Clarke, Martha Clarke, and Deborah Clarke £150 each. To the Vintners' Comp<sup>y</sup> a silver gilt salt of 60 ounces with my arms on it. To my niece Jane Allott al's Borston (sic) £30, free from control of her husb.; her son Lawrence Buston (sic), my godson, under age. To W<sup>m</sup> Caldwall, haberdasher, son of my brother Tho<sup>s</sup> Caldwall, £5. To John Allott £5. To S<sup>r</sup> Tho<sup>s</sup> Gorney, Knt., and his wife the lady Mary, my niece, £10 for mourning. My cousin W<sup>m</sup> Mounsey and his child<sup>n</sup> £40. Bequests to the various hospitals and prisons in London, and to poor of S<sup>t</sup> Michael's. To Anne and Marie the wives of my 2 sons W<sup>m</sup> and Daniel Caldwall £10 each. To my brother Geo. Duncombe a ring of 50s. To my son W<sup>m</sup> Caldwall my seal ring of gold which my brother fflorence Caldwall gave me, and to my son Daniel Caldwall the seal ring which I usually wear. Poor of Battersey £10. My servant and kinswoman Mary Watson £40. My kinsman and servant W<sup>m</sup> Caldwall £40. My cousin Tho<sup>s</sup> Wattson and his sister Katherine £5. My s<sup>d</sup> two sons W<sup>m</sup> and Daniel Caldwall ex'ors, to whom residue. My friends M<sup>r</sup> Rob<sup>t</sup> Ducy, Alderman of London, W<sup>m</sup> Man of Westminster, Esq., and my sons in law W<sup>m</sup> A'Court, John Withers, and John Duncombe, with John Childe, clerk of the Vintners'- Comp<sup>y</sup>, to be overseers. A monument similar to that for M<sup>r</sup> Philip Gunter to be erected in S<sup>t</sup> Michael's, Cornhill, at a cost of £30. Wit., Tho<sup>s</sup> Cæsar, Jo. Childe, Edmond Atmer, Rich<sup>d</sup> Broadley.

DANIEL CALDWALL of Horndon on the Hill, Essex, Esq. Will dated 12 Nov. 1634 ; proved 25 Nov. 1634 by Alice Caldwall the relict. (106 Seager.) To poor of Horndon my copyhold mess. in Horndon called Spilcockes, to be sold to make them a stock, or to buy an Almshouse. My cousins W<sup>m</sup> Caldwall and Tho<sup>s</sup> Caldwall £25 each. My servant Tho<sup>s</sup> Lovett £20. My freehold lands in Essex and elsewhere to my 4 dau'rs (under age), and each of them also to have an equal share of the money in the hands of my father Duncombe. Residue to my wife Alice, sole ex'trix ; she to have the education of those three little dau'rs which I have by her. My brother in law James Mayne, Esq., overseer. Wit., Jo. Hart, Tho<sup>s</sup> ffryer, Tho<sup>s</sup> Caldwall, Tho<sup>s</sup> Harper, Tho<sup>s</sup> Lovett, W<sup>m</sup> Crawley.

JAMES MAYNE, late of Bovingdon in the parish of Hemelhempsted, Herts, Esq., died in the par. of Allhallows Stayning, London, 16 Dec. 1642, or thereabouts. Nuncupative Will not long before his death ; proved 1 Jan. 1642 (1642-3) by Dorothy Mayne the relict. (7 Crane.) My wife sole ex'trix. My 2 dau'rs [names not given] £3000 each at ages of 14, out of my lands. My servants 20s. each. My man Sage £5. Poor of Bovingdon £5, and of Hitchin £5.

FLORENCE CALDWALL of St. Martin within Ludgate, Cit. and Haberdasher of London. Will dated 25 Oct. 8 Ja<sup>s</sup> I.; Codicil 11 July 10 Ja<sup>s</sup> I.; second Codicil 12 Sept. 1612 ; proved 11 Nov. 1612 by Marie Gourney. (91 Fenner.) To be bur<sup>d</sup> in S<sup>t</sup> Martin's, Ludgate, near my first wife Mary. To the Haberdashers' Comp<sup>y</sup> a mess. on Ludgate Hill, called the Angell, subject to certain rent charges to the poor of S<sup>t</sup> Martin's, Ludgate, and of Roulston, co. Staff., etc. To my wife Sibell Caldwall, in lieu of dower, certain messuages in S<sup>t</sup> Bride's, and also a mess. in S<sup>t</sup> Martin, Ludgate, called the Golden Dragon, in which W<sup>m</sup> Caldwall and John Waller now dwell as partners, and also half of my household stuff, etc. My corner house in Ludgate, in which I now dwell, to my da. Mary, wife of Tho<sup>s</sup> Gourney of London, Esq<sup>r</sup>, and also residue of my lands and ten'ts not otherwise bequeathed, rem$^r$, in default of issue, to my brother Lawrence Caldwall, Cit. and Vintner of London. Certain monies and goods due to my dau'r Mary Gourney, and to Florence Wild, by gift of their grandfather Wild, which my afores$^d$ wife and brother Lawrence Caldwall know of. My copyhold lands in Enfield, co. Midd., and in Southwark, Surrey, in the manor of parishe garden, to my nephew Richard Caldwall, son of my brother Thomas. Lands and ten'ts at Waltham Abbey, Essex, and Waltham Cross, Herts, to Lawrence Caldwall, another son of my brother Thomas. A house at Waltham Cross to Daniel Caldwall, one of the sons of my brother Lawrence. A tenem$^t$ on Ludgate Hill called the Queen's Arms to my s$^d$ da. Mary, rem$^r$ to W$^m$ Caldwall (son of my brother Thomas) for life, rem$^r$ to my godson Florence Caldwall, son of the s$^d$ William. To the Haberdashers' Comp$^y$, Vintners' Comp$^y$, Armorers' Comp$^y$, and Barber Surgeons' Comp$^y$ £100 each. Rings of 20s. to my sister Caldwall in Cornhill, my sister Caldwall of Rowleston, my sister Wild, my sister Wall, my sister Passemore, my sister Green, my sister ffainmere, my cousin Susan Court, my cousin Syndeny Clarke, my cousin Ann Caldwall, my cousin Eliz. Caldwall, my cousin Rich$^d$ Caldwall's wife of Rowleston, John Melborne, my cousin Elianor Wood, my cousin Bentley, my cousin Wardull's wife, M$^{ris}$ Underhill, fflorens Caldwall, fflorens Wilde, Mary Court, Cassandra Greene, my cousin Wythers' wife, my cousin Dubleday's wife, my cousin Dubleday, my cousin Court, and my brother Passemere. My sister Allatt £5. My sister Sheppard £5. My cousin Rich$^d$ Caldwall, son of my brother Thomas, £10. I forgive my cousin Tho$^s$ Caldwall what he oweth me. Bequests to prisons, and to poor of S$^t$ Bride's, S$^t$ Dunstan's, and S$^t$ Martin, Ludgate. My wearing apparel to my brother Lawrence Caldwall, my cousin Court, my brother Sheppard, my brother Wilde, my brother Passemere, my cousin Tho$^s$ Melborne, my cousin W$^m$ Caldwall, haberdasher. My seal ring of Arms to my brother Lawrence Caldwell. To my da. Marie Gourney £100 to her own use, as a gift, given to her by her grandfather M$^r$ Ottewell Wild. There is in my hands £200 and more, of the gift of my father in law M$^r$ Ottewell Wild, for me to bestow on my godson fflorens Wild, I therefore, in discharge of the same, give him £300 at his age of 24. The s$^d$ fflorens to be brought up at the University. My brother Wild and his children. To my da. Mary Gourney my coach and horses. Lease of land, etc., in Southwark to my cousin fflorens Caldwall, son of my cousin W$^m$ Caldwall. Rich$^d$ and Lawrence Caldwall (sons of my brother Thomas), M$^r$ Gilbert Rowlstone, M$^r$ Arthur Rowleston, the parson of Rowleston, M$^r$ Browne, attorney, my cousin Towne, John Shepard, Thomas Watson, Nich$^a$ Milborne of Foston, W$^m$ Clarke, and Jeromy Horoben of Burton to oversee my bequests to the schoolmaster, poor, etc., of Rowleston. My da. Marie Gourney ex'trix. My brother Lawrence Caldwall, my cousin Dubleday, my cousin Court, and my brother Passmor. Wit., Keagle Mathew, Law. Dawson, Edw$^d$ Browne, etc.

WILLIAM CALDWALL, late of London, Grocer. Will dated 1 Aug. 1607; proved 16 Jan. 1610 (1610-11) by the ex'ors. (1 Wood.) To the Schoolmaster of Rolleston £50. Poor of Rolleston. To repairs of church clock and bridge of Rolleston £10. A stone to lie upon me with my father and mother's picture, and the Caldwall arms, and upon it to be written such legacies as I have given to the poor and Freeschool of Rolleston, and for the same £3 6s. 8d. My sister Joane Allatte of ffoston and her children £20. To my brother Thomas Caldwall's children, viz., Lawrence, Elizabeth, and Dorothy £20 each, and to his other da$^s$ Margerie and Frances £10 each. To my cousin Alice wife of Richard Watson £15, and to their children £15. My godson W$^m$ Caldwall of London £26 13s. 4d. My cousin Arthur Caldwall of London, Apothecary, £20. My brothers fflorence Caldwall and Lawrence Caldwall 20s. each for rings. To my cousin Rich$^d$ Caldwall (son of my brother Thomas) £30, and to his the s$^d$ Richard's son and my godson W$^m$ Caldwall £20. My brother Sheppard 40s., and my sister his wife £3 6s. 8d., and to her children Thomas, Joane, Anne, and Jane £53 6s. 8d. My cousin Alice Keylinge and her children which she had by John Keylinge £5. M$^r$ Parson of Rolleston and my cousin Rob$^t$ Towne of Burton overseers. Poor of Rolleston and Onslow. Humfrey Caldwall 3s. 4d. My nephews Rich$^d$ Caldwall and Lawrence Caldwall ex'ors. No witnesses named.

## FINCH, FISHER, THROCKMORTON, AND DILKE FAMILIES.

### FROM FLY-LEAVES OF A BIBLE FORMERLY IN THE AYLESFORD LIBRARY.

S[r] Clement ffisher, sonn of S[r] Robert ffisher, Baronet, was married by Gilbert Shelden, Lord Arch Bishop of Canterbury, Desember 8th (1662), to Jane Lane, Daughter to Thomas Lane, Esq., of Bentley in the County Stafford.

S[r] Clement Fisher, Bar[tt], son of Thomas Fisher, Esq., of Walsh Hall in Mereden, & grandson of S[r] Rob[t] Fisher, Bar[tt], of Great Packington, was married to M[rs] Anne Jennens of Erdington, Daughter of Humphrey Jennens, Esq. (of the place afores[d]), by the Rev[d] M[r] Yardley, Vicar of Aston, at the Parish Church of Sheldon on the 16th of Feb[ry] 1685, & dyed the 9th of April 1729, leaving Issue only one Daughter Mary, which Mary was married at Great Packington on the 9th of Dec[br] 1712 (in his life time) to the Hon[ble] Heneage Finch, Esq., son of Heneage L[d] Guernsey, afterward Earl of Aylesford (in Kent), leaving all his Estate to the said Mary and her issue charged w[th] a Rent Charge to his younger & only surviving Robert (now S[r] Rob[t]) w[th] a Provision for his children (in case he sh[d] have any) w[ch] is not likely to happen, S[r] Robert being now well stricken in years.    1733.

Lettice Littleton, daughter of S[r] Edward Littleton and Dame Mary his wife, was born the 1st day of January and baptised y[e] x[th] day of y[e] same A[o] D'ni 1601.

Fisher Dilke, son of S[r] Thomas Dilke and Dame Mary his wife, was baptised the xxvij[th] day of February A[o] D'ni 1591.

George Fisher, sonn of S[r] Clement Fisher, Knight, was baptised the xxiiij[th] of May A[o] D'ni 1573.

Anne Fisher the daughter of S[r] Clement Fisher, Knight, was borne the xxix[th] day of May at 3 of y[e] clock in the after noone & baptised the vij[th] of June A[o] D'ni 1572. She was married to S[r] Thomas Dilke, Knight, the 5th day of January A[o] D'ni 1588.

Thomas Dilke, sonn of S[r] Thomas Dilke & Dame Ann his wife, was baptised the xxviij[th] day of June A[o] D'ni 1590; he was borne the eleventh June afores[d] betwixte tenne & eleuen of the clocke at night.

Lettice Dilke, daughter of S[r] Thomas Dilke & Dame Anne his wife, was baptised at Coleshall the 21[th] day of July Anno d'ni 1597.

Mary Fisher, daughter of S[r] Clement Fisher, Knight, was baptised the xx[th] day of August A[o] D'ni 1581. She was married to S[r] Edward Littleton, Knight, the xvj[th] of January A[o] D'ni 1598.

Clement Throckmorton, son of S[r] Clement Throckmorton & dame Lettice his wife, was baptised the ij[d] day of August A[o] D'ni 1604 1604 (sic).

S[r] Clement Throckmorton, Knight, & M[rs] Mary Kendall were married the xxj[th] of September A[o] D'ni 1568.

S[r] Robert Fisher, son of S[r] Clement Fisher, Knight, was borne the xxix[th] day of Novemb[r] & baptised the ix of December A[o] D'ni 1579.

Dame Mary Fisher, daughter to Francis Repington, Esquier, was borne the xxv[th] day of December A[o] D'ni 1543.

Edwarde Littleton, son of Sʳ Edwarde Littleton and Dame Mary his wife, was baptised the xixᵗʰ day of December Aº D'ni 1599.

---

Fisher Littleton, son of Sʳ Edwarde Littleton and Dame Mary his wife, was baptised yᵉ xᵗʰ day of December Aº D'ni 1600.

---

Clement Fisher, son of John Fisher, Esquier, was baptised the twentieth day of Nouember Aº D'ni 1538.

---

Lettice Fisher, daughter of Sʳ Clement Fisher, Knight, was borne the xxvi of Nouember Aº D'ni 1578 & baptised at Tamworth. She was married to Sʳ Clement Throckmorton, Knight, Aº D'ni 1602 the xxᵗʰ of July.

---

FROM FLY-LEAVES OF A BIBLE, 1741, FORMERLY IN THE AYLESFORD LIBRARY.

Ch. Guernsey, 1750.

Heneage our Eldest Son, Born July 4ᵗʰ O.S. 1751 at Isleworth. Christen'd the 13ᵗʰ of the same month. His Grandfather the Earl of Aylesford & the Earl of Winchilsea his Godfathers, & my mother Charlotte Dˢˢ Dowager of Somerset His Godmother.

Charles 2ᵈ Son, born in Grosvenor Square May 24ᵗʰ O.S. 1752. The Earl of Egremont & Charles Jennens, Esqʳ, his Godfathers ; the Marchioness of Granby his Godmother.

William Clement 3ᵈ Son, born May 27 N.S. 1753 in Grosvenor Square. Lᵈ Viscount Andover & yᵉ Rᵗ Honᵇˡᵉ William Finch his Godfathers ; Frances Dˢˢ of Somerset his Godmother.

Charlotte, born May 13ᵗʰ 1754 in Grosvʳ Square. Christen'd June yᵉ 9ᵗʰ. Her Grandmother Charlotte Dutchess of Somerset & Essex Dutchess of Roxburghe, Godmothers ; Sir William Courtenay, Godfather.

John, born May 22ᵈ 1755 in Grosvʳ Square. Christen'd June the 17ᵗʰ. Mary Countess of Winchilsea, Godmother ; John Marquess of Granby & William Earl of Dartmouth, Godfathers.

Edward, born April 26 1756 in Grosvʳ Square. Christen'd May 23. The Lady Frances Courtenay, Godmother ; The Honᵇˡᵉ Edward Finch & Percy Wyndham O'Brien, Godfathers.

Daniel, born April 3ᵈ 1757 in Grosvenor Square. Christen'd yᵉ 30ᵗʰ of the same month. The Countess of Northumberland, Godmother ; the Earl of Brooke & the Right Honᵇˡᵉ Henry Bilson Legge, Godfathers.

Seymour, born June 11 1758 in Grosvʳ Square. Christen'd yᵉ 8ᵗʰ of July. The Honᵇˡᵉ Mʳˢ Finch his Godmother ; the Marquiss of Rockingham & the Earl of Northumberland his Godfathers.

Henry Allington, born in Grosvenor Square Feb. 26 1760. Christen'd March 25ᵗʰ. The Countess of Egremont his Godmother ; the Earl of Suffolk and the Right Honᵇˡᵉ George Greville, Godfathers.

Frances, born in Grosvenor Square Feb. 9 1761. Christen'd March yᵉ 8ᵗʰ. The Countess of Dartmouth & Lʸ Charlotte Finch (the Lady of the Right Honᵇˡᵉ William Finch) the Godmothers, & Lord Warkworth, Godfather.

Maria Elizabeth, born at Packington Octʳ 7ᵗʰ 1766. Xtn'd Octʳ 29ᵗʰ. Maria Constantia the Countess of Suffolk & Mʳˢ Grenville, Godmothers, & Lᵈ Hyde, God-father.

Henrietta, born June 3ᵈ 1769 in Grosvenor Square. Christened the 25ᵗʰ June. The Rᵗ Honᵇˡᵉ Lady Andover & Harriet Lʸ Bingley, Godmothers, & Savile Finch, Esqʳ, Godfather.

---

FROM FLY-LEAVES OF BOOK OF COMMON PRAYER, 1671, FORMERLY IN THE
AYLESFORD LIBRARY.

Heneage ⎫ Finch.
Mary ⎭

Mary Fisher

Oct^br 1714 Gernsey.
July 1719 Aylesford.

I was married to my loving wife on the 9^th day of Dec^br 1712.  It has pleased
God to bless me with Issue—

Ann, born Oct^br 17^th 1713.
Heneage, born Nov^br 6^th 1715.
Mary, born March 1^st 1716-17.
Elizabeth, born Nov^br 28 1718.
Frances, born Feb. 4^th 1720-1.
Jane, born Dec^br y^e 4^th 1722.

Daughter Anne Christned Oct^br 24^th 1713.   Countess of Aylesford then Lady
Gernsey, M^rs Felicia Jennens, Godmothers ;  S^r Clement Fisher, Godfather.

Son Heneage Christned Nov^br 19^th 1715.   Earl of Aylesford, S^r Clement
Fisher, Godfathers ; Countess of Nottingham, Godmother.

Daughter Mary Christned March 14^th 1716-17.   Lady Mary Finch, Lady Lee,
Godmothers ; Charles Jennens, Esq^r, Godfather.

Daughter Elizabeth Christned Dec^br 11^th 1718.   Viscountess Scudamore, M^rs
Elizabeth Jennens, Godmothers ; Daniel Lord Finch, Godfather.

Daughter Frances Christned Feb. 21^st 1720-1.   Countess of Dartmouth, M^rs
Jennens (Bedford Walk), Godmothers ; Lord Bingley, Godfather.

Daughter Jane Christned Dec^br y^e 18^th 1722.   Countess Dowager of Aylesford,
Lady Digby, Godmothers ; Earl of Nottingham, Godfather.

---

My Lord

Yesterday morning Lady Charlotte complained of some little uneasiness,
about 10 o'clock in the evening she was much worse, & a little after one by the
assistance of a good woman from Richmond, she was safely delivered of a fine boy,
& both she & the child as well as can be expected.

I am, your dutiful son

GUERNSEY.

Isleworth July y^e 4^th 1751
½ after one Thursday morning.

---

LORD OR LAWARD.—Thomas Lord, b. about 1585 ; his wife Dorothy, b. about
1590 ; their children Richard, Thomas, Ann, William, John, Robert, Aymee, and
Dorothy emigrated to New England in 1635.  They were a wealthy and prominent
family.  Mrs. Dorothy Lord, widow of Thomas, used on the seal of her will the
arms given as those of the " Laward alias Lord " family—Argent, on a fess gules
between three cinquefoils azure a hind passant between two pheons or.  What part
of England was the original seat of that family, and who are now its principal
representatives ?   Can this Thomas Lord and his family be found in its pedigrees ?
Are there any printed pedigrees of the family which uses these arms ?  If so, where ?

MARVIN, MERVYN, MERVIN.—Matthew and Reinold, Reynold, or Reginald
Marvin, perhaps Mervin or Mervyn, emigrated to New England with their families
before 1648.  They are supposed to have been brothers.  In America they were
large landholders, took important parts in public affairs, and founders of leading
families.  Information is desired in relation to their birthplace and ancestry.

Replies to these queries are much desired immediately by Mrs. EDWARD
ELBRIDGE SALISBURY, New Haven, Connecticut, United States of America, in the
preparation of a large genealogical work.

# Upton.*

## ABSTRACTS OF WILLS AND RECORDS OF ADMINISTRATION.

94. William Upton of St. Giles in the Fields, Midd˟. Adm'on 31 Aug. 1704 to the relict Sarah.

95. John Upton, mariner, on board H.M. Ship "Monmouth." Nuncupative. 28 or 29 Sept. 1704. All I have to my messmate William Arnold. Adm'on 16 Nov. 1704 to said William Arnold. Deceased was late of King's Ship "Hampshire," but died in the "Monmouth," a bachelor. (246 Ash.)

96. *Hon.* Mary Upton *alias* Boyle† of Castle Norton, Ireland. Adm'on 17 Oct. 1706 to her husband Clotworthy Upton, Esq.

97. John Upton‡ of St. Olave's, Hart Street, London. Adm'on (C.P.C.) 8 Jan. 1706-7 to the relict Mary.

98. Arthur Upton of Castle Upton, co. Antrim, Ireland. Dated 1 Jan. 1706. Mentions son Clotworthy Upton;§ son John Upton,‖ who got a commission in the army; son Hercules Upton, merchant; son Thomas Upton, who is going to the bar; daughter Rebecca, and my married daughters. Proved in Dublin 20 June 1706. (Record Office, Dublin.)¶

99. John Upton of Hartley Wintney, co. Southampton. Adm'on 3 Feb. 1709-10 to the relict Susanna.

100. Ursula Upton,** widow, and relict of John Upton of Lupton, Esq., decᵈ. Dated 16 July 1708. To be buried near my said husband in our aisle in Brixham Ch.; to my sister-in-law Mrs. Sarah Lytcott a mourning ring; to my niece Mrs. Mary Peacock £20; to Mrs. Dorothy Sherwell my sister-in-law £10, and her father's and grandfather's pictures in the dining-room at Lupton; to my niece Mrs. Ursula Brooking my little watch and chain; to my chaplain Mr. George Brett three guineas; to Mrs. Ann Upton my kinswoman £20, and sundry articles Mr. Upton bought at her father's servey; to my servant Rebecca Upton £10; appoint my only son John Clerke executor, and my kinsmen and friends Mr. Thomas Power of Bideford, merchant, Mr. George Yard of Stoke, and Mr. William Lang of Woodish, gent., to be my trustees and assistant to said son; my nephew Mr. William Upton†† to be paid £50 I owe him; rings to my nephew Mr. William Brookins, my sister-in-law Mrs. Katherine Upton,‡‡ and my nieces Mrs. Mary Ligoe,§§ Mrs. Ann Brace,§§ and Mrs. Ann Bringhurst, Mrs. Mary Kingby,‖‖ Mrs. Jane Uvedale,¶¶ if she be alive, and Mrs. Sarah Long; sundry articles of dress, etc., to my nieces in this country,*** viz., my niece Warne, niece Mary Brookin, niece Power, niece Ursula Brooking, all my nieces Sherwell and my sister Sherwell; my linen etc., to my cousin Ann Upton and my cousin Beck [*sic,* query Keck]. Proved 14 Feb. 1709-10 by John Clerke, Esq., son and ex'or. (42 Smith.)

101. Moses Upton of Bridport, Dorset, innholder. Dated 30 Jan. 1709-10. To my wife Joane my dwelling-house, etc., in Athlington *alias* Allington, Dorset,

---

\* Continued from p. 96.

† No. 96 is identical with No. 86, *ante.* Her husband Clotworthy Upton was son of Arthur Upton who made will No. 98.

‡ His father was John Upton who made will No. 79. The relict Mary is No. 111, *post.* Nos. 110, 116, and 134 were his children.

§ The son Clotworthy was husband of Mary Upton, No. 96, *ante.*

‖ The son John Upton made will No. 128.

¶ This is the earliest Upton will recorded in Dublin.

** Widow Ursula Upton was daughter of Sir John Lytcott, and when she married John Upton in 1665 was "widow Ursula Clarke, aged 29." Her sister Jane was second wife of John Upton, No. 79, *ante;* and her sister Anne was wife of Secretary John Thurloe.

†† The nephew William was son of her husband's brother William Upton.

‡‡ Catherine Upton, *née* Otway, was wife of her husband's brother William Upton.

§§ Mary, wife of Thomas Ligoe, and Anne, wife of Francis Brace, were daughters of testatrix' sister Anne, wife of Secretary John Thurloe.

‖‖ "Kingby": Query Mrs. Mary Knightly daughter of testatrix' sister Jane by John Upton, No. 79, *ante.*

¶¶ Jane Uvedale was daughter of testatrix' sister Jane by John Upton, No. 79.

*** England. Testatrix had lived some years in Ireland.

for the rest of the term; to my daughters Anne and Elizabeth each £30 at 21 or marriage; to my daughter Abigail £20 at 21 or marriage; residue to son John, and appoint him executor. Overseers, John Derby, baker, and John Symmes, scrivener, both of Bridport, they to adm^r my estate during my son's minority. Codicil, 3 April 1710: to daughter Abigail £10 more; to wife and daughters Anne and Elizabeth sundry stuff. Adm'on 9 Nov. 1710 to said John Derby during the minority of said son and ex'or. (258 Smith.)

102. Jane Upton of Earl's Court, parish Warnbrough, Wilts, widow. Dated 5 Dec. 1709. To my nephew Abraham Brind of Hinton, Wilts, 5s.; to my nephew Richard Brind of London 5s.; to my nephew Isaac Brind £60, and all residue, including £10 due me from his brother said Abraham Brind, and appoint him executor. Proved 24 Sept. 1711 by ex'or. (195 Young.)

103. Francis Upton* of Christ Church, London, Doctor of Medicine. Adm'on 3 Nov. 1711 to the relict Sarah.†

## HILL OF LUDHUISHE, CO. SOMERSET.‡

EXCHEQUER, COURT OF AUGMENTATIONS, MISCELLANEOUS BOOKS, VOL. 106 (44), SOMERSET, P. 24. PUBLIC RECORD OFFICE (JUNE) 35 HENRY VIII.

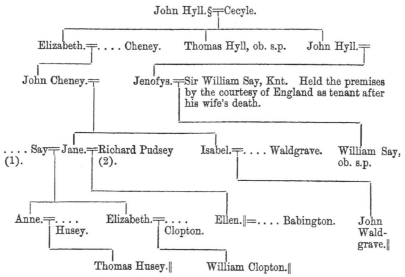

* Dr. Francis Upton was son of Ambrose Upton who was brother of John Upton who made will No. 79, *ante*.
† The relict Sarah Upton made will No. 123, *post*.
‡ Communicated by WILLIAM BOYD, Esq.
§ John Huyshe was seised of the Manor of Ludhuyshe, co. Somerset, and by his deed dated Tuesday the Feast of St. Peter and St. Paul, Hen. V., he thereof enfeoffed Hugh Cary, John Soithwood, parson of Spaxton, and Edward Culyforde to hold to them and their heirs for ever to the use of the said John Huyshe and his heirs, and the said Hugh Cary and Edward Colyforde, by deed dated 8 May 8 Hen. VI. [A.D. 1430], gave the said manor to John Hyll and Cecyle his wife, with remainder to Thomas, son of John Hyll and his heirs, and, them failing, to the right heirs of John Hyll.
‖ Gave and sold the premises to Edward Waldegrave, gent., who is called upon to declare by what title he held the said Manor, which the Court was informed ought to belong to the King by the attainder of Gertrude, late Marchioness of Exeter, to whom and to Lady Anne Bowser the said Manor descended as coheirs of Sir William Say, Knt. The Court decreed that the said Edward should have possession of the premises (June) 35 Henry VIII. (A.D. 1543).

Theise armes above depicted that is to saye gules a keepe or castell golde on A borduer
az ur penny Tourett of the grounde be the auncyent armes of the Borough of Dunheved
alias Launceston in the county of Cornewaill withe armes and creast was registred
confirmed and allowed in the tyme of the visytation of Cornewaill by me Roberte
Cooke als Clarencieulx esquier prinvypate herwault and Kinge of armes of the east
west and south parties of this realme of England from the ryver of Trent southwarde
vnto Thomas Crossly maior Thomas Hickes, Samson pyper, Robert Horge, Thomas
Gunnfrey, Stephyn Bennett, william Morten, John Sugers and Olyner Colley aldermen
of the same borough, And they the same armes and creast to vse beare and showe by them
And theire Surressors in lyke place and offyce for ever at theire Lyberty and pleasure
withont lett or interruption of any parson or parsons, In witnes wherof I the above
saide Clarencieulx Kinge of armes have herevnto subscribed my name and have
herevnto the seale of offyce the xxiij of July Ao dm 1573 And in the xv yere of the
reigne of oure soveraigne lady Elizabeth by the grace of god queue of england ffraunce
and Ireland Deffendor of the faythe &c

                                    Robt Cooke alias Clarencieulx
                                         Roy Darmes

ARMS OF THE BOROUGH OF DUNHEVED, OTHERWISE LAUNCESTON.
COPIED FROM THE ORIGINAL GRANT IN THE POSSESSION OF THE CORPORATION.

# Genealogp of Browne

## OF SHREDICOTE, PARISH OF BRADELEY, CO. STAFFORD

(Now represented by PEPLOE of Garnstone Castle, co. Hereford).

**D.** **George Browne** (eldest surviving son of Thomas Browne C and his wife Apollonia, of Shredicote, co Stafford, and Hungry Bentley, co. Derby) (b. at London? ; d. intestate ; bur. [in Bradeley Church,* co. Stafford] 22 April 1651-2. Letters of Administration granted to his widow Anne Browne, P.C.C., 6 May 1652). Inherited Shredicote under his father's will 1630. Arms : BROWNE *impaling* SKRYMSHIRE. *Quarterly*—1 *and* 4, *Gules, a lion rampant or within a bordure vaire,* for SKRYMSHIRE (granted 13 April 1584) ; 2 *and* 3, *Azure, a chevron between three flies argent,* for MUSCHAMP. Mar. Anne, dau. of Sir Thomas Skrymshire, Knight, of Aqualate, parish of Forton, High Sheriff of Stafford 1619 (bapt. [at Forton] 1 Sept. 1605 ; bur. [in Bradeley Ch.] 28 Jan. 1690-1). Bequeathed† the yearly interest of £5 for ever to poor of Bradeley. Administered her husband's estate 1652. Legatee under Apollonia Browne's will 1653, who bequeathed her xxs. to buy a ring. Issue:—

**E.** 1. Thomas Browne of Shredicote, eldest son. (*Vide infra*).
2. George Browne (bapt. [at Bradeley] 4 Aug. 1646 ; d. . . . .). Legatee under his aunt Apollonia's will 1659, who bequeathed him "two ewes and two lambs " and £50. Legatee under his sister Apollonia's will, who bequeathed him £10. Mar. (25 Oct. 1680) Mary Wickstead‡ (dead 1690 ?). Issue:—

**F.** 1. George Browne (d. . . . .). Legatee under Apollonia Browne's will 1690, who bequeathed him £20.
1. Anne (d. . . . .). Legatee under Apollonia's will 1690, who bequeathed her £20.

**E.** 1. Apollonia (bapt. [at Bradeley] 29 Nov. 1636 ; d. unmar.; bur. there 28 Jan. 1690-1 ; nuncupative will dated 22 Jan. 1690-1 ; pr. [at Lichfield] 3 July 1691. Bequeathed the yearly interest of £10 to poor of Bradeley for ever). Legatee under her aunt Apollonia's will, who bequeathed her "one feather bed wᶜʰ is in chamber com'only called Joannes chamber " and £50.
2. Margaret (bapt. [at Bradeley] 30 Jan. 1637-8 ; d. . . . .).
3. Elizabeth (bapt. [at Bradeley] 12 Aug. 1641 ; d. . . . .). Legatee under her aunt Apollonia's will 1659, who bequeathed her "two ewes and lambs " and £50. Legatee and co-executrix under her sister Apollonia's will 1690, who bequeathed her £5. Mar. John Phillips (d. . . . .). Legatee under Apollonia's will 1690, who bequeathed him £5. Issue:—

**F.** 1. Anne Phillips (d. . . . .). Legatee under Apollonia Browne's will 1690, who bequeathed her £40.
2. Mary Phillips (d. . . . .). Legatee under Apollonia Browne's will 1690, who bequeathed her £20.
4. Mary (bapt. [at Bradeley] 15 Aug. 1644 ; d. . . . .). Legatee under her aunt Apollonia's will 1659, who bequeathed her £250 and " a dyamond ring, one chynah dish, halfe of my weareing lynnen, one tye, a lockett, and a payre of pearle band strings." Legatee and

---

* "1651. Received by me Thos. Bird of Mʳˢ Browne for breaking up the Church floor for Mʳ Geo. Browne 0 *l.* : 3 : 4*d.*"—Parish Register of Bradeley.
† No will recorded at Somerset House or Lichfield.
‡ Probably of the Wickstead family of Nantwich, co. Chester. Only the date of the marriage is recorded in the Bradeley Register, where a space is left probably for the insertion of the name of the church at which the ceremony took place,

co-executrix under her sister Apollonia's will 1690, who bequeathed her 20 guineas. Mar. ([in Bradeley Ch.] 26 Dec. 1678) Lewis Dickenson "of Acton Trussel, Gent." (d. . . . .).

E. **Thomas Browne** (eldest son) of Shredicote (bapt. [at Bradeley] 23 March 1642-3 ; bur. there 10 Aug. 1728 ; will dated 31 Jan. 1722 ; pr. [at Lichfield] 16 June 1729 by John Stanley).  Legatee under his aunt Apollonia's will 1659, who bequeathed him "one peper mill w$^{th}$ all y$^e$ implem$^{ts}$ belonging thereto w$^{ch}$ were formerly fixed to y$^e$ house att Shredicoat," and £50. Legatee under his sister Apollonia's will 1691, who bequeathed him £5. Legatee under his son George Browne's will 1711, who bequeathed him the personal estate.  Mar. 1st ([at Forton, co. Stafford] 27 Aug. 1668 ; Marr. Licence by Bishop of Lichfield dated 13 July 1668) Mary Carr of Aqualate, parish of Forton (b. 1646 ; æt. 22 at marriage ; bur. [at Bradeley] 19 Dec. 1689) ; mar. 2nd (Marr. Licence at Lichfield dated 1707) Mary, dau. of . . . . and relict of . . . . Stanley (bur. [at Bradeley] 13 Aug. 1728 ; will dated 8 Dec. 1727 ; pr. [at Lichfield] by son John Stanley 16 June 1729).  Issue (by first marriage only) :—

  **F.** 1. George Browne of Shredicote (bapt. [at Bradeley] 29 Dec. 1670 ; d. unm. ; bur. there 7 June 1711 ; will dated 31 May 1711 ; pr. [at Lichfield] 15 June 1711 by the Rev. Walter Jennings and Thomas Pickstock the ex'ors).  Devised the Shredicote estate to be sold to his brother-in-law the Rev. Samuel Peploe, M.A., and of the proceeds of the sale £200 to be given to each of the four children of the Rev. Samuel Peploe, and the remainder to be equally divided between the children of the testator's brothers James and John Browne.

      2. James Browne* (bapt. [at Bradeley] 27 March 1672 ; dead 1711) ; mar. . . . ., and issue living 1711, legatees under their father's will, and under their uncle George Browne's will 1711.

      3. John Browne (bapt. [at Bradeley] 28 Aug. 1673 ; living 1711) ; mar. Eleanor . . . . (d. . . . .).  Issue :—

      **G.** 1. William Browne (bapt. 7 Aug. 1708 ; d. . . . .). ⎫
          2. Thomas Browne (bapt. 10 March 1712-13 ; d. . . . .). ⎪  All bapt.
          3. Edward Browne (bapt. 15 March 1715-16 ; d. . . . .). ⎪  at Bradeley,
          4. Joseph Browne (bapt. 26 Nov. 1717 ; d. . . . .). ⎬  and legatees
          5. Walter Browne (bapt. 22 Oct. 1719 ; d. . . . .). ⎪  under their
          6. Peter Browne (bapt. 20 July 1721 ; d. . . . .). ⎪  uncle George
          1. Elizabeth (bapt. 7 Sept. 1714 ; d. . . . .). ⎪  Browne's will
          2. Anna† (bapt. 11 July 1723 ; d. . . . .). ⎭  1711.

  **F.** 4. William Browne (bapt. [at Bradeley] 11 Feb. 1674-5 ; bur. there 10 May 1675).

      1. Ann (bapt. [at Bradeley] 7 Oct. 1669 ; bur. [in Chester Cathedral] 20 Jan. 1758) ; mar. the Rev. Samuel Peploe‡ (b. 1668? ; d. 21 Feb. ; bur. [in Chester Cathedral, M.I.] 28 Feb. 1752 ; will dated 24 April 1749 ; pr. [at York] 7 May 1752).  Entered as a Battler of Jesus Coll., Oxford, 12 May 1687 ; graduated in Arts, B.A. 12 March 1690 ; M.A. 19 Oct. 1693 ; in Divinity, B.D. (Lambeth)§ 10 March 1718.

---

    * There is a will of James Browne, dated 27 April 1701, pr. at Lichfield by Margaret Phillips 24 May 1701, which might be identical with above.
    † Query married (in Bradeley Church) 24 May 1743 Thomas Ellits.
    ‡ In the matriculation register of Oxford he is described as aged 18, son of Palmore Peploe of Dawley Parva, co. Salop.  No further information could be obtained regarding his ancestry.
    § The Rev. Dr. Gastrell, as Bishop of Chester, "conceived it his duty to refuse to admit the Rev. Samuel Peploe to the Wardenship of Manchester, to which he had been nominated by the Crown, and for which, on the recommendation of the Primate, he had qualified himself by the Lambeth degree of B.D., instead of proceeding regularly at his University, as he himself had originally intended.  It was not probable that Mr. Peploe could have experienced any difficulty in obtaining his degree at Oxford, and the Bishop of Chester, at the same time that he insisted

Admitted to Holy Orders. Instituted to the Rectory of Kedleston, co. Derby, 3 May 1695, which he resigned in 1700. Presented to the living of Preston, co. Lanc., 6 May 1700, which he held until 1727. While at Preston in 1715, during the rebellion in favour of the Old Pretender, he marched out against the rebels and distinguished himself by a loyal attachment to the cause of King George I. His Majesty thereupon appointed him to the Wardenship of the Collegiate Church of Manchester, to which he was presented 16 Feb. 1715. He was nominated to the Bishopric of Chester 4 April 1726, and consecrated in St. Margaret's, Westminster, Lord Bishop of Chester,* 12 April 1726, which see he held until his decease. Arms : *Gules, three mitres labelled or* (Diocese of Chester) ; *impaling, Azure, a chevron raguled counter-raguled between three bugle-horns or* (for PEPLOE) ; *and* PEPLOE *impaling* BROWNE. He was author† of :—(1) 'A sermon [on 2 Samuel xv. 4] preached at the Assizes held at Lancaster,' Lond., 1710, 8vo ; (2) 'God's peculiar care in the preservation of our religion and liberties : a sermon [on 1 Samuel xii. 7] preached at Lancaster Assizes, etc.,' Lond., 1716, 8vo ; (3) 'A sermon [on Matthew xxv. 40] preached at the anniversary meeting of the children educated in the Charity Schools of London,' Lond., 1730, 4to ; (4) 'A collection of curious papers containing First a new method of reasoning,' 1730 (?), 4to ; (5) 'A sermon [on Matthew x. 34] preached before the Lords Jan. 30, 1732,' Lond., 1732, 4to; 2nd edit., Lond., 1733, 4to; (6) 'Popish Idolatry : a strong reason why all Protestants should zealously oppose the present Rebellion : a sermon [on 1 Corinthians x. 14],' Lond., 1745, 8vo. Issue :—

1. Samuel Peploe (only son and heir).
1. Mary (living 1711), mar. Francis Jadrell, Esq., of Yeardsley.
2. Anne (living 1711), mar. James Bayley, Esq. (d. 1769 ?). Constituted Registrar of Chester 9 Aug. 1745, which he held until 1769.
3. Elizabeth (living 1711), mar. John Bradshaw, Esq., of Manchester.

*(To be continued.)*

---

on qualification by the regular degree, offered his interest to obtain it, if any unforeseen difficulty should occur. The matter was, however, carried to the King's Bench and a decision given against the Bishop, who thereupon published 'The Bishop of Chester's case, with regard to the Wardenship of Manchester, in which it is shewn that no other degrees but what are taken in the University can be deemed legal qualification for any Ecclesiastical preferment in England.' After the publication of this at Oxford, the University decreed, in full convocation, 22 March 1720, that solemn thanks should be returned to the Bishop for having so fully asserted the rights, privileges, and dignities belonging to the University degrees in this book."—Ormerod's 'Hist. of Chester,' p. 80.

The cause was first tried at the Lancaster Assizes 13 Aug. 1722. The argument in favour of the Archbishop's right to grant the degree (which dates from 25 Hen. VIII., 1534) was, it is said, conducted with "much learning and research." The notes for the instruction of Counsel are with Bishop Chandler's papers in the British Museum (Add. MS. 6489). The hearing occupied fifteen hours (Lambeth MS. 1133). The case was then carried by appeal before the King's Bench, where it was decided in favour of the Archbishop 23 May 1725. By a curious coincidence the Rev. Samuel Peploe succeeded his adversary (Dr. Gastrell) in the Bishopric of Chester.

* In a 'Peerage Directory,' 1727 (reprinted in the 'Genealogist', 1884, vol. i., p. 49), Dr. Peploe, Bishop of Chester, is mentioned as living in Queen Street, London. There is a portrait of Bishop Peploe at Garnstone Castle, co. Hereford.

† The publications here given are in the British Museum. They doubtless form only a small portion of his Lordship's works. The late Very Rev. J. S. Howson, D.D., Dean of Chester, informed me that Mr. Peploe's Sermons were much admired at the time by the Duke of Cumberland, who, upon hearing Mr. Peploe preach before he had obtained preferment, was graciously pleased to declare that he who was now " peep-low " should be made to " peep-high ; " an exhibition of His Grace's wit of such intense brilliancy and captivating delicacy that we cannot wonder at its being so long and faithfully remembered.

# Annotations to the Heraldic Visitation of London, 1633.

## Gore.

REGISTERS.

HACKNEY.

### Marriages.

| | | |
|---|---|---|
| 1593 | Aug. 20 | John Goore [Gore] & Anne Bougdler [Bowdler]. |
| 1621 | Aug. 21 | Wᵐ Priestley of Gray's Inn, Midd., esq., & Hester Gore of Trinity Lane, Lond. |
| 1627 | July 31 | Wᵐ Briggs of Gray's Inn, esq., & Sarah Gore, da. of Sir John Gore, Knt., Alderman of London. |

### Baptisms.

| | | |
|---|---|---|
| 1556 | Aug. 22 | Thomas Gore. |
| 1557 | Nov. 8 | John Gore. |
| 1559 | Nov. 12 | George Gore. |
| 1561 | April 7 | John Gore. |
| 1563 | July 26 | Elizabeth Gore. |
| 1564 | Nov. 21 | Jane Gore. |
| 1566 | Nov. 14 | Joane Gore. |
| 157$\frac{6}{7}$ | Feb. 10 | Anne Gore. |
| 1628 | April 16 | William s. of Wᵐ Prisley [Prestley], esq., & Hester his wife. |
| 1631 | Sep. 29 | Martha d. of Wᵐ Gore, vintner. |
| 1633 | Oct. 20 | James s. of Wᵐ Gore, vintner, & Eliz. his wife. |
| 1636 | April 25 | William s. of William Gore, glover. |
| 1637 | Oct. 20 | Thomasine d. of Wᵐ & Margᵗ Gore. |
| 1639 | June 29 | James s. of Wᵐ & Margᵗ Gore. |
| 1640 | Nov. 18 | William s. of Mʳ Wᵐ Gore & Margaret his wife. |
| 1641 | April 18 | Robert s. of William & Eliz. Gore. |
| 1642 | Oct. 8 | John s. of William & Margaret Goore. |
| 164$\frac{2}{3}$ | Mar. 3 | John & Elizᵗʰ twins of Wᵐ & Ann Goer. |

### Burials.

| | | |
|---|---|---|
| 1595 | June 3 | Mary Goore, widow. |
| 1624 | Sep. 7 | Ann Gore, spinster. |
| 1629 | Nov. 13 | Ellen wife of John Gore. |
| 1634 | Sep. 8 | James Gore, a child. |
| 1640 | Nov. 19 | William Gore. |
| 164$\frac{3}{4}$ | Feb. 11 | William Gore. |
| 1644 | July 1 | Margaret Goore. |
| 16$\frac{50}{51}$ | Mar. 13 | John Goore, died 12 Mar. |
| 1661 | June 30 | Anne Goore, senʳ, from Well Street. |
| 1662 | April 17 | James Gorre, from London. |

### ST. MARY MAGDALEN, MILK STREET.

#### Marriage.

| | | |
|---|---|---|
| 1618 | Dec. 21 | Ralph Gore & Agnes Merricke. |

#### Baptisms.

| | | |
|---|---|---|
| 1619 | Dec. 16 | Ann d. of Ralph & Agnes Gore. |
| 1621 | April 17 | John s. of Ralph & Agnes Gore. |
| 1624 | July 26 | Ann d. of Ralph & Agnes Gore. |
| 162$\frac{6}{7}$ | Mar. 21 | Ralph s. of Ralph & Agnes Gore. |
| 1627 | Aug. 2 | Ann d. of Ralph & Agnes Gore. |

*Burials.*

| | | | |
|---|---|---|---|
| 1607 | Dec. | 23 | M$^{r}$ Jarrard Gore. |
| $160\frac{7}{8}$ | Feb. | 20 | M$^{rs}$ Ellen Gore. |
| 1617 | June | 5 | M$^{r}$ Robert Gore, merch$^{t}$ taylor. |
| 1624 | July | 31 | Ann d. of Ralph Gore. |
| 1637 | April | 25 | An infant of Ralph Gore. Old vault. |
| 1637 | Sep. | 8 | Ralph Gore. Old vault in South Aisle of the Church. |

St. Anne, Blackfriars.

*Marriages.*

| | | | |
|---|---|---|---|
| 1620 | July | 9 | William Gore & Elizabeth Ley. |
| 1627 | July | 30 | John Adie & Elizabeth Goare. |

St. Bartholomew, Exchange.

*Marriage.*

| | | | |
|---|---|---|---|
| $159\frac{7}{8}$ | Feb. | 20 | Francis Gore & Dorothy Eaton. |

St. Giles, Cripplegate.

*Marriages.*

| | | | |
|---|---|---|---|
| 1567 | Dec. | 15 | Ralph Goare & Hellen Berick. |
| 1601 | June | 1 | Samuel White & Elizabeth Gore. |
| 1619 | Nov. | 3 | William Goer & Jane Spicer. |
| 1635 | Nov. | 18 | William Gore & Anne Rayner. |

*Baptisms.*

| | | | |
|---|---|---|---|
| 1602 | Sep. | 19 | Ann d. of Robert Gore, button maker. Query, if not buried as "Agnes" on the 21st. |
| 1725 | Oct. | 10 | Samuel s. of Samuel Gore, gent., & Mary, bo. 28 Sep. |
| 1728 | Oct. | 6 | Michael & Samuel sons of Samuel Gore. |

*Burials.*

| | | | |
|---|---|---|---|
| 1602 | Sep. | 21 | Agnes d. of Robert Gore, button maker. |
| 1654 | Oct. | 16 | Thomas s. of Henry Gore, weaver, thrush. |
| 1728 | Oct. | 23 | Michael s. of Samuel Gore, gent., conv$^{s}$. |
| 1733 | May | 30 | Samuel Gore, postman, fever. |

St. Mary Aldermanbury.

*Marriages.*

| | | | |
|---|---|---|---|
| 1594 | May | 27 | William Goare & Margaret Tyllnye. |
| 1615 | Nov. | 16 | Stephen Smith & Mary Goare. |

*Baptisms.*

| | | | |
|---|---|---|---|
| $15\frac{89}{90}$ | Jan. | 23 | Elkana d. of M$^{r}$ Jarrat Goare, jun$^{r}$, merch$^{t}$. |
| 1595 | Aug. | 6 | Jerrard s. of M$^{r}$ Gerrard Gore, jun$^{r}$, merch$^{t}$. |
| $159\frac{6}{7}$ | Feb. | 27 | William s. of M$^{r}$ Jerrard Goare, jun$^{r}$, merch$^{t}$. |
| 1599 | Dec. | 9 | Richard s. of Jerrard Goare, jun$^{r}$, merch$^{t}$. |
| 1602 | June | 27 | Anthony s. of M$^{r}$ Jerrard Goare, jun$^{r}$, merch$^{t}$. |

*Burials.*

| | | | |
|---|---|---|---|
| 1541 | April | 14 | Wyneford Goare. |
| $159\frac{6}{7}$ | Feb. | 7 | Elkana d. of M$^{r}$ Gerrard Goare, jun$^{r}$, merch$^{t}$. |
| 1603 | April | 2 | Anthony s. of M$^{r}$ Jerrard Goare, merch$^{t}$. |
| $160\frac{5}{6}$ | Mar. | 1 | Mary Goare. |
| 1614 | Mar. | 27 | M$^{r}$ Jerrard Goare, merch$^{t}$. |

St. Bartholomew the Less.

*Marriage.*

| | | | |
|---|---|---|---|
| 1647 | April | 20 | John Gore, of Heton, & Constance Dale, widow. |

ST. BRIDE'S.

*Marriages.*

1694  Nov. 18  Samuel Phillips, bach<sup>r</sup>, & Elizabeth Gore, sp<sup>r</sup>.  Lic.
1704  Nov. 23  John Gore, wid<sup>r</sup>, & Ann Sundry, sp<sup>r</sup>.  Lic.

*Burials.*

1620  Dec. 21  Robert Goore.
1624  April 19  Henry Goore, prisoner from the Fleet.

(*To be continued.*)

## MONUMENTAL INSCRIPTIONS OF HOLY TRINITY, BRADFORD-ON-AVON, CO. WILTS.*

NORTH AISLE.

*A painted window, Adoration of the Magi and Shepherds :* At rest | Nov. 5, 1876, | Aged 62. | At rest Dec<sup>r</sup> 1, 1877, | Aged 53. | At rest | Oct. 28, 1877, | Aged 32. | To the glory | of God and in | loving memory of | Emanuel Taylor | 20 years churchwarden of this parish. | Sarah Augusta Taylor | his beloved wife. | Charlotte Augusta Sparks | their only daughter.

Frances Taunton, 2<sup>nd</sup> Daughter and 6<sup>th</sup> Child | of the Rev<sup>d</sup> Robert Taunton, LL.D., and Frances his Wife, | deluding the fond hopes of Relatives who anticipated | in her opening graces the loveliness of personal charms | and still more captivating loveliness of mind, fell | an early Victim to Consumption on the 24<sup>th</sup> of May, 1803, | Aged 16 Years. | Elizabeth Weekes Taunton, eldest Daughter | and 3<sup>rd</sup> Child of the Rev<sup>d</sup> Robert Taunton, LL.D., and | Frances his wife, having thro' a long and severe trial | of debilitated health evinced a pious resignation to | the decrees of Providence, only exceeded by the warm | benevolence with which she ever interested herself | to assuage the cares and sufferings of others, | She departed this Life on the 11<sup>th</sup> of March, 1815, | Aged 33 Years. | Richard Hobbs Taunton, fifth Son and seventh Child of the Rev<sup>d</sup> Robert Taunton, LL.D., and | Frances | his Wife, Lieut<sup>nt</sup> in H.M. 23<sup>rd</sup> Light Dragoons, fell a | Victim to the Cholera Morbus, which so fatally ravag'd | the British Camps in India in the Pendaree War, on the | 19<sup>th</sup> of May, 1819, Aged 30 years.  On the 17<sup>th</sup> of | the same Month this young Officer in high health and spirits | wrote to his friends that the fatal | disorder had disappeared from the Camp. —— About 7 | o'clock in the Morning of the 19<sup>th</sup>, he was himself seized | with it and before Noon he lay a Corpse.

John Hearne Taunton Esq<sup>re</sup>, | third son of | the Rev<sup>d</sup> Robert Taunton, | and Frances his wife, | died on April 15<sup>th</sup> 1852, | aged 69 years and sixteen days.

Rev<sup>d</sup> Robert Taunton, LL.D., | Having adorned a strong and comprehensive mind, | With useful and extensive Knowledge, | Having conscientiously discharged the Duties of | Husband, Father, Friend, Citizen and Christian, | Departed to seek his Reward | July 17<sup>th</sup>, 1797, Aged 57 Years. | The afflicted mother of his eight helpless orphans | Erected this Monument | To his Memory. | Their departure is taken for misery | and their going from us to be utter Destruction | but they are in peace. | Frances Taunton, Relict of the | Rev<sup>d</sup> Robert Taunton, LL.D., and Daughter | and Coheiress of Leonard Cropp Esq<sup>re</sup> | of the County of Hampshire, having with a rare | and happy union of masculine good sense | and maternal tenderness, Religiously fulfilled | the sacred trust of Education, which devolved on her | by the decease of her husband and brother, | bequeathing to her Children a faithful pattern | of that warm benevolence in action | and that pious resignation in affliction | which Christianity enjoins, | departed this Life | on the 25<sup>th</sup> of Nov<sup>r</sup>, 1819, | Aged 67 Years.

* Continued from p. 102.

*A brass,\* thereon figures of a man and woman ; out of the mouth of the former*
*" Sancta Trinitas un' de' ;" out of that of the latter "Miserere nobis":* Off yoʳ charite
pray for the soules of Thomas Horton & Mary his wyffe which | Thom's was su'tyme
ffunder of this chawntry And decessid the . . . . day of . . . . Anᵒ d'ni ᴍᵒ ᴄᴄᴄᴄᴄᵒ |
. . . . & yᵉ sayd Mary decessid yᵉ . . . . day of . . . . Anᵒ ᴍᵒ ᴄᴄᴄᴄᴄᵒ . . . . on whos soules
Jhu have mercy. | Jhu. mercy | Lady helpe.

Sacred to the Memory of | Mʳ John Renison, Clothiere of this Town, | and
Anne his Wife, She departed this Life | in humble hopes of a blessed immortality, |
18ᵗʰ November, 1793, | Ætat : 48. | He also departed this Life the 4ᵗʰ of | February,
1816, Ætat : 71. | In every relation of Life he was a | strictly upright, conscientious,
and | honest Man, beloved and respected | by all who knew him. | Filial gratitude
and affection hath raised | this Monument to perpetuate the | remembrance of such
worthy Parents.

Arms : THRESHER ; impaling, Sable, crusily, a lion rampant argent between two flaunches
ermine, LONG of Whaddon.

Juxta | Hoc Marmor | Depositum jacet | Quicquid mortale fuit | Johannis
Thresher, Armig : | Edvardi Thresher, Filij unici, | Qui vividos aliquot juventæ
annos | Londini, inter Juris peritos exegit, | Legum studijs enixe imcumbens, | In
his | Miro Ingenii acumine, et viribus ditatus, | Tam feliciter, et mature claruit, | Ut
plerisq' sui Temporis usq' celeberrimis, | hisce studijs Famam sectantibus, | multum
præcelluisse merito diceretur, | Fori Decus grande | In ipso Honorum aditu |
Famæq' crescentis | Flore nitentem, | cum jam Filium fœtus videret, | Obijt
Pater | Huic dum viveret, | Ingenium insigne, et præclarum | Integritas inviola-
bilis, | Aliæq' optimæ Indolis Dotes, | Gratiæ et Honoris apud omnes, | Plurimum
conciliarunt | Commercium, | ad Parochiam de Bradford, et Villas circumjacentes |
Peculiariter respiciens : | (Heu! priscam Angliæ Gentis Gloriam | Vellus aureum) |
Prosperis et honestis Artibus excoluit, | Et sibi et Patriæ. | Mortuo Patre, Johannes,
Filius | (Jam Sepulchri | Ut prius Ingenij particeps) | Privata publicis anteponens, |
Ad Sedes paternas solum natale, | Huc jubens secessit, | Hic Otio indulgebat, | Sibi
gratissimo, honesto, tamen ac utili : | Amicis, quippe Patriæq' | Strenue consulens, |
Hic Liberalitate, Benevolentia, ac Candore, | Pariter notabilis, | Apud omnes
multum desideratus | Supremum Naturæ debitum solvit. | De Ellen uxore ejus,
Filia Henrici Long de Melksham | Armig : de Ellen, sorore & Cohærede Johannis
Trenchard, | nuper de Cutteridge, Com. Wilt. Armig : sex suscepit Filias, | quarum
solum quatuor huic superesse vivebant, viz., | Ellen, Dyonisia, Elizabetha, et Maria.

Obijt { Pater die 18 Feb. 1725, Ætat. 65.
{ Filius die 17 Aug. 1741, Ætat. 52.

Filij Conjugis dilecti Vidua Hoc Marmor | Utriusq' Memoriæ Sacrum Pientissime
posuit.

\* Vid. Kite's ' Monumental Brasses of Wiltshire,' p. 51.

Sacred | to the Memory of | Edward Baily of Ashley, Gent: | he died October ye 18th 1760, Æt. 80. | Also Ann his Wife, | Eldest Daug[r] of William Harding | of Broughton Gifford, Gent : | (in this County) | she died December ye 29th, 1759, Æt. 75. | Also Edward Fisher, Second Son of | William and Margaret Fisher, | he died April ye 5th, 1761, Æt. 4. | Also Ann Lewis, Relict of the | Rev[d] John Lewis of Whaddon, | (in this County), | she died November ye 8th, 1758, æt. 40. | Also to the Memory of M[rs] Margaret Fisher, | Wife of M[r] William Fisher, | (and Daughter of the abovesaid | Edward and Ann Baily,) | she died May the 30th, 1796, | Aged 71 Years.

Sacred to the Memory of | Charles Timbrell Esq[r] | who died August 20th, 1821, aged 60 Years. | His many virtues as a | Husband, Father, Friend, and Master, | will ever live in the remembrance | of those who knew him. | Also of his Daughter, | Ann Timbrell, | who died March 9th, 1806, aged 10 Years. | And four Daughters | who died in their Infancy. | Also of Ann Timbrell, Relict of the said | Cha[s] Timbrell Esq[r], who died Jan[ry] 29th, 1831, | Aged 61 Years, whose tenderness and anxiety as a | Wife and Parent, whose piety as a Christian, | and benevolence to the poor gained her the | Esteem of all who knew her.

Arms : Quarterly gules and argent, in the first and fourth quarters an escallop of the second ; impaling, Sable, a fess ermine between three bells, BELL.
Crest : A lion's head erased.

Near | this tablet are | deposited the remains | of the Rev[d] Edward Bowles, | late Vicar of this parish, | He departed this life the | first day of February, 1808, | in the 48th year | of his age.

Arms* : Or, a chevron between in chief three bees volant and in base as many torteaux gules ; on a shield of pretence, Or, on a chevron between three demi-lions rampant gules as many cross-crosslets argent, STEVENS.
Crest : A bull's head erased.

Near this Monument are Interred | the remains of Ann Bailward | late of this place, Widow, | who departed this life | the 25th day of July, 1788, | Aged 75 Years. | Also of Samuel Bailward late of | Horsington in the County of Somerset, Esq[re], | her Son, | who died the 9th day of April, 1800, | Aged 53 Years. | Henry Methuen Bailward Esq[re], | of the Royal Navy, | Son of the above Samuel Bailward, | died July 1st, 1812, Aged 24 Years. | Mary Anne, eldest Daughter | of the above Samuel Bailward, | died August 18th, 1825, | Aged 45 Years. | Anna Maria, Relict of the above Samuel Bailward | and only Child of the late William Stevens, | of Frankley House in this Parish, Esq[re], | where she departed this life the 21st of May, 1837, Aged 78 Years. | In her the Poor lost a kind and liberal Friend whose ear and hand | were ever open to their wants.

*A large slab with four panels.*

Arms : A demi-virgin proper full-faced crowned with an eastern crown, MERCERS' COMPANY.
Crest : A nag's head (looking sinister) couped, BAILY.

This burial place and tombe was Erected by William Baily of this Towne Mercer. | Also | Here Lyeth ye Body of | William Baily of this Town | Mercer who Departed this | Life ye 25th Day of March | Anno Domini 1712 | Aged 68 Yeares.

Arms : Sable, a mullet argent, on a chief or a fleur-de-lys gules.

To Perpetuate the Memory | of a Truly Pious, Virtuous, Affectionate, Good Wife, | Susannah Rogers, | Who Died May the 1st, 1755, | Aged 22 Years. | This Monument was Erected Anno Dom' 1756.

* Near this at one time was a *Hatchment* with the above arms.—' Wilts. Arch. Mag.,' v., 235.

*A brass plate :* Neare this place lyeth the body of M<sup>r</sup> Michaell Tidcombe who deceased ye 26 day of July An° Dom' 1662.

Tidcombvs tvmvlo jacet hoc Michaelis in alto,
Sospes dum clangit bvccina, ' Svrge,' manet.

Also neare this Place lieth ye Body of Sarah ye Daughter of ye said Michaell Tidcombe, who Deceased ye 11<sup>th</sup> Day of July, An° Dom. 1661. (M.I.)*

## Bacon Wills.†

### FROM IPSWICH REGISTRY.

T. In the name of God, Amen. In the sixtene daie of ffebruarie And
Will'm Bacone. in the seavnthe yeare of the Raigne of our Sou'aigne Kynge James of England ffraunce & Ireland And of Scotland the xliij<sup>th</sup> I William Bacone of Coddenham in the Countie of Suff. Yeoman being verie sicke in Bodye but in p'fect mynde & remembraunce (thankes be given unto Allmightie God) I doe ordaine and make this my last will and Testament in manner and forme followinge ffirste I Commytt my sowle unto the merciefull handes of Allmyghtie God my heavnlie ffather and to Jesus Christe my only Saviour and Redemer beleavinge stedfastlie throughe his passion and pretious bloudsheddinge to have free forgivenes of all my sinnes, And my Bodye unto Christian buryall when it shall please god to call me out of this worlde. It'm I give and bequeathe unto Rose my daughter all that my Tenementt and Landes in Creatting and Coddenham which I hould by free dede To have and to houlde to my saide daughter and hir assignes untill Rose Ballett my grandchilde shall accomplishe hir age of Twentie yeares. It'm I give all that my saide Tenement unto the saide Rose my grandchilde with all the saide Landes aforesaide when she shall accomplishe hir saide age of Twentie yeares To have and to houlde the saide Tenement and Landes aforesaide unto the saide Rose my grandchilde and hir heires for ever from the tyme of hir saide age aforesaide. Allsoe my mynde and will is that my saide daughter shall Conveye and assuer All that my Tenement and Landes in ffackenham which I houlde by Coppie of Court Roull unto Susan Ballett my grandchilde. It'm I give unto Michaell Bacon the sonne of my brother Richard Bacon the full and whole somme of Tenne Powndes of good monye To be payde unto him by my Executors within one year next after my decease. It'm I give unto William Bacon the sonne of my brother Michaell Bacon Tenne Powndes of good monye to be paide unto him by my saide Executors within one yeare next after my decease. It'm I give unto Michaell Bacon the sonne of my brother Thomas Bacon ffive Powndes of good monye to be paide unto him by my executors within one yeare next after my decease uppon Condic'on That he the saide Michaell Bacon or his assignes shall paye or cause to be paide unto Susan his sister the som'e of ffive powndes whiche he is to paie hir as a Legasie given unto hir by my saide brother Thomas Bacon Provyded that yf he have payde the saide v<sup>li</sup> or that yf he doe paye the saide v<sup>li</sup> unto the saide Susan yf shee be yet livinge That then I will this my guifte of ffive powndes to be paide unto the saide Mychaell or otherwyse I will the sayde ffive powndes shalbe paide unto the saide Susanne by my saide Executors Allwaies Provyded that yf the saide Susann be departed that then I wyll the sayde v<sup>li</sup> to be paide unto the saide Michaell by my saide Execut' within one yeare after my decease as aforesaide. Allsoe I give unto the sayde Susann ffive Powndes of good monye to be paide unto her by my saide Executors w<sup>th</sup>in one yeare after my decease. It'm I give unto Joahne Wade of Helmyngham the daughter of Thomas Bacone the somme of Twentie Shillings of good monye to be paide unto hir by my saide Executors w<sup>th</sup>in one yeare next after my decease yf she be then livinge. It'm I give unto the wyef of      (*sic*) Steggall of Ashbockinge twentie shillinges within one monethe next after my decease to be paide by my Executors. It'm I give unto Judithe Bullyne my servaunt fortye shillinges of good monye w<sup>th</sup>in one

---

* (M.I.) signifies that the Arms or Monuments to which these letters are attached are destroyed or illegible, and therefore are supplied from the rare printed ' Monumental Inscriptions of Wiltshire, 1821.'        † Continued from p. 100.

yeare next after my decease to be payde unto hir by my saide Executors.   It'm I
give unto fortye of the poorest people whiche be nowe dwellinge in the towne of
Coddenham aforesaide ffortie shillings of good monye (that is to saye) to everie one
of them xij^d To be paide unto them by my saide Executors att the tyme of my
buryall being Inhabitants or howshoulders.   It'm I give twentie shillinges of good
monye to be paide unto the poore people of Coddenham aforesaide to be paide unto
them by my saide Executors within one yeare after my decease And soe for the xx^s
Everie yeare untill the sum'e of Three Poundes be fullye paide Allwaies Provyded
That yt shall please God to call me out of this worlde in anye other Towne That
then the saide guifte to be voyde whiche was to be given unto the saide poore
people in Coddenham aforesaide.   It'm I ordaine and make Rose my daughter my
sole and onely Executrixe Requiringe hir And my sonne in Lawe John Ballett hir
husbonde to see this my last will proved accordinge unto the due course of Lawe
And allsoe to dischardge and paye all suche guiftes and Legasies As is sett downe
in this my will and Testament And all the Resydewe of my goodes Ready monye
Leases Cattells and Chattells with all my Jewells and plate I give unto my saide
daughter Rose and hir assignes for ever Provyded and my mynde & will ys That yf
my saide daughter shall not prove this my saide wyll within three monethes next
after my decease And be come my Executrixe with the consent of hir sayde husbande
That then I ordayne and make thaforesayde Myhell Bacon the sonne of Richard
Bacone my brother my onely Executor And that then I will the saide Myhell shall
have houlde occupye and enioye all that my Lease in Coddenham with all the Tearme
of yeares yett to Come and unexpyred uppon Condic'on that he the saide Myhell or
his assignes shall paye and discharge All suche guifts and Legasyes as are sett downe
in this my last wyll and Testament.   In wittnes hereunto I have sett my hands
and Seale.   Sign' WILLI'MI BACON.   Witnes EDM : CLARKE.
    Proved at Ipswich 29 March 1610 by Rose Ballett.

*(To be continued.)*

# Dalison Notes.*

[Easter 17 Edw., A.D. 1289.]
Lincoln scilicet.
    Simon filius Galfridi de Hakethorn' per attornatum suum petit versus Adam de
Torkesey et Aliciam uxorem ejus quadraginta et duas acras terre, etc., in Hakethorn
et Herpeswell.   Et versus Rogerum Dalizun et Agnetem uxorem ejus quadraginta
et duas acras terre, duas acras prati et dimidiam et tres partes duorum mesuagiorum,
cum pertinentiis, in eisdem villis, etc., us jus, etc., per breve de consanguineo.
    Et Adam et alii per attornatum suum veniunt, etc.   Dies datus est eis hic in
Octabis Sancti Johannis Baptiste, etc.
                                        De Banco Roll, Edw. 1, No. 80, m. 71 d.

[Mich., 17-18 Edw. 1, A.D. 1289.]
Lincoln scilicet.
    Simon filius Galfridi de Hakethorn' petit versus Rogerum Dalizun et Agnetem
uxorem ejus unum toftum, quadraginta et duas acras terre, etc., in Hakethorn et
Herpeswell.   Et versus Galfridum filium Johannis Cobbyng quadraginta et duas
acras terre, etc., in eisdem villis ut jus, etc., de quibus Agnes filia Willielmi de
Hakethorn' consanguinea ipsius Simonis cujus heres ipse est fuit seisita in dominico
suo ut de feodo die quo, etc.
    Et Rogerus et alii veniunt.   Et Rogerus et Agnes de tenementis versus eos
petita dicunt quod ipsi non tenent integre predicta tenementa quia dicunt quod
quidam Bartholomeus Peke tenet inde unam acram terre et quartam partem unius
acre prati.   Et quidam Hugo de Hakethorn tenet inde unam acram terre et dimidiam.

* Continued from p. 103.

Dicunt etiam quod ipsi non tenent de predictis tribus partibus duorum mesuagiorum nisi quartam partem unius mesuagii tantum. Et Galfridus pro se dicit quod non tenet integre predicta tenementa, etc., quia dicit quod quidam Hugo de Hakethorn tenet inde dimidiam acram terre et dimidiam acram prati ; et quoad tres partes predictorum mesuagiorum dicit quod ipse non tenet inde nisi quartam partem unius mesuagii in Herpeswell, et terciam partem unius mesuagii in Hakethorn, nec tenuerunt die quo predictus Simon breve suum versus eos impetravit, scilicet, vicesimo quarto die Octobris, anno Regis nunc, sextodecimo. Et de hoc ponunt se super patriam. Et Simon similiter. Ideo preceptum est Vicecomiti quod venire faceret hic in Crastino Purificationis Beate Marie, nisi Justiciarii ad assisas capiendas assignati prius, etc., xij, etc.

De Banco Roll, Edw. 1, No. 82, m. 45.

[18 Edw. 1, A.D. 1289-1290.]
Feodum de Honore Lancastrie.
De Matillide Dalazoun tenente dimietatem feodi in Langeton quam Willielmus Blaunchard quondam tenuit . . . . C . . . .

Exchequer Lay Subsidies, Lincoln, 135-1, Roll 2 d.

Lincoln.
Juratores dicunt quod locus qui vocatur Lemerkes Enges apud Lenediholmes in Netleton non est separale Matilde que fuit uxor Johannis de Dalazun immo communa pasture Andree de Orewell de Netleton (et pene xx aliorum qui implacitati quolibet tercio anno. Et quod illo anno et tempore depasti sunt predictam pasturam fuerunt) et placeam communa sua fuit, etc. Ideo ipsi sine die et Matilda in misericordia.

Coram Rege Roll, Hill., 26 Edw. 1, Roll 29, A.D. 1298.

Essonia capta . . . . die Veneris proxima post Quindenam Sancti Michaelis anno regni Regis Edwardi xxxij.
Lincoln scilicet.
Willielmus filius Willielmi Delason de Fulnehtby verus Petrum filium Willielmi Delason de Fulnehtby de placito assise mortis antecessoris per Johannem Cut die Lune proxima post Festum Epiphanie Domini.

Assize Roll, Divers Cos., N-2-13 1, m. 55, 16 Oct. A.D. 1304.

Adhuc de assisis captis apud Lincoln . . . . die Lune proximo post Festum Omnium Sanctorum, anno regni Regis Edwardi, tricesimo.
Assisa venit recognitura si Rogerus filius Cristiane Moris, Frater Alanus Bonde, Bartholomeus Mawe, Ricardus Ollesone, Johannes Godknape, Willielmus filius Gadardi, Robertus Le Lung', Godardus Colnel, Willielmus Remay, Laurencius Madelunsone, Robertus de Wadyngham et Alicia uxor ejus, Henricus Haldan, Willielmus Stag', Hugo Le Fisshere, Johannes filius Ricardi Le Clerk, Rogerus de Alenzun . . . . Johannes le Creuequor, etc., disseisiverunt Osbertum Motekan de communa pasture sue in Hakethorn que pertinet ad liberum tenementum suum in eadem villa post primam, etc.
Et Rogerus et alii non venerunt. Ideo capiatur assisa versus eos per defaltam, etc.
Postea ponitur in respectum usque diem Jovis proximum post Festum Sancti Hillarii apud Staunford pro defectu . . . . Juratorum. Ideo ipsi in misericordia, etc.
Eadem assisa venit recognitura si Rogerus filius Cristiane Mous, etc., [ut supra] disseisiverunt Johannem de Alenzun de Hakethorn de communa pasture sue in Hakethorn que pertinet ad liberum tenementum suum in eadem villa post primam, etc. Et Laurencius et Rogerus de Alenzun in propria persona sua venerunt. Et alii non venerunt. Et Laurencius et Rogerus nichil dicunt quare assisa remaneret. Ideo capiatur assisa versus eos, et versus alios capiatur assisa per defaltam, etc. Postea ponitur in respectum usque diem Jovis proximum post Festum Sancti Hillarii apud Staunford pro defectu . . . . Juratorum qui non venerunt. Ideo ipsi in misericordia, etc.

Assise capte apud Staunford . . . . die Jovis proxima post Festum Sancti Hillarii anno regni regis Edwardi, xxxj°.

Johannes de Alenzun de Hakethorn qui tulit breve nove disseisine versus Rogerum filium Cristiane Mous et alios de communa pasture in Hakethorn non est prosecutus.   Ideo predictus Johannes et plegii sui in misericordia, etc.

Assize Roll, Divers Cos., N-2-12 2, m 9 d., m. 26 d., [5 Nov. A.D. 1302].

*(To be continued.)*

## NOTES AS TO FAMILY OF BOWKER OR BOOKER.*

REGISTERS OF BLACKLEY CHAPEL, MANCHESTER.†

### Baptisms.

| | | | |
|---|---|---|---|
| 1655 | Aug. | 5 | James son of James Bowker of Cromsel. |
| 1657 | May | 27 | William son of Robert Bowker of Moston. |
| 1657 | June | 28 | Samuel son of James Bowker of Crumpsall. |
| 1657 | Dec. | 13 | William son of William Bowker of Crumpsall. |
| 1670 | April | 12 | Margarett daughter of Mr James Bowker of Blakeley.‡ |
| 1673 | Dec. | 21 | John sonn of Robert Bowker of Blakeley. |
| 1677 | Feb. | 10 | Mary daughter of William Bowker of Crumsall. |
| 1692 | Feb. | 23 | James ye son of R't Bowker of Cromsal. |
| 1702 | April | 19 | Katherine ye daughter of John Bowker of Cromsall. |
| 1702 | Nov. | 7 | Joseph son of Robert Bowker of Crompsall. |
| 1722 | Nov. | 18 | James son of Mary Bowker of Crompsall. |
| 1724 | Oct. | 11 | Mary daughter of Joseph Bowker of Crompsall. |
| 1725 | April | 18 | James son of Peter Bowker of Cromsale. |
| 1726 | Sep. | 18 | Thomas son of James Bowker of Blakeley. |
| 1742 | Nov. | 19 | John son of James Bowker of Ormshill Road. |
| 1743 | June | 24 | Robert son of Francis Bowker of Blakeley, weaver. |
| 1744 | June | 24 | Elizabeth daughter of John Bowker Junr of Ormshill in Cheetham. |
| 1746 | July | 27 | Mary daughter of Francis Bowker of Blakeley, weaver. |
| 1746 | Aug. | 3 | Alice daughter of Francis Bowker of Blakeley, weaver. |
| 1748 | Mar. | 19 | Ellin daughter of Francis Bowker of Newton, weaver. |
| 1771 | July | 25 | Susanna daughter of Samuel Bowker of Crumpsall, weaver. |
| 1771 | Nov. | 3 | Ann daughter of Charles Bowker of Crumpsall, weaver. |
| 1771 | Sep. | 5 | Hannah daughter of Charles Bowker of Crumpsall, weaver. |
| 1775 | Mar. | 25 | Samuel the son of Samuel Bowker of Crumpsall, weaver. |
| 1775 | June | 16 | Samuel the son of Samuel Bowker of Crumpsall, weaver. |
| 1775 | Nov. | 5 | John son of Robert Bowker of Crumpsall, weaver. |
| 1776 | June | 16 | John son of Charles Bowker of Crumpsall, weaver. |
| 1776 | Sep. | 21 | John son of Samuel Bowker of Crumpsall, weaver. |

### Marriage.

| | | | |
|---|---|---|---|
| 1732 | Jan. | 16 | Henry Bowker of Manchester and Elizabeth Shelmerdine of the same married by licence. |

### Burials.

| | | | |
|---|---|---|---|
| 1655 | Jan. | 4 | Margaret Bowker wife of Robert Bowker of Moston. |
| 1658 | Nov. | 6 | Robert Bowker of Moston. |
| 1659 | Sep. | 14 | Richard son of Robert Bowker of Cromshall. |
| 1666 | July | 29 | Elizabeth wife of Ralphe Bowker of Blakley. |

* Communicated by CHARLES E. B. BOWKER, Esq.
† Extracted by the Rev. GEORGE BOOKER, M.A.
‡ In a list of ministers conforming in 1662 occurs the name of James Booker of Blackley, Assistant Minister of the Chapel.   Whether his conformity secured him a continuance there does not appear.   A minister of this name is found ten years later at Sowerby, near Halifax. (The Rev. John Booker's 'History of Blackley Chapel,' p. 70.)

| 1669 | April 16 | Elizabeth Booker of Croomshall. |
| 1670 | May 26 | John sonne of William Bowker of the Harpurhey. |
| 1671 | Oct. 7 | John Boouker of Moston. |
| 1672 | Oct. 30 | Georg Boucker son of Robert Boucker of Blackley. |
| 1673 | Feb. .. | Joseph son of William Boouker of the Harperhey. |
| 1676 | Sep. 11 | William Bowker of the Harpurhey. |
| 1704 | June 24 | Mary Bowker, widow. |
| 1744 | April 25 | Robert son of Francis Bowker of Blackley, weaver. |
| 1770 | April 9 | Martha wife of Joseph Bowker of Moston, weaver. |
| 1779 | Oct. 12 | James Bowker of Crumpsall, weaver. |

These Notes are in continuation of the series commenced by the "Prestwich Entries" in Vol. IV., New Series, p. 316.

### MONUMENTAL INSCRIPTION.

*On a mural tablet at the western extremity of the north aisle of Blackley Chapel.*

Sacred to the memory of Robert Bowker of Bowker Bank who died Sep. 26th 1797 aged 64 years. Of Sally his wife who died May 29th 1825 aged 88 years. And of Esther their daughter who died June 16th 1796 aged 17 years. Also of Henry Hill Bowker son of John and Eliza Bowker of Polefield in the parish of Prestwich, and grandson of the above, of Brazenose College Oxford, whose early promise of future usefulness in life was cut short by death on the 26th of Nov. 1838 in the 24th year of his age. And of Lucy daughter of John and Eliza Bowker of Polefield who died May 5th 1824 aged 6 months.

The following notes* have been furnished by ALEXANDER BROWN, Esq., of Norwood P.O., Nelson County, Virginia, U.S.A.

Michael Booker was killed by the Indians at Lieut. Gib's Plantation, James River, Virginia, March 22, 1621-2.

Rev. James Bowker was Rector of Kingston Parish, Gloucester County, Virginia, 1677–1691; of St. Peter's Parish, New Kent, Virginia, 1698–1703.

Rev. Ralph Bowker, a Minister in Virginia from 1700–1719.

Edward Booker, a Member of the Virginia House of Burgesses in 1736.

William Booker of Prince Edward County, Virginia, a Member of the Revolutionary Convention which met at Williamsburg, Va., in May 1776.

---

## MONUMENTAL INSCRIPTIONS FROM THE BURIAL-GROUND OF ST. GEORGE, HANOVER SQUARE,† NEAR MARBLE ARCH.‡

William Cox, son of Richard & Ann Cox, of this parish, died Feb. 19, 1817, in his 19th year.

———

M[r] Joseph Warburton of Mount Street, died Sep. 14, 1817, aged 67.   M[rs] Elizabeth Warburton, wife of the above, died Feb. 3, 1826, aged 73.

———

M[rs] Cecilia Brown, died 11 Sept. 181[2 ?] in her 79th year.

———

M[r] William Turnham, died 14th Jan. 1835, in his 62nd year.
Susannah, relict of the above William Turner, died November 26, 1842, aged 59.

———

M[rs] Mary Rider, died March 12, 1817, aged 55.

———

* Needless to say these American extracts do not relate to the Blackley Entries, but are only printed for general genealogical information.
† This ground was opened in 1764. It has been closed for interments several years.
‡ Communicated by F. S. SNELL, Esq., M.A.

Mary, wife of George Hutchinson, died Nov. 11, 1844, aged 54.

M$^r$ William [Peercy?], died 28 Dec. 1834, aged 51.

William Field, of Edwards Mews, Duke S$^t$, Winchester Square, died March 7, 1843, aged 60.

John Edmonds, Jun$^r$, died Feb. 6, 1841, aged 19 years, 9 months [*rest obliterated*].
M$^{rs}$ Emily Earnevale, died April 13, 1818, aged 33.

Miss Millicent Sheppard, died 14 March 1841, aged 14.
M$^{rs}$ Mellicent Keable, late of James S$^t$, Oxford S$^t$, mother of the above, died Sep. 26, 1843, aged 76 years.
M$^r$ Thomas Keable, husband of the above, died March 15, 1847, aged 85 years.

Ann, wife of William Small, of South Molton S$^t$, died May 2, 1840, aged 59 years.
M$^r$ William Small, husband of the above, died 20 June 1850, aged 76 years.

The family grave of S. & E. Sandall of Mount S$^t$.
M$^r$ Samuel Sandall, died Jan. 25, 1845, in his 54$^{th}$ year.
M$^{rs}$ Elizabeth Sandall, wife of the above, died June 3, 1853, in her 68$^{th}$ year.
Also the following children of above:
Henry William, died April 20, 1848, aged 12 months.
Henry, died Jan. 10, 1820, aged 11 months.
Caroline, died March 5, 1822, aged 15 months.
George, died Jan. 10, 1825, aged 1 month.
Georgina, died May 19, 1829, aged 2 months.

M$^r$ John Rimbron Jones, of 7 Robert S$^t$, Grosvenor Square, died June 23, 1844, aged 52.
Also his son Joseph Rimbron Jones, died June 13, 1844, aged 16.

William Hoad, died June 3, 1841, aged 40.
Matilda Clarke, wife of William Clarke, & sister-in-law of the above, died June 17, 1848, aged 40.

James Storier, died March 6, 1841, aged 49 years.
This stone erected by his affectionate widow . . . . [*worn off*].

M$^r$ John Merry, late of No. 29, Gilbert S$^t$, Grosvenor Square, died 4 June 1840, aged 36.

Thomas Batt, died October 1, 1818, aged 51.
Elizabeth Batt, wife of the above, died June 4, 1830, aged 76.
Eliza, daughter of the above, late wife of W. H. Cooper, died 4 August, 1832, aged 37.

Ann Green, died 7 June 1841, aged 24.

Margaret Maclean, relict of the late Major Maclean, formerly of Berwick-on-Tweed, died 4 Feb. 1841, aged 81 years.
Also her grandson Archibald Lapslie Barrow, died 5 May 1843, aged 2 years, 9 months.

M<sup>rs</sup> Ann Elder, died January 5, 1818, aged 63.
M<sup>r</sup> William Elder, husband of above, died June 6, 1818, aged 57.

Frederick Elsegood, died Nov. 30, 1817, aged 11 months, 2 weeks.
John Elsegood, died Dec. 25, 1822, aged 2 years, 10 months.
John Elsegood, died Aug. 10, 1824, aged 6 months, 6 days.
George Elsegood, died May 30, 1834, aged 12 years, 4 months, 24 days.
Francis Charles Elsegood, died December 11, 1841, aged 28.·

M<sup>rs</sup> Leah Smith, wife of Richard Smith, of Malpas, Cheshire, died 7 Feb. 1841,
aged 38.

Miss Mary Ann Evett, died Feb. 22, 1842, aged 28, daughter of John & Elizabeth
Evett, of South S<sup>t</sup>, Grosvenor Square, who are interred near this place.
John Sutherland Evett, son of M<sup>r</sup> George Evett, brother of the above, died 24 Feb.
1845, aged 5 months.
Charlotte Elizabeth Evett, wife of the above George Evett, died 18<sup>th</sup> April 1846,
aged 30.

Henrietta Wallis, daughter of Benj. & Henrietta Wallis of this parish, died March
12, 1818, aged 3 years, 8 months.
Benjamin Wallis, father of the above, died 26 April 1846, aged 75.

James Bowles, died 17 Dec. 1844, aged 47.

This stone is erected by an only daughter to the memory of her beloved father
George Hill, died 29 Dec. 1843, aged 83.

M<sup>r</sup> Samuel Dummer, died 22 Feb. 1842, aged 54.
Mary wife of Tho<sup>s</sup> Cass Esquire, died 6 January 1830, aged 85.
M<sup>rs</sup> Ann Morton, sister of the above, died 6 March 1838, aged 78.
M<sup>rs</sup> Margaret Webb, died 9 March 1841, aged 79.
Mary Ann Houghton, died 4 Sep. 1840, aged 34.
M<sup>r</sup> Tho<sup>s</sup> Cass, of Knightsbridge, died Sep. 10, 1817, aged 78 years ; an inhabitant
of this parish upwards of fifty years.

M<sup>r</sup> William Field, died Oct. 21, 1816, aged 66.

Elizabeth Evans, daughter of William & Sarah Evans, of Swallow Street, born
June 11, 1814, died May 21, 1817.
John Evans, son of the above, born Nov. 1, 1816, died Feb. 6, 1818.
Samuel Evans, son of the above, born Dec. 15, 1819, died Feb. 19, 1821.
M<sup>rs</sup> Sarah Evans, mother of the above, died April 9, 1831, in her 52<sup>d</sup> year.
M<sup>r</sup> William Evans, husband of the above, died June 29, 1844, aged 78.

Ellen Mivart, wife of Jas. Mivart, Jun<sup>r</sup>, died Oct. 21, 1814, aged 34.

M<sup>rs</sup> Elizabeth Stikeman, died 19 Jan. 1814, aged 34.
Ann Maria Stikeman, died 6 Feb. 1817, aged 34.

William Evans, Jun<sup>r</sup>, died 11 Dec. 1843, aged 33.

Augusta, aged 6 years & 8 months, suddenly torn from gay existence & from her
inconsolable parents, by a domestic accident, 6 July 1816.
Edward Henry, died April 1812, aged 9 months.
Both children of Sir Richard Phillips of the City of London.

M<sup>r</sup> William Gattie, of New Bond S<sup>t</sup>, died 30 Oct. 18[1 ?]4, aged 64 years.
Miss Caroline Gattie, daughter of the above, died June 16, 1821, aged 28.
M<sup>rs</sup> Ann Gattie, widow of the above, died April 29, 1830, aged 68.

M<sup>r</sup> Alexander Leslie, late of Conduit S<sup>t</sup> in this parish, died June 30, 1823, in his
    57<sup>th</sup> year.
Sarah May Leslie, died Feb. 16, 1819, aged 10 days.
John Alexander Leslie, died March 12, 1822, aged 20 months ; grandchildren of
    the above.

(To be continued.)

## GRANT OF ARMS TO ROBERT TOOTH, ESQ., 1854.

To all and Singular to whom these Presents shall come Sir Charles George
Young Knight Garter Principal King of Arms and James Pulman Esquire
Clarenceux King of Arms of the South East and West parts of England from the
River Trent Southwards send greeting : Whereas ROBERT TOOTH of Swifts in the
parish of Cranbrook in the County of Kent and of the City of London Merchant
hath represented unto the Most Noble Henry Charles Duke of Norfolk Earl
Marshal and Hereditary Marshal of England Knight of the Most Noble Order of
the Garter That upon an examination of the Records of the College of Arms it does
not appear that Armorial Ensigns have hitherto been established to his Family and
being unwilling to bear any without unquestionable authority He therefore requested
the favor of his Grace's Warrant for Our granting and assigning such as may be
proper to be borne by him and his descendants with due and proper differences
according to the Laws of Arms : And forasmuch as the said Earl Marshal did by
Warrant under his hand and seal bearing date the thirtieth day of March last
authorize and direct Us to grant and assign such Armorial Ensigns accordingly
Know ye therefore that We the said Garter and Clarenceux in pursuance of His
Grace's Warrant and by virtue of the Letters Patent of our several offices to each
of Us respectively granted do by these Presents grant and assign unto the said
ROBERT TOOTH the Arms following that is to say Gules a demi gryphon segreant
between three Feathers Argent : And for the Crest on a Wreath of the Colours A
gryphon segreant gules semé of Mullets and holding in the sinister claw a Feather
Argent as the same are in the margin hereof more plainly depicted to be borne and
used for ever hereafter by him the said ROBERT TOOTH and his descendants with
due and proper differences according to the Laws of Arms. In witness whereof
We the said Garter and Clarenceux Kings of Arms have to these Presents subscribed
our names and affixed the Seals of Our several offices this fourth day of April in
the seventeenth year of the Reign of Our Sovereign Lady Victoria by the Grace of
God of the United Kingdom of Great Britain and Ireland Queen Defender of the
Faith etc. and in the year of Our Lord One thousand eight hundred and fifty-four.

    CHAS : GEO : YOUNG, Garter.        J. PULMAN, Clarenceux.

SKINNER (New Series, Vol. II., p. 188).—John Skinner, born 27 Aug. 1671, was
son of another John Skinner of Austin Friars, London, by Susanna, daughter and
coheiress of Robert Brinley. See Hutchins' ' Co. Dorset,' vol. ii., p. 609, Skinner of
Dewlish ; and this family of Skinner is referred to at vol. iii., pp. 207, 209, 210,
and 212. Can any one add to the Skinner pedigree as it appears in ' Mis. Gen. et
Her.' and in Hutchins' ' History of Dorsetshire ' ?

National Conservative Club,        REGINALD STEWART BODDINGTON.
    9 Pall Mall, S.W.

# Genealogy of Browne

## OF SHREDICOTE, PARISH OF BRADELEY, CO. STAFFORD

(Now represented by PEPLOE of Garnstone Castle, co. Hereford).*

**Samuel Peploe** (b. 1699 ? ; d. 22 Oct.; bur. [in Chester Cathedral, M.I.] 30 Oct. 1781, æt. 82 ; will dated 1 Sept. 1781, pr. [at Chester] 23 March 1782). Entered Wadham Coll., Oxford, 29 April 1723. Graduated† in Civil Law, B.C.L. 29 Oct. 1726, and D.C.L. (as a grand compounder) 2 July 1763. Admitted to Holy Orders ; installed Prebendary of Chester Cathedral (6th stall) 4 July 1727. Succeeded his father in the living of Preston 10 July 1727. Presented to the living of Northenden, co. Chester, 13 Nov. 1727. Collated Archdeacon of Richmond 4 June 1729. Succeeded his father in the Wardenship of Manchester, and presented thereto 30 March 1738. Rector of Tattenhall, co. Chester, 16 April 1743, which living he held until his decease. Created Chancellor of Chester by patent from his father 5 Aug. 1748. Bequeathed £200 upon trust for the poor of Tattenhall, of which £10 10s. 10d. is distributed every Christmas in clothing ; also £200 to the poor of Northenden, of which £10 10s. 8d. is given away at Easter in clothing. Arms : *Azure, on a chevron raguled counter-raguled between three bugle-horns stringed or, a mitre with labels of the field ; on a canton ermine a crosier or and a sword gules in saltire, the former surmounted by the latter.* Crest : *On a wreath of the colours a ducal coronet or, therein a reindeer's head gules antlered gold, charged on the neck with a human eye shedding drops of tears proper ;* granted and confirmed by R. warrant from the Earl Marshall, dated 21 Feb. 1753. Mar. 1st, Anne, dau. of the Rev. Thomas Birch, M.A., Rector of Hampton Bishop, co. Hereford, and Vicar of Preston, co. Lancaster (younger brother of John Birch, Esq., M.P., Colonel in Parliamentary Army, and 3rd son of Samuel Birch, Esq., of Ardwick, Manchester, descended from Birch of Birch, co. Lancaster). Issue :—

1. John Peploe. (See *infra*.)
   Mar. 2nd (10 Oct. 1774), Rebecca, dau. of Edward Roberts, Esq., Deputy Registrar of Chester (born 1720 ? ; d. s.p. 29 Oct. ; bur. in Chester Cathedral 2 Nov. 1779, æt. 59. Will dated 13 Aug. 1779, pr. 22 June 1782, P.C.C. [309 Gostling]).

**John Peploe** (son and heir) (b. 1742 ? ; d. 26 Jan. 1805, æt. 63 ; bur. at Weobley, co. Hereford, M.I. Will dated 20 July 1803, codicil 17 Dec. 1804, pr. P.C.C. 28 Feb. 1805). Succeeded, on the death of his uncle, Samuel Birch, Esq., Barrister-at-Law, in 1752 to Garnstone estate, co. Hereford. Assumed the additional surname and arms of BIRCH by Act of Parliament ; High Sheriff, co. Hereford, 1768. Mar. (Oct. 1764) Anne, d. and h. of William Clowes, Esq., of Hunt's Bank, Lancashire (b. 1744 ? ; d. [at Cheltenham] 6 May 1820, æt. 76 ; bur. at Weobley, M.I.). Issue : —

1. Samuel Peploe (only son).
1. Anne (bapt. [at Garnstone] 18 Aug. 1765 ; d. 1846, æt. 83 ; bur. at Weobley, M.I.). Mar. ([at St. George's, Hanover Square] 2 June 1790) Daniel Webb, Esq., of Audley Square, London (b. . . . . . ; d. [at Tunbridge Wells] 3 April ; bur. [at Horsemonden, Kent] 7 April 1828). Issue :—
   1. Daniel Peploe Webb (eldest son).
   2. John Birch Webb. (See *infra*.)

* Continued from p. 115.
† The degrees of B.C.L. and D.C.L. are the only ones I can find officially recorded by the University of Oxford. In the grant of arms in 1753 he is described as B.D., and in his monumental inscription in Chester Cathedral as LL.D.

3. George Samuel Webb of Wexford, Ireland (b. 1 Dec. 1805; bapt. [at
Lovell Hill, near Windsor] 1 Jan. 1806; d. 8 Jan., bur. [at Wexford]
8 Jan. 1841). Mar. Anna, dau. of Henry de Rinzy, Secretary to the
Grand Jury, co. Wexford (d. . . . .). Issue:—
  1. Mary Ann (bapt. [at Baltinglass, co. Wexford] 30 June 1839; d.
  . . . .); mar. William Croker Harvey, Esq. (b. . . . . ; d. . . . .),
  Treasurer of co. Wexford.
    1. Anne (d. unm. 1875; bur. in Cheltenham Cemetery).
    2. Mary Ann (living 1888); mar. ([at Broadwater, Sussex] 8 Nov. 1823)
    John Mapes Ensor, Esq., of Rollesby Hall, co. Norfolk (b. 1796;
    d. 1852). Issue :—
      1. John Mapes Webb Ensor, of Rollesby Hall (d. 1855).
      2. Charles Peploe Smith Ensor, now of Rollesby Hall (living 1888.
      Vide Burke's 'Landed Gentry').
      3. Mary Ann.
    3. Elizabeth (b. 1800; d. unmar. 1880; bur. at Cheltenham).
    4. Caroline (d. . . . .); mar. (1837) John Jordaine Dennett, Esq.,
    of Southampton Town (d. s.p. Nov. 1842).
  2. Mary (b. 1769?; d. unm. 1830, æt. 61; bur. [at Hunt's Bank]. M.I.
  Weobley Church).

**Samuel Peploe** of Garnstone Castle, co. Hereford (b. [at Hunt's Bank]
1 July 1774; d. 24 April 1845, æt. 71 years; bur. Weobley; M.I. Will
dated 22 July 1831); mar. (15 March 1796) Katherine Frances, eldest dau.
of Sir George Cornewall, 2nd Bart., of Moccass Court, co. Hereford (b.
1772?; d. s.p. 21 March 1831, æt. 59; bur. [at Weobley. M.I.]). Succeeded by his nephew :—

**Daniel Peploe Webb** (b. 21 Feb. 1794; d. unm. April 1866; bur. Weobley;
M.I.). Assumed the surname and arms of PEPLOE (to quarter Peploe, in
1st quarter, with Webb) by Royal Licence 17 May 1845, on succeeding to
Garnstone. High Sheriff, co. Hereford, 1845. Succeeded by his brother :—

**John Birch Webb** (b. 9 Sept. 1801; bapt. [at Court Lodge, co. Kent]; d.
26 Jan. 1869; bur. [at Weobley]; M.I.). Graduated at Oxford. Admitted to Holy Orders. Instituted to living of Weobley 1825. Assumed
the surname and arms of PEPLOE by Royal Licence 26 June 1866, on succeeding to Garnstone. Mar. ([at Ludlow, co. Salop] 3 Jan. 1828) Annie,*
2nd dau. of John Molyneux, Esq., R.N. (brother of Sir Thomas Molyneux,
Bart., of Castle Dillon, co. Armagh) (b. 1805; d. 1880; bur. at Brompton
Cemetery). Issue :—
  1. Daniel Peploe Webb Peploe of Garnstone. (See infra.)
  2. Augustus Henry Webb† of Chadnor Villa, Cheltenham (b. 1 July, bapt.
  [at Weobley] 12 Sept. 1834; d. [at Cheltenham] 25 Sept. 1886. Late
  Captain R.N. Entered the Royal Navy 1846. Served in the Burmese War of
  1852-3; in the Baltic and Crimea 1854-5; for which services he had four
  medals and three clasps; retired 1874. Mar. ([at St. Mary's, Tenby] 28 Nov.
  1867) Frances Capel, dau. of Colonel J. G. William Curtis (H.E.I.C.S.),
  C.B., of Tenby (living 1888). Issue :—

---

* Mrs. John Birch Webb was authoress of the following works :—'Naomi' (1841); 'A Tale
of the Vaudois' (1842); 'The Beloved Disciple' (1848); 'Julamerk' (1849); 'The Martyrs of
Carthage' (1850); 'Idaline' (1854); 'Marco Griffi' (1859); 'Blind Ursula' (1860); 'My Life
in the Prairie' (1860); 'Helen Mordaunt' (1860); 'Loyal Charlie Bentham' (1861); 'Arthur
Merton' (1863); 'Alypius of Tagaste' (1865); 'Ishmael the Yezidee' (1865); 'The Lawgiver,
etc.' (1865); 'Benaiah' (1865); 'The Stitch in Time' (1866); 'Pomponia' (1867); 'The Five
Pound Note, etc.' (1874); 'The Pilgrims of New England' (1874); 'The Lovells' (1874);
'I Know' (1879), etc.
† Captain Webb has not taken the name of Peploe.

1. John Curtis Webb (b. 29 Oct. 1868; bapt. at St. Mary's, Tenby; living 1888).
2. Daniel Cecil Webb (b. 10 March 1874; bapt. SS. Philip and James, Leckhampton; living 1888).
3. Roger Cunliffe Hastings Webb (b. 10 Dec. 1876; bapt. St. Mary's, Tenby; d. Jan. 1877).
4. Edmund Melville Webb (b. 17 Aug. 1878; bapt. St. Mary's, Tenby; living 1888).
1. Dorothy Emily (b. 28 Dec. 1875; bapt. St. Mary's, Tenby; d. Jan. 1877).
2. Millicent Grace (bapt. St. Mary's, Tenby; living 1888).
3. Ellen Eugenia (b. 24 Oct. 1881; bapt. Christ Ch., Cheltenham; d. May 1882).
3. Hammer William Webb-Peploe (b. 1 Oct., bapt. [at Weobley] 15 Nov. 1835; living 1888); of King's Pyon House, co. Hereford, and Vicar of St. Paul's, Onslow Square, London. Entered Pembroke College, Cambridge, Oct. 1856. Graduated in Arts, B.A. June 1859, and M.A. 1877. Admitted to Holy Orders 1863. Presented to the Vicarage of St. Paul's, Onslow Square, Oct. 1876, and instituted thereto Dec. 1876. Mar. ([in St. Paul's, Avenue Road, London] 11 April 1863) Frances Emily, eldest dau. of the Right Hon. Lord Justice Lush of London (living 1888). Issue :—
1. John Harold Webb-Peploe (b. 9 March 1864; bapt. at Weobley, co. Hereford; living 1888).
2. Robert Murray Watkin Webb-Peploe (b. 13 Nov. 1865; bapt. at Weobley; living 1886).
3. Francis Hammer Webb-Peploe (b. 1 May 1867; bapt. at Weobley; living 1888).
4. Henry Guy Webb-Peploe (b. 4 Nov. 1868; bapt. at King's Pyon; d. Dec. 1876).
5. Howard Melville Webb-Peploe (b. 12 Feb. 1870; bapt. at King's Pyon; living 1888).
6. Edward Alec Webb-Peploe (b. April 1874; bapt. at King's Pyon; d. Sept. 1874).
1. Elizabeth Maud (bapt. at King's Pyon; living 1888).
2. Constance Annie (bapt. at King's Pyon; d. Feb. 1887).
1. Charlotte Anne (b. 14 May; bapt. [at Weobley] 8 June 1831; d. 31 Jan.; bur. 3. Feb. 1842).
2. Gertrude Elizabeth (bapt. at Weobley; living 1888). Mar. ([at King's Pyon] 19 Nov. 1861) the Rev. John Hearn Poppelwell (b. 21 Feb. 1829; living 1888). Entered University College, Durham, 1847. Graduated in Arts, B.A. 1851, M.A. 185–. Admitted to Holy Orders. Presented to the living of St. Martin's, Haverfordwest, Nov. 1879. Issue :—
1. Henry Frank Webb Poppelwell (b. 24 July 1863; living 1888).
2. Charlie Thomas Digby Webb Poppelwell (b. 3 Jan. 1865; living 1888).
3. Herbert George Stuart Webb Poppelwell (b. 8 July 1866; d. 31 March 1867).
3. Eleanora Maria (bapt. at Weobley; living 1888). Mar. ([at King's Pyon] 28 May 1857) Thomas Myers Croome, Esq., of Cainscross House, Stroud, co. Gloucester (b. 24 April 1834; d. 15 Jan., bur. at Cainscross 20 Jan. 1883). Issue :—
1. Arthur Capel Molyneux Croome (b. [at Northfield House] 21 Feb., bapt. [at the Slad] 17 April 1866; living 1888).
1. Alice Nora (b. [at Greenhouse Court] 19 May 1858; bapt. at the Slad; d. 15 April 1864).
2. Ethel Nora (b. at Northfield; bapt. at the Slad; living 1888).
3. Ella Mabel (b. and d. [at Northfield] 15 Sept. 1869; bapt. and bur. at the Slad; d. 19 Jan. 1870).

4. Geraldine Maud (b. at Northfield ; bapt. at the Slad ; d. 12 Oct. 1887).
4. Ella Mary Ann (bapt. at Weobley; living 1888). Mar. ([at Berne, Switzerland]
  7 June 1870) the Rev. William Henry Hutchinson (b. 2 Nov. 1836 ; living
  1888). Entered Pembroke College, Cambridge, Oct. 1857. Graduated in
  Arts, B.A. 1860, M.A. 1862. Admitted to Holy Orders 1860. Curate
  of Leckhampton 1860-62. Curate of St. Mark's, Gloucester, 1862-64. Presented to the living of SS. Philip and James, Leckhampton, co. Gloucester,
  Aug. 1864, and instituted thereto Oct. same year. Surrogate and Rural
  Dean of Cheltenham 1884. Issue :—
    1. Ernest Hammer Peploe Hutchinson (b. 17 July ; bapt. 11 Aug. 1871 ;
       living 1888).
    1. Stella Mabel Hutchinson (living 1888).
    2. Florence Ella Molyneux Hutchinson (living 1888).

**Daniel Peploe Webb Peploe** (eldest son) of Garnstone Castle, co. Hereford
  (b. 15 Feb., bapt. [at Weobley] 4 July 1829; d. [at Florence, Italy]
  4 Nov. 1887, bur. at Weobley). Late Major 4th Dragoon Guards; J.P. and
  D.L., co. Hereford. Served throughout the Crimea. Returned M.P. for co.
  Hereford 3 Feb. 1874–1880. Mar. (22 June 1860) Eliza Debonnaire
  Theophila, youngest dau. of Sir Thomas Theophilus Metcalfe, 4th Bart., of
  Fern Hill, Berkshire (living 1888). Issue :—
  1. Daniel Henry Theophilus Peploe (eldest son) of Garnstone Castle.
  2. Fitzgerald Cornewall Peploe (b. 5 Sept. 1862 ; living 1888).
  3. Hugh Metcalfe Scott Peploe (b. 22 Sept. 1863 ; d. 7 July 1869).
  1. Evelyn Theophila (d. 22 May 1873).
  2. Winifred Theodora Debonnaire (living 1888).

**Daniel Henry Theophilus Peploe** (eldest son) of Garnstone Castle, co. Hereford (b. 24 April 1861 ; living unm. 1888).

The arms assigned to the Peploe family as emblazoned in the Heralds' College
are :—
    ARMS.—*Quarterly : 1 and 4, Azure, on a chevron raguled counter-raguled or,
    between three bugle-horns or, and stringed or, a mitre with labels of the field ; on
    a canton ermine a crozier or and sword in saltire gules, the former surmounted by
    the latter*, for PEPLOE ; *2 and 3, Or, a cross paly sable and azure, in the first and
    fourth an eagle displayed sable*, for WEBB.
    CRESTS.—*A ducal coronet or, issuant therefrom a reindeer's head gules, attired
    gold, charged on the neck with a human eye shedding drops of tears proper*, PEPLOE.
    *An eagle displayed sable semée de fleurs-de-lis or, and in the mouth a trefoil vert*,
    WEBB.

---

MONUMENTAL INSCRIPTIONS FROM THE BURIAL-GROUND OF
  ST. GEORGE, HANOVER SQUARE, NEAR MARBLE ARCH.*

Joseph Hughes, formerly of South Audley St, & late of King St, St James, died
  Oct. 23, 1843.
This stone is erected by Eliza, his second wife, who after a short union with the
  kindest & most tender husband, happy, though chastened with affliction was
  doomed by Providence to early widowhood.
In the same grave are deposited the remains of Mary Wells, his daughter, died
  April 3, 1832, aged 5 months, and Amiretta, his first wife, died May 15,
  1839, aged 35.

Ann Penn, daughter of Samuel & Ann Penn, of this parish, died Dec. 19, 1814,
  aged 3 years 3 months.

* Continued from p. 128.

Samuel Penn, father of the above, died April 13, 1815, in his 30th year.

M$^r$ John Hall, of New Bond S$^t$, died Oct. 5, 1814, aged 63.

Susannah Jane, daughter of Chris$^r$ & Alice Lawson, died Oct. 6, 1811, aged 13 months 6 days.

M$^r$ John Read, Mathematical Instrument Maker . . . [W . . . alle . . .] in Lancashire, died at Knightsbridge, where he had resided near sixty years, died 22$^{nd}$ Sep. 1814, in his 88$^{th}$ year. [*Long eulogy, etc., barely legible.*]

Thomas Colman, of Mount S$^t$, in this parish, died August 20, 1814, aged 52.
M$^{rs}$ Eliz$^h$ Colman, wife of the above, died Feb. 1, 1823, aged 73.
Master Joseph Colman, grandson of the above, died Sep. 24, 1821, aged 1 year & 7 months.
George Edwin Colman, died Jan. 1, 1830, aged 6 years & 2 months.
M$^r$ Joseph Colman, father of the above children, died April 5, 1831, aged 43.

Eliza Turner, died Dec. 4, 1814, aged 8.
M$^r$ Joseph Turner, late of Piccadilly, died August 25, 1825, in his 57$^{th}$ year.

M$^r$ Ralph Soulsby, died 11 Dec. 1827, aged 59.
M$^{rs}$ Ann Soulsby, widow of the above, died April 12, 1852, aged 79.

M$^{rs}$ Ann Jackson, daughter of Samuel & Eliz$^{th}$ Jackson, died March 26, 1823, aged 37.

Ann Evans, spinster, daughter of Jas. and Ann Evans, died April 26, 1826, aged 57.
James Evans, father of the above Ann Evans, died 14 Jan. 1830, aged 62.

Harriet Louisa Holloway. [*The rest of the inscription is hidden by the stem of a tree.*]

M$^{rs}$ Elizabeth Lavenu, died Jan. 15, 1814, in her 42$^{nd}$ year.
Augusta Maria, daughter of the above, died Nov. 4, 1801, in her 7$^{th}$ year.
M$^r$ Lewis Augustus Lavenu, husband of the above, died Aug. 17, 1818, in his 51$^{st}$ year.

M$^{rs}$ Phebe Gilbert, wife of M$^r$ Thomas Gilbert, of Hamilton Street, Piccadilly, died Sep. 21, 1805, aged 43.
Also the above Thomas Gilbert, died Dec. 12, 1805, aged 46.

Eliz$^{th}$ Woods, born Jan. 3, 1813, died Feb. 9, 1817, aged 4 years 1 month 6 days; daughter of John & Eliz$^{th}$ Woods, of Grosvenor Mews, Bond Street.

M$^{rs}$ Charlotte Vanderant, died April 6, 1805, aged 61.

Susannah, wife of M$^r$ John Butcher, of this parish, obiit Dec. 10, 1805, Ætat. 36.
Lucretia Butcher, daughter of the above, died 17 April 1808, aged 10 years 4 months.
Mary Butcher, died May 19, 1810, aged 11.
M$^r$ Cha$^s$ Butcher, son of the above, died May 22, 1825, aged 23.
Thomas John Butcher, son of the above, died Nov. 7, 1835, aged 39.

Mary Blackburn, wife of Henry Blackburn, of York Hospital, Chelsea, died 13 Dec. 1815, in her 60$^{th}$ year.

William Henry Blackburn, son of the above, died 29 Aug. 1814, in his 17th year.
Also of the above Henry Blackburn, died 1st March, 1816, aged 53.

Ann Pawson, died 16 April 1809, in her 28th year.

Thomas Waller Barrow, died Aug. 3, 1816, aged 5 years & 8 months.

H. G. Obiit Dec. 8, 1805, aged 2 years.
William Francis Greene, obiit April 4, 1808, aged 6 years.
William Francis Green, obiit March 7, 1833, aged 63 years.

Mary Holl, wife of Benjamin Holl, late of the Navy Office, died 3 Nov. 1803, aged 63.

.....................................................[*obliterated*].
Charlotte Mary Pringle Mackenzie, daughter of the above, died April 11, 1814, aged 24.

Richard Pouncett Webb, of this parish, died July 6, 1798, aged 51.
Alice Webb, wife of the above, died Feb. 23, 1810, aged 58.

Matthew Musgrave [Gent. ?], died Sep. 3 [176– ?], aged 68.    [*Rest worn off.*]

Philip Henry Reilly, died 28 Feb. 1821, aged 53.

George Catford, died Dec. 28, 1824, in his 46th year.
Elizabeth Catford, widow of the above, died Feb. 5, 1843, in her 66th year.

John Chittleburgh, of this parish, died 21 Dec. 1810, aged 59.

Clementina, daughter of Cha[s] Tho[s], & Caroline Sutton, died July 6, 182[–], aged 6 years.
Also the above named Caroline Sutton, died Sep. 27, 1824, in her 25th year.
Edward George Sutton, son of the above, died Feb. 24, 1825, aged 8 months.

.....................................................[*several lines illegible*].
.........and Henry his Brother, ob. 2 Aug. 1811, aged 11 weeks.
Emma Flicker, sister of the above, died Nov. 7, 1819, aged 2 years.

M[r] Henry Augustus Capps, late of Baker S[t], Portman Square, died January 4, 1832, aged 35 years.

Robert Hume, died 17 Jan. 1823, aged 50 years.    Also three of his children, died in their infancy.

Elizabeth, daughter of Samuel and Maria Langton, aged 17 months.
Alice Langton, born Nov. 13, 1810, died Jan. 15, 1811, aged 9 weeks.
M[r] Samuel Langton, father of the above, died March, 21, 1812, aged 66 years.
Hannah Gregory, died March 12, 1853, aged 68 years.
Maria Langton, wife of the above named M[r] Samuel Langton, died Aug. 26, 1853, in the 76th year of her age.

Henry, son of Captain Thomas, & Mary Anne Crosse, died in Upper Montague Street, Jan. 11, 1823, aged [    ] weeks.

John Best Webb, Esq., died Nov. 30, 1851, aged 72 years.
Mary Jane Webb, second wife of the above, died July 26, 1843, aged 61 years.

(*To be continued.*)

# Bacon Wills.*

FROM IPSWICH REGISTRY.

T.
Thome Bacon
sen'.

In the name of God, Amen. The Eleaventhe daye of September in the yeare of our Lorde God One Thowsand Sixe hundred and Eleaven I Thomas Bacon th'elder of Ringshall in the Countie of Suff. and within the dyocs of Norw^ch beinge sicke in bodye but in good and p'fecte Remembrance (Prayse and Lawde be unto Allmightie God) doe ordayne constitute and make this my Testament concerninge herein my Last will in manner and forme followinge ffirste I Bequeathe my Sowle into the hands of Allmightie God my maker Trustinge in the meritts and passion of his sonne Jesus Christe my onelie Saviour and Redemer to have fre Remission of all my Synnes and my Bodye I will it to be buryed in the parishe Churche yarde of Ringshall aforesaid Concern-ynge my worldlie Goodes I will them as hereafter followethe Item I give and bequeathe unto the poore people Inhabitinge with in the parishe of Ringshall abouesaide twelue pence Currant Inglishe money And to be distributed amongest them uppon the daie of my buryall at the discretion of my Executrice. It'm I give and bequeathe unto Alice my wief all that my dwellinge howse wherein I nowe dwell as Hall Parlour Butterye and Dayry with the yarde next betwen my said howse and the highe waye and soe directlie upp even from the west end of my saide howse unto the Grippe thereby and one rode bredithe rownd aboute my saide howse with free libertie of Ingresse egresse & Regresse unto and from the heghe waie thoroughe the rest of the Rest (sic) of my Lande for her Usuall waie as it is now used To have and to houlde to her dueringe her naturall lief Shee maytayninge my saide howse in sufficient Rep'ations And after her deceasse I give the saide howse & yard aforesaide unto Robert my sonne and his heires for ever. Item I give and bequeathe unto Alice my wiffe All my movable goodes whiche are within my forsaide howse except my Greate Chist whiche was my ffathers whiche my will and mynde is that Robert my sonne shall have it. It'm I geve and bequeathe unto Robert my sonne All the Use of my Landes and howses not before geven To haue and to houlde to him and to his heires for eu' p'sentlie after my decease he his heires or assignes yeildinge and payeing there out as hereafter shalbe expressed more at lardge. It'm I will y^t Robert my sonne his heires or assignes shall paye out of my saide Lands before given him ffower Powndes Currant Inglishe money yerlie every yeare one yere after an other unto Alice my wife or her assignes dueringe hir naturall lief and to be paid quarterlie that is w^th in one quarter of one year next after my decease twentie shillinges and soe to continew in payment everye quarter of A yere then followinge twentie shillinges dueringe the naturall lief of Alice my wief. It'm I will that Robert my sonne his heires or Assignes shall paye owt of my Landes before geven him unto Susann my daughter Sixe pownds thirtene shillings & ffower pence current Inglishe money in forme followinge that is w^thin one yere next after the decease of Alice my wief yf shee live soe longe three pownds sixe shillings & eight pence And the second yeare next after the decease of Alice my wief yf shee live soe longe other Three Powndes sixe shillings & eight pence. It'm I will that Robert my sonne his heires or Assignes shall paye out of my Landes before given him unto Marye my daughter Sixe Powndes thirtene shillings & fower pence currant Inglishe money in forme followinge that is within the Third yeare next after the decease of Alice my wyfe yf shee live soe longe three Pownds sixe shillings & eight pence And the ffowrth yeare next after the decease of Alice my wief yf shee live soe longe other Three Poundes Sixe shillinges & eight pence in full payment of the saide vj^li xiij^s iiij^d. It'm I will that Robert my sonne his heires or Assignes shall paye owt of my Landes before geven him unto Anne my daughter Tenn Powndes currant Inglishe monye in forme followinge that is the fyfthe yeare next after the decease of Alice my wief if my saide daughter live soe longe ffive Powndes and the

* Continued from p. 122.

Sixte yeare next after the decease of Alice my wief yf my saide daughter live soe longe other ffive Powndes in full payment of the foresaide Tenn Powndes. It'm I will that Rob'te my sonne his heires or assignes shall paye owt of my Landes afore given him unto Thomas my sonne Tenne Powndes of Currant Inglishe monye in forme followinge that is the Seaventhe yeare next after the decease of Alice my wife yf my said sonne Thomas live soe longe five powndes And the eighte yeare next after the decease of Alice my wief yf my saide sonne Thomas live soe longe other ffive Powndes in full payment of the saide Tenne Powndes. It'm I will that Robert my sonne his heires or Assignes shall paye owt of my Landes before geven him unto Thomas Ryvett my grandchilde twenty shillings currant Inglishe monye when he come unto the age of one and twentie yeares yf he live soe longe. It'm I will and yˢ is my mynde yf that Rob'te my sonne his heires or Assignes shall fayle in payment of all suche som'es of money whiche I have willed before to be payd owt of my Landes before given him Contrarye to this my will and mynde Then I will & mynde (sic) is that the p'tie or p'ties whiche shall not be payde in p'te or in the whole shall enter into all the Landes before given unto Robert my sonne And the same to have holde & possesse untill the saide p'tie or p'ties before saide shall be fullie paide accordinge unto this my will Provyded allwayes and it is my will That Whereas I haue geven as aforesaid my Landes unto Robert my sonne p'sentlie after my decease my mynde is that yf anye Corne shalbe standinge or beinge upon the same Landes that my Executrice shall take of the Corne and therewᵗʰ paye my debtes. It'm I will and yt ys my mynde that Alice my wyfe shall haue all my Corne Haye Swyne Neats Bullocks Wennells Horses Mares Tumbrell Carts Plowghs and traics Harrowe and barrowe and all my monye whiche I haue and is dewe unto me And with the same paye my debtes and bringe my bodye honestlie unto the grownde And of this my Testament and last will I ordayne Constitute and make Alice my wief my sole Executrice hopinge she will prove this my will and p'forme soe muche as is to be p'formed by her accordinge to this my will and Testament that is my last will and testament I haue hereunto sett my hande and Seale. It'm It is my will and mynde that whereas I haue geven all that my dwellinge howse as aforesaide unto Alice my wife and fower Powndes yearelie to be paid hir dueringe her naturall lief my wyll and mynde ys yf Alice my wief doe marrye at anie tyme after my decease Then my will and mynde is that the Legasie & guiftes before given hir shalbe utterlie voyde And to be dispossessed owt of the saide howse and to haue fortye shillings a yeare yerly to be paide her owt of my said Landes by Robert my sonne his heires or Assignes and quarterlie to be paide by equall portions. These beinge witnesses unto the Confirmynge of this will John Wellam Edmund Wellam his m'ke and me William Sparrowe with others. Sign' Thome Bacon.

Proved at Ipswich 10 October 1611.

(*To be continued.*)

## Baldwin.

### Vincent's Salop.

Joh'es Bawdewyn de Didlebery⫟Anna filia et hæres Ricardi L'infant.
in com. Salop.

Thomas Bawdewyn de Didlebery in com. Salop.⫟

Will'us Bawdewyn de Didlebery⫟Alicia fil. et hæres Willimi Wigley.
in com. Salop.

A

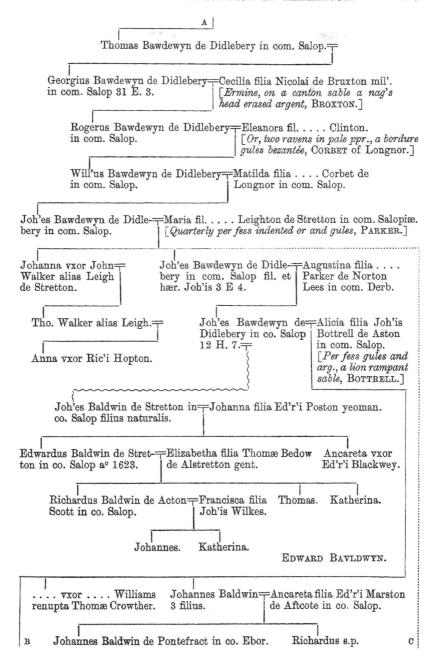

A |

Thomas Bawdewyn de Didlebery in com. Salop.⊤

Georgius Bawdewyn de Didlebery⊤Cecilia filia Nicolai de Bruxton mil'.
in com. Salop 31 E. 3.      | [*Ermine, on a canton sable a nag's*
     | *head erased argent,* BROXTON.]

Rogerus Bawdewyn de Didlebery⊤Eleanora fil. . . . . Clinton.
in com. Salop.      | [*Or, two ravens in pale ppr., a bordure*
     | *gules bezantée,* CORBET *of* Longnor.]

Will'us Bawdewyn de Didlebery⊤Matilda filia . . . . Corbet de
in com. Salop.      | Longnor in com. Salop.

Joh'es Bawdewyn de Didle-⊤Maria fil. . . . . Leighton de Stretton in com. Salopiæ.
bery in com. Salop.      | [*Quarterly per fess indented or and gules,* PARKER.]

Johanna vxor John⊤      Joh'es Bawdewyn de Didle-⊤Augustina filia . . . .
Walker alias Leigh |      bery in com. Salop fil. et | Parker de Norton
de Stretton.      hær. Joh'is 3 E 4.      Lees in com. Derb.

Tho. Walker alias Leigh.⊤      Joh'es Bawdewyn de⊤Alicia filia Joh'is
     Didlebery in co. Salop | Bottrell de Aston
Anna vxor Ric'i Hopton.      12 H. 7.⊤      in com. Salop.
     [*Per fess gules and*
     *arg., a lion rampant*
     *sable,* BOTTRELL.]

Joh'es Baldwin de Stretton in⊤Johanna filia Ed'r'i Poston yeoman.
co. Salop filius naturalis.

Edwardus Baldwin de Stret-⊤Elizabetha filia Thomæ Bedow      Ancareta vxor
ton in co. Salop aᵒ 1623. | de Alstretton gent.      Ed'r'i Blackwey.

Richardus Baldwin de Acton⊤Francisca filia      Thomas.      Katherina.
Scott in co. Salop. | Joh'is Wilkes.

Johannes.      Katherina.

EDWARD BAVLDWYN.

. . . . vxor . . . . Williams      Johannes Baldwin⊤Ancareta filia Ed'r'i Marston
renupta Thomæ Crowther.      3 filius. | de Aftcote in co. Salop.

B      Johannes Baldwin de Pontefract in co. Ebor.      Richardus s.p.      C

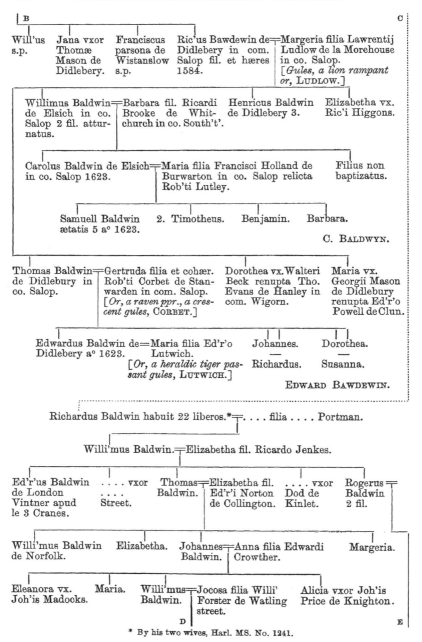

| B | | | | | C |

Will'us s.p. | Jana vxor Thomæ Mason de Didlebery. | Franciscus parsona de Wistanslow s.p. | Ric'us Bawdewin de=Margeria filia Lawrentij Didlebery in com. Salop fil. et hæres 1584. | Ludlow de la Morehouse in co. Salop. [*Gules, a lion rampant or*, LUDLOW.]

Willimus Baldwin=Barbara fil. Ricardi  Henricus Baldwin  Elizabetha vx.
de Elsich in co. | Brooke de Whit- de Didlebery 3.  Ric'i Higgons.
Salop 2 fil. attur- | church in co. South't'.
natus.

Carolus Baldwin de Elsich=Maria filia Francisci Holland de  Filius non
in co. Salop 1623. | Burwarton in co. Salop relicta  baptizatus.
Rob'ti Lutley.

Samuell Baldwin  2. Timotheus.  Benjamin.  Barbara.
ætatis 5 a° 1623.
                                    C. BALDWYN.

Thomas Baldwin=Gertruda filia et cohær.  Dorothea vx.Walteri  Maria vx.
de Didlebury in | Rob'ti Corbet de Stan-  Beck renupta Tho.  Georgii Mason
co. Salop. | warden in com. Salop.  Evans de Hanley in  de Didlebury
[*Or, a raven ppr., a cres-*  com. Wigorn.  renupta Ed'r'o
*cent gules*, CORBET.]  Powell de Clun.

Edwardus Baldwin de=Maria filia Ed'r'o  Johannes.  Dorothea.
Didlebery a° 1623. | Lutwich.  ―  ―
[*Or, a heraldic tiger pas-*  Richardus.  Susanna.
*sant gules*, LUTWICH.]
                                    EDWARD BAWDEWIN.

Richardus Baldwin habuit 22 liberos.*=. . . . filia . . . . Portman.

Willi'mus Baldwin.=Elizabetha fil. Ricardo Jenkes.

Ed'r'us Baldwin  . . . . vxor  Thomas=Elizabetha fil.  . . . . vxor  Rogerus =
de London  . . . .  Baldwin. | Ed'r'i Norton  Dod de  Baldwin
Vintner apud  Street.  de Collington.  Kinlet.  2 fil.
le 3 Cranes.

Willi'mus Baldwin  Elizabetha.  Johannes=Anna filia Edwardi  Margeria.
de Norfolk.  Baldwin. | Crowther.

Eleanora vx.  Maria.  Willi'mus=Jocosa filia Willi'  Alicia vxor Joh'is
Joh'is Madocks.  Baldwin. | Forster de Watling  Price de Knighton.
street.
                D                                    E

* By his two wives, Harl. MS. No. 1241.

BRASS PLATE INSERTED IN NORTH WALL OF CHANCEL,
DIDDLEBURY CHURCH, SALOP.

ARMS QUARTERLY.--1. BALDWYN. ARGENT A SALTIRE SABLE.
    2. WIGLEY. BARRY OF SIX AZURE AND ARGENT A CHIEF ERMINE.
    3. CHILDE. GULES A CHEVRON ERMINE BETWEEN THREE EAGLETS CLOSE ARGENT.
    4. ACHELEY. PER PALE GULES AND OR A FLEUR DE LIS COUNTERCHANGED.

CREST ON A MOUNT VERT A COCKATRICE WITH WINGS ADDORSED ARGENT BEAKED COMBED DUCALLY
    GORGED AND LINED OR.

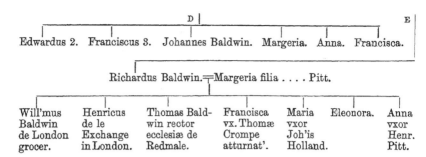

| D \| | | | | | | E \| |
|---|---|---|---|---|---|---|
| Edwardus 2. | Franciscus 3. | Johannes Baldwin. | Margeria. | Anna. | Francisca. | |

Richardus Baldwin.⊤Margeria filia . . . . Pitt.

| Will'mus Baldwin de London grocer. | Henricus de le Exchange in London. | Thomas Baldwin rector ecclesiæ de Redmale. | Francisca vx. Thomæ Crompe atturnat'. | Maria vxor Joh'is Holland. | Eleonora. | Anna vxor Henr. Pitt. |
|---|---|---|---|---|---|---|

## DIDDLEBURY.
### *Brass, north wall.*

QVI MARE QVI FERRVM DVRÆ QVI VINCVLA TVRRIS
QVONDAM TRANSIVIT NVNC INGENS ATROPOS OCCA
NOMEN SI QVÆRAS SOBOLES QVOT QVÆ FVIT VXOR
OCCVBVIT QVANDO QVÆ SVBSVNT HÆC TIBI MO'STRA'

Arms : Quarterly of four : 1. BALDWIN ; 2. WIGLEY ; 3. CHILDE ; 4. ACHELEY.
Crest : BALDWIN ; and on a smaller shield, BALDWIN impaling LUDLOW, a lion rampant.

THOMAS PRIMOGENITVS RICHARDI BAWDEWIN DE
DIDLEBVRIE ET MARGIRIÆ VXORIS EIVS FILIÆ LAW-
RENCII LVDLOWE DE MOREHOWSE DVXIT IN VXORE'
GERTRVDAM FILIAM ROBERTI CORBET DE STAND-
WARDINE DE QVA GENVIT TRES FILIOS EDWARDVM
IOHANNEM ET RICHARDVM ET DVAS FILIAS DORO
THEAM ET SVZANNA' ET VALEDICIT MVNDO ⎫ ET OBIIT
ANNO D'NI 1614 ÆTATIS SVÆ LXVIII.  ⎬ 4 APRILIS
                                     ⎭   1623.

## Cullum.*

THE BOOKE OF COMMON PRAYER, 4to, Robert Barker, 1615.

*On the first page :* Ann Wyatt.†    Mary Skiner.
*On last page :* John the Son of John and Susan Cullum was Baptised in
Hawsted Chappell July the nineteenth in the Year One Thousand Seven Hundred
& Thirty three Being Thursday, & was then And there Baptised by me John Smith
The Vicar of Stetchworth and Curate of Nowton, the Former in Cambridgeshire
and Dioces of Ely, the Latter in the County of Suffolk & Dioces of Norwich.

THE BOOK OF COMMON PRAYER, Cambridge, John Hayes, 1670, folio.
### *First Page.*

Edw[d] Isaac Jackson & Mary Ray was Married Aug. 3[d] 1720.
    Theophila, the Daughter of Edw[d] Isaack Jackson & Mary his wife, was born on
the 2[d] of June 1721, at Nine in the Evening, and was baptized y[e] 22[d]. Her
Godfather was M[r] Matt. Isaack. Her Godmothers : M[rs] Elizabeth Ray, Sen[r], and
M[rs] Palgrave Isaack.
    Walter Isaack Jackson, son of Edw[d] Isaack Jackson and Mary his wife, was
born on the 16 of June 1722, between the hours of 11 and 12 in the Morning, and

---

* Communicated by G. MILNER-GIBSON-CULLUM, Esq., F.S.A.
† Afterwards wife to Sir Jasper Cullum, Bart.

was baptized the 3<sup>d</sup> of July. His Godfathers was M<sup>r</sup> Walter Ray & M<sup>r</sup> Giles Isaack. His God Mother: M<sup>rs</sup> Eliz<sup>th</sup> Ray of Denham.

Elizabeth, Daughter of Edw<sup>d</sup> Isaack Jackson & Mary his wife, was born the 1<sup>st</sup> of September 1723, at seven in the Evening, and was baptized y<sup>e</sup> 19. Her Godfather was the Rev<sup>d</sup> M<sup>r</sup> Rob<sup>t</sup> Butts. Her Godmothers: M<sup>rs</sup> Marg<sup>t</sup> Ray of Haughley & M<sup>rs</sup> Eliz. Ray, Jun<sup>r</sup>.

---

Thomas Gery Cullum was born at Hardwick House, near Bury S<sup>t</sup> Edmunds, Suffolk, November the 30<sup>th</sup> in the year of our Lord 1741.

---

Robert Hanson and Elizabeth Jackson were married at Weatherden (*sic*) in Suffolk by the Rev. M<sup>r</sup> Richard Ray on Monday the 14 of May 1744. She ob. 7<sup>th</sup> Oct<sup>r</sup> 1760, etat. 38<sup>th</sup>. He ob. Nov<sup>br</sup> 1765.

Mary, a daughter of the s<sup>d</sup> Robert and Elizabeth, was born the 28 of Jan., about 8 in the morning, being Monday, in the year 1745, and christned at the Low Church in Kingston upon Hull on the 1<sup>st</sup> of March following. Her sureties were her Grandfather Hanson, her Grandmother Jackson, and M<sup>rs</sup> Eliz. Levett of Normanton, her Great Aunt by Marriage.

Ann, a Daughter of the s<sup>d</sup> Rob<sup>t</sup> and Eliz., was born on Wednesday the 29<sup>th</sup> of March 1749, about two at noon, and was christned at the Low Church aforesaid on the 3<sup>d</sup> of May following. Her sureties were her Grandfather Jackson, her Grandmother Hanson, & M<sup>rs</sup> Ann Ray, her Great Aunt.

Thomas, a son of the s<sup>d</sup> Robert and Eliza, was born on Monday the 12 of August 1751, about eight in the morning, and christned at Melton in the parish of Welton on the 18<sup>th</sup> of Sept<sup>r</sup> following. His sureties were Thomas Fell, Esq<sup>r</sup>, M<sup>r</sup> Tho<sup>s</sup> Levett his great uncle, and Miss Theophila Jackson his Aunt.

Levet, a son of the same Rob<sup>t</sup> and Eliza, was born on Tuesday the 31<sup>st</sup> of December 1754, ab<sup>t</sup> five in the morning, and christned at Melton afores<sup>d</sup> on the 8<sup>th</sup> of January following. His sureties were W<sup>m</sup> Wilberforce, Esq<sup>r</sup>, Rev<sup>d</sup> Bernard Mills, & M<sup>rs</sup> Ann Ray.

---

Thomas Gery Cullum and Mary Hanson were married at Bury S<sup>t</sup> Edmunds (in S<sup>t</sup> Mary's Church) in Suffolk, by the Rev<sup>d</sup> Sir John Cullum, on Thursday the 1<sup>st</sup> of September 1774.

John, son of Thomas Gery and Mary Cullum, was born on Wednesday the sixteenth of October, between the hours of eight & nine in the evening, in the year one thousand seven hundred and seventy six, and christned at S<sup>t</sup> Mary's Church, by the Rev<sup>d</sup> M<sup>r</sup> Sharp, February 6<sup>th</sup> 1777. His sureties were his uncles the Rev<sup>d</sup> S<sup>r</sup> John Cullum, B<sup>t</sup>, & Levett Hanson, Esq<sup>r</sup>, & His Grandmother Lady Cullum. Died October 26, 1788.

Thomas Gery, Son of Thomas Gery and Mary Cullum, was born on Thursday twenty-third of October, about Twelve o'clock at noon, in the year One Thousand Seven Hundred and Seventy seven, and Christned at S<sup>t</sup> Mary's Church, by the Rev<sup>d</sup> M<sup>r</sup> Craske, on December the 19<sup>th</sup> in the above year. His sureties were Charles Kent, Esq<sup>r</sup>, of Fornham, & John Leathes, Esq<sup>r</sup>, of Bury, & his great aunt M<sup>rs</sup> Katherine Hanson of Normanton in Yorkshire.

John Palmer, son of Thomas Gery and Mary Cullum, was born on Sunday May the 18, 1783, about 9 o'clock in the morning, and christned at S<sup>t</sup> Mary's Church on Thursday June 19<sup>th</sup> in the above year by the Rev M<sup>r</sup> Craske. His sureties were his uncles the Rev. S<sup>r</sup> John Cullum, B<sup>t</sup>, and Ashley Palmer, Esq., and his great aunt M<sup>rs</sup> Elizabeth Hanson of Normanton in Yorkshire.

Susanna, daughter of S<sup>r</sup> Thomas Gery Cullum, Bar<sup>t</sup>, and Dame Mary his wife, was born on Saturday March the 3, 1787, about two o'clock in the morning, privately baptized Sunday March the 11<sup>th</sup>, and baptized in S<sup>t</sup> Mary's Church Wednesday July the 23rd 1788. Her sureties were her aunts M<sup>rs</sup> Palmer & M<sup>rs</sup> Vernon, & the Rev<sup>d</sup> George Ashby, Rector of Barrow in Suffolk, & Charles Miller, Esq., late of Fort Marlboro' in the East Indies. Died May 20, 1805.

# Langley Pedigree—Pedigree C. (*Vide* Vol. II., p. 274.)

## LANGLEYS OF YORKSHIRE.

Henry Langley of Dalton, co. York. Mentioned in his brother = ....fl..... Kaye of Woodsome, co. Ebor. Thomas the Lord Chancellor's will.

1. Thomas Langley of Rathorpe Hall. Ob. 28 April = Margery, fil. .... Womb- 2. Robert Langley = .... fl. 3. Henry Langley, 10 Hen. VIII. Inq. p.m. 28 Aug. 10 Hen. VIII. | well of Wombwell. of Langley. | .... æt. 10, 16 Hen. VI.

George = .... Langley. | fil.

Richard Langley of Rathorpe Hall. Aged 14 in 10 Hen. VIII. Ob. 24 Sep. = Joan, fil. .... Beaumont 1587. Inq. p.m. 4 May 30 Hen. VIII. Will proved 1 July 1539. of Mirfield.

William = .... fl. Langley, | .... See Pedigree **B.**

Richard Langley. Nat. 1529. Ob. 1 Dec. 1586. = Agnes, fil. Agnes, fil. Wil = Thomas Robert = .... Richard liam Tate (or Langley. Langley. | fil. Hansby of Yates). .... Malton.

Katherine = Thomas Leigh Langley. of Boothes.

Margaret Alice Jane Isabel Langley, Margaret Catherine = .... Langley. Langley. Langley. ux. William Langley. Langley. | Hodgson. Foster of Evers- — | fil. wick. Agnes Langley.

Marmaduke = Ursula, fil. John Rudston of Christopher = Arthur = .... Dolman of Hayton, Esq., by Margaret Langley of | Langley of | fil. Pocklington. his wife, fil. John Trollope Millington. | Rathorpe | Mar. 2. of Thornley, co. Durham. Nat. 1569. | Hall. |

A         B

Richard Langley of Rathorpe Hall.=....fil.....

Arthur Langley of Rathorpe Hall.  Ob. June 1659.=Dorothy, fil. William Cartwright, Clerk of Assize for co. of York.

2. Sarah Langley.

3. Elizabeth=John Brown Langley.  of Leeds.

4. Winifride=William Swale Langley.  of Kippus.

5. Catherine=John Dixon Langley.  of Lepton.

6. Grace Langley.

1. Richard Langley of Rathorpe Hall, æt. 61, 2 April 1666.=Mary, fil. William Bentley of Heptonstall, co. York.

1. Mary=John Fox of Langley.  Scarborough.

2. William Langley.

2. Barbara=William Brooke of Langley.  Heckmondwyke.

5. Sarah Langley.

1. Arthur Langley=Sarah, fil. William of Rathorpe Hall.  Garlicke of Dinting, Nat. 1634.  co. Derby.

2. John Langley.

1. Susannah=Phillip Rippon Langley.  of Darlington.

Dorcas Langley.

3. Mary=John Wilson Langley.  of Thornhill.

4. Catherine Langley.

William Langley=Elizabeth, fil.....Brentnell of Rotherham.  of Wallingweth.

John Langley.

John=Sarah Turner.  Langley.

John Bell=Elizabeth=Richard of Shef-  Langley.  Thompson field.  of Sheffield. Mar. 2.  Mar. 1.

Walter Langley of Rotherham.  Nat. 1699.  Ob. s.p. 1 Jan. 1780.  Sep. at Rotherham.

Richard.  William.  —  —  William.  Hannah.  All died in infancy.

Ann Langley.=John Barton Ob. 31 Oct.  of Rotherham. 1733.

*Ric: Langley*

σ

Mary, fil. Michael Wentworth=Richard Langley of Millington. ...; fil....=Francis Langley of Great Langton,
of Wooley.      Occurs 1612.      Robinson.     co. Ebor.  Ob. c. 1636.

William Brigham of Wyton.=Ursula     Richard     Ferdinand=Mary Langley.=Sir Brian Stapleton
Ob. c. 1670.     Langley.     Langley.     Thweng.      of Hirst. Mar. 1.

2. Jane Langley. Mar.
1 .... Richardson of
Kirkby. Mar. 2 Richard
Mason.

1. Anne Langley. Mar.
1 .... Conyers of Rawker.
Mar. 2 John Fall.

Anne Langley. Mar.
1 .... Mar. 2 ....
Osborne. Mentioned
in brother Thomas
Langley's will.

Muriel Langley.=Richard
Mentioned in    Robinson
brother Thomas  of Cundall,
Langley's will.  co. Ebor.

2. Charles=Mary,
Langley.   fil.
      ....

1. Christopher   2. George=Anne, fil. Christo-   3. Francis   4. John   Mary
Langley of    Langley  pher Danby of   Langley  Langley  Lang-
South Cowton.  of Great  Great Langton.  of Little  of Lang-  ley.
         Langton.               Danby.    ton.

4. George Langley=Anne Robinson.
of Northallerton,  Nup. at Kirkby-
co. York.      Fleetham, co.
           York, 4 Dec. 1666.

3. Francis Langley,=....
Citizen of London.  fil.
             ....

Francis Langley. Mentioned in
uncle Thomas Langley's will.

1. Thomas Langley of North Grimston. Aged 41, 10 Sept. 1666. Ob. 27 Jan. 1694.=Elizabeth, fil. Henry
Sep. at North Grimston 31 Jan. 1694. M.I. Will dated 10 Feb. 1691. Codicil   Metcalfe of Hull
dated 18 June 1693. Probate at York 18 June 1695.               Mentioned in husband's will. Ob.
1 Aug. 1697, æt. 63.
Sep. at North Grim-
ston.

*Tho. Langley* [signature]

D

D

1. Henry Langley. Nat. 1656. Ob. vitâ patris.

2. Thomas Langley of North Grimston. Nat. 1665. Ob. 1 Nov. 1723. Executor of his father's will. Sep. 5 Nov. 1723 at North Grimston, æt. 58. Will dated 24 Dec. 1722. Codicil dated 8 Aug. 1723. Probate at York 14 Feb. 1724.

3. George Langley.

1. Anne Langley.=Phillip Seaman Mentioned in father's will. | of West Elley, co. York. Defunct 1691.

5. Frances Langley. Ob. s.p.

2. Frances Langley. Ob. vitâ patris.

3. Elizabeth Langley.=Richard Fothergill Living 1772 Mentioned in fa—r's will. | of London.

4. Mary=Edward Hutchinson of Wykeham Langley. | Abbey, co. York. Ob. Intest. Adm. granted 6 Feb. 1719.

Richard Hutchinson Langley of Wykeham Abbey. Assumed name=Elizabeth, fil. et hær. Boynton Boynton of Rawcliffe, co. York, and arms of Langley under will of his uncle Thomas Langley. Ob. 7 | Esq., by Elizabeth his wife. Ante-nuptial settlement dated 6 Dec. 1755. Will dated 17 March 1755. Probate at York 31 Dec. 1755. | Nov. 1724. Executrix of husband's will 1755.

Frances Langley. Ob. 28 April 1817, æt. 79. Sep. in York Minster.

Anne Langley. Ob. at the Manor House, St. Marygate, co. York, 3 Dec. 1803. Sep. in York Minster 9 Dec. 1803. M.I.

John Dealtry, M.D. Mentioned in brother-in-law Boynton Langley's will. Ob. 25 March 1773. Sep. in York Minster 30 March 1773, æt. 65. M.I.

Mary=Elizabeth Langley. Mentioned in her father's will. Ob. at Bradenham House, co. Buckingham, 28 Aug. 1812. Sep. in York Minster 15 Sept. 1812. M.I.

3. William Langley. Mentioned in his father's will.

1. Boynton Langley of Wykeham Abbey. Ob. 5 Jan. 1772. Will dated 11 Dec. 1769. Mentioned in his father's will. Probate at York 29 Jan. 1772.

=Mary, fil. Sir William Foulis, Bart. Nup. 19 May 1760. Executrix of husband's will 1771.

2. Matthew Langley. Mentioned in father's will, and in brother Boynton's will.

Richard Langley of Wykeham Abbey.=Dorothy, fil. Henry Willoughby, Sheriff of Yorks. 1786. Ob. s.p. 27 | 5th Lord Middleton. Nat. 18 Jan. 1817. Sep. in York Minster 4 | July 1758. Nup. 24 Nov. 1784. Feb. 1817. Will dated 10 May 1810, | Ob. 13 April 1824. Sep. in York two codicils 26 March 1813 and 4 Jan. | Minster 21 April 1824. M.I. 1817. Probate (York) 20 March 1817. | Executrix of husband's will. Probate (London) 3 April 1817.

Mary Langley. Mentioned in brother Richard's will. Ob. 13 and sep. 19 Nov. 1811 in York Minster, æt. 48. M.I.=Robert Royds of Easthorpe Park, co. York, Esq., Ob. Feb. 1815. Sep. in York Minster, M.I., æt. 57. Mentioned in brother-in-law Richard Langley's will.

# Genealogy of Browne.*

CONFIRMATION OF ARMS TO THE VEN. SAMUEL PEPLOE, B.D.,
ARCHDEACON OF RICHMOND, 23 FEB. 1753.†

To All and Singular to whom these Presents shall come, John Anstiś Esquire Garter Principal King of Arms, and Charles Townley Esquire Norroy King of Arms of the North parts of England from the River Trent Northwards send Greeting. Whereas the Reverend Samuel Peploe, B.D., Chancellor of the Diocese of Chester and Warden of Manchester College in the County Palatine of Lancaster, hath represented unto the Right Honourable Thomas Earl of Effingham Deputy (with the Royal Approbation) to the Most Noble Edward Duke of Norfolk Earl Marshal and Hereditary Marshal of England, That his Father the late Right Reverend Doctor Samuel Peploe Lord Bishop of Chester did bear and use for his Arms—Azure a Chevron Counter Embattled between three Bugle Horns Or, and for the Crest, Out of a Ducal Coronet Or, a Rain Deer's Head Gules, Antler'd Or, as his Ancestors heretofore had done, but being desirous to have some Additional bearing thereunto to perpetuate the singular Loyalty of his Father to his late most Sacred Majesty King George the First at the Battle of Preston in Lancashire in the year 1715 and also his advancement in the Church on that Account, did therefore request his Lordships Warrant for our devising Granting and Assigning unto him and his Descendants and to the other Descendants of his said Father such Arms and Crest accordingley and that the same may be registred in the College of Arms, as a perpetual Memorial thereof. And for as much as his Lordship duly considering the Premises did by Warrant under His Hand and Seal bearing date the twenty first day of February instant, Order and Direct us to Devise Grant and Assign unto the said Samuel Peploe and the Descendants before mentioned such Arms and Crest as may be lawfully born by him and them, Know Ye that We the said Garter and Norroy in pursuance of the Consent of the said Earl of Effingham and by Virtue of the Letters Patent of Our several offices to each of us respectively Granted under the Great Seal of Great Britain have devised and Do by these Presents Grant and Assign to the said Samuel Peploe, the Arms following, Viz$^t$, Azure on a Cheveron Embattled Counter Embattled, between three Bugle Horns Stringed Or a Mitre with Labels of the Field, On a Canton Ermine a Crosier Or and a Sword Gules in Saltire, the Former Surmounted by the Latter, And for the Crest, On a Wreath of the Colours a Ducal Coronet Or, therein a Rein Deer's Head Gules Antler'd Gold, Charged on the Neck with an Human Eye

---

* Continued from p. 132.

† The engraving is a *facsimile* of the sketch of arms from the copy of the grant as entered in the books of the College.

shedding Drops of Tears proper, as the same are in the Margin hereof more plainly depicted. To be born and used for ever here-after by him the said Samuel Peploe and his lawfull Descendants and also by the Lawfull Descendants of his said Father the late Right Reverend Doctor Samuel Peploe, Lord Bishop of Chester, deceased, with due and proper differences, according to the ancient Usage and Custom of Arms, without the Lett or Interruption of any Person or Persons whatsoever.  In Witness whereof We the said Garter and Norroy Kings of Arms have to these Presents subscribed our Names and affixed the Seals of Our several offices the twenty third day of February in the twenty sixth year of the Reign of Our Sovereign Lord George the Second by the Grace of God King of Great Britain, France, and Ireland, Defender of the Faith and so forth and in the Year of Our Lord God one thousand seven hundred and fifty three.

JOHN ANSTIS, Garter                    CHARLES TOWNLEY, Norroy
Principal King of Arms.                         King of Arms.

Examined by JAS. LANE, Richmond, Regr.

## Monumental Inscriptions.

The following inscriptions are upon monuments in the nave of Chester Cathedral, behind the nearest pillar to the choir in the south range :—

1. Monument to Bishop Peploe, of Derbyshire marble, decorated with cherubim and foliage. Above the inscription are the arms of the diocese, impaling Peploe : Gules, three mitres proper ; impaling, Azure, a chevron raguled between three bugles strung or.

Juxta dormit,
beatam expectans resurrectionem,
reverendus admodum in Christo Pater
Samuel Peploe, S.T.P.
olim ecclesiæ Kedlastoniæ prope Derbiam rector,
tum vicarius Prestonensis in agro Lancastriæ,
mox optimo favente principe,
Collegii Mancinensis guardianus
reliquos deinde, quos plurimos produxit, annos,
Episcopus Cestriensis.
Ampliora adeo non cupide expetivit, ut
ultro oblatis carere mallet.
Qualis erat, supremus dies indicabit
Obiit 21ᵐᵒ die Februarii,
Anno salutis humanæ
MDCCLII,
ætatis suæ
LXXXIV.

2. A pyramidal marble monument by Nollekens.  Above the inscription a boy weeping over an urn.  Arms : Azure, on a chevron raguled or a mitre sable, on a canton ermine a sword and crosier in saltire or.  Crest : A reindeer's head gules, attired or, issuing from a ducal coronet.

Sacred
to the memory of Samuel Peploe, LL.D.,
Chancellor of the Diocese of Chester, and Warden
of the Collegiate Church in Manchester.
He died Oct. 22, 1781.
Aged 82 years.

## MONUMENTAL INSCRIPTIONS OF HOLY TRINITY, BRADFORD-ON-AVON, CO. WILTS.*

### SOUTH AISLE.

Memoriæ | Ricardi Whatly, hujus Parochiæ, Armigeri ; | Eleanor, Uxoris ejus, et Progenei subnumeratæ : | quorum Reliquiæ prope deponuntur Hoc | Marmor, sola deplorante Filia erectum, | Sacrum est. | Ricardus, Pater, obiit 4ᵗᵒ Novˢ, 1782, Ætatˢ 73. | Eleanor, Uxor, obiit 10ᵐᵒ Decˢ, 1786, Ætatˢ 61 ; | et Progenies, vizᵗ : | Anna, 9ᵐᵒ Decˢ 1756, | Mense Ætatˢ 9. | Maria, 30ᵐᵒ Janⁱⁱ, 1765, | Ann Ætatˢ 11. | Ricardus, 7ᵐᵒ Octˢ 1774, | Ætatˢ 14. | Johannes, 23° Maii, 1779, | Ætatˢ 25. | Gulielmus, 28° Novˢ 1781, Ætatˢ 16. | Eleanora, 16° Nov. 1787, | Ætatˢ 20.

* Continued from p. 121.

A bomb fired, thereon inscribed in Gothic character the capital-letter S.—Ratio ultima Regum.
*Near this place are buried | Henry Shrapnel | of this Parish, who died An°
1688. | Also | Elizabeth, his Wife, who died An° 1676. | Also Zachariah Shrapnel, |
who died An° 1723. | Also | Zachariah Shrapnel, | who died Jan^ry 28, 1761, | Aged
67. | Joseph Shrapnel, Obiit May 8^th, 1756, Ætat. one Year. | Joseph Shrapnel,
Obiit Jan^ry 26, 1759, only three Weeks. | Lydia Shrapnel, Obiit Aug^st 23, 1766,
Ætat. 10 Years. | Ann Shrapnel, Obiit March 26, 1787, | Ætat. 33. | Elizabeth
Warren, daughter of | Zachariah and Lydia Shrapnel, | Obiit April 15, 1796,
Ætat. 38. | Zachariah Shrapnel, Obiit May 5, 1796, Ætat. 71. | Lydia Shrapnel,
his wife, Obiit Mar^h 1797, Ætat. 70. | In Memory of the Rev^d Joseph Shrapnel, |
Obiit Nov^r 9^th, 1821, Ætat. 61. | Also to the Memory of | General Henry Scrope
Shrapnel, | Colonel Commandant 6^th Battalion of Artillery, | Obiit 13^th March 1849,
Ætat. 80 Years. | Also of Esther, his Wife, | Obiit 13^th September, 1852, | Ætat.
.. Years, | and was Interred in the Chancel | of this Church.

Arms : DEVERELL.

Sacred to the memory of | Amelia, wife of John Deverell Esquire | of Franck-
leigh, | departed this life 29^th June, 1846, Aged 35. | Also of the above named |
John Deverell Esquire | of Franckleigh, barrister-at-law, | died April 26^th, 1876,
Aged 63.

In Memory of | Caroline, | Wife of M^r William Gaisford | of Seend, in this
County, | who died July 1^st, 1813, | Aged 33 Years. | Likewise | of their Infant
Daughter, | Caroline, | who died August 23^rd, 1813, | Aged 6 months.

In Memory | of George Bethell Esq^re | who died March 26^th, Anno Dom: 1795, |
Aged 65. | This Marble in filial Affection is raised | by his surviving three
Daughters ; | He was uniformly respected as | A Man of strict Integrity ; | an
upright Magistrate ; | And the poor Man's Friend. | Sacred also to the Memory |
of Sarah his Wife | who departed this Life | January 7^th, 1777, Aged 32. | And of
Elizabeth their Daughter | who died an Infant.

In Memory of Elizabeth | Wife of James Bethell, Gent., of Lady Down ; |
departed this life Feb. 27^th, 1820, | in the 53^rd year of her Age. | Also Samuel,
second son of | James and Elizabeth Bethell, | who died Feb. 7, 1831, in the 32^nd
Year of his Age. | Beneath this humble tribute of Affection | are also deposited the
Remains of | James Bethell who died April 14^th, 1831, | in the 66^th Year of his Age.

Arms : A wolf rampant collared and chained, in chief three crosses patty fitchy.
Crest : A goat's head erased.

In a Vault near this Monument | are interred the Remains of | Thomas Bush
Esq^re, | who after leading a virtuous | and exemplary Life | died November 21^st,
1809, Aged 68, | beloved and respected by all who knew him. | He was a good
Christian, | an affectionate Husband, | an indulgent Father, a sincere Friend, | an
active Magistrate, | and a valuable Member of Society. | Also the Remains of Mary
his wife | who died on the 16^th of January, 1824, | Aged 69 Years.

Under the Tomb | Opposite the Door beneath | Lye the Bodies of | John
Rogers, A.M., | His Dear Wife Elizabeth, | and several of his Family. | He was
Fourty three Years Vicar of this Parish, | And Died April 20^th, 1754, in the 76^th
Year of his Age.

Arms : ROGERS.          Crest : A fleur-de-lys gules.

* There is the following *Hatchment* in the *North Aisle :* Quarterly—1, Crusily, a lion
rampant ; 2 and 3, Quarterly, i and iv, Argent, a bend or ; ii, Azure, a saltire or ; iii, Azure, on a
saltire or two bars gules ; 4, Gules, a fess ermine between three nag's heads erased or ; over all
on an escutcheon a bomb fired.  Crest : Out of a coronet or a plume of ostrich-feathers.  Ratio
ultima regum.  General Shrapnel was the inventor of the Shrapnel shell.

L 2

*On a white marble monument a woman sitting in mournful attitude, underneath is the parable of the good Samaritan carved in relief:* In the family Vault | in the adjoining Church Yard | are deposited the remains | of Thomas Timbrell Esq^re | who departed this Life | on the 23^rd day of April, 1815, | Aged 83 Years. | Likewise Elizabeth, | Wife of the above Thomas Timbrell, | who died on the 8^th day of March, 1805, | Aged 77 Years.

*Arms : TIMBRELL.        Crest : A lion's head erased quarterly gules and or.

To the memory | of Robert Davis, surgeon, | of Woolley Hill, near this town : | who died May the 3^rd, 1790, aged 52 years. | Also of Susanna, his Wife, who died Jan^y 14^th, 1826, aged 80 years. | Also of Susanna Davis, their daughter, | who died Jan^y 30^th, 1798, aged 21 years. | Also of Robert and Thomas Davis, | sons of the above Robert and Susanna Davis, | both of whom died infants.

Sacred to the memories | of John Deverell, Gent., | of Frankly in this parish : | who departed this life | July 5^th, 1785, | aged 64 years. | William Morford Deverell, | son of the above John Deverell, | who died January 2^nd, 1787, | aged 22 years. | Mary, wife of the above | John Deverell, | who died January 25^th, 1802, | aged 72 years. | Mary Anne Deverell, | grand-daughter of the aforesaid | John and Mary Deverell, | who died October 21^st, 1805, | aged 5 years and 8 months. | John Deverell Esq^re, son of the above | John and Mary Deverell, who died May 21^st, 1829, | aged 68 years ; | In him was found a dutiful son, | the best of husbands, a good neighbour ; | He lived and died generally esteemed | and respected. | Also of | Mary Deverell, relict of the above John Deverell, Esq^re, | who died April 4^th, 1837, | aged 68 years.

Arms : DEVERELL.

*A white marble monument, a woman mourning over an urn on which hangs a medallion portrait of a man, an angel pointing upwards :* Underneath are deposited | The Remains of | Francis Smith, Lieut^ General | of his Majesty's Forces, | And Colonel of | The 11^th Regiment of Foot, | Who died November 7^th, 1791, | Aged 68 Years.

Arms : Azure, two bars between three pheons or.
Crest : Two arms embowed, vested azure, cuffed or, holding in the hands proper a pheon of the
    last.

Arms : A chevron gules between three hurts.
Crest : A lion's head erased pierced through the mouth with an arrow.

Sacred to the memory of | John Baskerville, Esq : | of Woolley : eldest son of | John and Hester Baskerville ; | he died at Bath, December 20 : 1837, | aged 65 years.

Arms : BASKERVILLE impaling WEBB.
Crest : A falcon's head erased pierced through the beak with an arrow.

Near this place are deposited the | Remains of John Baskerville Esq^re, | many Years a Deputy Lieutenant | for this County, | who died March 15^th, 1800, Aged 54 ; | He was a just and upright Man, | and a sincere Friend. | Also the Body | of Joseph Baskerville Esq^re, | Second and youngest Son of the | above John Baskerville, | who died October 7^th, 1812. | Also the Body of Hester, | Wife of the above John Baskerville, | She departed this life | December 16^th, 1819.

In memory | of Iohn Ferrett Esq^re, | Born in this Town March the 15^th, 1702, | And Died May the 12^th, 1770, | Aged 68 Years. | On whose Soul O Blessed Lord God have mercy.

There needs no Epitaph this good Man's worth to raise ;
Name him but only and you record his Praise.

* The second and third quarters and the escallops are here *or*, not *argent*.

Arms : TUGWELL ; impaling, Sable, a stag at gaze within a bordure quarterly ermine and erminois, JONES.
Crest : TUGWELL.

To the memory of | Thomas Tugwell Esq : | of Woolley House | in this parish, | a deputy lieutenant and | a magistrate for this County, | obiit 18 : of April, A.D. 1833. | Æt 64 years. | His remains are interred in a vault | in South Wraxhall churchyard | in this parish.

----

Arms : Or, a bend gules.

Near this Place lieth the Body of | Edward Cottle | of Bradford-Leigh, who departed | this life Feb^ry 14^th, 1718, Aged about 52 Years. | Also | the Body of Edward Cottle Jun^r, Son of | the above named Edward Cottle & Ann | his Wife, who died Feb^ry 15^th, 1727, Aged 27 Years. | Also | the Body of Ann, Wife of Edward Cottle | Sen^r, who died March 13^th, 1728, | Aged 62 Years. | Richard, Son of Edward & Ann Cottle, | died Feb^ry 16^th, 1736, Aged 31 Years. | Edward, Son of Richard & Mary Cottle, | died March 25^th, 1758, | Aged 26 Years. | Also In Memory of Mary, Wife of | Richard Cottle, who died May | the 30^th, 1773, Aged 69 Years.

----

SOUTH CHANCEL ARCH.

Near | this Place are deposited | the Remains of | M^r Walter Browne, | who departed this Life | August 1^st 1769 : | in the 52^nd Year of his Age.

(*To be continued.*)

----

# Dalison Notes.*

Assise capte apud Staunford . . . . die Lune proxima post Epiphaniam Domini, anno regni Regis Edwardi filii Regis Henrici, xxxiij°.
Lincoln scilicet.
Petrus filius Willielmi de Alazon qui tulit breve mortis antecessoris versus Willielmum filium Willielmi de Alazon de Fulnetby et Johannem Russel de Stenyngod et Margaretam uxorem ejus de tenementis in Reddebourne non est prosecutus.    Ideo ipse et plegii sui de prosequendo in misericordia, videlicet, Gilbertus filius Thome de Houton et Walterus de Rende de eadem, etc.
Assize Roll, Divers Cos., N-2-13 1, m. 38, [11 Jan. A.D. 1305].

----

Lincoln.
Iidem consignantur ad assisam nove disseisine capiendam quam Matillis Dalazun arrainiavit versus Alexandrum de Insula et Agnetem uxorem ejus de tenementis in Clisceby.
Patent Roll, 1 Edw. 2, p^t 2, m. 48 d., [A.D. 1307-1308].

----

Lincoln scilicet.
Johannes Dalazun, per attornatum suum, optulit se iiij die versus Willielmum Le Vendur de Herpeswell, Robertum Le Vendur de Herpeswell, etc., de placito quare cum custodia unius mesuagii et unius carucate terre, cum pertinentiis, in Hakethorn, usque ad legitimam etatem heredis Johannis le Crevequer ad ipsum Johannem Dalazun pertineat, eo quod predictus Johannes le Crevequer terram suum de eo tenuit per servicium militare, ac idem Johannes Dalazun in pacifica seisina ejusdem custodie diu exstiterit ; predicti Willielmus Le Vendur, etc., ipsum Johannem Dalazun a custodia illa vi et armis ejecerunt, etc.    Et ipsi non venerunt, etc.    Et preceptum est Vicecomiti, etc., quod habeat corpora eorum hic a die Sancti

* Continued from p. 124.

Johannis Baptiste in xv dies, etc. Ad quem diem Vicecomes non misit breve. Ideo preceptum est Vicecomiti, etc., quod habeat corpora eorum hic a die Sancti Hillarii in xv dies, etc.
De Banco Roll, Edw. 2, No. 1 [Hilary, 1 Edw. 2, A.D. 1308], m. 137 d.

Lincoln scilicet.
Simon filius Galfridi de Hakethorne ponit loco suo Willielmum de Chartres versus Galfridum filium Hugonis de Hakethorn et Rogerum filium Willielmi Dalazun de placito terre.
De Banco Roll, Edw. 2, No. 3.
Attorney Roll, m. 17 d., Trinity, 1 Edw. 2, [A.D. 1308].

Lincoln scilicet.
Petrus de Alazun ponit loco suo Willielmum de Chartres versus Johannem Gascryk* de Barton et Petrum le Provost de placito detentionis averiorum.
De Banco Roll, Edw. 2, No: 5.
Att. Roll, m. 13 d., [Mich., 2 Edw. 2, A.D. 1308].

Adhuc de essoniis captis apud Sanctum Botulphum (die Lune proxima post Festum Sancti Petri Advincula, anno regni Regis Edwardi filii Regis Edwardi, secundo).
Lincoln.
Matillis Dalazon querens versus Alexandrum de Insula et Agnetem uxorem ejus de placito assise nove disseisine per Adam Prat. Die Lune proxima post Festum Sancti Andree Apostoli apud Staunford.
Alexander de Insula querens versus Matillidem que fuit uxor Johannis Dalazon de Lagheton, Johannem filium Johannis Dalazon, Walterum Le Sergaunt de Nettelton et Adam Le Pynder de Lagheton de placito assise nove disseisine per Ricardum Prat. Die Lune proxima post Festum Sancti Andree Apostoli apud Staunford.
Assize Roll, Divers Counties, N-2-14 5, m. 7, [5 August A.D. 1308].

Assise capte apud Sanctum Botulphum .... die Lune proxima post Festum Sancti Petri Advincula, anno regni Regis Edwardi filii Regis Edwardi, secundo.
Assisa venit recognitura si Johanna que fuit uxor Simonis de Kirketone, etc., disseisiverunt Alanum de Tiryngtone de Langeton et Evam uxorem ejus de libero tenemento suo in Humbelok, etc. Ideo capiatur assisa. Set ponitur in respectu pro defectu recognitorum, scilicet, Radulphi de Bateyate, Johannis de Neubell, Petri Dalazoun de Fulneteby, etc.

m. 8.

Lincoln scilicet.
Dies datus est Petro Dalazoun de Folneteby querenti et Johanni de Gaskerik seniori de placito detencionis averiorum in Octabis Sancte Trinitatis, etc.
De Banco Roll, Edw. 2, No. 6 (Rotulus Prece Parcium), m. 6, [Hil., 2 Edw. 2, A.D. 1308-9].

Matillis que fuit uxor Johannis de Alazun de Laghton per Radulphum Faunel attornatum suum optulit se quarto die versus Philippum filium et heredem Normanni Dercy de placito quod esset hic ad hunc diem ad warantizandum ei unum toftum et unam bovatam terre et dimidium, duas acras prati et dimidium cum pertinentiis in Hauneworth juxta Hakethorn que Idonia de Morwode in curia Regis hic clamat ut jus, etc. Et unde, etc. Et ipse non venit. Et habuit diem per essoniatorem suum hic ad hunc diem, etc. Judicium. Capiatur de terra predicti Philippi in manum domini Regis ad valenciam, etc.
De Banco Roll, Edw. 2, No. 10, m. 264, Mich., 3 Edw. 2, [A.D. 1309].

* *Bascrik* in the Record.

# Annotations to the Heraldic Visitation of London, 1633.

## Gore.*

### REGISTERS.

#### ALLHALLOWS, LOMBARD STREET.

##### Marriage.

1665  April  8   William Gore, esq., of Gray's Inn, & Mary Chappell, of S$^t$ Peter's Cheap.

#### St. Peter ad Vincula (Tower).

##### Burials.

1788  May  23   Elizabeth Maria d. of John Gore, esq., Dep$^y$ Gov$^r$ of y$^e$ Tower, in Chapel under family pew.

1791  June  17   Bellamin, ux. John Gore, esq., Dep$^y$ Lieut. of the Tower, in Chapel.

1794  Mar.  14   John Gore, esq., Dep$^y$ Gov$^r$ of the Tower.

#### St. Martin Outwich.

##### Marriage.

1689  Nov.  5   John Gore, of St. Andrew Undershaft, & Elizabeth Peterson, of the same.

##### Baptisms.

1725  April 27   John s. of John & Hannah Gore.
1727  April 19   Elizabeth d. of John & Hannah Gore.
1729  June 26   Katharine d. of John & Hannah Gore.
1731  May  26   Ann d. of John & Hannah Gore.
173⁴⁄  Feb.  21   Susanna d. of John & Hannah Gore.

##### Burial.

1716  Oct.  27   Jane Gore.

#### St. Margaret's, Lothbury.

##### Marriage.

158⁶⁄  Jan.  29   Thomas Goore & Julian Horne.

##### Burials.

1623  July  28   Francis Gore, gent.
167⁴⁄  Jan.  22   Thomas s. of Christopher Gore.   N. Aisle.
1688  June 23   Christopher Gore.   N. Aisle.
1739  Dec.  19   Elizabeth Gore.   Midd. Chancel.

#### St. Alphage.

##### Marriages.

1630  Mar.  30   Nicholas Conway & Jane Gore.
1717  July  30   John Gore, of S$^t$ Olave, Hart Street, & Hannah Sambrooke, of S$^t$ Michael Basishaw.   Lic.

#### St. Sepulchre.

##### Marriages.

1737  Dec.  14   James Gore & Frances Taylor.   Lic.
1750  Dec.  13   Francis Gore & Susannah Hinde.

* Continued from p. 118.

*Burials.*

1662  Nov.  19  Sara Gore.
1673  Aug.  10  Elizabeth Gore, widow.
1680  July  22  (*blank*) son of Tho⁸ Gore.
1681  May  10  Thomas Gore.

### St. Mary Abchurch.

*Baptism.*

1583  June  16  William s. of Francis Gore.

*Burials.*

1592  July  16  Elizabeth d. of Francis Gore.
1597  Sep.  20  Jone wife of Francis Gore.
1616  July  19  Francis Gore.
1617  April  12  Julian Gore.

### St. Mary Aldermary and St. Thomas Apostle.

(See Harleian Publications.)

### St. Peter le Poor.

*Marriages.*

159⁴⁄₅  Jan.  21  William Gore & Joane Lee.
1658  Dec.  5  Thomas Warner & Mary Gore.

### Allhallows Staining.

*Marriages.*

169½  Jan.  14  George Abbott, of Cogshall, Essex, & Elizabeth Goare, of St.
                 Andrew's, Holborn.  Lic.
1697  Nov.  2.  Joseph Crampthorne, of Sawbridgeworth, & Mary Gore, of Gilston,
                 both in Herts.  Lic.

### St. Michael Royal or St. Michael Paternoster Royal, Vintry Ward.

*Marriages.*

1647  April  19  Francis Goore & Margaret Bromley.
1656  Aug.  21  Capt. John Tinkar & Elizabeth Gore.
16⁶⁰⁄₆₁  Feb.  7  Mʳ Gerrard Goare & Mʳˢ Anne Russell.

### St. Dunstan in the East.

*Marriage.*

1608  Oct.  9  Richard Gore & Jevyn Allen.

*Burials.*

16¹³⁄₁₄  Jan.  29  William Gore.
1634  Dec.  10  Edward Gore.

### St. Olave, Hart Street.

*Marriages.*

1647  April  22  Sir John Goare & Mʳˢ Bridgitt Lee, married in yᵉ house.
1704  May  29  Joseph Mellish, esq., of co. Nott., & Madam Dorothy Gore d. of
                 Sir Wᵐ Gore, of this parish.  Lic.

*Baptisms.*

157⅔  Jan.  7  Christian d. of Edward Goore.
169⅔  Jan.  31  Ann d. of Sir Wᵐ Gore, Knt., & Dame Eliz.
1694  May  31  Robert s. of Sir Wᵐ Gore, Knt., & Dame Eliz.
1695  July  16  Thomas s. of Sir Wᵐ Gore, Knt., & Dame Eliz.

*Burials.*

1698 July 25 M<sup>rs</sup> Elizabeth Gore.
170⅚ Mar. 14 The Lady Elizabeth Gore, bur<sup>d</sup> at Tring, Hertfordsh.
170¼ Jan. 29 Sir W<sup>m</sup> Gore, bur<sup>d</sup> at Tring in Hertfordsh.

### ALLHALLOWS THE LESS.

*Marriage.*

1626 April 18 Philip Jermine & Mary Goare.

## Bacon Wills.*

### FROM IPSWICH REGISTRY.

Testamentum
Cathrine Baken
de Birstall.
    In the name of God, Amen. The xxx<sup>th</sup> daye of August One Thowsand six hundred & Twelve I Catren Baken the wife of Thomas Baken of Birstall in the Countie of Suff. & in the diocs of Norw<sup>ch</sup> beinge whole of mynde & of good and p'fecte Remembrance thankes be to Almyghty God doe ordeyne this my last will and Testament Revokinge all others ffirst I geve & bequeathe my sowle to Almighty God my Creator & to Jesus Christe my Saviour and Redemer trustinge to have forgevenes of all my Synnes & to be saved by his only meritts & death & by noe other meanes & my bodye to be buried in the Churchyarde of Birstall. Item I geve unto Thomas Baken my yongest sonne all my land lyinge in Winston & fframsden caled hokstenffeild & ffoxes medowe w<sup>th</sup> th'appuretenancs therto belonginge after the death of Thomas Bacon my husbande for my mynde is that my husbande Thomas Baken should haue this lande terme of his life And I doe ordeyne my husbande Thomas Bakon my sole Executor. In witnes wherof I have setto my hande this Daye & yere aboue written. The marke of CATREN BAKEN. Red & delivered in the p'sence of Will'm Brades and Isacke Abbott.

    Proved at Ipswich 22 June 1613.

Testamentum
Thome Bacon
de Woodbridge.
    In the name of God, Amen. The fifteenth daye of October in the yere of o<sup>r</sup> Lorde God 1613 and in the Eleventh yere of the reigne of o<sup>r</sup> Sovereigne Lorde Kinge James of Englande ffraunce and Irelande and of Scotlande the seven and ffortyth I Thomas Bacon of Woodbridge in the County of Suff. being sicke in body but in good and p'fecte remembrance thanks be to God doe make and ordeyne this my testament Conteyninge therein my last will in manner and forme followinge ffirst I comytt my sowle into the hands of Almighty God & I will my bodye shalbe buryed in the Church yarde of Woodbridge aforesaid or else where yt shall please God to appoynte And as Concerninge my worldlye goods ffirst I geue and bequeath unto Henry Bakon my sonne Twentie Pownds of good & Lawfull money of Englande to be payde by myne Executrix w<sup>th</sup>in six month after my decease out of the money that is dewe unto me from John Chandler of Sutton. Item give unto my said sonne Henrye my blacke Cowe or fower Pownds of lawfull money of Englande at the Choyse of the saide Henrye to have the same uppon Michaelmas daye next followinge after my decease. Item I give and bequeath to Elizabeth Bacon my daughter twenty pownds of good and lawfull Englishe money to be paide by myne Excutrix w<sup>th</sup>in half A yere after my dep'ture out of this life. Item I geue & bequeath unto the said Elizabeth my byble. Item I geue & bequeath unto Alice my wife all the rest of my moveable Goodes that are unbequeathed she payinge all my Debtes w<sup>ch</sup> I owe And of this my last will and testament I make and ordayne Alice my wife my sole Executrix to se this my will executed accordinge to my trewe intent and meaninge And my Kynesman Gregory Nicholls supravisor. In witnes whereof I have hereunto sett my hande the daye and yere first aboue wretten. Sign' THOME BAKON. Witnes hereunto Gregorye Nicholl and Thomas Richer.

    Proved at Ipswich 4 November 1613.

* Continued from p. 136.

MONUMENTAL INSCRIPTIONS FROM THE BURIAL-GROUND OF
ST. GEORGE, HANOVER SQUARE, NEAR MARBLE ARCH.*

Elizabeth Webb, daughter of the above John Best Webb, Esq., & Mary Jane his
wife, died July 6, 1830, aged 4 years.
Marianne Smale Murch, died 15 April, 1806, aged 3 years & 5 months.
George Murch, Jun^r, died 24 Sep. 1809, aged 19.
M^rs Elizabeth Webb, wife of John Best Webb, of Piccadilly, died July 4, 1824,
aged 40.
Elizabeth Webb, daughter of the above [John Best] Webb. [*Rest of inscription
hidden by a footstone.*]

———

Edward Hoskins, Esq., of Conduit Street in this parish, died June 20, 1822, aged
63 years.

———

M^r William Parker, late of North Bank, Regent's Park, for upwards of 25 years
and to the period of his decease an officer of this parish, died 31 May 1843,
aged 67 years.
Sarah, his wife, died 10 August 1830, aged 40 years.    Also of their following
children :
Jeffery, died April 1824, aged 10 months.
Decimus, died August 25, 1830, aged 3 months.
John George, died May 1831, aged 13 years.
Henry, died May 15, 1843, aged 23 years, and was buried in the island of Kishm
in the Persian Gulf.

———

............................................[*several lines illegible*].
Amelia Harriet Auriol, their youngest daughter, born 2 [7 ?] Feb. 1805, died 18
Jan. 1819.

———

Lionel Dormond, died Feb. 1, 1837, in his 51^st year.
William Lionel Dormond, nephew of the above, died May 9, 1844, in his 23^rd year.
Mary Dormond, mother of the above William Lionel Dormond, died 6 Dec. 1851,
in her 68^th year.

———

M^rs Ann Dunn, died 14^th May 1823, in her 46^th year.

———

Sarah Ann, daughter of William & Sarah Owen, of New Bond Street, died June 7,
1838, aged 1 year and 2 months.
M^r Thomas Glyndwr Owen, of New Bond Street, died June 13, 1838, aged 28
years.
Edward, son of the above named Thomas Glyndwr Owen, died June 18, 1838, aged
1 year and 8 months.
Thomas Glyndwr, son of the above named Thomas Glyndwr Owen, died Oct. 13,
1850, aged 11 years and 8 months.

———

Caroline Ann [Smythe ?], died July 24, aged 2 years and 11 weeks.
Robert Greathead [      ], died Oct. 10, 1822, aged 64 years.
Sarah, relict of the above Robert Greathead, died June 16, 1842, in her 74^th year.

———

M^r James John Cuthbertson, died Jan. 16, 1831, aged 28.
Rosa Sarah Cuthbertson, youngest daughter of the above, died Dec. 29, 1832, aged
2 years, 8 months, 9 days.

———

James Swinton, Serjeant Major of his Majesty's First Battalion, 36^th Regiment,
died 18 Dec. 1814, aged 44.    Monument erected by his widow.

* Continued from p. 134.

M<sup>rs</sup> Ann Gadd, wife of M<sup>r</sup> James Gadd, of [Down ?] Street, in this parish, died
13 April, 1833, in her 71<sup>st</sup> year.
James Gadd, son of James and Ann Gadd, died 4 Feb. 18[2 ?]3, aged 26.
M<sup>r</sup> James Gadd, husband of the above Ann Gadd, died June 27, 1835, aged 66.
M<sup>r</sup> William Gadd, died Oct. 3, 1837, aged 38.
John Gadd Halford, died April 19, 1852, aged 26.

———

M<sup>r</sup> Richard Bickerstaff, died Jan. 30, 1837, aged 59.
M<sup>rs</sup> Isabella Bickerstaff, widow of the above, died Dec. 18, 1837, aged 65.

———

M<sup>r</sup> Stephen Dykes, late of this parish, died 29 Jan. 1829, aged [41] years.

———

Josephine Auvray, born Nov. 3, died Dec. 16, 1846.
Melanie [Melante ?] Auvray, born June [　] died April [　] 1848.

———

John Woollams Esq. died Jan. 22, 1834, aged 56.

———

M<sup>rs</sup> Margaret Essex, died 20 April 1822, in her 83<sup>rd</sup> year.

———

Mary Ann Tildesley, wife of Thomas Pawson Tildesley, died Aug. 13, 1825,
aged 26.
Mary Ann Fidelia Tildesley, daughter of the above, died Aug. 16, 1825, aged
4 months.
M<sup>r</sup> Edmund Hall, father of the above, died Nov. 30, 1828, aged 62.
Thomas Pawson Tildesley, died June 6, 1848, aged 52.

———

Susannah Mary Read, died June 10, 1822, aged 5 months.
Elizabeth Margaret Read, died June 27, 1822, aged 2 years ; daughters of John &
Mary Read, of Upper Brook Street, Grosvenor Square.
M<sup>r</sup> Stephen Read, grandfather to the above children, died Jan. 13, 1825, in his
68<sup>th</sup> year.

———

M<sup>rs</sup> Mary Hammond, died 13 July 1822, in her 47<sup>th</sup> year.
M<sup>r</sup> Robert Hammond, husband of the above, formerly of Mount Street, Grosvenor
Square, died 23 Jan. 1830, in his 66<sup>th</sup> year.
Also of six of their children.
Also M<sup>rs</sup> Caroline Hammond, died 11 July, 1837, in her 24<sup>th</sup> year ; the beloved
wife of M<sup>r</sup> William Hammond, of Oxford Street.

———

M<sup>rs</sup> Susannah Bellerby, died 26 May, 1838, aged 33 ; the beloved daughter of the
late M<sup>r</sup> Robert Hammond, of Mount Street, in this parish. This stone was
erected to her memory by her brother Robert.
Mary, the beloved wife of M<sup>r</sup> Robert Hammond, of York Street, Westminster, died
3 Oct. 1849, in her 52<sup>nd</sup> year.
M<sup>r</sup> Robert Hammond, husband of the above, of York Street, Westminster, eldest
son of Robert Hammond, of Mount Street, Grosvenor Square, died 28 Nov.
1853, in his 60<sup>th</sup> year.

———

William Blackborow, died May 13, 1825, aged 30.

———

M<sup>rs</sup> Hannah Jupp, wife of M<sup>r</sup> Edmund Jupp, of this parish, died 26 Oct. 1807,
aged 64.

———

John Lewis Esq. late of this parish, died April 16, 1821, aged 68.

———

Amy, daughter of Anthony & Mary Francis, died 6 Nov. 1830, aged 15.
Mary Francis, died 10 March 1851, aged 64.
Anthony Francis, died 12 June 1851, aged 66 ; parents of the above Amy Francis.

# Upton.*

## ABSTRACTS OF WILLS AND RECORDS OF ADMINISTRATION.

104. Joane Upton† of St. Margaret's, Westminster, widow.    Dated 13 Nov. 1710.   To be buried in the church of Stoke Newington, Midd$^x$, in the vault where my dear dec$^d$ husband lies ; funeral charges not to exceed £200 ; to my son-in-law Anthony Upton, Esq.,‡ £100 ; to my grandsons§ William and John Upton each £50 ;  to my daughter Elizabeth Farrington‖ £80;  to my granddaughter Elizabeth Phill¶ £20 for piece of plate ; to my grandson Thomas Sayer £80 in trust to pay to my daughter Mary Knightley** the interest thereof for her life, the principal at her death to go to said Thomas Sayer ; †† to Dorothy Sayer†† my granddaughter £20 for piece of plate ; to my daughter Jane Uvedale‡‡ £80 ; to Jane Cox my granddaughter £20 for piece of plate ; said legacies amounting to £500 to be paid out of money now in the hands of my grandson Robert Cox of Basinghall Street, Factor ; to the Hon. the Countess of Westmoreland§§ my diamond locket with my late husband's and my hair in it, and also the medal of the Seven Bishops in a box lined with velvet ; to my daughter Mary Upton‖‖ one side of my diamond crozier, a silver fork with my husband's and my arms engraved on it, and my yellow sticht petticoat ; to my daughter Elizabeth Farrington the other side of said crozier, some plate, etc. ; to my granddaughter Dorothy Sayer the middle part of said crozier, now in the possession of my daughter Mary Knightley, and sundry plate ; to said Mary Knightley interest on £50 ; to my daughter Jane Uvedale sundry jewels, etc. ; to my grandson Daniel Farrington my husband's original picture, the great escutcheon, etc. ; to my grandson John Uvedale a silver tankard ; to my said grandson Thomas Sayer a tankard and £200 ; to Thomas Uvedale my grandson £10 for plate ; to my son Anthony Upton £50 for a ring ; to my grandsons Richard, Nicholas, Anthony, and Lytcott Upton, the four younger children of my son [her step-son] John Upton, dec$^d$, each £25 at 21 ; to Col. Hales, now Governor of Chelsea College, my best diamond ring, and to his lady a silver porringer, diamond locket, sable tippett, etc. ; to Capt. John Goodwyn, nephew to said Col. Hales, a silver candlestick, and to his sister Elizabeth Goodwyn a silver chafing dish ; to my sister Anne Gibbs¶¶ £20 for mourning, sundry jewels, etc., and my gold seal with my arms engraved upon it, being 3 Pine Apples, etc., for her life, same to go on her death to Mrs. Chamberlayne, now wife of John Chamberlayne, Esq., one of my ex'ors ; to said John Chamberlayne, his heirs, etc., all those lands, etc., in Frampton or elsewhere, Gloucester, which came to me by a will, fine and recovery made, etc., by Edmond Clifford, late of Gray's Inn, Esq., dec$^d$ ; and whereas there is now £1200 lent on said premises by me and my sister Ann Gibbs equally, etc., Mr. Chamberlayne shall pay said sister £10 more per annum for life ; to granddaughter Dorothy Sayer a cabinet, china, plate, jewels, and £100 ; to my granddaughters Mary, Elizabeth, and Ursula Uvedale plate, jewels, etc. ; to Thomas

* Continued from p. 112.
† The testatrix, *née* Stow, having survived two husbands, Agar and Meggs, became third wife, and ultimately widow, of John Upton who made will No. 79, *ante*. She bore him no children.
‡ Anthony Upton was her husband's son.
§ William and John Upton (No. 110, *post*) were sons of her husband's son John, No. 97, *ante*.
‖ Elizabeth Farrington was daughter of testatrix' husband John Upton.
¶ Elizabeth Phill was daughter of Elizabeth Farrington.
** Mary Knightley, wife 1st of John Sayer, 2nd of Richard Knightley, was daughter of testatrix' husband John Upton.
†† Thomas and Dorothy Sayer were children of said Mary Sayer *alias* Knightley.
‡‡ Jane Uvedale, *née* Upton, was her husband's daughter.
§§ Doubtless Rachel, only daughter and heiress of Mr. Alderman Bence of London, and widow of Vere (Fane), 4th Earl of Westmoreland. N.B.—The first wife of John Upton, husband of the testatrix, was Elizabeth Bence.
‖‖ Mary Upton, *née* Warren, was widow of John Upton, step-son of the testatrix.
¶¶ See third note on will No. 79, *ante*.

Fryer and Millicent his wife £50 ; to William Messindue £40, and to his aunt Mrs. Green £10 ; to said Mr. Chamberlayne £550 of £800 he owes me, he to pay his now wife Elizabeth £100 ; to John Wade of London, stuffman, £50, and same to my niece Elizabeth* Wade his wife; to Honora Beanes £50 ; to my cousin Archer's† four daughters each £10 ; to Mrs. Margaret Austin, formerly called Agar, £10 ; to Mrs. Alice Newlove £5 ; to poor of St. Mary Bridsman in Canterbury £20, to be disposed by Mr. Moses Agar, alderman, of Canterbury; to Mary Collins £5 ; to Margaret Leigh, widow, £5 ; to poor of St. Marg<sup>ts</sup>, Westm<sup>r</sup>, £5, and of Stoke Newington £5 ; to William Plumer, son of Elizabeth Plumer, widow, late of St. John's Hospital without Northgate in Canterbury, £10 ; to Mr. Robert Cox of Basinghall Street, Factor, £50 ; to Mr. Radford and wife £20 he owes me ; to Samuel Paynter £200, and his mother £50 ; to my cousin Stow's three daughters Anne Millway, Judith Webb, and Elizabeth Paskall each £30 ; to my cousin Colley's son and daughter each £30 ; to Mrs. Mansell of Chelsea, Midd<sup>x</sup>, widow, and her daughter Mary Mansell, each £50 ; to Mrs. Unton English £10 ; to Mrs. Gibbs of Gloucester City £10 for plate ; to my cousin Keck's‡ two daughters each £10 to put them out apprentices; to my granddaughter Margaret James *alias* Newton £10, etc. ; and to her eldest son Robert James, Esq., £100, plate, etc., and to his wife linen, etc. ; to Elizabeth Richardson, daughter of said Margaret James, £30, plate, etc. ; to Margaret and Katherine, other daughters of said Margaret James, each £60, plate, etc. ; to Ostrick and William James, younger sons of said Margaret, each £20 ; to Mr. Holford and Joanna his wife £100, residue of my household goods, etc. ; to said Joanna jewels, etc. ; to my grandson Holford all my books ; to said Mr. Chamberlayne and my grandsons Thomas Sayer, John Upton, and John Uvedale all money due me from Joseph and Nathaniel Horneby (£1600 and upward) equally ; to said Moses Agar and Edward Agar each £10 ; an annuity of £28 for 90 years to be sold, and of the proceeds the interest on £150 devoted by a long bequest to pay for the preaching of five sermons annually for ever in the Collegiate Church of St. Peter's, Westm<sup>r</sup>, and to certain charities ; £200 to be put out, etc., and the interest applied to apprentice annually one poor child from the Gray Coat Hospital in St. Marg<sup>ts</sup>, Westm<sup>r</sup>, one from the Green Coat Hospital, and a third from the Blue Coat ; £100 to propagate the Gospel in foreign parts ; to Stow Paskall £30 ; residue to John Chamberlayne of Westminster, Esq., and Thomas Sayer of Furnivall's Inn, Midd<sup>x</sup>, gent., and appoint them executors, and in case either or both die, my nephew John Wade of Cheapside, London, stuffman, and my grandson Robert Cox to succeed as ex'ors. Witnesses, Thomas French, porter of the College, *et al.* Codicil, 30 Aug. 1711 : Amends the bequest for preaching sermons ; to said cousin Colley's children, viz., Robert and Elizabeth, son and daughter of James Colley, late of Dover, £20 more to Robert, and £20 less to Elizabeth ; to Mrs. Anne Berry of Salisbury Lane of Rotherhill £20 ; to Mrs. Penning of Dean's Yard, Westm<sup>r</sup>, and her daughter Berry of same, both widows, each £10 ; to said Anne Milleway, Judith Webb, Elizabeth Paskall, and Stow Paskall each £20 more ; to said Honora Baynes £20 more, the sums given to her to be paid in trust to her brother Edward Agar ; after her death the interest to go to her youngest daughter ; to Dorothy English, sister of Mrs. Unton English ; my sister Anne Gibbs, now dec<sup>d</sup> ; revokes legacies to Mrs. Gibbs of Gloucester, etc. ; the locket which I gave to the Countess of Westmoreland, now dec<sup>d</sup>, to go to my said cousin Elizabeth Chamberlayne, and appoint her joint executor. Proved (C.P.C.) 3 Oct. 1713 by John Chamberlayne and Thomas Sayer, power reserved to Elizabeth ux. said J. C. Proved (D. and C. Westm<sup>r</sup>) 18 Jan. 1713-14 by Chamberlayne only. (D. and C. Westm<sup>r</sup>.)

*(To be continued.)*

* Elizabeth Wade was daughter of Gilbert Upton, brother of the testatrix' husband.
† Mary, daughter of Hugh Upton, brother of the husband of testatrix, married John Archer of London, merchant.
‡ Ann, daughter of Gilbert Upton, brother of the husband of the testatrix, married Edward Keck.

# Langley Pedigree—PEDIGREE D. *(Vide p. 141.)*

## THE BARONETS' BRANCH.

William Langley.=.... fil.....

George Langley of Stainton, co. Ebor.=Jane, fil. John Hall of Sherborne, co. Ebor.

Sir William Langley, 1st Bart., of Higham Gobion, co. Beds, and Sheriff=Elizabeth, sister of Hutton, co. York. Created Baronet 29 May 1641. Ob. 21 Aug. 1652 | Viscount Lumley. at High Holborn. Sep. 23 Aug. 1652 at St. Andrew's, Holborn.

Matthew Langley, ob. s.p.

John Langley, ob. s.p.

1. William Langley, ob. vitâ patris.

Sarah, fil. John Neale of Malden Ashe, co. Essex. Sep. at St. Margaret's, Westminster, 4 Nov. 1701. Executrix of her husband's will. Ux. 3.=Sir Roger Langley, Bart., nat. 1628. Sep. at St. Margaret's, Westminster, 4 Jan. 1699. Will dated 20 Sept. 1697. Codicil dated 22 Feb. 1697-8. Second codicil dated 17 Oct. 1698. Probate dated 10 Jan. 1698-9. Ux. 2, Barbara, fil. and coh. Sergeant Chapman and relict . . . Hobson. Mar. lic. dated 10 April 1672. Nup. 16 April 1672 at St. Bartholomew the less, London.=Mary, fil. Thomas Keightley of Hertingfordbury, co. Herts, Esq., by Rose his wife, fil. Thomas Evelyn of Long Ditton, co. Surrey, Esq. Mar. lic. dated 26 April 1647. Ux. 1.

From Visitation of Yorkshire, 1666.

A

B

B |

A |

Sarah Langley, bap. 20 Feb. 1684-5 at St. Andrew's, Holborn. Mentioned in her father's will.

Mary Langley.

David Langley, bap. at St. Margaret's, Westminster, 24 June 1688. Ob. 1708. Mentioned in his father's will.

Judith, fil. et hær. .... De la Hay of Westminster. Nup. at St. Augustine's, London, 30 Nov. 1717. Sep. 17 Jan. 1740. = John Langley, Major, bap. at St. Margaret's, Westminster, 25 May 1687. Battle of Malplaquet. Mentioned in father's will. Ob. 9 and sep. 18 Aug. 1741.

1. William Langley, ob. inf.

Elizabeth Langley.

Frances Langley.

1. William Langley. Mar. lic. dated 16 Sept. 1667. Ob. vitâ patris. = Isabella, fil. Sir John Griffith, Kt., of Brith, Kent. Nup. 2d 14 May 1687. Mentioned in her second husband's will and legatee under her son William's will. Ob. Jan. 1715. = Robert Edgworth, Esq., administrator of his wife Isabella's estate. Mar. 3.

Thomas, fil. William Barnes of East Winch, co. Norfolk, Esq., by Ann, fil. Thos. Coppin of Marketcell, co. Beds, Esq. Mar. 2.

Richard Langley. — Thomas Langley.

Roger Langley, sep. at St. Martin's in the Fields 12 Nov. 1681.

Mary Langley. = William Prescott of Essex.

Rose Langley. = Peter Priaux of London.

1. Sir Roger Langley, Bart. = Mary, fil. Stanislaus Browne of Eastbourne, Esq. Ob. 19 Sept. 1721. Mentioned in paternal grandfather's will.

2. William Langley of Elwick. Ob. 1707. Devisee in fee of East Winch Estate under will of his stepfather Thos. Barnes. = Margaret, fil. ...., Sutton of Barbadoes, and relict of Abraham Jaggard. Renupt. Richard Hyde of St. Dionis Backchurch 4 Nov. 1708. Mar. 3. Ex'trix of second husband's will. Ob. Feb. 1719.

Isabella Langley, nup. at Lincoln's Inn Chapel 23 Aug. 1724. = William Ettricke of High Barnes, co. Durham, Esq. Devisee of East Winch Estate under her father's will.

Charles Langley, ob. inf.

*Isabell Ettricke*

From a Deed dated 10 Feb. 1727.

*Wm Ettricke*

From a Deed dated 10 Feb. 1727.

C

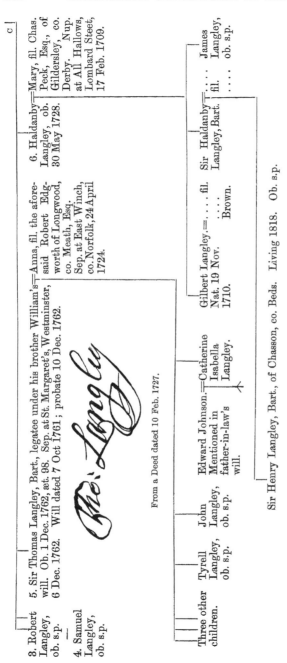

c |

8. Robert Langley, ob. s.p. —

4. Samuel Langley, ob. s.p.

6. Haldanby Langley, ob. 30 May 1728. = Mary, fil. Chas. Peck, Esq., of Gildersley, co. Derby. Nup. at All Hallows, Lombard Steet, 17 Feb. 1709.

5. Sir Thomas Langley, Bart., legatee under his brother William's will. Ob. 1 Dec. 1762, æt. 98. Sep. at St. Margaret's, Westminster, 6 Dec. 1762. Will dated 7 Oct 1761; probate 10 Dec. 1762. = Anna, fil. the aforesaid Robert Edgworth of Longwood, co. Meath, Esq. Sep. at East Winch, co. Norfolk, 24 April 1724.

James Langley, ob. s.p.

Sir Haldanby Langley, Bart. = .... fil. .... Brown.

From a Deed dated 10 Feb. 1727.

Gilbert Langley. = .... fil. .... Brown. Nat. 19 Nov. 1710.

Edward Johnson. Mentioned in father-in-law's will. = Catherine Isabella Langley.

Tyrell Langley, ob. s.p.

John Langley, ob. s.p.

Three other children.

Sir Henry Langley, Bart., of Chasson, co. Beds. Living 1818. Ob. s.p.

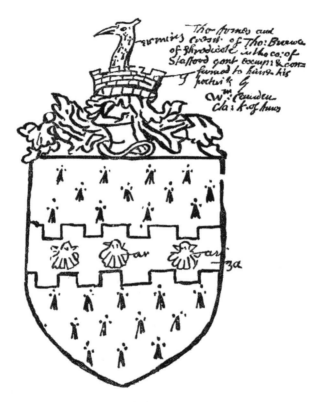

BROWNE ARMS.

Fig. 1.

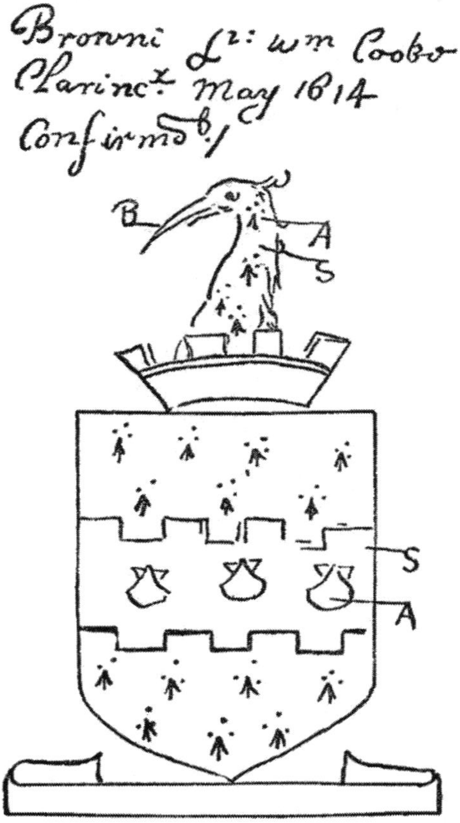

BROWNE ARMS.

Fig. 2.

# Genealogy of Browne.*

Extract from a Manuscript† containing " Church Notes in co. Stafford, 1679–80," recording an inscription upon a slab in Bradeley Church, to the memory of Thomas Browne, Esq., of Shredicote. The slab has since disappeared.

"In Bradeley Church
" A monument fixt to the upper end of the body of the Church next the Chancell, on the north side of yᵉ Navis Ecclesiæ over ag'st the Pulpit.  The Effigies of a man and woman kneeling with these arms for him,‡ and upon a prostrate gravestone this Inscription :—

> Hic jacet humatum corpus Thomæ Browne, dum vixit nuper de Shredicot, Almæ Curiæ Cantuariensis de Arcubus§ London, procuratorum generalium unius ; nec non Cœnobi D'ni Regis Jacobi in Charterhouse London fundati, Gubernatorum unius per ipsum fundatorem nominati, qui fatis cessit, 5 die Aprilis 1633, ætatis suæ 71, et post se reliquit Apolinam conjugem mœtissimam sexo‖ proles vizᵗ 4 filios ac duas filias."¶

This Thomas Browne is further commemorated in the following graceful decasyllabic lines in incised letters upon a large plate above the kneeling effigies of Thomas Browne and his wife. The plate is still evident.

P. M. S.
PEACE TO THY BETTER PARTE, ALL THAT DID KNOWR
THEE LIVINGE SHARE AS LIBERALLIE THEIR WOE,
AS THE POORE DID THY ALMES, THE RICH THY GRACE,
DISCOVRSE, AND CONVERSE, WHO NOW FILLS THY PLACE?
ORACVLOVS BROWNE! THY COVNTREY DOTH NOT CALL
VPON THEE BY ONE VERTVOVS STILE, BVT ALL +
RELIGION MOVRNES, AND HOSPITALITIE
(IN THY DEATH MADE AN ORPHAN) WEEPES FOR THEE
THY CALLING IVSTLIE MERITED THE NAME
OF CIVILL, THOV DIDST LIVE, AND DIE THE SAME +
THE GENERALL VOICE PROCLAIMES ITT + EACH MANS CAVSE
IN THEE STOOD SAFE + THOV PILLAR OF THE LAWES + .

---

## Browne Coat Armour.

The earliest record of the Brownes of Caverswall, and afterwards of Shredicote and Hungry Bentley, being entitled to bear " coat armour " is a confirmation of arms and crest by Sir William Camden, Clarencieux King of Arms, in May 1614, to Thomas Browne of Shredicote, co. Stafford, of which a facsimile is given (Fig. 1—see Plate) from the records of the College of Arms.  (M. 2, fo. 3.)

And there is another tricking (Fig. 2—see Plate) in the same records (Ed. N. 5670, B.) which states, erroneously, that the grant was made by " Sir Wᵐ Cooke, Clarencˣ " ; no one of that name having held the office of Clarencieux.

But Sir William Camden's *original* record of the grant or confirmation is in the Harleian MSS. at the British Museum, where, in MS. No. 6095, fol. 31, is the following sketch by Sir William Camden (Fig. 3, p. 162).  The volume is endorsed " Grants of Arms," and the written title-page is as follows :—

---

* Continued from page 146.

† The following is the reference to this MS. in the William Salt Library at Stafford : "147. Dugdale, Sir William.  A Memorandum Book in his hand containing account of various work done.  Diary of his Proceedings, Church Notes, in the co. of Stafford, &c., 1679—1680."  The Librarian states that the MS. is not in the handwriting of Sir William Dugdale, but of his clerk, Gregory King, who afterwards became Rouge Dragon Pursuivant.

‡ A tricking of the Browne arms is here given.
§ *Sic*, should be *Arctubus*.       ‖ *Sic*, should be *sexto*.
¶ The translation : "Here lies buried the body of Thomas Browne, during his lifetime of Shredicot, one of the Proctors of the Canterbury Court of Arches in London ; also one of the Governors of the Monastery of Charter House of our Lord King James, founded in London, nominated by the Founder himself.  He died the 5ᵗʰ day of April 1633 in the 71ˢᵗ year of his age, leaving behind him his most disconsolate widow Apolina, and six children ; namely four sons and two daughters."

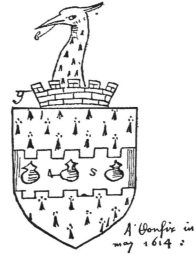

Fig. 3.

In this manuscript the grants are distinguished from the confirmations by having the word "patten" (patent) written above them.

At the Visitation of Derbyshire made by Sir William Dugdale in 1663, Edmund Browne and William Browne, sons of Thomas Browne above, certified the pedigree entered (Vincent C. 34, Coll. Arms). This pedigree is endorsed : " Respite taken for proofe of these Armes : but no proofe made." And then, in a later hand : " But vide M. 2 fo. 3 in Coll. Arms," referring to Camden's grant (Fig. 1—see Plate).

Also in the same MS., folio 90, is the following :—

> "The names of such persons residing in the County of Derby as had respit given them to make proofe of the Armes they pretend to.
>
> Wirksworth  ⎱ EDM. BROWNE of
> Hundred      ⎰ Hungry Bentley."

Adding that " no proofe was made within the time Limited."

At the Visitation of London made by Sir Henry St. George (Coll. Arms, K.G. 75) 30 June 1687, Rupert Browne of London certified the pedigree and arms entered, from his father the last-mentioned Edmund Browne.

No instance has been met with of the Brownes of Caverswall, the ancestors of the Shredicot and Hungry Bentley families, having made use of coat armour, as in the sealing of wills and so forth ; and it is very probable that when Thomas Browne came to London to study the law he adopted the coat of arms which was afterwards confirmed to him by Sir W. Camden as above. Had his family borne coat armour before him, he would have been able to make proof of it, and there would not have been any necessity for having the coat of arms confirmed to him anew.

The correct description and blazonry of the crest and arms as granted to Thomas Browne can only be obtained from Sir W. Camden's original sketch (Fig. 3). In nearly all of the subsequent "trickings" the arms and crest have, through negligence or ignorance, been incorrectly delineated. They are :—

THE CREST : Out of a mural coronet (of five battlements) gules, a stork's head issuing ermines beaked azure.

[In Camden's original sketch (Fig. 3) five battlements are given and should be retained. In Figures 1 and 2 only four are given ; and in the official Visitations of 1663 and 1687 three only are shewn. It should also be observed that the stork's head is ermines (white spots upon black ground), and not ermine (black spots upon white ground) as the shield. In Camden's original tricking no mention is made of the blazonry of the stork's head, but as it is registered ermines in the College of Arms, such proof may suffice.]

THE ARMS: *Ermine, on a fess embattled counter-embattled (five battlements above) sable three escallop shells argent.*

The arms of Thomas Browne are thus emblazoned (1633) above his tomb in Bradeley Church, co. Stafford, impaling the arms of Southaicke in right of his wife.

*(To be continued.)*

# Upton.*

## ABSTRACTS OF WILLS AND RECORDS OF ADMINISTRATION.

105. John Upton of New Castle in the county of Limerick, gent. Dated 8 Dec. 1712. Whereas Col. Thomas Holms of Killmallock, co. Lim^k, did by lease dated 28 July 1694 grant unto me, etc., all and singular the towns and lands of Ballynaberny, Ballymenagh, Glenstare, and Curragh-ne-Mullaght,† for and during the natural lives of George Upton, Samuel Upton, and John Upton, junior, and every of them, under the yearly rent of £95 per annum, with a covenant that on death of either of the said three lives he, the said Coll. Thomas Holms, his heirs, etc., shall, in consideration of £47 10s. 0d., grant unto me the said John Upton, my etc., the said lands by a new lease for the two surviving lives and such other life as I, etc., shall then name, etc. ; provides for renewing the lease from time to time, for dividing the rent and fine among his legatees, and for securing them against the persons in whose name the lease may hereafter be held.   To my son George Upton and heirs of his body the lands of Ballyneanagh granted me in said lease, he to pay £30 of the said rent and £15 towards the renewal of the lease.   To my son Samuel and heirs of his body all that part of Glanstare granted in said lease, he paying £15 of the rent ; in case my son Samuel die without issue, then said land to descend to the next of his younger brothers and the heirs of his body, and for want of such to such younger brother as shall be then living and his heirs that shall have no part of said lands from me.   To my son John Upton and heirs of his body said lands of Curragh-ne-Mullaght, he paying £30 of the rent and £15 of the renewal ; if he die without issue, then to the next of his younger brothers, etc., as above.   Son Samuel, etc., to pay £7 10s. of the renewal charge.   To my son Samuel Upton all that part of Glanstare which I hold from Mr. John Marshall by lease ; if son Samuel die, then same to go as above.   To my son Samuel all the title, etc., I have in a part of Glanstare which I purchased from Capt. Nicholas Bourke by deed dated 5 March 1706, being 15 acres ; also upper and lower Ballyhennies, Farren Mullen, and Rathna-Connery, being part of the lands granted me by Sr William Courtney by lease ; the said Samuel to pay the rent of £35 and the proportion of duties payable by said lease, and to build the house and plant the orchard as provided in the lease ; in case of his failure so to do, this property to revert to my executors for the use of such of my children as I have given my stock and other farms to.   To my six sons John, Conyers, Edward, Charles, William, and Jonathon all my mortgages, farms, money, debts due me, and other personal fortune and stocks, the same to be managed by my ex'ors for my said six sons till 21 respectively, each to have his portion at 21 ; ex'ors to have power to advance money to put these sons to a profession or employment.   Whereas £20 was paid to my son Conyers Upton's master when he was apprenticed, and £4 to redeem a year of his apprenticeship, my ex'ors to advance my son Conyers money to set up his trade.   To my son George 30 cows, but if George does not take up the bonds perfected to Mr. Giles on account of his marriage, he shall not have the cows nor the abatement in the rents of Ballyneany, but shall pay £32 per annum thereout ; to my son John Upton 40 cows out of my stock, if he should chance to marry, etc. ; my son George not to have said land or cows till he deliver to my ex'ors the bonds

* Continued from p. 157.
† *Id est*, " The coarse, high field," now called " Ashgrove."

M 2

which I have passed to Mr. Giles, the said George's father-in-law, on account of
said George's marriage ; to my son William Upton and heirs of his body said lands
of Ballynaberny, he paying £20 of the rent and £10 for the renewal ; if he die
without issue, then the same to descend, etc., as above ; to William certain cows
and the 15 acres in Glanstare given to Samuel, unless Samuel pay a bond of £23 ;
son John's 40 cows to be charged to him as part payment of his share of the residue.
Refers to marriage of son George to his now wife, daughter of said Rev[d] Stephen
Giles.   Whereas I have several farms by leases which will soon determine, my ex'ors
to do their utmost to renew the same for the benefit of my said six sons John,
Conyers, Edward, Charles, William, and Jonathon.   Appoint Thomas Boles of
Morigg, co. Cork, gent., Samuel Upton of Killabrahir, said co., gent., and John
Upton of New Castle, co. Lim[k], gent., executors.   Whereas I in previous clauses
ordered that in case my son Samuel die without issue, etc., I wish said Samuel to
enjoy said lands of Glanstare to him and his heirs without said limitation.   Witnessed by John Andrews, Paul Mohir, and Gerald Fitz Gibbon.   Proved at the
City of Limerick 20 March 1713 by said Thomas Boles and John Upton, said
Samuel Upton of Killbrahir, co. Limerick (sic), "progener," named in said will,
renouncing.   (Record Office, Dublin.)

106. Thomas Upton of Stepney, Midd[x].   Adm'on 20 June 1717 to Sherman
Godfrey, principal creditor.

107. Jonathan Upton of St. Edmund the King, London.   Adm'on 19 March
1717-18 to the relict Mary.

108. Anthony Upton* of Lincoln's Inn, Midd[x], Esq., but at present residing at
Grays in same county.   Dated 4 June 1718.   Appoint my sister Mrs. Mary
Knightley and my nephew Capt. William Upton[†] executors, and give each £50 ;
to my brother Capt. Richard Knightley my two cases of pistols and 20s. for a ring ;
to my brother Mr. Thomas Uvedale and each of his children and grandchildren,
comprehending Mr. Philip Beach, each 20s. for a ring ; to my sister Mrs. Mary
Upton, widow of my late brother Mr. John Upton,[‡] £10 and 20s. for a ring, and
to her son, my nephew, Mr. John Upton,[§] 20s. for a ring; to my sister Mrs.
Elizabeth Farrington, Daniel Farrington, Esq., her son, Mrs. Elizabeth Phill, her
daughter, and Mrs. Elizabeth Phill the younger, her granddaughter, each 20s. for
a ring ; to Mrs. Dorothy Sayer, daughter of my sister Knightley, 20s. for a ring,
and the choice of my best East India nightgowns; to Mr. Charles Molloy his father's
picture; all the family pictures which hang in my chambers at Grays to my
nephew and ex'or Capt. William Upton, the large diamond ring I bought of
Mr. Cuddon, and the seal ring with a black stone cut with my father's coat of arms,
etc.   Proved 10 July 1718 by Mary ux. Richard Knightley, Esq., and William
Upton, Esq.   (C.P.C., 151 Tennison.)

109. Nicholas Upton,‖ who died at Bombay in the East Indies, a bachelor.
Adm'on 23 Jan. 1721-2 to his mother Mary Upton, widow.

110. John Upton¶ of St. Peter le Poor, London, bachelor.   Adm'on (C.P.C.)
5 Oct. 1722 to John Upton, principal creditor, Mary Upton,** widow, mother of
dec'd, and William Upton and Anthony Upton,†† brothers of dec'd, renouncing.

111. Mary Upton‡‡ of St. Helen's, London, widow.   Adm'on (C.P.C.)
17 Dec. 1724 to her son William Upton.

112. Nathaniel Upton of Fitzhead,§§ Somerset, bachelor.   Adm'on 20 Sept.

* The testator was son of John Upton who made will No. 79.
† Capt. William Upton was son of testator's brother John, No. 97, by his wife Mary Upton,
No. 111.
‡ See note †, above.
§ The nephew John Upton is No. 110, post.
‖ The deceased was son of John Upton, No. 97, and Mary Upton, No. 111.
¶ This John Upton was son of John Upton, No. 97, ante.
** Widow Mary Upton is No. 111, post.
†† The brother Anthony Upton made will No. 134.
‡‡ Mary Upton was widow of John Upton, No. 97, ante.
§§ He was son of Nathaniel Upton, No. 84, ante.

1725 to Anne ux. William Bruford, Catherine ux. Henry Manning, and Sarah Upton, spinster, sisters of dec[d], Anne Upton, widow, mother of dec[d], being cited and not appearing.

113. John Upton of St. Margaret's, Westminster, Midd[x], bachelor. Adm'on 11 Feb. 1726-7.

114. John Upton* of North Reading, Mass., New Eng. Dated 29 Aug. 1720. To my son John Upton 5s.; to my son-in-law James Stimpson, or his heirs by my daughter that is dec[d], 5s.; to my daughter Mary Mackentier £3; to my son Ezekiel Upton £3; to my daughter Elizabeth £12, £2 per annum; to my son Joseph 5s., my father having already by will given him "a valuable quantity of land;" to my son Jonathan all my personal estate out of doors and all apparel, and appoint him executor; to my daughter Hephzibah £10 and all the household goods. Proved 6 Nov. 1727. (Middlesex Probate Records, xviii., 447.)

115. Thomas Upton of St. James, Westminster, Midd[x]. Adm'on 19 Aug. 1730 to the relict Jane.

116. Richard Upton,† merchant and mariner. Dated on board ship "Compton," 7 Jan. 1728-9. Appoint executors Robert Adams and Richard Mead, Esq[s], and to each £20 for mourning; to my brothers William, Anthony,‡ and Lytcott Upton each £50; residue to my daughter Ann Upton. Proved 11 Sept. 1730 by Robert Adams, Esq., surviving ex'or. (267 Auber.)

117. Richard Upton of Falmouth, Cornwall. Adm'on 15 Jan. 1731-2 to Wm. Pye, Esq., Robert Culverden, John Williams, jr., Esq., and Abraham Hull, surviving ex'ors named in the will of Hudson Upton,§ dec[d], while he lived son of said Richard Upton, dec[d], for that Elizabeth Upton, widow, relict of said Hudson Upton, died before administering; Elizabeth Hull, widow, daughter of said Richard Upton, dec[d], having renounced.

118. Ann Upton of Woburn Abbey, Bedford, spinster. Dated 18 April 1725. To my niece Elizabeth Watts and her husband Henry Watts £10; to my niece Anne Smelt and her husband Richard Smelt £10; to my niece Mary Oriell £5; to my nephew Nicholas Bullingham 20s. for ring; to my sister Eleanor Pitts my annuity for 99 years for her life, remainder to my said niece Anne Smelt and her two sons; residue to said Eleanor Pitts, and appoint her executrix, but if she die, then said Anne Smelt to be exec'x. Proved 15 Nov. 1733 by Anne ux. Richard Smelt. (302 Price.)

119. William Upton of Haslemere, Surrey. Adm'on 17 Feb. 1735-6 to his son William Upton,‖ the relict Joan renouncing. Adm'on de bon. non 19 Feb. 1745-6 to Joan Denyer, widow, daughter of dec[d]; said William Upton, son and adm[r], now also dec[d].

120. John Upton of Portsmouth, Southampton, gent. Dated 20 Aug. 1734. To Sarah wife of Matthew Grover of Portsmouth, mason, and Alice wife of William Smith of same, glazier and plumber, my dwelling-house on the north side of the upper end of the High Street in Portsmouth (which was given me by my good friend and relation Sir John Suffield of Widley, South[ton], K[t], by deed dated 5 and 6 Feb. 1730-1), for their lives and the life of the longest liver, remainder to Sarah, Mary, and Thomas Collier, children of Thomas Collier, shipwright, and William and Edward Smith, sons of said William and Alice Smith, and any other children they may have, as tenants in common, each at 21 or marriage; residue to said Sarah Grover and Alice Smith equally, and appoint them executrices. Proved 29 Oct. 1736 by said Alice ux. William Smith and said Sarah widow of said Matthew Grover dec[d]. Adm'on de bon. non 20 Dec. 1743 to Wm. Smith, husband

---

* Testator was son of John Upton who made will No. 90.
† Capt. Richard Upton was son of John Upton, No. 97, ante.
‡ The brother Anthony Upton made will No. 134.
§ Query: Was Hudson Upton son of Elizabeth Hudson who was licensed Jan. 14, 1669-70, to marry Richard Upton of Stepney, Midd[x], gent., bachelor, aged about 23?
‖ I suppose the son William made will No. 130. See also No. 30, ante.

of said Alice now dec<sup>d</sup>, of goods unadministered by her and by said Sarah Grover (late Sarah Wing ux. Thomas Wing), she having died intestate. (230 Derby.)

121. Richard Upton of St. Nicholas, Deptford, Kent, innkeeper and victualler. Dated 31 May 1736. To Richard my son of same parish, baker, 1s. ; to my father John Upton 1s. ; residue to my wife Elizabeth, and appoint her executrix. Proved 15 Aug. 1737 by exec'x. Adm'on *de bon. non* 24 Jan. 1739-40 to James Feltham, husband and adm<sup>r</sup> of Elizabeth Feltham *alias* Upton,* said exec'x. (193 Wake.)

122. Nathaniel Upton of Christ Chuch, Midd<sup>x</sup>, bachelor. Adm'on 11 Oct. 1738 to Samuel Oulddred, principal creditor.

123. Sarah Upton,† widow of Dr. Upton, dec<sup>d</sup>. Dated 16 Aug. 1727. To be buried in Christ Church, London, near my said husband, without escutcheons or pall bearers, and no monument or inscription over me. Appoint my dear son John Upton of London, merchant, sole executor ; to my granddaughter Mrs. Sarah Upton £1000 Bank stock, she not to marry without consent of her father Colonel Upton‡ of Ireland and her mother my daughter Mary Upton wife of said Col. Upton ; to my grandson Francis Upton one of the sons of said Col. Upton £300 ; to my daughter Mary Upton the picture of my father-in-law Mr. Upton§ for life, and then to my granddaughter Mary Upton ; all residue to my said son and ex'or John Upton. Codicil, 19 Feb. 1733-4 : Said £1000 to be paid to said Mrs. Sarah Upton without any restrictions. Codicil, 16 May 1734 : Considering the inconvenience of being carried from Bath, where I probably shall end my days,‖ I now direct to be buried in the churchyard at Weston near Bath, as near Mrs. Boteler's burying place as may be. Adm'on 16 Oct. 1739 to Ralph Allen, Esq., Attorney of said John Upton, son and ex'or named, now residing in Egypt. (220 Henchman.)

124. Elizabeth Feltham *alias* Upton¶ of St. Nicholas, Deptford, Kent. Adm'on 24 Jan. 1739-40 to her husband James Feltham.

125. William Upton** of Salem, Mass., N.E. Dated 13 April 1739. To each of my sons William, James, Francis, Edward, and Richard 5s. ; to my son Timothy my half part of the house and land in the Middle precinct in Salem which I hold in common with my son James; to my son Caleb 5s. ; to my daughter Mary Rich 5s. ; to my daughter Dorcas 5s., household goods, etc. ; residue, including Bear meadow in Reading, about four acres, all my stock of creatures, etc., to my son Paul, and appoint him executor. Proved 10 March 1739-40. (Middlesex Probate Records, xxiv., 97.)

126. Rebecca Upton†† of Lampton, Midd<sup>x</sup>, spinster. Dated 7 Aug. 1739. All personalty to my dear nephew Mr. Arthur Upton, son of my late brother Ambrose Upton, and appoint him executor. Proved 12 March 1739-40 by ex'or. (95 Browne.)

127. John Upton, heretofore of Falmouth, Cornwall, but since residing at Madras, East Indies, bachelor. Adm'on 29 Oct. 1740 to his sister Ann Upton, spinster, next of kin.

128. Colonel John Upton‡‡ of Castle Upton, co. Antrim, Ireland. Dated 17 Oct. 1733, with codicil 28 Nov. 1738. Mentions my brother Clotworthy Upton, dec<sup>d</sup> ; my brother Thomas Upton; my brother-in-law John Upton§§ of London, merchant; my wife Mary ; §§ my sons Arthur, Francis, and Clotworthy Upton ;‖‖ my daughter Sarah

* Elizabeth Feltham *alias* Upton is No. 124, *post*.
† Sarah Upton, *née* Norman. See third note under will No. 80. Her husband was Dr. Francis Upton, No. 103, *ante*.
‡ This Col. John Upton made will No. 128.
§ *Id est*, Rev. Ambrose Upton, Canon of Christ Church, Oxford.
‖ She is described in the Calendar as dying at Bath.
¶ Elizabeth Feltham was widow of Richard Upton who made will No. 121.
** The testator was son of John Upton who made will No. 90.
†† The testatrix was sister of Dr. Francis Upton, No. 103, *ante*, and daughter of Rev. Canon Ambrose Upton.
‡‡ Col. John Upton was son of Arthur Upton who made will No. 98, and brother of Clotworthy Upton named as adm<sup>r</sup> in Nos. 86 and 96, *ante*.
§§ Testator's wife Mary and brother-in-law John Upton were children of Dr. Francis Upton, No. 103, *ante*, and Sarah Upton who made will No. 123.
‖‖ The son Clotworthy Upton became 1st Baron Templetown.

ux. Thomas Perrot of Bath, Esq. ; my daughter Mary ux. Sam. Campbell of Mt. Campbell, co. Louth ; and my daughter Anna-Letitia. Proved 4 March 1741. (Record Office, Dublin.)

129. Arthur Upton of Shoreditch, Midd<sup>x</sup>, gent. Dated 23 Jan. 1733-4. To my affectionate mother-in-law Mrs. Jarvis a guinea ring ; residue to my wife Barbara, and appoint her executrix. Proved 16 May 1744 by exec'x. (135 Austis.)

130. William Upton,* the elder, of Haslemere, Surrey, mercer. Dated 28 Aug. 1745. Whereas I have surrendered my customary tenement called Deane and sundry lands, etc., in the manor of Linchmere, I now give the same to Sarah my wife and friend James Simmons of Frinsham, Surrey, papermaker, in trust to sell the same and discharge the legacies bequeathed by my late uncle John Steer to my brothers and sisters ; to John my son my freehold lands in Liss, co. South<sup>ton</sup> ; my household goods equally to my said wife and son John and my daughters Dorothy and Elizabeth ; to William my son £5 ; to said daughter Dorothy £50 at 21 ; to said daughter Elizabeth £150 at 21. Whereas my son William is entitled to the messuage, etc., where I now dwell immediately on my death, I give him also £16 *per annum* for life. Appoint said son John executor. Proved 1 March 1745-6 by ex'or. (103 Edmunds.)

131. James Upton on board H.M. Ship "Royal Sufferance." Dated 22 June 1744. All to friend Francis Brooks of St. John's, Wapping, Midd<sup>x</sup>, and appoint him executor. Proved 14 May 1747 by ex'or. (138 Potter.)

132. Charles Upton† of Hampton, Midd<sup>x</sup>, late Commander of H.M. Sloop the "Mortar." Dated 7 Aug. 1749. All my estate to my wife Isabella, and appoint her executrix. Proved 10 Aug. 1749 by exec'x. (268 Lisle.)

133. James Upton,‡ Clerk, of Hill Bishops, Somerset. Dated 2 Oct. 1744. All my estate to my wife Mary,§ and appoint her executrix, she paying my debts and legacies ; to my daughter Ann, now ux. John Tripp, Esq., the remainder of her fortune unpaid at my death ; to Charles my son, now in the Sea Service, £50 ; to Samuel my youngest son £40 ; to my daughter Mary, on whom my Woodford estate in parish Monk Silver is settled, £10 and my furniture in the parsonage of said place. Proved 22 Nov. 1749 by exec'x. Adm'on *de bonis non* 26 June 1754 to Francis Upton, Clerk, and Samuel Upton, ex'ors of said Mary Upton, exec'x, now also dec<sup>d</sup>. (359 Lisle.)

134. Anthony Upton‖ of London, gent. Dated 17 Sept. 9 George (1722) [*sic*]. To my cousin John Upton¶ of London, merchant, £40 for mourning ; to Thomas

---

* See note on abstract No. 119, *ante*.

† Capt. Charles Upton was son of Rev. James Upton who made the will next following. Perhaps his widow made will No. 137.

‡ The testator, the learned editor of Aristotle and Ascham, and doubtless the most scholarly man who ever bore the Upton name, deserves more than passing notice. I have been unable to learn his parentage. He is said to have been born in Cheshire in 1670, and was elected a Fellow in King's College, Cambridge, from Eton. He was incumbent at Eaton College, Bucks, in 1717 ; at Ilminster, Somerset, 1724-5 ; and at Bishop's Hull, Somerset, 1731, 1737, and when he made his will. He died in 1745, having had children as follows :

I. James, matric. at Balliol Coll., Oxford, June 4, 1717, aged 16 ; M.A. Nov. 25, 1723.

II. John, born at Taunton, Somerset, 1707 ; matric. at Merton Coll., Oxford, March 15, 1724-5, aged 17 ; B.A. Exeter Coll. July 7, 1730 ; M.A. May 10, 1732. He was prebendary of Rochester, and an author of note, editing Arian's 'Epictetus' in 1737 and 'The Faërie Queene' in 1758. He died in 1760.

III. George, matric. at Exeter Coll. April 1, 1731, aged 17 ; B.A. Oct. 12, 1734 ; M.A. June 10, 1737 ; called "Rev." 1751.

IV. Francis, matric. Exeter Coll. July 6, 1737, aged 19 ; B.A. June 30, 1741 ; M.A. April 13, 1744 ; B.D. Dec. 9, 1755 ; called "Rev." 1754.

V. Mary.

VI. Ann, married John Tripp, barrister-at-law, J.P., etc. From her descended the present Tripp family of Huntspill and Sampford Brett, Somerset. See Burke's 'Landed Gentry.'

VII. Charles, Commander R.N. He made will No. 132.

VIII. Samuel, youngest son. He was of age in 1751.

§ The widow Mary Upton made will No. 139.

‖ The testator was son of John Upton, No. 97, and Mary Upton, No. 111.

¶ The cousin John Upton was testator's second-cousin, and son of Dr. Francis Upton, No. 103.

Rous of Newgate Street, London, druggist, £10 for mourning ; residue to my mother Mary Upton and my brothers Captain William Upton, Captain Richard Upton,* and Lytcott Upton equally ; appoint said brother Captain Richard Upton and said cousin John Upton executors.  Adm'on 19 Dec. 1749 (testator called " of St George the Martyr, Middx") to Ann Upton, spinster, a creditor, for that John Upton, the surviving ex'or named, had renounced, and William Upton the brother and only surviving residuary legatee first renouncing, said Mary Upton the mother and Richard and Lytcott Upton the brothers of decd dying in testator's lifetime. (290 Lisle.)

135.  Thomas Upton.  "Writ with my own hand at the siege of marushes [query " Mauritius "] 21 June 1748."  To my two sons John and Martin Upton my houses, lands, etc., in Bidburrough, Kent, and to them and my two daughters Sarah and Mary Upton all my personalty equally, but my wife Sarah to have the use of all till my youngest child be 21, or until she marry again, in which case said children to have their portions at once.  Adm'on 14 May 1750 to the relict Sarah (testator called late of Bidborough, Kent, and late Master at Arms belonging to H.M. Ship " Deptford").  (108 Greenly.)

136.  George Upton of St. Mary, Islington, Middx, carpenter.  Dated 4 Aug. 1750.  My freehold estate in Islington to Anne Thorn, now living with me, for her life ;  to my brother Joseph Upton† and John Bowsteridge of Upper Halloway, Middx, farmer, said real estate after death of said Ann Thorn, and all other estate to use of my grandson Alexander Upton Burges when 21, remainder to my right heirs ; I confirm to William Burges my son-in-law £600 laid out in the name and to the use of my late daughter, the same to be regarded as part of her portion ; to the eldest son of my brother Robert £10 ; to Joseph Upton son of my brother Richard £10 ; residue to said Ann Thorn, and appoint her and my said brother Joseph Upton and said John Bowsteridge executors.  Proved 31 Aug. 1750 by said Ann Thorn, widow, Joseph Upton, and John Boustred alias Bowsteridge. (281 Greenly.)

137.  Isabella Upton‡ of Shipnash, parish Abbots Langley, Herts, widow.  Dated 3 Sept. 1750.  To my sister Sarah Moon £5 when 21 ; to John Gibson of Bread Street, London, gent., £5 and all residue, and appoint him executor.  Proved 15 Sept. 1750 by ex'or.  (310 Greenly.)

138.  John Upton of St Mary, Islington, Middx.  Adm'on (C.P.C.) 11 May 1751 to the relict Mary.

139.  Mary Upton,§ widow.  Dated 3 Jan. 1750-1.  To my granddaughter Mary Tripp £200, and my granddaughter Ann Tripp £100, and my grandson James Upton Tripp £100, being children of John Tripp, Esq., and my daughter Ann, and for this I charge my mortgage on Mrs. Susannah Tithill's estate in parish Hillbishops, and appoint my son the Rev. Mr. George Upton to receive the same to their use during their minority, and to him £50 ; to my daughters Mary Upton and Ann Tripp sundry plate, furniture, etc. ; to be buried in the chancel of Hill Bishops near my dear late husband ; appoint my sons Francis and Samuel Upton executors.  Proved 27 Aug. 1751 by both ex'ors.  (248 Busby.)

140.  Thomas Upton of Bromley, Kent, bachelor.  Adm'on 27 July 1754 to his brother George Upton, his mother and next of kin Obedience Upton, widow, renouncing.

(*To be continued.*)

---

* The brother Richard Upton made will No. 116.
† The brother Joseph Upton made will No. 143.
‡ See note on will No. 132, *ante.*
§ Mary Upton was widow of Rev. James Upton who made will No. 133.

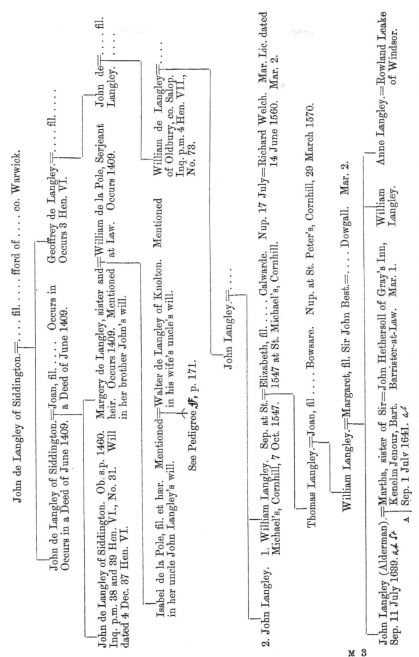

**Langley Pedigree**—Pedigree C. (*Vide* Vol. II., p. 274.)

LANGLEYS OF SIDDINGTON-LANGLEY AND LONDON.

John de Langley of Siddington.=.... fil. .... fford of .... co. Warwick.

John de Langley of Siddington.=Joan, fil. .... Occurs in a Deed of June 1409.

Geoffrey de Langley.=.... fil. .... Occurs in Occurs 3 Hen. VI. a Deed of June 1409.

Margery de Langley, sister and=William de la Pole, Serjeant heir. Occurs 1409. Mentioned at Law. Occurs 1409. in her brother John's will.

John de=.... fil. Langley.

William de Langley=.... of Oldbury, co. Salop. Inq. p.m. 4 Hen. VII., No. 73.

John de Langley of Siddington. Ob. s.p. 1460. Inq. p.m. 38 and 39 Hen. VI., No. 31. Will dated 4 Dec. 37 Hen. VI.

Isabel de la Pole, fil. et hær. Mentioned in her uncle John Langley's will.

Mentioned=Walter de Langley of Knolton. in his wife's uncle's will.

Mentioned

See Pedigree **F**, p. 171.

John Langley.=....

1. William Langley. Sep. at St. Michael's, Cornhill, 7 Oct. 1547.

=Elizabeth, fil. .... Calwarde. Nup. 17 July=Richard Welch. Mar. Lic. dated Sep. at St. 14 June 1560. Mar. 2. Michael's, Cornhill. 1547 at St. Michael's, Cornhill.

Thomas Langley.=Joan, fil .... Bowsare. Nup. at St. Peter's, Cornhill, 29 March 1570.

William Langley.=Margaret, fil. Sir John Best.=.... Dowgall. Mar. 2.

2. John Langley.

John Langley (Alderman).=Martha, sister of Sir=John Hethersoll of Gray's Inn, Sep. 11 July 1689. Kenelm Jenour, Bart. Barrister-at-Law. Mar. 1. Sep. 1 July 1641.

William Langley.

Anne Langley.=Rowland Leake of Windsor.

M 3

A|

**1. Grillagon Langley.** Bap. at St. Peter's, Cornhill, 24 July 1608. Nup. 4 May 1640 at St. Antholin, London. = **Jeffrey Howland.** Sep. 24 Sept. 1679.

**2. Anne Langley.** Bap. at St. Peter's, Cornhill, 25 Nov. 1610. Ob. 25 Feb. 1630. Sep. at St. Peter's, Cornhill, 1 March 1630.

**3. Elizabeth Langley.** Bap. at St. Peter's, Cornhill, 19 May 1615. = **William Limbery** of London, Merch^t.

**4. Judith Langley.** = **Obediah Sedgwick,** B.D.

**5. Martha Langley.** Bap. at St. Peter's, Cornhill, 24 Feb. 1621. Ob. 19 Aug. 1630. Sep. at Much Baddow, co. Essex.

---

**1. Andrew Langley.** Nat. 1606. Sep. at St. Peter's, Cornhill, 1608.

**2. John Langley.** Nat. 17 March 1612. Bap. at St. Peter's, Cornhill, 28 March 1613. Mentioned in his son Sir Richard's will. = **Elizabeth,** fil. .... Middleton. Nup. 14 Sept. 1640.

**3. Richard Langley.** Nat. 1619. Ob. Sept. or Oct. 1659. Sep. at Basinghall Street. = **Amy,** fil. Thomas Mane.

**4. Andrew Langley.** Bap. at St. Andrew's, Cornhill, I Aug. 1624. Sep. at St. Peter's, Cornhill, 8 Dec. 1659. = .... fil. Ux. 2.

**5. Philip Langley.** Bap. at St. Peter's, Cornhill, 22 Nov. 1627. Sep. at St. Peter's, Cornhill, 28 Oct. 1670.

---

Anne Langley. | Elizabeth Langley.

John Langley. = Mary Menlangley.

Richard Langley. Bap. at St. Mary Aldermanbury 7 Sept. 1648. Sep. at St. Mary Aldermanbury 22 April 1650.

Thomas Langley. Bap. at St. Mary Aldermanbury 8 June 1650. Mentioned in cousin Samuel's will.

---

**2. Andrew Langley.** Ob. s.p. Mentioned in brother Samuel's will.

**3. Phillip Langley.** Ob. s.p.

**5. James Langley.** Bap. at St. Peter's, Cornhill, 11 May 1645. Ob. s.p. Sep. at St. Peter's.

**6. William Langley.** Ob. s.p.

**7. Samuel Langley.** Ob. s.p. Will dated 9 Feb. 1693. Prob. 15 Oct. 1697 and 19 Nov. 1697.

**8. Nathaniel Langley.** Ob. s.p. Sep. at St. Peter's, Cornhill, 21 Nov. 1672.

---

**4. Sir Richard Langley, Kt.** Nat. 1644. Knighted 6 March 1672. Sep. at St. Peter's, Cornhill, 19 Feb. 1678. Will dated 8 Feb. 1678; probate dated 30 Oct. 1678. Ob. s.p. = **Cecill,** fil. Andrew Ellis of Abrey, co. Flint, Esq., by Frances, 2nd da. of James Fiennes, second Viscount Say and Sele. Nupt. 1° at Westminster Abbey 13 March 1673. Ob. 22 July 1715 at Bath, æt. 57. Sep. at Broughton, co. Oxford. M.I. Probate of Will 3 Aug. 1715. = **William, fil. William, Esq.,** Fiennes. Mar. 2.

**1. John Langley.** Bap. 19 May 1642. Ob. s.p. Sep. 24 Dec. 1655.

---

**1. Martha Langley.** Bap. at St. Peter's 3 March 1644. Sep. at St. Peter's 7 March 1644.

**2. Jane Langley.** Sep. at St. Peter's 5 Feb. 1650.

**3. Elizabeth Langley.** Ob. 27 Sept. 1724. Sep. at Chelsea. Mentioned in brother Samuel's will. = **Sir Hans Sloane,** Bart. Mar. 2. Mar. Lic. dated 9 May 1695. Ob. 11 Jan. 1753. Sep. at Chelsea 18 Jan. 1753. M.I.

**Fulk Rose** of Jamaica, Esq. Mentioned in Samuel Langley's will.

**4. Martha Langley.** Mentioned in brother Samuel's will. = **Matthew Skevington** of Newton Blossonby, co. Bucks.

**5. Jane Langley.** = .... Swymmer of Jamaica.

PEDIGREE **F.** (*Vide* Vol. II., p. 274.)

## LANGLEYS OF KNOLTON, KENT.

Benedict de Langley.=....fil.....

John de Langley.  Margaret de Langley.  Agnes de Langley.

Richard de Langley.=....fil.....

William de Langley, ob. 6 Ed. III.=Christian, fil. et hær. John de Sandhurst, Lord of the Manor of Knolton.

William de Langley of Knolton, Sheriff of Kent 21, 23, and 25 Ed. III.=....fil.....

William de Langley of Knolton, Sheriff of Kent 4 Hen. V.=....fil.....

William=Lucia, fil. de Lang-  Richard ap ley.  Lese.

Sir=John Norton. Mar. 1.

Joan de Langley, ob. 31 Oct. 1431. Sep. at Sheldwick, co. Kent. Ux. 1.=William Marys, Esquire of the Body to Henry V., Sheriff of Kent 21 Hen. VI. Ob. 31 Aug. 1459. Sep. at Preston, near Faversham.=Joan, fil. Bartholomew Bourne of Sharsted in Doddington. Ux. 2.

Walter de Langley of Knolton. Ob. 4 March 1470. Sep. at Grey Friars, London. M.I. Will dated 25 Feb. 9 Ed. IV.; probate 9 March 1470.=Isabella, fil. et hær. William de la Pole. Mentioned in husband's will. Ob. 1474. Inq. p.m. 14 Ed. IV., No. 40. See Pedigree ©, p. 169.

Richard de=Anne,=William Langley.  fil.  Darell.
....

John=Mabel Alden Lang- of ley. Alden.

A

A |

Elizabeth, fil. John Isaacs of Patricksbourne, co. Kent. = 1. William de Langley of Knolton. Mentioned in will of maternal great-uncle John Langley, and in father's will. Ob. 1482. Esch. 4 Hen. VII., No. 72. = Joan, fil. Sir John Lisley of Hampole, co. Kent, Kt. Ux. 1.

Elizabeth Langley, ob. s.p.

John Langley of Knolton. Ob. s.p. 3 Nov. 1518. Inq. p.m. 11 Hen. VIII., No. 92. = Jane, fil. Sir Thomas Peyton of Iselham by Joan = Sir Edward Ryngeley, his wife, fil. .... Calthorpe. Sep. at Sandwich, Kt. Will dated 24 co. Kent, Dec. 1551. Will dated 14 Dec. 1551. July 1543. Mar. 2.

Joan, fil. John Tame of Fairford, co. Gloucester. Ux. 1. = Edmond de Langley of Siddington-Langley. Mentioned in will of maternal great-uncle John Langley, and in father's will. Will dated 13 Feb. 1489; probate 24 May 1489. Inq. p.m. 6 Hen. VII. = Elizabeth, fil. .... Tracy. Mentioned in husband's will. Ux. 2.

Roger de Langley. Mentioned in father's will.

Thomas = Alice Langley, aged 30 = John Euerdon. in 1519. Mentioned in Huntley. father's will. Mar. 2.

Walter Langley, aged 5 in = Anne, fil. Sir Thomas Hunger-6 Hen. VII. Ob. s.p. 1503. ford by Elizabeth his wife, da. Mentioned in father's will. of John Hall of Salisbury.

Roger = Christian Langley, aged = William Wigs-36 in 1519. Mentioned Pye. ton. in father's will. Mar. 1.

Henry, fil. John Kettleby = Isabel Langley, aged 40 in 1519. = Edward of Kettleby, co. Lincoln. Mentioned in father's will. Scudamore. Ob. 31 Hen. VIII. = Mar. 2. .... Lymerk. Mar. 3.

Matilda = John Weeks of Dursley, Langley. co. Gloucester, Esq.

John Langley, Lord of Grimscote, co. Northampton. Mentioned in = Elizabeth, will of maternal great-uncle John Langley, and in father's will. fil. ....

John Langley, ob. s.p.    Ellenor Langley. = John Clarell.

For later Warwickshire Pedigrees, see Vol. II., pp. 337-339.

## MONUMENTAL INSCRIPTIONS OF HOLY TRINITY, BRADFORD-ON-AVON, CO. WILTS.*

### North Chancel Arch.

Near this place are deposited the remains | of Samuel Cam, one of his Majesty's Justices | of the Peace for the County of Wilts, | He departed this Life Nov<sup>r</sup> 7<sup>th</sup>, 1792, Aged 78 Years. | By his first Wife, Elizabeth Cam, he had | ten Children. They and their Mother together with | Elizabeth Cam, one of his three Daughters | by his last Wife Mary Cam are buried with | him in the same Grave. | Mary Cam and his other two Daughters by her | Charlotte and Harriot Cam are buried | in the Sepulchral Ground belonging to Lownes-mead | Chapel, Bristol. | Maria Theresa Cam, one of his Daughters by | Elizabeth his Wife, married | M<sup>r</sup> Isaac Hillier, by whom she had a Family. | Charlotte Cam, one of his three Daughters | by Mary his Wife, married | Benjamin Hobhouse, Barrister-at-Law, | by whom she had several Children. | By him this Monument was erected A.D. 1791.

### On Floor of Nave.

Walter Burcombe died Nov<sup>r</sup> 17<sup>th</sup>, 1814, | Aged 33 years. | Richard Burcombe. | Elizabeth, Wife of W<sup>m</sup> Goodall Burcombe, | died Sep<sup>t</sup> 25, 1797, Aged 56 years. | W<sup>m</sup> Goodall Burcombe died August 8<sup>th</sup>, 1816, | Aged 75 years. (M.I.)†

Underneath this Stone are Deposited the Bodies of | John Lea & Susanna his Wife, | He died December . . . . | She 2 Feb. 1730, Aged 67. (M.I.)

Also near this place are Deposited the Bodies of | David Lea and Will<sup>m</sup> Lea, Sons of the abovesaid | John and Susanna Lea. David Departed this life the . . | Nov. 1772, Aged 67 years. W<sup>m</sup> Nov. 15<sup>th</sup>, 1776. (M.I.)

Here Lyeth the Body of Esther Cooper, Wid<sup>w</sup>, | who Departed this life December 31 Anno Dom' | 1707, Aged 96 years. | Also Here Lyeth the Body of Richard Cooper of | Bradford, Clothier, Son of the said Esther Cooper, | who Departed this life February ye 6<sup>th</sup> Day, Anno | Dom', 1723, Aged 74 years. (M.I.)

Here Lyeth the Body of Robert Cooper, who departed | this Life the 29 Day of Feb. 1631, Ætatis suæ 55. (M.I.)

Here lyeth the Body of Martha, Daughter of Richard | and Mary Edwards. She Departed this life May the | 10, A.D. 1740, Aged 22. (M.I.)

Here lyeth the Body of John Whatly of this Parish, | who died Aug. 8, Anno Dom. 1717, Aged 46 years. (M.I.)

### On Floor of North Aisle.

Hic jacet Johannes Jones, Filius Johannis Jones de | Bradford, Pharmacopolæ. Qui Obijt Primo die Aprilis | Anno Dom. 1703, Ætatis suæ 9. (M.I.)

Hic sepultus est Johannes Jones, de Bradford, nuper Pharmacopola. Qui Obijt Sexto die Februarij, Anno | Dom. 1709, Ætatis Suæ 44. (M.I.)

Here lies the Body of Daniel Jones, who died Dec. | 1732, Aged 57. | And that of Elizabeth his wife, who died April 28<sup>th</sup>, | MDCCL, Aged 75. | Likewise the Body of Daniel Jones, their Son, who | died June 9<sup>th</sup>, MDCCLXX, Aged XLVIII. (M.I.)

* Concluded from p. 149.

† (M.I.) signifies that the Arms or Monuments to which these letters are attached are destroyed or illegible, and therefore are supplied from the rare printed ' Monumental Inscriptions of Wiltshire, 1821.'

Here Lyeth the Body of Daniel Jones, who De | parted this life December ye 2ᵈ, A.D. 1732 | Aged 58 years.  (M.I.)

Joseph Wood died March the 29, 1725. | Mary, Wife of Simon Wood, died Feb. 21, 1763. | William, Son of Simon and Sarah Wood Died May | the 24, 1765. | Wᵐ Wood, Son of the said Joseph Wood, died | December 1767. | Thomas Baskerville Departed this life September ye | 4ᵗʰ, 1779.  (M.I.)

*A brass plate :* Here lyeth the Body of Rosewell Smithfield, Son | of Rosewell Smithfield of this Parish, Clothier.  He | Departed this life July 22, 1726, Aged 17 years. | Also here Lyeth the Body of Elizabeth Smithfield, | Mother of the said Rosewell Smithfield, who died ye | 17ᵗʰ Feb. 1742, Aged 70.  (M.I.)

### HATCHMENT IN NORTH AISLE.

Arms : Per fess sable and argent, in chief a royal crown or, in base a lion passant of the first, JONES ; impaling, Sable, crusily, a lion rampant argent, LONG.  (M.I.)

### WEST SIDE OF SOUTH PORCH.

Underneath | this Place Lyeth | the Body of | John Shrapnell, | who Departed | this Life, January | the 4ᵗʰ, 1729, | Aged 55 Years.

## MONUMENTAL INSCRIPTIONS FROM THE BURIAL-GROUND OF ST. GEORGE, HANOVER SQUARE, NEAR MARBLE ARCH.*

Mʳ John Burniston, died 3 Nov. 1828, in his 39ᵗʰ year.
Mʳ William Hutchings, died 10 Aug. 1837, in his 51ˢᵗ year.

Mʳ Jonathan Gordeux [or Cordeux ?], died March 20, 1796, aged 47.

Mʳ Francis Hagan, died Oct. 20, 1809, aged 32.
Henry John Hagan, died Sep. 10, 1839, aged 1 year, 9 months.
Edith Hagan, died Aug. 24, 1853, aged 49.

Mʳ John Deakin, died Jan 1, 1827, aged 47.

Mʳ John Allan, late of [Greek ?] Street, in this parish, [carpenter ?], died March 5, 1824, aged [43 ?].

Mʳ Richard White, died Jan. 4, 1831, aged 78.
Sarah Ann, widow of the above, died Aug. 19, 1839, in her 77ᵗʰ year.

Mʳ Joseph Rutledge, of Avery Row, in this parish, died Aug. 11, 1841, aged 57. Also near this spot are interred eight of his children, who died in their infancy ; and in the ground attached to the chapel in Tottenham Court Road, lies the body of Joseph, son of the above, born March 7, 1818, died May 14, 1833.
Mʳˢ Elizabeth Rutledge, widow of the above, died Nov. 12 1843, aged 58.

* Continued from p. 155.

..............daughter of.........[and Ann Wordsworth].............New Bond Street, in the parish of S^t George, Middlesex, died 28 Oct. 1801, aged .. years, .. months, .. days.

Also Eliza, daughter of the above, died 25 May, 1804, aged 1 year, 5 months, 7 days.

Ann, daughter of the above, died 9 June 1805, aged 6 months, 6 days.

Also the above Ann Wordsworth, died 10 May, 1808, aged 42.

---

Edward Fennah, late of the parish of S^t Marylebone, died Oct. 13, 1833, aged 25.

Susannah, mother of the above Edward Fennah, died Aug. 26, 1838, aged 59.

Thomas Fennah, husband of the above Susannah Fennah, died Jan 31, 1842, aged 70.

---

M^rs Mary Ann Philliston, wife of M^r Charles Philliston, of this parish, died Sep. 30, 1824, in her 65^th year.

Also the above M^r Charles Philliston, died Dec. 15, 1835, aged 70.

Also M^r Charles Philliston, son of Charles and Mary Philliston, died July 4, 1837, aged 37.

Also M^rs Jane Philliston, second wife of M^r Charles Philliston, died July 28, 1848, aged 76.

---

John Hiett, of the parish of S^t George, Hanover Square, died 13 Oct. 1791, in his [75^th or 73^rd?] year.

---

James Hamstead, died Jan. 19, 1840, aged 59.

Susannah Hamstead, wife of the above, died 27 Oct. 1848, aged 68.

---

Elizabeth Ann Williams, daughter of Richard and Elizabeth Williams, of Oxford Street, in this parish, died March 25, 1825, aged 11 months.

Also the above named M^rs Elizabeth Williams, died 11 April, 1833, aged 38.

---

M^r John Williams, died July 23^d 1808, aged 67.

Mary Williams, died 6 Dec. 1814, aged 60.

---

Francis Belcher Allen, son of F. B. and M. A. Allen, and grandson of the above, died April 11, 1824, aged 7 months, 3 weeks.

Ellen Allen, died April 1, 1831, aged 4.

Rosetta Allen, died April 25, 1831, aged 2.

M^r Francis Belcher Allen, died Jan. 6, 1851, aged 67.

---

Francis Hackwood, for many years a member of the Royal Society of Musicians, died April 8, 1821, aged 87.

---

M^rs Clara Towns, wife of Thomas Towns, of this parish, died Dec. 6, 1832, aged 26.

---

M^r Joseph Knight, died Dec. 19, 1834, in his 34^th year.

M^rs Ann Moore, died Oct. 13, 1840, aged 72.

---

M^rs Mary Kekwick, died 25 Dec. 1830, in her 79^th year.

---

M^rs Mary [Stevens ?], died 11 March, 1808, aged 55.

Robert Harbottle, son of M<sup>r</sup> William Harbottle, of Anick Grainge, Northumberland,
    died July 2 [4 ?] 1807, aged 20.
William Clarke, died 3 Aug. 1830, aged 70.
M<sup>rs</sup> Elizabeth Clarke, relict of the above, died 1 Nov. 1842, aged 64.

---

F. S. H., died April 25, 1806, aged 4 months.

---

M<sup>r</sup> David Torrane, Yeoman of the Guard in the [Reigns ?] of King George the
    II & III, died [5 ?] March 1778, in his 7[2 ?]<sup>nd</sup> year.
[Elizabeth ?], wife of the above M<sup>r</sup> David Torrane, died Dec. 20, 1782, in her
    7[ ]<sup>th</sup> year.

---

. . . . len of Old [Bond Street ?] . . . . 1806, aged 52.

---

M<sup>r</sup> David Wernham, died Dec. 1, 1800, aged 62.
M<sup>rs</sup> Mary Wernham, wife of the above, died July 23, 1830, aged [89].

---

Joseph Emmerson, died June 17, 1823, aged 39.
Margret, wife of the above, died Nov. 14, 1838, aged 58.    Inscribed by their
    bereaved children.
Also John Phillips Morgan, son-in-law of the above died 27 July 1843, aged 31.
George Emmerson, son of the above, died Feb. 15, 1850, aged 38.

---

M<sup>rs</sup> Elizabeth Downs, died Oct. 7, 1806, aged 53.
William Maginnis, died July 20, 1814, aged 32.
M<sup>rs</sup> Marion Maginnis, mother of the above William Maginnis, died April 10, 1829,
    aged 69.
Catherine Mullord, died May 9, 1830, aged 78.

---

M<sup>r</sup> Charles Lawton, Sadler, of this parish, died 17 Jan. 1809, aged 77.
M<sup>rs</sup> Ann Lawton, wife of the above, died May 22, 1817, aged 89.

---

M<sup>r</sup> John Clayton, died Aug. 5 1807, aged 51.

---

M<sup>r</sup> John Louis Calemard, died 25 Nov. 1808, aged 55.
M<sup>rs</sup> Angelique Pierrette Calemard, his wife, died 6 April 1822, aged 56.
Jane Frances Duding, sister to the above, died July 26, 1837, aged 67.    Requiescat
    in pace.

---

. . . . . . . . . . . . . .M<sup>r</sup> James [Alcorn], died [    ] Oct. 1805, aged 62.
M<sup>r</sup> James Alcorn, nephew of the above, died Nov. 22 1807, aged 26.
James Henry Alcorn, infant son of the last named James [Alcorn], aged 18 weeks.

---

M<sup>r</sup> Robert Grant, late of this parish, died Oct. 2, 1814, aged 58.
Miss Ann Grant, daughter of the above, died March 17, 1824, aged 28.
Lieut. James Grant, R.N., died Sep. 30, 1829, aged 43.
M<sup>rs</sup> Ann Grant, died 21 June 1834, aged 77.

---

M<sup>r</sup> John Hewlett, late of Thomas Street, Oxford Street, died 2 June, 1837, in his
    59<sup>th</sup> year.
M<sup>r</sup> John Hewlett, son of the above, died 15 July 1842, in his 40<sup>th</sup> year.

---

Master James Charles Lawton, died 11 July 1808, aged 15.
James Lawton, father of the above, died April [14 ?] 1817, aged 58.

*(To be continued.)*

IOHN CONDUITT Esq.

Charles C. Barton

## Pedigree of Barton.*

Richard Barton of Brigstock, co. Northampton. Will dated 13 Dec. 1608, in which he desires to=Katherine, his wife, living 1608.
be buried in the parish church of Brigstock aforesaid, and proved 18 May 1609 at Peterborough.

- Richard Barton of Brigstock,=Katherine, da. of Henry Sawyer of Ketter-ing, co. North'ton. Marriage settlement dated 31 Aug. 35 Eliz., 1593. | eldest son. Proved his father's will 1609.
- Thomas Barton. Had a da.=Katherine. Both living in 1608.
- Giles Barton. Living 1608.
- Eleanor, wife of ... Laxton, 1608.
- Daughter, wife of Thomas Fletcher. Both living 1608.

Thomas Barton of Brigstock aforesaid, eldest son. Buried there 31 Aug. 1658.=Katherine, 2nd da. of Thomas Palmer of Carlton, co. North'ton, and sister of
Will dated 28 Aug., and proved 26 Nov. 1658 in C.P.C. | Sir Geoffry Palmer, Kt. and Bart., Attorney-General to King Charles II.

- Captain Thomas Barton=Alice ... his wife. Died 22 and was bur. 24 April 1711, æt. 86, at Brigstock. M.I. Will dated 3 March 1710, and proved 30 May 1711 at Peterborough. | of Brigstock aforesaid, eldest son. Died 29 Feb. and was buried there 2 March 1704-5, æt. 85. M.I. Will dated 10 Dec. 1703; proved 5 April 1705 in C.P.C.
- Edward Barton, formerly of Brigstock, and subsequently of Grafton Under-wood, co. North'ton, gent. Living 1676, æt. 54.
- Elizabeth, mar. Thomas Dudley of Brigstock. Both living in 1658 and 1667.
- Daughter, mar. ...Goulburn, and both living in 1658.
- Margaret. Living 1658, unmarried.
- Frances. Living 1658, unmarried.
- Thomas Maydwell=1st wife, Katherine. Mar. 19 July 1657 at Brigstock. Bur. 20 May 1660 at Kettering. | of Kettering, co. Northampton. Living 1658.

### All bapt. at Brigstock.

- Anne, eldest da. Bapt. 4 July 1649.
- Catherine, 2nd da. Bapt. 13 Sept. 1650. Living 1710. Wife of .... Porter.
- John Norrgreaves=Mary, 3rd da. Born 18 Oct. 1654. Mar. 11 Feb. 1674-5 at Brigstock aforesaid. Died before 1710. | of Brigstock aforesaid. Bur. there 11 April 1682.
- Major Thomas Manning=Alice, 4th da. Born 21 May 1666. Bur. at Brigstock 25 Feb. 1738-9. Will dated 11 Feb. 1738-9; pr. 13 March following in C.P.C. | of Oundle, co. North-ampton. Mar. in 1671 at Brigstock. Died 16, and was bur. there 18 Aug. 1705. M.I. 1st husband.
- Born=Thomas Hunt of Oundle aforesaid. A Captain in a Regiment of Horse commanded by Richard, Lord Cobham. Mar. there 31 Jan. 1716. Bur. 30 Aug. 1728 at Brigstock. Adm'on granted 26 Sept. 1728 to Alice, his widow, in C.P.C. 2nd husband.

- Thomas Barton of Brigstock, and of Exton, co. Rutland, eldest son.=Mary Dale of Exton, co. Rutland, spinster. Mar. there 13 May 1669; also registered at Brigstock. Buried 1 March 1722 at Exton aforesaid. | Bapt. 16 June 1652 at Brigstock. Bur. 19 Sept. 1690 at Brigstock aforesaid. Adm'on granted May 1692 to Mary Barton, his widow, in C.P.C.
- John Barton, 2nd son. Born 1 April 1658. Bapt. at Brig-stock. Bur. 11 Sept. 1659 at Brigstock.

\* Communicated by the Rev. T. S. HILL, Thorington.

B                             B

Major Noel Barton,=Frances afterwards Colonel, .... of Exton aforesaid. Buried Bapt. 7 Sept. 1674 28 Dec. at Exton. Will dat. 1739 at 2 Nov. 1706, and pr. Exton 13 Jan. 1714-15 in aforesaid. C.P.C.

John Barton. Bapt. 2 June 1673 at Brigstock.

Matthew Barton, Bapt. 24 April 1672 at Brigstock. Bur. at St. James's, West-minster, 20 March 1725-6. Will dated at St. Martin's in the Fields, co. Middx., 25 Oct. 1724; pr, 13 May 1726 in C.P.C.

Edward Barton, 2nd son. Bapt. April 1671 at Brig-stock.

A |

Thomas Barton of Brigstock aforesaid,=Elizabeth, 2nd da. of the above and of Preston, co. Rutland, Attorney Robert Barton and Elizabeth at Law, eldest son. Bapt. 25 April 1670 Pilkington. Bapt. 30 May 1667 at Brigstock, registered at Exton. Bur. at Brigstock. Mar. 26 July 1694 28 Dec. 1723 at Exton. Will dated at Rushton, co. Northampton. 28 Jan. 1722-3, and proved 14 April Died at Uppingham, and was 1724 in C.P.C. buried 19 Nov. 1731 at Exton.

All bapt. at Brigstock.

Catharine, bapt. 22 April 1700. Un-mar. 1723 and 1739.

Elizabeth, bapt. 11 Jan. 1697-8. Un-mar. 1723 and 1739.

Mary, bapt. 24 July 1696, and buried 11 Sept. following at Brigstock.

Knightley Matthew Barton, born 1 and bapt. 28 Oct. 1708. Living 1723.

Edward Barton, born 19 Aug. and bapt. 11 Sept. 1706. Died 16 and bur. 17 July 1710 at Brigstock. M.I.

Robert Barton, bapt. 27 May 1703, and bur. 23 March 1704-5 at Brigstock.

Thomas Barton, eldest son, bapt. 4 June 1696. Living in 1723.

John Barton, bapt. 21 Jan. 1701-2.

Robert Barton, bapt. 12 Aug. 1708 at Exton.

Elizabeth, da. of Rev. James Turner, Rector of Garthorpe, co. Leicester. Bur. at Exton aforesaid 9 Oct. 1800, aged 90 years.

Rev. Baptist Noel Barton, A.M., Rector of Cottesmore, Vicar of Exton, and Rector of Wing=Elizabeth, all in co. Rutland. Domestic Chaplain to Philip, Earl of Harborough. Sometime Chaplain to Clare Hall, Cambridge. A.B. 1728. A.M. 1733. Bapt. at Exton 7 Sept. 1707. Died 20 June 1762. Buried at Exton aforesaid, aged 55 years. M.I.

Mary, Alive 2 Nov. 1706. Bur. 1 Oct. 1709 at Exton aforesaid.

C |

Frances,=Rev. Richard 4th da. Williams, Vicar of Oakham, co. Rutland.

D

Thomas=Elizabeth Barton. ....

1. Elizabeth, bapt. 10 June 1737 at Exton aforesaid. Died unmar.

2. Mary, bapt. 8 Feb. 1739 at Exton afore-said. Died unmar.

3. Catharine. Died unmar.

Robert Barton, ob. s.p.

Catharine, ob. s.p.

Elizabeth, ob. s.p.

James Barton,=Mary, da. of bapt. 9 Oct. ... 1738 at Exton Crawford of aforesaid. Swineshead, co. Lincoln.

John Barton, bapt. 19 Sept. 1734 at Exton aforesaid. Ob. s.p.

Matthew Barton, A.M. Fellow of Clare Hall, Cam-bridge. A.B.1763. A.M. 1766. Died unmar.

Rev. Baptist Noel Barton, A.M., Vicar of Lavington, co. Bucks. Sometime Fel-low of Clare Hall, Cam-bridge. A.B. 1755. A.M. 1758. Bapt. 15 Aug. 1733 at Exton aforesaid.

B

Rev. Matthew Barton, A.M., Rector of Clipsham, co. Rutland. Sometime of St. John's College, Cambridge. A.B. 1797. A.M. 1819. Only son. Bapt. at Swineshead aforesaid 15 April 1774.

Frances, youngest da. Born 1792.

Rev. Richard Williams, A.M., Vicar of Oakham aforesaid. Sometime of St. John's College, Cambridge. A.B. 1802. A.M. 1806. Died unmar.

Mary, eldest da.=Rev. James Inman, D.D., Of the Royal Naval College, Portsmouth. Sometime Fellow of St. John's College, Cambridge. A.B. 1800. Died 1859. Born 1782 at Colsterworth, co. Lincoln. A.M. 1805. Died 1871.

D

C

Rev. Matthew Williams Barton, A.M., of Thwing, co. York. Formerly Head Master of the Grammar School, Chipping Campden, co. Gloucester, and sometime Master of Queen Elizabeth's Hospital, Bristol. Sometime of St. John's College, Cambridge. A.B. 1833. A.M. 1847. 2nd son. Born 25 April 1810. Bapt. at Edmonthorpe, co. Leic. Died 3, buried 6 Jan. 1883 at Bow Cemetery, London, aged 73, unmar.

Rev. John Barton, 4th and youngest son, of Kirk Langley, co. Derby. Formerly Incumbent of St. Anne's, Derby. Born 29 March at Edmondthorpe, co. Leicester. Bapt. 5 May 1813 at Portsmouth. Died 17, buried 19 June 1875 at Kirk Langley aforesaid, aged 62.

=Mary, eldest da. of John Harrison, Captain in the Royal Navy, of Luton, co. Kent. Married 22 July 1851 at the Parish Church, Margate, co. Kent.

Frances Mary, born 27 Aug. 1807 at Burton Coggles, co. Lincoln, and bapt. there. Died unmarried, aged about 28 years.

James, 1st son, born 1808 at Oakham, co. Rutland. Died in infancy.

Mary, born 8, bapt. 17 May 1814 at Havant, co. Hants. Died aged about 12 years.

Richard, 3rd son, born 26 Jan.. bapt. 3 Feb. 1812 at Edmondthorpe aforesaid. Died in infancy.

Elizabeth, born 29 April 1818, bapt. at Portsmouth. Died unmarried, aged about 43 years.

Georgiana Sara Pankhurst; only child, born 11 Sept. 1852.=George Bainbridge Barrington Bapt. at Kirk Langley aforesaid. Married 6 Oct. 1881 at of Kirk Langley aforesaid. Belper, co. Derby.

Elizabeth, da. of George Pilkington of Stanton-le-Dale, co. Derby,=Robert Barton of Brigstock, co.=Hannah, da. of Rev. Barnabas Smith, Rector of North by Elizabeth, da. of Thomas Haslewood of Belton, co. Rutland, Northampton, gent. Bur. there Witham, co. Lincoln, and half-sister of the celebrated 5th son of Edward Pilkington of Stanton aforesaid and Mildred 22 Sept. 1693, æt. 63. M.I. Will Sir Isaac Newton, Kt. Bapt. there 7 Sept. 1652. Morgan his wife. Buried 4 Feb. 1674-5 at Brigstock. 1st wife. dated 2 Sept., and proved 2 Oct. Executrix and proved her husband's will in 1693. 1693 in C.P.C. Living a widow 1695. 2nd wife.

Robert Barton, only son by 2nd wife. Lieut.-Colonel=Catharine Greenwood=Col. Robert Gardner of the City of Westminster, in Colonel Cave's Regiment, Hill's Brigade. Bapt. Proved will of her 2nd and of Carrickfergus in Ireland. Will dated 22 21 Aug. 1684 at Brigstock. Lost in the 26 Lawrence, husband 16 May 1729. Aug. 1728; proved 16 May 1729. His only child Canada, in 1710-11. Adm'on granted 26 April 1712 Party to her daughter's Joanna mar. Rev. Cutts Barton, D.D., Dean of to Catharine his widow in C.P.C. 1st husband. marriage settlement 28 Bristol, and Rector of St. Andrew's, Holborn. Dec. 1741. 2nd husband.

Hannah, da. by 2nd wife, bapt. 16 Nov. 1678 at Colsterworth, co. Lincoln, and was bur. 19 Feb. 1681-2 at Brigstock.

E　　F　　G

G

Catharine, only da., aged 23 in 1733, and then mar. to Frederic Burr. He was living 1741 and 1764. Died at Miles Court, Bath, 1789.

Robert Barton, 2nd son, born 23 Oct., and bapt. 21 Nov. 1709 at Brigstock. Living 1741.

=Elizabeth, 2nd da. of Rev. Jeffery Ekins, M.A., Rector of Barton Segrave aforesaid. Born 20 Oct. 1735. Died 2, and bur. 8 Dec. 1804 at Fulham, co. Middx. M.I.

=Major Newton Barton of Langley, co. Bucks, and of Irthlingborough, co. Northampton, Aide-de-Camp to General Honywood. Mar. 9 June 1758 at Barton Segrave aforesaid. Died at his house in Milsom Street, Bath, Oct. 1768. Will dated 15 Sept. 1764, and proved 4 Nov. 1768 in C.P.C. 1st husband.

John Hatsell of Marden Park, near Godstone, co. Surrey, Clerk of the House of Commons, and Bencher of the Middle Temple, London. Mar. 13 Jan. 1778 at Worting, co. Southampton. Died 15, and buried 24 Oct. 1820 in the Temple Church, London, æt. 79, 2nd husband.

---

Robert Barton, a Captain in the 76th Regiment of Infantry, eldest son. Died in India 17 July 1794.

Newton Barton, 2nd son. Living 1764.

Charles William Newton Barton, Private Secretary to Henry Addington, 1st Viscount Sidmouth. Sometime Fellow of New College, Oxford. 2nd and youngest son. Bapt. at Windsor, co. Berks, 6 March 1762. Drowned at Worthing, co. Sussex, 4 June 1808, æt. 46, unmar. Buried at Broadwater, co. Sussex, on the 9th. M.I. Will, in which he describes himself as Newton Barton only, dated 29 May ; pr. 22 June 1808 in C.P.C.

=Mary, eldest da. of Allen Young of Orlingbury, co. Northampton. Bapt. there 19 Nov. 1755. Mar. there 17 Feb. 1789, Died at Stanwick, co. Northampton, 9, and buried 17 May 1849, æt. 94, at Orlingbury.

Rev. John Barton, M.A., Vicar of Sonning, co. Berks, 1792, and Rector of Chiddingfold, co. Surrey. Chaplain to the House of Commons 1801, and Prebendary of Canterbury Cathedral 1802. Sometime Fellow of New Coll., Oxford. Died s.p. at Sidmouth, co. Devon, 17 Feb. 1803, æt. 44. Buried in Exeter Cathedral. M.I. at Exeter and at Sonning. Will dated 1 May 1800 ; proved 18 March 1803 in C.P.C.

---

John Conduitt of Cranbury Lodge in the Parish of Otterbourne, co. Southampton. M.P. Master of the Mint 1727. Died 23 and buried 29 May 1737, æt. 49, in Westminster Abbey. M.I.

=Katharine, da. by 2nd wife, bapt. 26 Aug. 1717 in Russell Court Chapel. Died 20 and buried 29 Jan. 1739-40, æt. 60, in Westminster Abbey. M.I. Will dated 23 July 1739 ; proved 10 Feb. 1739-40 in C.P.C.

John Warner of Geddington, co. Northampton.

=Margaret, da. by 2nd wife, bapt. 7 June 1687 at Brigstock. Mar. by licence 10 May 1709 at Brigstock.

Marriage licence at the Faculty Office dated

John Wallop, commonly called Viscount Lymington, M.P. for Andover, eldest son of John, 1st Earl of Portsmouth, and father of John, 2nd Earl. Born 3 Aug. 1718. Died v.p. 19 Nov. 1749. Buried at Farley, co. Southampton.

=Catharine, only child and heir, 7 and married 8 July 1740 at St. Andrew's, Holborn, aforesaid, he aged about 21 and she 19 and a spinster. Died 15 April, and bur. 4 May 1750 in Westminster Abbey.

See Peerage.

E

F

## Barton Pedigree—continued.

All bapt. at Brigstock.

**E**

Rev. Geoffry Barton, A.M., Rector of Rushton, co. Northampton. Sometime Fellow of Trinity Coll., Camb., A.B. 1683. A.M. 1687. Eldest son. Bapt. 24 March 1660-1. Died 4 and bur. 6 April 1725 at Rushton. Adm'on granted 31 May 1725 to Elizabeth his widow in C.P.C. = Elizabeth, 5th and youngest da. of Richard Lockwood of Gayton, co. Northampton, by Susannah his wife, only da. and heir of Edward Cutts. Born 29 March 1680. Bur. 10 Sept. 1762 at St. Andrew's, Holborn. Will, in which she is described as of St. George's, Bloomsbury, co. Middx., widow, dated 1 Aug. 1756, and proved 19 Oct. 1762 in C.P.C.

Robert Barton, 2nd son, bapt. 30 Sept. 1665. Bur. 20 Jan. following at Brigstock.

Susannah, eldest da., bapt. 25 May 1664. Mar. Wollysborn Sill, gent. She died 21 Dec. and was bur. 22 Dec. 1686, æt. 23, at Brigstock. M.I.

Elizabeth, 2nd da., bapt. 30 May 1667. Mar. 26 July 1694 Thomas Barton, eldest grandson of her uncle Captain Thomas Barton, v. supra.

---

Lyon Falkener of Uppingham, co. Rutland, and of Clement's Inn in the par. of St. Andrew, Holborn, Attorney at Law. Died at Oundle 18 and bur. 20 Sept. 1722 at Uppingham. Will dated 11 Sept. 1722 ; proved 22 March following in C.P.C. = Mary, 3rd da., bapt. 8 Jan. 1668-9. Mar. 13 Oct. 1706 at Barton Segrave, co. Northampton. Living 1733.

Rev. Alexander Ekins, Rector of Barton Segrave, co. Northampton. Bur. there 3 June 1703. 1st husband. = Jane, 4th da., bapt. 9 June 1670. Mar. circa 1694. Bur. 5 Feb. 1732-3 at Brigstock. M.I. = Thomas Manning of Oundle, co. Northampton. Mar. 16 Jan. 1710 at Brigstock, and buried there 10 Oct. 1737. Adm'on granted in C.P.C. 10 March 1738 to his son Thomas, his relict Mary Manning renouncing. 2nd husband.

William Lisle of Evenley, co. Northampton, eldest son of Colonel William Bowles of Evenley. M.P. for Brackley, co. Northampton. Born 1666. Died v.p. before 1716. = Barbara, 5th da., bapt. 23 Feb. 1673-4. Mar. 13 Feb. 1695 at Rushton, co. Northampton.

---

All bapt. at Rushton.

Rev. Jeffery Barton, D.D., Rector of St. Andrew's, Holborn, co. Middx., and Rector of Black Notley, co. Essex, 1725. Domestic Chaplain to Robert, Lord Walpole. Sometime Fellow of King's College, Cambridge. A.B. 1721. A.M. 1725. Eldest son. Born 24 Sept. 1698. Died unmar. 7 Sept. 1734. Bur. at Black Notley. Adm'on granted to his brother Cutts 5 Dec. 1734 in C.P.C.

Charles Barton, 2nd son, born 21 Jan. 1700-1. Died between 1710 and 1712.

The Very Rev. Cutts Barton, D.D. = Joanna Gardner.

See Pedigree **A**, p. 183.

Robert Barton of Rownhams, co. Southampton. Appointed Consul at Grand Cairo in 1732. 4th son. Born 19 May 1708. Died s.p.s. 3 April 1798. Bur. in the Abbey Church, Romsey, co. Southampton, æt. 90. M.I. Will dated 21 Jan. 1792, and proved 21 April 1798 in C.P.C. = Delitia, sister of George Bridges of Siddington, co. Gloucester. Married before Sept. 1733. Died 15 May 1789, æt. 75. Buried in the Abbey Church, Romsey, aforesaid 26 of same month. M.I.

---

John Barton of the Tower of London, 6th son. Born 14 May 1715. Died unmarried, and was bur. at St. Andrew's, Holborn, 1 Dec.1785,

George Barton, Consul at Cyprus, 5th son. Born 9 Aug. 1711. Died unmar. 17 April 1739. Bur. at the Church of St. Lazarus in Cyprus. Will dated 16 April 1739 ; proved in Cyprus 27 Sept. 1742, and in C.P.C. 1 March 1743. M.I

Matthew Barton of Hampstead, co. Middx. An Admiral in the Royal Navy. 7th son. Born 2 Aug. 1716. Died s.p. at Hampstead, and was buried 6 Jan. 1796 at St. Andrew's, Holborn. Will dated 13 April 1795, and proved 5 Jan. 1796 in C.P.C. = Rachel, sister of Abraham Brook of Hinton St. George, co. Somerset. Bur. 25 Jan. 1813, æt. 69, at Hampstead. M.I. Will dated 5 July 1806 ; proved 6 March 1813.

Elizabeth, eldest da., born 16 Dec. 1699. Died before 1713.

Susanna, 2nd da., born 6 July 1702. Buried 3 May 1725 at Rushton, unmar,

N

H

H

Catharine, 3rd da., born 1 Nov. 1709.

Elizabeth, 4th da., born 19 March 1712-13.

Matilda, 5th da.,

Anne, 6th da., born 29 June 1720.

Frances, 7th and youngest da., born 17 Nov. 1724, and bur. 18 Aug. 1787 at St. Andrew's, Holborn.

Rev. Montagu Barton, M.A., Rector of Stoke Dry, co. Rutland, = Dorothy, da. of Samuel Blackwell 1742, and Rector of Stourton, co. Wilts, 1755. Chaplain to the Royal Artillery. Sometime Fellow of King's Coll., Cambridge. A.B. 1740. A.M. 1749. 8th and youngest son. Born 16 Sept. 1717. Bur. 27 April 1790 at Stourton. M.I. Adm'on granted April 1791 to his son Montagu in C.P.C. — of Hatton Garden in the parish of St. Andrew, Holborn. Mar. there 18 Oct. 1750, and buried 20 March 1756 at Stourton.

Henry Hoare Barton, 2nd son, bapt. 20 Feb. 1755 at St. Andrew's, Holborn.

Rev. Edward Salter, M.A., Rector of Strathfieldsaye, co. Southampton, and Prebendary of Winchester. Died 23 and bur. 30 May 1812 in Winchester Cathedral. M.I. Will dated 16 Dec. 1809, and proved 26 June 1812 in C.P.C. = Delitia, eldest and only surviving da., bapt. 25 Aug. 1753 at Saint Andrew's, Holborn. Married at Stourton aforesaid 18 May 1778. Died 3 and bur. 9 Feb. 1833 at Iron Acton, co. Gloucester. M.I. in Winchester Cathedral. Will dated 26 May 1821, and proved 13 March 1833 in C.P.C.

Ann Dorothy, 2nd and youngest da., bapt. 18 Mar. 1756 at Stourton, and bur. there 23 Dec. following.

---

Rev. Montagu Barton, A.M., Rector = Caroline Louisa, da. of of Stourton, co. Wilts, 1790. Rector of Broad Clyst, co. Devon, 1795. Sometime of Trinity Coll., Camb. Eldest son. Bapt. 25 Aug. 1752 at St. Andrew's, Holborn. Died 16 and bur. 22 May 1819, æt. 66, at Broad Clyst aforesaid. M.I. Will dated 3 June 1817, and proved 10 Aug. 1819 in C.P.C. — William Hayter of Newton Toney, co. Wilts. Mar. there 4 Aug. 1781. Died at Budleigh Salterton, co. Devon, 2, and bur. 10 Oct. 1834, æt. 65, at Broad Clyst aforesaid. M.I. Will dated 3 Aug. 1881; pr. 3 Nov. 1884 in C.P.C.

George Robert Salter, 2nd son, born 1 Aug. 1781. Bur. 2 Feb. following at Strathfieldsaye aforesaid.

Rev. Edward Montagu Salter, M.A., Rector of Wood Norton, co. Norfolk, 1825. Sometime Student of Christ Church, Oxford. B.A. 1813. M.A. 1815. 4th son. Born 12 May, bapt. 5 June 1790. Died unmar. 31 March and bur. 8 April 1845 at Wood Norton. M.I. Will dated 18 Feb. and pr. 19 April 1845 in C.P.C.

Rev. John Salter, M.A., Rector of Iron Acton, co. Gloucester, and Hon. Canon of Bristol Cathedral. Formerly Student of Christ Church, Oxford. B.A. 1814. M.A. 1817. 5th and youngest son. Born 18 Aug. and bapt. 4 Sept. 1791. Died 9 Feb. 1877, aged 85.

_All bapt. at Strathfieldsaye._

Rev. Thomas Salter, B.A., Rector of Ibberton, co. Dorset, 1813. 3rd son. Born and bapt. 14 Aug. 1788. Died unmar. 25 Dec. 1854. Bur. at Sway, co. Southampton. Adm'on granted 25 April 1855 in C.P.C.

Catharine, 3rd and youngest da., born 19 Jan. and bur. 14 May 1784 at Strathfieldsaye.

Henrietta, 2nd da., born 5 Nov. and bapt. 6 Dec. 1782. Died unmar. 8 and bur. 15 April 1843 at Iron Acton aforesaid. Adm'on granted 13 May 1843 in C.P.C.

---

Robert Montagu Barton, only child, bapt. 23 Oct. 1792 at Stourton aforesaid. Died unmar. 6 Sept. 1835. Bur. at Broad Clyst aforesaid. M.I. Adm'on granted 2 Oct. 1835 in C.P.C.

Edward Salter, eldest son, born 8 and buried 16 March 1780 at Strathfieldsaye aforesaid.

Delitia, eldest da., born 13 March and bapt. 11 April 1779. Died unmar., in Suffolk Square, Cheltenham, 4, and buried 11 March 1859 in the New Burial Ground at Cheltenham. M.I. Will dated 30 April 1845 and proved 30 March 1859 in C.P.C.

# Barton Pedigree—Pedigree A. (*Vide* p. 181.)

The Very Rev. Cutts Barton, D.D., Dean of Bristol, Rector of St. Andrew's, Holborn, co. Midx., 1734, and of Little Laver, co. Essex, Chaplain to H.R.H. Frederic, Prince of Wales. Clerk of the Closet to H.R.H. the Princess Dowager of Wales 1765. Sometime of St. Peter's College, Cambridge. A.B. 1727. A.M. 1732. D.D. 29 Nov. 1756. 3rd son. Born 5 Oct. 1706. Died 10 Dec. 1780. Buried at Langley, co. Bucks. M.I. Adm'on granted 5 Feb. 1781 to his son Charles, and again in Nov. 1806 in C.P.C. **=** Joanna, only child and heir of Colonel Robert Gardiner of Carrickfergus in Ireland, and of the City of Westminster, by Catharine his wife, widow of the above Colonel Robert Barton. Marriage settlement dated 28 and mar. 29 Dec. 1741 at St. Andrew's, Holborn. Died 2 and buried there 8 Feb. 1774.

All bapt. at St. Andrew's, Holborn.

**Montagu Barton,** eldest son, bapt. 23 Aug. 1743. Bur. 30 Jan. following at St. Andrew's, Holborn.

Sarah, eldest da. of Nicholas Pearse of Woodford, co. Essex, born 26 Sept. 1763. Mar. at St. Andrew's, Holborn, 21 May 1785. Died s.p. 4 and buried 9 Nov. 1797 at Woodford aforesaid. 1st wife. **=** Rev. Charles Barton of Rownhams, co. Southampton, M.A. Rector of Deene, co. Northampton, 1777. Rector of St. Andrew's, Holborn, 1781. Sometime of Christ Church, Oxford. B.A. 1773. M.A. 1776. 2nd son. Born 23 Feb. and bapt. 2 April 1751. Died at Bath 29 Dec. 1805. Buried 10 Jan. following at St. Andrew's, Holborn. M.I. Will dated 4 May 1805, and proved 17 Jan. following in C.P.C. **=** Harriet, 3rd da. of Matthew Carrett of Hatton Garden in the parish of St. Andrew, Holborn. Born at Lisbon 26 Aug. 1763. Mar. at St. Marylebone 27 March 1799. Died 30 April and buried 5 May 1855, æt. 92, at Bradford Peverill, co. Dorset. M.I. Will dated 27 Feb. 1847, and proved 18 June 1855 in C.P.C. 2nd wife.

**Matthew Barton,** 3rd son, twin with Robert, bapt. 26 Oct. 1753. Bur. 3 June 1765 at St. Andrew's, Holborn.

Robert Barton of Burrough House in the parish of Northam, co. Devon. Vice-Admiral of the Red. 4th son, twin with Matthew. Bapt. 26 Oct. 1753. Died 16 and bur. 23 Dec. 1831 at Meavey, co. Devon. M.I. Will dated 23 Oct. 1831, and pr. 13 March 1833 in C.P.C. **=** Anne Maria, only child and heir of Henry Downe of Burrough House aforesaid, Colonel of the North Devon Volunteers, and a Deputy Lieutenant for Devonshire; sometime in the 5th Regiment of Foot. Born at Burrough House, and bapt. at Northam 28 Sept. 1766. Mar. there 31 Oct. 1786. Died 28 Jan. and bur. 4 Feb. 1828 at St. John's, Withycombe, co. Devon. M.I.

John William Barton, a Captain in the 1st Somerset Militia, and a Deputy Lieutenant for Somersetshire. 5th and youngest son. Born 27 Feb. and bapt. 14 April 1757. Died 13 and buried 19 Nov. 1821 at St. James's, Bath, co. Somerset. Will dated 9 Jan. 1817, and proved 27 Feb. 1822 in C.P.C. **=** Mary, eldest da. of Thomas Dorey of Bath, co. Somerset. Born 23 Dec. 1785. Died 28 March and bur. 4 April 1856, æt. 71, at Britford, co. Wilts. M.I. Adm'on granted 12 Nov. 1856 in C.P.C.

**Mary Ann,** only child, bapt. 6 Dec. 1809 at St. Michael's, Bath. Mar. 14 March 1822 at St. Mary-le-Port, Bristol. Died 19, bur. 26 June 1856 at Britford, co. Wilts. M.I. Adm'on granted 7 Nov. 1866 in C.P.C. **=** Rev. Richard Humphry Hill of Dilton, co. Wilts, A.B. Vicar of Britford, co. Wilts, 1849. Born 6 July 1800, and bapt. 27 Jan. 1805 at Bathwick, Bath. Sometime of St. John's College, Cambridge. A.B. 1827. Died 4 and bur. 8 Feb. 1868 at Britford aforesaid. M.I. Adm'on granted 1868 in C.P.C.

A | B

Matthew Turton Barton, 2nd son. Bapt. June 1792, died 12 May 1793, both at Bishopstoke, and bur. there.

Anne Maria, 1st da., bapt. at Northam aforesaid July 1789. Mar. at St. David's, Exeter. Died 14 and bur. 23 Dec. 1831 at Meavey, co. Devon, s.p.
= Rev. John Abbott, Rector of Meavey aforesaid.

Elizabeth, 2nd da., bapt. Nov. 1790 at Bishopstoke. Mar. 12 Dec. 1810 at Northam aforesaid. Died 19 Feb. 1814. Buried at St. John in the Wilderness, Exmouth, co. Devon.
= Francis Stanfell, a Captain in the Royal Navy. Died 14 Dec. 1831. Bur. at St. Lawrence, Exeter,

Delitia Montagu, 3rd and youngest da., bapt. April 1794 at Northam aforesaid. Mar. 27 May 1820 at St. Sidwell, Exeter. Died 17 June 1836. Bur. at Northam aforesaid.
= Thomas Wren, Major H.E.I.C.S. Deputy Lieutenant co. Devon.

Robert Cutts Barton, a Captain in the Royal Navy. Of Burrough House aforesaid. Bapt. at Northam, co. Devon, 1788. Died 1827, and bur. in the nave of the Cathedral, Salisbury.
= Rebecca Lopes, da. of ... Franco. Mar. at St. David's, Exeter, and bur. at Bickley, co. Devon.

Henry Downe Barton of Southern-Hay Place, Exeter, 3rd and youngest son. Born 8 Nov. and bap. Dec. 1801 at Northam, co. Devon.
= Margaret, da. of Forbes MacBean Chevers, M.D., of Richmond; widow of James Webster, H.E.I.C.S., of Shonlden Lodge, Deal. Mar. at Walmer, co. Kent, 24 Sept. 1839.

Henry Downe Chevers Barton, Lieutenant in the 57th Regiment of Infantry, eldest son. Bapt. March 1841; died 1 April 1872, unmarried; and buried—all at St. David's, Exeter.

Robert Montague Barton, 2nd son, bapt. 30 Aug. 1842 at St. David's, Exeter.

Francis Forbes Barton, 3rd and youngest son, bapt. Sept. 1843 at St. David's, Exeter. Died unmar. 5 Dec. 1869, and bur. at St. David's aforesaid.

Emily Kate, eldest da., bapt. Aug. 1845 at St. David's aforesaid.

Delitia Amy, 2nd and youngest da., born Dec. 1849. Bapt. Jan. 1850 at St. David's aforesaid. Died Dec. following, and buried at St. David's.

Henry Charles Benyon Barton of Bays Hill Lawn, Cheltenham, co. Gloucester, and of Burrough House, co. Devon, aforesaid.
= Mary Ann, da. of ... O'Neile of Barbadoes, Mar. at Chel-tenham 1841.

Elizabeth, 1st da., born 1823. Died 1841, unmar.

Katherine Frances, 2nd and youngest da., born 1824.
= William Rennell Coleridge of Salston Ottery St. Mary, Devon. Major in South Devon Militia.

Joanna, eldest da., born 15 and bapt. 17 Sept. 1744. Bur. 14 May 1752 at St. Andrew's, Holborn.
= John Crofts of the par. of St. Augustine in Bristol.
= Elizabeth Catharine, 2nd da., born 31 Aug. and bapt. 6 Sept.1745. Mar. at St. Andrew's, Holborn, 10 March 1766. 2nd wife.

Rev. Thomas Bowen, A.M., Rector of Pulham St. Mary the Virgin with St. Mary Magdalene, co. Norfolk, 1765. Sometime of Trinity College, Cambridge. A.B. 1759. A.M. 1762. Died 1 and bur. 8 Dec. 1807 at Pulham. M.I. Will dated 27 Aug. 1803, and proved 21 Jan. 1808 in C.P.C.
= Frances, 3rd da., bapt. 23 Nov. 1746. Mar. at St. Andrew's, Holborn, 3 April 1769. Died at East Bergholt, co. Suffolk, 11, and bur. 19 Jan. 1825 at Pulham St. Mary aforesaid. M.I.

Rev. John Crofts, M.A., Rector of Great Berkhampstead, co. Hertford. Sometime of Christ Church, Oxford. B.A. 1789. M.A. 1792. Died unmar. 15 and bur. 21 Jan. 1851, aged 82. Will dated 8 July 1849, and proved 3 Feb. 1851 in C.P.C.

C

Susanna Elizabeth, 5th and youngest da., born 11 Dec, 1760, bapt. 8 Jan. following. Bur. at St. Andrew's, Holborn, 8 Feb. 1764.

A

Thomas Watts of Beaumont Lodge in the parish of—Mary Ann, 4th da., bapt.=Henry Brooksbank of Chesterfield Street, Old Windsor, co. Berks, and of Craig's Court, 21 April 1755. Died s.p. May Fair, in the parish of St. George, Charing Cross, co. Middx. Mar. 6 May 1785 at in Harley Street in the Hanover Square, co. Middx. Mar. at St. St. Andrew's, Holborn. Died 3 and bur. 11 Sept. parish of St. Marylebone, Marylebone 7 March 1801. Died 18 April 1798, æt. 67, at Sunninghill, co. Berks. Will dated and was buried 12 Feb, 1847. Bur. at Boulogne-sur-Mer, France, 18 April 1797, and proved 1 Oct. 1798 in C.P.C. 1821 at St. Andrew's, born, 8 Feb. 1764. 1st husband. Holborn, æt. 66, 2nd husband.

Hastings Nathaniel=Mary Anne, 2nd and youngest da., Middleton of Brad- born 2 Feb. and bapt. 2 May 1804. ford Peverill, co. Mar. 9 Sept. 1834 at St. John's, Dorset, and of the Paddington, co. Middx. Died at Inner Temple, Lon- St. Leonard's-on-the-Sea 24 and don, Barrister-at- bur. 29 Dec. 1866 at Bradford Law. A Deputy Peverill aforesaid. M.I. Lieutenant for the County of Dorset.

Charles Cutts Barton=Emilia Ann, eldest da. of of Rownhams afore- Hastings Nathaniel Mid- said, only son and dleton of Charles Street, heir, born 2 April and St. James's Square, co. bapt. 12 May 1802 at Middx. Born 18 March St. Andrew's, Holborn. 1805. Mar. at Speldhurst, Sometime of Christ co. Kent, 20 June 1826. Church, Oxford. B.A. Died 13 Sept. 1850 at 1824. M.A. 1830. Stuttgart in the Kingdom of Wurtemburg, and bur. there. M.I.

Rev. Peter Cotes, M.A.,=Harriet Elizabeth, Rector of North Lichfield, eldest da., born 21 co. Southampton. Some- Feb, bapt. 27 March time of Wadham College, 1801 at St. Andrew's, Oxford. B.A. 1821. M.A. Holborn. Married in 1827. Died 24 and bur. Paris 6 Nov. 1830. 30 Aug. 1865 at North Died 9 Feb. 1832, Lichfield. M.I. Will and bur. at Shaw, co. dated 26 Nov. 1864; pr. Berks. M.I. 1 Nov. 1865 in C.P.C. 1st wife.

Julia Harriett, only child, born 30 Nov. 1831; bapt. 13 Oct. following at Shaw aforesaid. Died unmar, 15, and bur. 22 Nov. 1864 at North Lichfield aforesaid. M.I.

Hastings Burton Middleton=Charlotte Lucia, eldest of the Middle Temple, Lon- da. of Rev. Charles Old don, 2nd son, born 30 Sept.; Goodford, D.D., Provost bapt. 10 Nov. 1839 at Betch- of Eton Coll., co. Bucks. worth, co. Surrey. Some- Mar. 16 June 1873 at time of Magdalene College, Chilton Canteloe, co. Oxford. B.A. 1863. M.A. Somerset. 1868.

William Frederic Middleton, a Lieut. in 13th Regiment of Foot, 3rd and youngest son. Born 8 May; bapt. 11 June 1841 at Betchworth aforesaid. Died at Sand- gate, co. Kent, 17, and bur. 23 Aug. 1867 at Bradford Peverill. M.I.

Georgina Mary Anne, eldest da., born 20 March; bapt. Aug. 1836 at Reigate, co. Surrey. Died 28 Sept. and bur. 4 Oct. 1855 at Bradford Peverill. M.I.

E

Hastings Edward Middleton, eldest son, born 28 June; bapt. 2 Aug. 1837 at St. John's, Paddington. Died 9, and buried 16 May 1838 at Kensal Green Cemetery, co. Middx.

D

D | E

Rev. Osmond Fisher, M.A. (eldest son of Rev. John Fisher, Archdeacon and Canon Residentiary of Salisbury Cathedral), Vicar of Elmstead, co. Essex, 1857. Rector of Harlton, co. Cambridge, 1867. Fellow of the Geological Society, Sometime Fellow of Jesus College, Camb. A.B. 1841. A.M. 1844. = Maria Louisa, 2nd da., born 22 July, and bapt. 2 Sept. 1838 at Reigate aforesaid. Mar, 7 April 1858 at Puddletown, co. Dorset. Died 15, and bur. 20 July 1867 at Harlton aforesaid.

Rev. Francis Sterry, M.A., Rector of Poltimore, co. Devon, 1869. Sometime of Exeter Coll., Oxford. = Augusta Emily, 3rd da., born 23 Dec.1842; bapt. 17 March following at Reigate aforesaid. Mar. 19 May 1864 at St. Leonard's-on-the-Sea, co. Sussex.

Arthur John Goodford, eldest son of Rev. Charles Old Goodford, D.D., Provost of Eton College aforesaid. = Harriet Elizabeth, 4th and youngest da., born 18 Oct.; bapt. 28 Nov. 1845 at Worthing, co. Sussex. Mar. 2 Aug. 1875 at Bradford Peverill, co. Dorset.

Charles Hastings Barton of Maryborough, formerly of Tanunda, Queensland, Australia. Mar, there lia, eldest son. Born 11 Dec. 1828. Bapt. at Vevey in Switzerland. Sometime of Christ Church, Oxford. B.A. 1862.
— 1 wife, Catherine Basedow of Tanunda, in Australia. Mar, there 18 March 1859. Died 29 July 1863, and bur. there. M.I.
= Elizabeth Basedow of Tanunda aforesaid.

Newton Barton, Major-General (retired). Bengal Staff Corps. Sikh War medal. Indian Mutiny medal. 1st and 2nd Afghan Campaign medal. 2nd son. Born 16 Aug., and bapt. 21 Sept. 1831 at St. Mary's, Marylebone, co. Middx. = Edith Catharine, eldest da. of Henry Vansittart of the Bengal Civil Service. Mar. 26 Dec. 1868 at Christ Church, Missourie, in the East Indies.

Charles Frederick Barton, born May 1860, and bapt. at Tanunda aforesaid.

Harriet Catharine, eldest da., born in 1861. Died in 1862.

Catharine, 2nd da., born in 1862.

Harriet, 3rd da., born in 1863.

Lizzie, born 1866.

Johanna, born 1869.

Newton, born 1870.

Minna, born 1872.

Octavia Augusta, born 1873.

Laura Irene, born 1876.

John, born 1878.

Montagu Barton, late a Major in the 86th Regt. of Foot. Born 18 Nov. 1832. Bapt. 10 Feb. following at Walton-on-Thames, Surrey.
= Sarah, 2nd da. of Frederick Smyth, of Tenby, co. Pembroke. Born 19 July 1835. Bapt. at St. Mary, Tenby, and mar. there 19 Aug. 1858. Died 20 March 1869, and bur. there. M.I.
= 2nd wife, Susan Maria, 2nd da. of Rev. Frederick Graeme Middleton, M.A., Rector of Medsted, co. Hants. Mar. 13 Jan.1874 at St. Michael's Church, York Town, co. Surrey.

Augustus Purling Barton of Monressor, near Bundaberg, Queensland, Australia, 4th son. Born 26 Aug. 1834 at Munich, Bavaria. Baptism registered in the Bishop of London's Office, Doctors' Commons, 4 Aug. 1843. = Geraldine De Courcy, 2nd da. of Rev. Maurice Atkins Cooke Collis, D.D., Rector of Clonmel, Queenstown, co. Cork. Mar. at Queenstown 9 Feb. 1869. Died 31 Dec. 1884 in Queensland.

Caroline Delitia.

Robert Maurice Barton, born Feb. 1870.

Hugh Barton, born June 1876.

Geraldine de Courcy, born June 1873.

Maud, born April 1875.

Alice, born Jan. 1880.

D | F

D

F

Charles Frederick Montagu Barton, eldest son, born 21 Nov. 1861. Died 30 Jan. following. Bur. in the Military Cemetery, Keishama Hock, British Caffraria, South Africa. M.I.

Geoffry Travers Barton, 2nd son, born 12 June 1864. Died 10 March following. Bur. at St. Mary, Tenby, aforesaid. M.I.

William Henry Nathaniel Barton, 3rd son, born 12 Jan. 1866, and bapt. at Boldre, co. Southampton. Died Aug. following, and bur. in Mount Jerome Cemetery, Dublin. M.I.

Newton Hastings Barton, 4th son, born 3 May 1868. Bapt. at St. Issell's, co. Pembroke.

Emily Louisa, eldest da., born 3 Aug. 1859. Bapt. at Keishama Hock, Pietermaritzburg, Natal, South Africa.

Harriett Anne, 2nd da., born 1 Aug. 1860. Bapt. at the Military Chapel, Keishama Hock aforesaid.

Annie Augusta, 3rd da., born 18 Nov. 1862. Bapt. at the Parish Church, East London, South Africa.

Nathaniel Cox Barton, Lieut. in the Royal Navy. 5th son. Born at Pesth, in Hungary, 22 March, and bapt. 26 July 1837 at Dresden. Died s.p. at Toynes 4 May 1868. Bur. at Shanegolden, co. Limerick. M.I. Adm'on granted 13 Oct. 1868 in C.P.C. = Jane, eldest da. of Rev. Maurice Atkins Cooke Collis, D.D., Rector of Clonmel aforesaid. Mar. at Fermoy, co. Cork, 13 Dec. 1866.

Robert Crofts Barton, of Toweran, Queensland aforesaid, 6th son, born 6 Oct. 1830 at Dresden in Saxony. Baptism registered in the Bishop of London's Office aforesaid 4 Aug. 1843. Died 10 Aug. 1887 in Queensland. = Anna, 4th da. of Rev. Robert Francis Bute Rickards, Vicar of Constantine, co. Cornwall. Mar. there 27 Sept. 1871.

Geoffry Barton, Colonel 7th Royal Fusiliers. Ashantee War; medal and clasp; South Africa, 1879, medal and clasp; Egypt, 1882; Soudan, 1885, medal and two clasps, Khedive star, 4th class Osmanich. 7th son. Born 22 Feb. 1844 at Stuttgart aforesaid. Baptism registered in the Bishop of London's Office aforesaid 3 March 1845.

William Henry Barton, 8th and youngest son, born 22 Jan. 1848. Died Aug. following. Bur. at Baden Baden in Germany. M.I.

Emilia Harriet, eldest da., born 6 March, and bapt. 10 April 1830 at St. Mary's, Marylebone.

Robert Geoffry. Noel. Lionel Salter. Violet Kathleen. Amy Grace.

Rev. William Eyre Hussey, M.A., of the Hall, Salisbury, co. Wilts, Vicar of Lyneham, in the same county, 1866-1887. Sometime of Christ Church, Oxford. B.A. 1862. M.A. 1866. Rector of Bromsberrow, co. Gloucester, 1887. = Katherine, 2nd da., born 1840 at Dusseldorf, Rhenish Prussia. Baptism registered in the Bishop of London's Office aforesaid 4 Aug. 1843. Mar. 1 June 1864 at Boldre, co. Southampton.

Carolina Delitia, 3rd da., born 27 Sept. 1841 at Dusseldorf aforesaid. Baptism registered at the Bishop of London's Office aforesaid 4 Aug. 1843. Died 27 March 1848. Bur. in Stuttgart aforesaid. M.I.

Harriett Anne, 4th da., born 23 Oct. 1842 at Stuttgart aforesaid. Baptism registered in the Bishop of London's Office aforesaid 4 Aug. 1843.

Augusta Lucretia, 5th and youngest da., born 16 Jan. 1846 at Stuttgart aforesaid. Baptism registered in the Bishop of London's Office aforesaid 29 Dec. 1846.

## Barton Evidences.

### Court Rolls.   Exchequer Augmentations, Portf. 5.

1514, 1515   Henry Barton.
1514, 1515, 1517, 1536, 1537, 1545   John Barton.
1517   John Barton and Alice his wife.
1537   John Barton and Joly his wife.
1537   Margaret Barton.
1515, 1588   William Barton.
1590   William Barton, Sen<sup>r</sup>, and Elizabeth his wife, Richard Barton his son, William Barton, Jun<sup>r</sup>, and Elizabeth his wife, son of William Barton, Sen<sup>r</sup>, and brother of Richard.
1588   Richard Barton.

### Patent Rolls.   Palmer's Indices.

1557   John Barton the elder.
1632   Rev<sup>d</sup> John Barton of Howicke, aged 40.
1632-3   Thomas Barton.
1633-4   Thomas Barton and Rev<sup>d</sup> John Barton, son of Richard (then alive) with brother and sister (wife of . . . . Atkinson), both alive.

Rev<sup>d</sup> Godfrey Barton, Vicar of Brigstock, was buried there 1698.

John Barton, "the elder," became with others tenant of the Manor of Brigstock under the Crown (the manor of Brigstock being part of the Queen's dowry). The manor was afterwards held by Richard Barton, who died 1609, by Thomas (died 1658), by Thomas (died 1704), who in 1703 gave his interest in the manor to his daughter Alice, wife of Thomas Manning. Alice Manning, then widow of Thomas Hunt, sold her interest to the Duke of Montague 1729.

# Upton.

## ABSTRACTS OF WILLS AND RECORDS OF ADMINISTRATION.*

141. Jane Upton† of Oxford, widow.   Dated 20 April 1752.   Whereas my late mother Mrs. Mary Wright by her last will gave to my brother Mr. William Wright £100 which he declared was in trust for me exclusive of my late husband, and whereas, after the death of my said brother, my sister Wright, his exec'x, by a note dated 17 April 1722 did acknowledge that she had £250 principal and interest of said £100, I now dispose of same to my nephew Henry Wright in return for the receipts of mine he can shew since the death of my son William Upton ; to my son Thomas Upton £5, and to his wife my damask gown, etc. ; to my nephew Mr. John Wright the pictures of my father and mother ; to my nephew Mr. John Dewe my brother Richard Dewe's picture ; if I die in Oxford, to be buried in St. Peter's Church by my dear mother ; appoint my son Arthur sole executor.   Affidavits 26 Nov. 1755 of Mary wife of Arthur Upton of Ealing, Midd<sup>x</sup>, and John Wright the younger of the city of Oxford, Esq., to writing of testatrix.   Proved 26 Nov. 1755 by Arthur Upton, son and ex'or.   (300 Paul.)

142. Henry Upton, midshipman on board H.M. Ship "Firebrand."   Dated 1 July 1740.   All my goods and estate to Susannah my wife, of St. Anne's, Limehouse, Midd<sup>x</sup>, and appoint her executrix.   Affidavit 23 Jan. 1756 that testator, late of St. Anne's, Limehouse, Midd<sup>x</sup>, died on or about the 16th inst.   Proved 4 Feb. 1756 by exec'x Susannah Upton, widow.   (54 Glazier.)

143. Joseph Upton‡ of Newington Green, parish St. Mary, Islington, Midd<sup>x</sup>. Dated 3 April 1756.   To my unhappy son George Upton £100 and no more, to be paid him by 12s. a month, and on condition he execute a general release to my ex'ors ; to my kinsman Thomas Ludgate§ of said Newington Green £30 and all my estate and interest in the farm near Newington Green rented of Peter Messers, Esq. ; residue

* Concluded from p. 168.
† Jane Upton, _née_ Wright, was widow of Ambrose Upton, Esq., a brother of Dr. Francis Upton, No. 103, _ante_.
‡ The testator, who was buried at Stoke Newington, Middx., 10 April 1756, was brother of George Upton who made will No. 136.
§ Thomas Ludgate of Hornsey, Middx., married Susanna Upton of Stoke Newington, spinster, 19 Nov. 1751.

of my estate to be converted into money, and two-thirds thereof to use of the child or children of my son-in-law John Palmer* of Newington Green, and the other third to my daughter Susan wife of said John Palmer; appoint executors my kinsman John Bowshed [? Bowstred] of Upper Holloway, Midd<sup>x</sup>, farmer, and friend John Wallbank of Highbury Barn, Midd<sup>x</sup>, farmer. Proved 8 April 1756 by both ex'ors. (124 Glazier.)

144. Henry Upton of Crookeston, Southampton, labourer. Dated 24 Sept. 1753. To Thomas my son my leasehold messuage in which I dwell in Cookeston, household goods, etc. ; to Jane Piper my daughter £12 ; residue to George my eldest son, and appoint him executor. Proved 13 April 1758 by ex'or. (136 Hutton.)

145. Thomas Upton of St. John's, Wapping, Midd<sup>x</sup>. Adm'on 30 May 1758 to the relict Sarah.

### NOTE.

The foregoing abstracts include every Upton will and administration recorded in London prior to the year 1758. Probably as many more may be found in the local registries of the different dioceses of England and in the courts called "Peculiar." I have memoranda of the will of Hugh Upton of Brixham, dated 1624, proved at Exeter ; and of wills, all proved at Chester, of the following persons, viz., John Upton of Winslow, 1582 ; Lawrence Upton of Prestbury, 1606 ; John Upton of Danerow, yeoman, 1629 ; and John Upton of Bollinfer, husbandman, 1641.

There were but fourteen Upton wills recorded in Dublin prior to the year 1800. Of the makers of these, three were of the Castle Upton family (viz., Nos. 98 and 128, *ante*, and Arthur Upton, whose will, dated 8 April 1763, proved 10 Nov. 1769, mentions only his wife Sarah) ; six, of whom the earliest is No. 105, *ante*, were of co. Limerick ; two of Cork ; two of Dublin ; and one of co. Tyrone.

---

### FROM THE DISTRICT REGISTRY AT LINCOLN.†

146. Thomas Upton of Honyngton. Dated 2 Feb. 1530. To be buried in church of St. Wylfryde of Honyngton. Bequests to High Altar there and to o<sup>r</sup> Ladye warke of Lyncoln ; to Margaret Ham my best gowne ; to my brother William Upton my best doblet and a pare of hose; to the iii sonys of Richerd Upton ; to my brother Richerde a mare and a fele [? filly], a frese cot, an ax and a wymbell ; to John Roper ; to John Glasyer my best bonnet ; to Robert Bevercots a bonnet ; to the chylde y<sup>t</sup> my wyffe is wythall ; to Schelton churche. Residue to my wife Elizabeth, and appoint her exec'x. Witnesses, Sir Alexander Mannyng, William Bothby, John Bothby, John Sutton, Robert Bevercots. Proved at Grantham *ult.* Feb. 1530. (1520–31,‡ 308.)

147. Nicholas Upton§ th'elder esqwyer of Northolme besyde Waynflete. Dated 8 Jan. 1533, 24 Henry VIII. To the iiij orders of frerys of Boston x<sup>s</sup> each ; to Chantry prestes of Corpus Xti in Boston x<sup>s</sup> for a trentall ; x<sup>s</sup> to the frerys in Boston to syng a trentall for me at Scala Celi ; to Northolme church vi<sup>s</sup> viij<sup>d</sup> ; to All Hallowys in Waynflete iij<sup>s</sup> iiij<sup>d</sup> ; to my sonne Nicholas my swanne marke w<sup>t</sup> the halffe barrys for terme of hys lyffe with remainder to my sonne John ; to sonne Hamond my swanne marke w<sup>t</sup> ij halffe mounes ; to sonne John my swanne marke w<sup>t</sup> the barre and iij nykks. Residue to sonne John, he to pay xxx<sup>li</sup> equally to Isabell and Barbara daughters of Robert Barret‖ at lawful age. All my lands in the parts of Lyndesey, co. Lincoln, to son John Upton¶ in tail, he to fynde a preste to synge for my soule, bothe my wyffes soulys and my father and mother and all Xten

---

* John Palmer of Stoke Newington married Susanna Upton of the same, spinster, April 12, 1744.

† The following are abstracts (received too late to appear in their proper place, chronologically) of all the Upton wills recorded in the District Registry at Lincoln, from its beginning in 1507 to the year 1750.

The Episcopal Registers of the Diocese of Lincoln (which, before the Reformation, comprised the counties of Lincoln, Rutland, Leicester, Northampton, Oxford, Buckingham, Bedford, Hertford, and Huntingdon) contain no Upton wills between the years 1280 and 1547.

‡ The volumes of these Registers are designated by the years which they include.

§ The testator is that Nicholas Upton described in the Visitation of 1564, printed on a previous page, as marrying first Alice Flite and second Margaret Sutton.

‖ Robert Barret was the first husband of testator's daughter Dorothy.

¶ The son John Upton made will No. 148.

soulys for xx<sup>ty</sup> yeres. Remainders over to son Hamond* and then to Isabell and Dorothe my dau'rs. Bequest to the repair of highway between Waynflet and Spillesby,—remainder to Richerd Wolmer and Isabell my daughter. To my sonne Nicholas x markes yerely unto suche season as he be promotyd by the Religion of St. John† and take the profetts theruppon; to sonne Hamond x<sup>li</sup> yerely for life in full satisfaction of Richmonde fee. All my lands in Holland [co. Lincoln] to my son John in tail; to my brother Adryan Upton xl<sup>s</sup> yerely for life. Ex'ors my sonne John Upton and Mr. doctor Smyth warden of the Gray frerys in Lincoln; supervisor my cosen John Lytylbery. Witness these men foloyng, John Lytylbery esqwyer, Richerde Wolmer esqwyer, John Upton gent, John Skupholm preste, John Johnson preste, William Vavosore gent, w<sup>t</sup> many other. Proved at Parteney x Nov. 1533 by John Upton, power reserved to Doctor Smyth. (1532–4, 210.)

148. John Upton,‡ esquyer, mayd at Northolme besyde Waynflete 17 July 26 Henry VIII. (1534). Lands in Northolme, Waynflete All Hallowys, Waynflete St. Marye, ffryskeny, Croft, Thorpe, and Ingolmellys to wife Elizabeth§ for life, in full recompense of her firste joynter and dower, she to fynde a preste for xx yeres according to the will of my fader; son Nicholas to have to hys exhibicion to he cum to the age of xxj yeres x<sup>li</sup> yerely out of lands in Legborne, Carleton, Reston, Gayton, and Thedilthorpe; ccc marks to be taken for payment of my debts; to my hunkill Adryan Upton xxxvj<sup>s</sup> viij<sup>d</sup> yerely for life besyde x<sup>s</sup> of my father bequeste;|| to cosyn John Lytylbery and cosyn Thomas Moygne xl<sup>s</sup> yerely each for life. To be buryd where it shall please God (sic). Bequests to o<sup>r</sup> Ladye of Lincoln and the iiij orders of frerys of Boston; to Anchorys of Boston iij<sup>s</sup> iiij<sup>d</sup>; to St. Thomas' churche of Northolme; appoint my wife Elizabeth exec<sup>x</sup>; xl<sup>li</sup> to be taken out of my lands for my funerallys and other days; my syster Dorothe Hatclyff ¶ xx<sup>ty</sup> marks over and besydes xxx<sup>li</sup> appoynted to her children by the laste will of my fader, yff she be good to my wyffe. Witnesses, Sir John Copuldyke, Kt., John Lytylbery, Esq., David Coward, doctor in medicens, Thomas Lytilbery, gent., Sir Robert Smyth, preste, Richerde Hartypole, and William Johnson, with many others. Proved at Lincoln 3 March 1534 by exec'x. (1534 et divers, 9.)

149. Valentine Upton** of Northolme, Esq. Dated 1 Dec. 1616. Mentions daughter Frances,†† aged under 12; son Hamond Upton;‡‡ uncle Ambrose

* The son Hamond Upton made will No. 12.

† This is, of course, the distinguished Knight of the Order of St. John of Jerusalem, Sir Nicholas or the Chevalier Upton, whom the Uptons of Devonshire have long been prone to claim as a fair branch from *their* family tree. He is called " Knight of the Rodes " in the Lincoln Visitation of 1564. He did not long remain in Lincolnshire to attend to his " swannes," but was soon " promotyd by the Religion," and early became one of the most valiant Knights of the Order. Even a search of the records at Malta does not disclose many facts regarding him. If it is true, as has been stated, that he made an attack on the famous corsair Dragut at Tarsheu in Malta in 1546, that may have been the service for which he was rewarded by being chosen, Oct. 5, 1547, " Auditor Computorum " for the " venerable Language of England." Nov. 15, 1547, he was appointed, by Grand Master Omedes, " Commander of Repton (or Ripston) in the Language of England," and shortly after he was exalted to the dignity of Turcopolier—the third dignitary in the Convent; one entry states that the Grand Master and Counsel chose him, " Nicolaum optum," " in locum tenentem Turcopulerij seu turcopuleriatus " 22 Dec. 1547, while another says they chose " nicolaum octum " " in tercupulerium relegionis " 5 Nov. 1548. In 1551 Dragut attempted to land in Malta, but was repulsed by the knights headed by Upton; and upon that occasion he added greatly to his laurels. He is said to have died in July of that year, probably of sunstroke, though one account says " of his wounds."

‡ Testator was eldest son of Nicholas Upton who made will No. 147.

§ The wife Elizabeth was daughter of William Copledike.

|| Sic, but the father bequeathed Adryan 40s. *per annum.*

¶ Dorothy had formerly been wife of Robert Barret, mentioned in will No. 147.

** The testator was son of Hamond Upton who made will No. 17.

†† This Frances Upton, who died at Northolme in 1643, had by her husband, Rev. Everard Dighton, a daughter Mary, born at Northolme 1639 (who married Thomas Dobbs and had issue Thomas and Mary), and an only son William, born at Croft 1641, who died *s.p.* 1702. Everard Dighton married (second) widow Frances Saltmarshe, and (third) Frances Andrewes, widow, daughter of Edward, second son of Lord Willoughby of Parham, the gallant defender of Barbadoes against the fleet under Sir George Ayscue.

‡‡ The son Hamond Upton made will No. 31.

Upton;* sister Standish.† Appoint John Piggot, Esq., William Lanckton, Esq., and William Suadring, Esq., ex'ors, and Sir Thomas Grantham, Kt., supervisor. Adm'on granted 31 Dec. 1616 to Frances Ayscough of Sotby, widow, mother of deceased, and Walter Dacres of Sotby, husband of Dorothy, sister of deceased, principal creditors. (1616, 191.)

150. Henry Upton of Hough on the Hill, yeoman. Dated 19 Jan. 1626. To be buried in Hough church. To daughters Elizabeth Alvey and Parnell Gelstrope x$^{li}$ each ; to sonne in law William Andrew v$^{li}$, and to Dorothye his nowe wiefe xx$^s$ ; to their daughter Elis$^{th}$, my goddaughter ; to poor of Hough xxx$^s$; poor of Gelson x$^s$ ; poor of Brandon v$^s$ ; to kinsman John Crayle of Broughton xx$^s$ ; to John Newis of Blanckney xx$^s$ ; to the church a new communion cloth ; to maidservants Marie Sewell and Marie Kemp, each v$^s$. My house and lands in Hough and Gelson to my two sonnes in lawe James Gelstrope and Richard Alvey to be divided. To the four children of Richard Alvey; to the three children of James Gelstrope ; to Mr. Edmond Thorold of Hough xx$^s$ ; to Mr. Righton our minister xx$^s$; to two menservants xii$^d$ each. Residue to my two sonnes in law, and appoint them ex'ors. Signed by mark. Witnesses, Edmond Thorold, Mathew Righton, Robert Thorold, Augustine Bee, sen$^r$, and John Warinn. Proved at Lincoln 18 Dec. 1627 by ex'or. (1627, 194.)

151. William Upton of Whapload, husbandman. Dated 14 May 1630. To mother church of Lincolne iiij$^d$ ; to grandchild John Upton 2$^{li}$ at 21 ; to son John his two children 2$^{li}$ at 21 ; to sons Robert and William Upton iij$^s$ iiij$^d$ each. Appoint wife Isabell and daughter Ann exec'xs. Signed by mark. Witnesses, Robert Avelin and Thomas Sagar. Proved at Boston (Eng.) 24 May 1630. (1630, 599.)

152. William Upton of Moulton, husbandman. Dated 12 Dec. 1691. Mentions brother Andrew Upton. Bequest to son John Upton to be put out for his use, also a brown filly and a gun, also (at 14) a Bible that was his brother Andrew's. Bequest to daughter Sarah Upton at 21, also a box standing in the parlour. Appoint daughter Susannah exec'x, and my trusty and beloved friend John Aubins of Moulton guardian for my children. Signed by mark. Witnesses, Martin Heaton, Xtofere Eland, and (by mark) John Upton. Proved at Lincoln 3 Oct. 1692. (1692, B'k I., 46.)

153. Samuel Upton of Lusby, blacksmith. Adm'on‡ 18 April 1724 to George Howgrave of Horncastle,§ gent., principal creditor. Surety, Thomas Snelling of the same, merchant. Inventory annexed £25 14s. 6d.

154. John Upton of Whaplode Drove, husbandman. Dated 29 May 1725. Mentions Sarah Upton [? wife, illegible]. To sister Alice ffalkner £4 4s.; to mother Mary Marchent 5$^s$ ; James Hoolt to have his freedome and receive his rent, and have a coat and wascoat and briches, a paire of stokings and 2 shirts. Witnesses, John Phenix, R$^d$ ffaulkner. Seal illegible. [No probate annexed.] (1725, 241.)

155. Henry Upton of Swaton, grazier. Dated 28 April 1741. To sons Henry, John, Thomas, William, and Samuel £100 each at 18 ; to Martha and Mary Upton 3 score and teen poundes each at 18, they to be brought up by my wife. Sealed with a cornucopia. Witnesses, Hen. Upton, John Upton. Proved 9 Oct. 1741. (1741, . . .)

* This Ambrose Upton signed the Upton pedigree, printed on a preceding page, at the Visitation of Lincoln in 1634.

† This sister was wife of Thomas Standish. I suppose her name was Faith.

‡ The Act Books for the Archdeaconry of Lincoln (the greater part of the county), long lost and but recently discovered, contain administrations from the year 1558, but the index begins with the year 1700. The Act Books for the Archdeaconry of Stow contain administrations from 1530, and are indexed from 1580. The above, from the Lincoln Archdeaconry, is the only Upton administration in these indices.

§ The Horncastle Register mentions : "1560, June 13, Jhone Upton sepulta."

# The Regestrie booke off Bramefeide off all Christnyngs Weddyngs and Buryings ffrom The feast of Seynt Mychaell Tharkan'gell be ... in the xxxtie yeare of Kyng henrye viijth.

*On the inside of this leaf is written:*

Henry son of Regnold Rabet* and Alys his wife was baptized Feb. 28, 1563-4.
Anne daught[r] of Ranould Rabit and Alys his wife bap. July xix 1565.

| | | |
|---|---|---|
| Mary daught[r] of the same | . . . | „ Aug. 1566. |
| Regnould | do. . . . | „ April 1568. |
| John . | . . . . | „ July 1569. |
| George . | . . . . | „ Sep. 1570. |

*On the outside of the cover of the first book is written the following:*

In this Book is an account of the burial of John Denney,† Vicar of Bramfeeld, that wrote the Customs of Bramfield.

*On the inside of the cover is written:*

Y[e] yeare off o[r] lorde A M cccccLXV.

Lowe . . . . . . . . Syr ffransses Roovses curate off the p'reshe off . . . . olde youe shall knowe that I askede y[e] banes off Matrimone betwexte Rynolde Wese & Margrete Pake There [? three] Solame dayes & There ys no cavse ffovnde but y[t] you maye mary them accordyng to the laves of god & thys Reme no more to you at thys tyme but Jhesu preser you & kepe you In the lord god. Amen.

By me your frend to my lytyll poore Rychard Jaye vycar of bra'felde
the xxvi daye J'e Jhe' enkepe us all now & ever. Amen.

## The booke of Christenyngs w[t]in the seid Towne & p'ysh of Bramefeilde ffrome the ffeast of Seynt Mychaell Tharkan'gell being in the yeare off o .. lord god a Thowsand ffyve hundreth xxxixth And The xxxtie yeare of the Reign of King henrye theight.

1539. XXX° HEN. VIII.

| | |
|---|---|
| Nov. 14 | Thomas ffelaye sonne of John ffelaye and Olyfe his wyffe. |
| Nov. 26 | Roger Ameill sonne of John Ameill gent. and Dorythie his wyf. |
| Dec. | None was christened y[t] moneth. |
| Jan. 6 | John Neyle son'e of John Neyle and [blank] his wyff. |
| Jan. 22 | Edmond Watlyng sonne of Will'm Watlyng and [blank] his wyf. |
| Feb. 18 | Katheryne Robson dowghter of Hamond Robson and . . . . |
| Mar. 13 | Robart Palmer sone of Thomas Palm' and [blank] his wyf. |
| Mar. 15 | John Chapplayne sone of John Chapplayne and [blank] his wyffe. |
| Mar. 22 | Nycholes ffelaye sone of Rob't ffelaye and [blank] his wyfe. |
| April 12 | Margaret Watlyng dowghter of Edmond Watlyn' and Alice his wyfe. |
| April 19 | John Reve son'e of John Reve and [blank] his wyff. |
| May | None christened. |
| June 3 | Anne Melle dowght' of Rob't Mell and [blank] his wyf. |

| | |
|---|---|
| July 3 | Roger Ward sonne of Roger Warde and [blank] his wyf. |
| July 30 | Robart Knyght [and] Regynald Knyght bastards sones of Johnne Knyght wydowe. |
| 1539. | The holle yeare Christened xiiij Children, whereoff Men Children xi whereof Bastards ij, Women Children iij. |
| 1540. | In the yeare of our lord god A Thousand ffyve hundreth & ffortie & in the xxxj yeare of the Reign of King henry VIII[th] was Christened at Bramefeild as hereafter ffolloweth. |
| Nov. 10 | Edmond ffelaye of John ffelay and Olyff his wyfe. |
| Dec. 15 | Richard Clerke sone of Rob't Clerke and [blank] his wyff. |
| Feb. 22 | Alice ffarro' bastard dowghter of Agnes ffarro' wydowe. |
| Mar. 3 | Margerye Browne dowghter of Mathie Browne and [blank] his wyfe. |
| Mar. 18 | Margarite Thruston bastard dowghter of Alice Thruston singlewoman. |
| April 12 | Johnne Veysye bastard dowghter of M'garete Veysye, synglewoman. |

---

* The Rabett family still hold property in Bramfield. They are owners of the Bramfield Hall estate. In the park the decayed trunk of the "Bramfield oak" is still standing.

† There is, however, no mention of John Denney's burial in these Registers; the leaf on which the notice was written must have been taken out, or the writer of the notice must have assumed, without investigation, that his burial was entered herein. He was a resident vicar, and the register is continued into the days of his successors.

May 3 Johnne Veysye dowghter of Thomas Veysye yong<sup>r</sup> and his wyfe.

May 22 Edmond Watlyng sonne of Edmond Watlyng and Alice his wyfe.

May 25 Brygette Reve [and] Marthee Reve dowghters of Nycholes Reve and Annes his wyfe.

July 6 Elizabeth Ameill dowghter of John Ameill gent. and Dorythie his wyfe.

Aug. 20 Will'm ffelay son of Thomas felaye and [blank] his wyfe.

Sep. 17 Anne Veysie dowghter of Thomas Veysye and [blank] his wyfe.

Oct. 1 Thomas Borley sone of Robarte Borley and [blank] his wyffe.

The holle yere Christened xiv<sup>th</sup> Children, whereof Men Children 6, Women Children ix whereof Bastards iij.

1541. In the yeare of our lord god, etc., as before.

Nov. 24 ffr'nnc's Melle dowghter of Rob't Melle gent. and [blank] his wyff.

Jan. 15 Isabell Neile dowghter of John Neyle and [blank] his wyff.

Jan. 16 Nycholes Knyghts sone of Ric' Knyghts and [blank] his wyff.

April 5 Nicholes Coye sone of John Coye and [blank] his wyfe.

May 10 Anne Wryght dowghter of Henrye Wryght and Christyn his wyfe.

June 14 Joh'nne Warde dowghter of Rog' Ward and [blank] his wyfe.

This yeare Christened vj Children, whereof Men Children ij, Women Children iiij, Bastards n°.

1542. In the yeare of our lord god, etc., as before.

Nov. 30 Brygytte Ells dowghter of [blank] Ells and [blank] his wyffe.

Feb. 14 Anthony Game sone of Rob't Game and [blank] his wyff.

This yeare Christened ij Children, whereof Men Children one, Women Children one, Bastards n°.

1543. In the yeare of our lord god, etc., as before.

Feb. 2 Philippe Ameile dowght<sup>r</sup> of John Ameile gent. and Dorythie his wyfe.

Mar. 7 Joh'nn Robson dowght<sup>r</sup> of Hamond Robson and [blank] his wyff.

Mar. 10 Brygytt ffelay dowght<sup>r</sup> of John felay and Olyf his wyffe.

Mar. 12 Edmond ffarro' sone of Edmond ffarro' and [blank] his wyff.

July 26 Katheryn Knyghts dowght<sup>r</sup> of Ric' Knyghts and [blank] his wyf.

Sep. 25 Christyn Whyght and Joh'nne Whyght dowght's of Will'm Whyght and [blank] his wyf.

Sep. 28 John Ameile sone of Will'm Ameill and [blank] his wyffe.

This yeare Christened viij Children, whereof Men Children ij, Women Children vj, Bastards none.

1544. In the yeare of our lord god, etc., as before.

Jan. 2 Alice Tylar bastard dowght<sup>r</sup> of Alice Tyla<sup>r</sup>.

Feb. 12 Anne Melle dowght' of Henry Mell gent. and ffr'nnc's his wyf.

Mar. 7 Nycholes Walpule sone of Nic' Walpule the yonger and [blank] his wyfe.

Mar. 20 Katheryn Watson dowght' of Will'm Watson and [blank] his wyf.

April 2 Margery Wryght dowght' of Henry Wryght and Christyn his wyfe.

April 30 Nicholes ffelay sone of Thomas ffelay and [blank] his wyff.

May 1 Elyn Ameill dowghter of John Ameile and Dorythie his wyfe.

Sep. 4 Marye Burgs dowght' of Rob't Burgs gent. and [blank] his wyff.

Sep. 6 Alice ffelay dowght' of Robart ffelaye and [blank] his wyf.

Sep. 30 Olyff ffarro' dowght' of Edmond ffarro' and [blank] his wyffe.

This yeare Christened x Children, whereof Men Children ij, Women Children viij whereof Bastards one.

1545. In the yeare, etc., as before.

Oct. 8 ffr'nnc's Watlyng sone of Edmond Watlyng and Alice his wyffe.

Feb. 8 Nycholes ffelay sone of John ffelay and Olyff his wyffe.

Feb. 12 Henry Neyle sone of John Neyle and [blank] his wyff.

Feb. 17 Margaret Ameill dowght' of Will'm Ameill and [blank] his wyff.

This yeare Christened iiij Child'n, whereof Men Children iij, Women Children one, Bastards none.

1546. In the yeare of, etc., as before.

Nov. 24 John Watlyng sone of W<sup>m</sup> Watlyng and [blank] his wyffe.

April 12 Agnes Crispe dowght' of John Crispe and [blank] his wyf.

May 2 Robarte Robson and Margaret Robson sone and dowghter of Hamond Robson.

July 8 ffyllice Knyght dowght'of Ric' Knyghts and [blank] his wyf.

July 17 Dorythie Harp dowghter of Rowland Harp and [blank] his wyf.

Aug. 11 Margery ffelaye dowghter of Robart ffelay and [blank] his wyfe.

Aug. 14 John fford sone of John fford and Margery his wyf.

Sep. 16 Arthure Walpule and John Walpule son'es of Nycholes Walpule and [blank] his wyffe.

This yeare Christened x Children, whereof Men Children 5, Women Childre' 5, Bastards none.

1547. In The yeare of our lord god A Thousand ffyve hundreth fortie & vij & the ffirst yeare of the Reign of King Edward the vj<sup>th</sup> was Christened at Bramefeild as here After ffollowethe fromeMychaelmes to Mychaelmes being one holl yeare & halff & in y° last yeare of kyng henry the viij<sup>th</sup> & so to y° Ann'ncyac'on of oure ladye.

Dec. 6 John Watlyng y° vj day of Decemb' in the last yeare of the Reign of king henry viij<sup>th</sup> The Sone of Edmond Watlyng & Alice his wyffe.

*On the margin is written :* Not' the deathe of kyng henry viij^th And y^e Raign of king Edward y^e vj^th.

The xxviij^th daye of Januarie in the yeare of our lord god A Thousand ffyve hundreth ffortie and vj dep'ted this present lyff our moost Noble King Henry the viij^th and was Royallye buryed At Wynsore the xvi^th day of ffebruarie in the same yeare And The xxxi^th day of Januarie begane King Edward the Sext his Royall Raign in the yeare of oure lord god 1546.

Feb.  3  John Watson sone of Will'm Watson and [*blank*] his wyf.
Mar. 14  Thomas fforman sone of Thomas fforman and [*blank*] his wyfe.
[*blank*]  Jaspar Mell sonne of Henry Mell gent. and ffr'nnc's his wyfe.
June 25  George ffelay sone of Thomas ffelay and [*blank*] his wyfe.
July 19  Marye Burye dowghter of John Berye and [*blank*] his wyff.
Aug.  4  Margaret ffelowe dowghter of Rob't ffelowe and M'garet his wyff.
Aug. 13  Christofer ffarro' sone of Nycholes ffarro' and Agnes his wyf.
Aug. 25  Nycholes Gyrlyng sone of Robart Gyrlyng and Joh'nne his wyf.
Sep.  9  Joh'nne Wryght dowghter of Henry Wryght and Christyn his wyf.
Nov. 30  Mary Joyn' dowghter of John Joyn' and [*blank*] his wyff.

This yeare & halff Christened xi Children, whereof Men Children vij, Women Children iiij, Bastards none.

1548.  In the yeare of, *etc., as before.*

April 10  Richard Walpule sone of Nycholes Walpule the Yonger.
April 13  Edward Brynd sone of [*blank*].
May 12  Rob't fford sone of John fford and M'gerye his wyfe.
May 17  Joh'nne Hynds dowght' of Henry Hynd and [*blank*] his wyf.
May 27  Arthure Melle sone of Henry Melle gent. and ffr'nnc's his wyfe.
June  4  Paule Crispe sone of John Crispe and [*blank*] his wyffe.
Aug.  6  Samuell ffyske sone of Jaferay ffyske and Joh'nne his wyf.
Oct. 29  Robart ffelay sone of John ffelay and Olyf his wyff.
Feb. 18  Olyff Girlyng dowght' of Rob't Girlyng and Joh'ne Girlyng his wyf.
Mar.  8  Agnes Paycoke bastard dowghter of Alice Paycoke.
Mar. 10  Margaret Alderman dowghter of [*blank*] Alderman and [*blank*] his wife.

This yeare Christened xi Children, whereof Men Children vij, Women Children iiij whereof Bastards one.

1549.  In the yeare, *etc., as before.*

May 21  fflowrence Crispe dowghter of John Crispe and [*blank*] his wyf.
May 26  John Wryght bastard sone of Margaret Wryght.
May 29  Amos ffarro' sone of Edmond ffarro' and [*blank*] his wyf.

June  9  Dorythie ffelaye dowght' of Robart felay and M'garet his wyf.
June 26  Prudence Watlyng dowght' of Will'm Watlyng and [*blank*] his wyfe.
July  6  Margaret Bery dowghter of John Berye and [*blank*] his wyfe.
July 21  Marye Mell dowghter of Henry Mell gent. and ffr'nnc's his wyfe.
Aug. 20  Nycholes Ameile sone of John Ameile gent. and Dorythie his wyf.
Sep.  2  Gerytrude Neyle dowght' of John Neyle and [*blank*] his wyf.
Sep.  7  George Harp sone of Rowland Harp and [*blank*] his wyf.
Oct.  7  Esdras fforman sone of Thomas fforman and Joh'nn his wyf.
Nov.  3  Georg Cocke sone of Robart Cocke and [*blank*] his wyf.
Dec.  8  Habrah'm Watlyng sone of Edmond Watlyng and Alice his wyf.
Dec. 12  Anne Joyn' dowght' of John Joyn' and [*blank*] his wyff.
Jan.  6  Edward ffelay sone of Thomas ffelaye and Alice his wyf.
Jan.  7  Elizabeth ffelay dowghter of Rob't ffelay theld' and [*blank*] his wyf.
Jan. 29  Henry Wryght and Alice Wryght sone and dowt' of Henry Wryght and Christyn his wyffe.
Feb.  2  Margaret Walpule dowght' of Ric' Walpule thong' and [*blank*] his wyf.

This yeare Christened xix Children, whereof Men Children ix whereof Bastards one, Women Children x.

1550.  In the yeare, *etc., as before.*

April 20  Robart Calthrope sone of Anthony Calthrope.
May  5  Sicilie Thorton dowght' of Edmond Thorton.
June  7  Thomasyn fford dowght' of John fford and Margerie his wyf.
June 16  Richard Benet sone of W^m Benet and Elizabeth his wyf.
June 30  Joh'nne Garrold dowghter of Regynald Garrold and Alice his wyfe.
Aug. 18  Henry Wryght sone of Thomas Wryght and M'garet his wyf.
Sep. 15  Anne ffarro' dowght' of Nycholes ffarro' and Agnes his wyff.
Oct. 18  Ric. Pecke bastard sone of Agnes Pecke.
Jan.  1  Nycholes ffelay sone of Rob't ffelay and M'garet his wyff.
Jan. 12  Margaret Cocke dowghter of Ric' Cocke.
Feb. 24  Joh'nne ffarro' dowght' of Edmond ffarro'.

This yeare Christened xi Childre', whereof Men Children v whereof Bastards one, Women Children vj.

1551.  In the yeare, *etc., as before.*

May 11  Henry ffelay sone of John ffelaye and Olyf his wyffe.
May 15  Margaret Matles dowght' of Will'm Matles and Annes his wyfe.
May 25  Marye Sphanke dowght' of Henry Sphanke.

Aug. 26   Rachell Melle dowght' of Henry Melle gent. and ffr'nnc's his wyf.

Oct. 25   Brygett Thurton dowght' of Edmond Thurton.

Nov. 11   Marye Calthrope dowght' of Anthony Calthrope.

Dec. 21   Pacyence Walpule dowght' of Ric' Walpule.

Jan. 15   John ffreston sone of Ric' ffreston.

Jan. 18   Margaret Harp dowght' of Roland Harp.

Jan. 27   Henry Joyn' sonne of John Joyn'.

Jan. 29   John Benet sone of W^m Benet and Elizabeth his wyf.

Feb. 15   Chrystyn Thurlyng dowght' of Nyc' Thurlyng and Christyn his wyf.

Feb. 17   Grace fforman dowght' of Thomas fforman.

This yeare Christened xiij Children, whereof Men Children iiij, Women Children ix, Bastards none.

1552.   In the yeare, *etc., as before.*

May 16   Jaferye Reve sone of John Reve.

May 17   Nycholes fforman sone of Thomas fforman.

May 18   Olyff Garrold dowght' of Raynald Garrold and Alice his wyf.

June 29   Thobie Neyle sone of John Neyle.

July 12   Grace ffelay dowght' of Rob't felay theld' and M'garet his wyf.

July 20   Alice Alderman dowght' of [*blank*] Alderman.

Aug. 2   Elizabet Will'ms dowght' of John Will'ms and Katheryne his wyf.

Aug. 23   Jeremye Wryght sone of Henry Wryght and Christyn his wyf.

Sep. 21   Grace ffarro' dowght' of Edmond ffarro'.

Oct. 18   John Dowsyng sone of Thomas Dowsyng.

Nov. 22   Henry Girlyng sone of Robart Girlyng and Joh'n his wyf.

Feb. 27   Margaret fford dowghter of John fforde and M'gery his wyf.

This yeare Christened xii Children, whereof Men Children vj, Women Children vj, Bastards none.

1553.

*On the margin is written :* The Death of King Edward the Sext of that name And the begynnyng of Quens Marie hir gracyous Raign.

M^d. The Sixt day of Julie dep'ted out of this world the Noble Prynce Edward the vj^th of that name & dyed At grenewyche in the xvj^th yeare of his Aige & is buryed At westm' whose soule god take to his Infynyte m'cie Amen. And the xx^tie day of Julie 1553 was p'claimed & begane hir Raign our moost gracyous Sou'aign Ladye and Quene Marie hir grace then being at fframyngh'm in Suff.

Aug. 16   Joh'n Alderman dowght' of John Alderman.

Oct. 23   ffr'nnc's Will'ms dowght' of John Will'ms and Katheryn his wyff.

Oct. 24   Marye ffarro' dowght' of Nicholes ffarro' and Agnes his wyf.

Jan. 23   Alice Thurlyng dowght' of Nic' Thurlyng and Christyn his wyf.

Mar. 1   Mary Benet dowght' of W^m Benet and Elizabeth his wyff.

Mar. 22   Margaret Wryght dowght' of Thomas Wryght and M'garet his wyff.

This yeare Christened vi Children, whereof Men Children none, Women Children vi, Bastards none.

(*To be continued.*)

## 𝔊resham 𝔐emoranda.

Indenture 25 July, 12 Jac. I., 1614, between Thomas Gresham of Fulham, Esq., Richard Wenman of Frengford, co. Oxon, Esq., and Dame Elizabeth Garrard of Dorney, co. Bucks, widow.   Recites will of Emynne Ogle of Edmonton, widow, dated 18 Sep. 1554, whereby being seised in demesne as of fee of certain lands, messuages, and tenements in the parish of St. Stevens in London over against Moregate, she devised them to Edward Leeke of Edmonton, Gent., and his heirs for ever.   The said Edward Leeke, by deed indented dated 27 April 44 Elizabeth, conveyed said premises to Thomas Gresham and Richard Wenman and to the heirs of said Thomas Gresham for ever.   Conveyance by Thomas Gresham and Richard Wenman to Dame Elizabeth Garrard and her heirs for ever.

Signed   *Tho: gresham*

*RYCHARD WENMAN.*

Endorsed Gresham and Wenman to Lady Garrard, barg. and sale, 25 July

1614, 12 Jacob. I.    Memorandum of 18 Nov. 1614, witnessed by Thomas Maye, William Segar, Garter, Benjamin Drury, Jo. Kedemister.

Thomas Gresham of Fulham was eldest son of John Gresham of North End, Fulham, mercer, by Elizabeth, daughter and heir of Edward Dormer, and grandson of Sir John Gresham, Knight, Lord Mayor of London 1547.    He was baptized at St. Ethelbert, London.    Married, 1st, Isabel, daughter of . . . . Holt and relict of John Gibbons of Southwark ; and, 2ndly, Judith, daughter of Sir William Garrard of Dorney, co. Bucks, Knight ; she remarried at St. Giles in the Fields 24 April 1639 William Morley, and died 21 Dec. 1660.    He died at Fulham 11 July 1620. Will dated 8 July 1619 ; proved in P.C.C. 17 July 1620 (Soame 74).

Richard Wenman of Souldern and Fringford, co. Oxon, was son of William Wenman of Fringford, by Elizabeth, daughter of Stephen Power of Wilton, Oxon, and grandson of Sir Thomas Wenman of Carswell, co. Oxon.    He married, 1st, Amy, daughter of Edward Bond of Carswell ; and, 2nd, Elizabeth, daughter of Sir George Throckmorton of Fulbrook, co. Bucks.    In the chancel of Fringford Church is a stone upon the ground with this inscription : " Here lyeth ye body of Richard Wenman Esquire who dyed ye xi of February Anno D'ni 1637."    11 Sep. 1637.    Commission to Thomas Wenman, son and heir of Richard Wenman, to administer ; Elizabeth Wenman, the widow, having renounced.

Elizabeth Lady Garrard was widow of Sir William Garrard of Dorney, Knight (son of Sir William Garrard, Knight, Lord Mayor of London 1555), who died 17 Nov. 1607, and was buried at Dorney the 8 Dec. following (Fun. Cert. Coll. of Arms, 1-16, p. 255).    She was youngest daughter of Sir Thomas Rowe, Knight, Lord Mayor of London 1569, by Mary, eldest daughter of Sir John Gresham, Knight, Lord Mayor.    She was mother of Judith, second wife of Thomas Gresham of Fulham.    Her will (Byrde 110), dated 31 Dec. 1623, was proved in P.C.C. 22 Dec. 1624.    She mentions therein her daughter Judith Gresham.

Sir John Kedermister, Knighted at Hampton Court 3 Oct. 1609, was of Langley, co. Bucks, son of Edmund Kedermister by Anne, daughter of John Leigh, Esq., of Addington, Surrey.    He married Mary, eldest daughter of Sir William Garrard of Dorney, sister of Judith, wife of Thomas Gresham.    Her will (66 Goare), dated 20 Nov. 1631, was proved in the P.C.C. 6 May 1637.

Bargain and sale by Thomas Gresham of Braisborough, co. Lincoln, gentleman, and Ann Mackworth of Empingham, co. Rutland, widow, in consideration of £80 paid to Ann Mackworth, to Thomas Eayre of Ordsall, co. Nottingham, gent., and Thomas Davis of East Retford, in said county, yeoman, of messuages and tenements, etc., in Ordsall and Thrumpton, co. Nottingham, to them and their heirs for ever.    Dated 3 Sep. 44 Eliz., 1602.

Signed     *Tho: Gresham*

*ANN MACKWORTH.*

Witnessed in dorso by Edmunde Mackworth, George Mackworth, Tho. Atkinson, John Still, and To. Denman, R P, Richard Parnell, his mark, John Lawson.

Endorsed Mrs. Mackworth to Tho. Eyre, Tho. Davies, 44 Eliz.

Thomas Gresham was the eldest son of Paul Gresham of Walsingham Parva, co. Norf., by his first wife Elizabeth, daughter of Jeremiah Markham of Houghton, co. Notts.    He was born in 1550.    In the Parish Register of Braceborough are entries of burial of Thomas Gresham 19 Sep. 1612 and 8 Dec. 1616.

Anne Mackworth was sister of Thomas Gresham, and wife of George Mackworth of Empingham.

# 𝔘pton.*

## EXTRACTS FROM PARISH REGISTERS.†

### PRESTBURY, CHESHIRE.‡

#### *Married.*

| | | |
|---|---|---|
| 1565 | Nov. 10 | (Mottram.) James Upton and Jone Adshedde. |
| 1589 | May 20 | (Macclesfeilde.) Hughe Upton and Agnes Harvyė. |
| 1606 | Aug. 29 | (Newton.) Wm. Bennett and Isabel Upton. |
| 1625 | Mar. 15 | John Upton and Katheren Halle. |
| 1635 | Feb. 28 | (Bollington.) Hugh Upton and Marie Yearwood. |
| 1636 | May 19 | Thomas Upton and Dorothie Allen. |
| 1636 | Nov. 8 | (Pott Shrigley.) Richard Upton and Isabell Hulme. |

#### *Baptized.*

| | | |
|---|---|---|
| 1564 | May 21 | (Newton.) Sybell Upton. |
| 1565 | June 10 | (Butley.) Thomas Upton. |
| 1567 | July 5 | (Newton.) John Upton. |
| 1583 | Mar. 26 | (Newton.) Isabell Upton. |
| 1585 | Dec. 5 | (Newton.) Elizabeth Upton. |
| 1588 | Aug. 22 | (Newton.) Richarde Upton. |
| 1589 | Nov. 10 | (Prestburie.) John Upton. |
| 1592 | June 17 | (Prestburie.) Lawrence Upton. |
| 1594 | Dec. 30 | (Prestburie.) Thomas Upton. |
| 1595 | Dec. 25 | (Prestburie.) Thomas Upton. |
| 1595 | Mar. 8 | (Newton.) Robert Upton. |
| 1598 | Nov. 27 | (Prestburie.) John Upton. |
| 1609 | Feb. 28 | (Bollingeton.) Marie Upton. |
| 1616 | Oct. 27 | (Bollington.) Isabell *fil.* Ric'i Upton. |
| 1623 | April 25 | (Prestburie.) Thos. son of Thos. Upton. |
| 1625 | Oct. 29 | (Prestburie.) John *fil.* Thome Upton. |
| 1625 | Jan. 21 | (Newton.) Margrett *filia* Ric. Upton. |
| 1630 | Feb. 20 | (Prestbury.) Ellen Upton *fil.* Thome. |
| 1633 | July 18 | (Newton.) Marie *fil.* Ric'i Upton. |
| 1634 | April 10 | (Tiderington.) Marie Upton *als.* Yearwood. |
| 1636 | May 22 | (Bollington.) Richard son of Hugh Upton. |
| 1636 | June 5 | (Newton.) John son of James Upton. |

#### *Buried.*

| | | |
|---|---|---|
| 1565 | Oct. 2 | (Butleye.) Thomas Upton. |
| 1575 | May 10 | (Newton.) Ales Wyotte [Alice Wyatt] *als.* Upton, bastarde. |
| 1577 | Mar. 11 | (Newton.) Ric. Upton. |
| 1578 | Mar. 22 | (Newton.) Agnes Upton. |
| 1594 | Jan. 15 | (Prestburie.) Thomas Upton. |
| 1595 | *Tertio* Mar. | (Prestburie.) John Upton. |
| 1597 | Dec. 23 | (Tydrington.) John Upton. |
| 1598 | July 12 | (Newton.) Margearie Upton. |
| 1606 | June 20 | (Presburie.) Lawrence Upton. |
| 1608 | Feb. 2 | (Bollington.) Jone Upton. |
| 1610 | Nov. 19 | (Newton.) Robert Upton. |

* Continued from p. 191.
† In most instances all Upton entries prior to the middle of the last century were extracted, but in a few cases the Registers were searched only for particular entries.

‡ Prestbury is the mother-church of an extensive parish, comprising a large portion of the Hundred of Macclesfield. At present it includes thirty-two townships, one of which is named Upton. Where mentioned, the names of these townships are given in parentheses, following the date. The Registers of this parish were searched only to the year 1636.

| 1610 | Jan. 15 | (Newton.)   Margarette Upton. |
| 1622 | Mar. 30 | (Presburie.)   John son of Thomas Upton. |
| 1625 | Feb. 8 | (Newton.)   Margrett Upton. |
| 1627 | June 22 | (Bollington.)   Richard Upton. |
| 1635 | Aug. 31 | (Bollington.)   Thomas son of Hugh Upton. |
| 1636 | June 21 | (Newton.)   John son of James Upton. |

## BRIXHAM, DEVONSHIRE.
### Married.

| 1583 | April 4 | Mr. Xpher Hody and Mrs. Elizabeth Upton. |
| 1585 | Nov. 22 | John Upton and Grace Shutt. |
| 1585 | Nov. 28 | William Russell and Joan Upton, widow. |
| 1595 | Sep. 15 | Henry Mylman and Grace Upton. |
| 1610 | Nov. 16 | Xtopher Cade and Joan Upton. |
| 1614 | May . . | John Heale and Elizabeth dau. of Mr. Arthur Upton. |
| 1638 | Oct. 9 | Mr. John Vaughan and Mrs. Elizabeth Upton. |
| 1642 | July 19 | Mr. John Champneis and Mrs. Anne Upton. |
| 1653 | June 28 | Master Samuel Thomas of Dartmouth and Mrs. Phillip Upton of Lupton. |
| 1654 | April 10 | Mr. William Langdon of Brixham and Mrs. Dorothy Upton of Plymouth. |
| 1671 | Nov. 10 | Mr. John Brooking and Mrs. Mary Upton. |
| 1732 | Jan. 23 | Matthew Upton and Anne Varrell. |

### Baptized.

| 1589 | Oct. 28 | John son of John Upton. |
| 1591 | July 15 | William son of Mr. Arthur Upton. |
| 1592 | Sep. 6 | Henry son of Mr. Arthur Upton. |
| $16\frac{1}{6}$ | Jan. 22 | Elizabeth dau. of John Upton. |
| 1616 | Sep. 22 | John son of John Upton, Esq. |
| 1631 | June 5 | Gartery dau. of John Upton, Esq. |
| $163\frac{3}{4}$ | Jan. 1 | Hugh son of John Upton, Esq. |
| 1634 | Sep. 7 | Thomas son of John Upton, Esq. |
| 1639 | Aug. 15 | John son of Mr. Arthur Upton. |
| 1641 | Mar. 30 | Arthur son of Mr. Arthur Upton. |
| 1667 | June 1 | Arthur son of Mr. Arthur Upton ; born 26 May. |
| 1729 | Sep. 29 | James son of John and Anne Upton. |
| 1733 | Nov. 27 | Matthew son of Matthew and Anne Upton. |

### Buried.

| $156\frac{7}{8}$ | Feb. 4 | Annys Upton. |
| 1573 | July 5 | Anne wife of Mr. John Upton ye yonger. |
| 1575 | July 1 | William son of Nicholas Upton *alias* Beter.* |
| 1580 | Nov. 15 | Nicholas Upton *alias* Beter.* |
| 1582 | June 16 | Mr. John Upton. |
| 1582 | Oct. 9 | Mistress Jane Upton. |
| $15\frac{88}{90}$ | Feb. 16 | Mr. Matthew Upton. |
| $159\frac{1}{2}$ | Feb. 12 | John Upton. |
| 1592 | April 19 | William son of Mr. Arthur Upton. |
| $159\frac{4}{5}$ | Feb. 14 | Mrs. Gartery Upton. |
| 1600 | Aug. 4 | Mr. John Upton. |
| 1603 | April 6 | John Upton. |
| 1610 | July 8 | Mrs. Anne Upton. |
| 1612 | June 17 | Mrs. Catherine Upton. |
| 1614 | Oct. 27 | Gartred Upton. |
| $16\frac{17}{18}$ | Mar. 11 | Mr. Arthur Upton. |

* An explanation of this "*alias* Beter" would be interesting.

| 163¼ | Jan. | 1 | Mr. Hugh Upton. |
| 1641 | Sep. | 12 | John Upton, Esq. |
| 164¾ | Feb. | 20 | Mrs. Dorothy Upton. |
| 1645 | Aug. | 18 | Mrs. Elizabeth Upton, child. |
| 166½ | Mar. | 5 | Arthur Upton, Esq. |
| 1669 | Sep. | 1 | Mr. Anthony Upton, merchant. |
| 1685 | Dec. | 17 | Mrs. Elizabeth Upton, gentlewoman. |
| 1687 | Sep. | 20 | John Upton, Esq. |
| 1687 | Oct. | 17 | Mrs. Ursula Upton dau. of John Upton, late dec'd, buried (*sic*, ? died) in St. Dunstan's in ye East in London, and brought home to be buried. |
| 1719 | June | 4 | Mrs. Anne Upton. |

### TRINITY CHURCH, EXETER, DEVONSHIRE.

*Married.*

| 1590 | May | 30 | John Upton of Haccombe and Ellen Podgcombe of Doewseignton ; by licence. |

*Baptized.*

| 1606 | Jan. | 8 | Rebecca dau. of Robert Upton. |

### MODBURY, DEVONSHIRE.

*Married.*

| 1615 | July | 28 | Arthur Upton and Mary Stradling. |

### NEWTON FERRERS, DEVONSHIRE.

*Married.*

| 1605 | June | 17 | George Upton, Esq., and Susanna Spurr. |
| 1632 | Nov. | 29 | Richard Drake, gent., and Eliz. Uppeton. |
| 1641 | May | 25 | Richard Loves and Frances Uppeton. |
| 1654 | Nov. | 27 | William Uppeton and Joane Hillersdon. |

*Baptized.*

| 1600 | Jan. | 23 | George son of George Upton. |
| 1606 | July | 1 | John son of George Upton. |
| 1607 | Sep. | 10 | Jane dau. of George Upton. |
| 1609 | Aug. | 20 | Nicholas son of George Upton. |
| 1611 | May | 19 | Warwick son of George Uppeton. |
| 1613 | May | 2 | Mark son of William Uppeton. |
| 1615 | June | 15 | Elizabeth dau. of William Uppeton. |
| 1616 | Aug. | 25 | Richard son of William Uppeton. |
| 1617 | Feb. | 1 | Amie dau. of William Uppeton. |
| 1619 | July | 4 | Phillip dau'r of Will. Uppeton and Amye his wife. |
| 1620 | Nov. | 1 | Mary dau'r of Will. Uppeton and Amye his wife. |
| 1621 | Oct. | 21 | Honor dau'r of Will. Uppeton and Amye his wife. |
| 1622 | Mar. | 9 | Izable dau. of Will. Uppeton. |
| 1625 | May | 6 | John son of W. Uppeton and Amy his wife. |
| 1626 | May | 23 | Jane dau'r of W. Uppeton and Amy his wife. |
| 1637 | Dec. | 10 | Amye dau. of Marke Uppeton and Darotie his wife. |
| 1642 | May VIII | | Marke son of Marke Uppeton and Darotie his wife. |
| 1667 | Mar. | 12 | John son of Will. Uppeton and Joan his wife ; born 6 March. |
| 1692 | July | 22 | Elizabeth dau'r of John Uppeton, gent., and Thomazin his wife ; born 14 July. |
| 1694 | [Aug. | 31] | Mary dau'r of John Uppeton, gent., and Thomazin his wife bapt. last day of August. |

*Buried.*

| 1600 | Jan. 23 | Phillippe wyfe George Upton. |
|------|---------|------------------------------|
| 1608 | Sep. 8 | Jane dau. George Upton. |
| 1611 | Dec. 27 | George Uppeton, Esq. |
| 1644 | April 15 | Marke Uppeton, gent. |
| 1648 | June 7 | William Upton, Esq[re]. |
| 1649 | Aug. 12 | Amy wife Will. Upton, Esq. |
| 1660 | July 22 | M[tris] Amey Uppeton. |
| 1668 | July 23 | M[tris] Dorothey Uppeton, widdoe. |
| 1680 | April 22 | Marke Uppeton, gent. |
| 1690 | April 23 | Joan wife William Uppeton. |
| 1702 | June 1 | John Uppeton, gent[n]. |
| 1709 | Dec. 6 | William Uppeton, Esq[re]. |
| 1724 | Feb. 12 | Thomasin Uppeton, gentlewoman. |

## ST. PETROCK'S, EXETER, DEVONSHIRE.
*Married.*

1667   Nov. 26   John Upton and Ales Hooker.

## WOODBURY, DEVONSHIRE.
*Married.*

163⅞   Jan. 26   Arthur Upton and Elizabeth Haydon.

## YEALMPTON, DEVONSHIRE.
*Married.*

1652   . . . . .   Francis Collin and Honor Upton.

*Baptized.*

1642   . . . . .   John and Loaxe children of John Uppeton.
1646   . . . . .   Oliver son of John Uppeton.

## HORNCHURCH, CO. ESSEX.
*Buried.*

1744   April 15   Thomas Upton.

## ROXWELL, CO. ESSEX.
*Buried.*

1780   . . . . .   Edward Upton, a traveller.

## GREENWICH, CO. KENT.
*Baptized.*

1680   Nov. 4   Mary dau. of Capt. Rich[d] Upton and Elizabeth.
1685   July 25   John son of Mr. John Upton, merchant, and Mary.

*Buried.*

167⅚   Feb. 8   Elizabeth dau. of Mr. Upton.
1677   June 14   Child of Mr. Rich[d] Upcot *alias* Upton.
1680   Nov. 15   Mary dau. of Mr. Upton.
1681   Oct. 24   Mr. Upton, senior.

## CROFT, CO. LINCOLN.
*Married.*

1638   April 23   Everard Dighton, Vicar of Croft, and Frances dau. of Valentine Upton of Northolme, Esq.

*Baptized.*

1644   June 6   Frances dau. of Hamond Upton, Esq., and Lucy; born 1st at Northolme.

## CHELSEA, CO. MIDDLESEX.

*Married.*

1634 Dec. 7 Nathaniel Besbeech and Elizabeth Upton, both of Feversham, Kent ; by licence.
1703 Nov. 18 Jonathan Upton of St. Edmund the King and Mary Lockwood of Chelsea.

*Baptized.*

1696 Sep. 17 Mary dau. of Mr. Ambrose Upton and Jane.

## CHISWICK, CO. MIDDLESEX.

*Married.*

1702 April 23 Richard Waterman of Ealing and Margaret Upton of Richmond, Surrey, both single. Licence.

*Buried.*

1815 Jan. 13 John Upton, Lieut. of the late 72$^d$ or Royal Manchester Volunteers, Turnham Green, aged 54.

## HACKNEY, CO. MIDDLESEX.

*Buried.*

166$\frac{4}{5}$ Mar. 6 Mrs. Ann Upton, a young gentlewoman.

## ST. ANDREW'S, HOLBORN, CO. MIDDLESEX.

*Married.*

1574 June 15 Nicholas Upton, gent., and Katherine Madoxe.
1695 April 4 John Wolfe of Northall, Mid$^x$, Clerk, and Ann Upton of this parish.

*Baptized.*

1722 Dec. 19 Ann dau. of Richard Upton, Esq., and Sarah, Bartletts Buildings.

*Buried.*

1581 June 16 Thomas Upton of Lincoln's Inn, gent.
1645 May 5 Hamond Upton, Esq., of Northam, co. Lincoln ; died 4$^{th}$ at Richard Whitlock's house above Fetter Lane.
1694 July 19 William Upton, gent., Hatton Garden.

## ST. GEORGE'S, BLOOMSBURY, CO. MIDDLESEX.

*Married.*

1788 May 27 John Prior of Fairford, co. Gloucester, widower, and Elizabeth Upton of this parish, spinster. Licence.
1805 Feb. 23 James Upton, Esq., of St. Mary Cole Abbey, London, widower, and Mary Brotherson of this parish, spinster. Licence.

## ST. GILES IN THE FIELDS, CO. MIDDLESEX.

*Baptized.*

168$\frac{1}{2}$ Jan. 26 Elizabeth dau. of Paul and Elizabeth Upton.
1689 July 1 Mary dau. of John and Phillis Upton.
1694 Aug. 15 John son of Mr. John Upton and Mary.
1711 Dec. 16 Richard son of Richard and Elizabeth Upton.
1712 April 10 Sarah dau. of John and Mary Upton.
1713 Dec. 29 Dorothy dau. of John and Mary Upton.
1714 Sep. 22 Elizabeth dau. of Thomas and Ann Upton.
17$\frac{14}{14}$ Feb. 8 Arthur dau. of John and Mary Upton.
1718 May 12 Sarah dau. of Thomas and Sara Upton.

| 1718 | Aug. 29 | Mary dau. of John Upton, Esq., and Mary ; born 14th. |
| $17\frac{19}{20}$ | May 2 | Thomas son of Thomas and Ann Upton. |
| 1721 | April 13 | Clotworthy son of Col. John Upton, Esq., and Mary; born 14th March. |
| 1721 | April 28 | John son of John and Jane Upton. |
| 1722 | Oct. 21 | Ann Letitia dau. of John Upton, Esq., and Mary; born 27th Sep. |
| $174\frac{1}{2}$ | Jan. 4 | Mary dau. of Robert and Elizabeth Upton ; born 2[d]. |
| 1743 | Oct. 2 | Henry son of William and Mary Upton. |
| 1745 | April 30 | Henry son of William and Mary Upton. |
| 1751 | June 27 | Mary dau. of Joseph and Eleanor Upton. |
| 1753 | Jan. 16 | Sarah dau. of James and Elizabeth Upton. |
| 1754 | Feb. 22 | Hannah dau. of Joseph and Elinor Upton. |

*Buried.*

| 1657 | Aug. 23 | John Upton. |
| $16\frac{78}{80}$ | Feb. 4 | James Upton. |
| 1704 | Aug. 19 | William Upton. |
| $17\frac{13}{14}$ | Jan. 30 | Dorothy dau. of Col. John Upton, carried away. |
| 1719 | June 11 | Mrs. Ann Upton. |

### ST. MARTIN IN THE FIELDS, CO. MIDDLESEX.

*Married.*

| 1635 | June 25 | Hamond Upton of Wainfleet, co. Lincoln, Esq., and Lucy Browne of East Kirkby, co. Lincoln. Licence. |

*Buried.*

| 1722 | May 20 | Grace Upton, woman. |
| 1741 | Sep. 25 | Capt. William Upton, man. |

### ST. MARYLEBONE, CO. MIDDLESEX.

*Married.*

| 1690 | Oct. 5 | John Upton and Ann Abbott. |

(*To be continued.*)

---

## ENGLISH INSCRIPTIONS IN THE LITTLE CEMETERY OF GRIANTE, NEAR CADENABBIA, LAKE OF COMO.*

In
loving memory of
Lawrence Harman Crofton
youngest son of the late
Morgan Crofton, R.N.
born Sept. 30th 1834
died Oct. 8th 1874
at Cadenabbia
from the effects of an accident.

---

Grace
second daughter of the late
John Armstrong first Bishop of Grahamstown
born June 20 . 1852
died June 7 . 1875.

* Communicated by G. MILNER-GIBSON CULLUM, Esq., F.S.A.

In loving memory
of
John Williamson
of Villa Guiseppina
and Westoe, South Shields.
Born 25 Sep : 1825
died 9 July 1887.

---

In memory of
Harriet Scratton
eldest daughter of the late
John Bayntun Scratton Esq.
and of Harriet his wife
of Milton Hall
In the parish of Prittlewell
and county of Essex
in England.
She departed this life
at Cadenabbia
2nd June 1844
aged 30 years.

---

(An Irish Cross.)
To the memory of
Lieutenant Colonel
Richard Hillman Daniel
Commanding 18th " The Royal Irish Regiment."
born 3[d] March 1830
died 21st May 1878.
Erected by his brother officers.

---

In memoriam
George Sherbrooke Airey R.N.
third son of Sir George Airey K.C.H.*
and of his wife Catharine Talbot de Malahide
Born at Messina 1810.
Died at Cadenabbia September 28. 1880.
Spes mei Crux Christi.

## BODINGTON OF CHARLECOTE.

### REGISTERS OF CHARLECOTE, CO. WARWICK.

*Baptisms.*

1623   William Bodington the sonne of Thomas Bodington was Baptized the eyght day of October in the yere above sayd: 1623.

1626   Annis Bodington the daughter of Thomas Bodington was Baptized the three and twentye day of July the yere 1626 as above said.

1628   Alicia Bodington filia Thome Bodington nata fuit decimo quinto die Octobris et baptizata decimo nono die eiusdem mensis Anno d'no 1628 et Regis Caroli quarto.

1631   Isabella filia Thome Bodington baptizata fuit vicesimo tertio die Octobris 1631.

* Is not this an error on the part of the Italian stonecutter for K.C.B. ?

1646 Thomas Boddenton the sonn of Thomas Boddenton and Elizabeth Boddento' baptized the third day of October 1646.

1648 John boddenton the sonne of Thomas and Elizabeth Boddenton was baptised the twelfe day of November 1648.

1652 Elizabeth Boddington the daughter of Thomas boddington and Elizabeth his wife was baptised y⁰ one and thirtieth day of Januarie 1652.

*Burials.*

1640 Elizabetha uxor Thome Bodington sepulta fuit vicesimo tertio die Octobris 1640.

1690 Susannah Bodington was Buryed the Twentieth day of August.

1694 Elizabeth Bodington was buryed the nine and twentieth day of January.

1723 Elizabeth Boddington was buried July y⁰ 28, 1723.

Is anything known of this family of Boddington, and can any one say who is its representative at the present time ?

*National Conservative Club,*    REGINALD STEWART BODDINGTON.
    *9 Pall Mall, S.W.*

# Dalison Notes.*

Assise capte apud Sanctum Botulphum .... die Jovis proxima post Festum Sancti Petri Advincula, anno regni Regis Edwardi filii Regis Edwardi, tercio.
Lincoln scilicet.

Johannes filius Roberti de Northkeleseye de Hakethorne et Clemencia soror ejus qui tulerunt breve assise nove disseisine versus Rogerum Dalazun et alios in brevi de tenementis in Hakethorn non prosecuti. Ideo predicti Rogerus et alii inde sine die, et predicti Johannes et Clemencia, et plegii sui, etc., in misericordia, videlicet, Simon filius Galfridi de Hackethorn et Thomas Le Feure de eadem.
Assize Roll, Divers Counties, N-2-14 5, m. 44, [4 August A.D. 1309].

Ascilia que fuit uxor Johannis de Alazoun, per Willielmum Bray attornatum suum, petit versus Radulphum Mouter de Covenham medietatem quatuor acrarum prati, cum pertinentiis, in Gernethorp, et terciam partem quatuor acrarum prati, cum pertinentiis, in Covenham ut dotem, etc.
Et Radulphus, per Hugonem de Keleby attornatum suum, venit. Et vocavit inde ad warrantum Willielmum de Alazoun, etc.
De Banco Roll, Edw. 3, No. 3, m. 66, Trin., 1 Edw. 3, [A.D. 1327].

Lincoln scilicet.

Ascilia que fuit uxor Johannis de Alazoun, per Willielmum Bray, etc., petit versus Radulphum Mouter de Covenham medietatem quatuor acrarum prati, cum pertinentiis, in Germethorp, et terciam partem quatuor acrarum prati, cum pertinentiis, in Covenham ut dotem, etc.
Et Radulphus per Hugonem de Keleby attornatum suum venit. Et vocavit inde ad warrantiam Willielmum filium Johannis de Alazoun, etc.
De Banco Roll, Edw. 3, No. 6, m. 74, Easter, 2 Edw. 3, [A.D. 1328].

Lincoln scilicet.

Ascilia que fuit uxor Johannis de Alazoun in misericordia pro falso clameo versus Johannem filium Ranulphi de Otteby de placito terre de tenementis in Suthelkyngton prout patet Termino Pasche anno regni Domini Edwardi nuper Regis patris, etc., decimo nono, rotulo clvj, etc.
De Banco Roll, Edw. 3, No. 7, m. 33 Trin., 2 Edw. 3, [A.D. 1328].

* Continued from p. 150.

Lincoln scilicet.

Willielmus de Allazun per Odonem de Bodekesham attornatum suum petit versus Walterum filium Simonis de Kynton unam bovatam terre, cum pertinentiis, in Ludyngton. Et versus Thomam filium Rogeri Preste de Botlesford in la vale unum toftum, cum pertinentiis, in eadem villa que Willielmus de Waterton dedit Willielmo Blaunchard in liberum maritagium cum Ascilia filia ejusdem Willielmi de Waterton, et que post mortem predictorum Willielmi Blaunchard et Ascilie et Willielmi filii eorundem Willielmi Blaunchard et Ascilie et Matillidis sororis ejusdem Willielmi filie eorundem Willielmi et Ascilie et Johannis filii ejusdem Matillidis, prefato Willielmo de Allazun filio predicti Johannis et consanguineo et heredi predictorum Willielmi Blaunchard et Ascilie descendere debent per formam donacionis predicte, etc.

Et Walterus per Willielmum de Drax attornatum venit. Et defendit ius suum quandocunque, etc. Et quia loquela alias remansit sine die per absenciam Justiciariorum, petit auditum resummonitionis loquele predicte.

Quo audito invenitur in eadem resummonitione variacionem inter originale et illam resummonitionem, etc. Ideo dictum est predicto Willielmo quod sequatur aliam resummonitionem si, etc.

De Banco Roll, Edw. 3, No. 8, m. 30 d., Mich., 2 Edw. 3, [A.D. 1328].

———

Essonia capta . . . . die Jovis proximo post diem Cinerum, anno regni Regis Edwardi tercii a conquestu, septimo.

Lincoln scilicet.

Ascilia que fuit uxor Johannis de Alazon de Laughton ponit loco suo Johannem de Elkynton vel Robertum de Yerdeburgh versus Johannem de Lungetoft, et Ricardum filium ejus, et Johannem Blaunchard, de placito assise nove disseisine.

Assize Roll, Divers Counties, N-2-18 5, m. 35 d., 23 Feb. A.D. 1333.

———

Assise . . . . capte apud Lincoln, die Jovis in septimana Pasche, anno regni Regis Edwardi tercii post conquestum, nono.

Lincoln scilicet.

Assisa venit recognitura si Willielmus Gunter et Matillis uxor ejus, Johannes Mareschal de Neuton juxta Sheldford, Cecilia que fuit uxor Willielmi Breton et Radulphus filius ejusdem Cecilie, Jacobus de Cantilupo et Willielmus Alisoun et Alicia uxor ejus injuste et sine judicio disseisierunt Adam Godewyn de Welyngoure Capellanum de libero tenemento suo in Welyngoure post primam, etc.

Et Johannes et Radulphus venerunt et alii non venerunt, set idem Radulphus respondit pro eis tanquam eorum ballivus et pro eis dicit quod ipsi nullam injuriam seu disseisinam inde fecerunt ; et de hoc ponit se super assisam. Et idem Radulphus . . . . vocat inde ad warrantum predictum Johannem Mareschal qui presens in Curia gratis ei warrantizat, et idem Johannes ut tenens per warrantiam suam dicit quod quidam Ricardus filius Albrede aliquando fuit seisitus de tenementis predictis in visu positis in dominico suo ut de feodo et inde obiit seisitus, post cujus mortem eadem tenementa descendebant eidem Matillidi nunc uxori ejusdem Willielmi Gunter et cuidam Alicie sorori ejusdem Matillde ut filiis et heredibus predicti Ricardi ; factaque post modum participacione eorundem tenementorum inter ipsas, predicta Alicia obiit. Et quidem Willielmus filius et heres ejusdem Alicie . . . . remisit, relaxavit et quietum clamavit totum jus suum et clameum quod habuit in tenementis predictis, etc.

Juratores dicunt super sacramentam suum quod predicti Willielmus Gunter et Matillis et Johannes Mareschal disseisierunt predictum Adam, etc.

Assize Roll, Divers Counties, N-2-18 5, m. 53 a., [1 April A.D. 1336].

*(To be continued.)*

o 3

# Wood of Hareston.

The family of Wood resided on their estate of Hareston in the parish of Brixton, Devonshire, from the 8th year of Edward III. till the present representative of the race sold the property, in portions, in the years 1868-69. There were nineteen descents of the Woods, from father to son, when John Wood left an only daughter, who married John Winter, a descendant of Sir William Winter, who commanded the "Vanguard" during the conflicts with the Spanish Armada. The Winter family were from Gloucestershire, and the name was originally spelt Wintour. The present representative of the families, Thomas Winter Wood of Plymouth, retook the name of Wood by royal letters patent, dated 12 Nov. 1850, and, by a strange though by no means uncommon caprice of fortune, sold the property a few years after as before mentioned.

The greater portion of the mansion house was destroyed by fire about the year 1700 ; but the chapel, embattled porch, and a few gables still remain ; the mullions, turrets, corbels, and facings are all of solid granite. The terminations of the granite label over the door of the entrance-porch bear the arms of Wood on the right side and of Fortescue on the left, clearly indicating that the house was built by John Wood in the reign of Henry VII., and who, in the family pedigree, is represented to have died in the 30th year of Henry VIII., after having been married to Jone Fortescue a great number of years.*

The house is now occupied as a farm homestead. There is an aisle in the parish church, surrounded by a carved screen, which is attached to the residence by a faculty from the diocese of Exeter, and was always preserved with jealous care, and repaired by the owners of Hareston.

The two first portraits painted by Sir Joshua Reynolds on his return to Plympton from the studio of Hudson, then the most famous portrait painter in London, with whom he had passed two years of close study, are still in possession of the Wood family.

Burke's 'Commoners' gives the descent of the Woods from the before-named John Wood, who married Jone Fortescue ; and the same authority also says "from the Woods of Hareston, Alderman Sir Matthew Wood, Bart., claims descent."

---

MONUMENTAL INSCRIPTIONS FROM THE BURIAL-GROUND OF ST. GEORGE, HANOVER SQUARE, NEAR MARBLE ARCH.†

M$^{rs}$ [Elizabeth Hallett] .... Jan. 16 181[-]. This stone erected by her disconsolate ....

Also Susannah [Hallett], daughter of the above, died Jan. 1802, aged 25.

M$^{rs}$ Harriett Powell, wife of M$^{r}$ Charles Martin Powell, daughter of the above, died July 23, 1810, aged 27.

M$^{r}$ Elijah Hallett, husband of the above M$^{rs}$ Elizabeth Hallett, died Sep. 10 183[-], aged 88.

---

M$^{r}$ Thomas Harris, of Green Street, Grosvenor Square, died Jan. 16, 1826, aged 62.

George Harris, son of the above, died June 10, 1806, aged 9 months.

M$^{rs}$ Elizabeth Blatchford Harris, wife of the above M$^{r}$ Thomas Harris, died April 30, 1833, aged 71.

---

M$^{rs}$ Sarah Parish, of Brigg, Lincolnshire, died 2 August 1826, in her 78$^{th}$ year.

---

* See Burke's 'Commoners,' vol. iv., p. 426.
† Continued from p. 176.

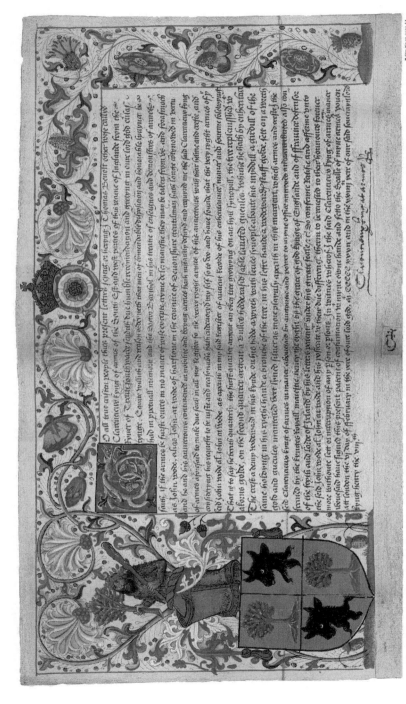

CONFIRMATION OF ARMS BY THOMAS BENOLT, CLARENCEUX, TO JOHN WODE OF HARSTONE, CO. DEVON, 1532.

M$^r$ John Harris of Queen Street, King's Road, Chelsea, died Nov. 30, 1842, aged [80 ?] years.

M$^r$ George Baylis, late of this parish, died August 10$^{th}$ 1816, aged 50.
Emma his daughter, died April 19$^{th}$ 1813, aged 1 year, 10 months, 6 weeks.
George Edward Baylis, grandson of the above, died July 18, 1838, aged 5 months 18 days, son of George and Eliza Baylis.
Edward Baylis, son of Edward & Ann Baylis, and grandson of the above, died 1 July 1839, aged 4 months.
M$^{rs}$ Elizabeth Baylis, wife of the above M$^r$ George Baylis, died 11 July 1847, aged 75.

Richard Savage . . . . . . . . Aug. . . . . . [1801 ?] aged 35.

Martha Jones, wife of Edward Jones of Craven Place, died Nov. 18, 1819, aged 71.
Also the above named Edward Jones, died Feb. 12 1837, in his 78$^{th}$ year.
M$^{rs}$ Sarah Garman, late of Bayswater, died July 24, 1841, in her 76$^{th}$ year.

Charles Lewis, died July 2$^{nd}$ 1811, aged 13 months, 19 days.
M$^r$ Richard Lewis, father of the above, died March 4$^{th}$ 1814, aged 36 years.

Rebecca Barnard, niece of James Wigg, Esq., died Nov. 29, 1805, aged 17.
James Wigg Esq. citizen of London, and late of Half Moon Street, died 28 Sep. 1806, aged 57.
M$^{rs}$ Mary Wigg, wife of the above named, died 25 Feb. 1784, aged 39.
Charles James & Mary Sparkes, son & daughter of Charles Sparkes, nephew of James Wigg Esq., who died in their infancy.
Elizabeth Ann Sparkes, died April 4, 1811, aged 8 years & 9 months.
Mary daughter of Charles & Maria Sparkes & beloved wife of John Laurie of Harley Street, died 23 April 1832, in her 21$^{st}$ year.
M$^{rs}$ Fanny Sparkes, died Jan. 26, 1836, in her 21$^{st}$ year.
Maria, wife of Charles Sparkes of Harley Street, died 16 May 1828, aged 52.
Robert Peter Laurie, died 17 Sep. [1835 ?] in his 34$^{th}$ year.

Charles John, son of Charles Henry & Charlotte Phillips, of Halfmoon Street, Piccadilly, died 14 Nov. 1826, aged 14.
Edward Henry Phillips, died 14 Feb. 1827, aged 7.
Robert Phillips, died 27$^{th}$ May 1827, aged 2.
John Phillips, died 9 Sep. [1843], aged 16.

M$^r$ James Williamson, of Park Street, Grosvenor Square, died June 6, 1824, aged 37.
M$^{rs}$ Sarah Williamson, relict of the above, died May 17, 1850, aged 64.

[. . . . Ratcliffe] wife of James Ratcliffe of South Molton Street, died 16 Oct. 1812, aged 33 years.
Louisa Amelia Ratcliffe, grand daughter of the above, died 10$^{th}$ July 1827, aged 3 years & 3 months. [*Rest of the inscription illegible.*]

William Childs, son of William & Mary Childs of North Audley Street, died March 23, 1821, aged 3 years & 6 months.
Eliza Childs, daughter of the above, died Aug. 1, 1822, aged 3 months.
Also the above named M$^{rs}$ Mary Childs, died Nov. 20 1826, aged 38.
Eliza Childs, daughter of the above, died Feb. 6, 1829, aged 2 years & 10 months.
Jane Childs, daughter of the above [. . . . 1838].
[Mary Ann Childs ? . . . . 1848.] [*Part of the inscription hidden by a footstone.*]

M<sup>r</sup> Jonathan Sampson, of South Street, Grosvenor Square, died Jan. 21, 1824
    aged [61 ?] years.
[M<sup>rs</sup> Ann (?) Sampson] wife [of the above ?] . . . . . . . .

M<sup>r</sup> John Place, died March 19 [1827] aged 67.

*(To be continued.)*

## GENEALOGICAL MEMORANDA RELATING TO
# The Family of Shuckburgh.*

KEY TO SITE OF MONUMENTS IN UPPER SHUCKBURGH CHURCH.

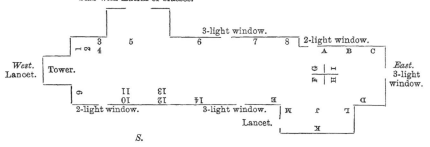

## Monumental Inscriptions.

UPPER SHUCKBURGH CHURCH.

*A on key plan.*

*Mural monument, north wall of chancel (with canopy, etc.), and upon it is a brass
with this inscription.*

Sacred
to the Memory of Anna Maria Draycott
Lady Shuckburgh the beloved and Lamented Wife
of Sir Francis Shuckburgh of Shuckburgh Bar<sup>t</sup>
by whom this tablet is erected, a tribute
of affection, yet rather in the Devoted hearts of
a sorrowing Husband, Children, and Friends,
than on the cold Monumental Marble be
engraven the Memorial of the Departed
There Reader, not here thou should'st seek
her Epitaph.
She died at Shuckburgh, on the VIIIth of
Nov<sup>r</sup> M<sup>o</sup>.V.CCC.XL.VI.
Lord be Thou our hope.

Arms at base : SHUCKBURGH, with Ulster badge in chief ; impaling DENYS, Argent, a cross patoncé
    gules between four fleurs-de-lis vert, on a chief azure a greyhound courant of the field.

---

* Communicated by C. G. S. FOLJAMBE, Esq., M.P.

B *on key plan.*

*Monument with medallion portrait on north wall, chancel.*

In Memory
Of Sir STEWKELEY SHUCKBURGH Baronet,
Son of S<sup>r</sup> JOHN SHUCKBURGH by ABIGAL
Daughter of JOHN GOODWIN Esq<sup>r</sup>.
In his private Capacity
He was a Steady & Sincere Friend,
A kind and indulgent Master :
In his publick
A zealous Advocate for the Liberties,
And a Faithful Dispenser of the Laws
Of his Country.
Perpetual Struggles with ill Health
Disabled him from exerting those Social Talents,
which would have indear'd him to Mankind :
But from those Struggles he took occasion to Shew
That hardest duty of a Christian
A Cheerful Submission to the Divine Will.
His retirement was Spent in improving his Mind
And preparing himself for Eternity.
He was exactly regular in the Duties of his Closet
And his behaviour in this house
Was an example of that Seriousness & Fervour,
which become the place of God's publick Worship.
He died at Bath unmarried the 6<sup>th</sup> of March 1759
Aged 47 Years.

Arms and Crest at base : SHUCKBURGH (Ulster badge on chevron).

---

C *on key plan.*

*Monument with medallion portrait within altar rails, north side.*

FRANCIS . SHVCKBVRGH . VIII . BARONET .
OB: OCT : XXIX . MDCCCLXXVI . ÆT. 87.

IN PATRIS DILECTI MEMORIAM, HOC MONVMENTVM
GEO : THO<sup>s</sup> FRA<sup>s</sup> SHVCKBVRGH, PIETATE SVA, PONI CVRAVIT.

At west end of this tablet :—
H. H. ARMSTEAD, A.R.A.

---

*Stained-glass two-light window on north side of chancel.*

In pious memory | of A. M. D. Lady Shuckburgh
this window Sir F. S. | dedicates to the Glory of God.

---

The east window of the chancel (three-light) is filled with modern stained glass, six subjects (events in the life of St. John the Baptist), but no memorial inscription.

The three-light window on the north side of the nave is filled with modern stained glass, six shields : Upper row—CLARE, KING EDWARD I., FERRERS, Gules, seven mascles or ; lower row—VERDON, SHUCKBURGH (with Ulster badge) impaling DENYS, HOLT. The Shuckburgh motto repeated in bend across the lights.

The three-light window on south side of the nave, also filled with modern stained glass, in tracery: 18 . F . S . 49 ; and in the lights, six shields : Upper row—DYSART, BEAUCHAMP, EARL OF WARWICK, LUNELL ; lower row—Quarterly, 1 NAPTON. 2 LUNELL, 3 SYDENHALL, 4 CARBONELL, and on an escutcheon of pretence SHUCKBURGH ;* EARL OF LEICESTER, Argent, a lion rampant vert ; FOXLEY, Argent, two bars gules.*  This window also has the Shuckburgh motto repeated in bend across the light.

A two-light window farther west, on south side of nave, with old stained glass, the Cruci-fixion in the tracery, and below are four shields, viz. :—

*Upper part of left-hand light.*

Shuckburgh arms and crest.

OMNIA . SUNT . HOMINIS . TENUI . PENDENTIA . ILLO ET . SUBITO . QUÆ . VALVERE . RUUNT .     [BVRGHE ANTHONIO . SHVKBVRGHE . ARMIGERO . DOMINO . DE . SHVK-VIR . VITÆ . INTEGRITATE . CELEBRI . EXITUQ' . PIO .     [FELICI . ET . CONJUGE SVO . AMANTISSIMO . QVI . MORTEM . OBIIT . PRIMO . DIE . APRIL AN'O D'NI 1593.     [MENSIS ANNA VXOR EIVS SECUNDA EX SKEFFINGTONIANI IN COMI TATU LECESTRIA FAMILIA NATA PRO PIGNORE PIETATIS IN MARITVM MŒRENS POSUIT 20 DIE MARTIJ ANNO D'NI 1593.

*Lower part of left-hand light.*

Shield : SHUCKBURGH, quarterly of six : 1, SHUCKBURGH ; 2, NAP-TON ; 3, CARBONELL ; 4, SYDENHALL ; 5, DYSART ; 6, LUNELL ; impaling, Gules, two bars argent, FOXLEY. Monogram : A. S. above shield, and date 1587 below it.

𝔇'ne ḥys tuis ⅾuoḃ. famuli | ḥanc junctis Anⅾonio Sⅾuckburg | Amen †

*Upper part of right-hand light.*

A shield.

Arms : SHUCKBURGH, quarterly of six : 1, SHUCKBURGH ; 2, NAPTON ; 3, SYDENHALL ; 4, LUNELL ; 5, CARBONELL ; 6, DYSART ; impaling SKEFFINGTON.

BENEDICAS . EAMQ' SIC TRANSIRE FACIAS PER BONA TEMPORA AUT NON AMITTAT Æ-TERNA.

*Lower part of right-hand light.*

Shield : Gules, two bars argent, FOXLEY.

Custoⅾire et regere et | is con in te requiescamus | ḥ Armiger †                                    et

The east window of the mortuary chapel, a lancet, is filled with stained glass representing the Resurrection of our Lord, but no memorial inscription. The west window, in the tower, a lancet, is filled with stained-glass emblems of the four Evangelists, etc., but no memorial inscription. There are also three windows filled with modern heraldic stained glass, which are now blocked on the inside by monuments ; one, a lancet, on north side of chancel, behind the monument to Sir Stewkeley Shuckburgh, 1759 ; another lancet, at east side of mortuary chapel, behind Sir Richard Shuckburgh's monument, 1656 ; a third, a two-light window, at south end of mortuary chapel, behind the large tomb to John Shuckburgh, 1631.

———

D *on key plan.*

*Mural monument within altar rails, south side.*

Hic requiescit Inter cognatos Cineres, Familiæ Suæ Decus et Dolor, Dominus JOHANNES SHUCKBURGH Baronettus, longo Parentum fanguine Nobilis, Virtutibus Nobilior fuis : eo enim Ingenii Candore, Morum svavitate,

* These are blazoned wrongly, but are so represented in the stained glass.
† These fragments of old glass have been put together and reglazed, and, as is evident, the two lower inscriptions have been wrongly glazed, the last words of each beyond the lead at | belonging each respectively to the other.
The Shuckburgh motto is repeated on these lights in bend, as in the other windows.

Animi Magnitudine,
Religionis Cultu
inclaruit,
Ut omnibus amabilis viveret,
Omnibus flebilis occideret.
Uxorem duxit Abigailem, Filiam
Georgij Goodwing de Latchford
In Comitatu Oxon, Armigeri,
ex quâ
Unum suscepit Filium, Filias decem.
Obijt octavo die Junij
Anno { D'ni 1724.
{ Ætat : suæ 41°.
Inscriptum hoc marmor
Desideratissimi Mariti Memoriæ
Vidua piè mœrens facrum esse voluit.

Arms at base : SHUCKBURGH, with Ulster badge on chevron ; impaling, Sable, two lions passant
in pale or, on a chief of the last three ogresses.

E *on key plan.*

*Mural monument with bust on south wall of chancel.*

Arms at top : SHUCKBURGH ; impaling, Chequy argent and sable, a fess gules.
(No Ulster badge.)

M. S.
Catharinæ Shuckburgh Hugonis Stewckley
Baronetti Filiæ, quæ ultra natalium splendorem
Suis eluxit virtutibus, ardentifsimæ ergo Deum
pietatis, Liberalitatis erga pauperes effufifsimæ,
Individui erga maritum amoris illustrifsimum
exemplar, quale nec præfens ætas æquare potutt*
nec Futura unquam antecedet. Eodem puerperio
Filio ex fe nato hæreditatem reliquet Temporariam
Sibi æternam acquifivit. Aug. 17 Anno Salutis
humanæ. 1683
Desideratifsimæ conjugi monumentum hoc
posuit Carolus Shuckburgh Bar^t Mœstissimus
Maritus.

F *on key plan.*

*Brass on floor of chancel, black-letter inscription above the figure of a woman.*

Arms at top : A chevron between three mullets pierced.†

𝕳𝖎𝖈 𝖏𝖆𝖈𝖊𝖙 𝕸𝖆𝖗𝖌𝖆𝖗𝖊𝖙𝖊 𝕮𝖔𝖙𝖊𝖘 𝖇𝖝' 𝕵𝖔𝖍'𝖓𝖎 𝕮𝖔𝖙𝖊𝖘 𝖋𝖎𝖑𝖎𝖎 & 𝖍𝖊𝖗𝖊𝖉'
𝕿𝖍𝖔𝖒𝖊 𝕮𝖔𝖙𝖊𝖘 𝖉𝖊 𝕳𝖔𝖓𝖎'𝖌𝖍𝖆𝖒 𝖆𝖗𝖒𝖎𝖌'𝖎 𝖖𝖚𝖔'𝖉𝖆' 𝖋𝖎𝖑𝖎𝖊 𝕿𝖍𝖔'𝖊 𝕾𝖍𝖚𝖐𝖇𝖚𝖗𝖗𝖌𝖍
𝕾𝖊𝖓𝖞𝖔𝖗 𝖉𝖊 𝕾𝖍𝖚𝖐𝖇𝖚𝖗𝖗𝖌𝖍 𝖆𝖗𝖒𝖎𝖌'𝖎 𝖈𝖚𝖎' 𝖆'𝖎𝖊 𝖕'𝖕'𝖎𝖊𝖙𝖚𝖗 𝕯𝖊𝖚𝖘 𝖆𝖒𝖊𝖓.

(*To be continued.*)

---

* Sculptor's error for *potuit*.
† This coat is fixed in error on this slab. It ought to be placed at the corner of the stone
on which is the brass of Anthony Shuckburgh.

# 𝔖trettell.*

ENTRIES FROM A BIBLE DATED 1663.   PRINTED AT CAMBRIDGE BY JOHN FIELD.
ON THE COVER ARE STAMPED THE LETTERS A. S., PRESUMABLY FOR
A(NNE) S(TRETTELL).

Anne Strettell daughter of Amos and Experience Strettell was born 23ᵈ of 12 mo
being the 7 day of ye weeke 169$\frac{4}{5}$.

Amos Strettell was born 1ˢᵗ 4 mo 1696.

Elizabeth Strettell 25ᵗʰ 7 mo the 7ᵗʰ day of ye week 1697.

Thomas Strettell was born 13ᵗʰ day of 7 mo ye 4ᵗʰ day of ye weeke 1699.

Ebenezer was born 27ᵗʰ 12 mo 1700.

Jacob was born 5ᵗʰ of ye 3 mo 1702.

Ebenezer departed this life 3 mo 1703.

Jacob dyed 11 mo at Robert Leckeys 170$\frac{3}{4}$.

Experience was born 23ʳᵈ 5 mo 1704.

Experience dyed 26 4 mo 1705.

Lydia Strettell was born 28ᵗʰ of 6 mo 4ᵗʰ day of ye weeke 1706.

Benjamin was born 23ʳᵈ of 9 mo 1ˢᵗ day 1707.

Experience Strettell wife of Amos Strettell departed this life 24ᵗʰ of 9ᵗʰ mo greatly
lamented.

Benjamin dyed 21ˢᵗ x mo 1708.

Amos Strettell son of Amos and Experience Strettell dyed the 30ᵗʰ of ye 11 mo 1712.

> Ann Strettell
> her bible
> Given her by
> John Tristrem.

Amos Strettell son of Hugh and Mary Strettell of Saltersley in Mobberly in
Cheshire in England was born the 24ᵗʰ day of ye 12ᵗʰ mo called ffebruary in
the year 1657 entered in ffrᵈˢ register book of Morley meeting in Cheshire.

Hee came to Ireland in the 1 mo called March 167$\frac{8}{9}$ hee took to wife Experience
Cappage daughter of Major Robert Cappage and Elezabeth his wife in a meeting
of the people called Quakers at Lambstone in the county of Wexford the 23ᵈ of
the 1 mo called March 169$\frac{3}{4}$.

Robert Strettell son of Amos and Experience Strettell was born in back lane Dublin
the 25ᵗʰ of xᵇᵉʳ ye 2ⁿᵈ day of ye weeke 1693.

Experience daughter of John & Anne Barclay was born ye 12ᵗʰ day of ye 4 mo
1715 between 7 & 8 in ye morning first day of ye weeke in Eustice Street
Dublin.

Christian was born 16 4 mo 1716 7ᵗʰ day.

Robert son of ye aforesaid 19ᵗʰ 1 mo 17$\frac{17}{18}$ the 4ᵗʰ day of ye weeke in Eustice Street
aforesᵈ.

Robert departed this life ye 3 mo following.

Anne was born ye 3ʳᵈ of 7 mo about 7 in ye morning and 5 day of ye weeke 1719.

Katherine was born 13ᵗʰ of ober 1720 ye 1ˢᵗ day of ye weeke.   She departed this
life 19ᵗʰ day of ye same.

Christian departed this life ye 5 ober 1721.   She dyed of ye small pox 11 days after
taken ill.

Patience was born ye 30 of 11 mo 1731 3ᵈ day soon after sun rise in ye morning.

John son of ye aforesaid was born 18ᵗʰ of ye 7 mo 1723 ye 4ᵗʰ day of ye weeke after
4 in ye afternoon.

Elizabeth was born 6ᵗʰ of 11 mo 17$\frac{25}{27}$ about $\frac{1}{2}$ an hour past 8 in ye morning ye 6ᵗʰ
day of the weeke in Eustice Street aforesaid.

* Communicated by J. F. FULLER, Esq., F.S.A.

# 𝕲𝖊𝖓𝖊𝖆𝖑𝖔𝖌𝖕 𝖔𝖋 𝕭𝖗𝖔𝖜𝖓𝖊.*

## 𝕰𝖛𝖎𝖉𝖊𝖓𝖈𝖊𝖘.

### CAVERSWALL.

CAVERSWALL REGISTERS.

1559   Margerie Browne was buryd the last day of January ann. 1559.
1561   Thomas Browne ye sonne of Will'm Browne was bapt. the xxij[th] day of Maie an'o p'dicto.
1561   . . . . Browne ye daughter of John Browne and his wife was bapt. xxj day of June 1561.
1562   Raffe Browne ye sonne of Raffe Browne and his wife was bapt. ye first day of Januarie in a'o 1562.
1562   Thomas Browne was buryed ye vij[th] day of Februarie a'o 1562.
1562   Raffe Browne and Marie Porter were marryed the x[th] daye of Februarie a'o p'd'cto 1562.
1563   Jois [Joyce] Browne the daughter of Will. Browne was bapt. ye xxv[th] day of Aprill in a'o p'd'cto.
1563   Margerie Browne the daughter of Raffe Browne was bapt. ye xxij daye of June in a'o p'd'cto.
1564-5   Anne Browne the daughter of . . . . [William Browne ?] was bapt. ye fourth day of . . . . [February ?] anno p'dicto.
1565   John Browne ye sonne of Raffe . . . . [Browne ?] was bapt. ye viij day of October in an'o 1565.
1566   Raffe Browne the sonne of Raffe Browne was bapt. the xvij[th] day of November ut supra. [Appended to this entry is a note in a later hand] pater R. Br., de Meere, gen.
1567-8   Elizabethe Browne the daughter of Will'm Browne was bapt. the xxvj[th] daye of Januarie a'o p'd'cto.
1568-9   Marie Browne the daughter of Raffe Browne was bapt. ye xv[th] daye of March anno 1568.
1569-70   Marie Browne was buryed ye . . . . day of Marche an'o p'd'cto.
1569-70   Marie Browne the daughter of Will'm Browne was bapt. the v[th] daye of Marche a'o p'd'cto.
1570   Grace Browne the daughter of Raffe Browne was bapt. ye viij[th] daye of Aprill a'o 1570.
1570   Grace was buryed ye xxx[th] daye of Julie a'o 1570.
1571   Margerie Browne the daughter of Will'm Browne was bapt. the xxvj[th] daye of Januarie a'o 1571.
1573-4   Alice Browne the daughter of Will'm Browne was bapt. the first daye of Januare ut sup[r].
1573-4   Will'm Browne the sonne of Raffe Browne was bapt. the v[th] daye of Maie ut sup[r].
1576   Thomas Browne the sonne of Raffe Browne and Maria his wife was bapt. the xiiij[th] daye of September a'o p'd'cto.
1584   Edward Morton and Margerie Browne were married the xv[th] day of June in a'o p'd'cto 1584.
1588   Edmu'de Wethering and Anne Browne were maried the iiij[th] daye of June a° p'd'cto.
1588   Will'm Lees and Elizabeth Browne were maryed the iiij[th] daye of August A'o D'ni 1588.
1591   Elizabeth Browne ye wife of Will'm Browne was buryed ye vx[th] [ix] daye of Aprill a'o p'd'cto.
1594   Will'm Browne and Marie . . . . [? Bobyn] were maried the xiiij[th] daye of Octobe in A'o D'ni 1594.
1594   . . . . [? Ralph] Bridgwood and Marie Browne were maried the xx[th] daye of Noyeber in a'o p'd'cto.
1598   Raulp Browne was buryed ye vx[th] [ix] daye of Maie a'o p'd'cto.
1598   Raupf the sonne of Raupf Browne and Dorothie his wife was bapt. ye xiiij[th] daye of Julij an'o p'd'cto.
1599   Dorothie Browne the daughter of Ralph Browne and Dorothie his wife was bapt. the x[th] daye of September anno p'd'cto.
1599-1600   Marie Browne the wife of Will'm Browne was buried the xxj[th] daye of Januarie a'o 1599.
1603   Will'm Browne was buryed the xxx[th] daye of Maie a'o 1603.

[Register deficient 1607—1613.]

1614   Thom[s] Browne filius Thom[s] Browne gent. et Clara uxor eius sepult fuit 8 die Sept'er 1614.
1615   Maria Browne vidua sepult fuit 7° die Aprilis a'o p'cto.
1615   Thoma[s] Browne filius Thoma Browne et Clara uxor eius baptizat fuit 10° die Sept. an'o p'd'o.
1617   Katherina Browne filia Thomæ Browne gent. et Clara uxor eius bapt. fuit 26° die Oct[r] a'o p'd'o.
1618   Dorothea Browne uxor Radulphi Browne gener. sepulta fuit decimo septimo die Augustij anno p'd'cto.
1618   Elizabetha Browne filia Radulphi et Joisae uxor eius baptizata fuit vicesimo septimo die September anno p'd'cto 1618.

* Continued from p. 163.

1618-19   Maria Browne filia Thome Browne et Clara uxor eius baptizata fuit 15° die March
          ut sup<sup>r</sup>.
1619   Dorothea ye daughter of Rauffe Browne gener. and Joyce his wyfe was baptized the xxvij<sup>th</sup>
       of June a'o ut supra.   [The name " Dorothea " is in different handwriting, and
       appears to be a later insertion.]
1621   Jane Browne the daughter of M<sup>r</sup> Ralph Browne & Joyce his wife was baptized July 29.
1621-2   Thomas Browne the sonne of John Browne & Bridget his wife baptized ye 5<sup>th</sup> die of
         February.
1622   Mary Browne the daughter of Ralph Browne and Joyce his wife baptized Decemb. 9.
1623-4   Raulfe Browne ye son of Raulfe Browne and Joyce his wife was baptized ffebrua. 21.
1625   Ellen Browne the daughter of Thomas Browne & Anne his wyfe was baptized the 27<sup>th</sup> of
       March.
1625   Raphe Browne the sonne of Raphe Browne was buryed the 29<sup>th</sup> of March.
1625   Raphe Browne the sonne of Raphe Browne aforesaid and Joyce his wife was baptized the
       8<sup>th</sup> day of Aprill.
1625   Ellen Browne ye daughter .of Thomas Browne and Anne his wyfe was buryed the i day of
       Julii an'o p'dicto.
1626   John the son of John Browne & Bridgett his wife was baptized Martii 25.
1626   John Browne the sonne of John Browne and Bridgett his wyfe was buryed the 28<sup>th</sup> day
       of March.
1626   John Browne ye sonne of Raphe Browne and Joyce his wife was baptized May 11<sup>th</sup>.
1626-7   Anne Browne the daughter of Raph Browne & of Joyce his wife was bap<sup>td</sup> 14 Maij.
1626-7   Ellin Browne the daughter of John Browne & Bridgett his wife was bapt. 5 August.
1628   Joyce Browne the daughter of Ra. Browne & Joyce his wife was bapt. 15 Junij 1628.
1629   Abigall ye daughter of Raph Browne & his wife was baptized ye 18<sup>th</sup> of October.
1630   Bridget Browne was buried May xxij.
1631   John Browne and Anne Woode were married Nov<sup>r</sup> 10.
1632-3   Joice Browne was buried Feb. 5<sup>th</sup>.
1633   .... daughter of John Browne & his wife was bapt. Maii the 9<sup>th</sup>.
1634   John Browne & Anne Sergeant were marryed August the 2<sup>d</sup>.
1634   Mary daughter of John Broome [Browne] & Anne his wife was baptized the 30 August
       1634.
1636   .... wife of Francis Browne was buried April 22, 1636.
1638   Raph the sonne of John Browne & Anne his wife was baptized the 30<sup>th</sup> December.
1640   Hugh Browne & Anne Till both of the parish of Carswall were marryed 12<sup>th</sup> Aprilis 1640.
1640   Thomas the son of Hugh Browne & Anne his wife was bapt. the 15<sup>th</sup> day of July Anno
       Domini 1640.
1641   Anne the daughter of Hugh Browne & of Anne his wife was baptized 24<sup>th</sup> of October
       a'o 1641.
1642   Raph Browne of the Meere gent. was buried 26<sup>th</sup> Aprilis An'o Do'ni 1642.

[Registers deficient 1643—1662 and 1665—1672.]

1693   November 9.   Brigitta filia Thomæ Brown et Prudentia uxoris ejus baptizata fuit, de Mear.
1695   Nov. 7.   Thomas filius Thomæ Browne & Prudentia uxoris natus fuit 7 Nov., bapt. 5 Dec.,
       de Meare.
1704   Martii 20.   Abigal filia Thomæ Brown & Prudentia ejus uxoris baptizata fuit.
1705   Maii 13.   Elizabetha filia Johannis Brown & Sarah ejus uxoris baptizata fuit.
1722   Thomas son of Thomas Browne & Hanna de Mear bapt. 25 Nov. 1722.
1743-4   Ralph Browne of Caughley, parish of Broseley, buried 20 March.

-------------

CHURCHWARDENS' ACCOUNTS.

THOMAS ASHBURIE  ⎫
GEORGE TOOTH     ⎬ Churchwardens 1626.
Ashburie served for Mr. Raph Browne.

-------------

Benjamin Warrilow churchwarden 1691, for Mr. Browne's house w<sup>ch</sup> he liveth in.

-------------

William the sonne of Thomas Heath, for the house he lives in, and ⎫
  Thomas Browne, for that house he lives in at Meare belongeinge ⎬ Churchwardens for the
  to Mr. Browne.                                                  ⎭ yeare 1695.

-------------

William Warrilow, for Mr. Browne's living in ye Mear held by Thomas Browne, 1720.

-------------

Mr. Littlehale, for Mr. Brown's old house pull'd down at Cookshill, 1723.

-------------

Copy of a Document recording the composition made by Ralph Browne of Caverswall, co. Stafford, and others, for not receiving Knighthood,* *temp.* Charles I.

To the Right Ho'ble Richard Lord Weston Lord Treasurer of England ; S'r Frauncis Cottington, Knt., Chancellor of his Ma'ties Court of Exchequer ; S'r Humfrey Davenport, Knight, Lord Chiefe Baron of the said Court ; and to the rest of the Barons there.

May it please yo'r Lo'pps :—

By vertue of his Ma'ties Com'ission, and the Instruc'ons thereunto annexed, and whereunto these P'sents are affixed, we have made composic'on for the Order of Knighthood and for issues lost w'th the p'ties hereafter named ; who for these causes have agreed to pay, and have paid to the Right Ho'ble Walter Aston, his Ma'ties Collector, the sev'rall sum'es of money hereafter menc'o'ed ; that is to say :—

| | | |
|---|---|---|
| Ralph Browne, of Carswall, Gent. | £10 | 0 | 0 |
| Mathew Moreton, of Engleton, Esq. | £17 | 10 | 0 |

etc., etc.

---

Copy of an Inscription upon a small copper plate at the head of a large slab,† let into the wall of the Chancel of Caverswall Church, co. Stafford :—

NEARE TO THIS PLACE LIETH THE<br>
BODIES OF IOHN BROWNE LATE OF HART-<br>
WALL GEN. WHO GAVE TO THE CHVRCH<br>
AND PORE OF THIS PARISH FIVE POVNDS<br>
YEARLEY FOR EVER HE DEPARTED THIS<br>
LIFE IN THE XXXIX YEARE OF HIS AGE<br>
AND WAS BVRIED DECEMBER THE XIIJ<br>
ANNO 1665 AND OF RALPH BROWNE<br>
LATE OF MEERE AND COOKSHILL HIS<br>
FATHER GEN. WHO GAVE TO THE CHVRCH<br>
AND PORE OF THIS PARISH THIRTY SHIL-<br>
LINGS YEARELEY FOR EVER HE DEPARTED<br>
THIS LIFE IN THE 72 YEARE OF HIS AGE<br>
AND WAS BVRIED APRLIL THE 14 ANNO 1670.

RES PATER ET NATO NATUS PATRIQ : ET EGEIU<br>
ATQ : DEA GENITOR NATUSQ : BENIGNE DEDERVN<br>
DIGNA LEGI SCRIBI DIGNA HÆC DIGNISSIMA DICI<br>
CONFVNDVNT LACHRYMIS SED SE MEA VERBA VALETI<br>
HÆC POSUI LIB VICAR. DE. CARS.

*Translation.*‡

Father (? God) and Son (? Christ) [gave] wealth to the son and father. And father and son gave liberally to the poor and to God. This is worthy to be written, and most worthy to be related. But my words mix themselves with tears. I placed it [here] by the permission of the Vicar of Caverswall.

And lower down on the said plate, in large incised letters :—

AN'O D'M'I 1670.

BLEST HERE AND NEAR<br>
IN PEACE DOE REST<br>
ALL THEY OF THESE<br>
THAT ARE DECEAST.

THO. BROWNE AND MARGERY<br>
RALPH BROWNE AND MARY<br>
RALPH BROWNE AND DOROTHY<br>
RALPH BROWNE AND IOYCE.

---

* 'Collections for a History of Staffordshire,' vol. ii., p. 13. The original document is in the Public Record Office.

† The small copper plate measures 12 by 9¼ inches. The slab to which the plate is fixed measures 6 feet 6 inches by 3 feet 6 inches. The whole of the inscription is now almost entirely hidden from view by a large monument to the late Lady St. Vincent, which has been erected in front of it. It is understood that the family burialplace was in the churchyard, outside the chancel, and immediately behind the inscription.

‡ This is the only sensible rendering which can be made of these very poor hexameters.

RALPH BROWNE ⎫
RALPH BROWNE ⎬
IOHN BROWNE ⎭

THE TWO FIRST BROWNES
OF CARSWALL WERE
BVT ALL THE REST WERE
OF THE MEERE
THE 4TH MADE THIS IN MEMORY
OF PARENTS POSTERITY.*

CHARITIES OF JOHN BROWNE AND RALPH BROWNE, 1666.

Copy of the tablet in the Vestry of Caverswall Church.

"Benefactions to the poor of this parish.

"John Browne late of Caverswall Gent. and Ralph Browne his Father, late of the Mear and Cookshill Gent. Left to the Poor of this Parish, for ever fourteen Acres of Land, called the Stevenstiches, in the Parish of Dilhorn, now let at the yearly Rent of Thirty Pounds, out of which two Pounds ten Shillings is to be paid Yearly for ever to the Minister for two Sermons, one upon th' 24th of June, and the other upon th' 13th of December."

The above tablet probably replaced an older one about 1832.

The Charity is composed of a gift of following lands :—

|                              | A. | R. | P. |
|------------------------------|----|----|----|
| Rowley Hill .................... | 1 | 3 | 30 |
| Upper Stephen Stiches ............ | 5 | 0 | 11 |
| Middle      ,,      ,,   ............. | 2 | 1 | 25 |
| Lower       ,,      ,,   ............. | 2 | 2 | 5 |
| Rowley Hill .................... | 2 | 0 | 26 |
| Total ............. | 14 A. | 0 R. | 17 P. |

A long report of this charity will be found in the 'Further Report of the Commissioners for Inquiring Concerning Charities,' 1825, Report xiii., pp. 356-7. The last Deed of Appointment of Trustees is dated 2 Sept. 1875. The total income now derived from the gift is £45 per annum : of which £42 10s. is distributed amongst the poor, and the remaining £2 10s. is paid to the Vicar of the parish, according to the donor's wishes, for preaching two sermons, the one upon 13 Dec., and the other upon St. John the Baptist's Day. There are about 100 donees, who at each half-yearly distribution receive sums varying from 1s. to 9s. They are carefully selected from the deserving poor of the parish, which contains over five thousand inhabitants.

Extract from Harl. MS. 1990, fol. 46-7 : Erdeswicke's ' View of Staffordshire' [1593—1603].

CAVERSWALL.

"Of Caverswall was Lord (as I take it) in R[ichard] 1st tyme one Thomas de Caverswall, Knt, who had issue Sr Richard de Caverswall, Kt, who had issue Will'm de Caverswall, which builded there a goodly Castle and Pools, the dam'es [dams] beinge of masonarye worke, and all his houses of office likewise, he had issue Rich' [de] Caverswall, who [lived] 19° E[dward] 3d [1435].

"ffrom the Caverswalls it came by descent to the Montgomeries, and from them to Gifford, from Gifford to Porte, and from Porte to my Lord of Huntingdon now owner thereof in the right of the Countesse his wife. The Castle† was lately in reasonable good repaire, but now is almost quite decayed by one Browne ffarmer of the demeanes which I think he p[ro]cured (if a man might guesse att the cause), lest the Lord should take a conceipt to lyve and soe take the demeanes from him."

(*To be continued.*)

---

* This word is almost defaced, and will probably soon become quite illegible.
† The Castle was rebuilt 1627—1630; it is said from a design by Inigo Jones. The present owner is Sir Joseph Percival Pickford Radclyffe, Bart., of Rudding Hall, York.

# The Register Book of Bramfield, co. Suffolk.*

**1554. In the yeare, etc., as before.**

June 8    Dorythie Melle dowght' of Henry Melle and ffr'nnc's his wyff.

June 16   Edmond Wryght and Marie Wryght sone and dowghter of Henry Wryght theld'.

June 25   Will'm Starke sone of Godfryde Starke and Agnes his wyff.

July 16    Will'm Cocke sone of Ric' Cocke.

Sep. 25   Nycholes Gyslyngh'm sone of John Gyslyngh'm and Joh'nne his wyf.

Oct.  2    Elizabeth ffreston dowght' of Ric' ffreston.

Oct. 23   Raynold Ameille sone of W^m Ameille.

Nov.  5    Rob^t ffolkerd and Marie ffolkerd sone and dowght' of W^m ffolkerd and Katheryn his wyf.

Nov. 12   Ric' Smyth sone of Rob^t Smyth.

Nov. 12   Agnes Richard dowghter of Ric' Richards and Margaret his wyf.

Dec. 11   Henry Dowsyn sone of Thomas Dowsyng and M'garet his wyf.

Dec. 25   Rog' ffelay sone of John ffelay and Olyf his wyff.

Jan.  6    John Joyn' sone of John Joyn' and Joh'nne his wyf.

Jan. 29   Rob^t fforman sone of Thomas fforman.

Feb. 18   Edmond Thurton sone of Edmond Thurton.

May 16   Renald ffelaye sone of Thomas and Alice his wyff.

June 19   Elizabeth Brokett dowghter of Robart Brokett and Margaret his wyf.

July 10   Marye Wace dowghter of [blank].

Aug. 15   Will'm Neylle sone of John Neylle.

A° p'mo Marie. This yeare Christened xxi Childre', whereof Men Children xiiij, Women Children vij, Bastards none.

**1555. In the yeare of our lord god A Thousand ffyve hundreth ffyftie & v & in the ffirst & ij^de yeares of the Reignes of king philipp & Quen Marie was Christened At Bramefeild as here followeth, viz.:**

Dec.  3    Will'm Gyslyngh'm sone of John Gyslyngh'm and Joh'nne his wyff.

Dec. 21   Joh'nne Clerke dowght' of Roger Clerke.

Mar.  5    Renald ffelay sone of Rob^t ffelay and Margerye his wyff.

Mar. 10   Philippe Benet dowght' of W^m Benet and Elizabeth his wyff.

April 20   Alice Richards dowght' of Ric' Richards and M'garet his wyff.

May  6    John Wolfleytt sone of Rog' Wolflet and Elizabeth his wyff.

May 12   Anthony West sone of Will'm West and Margery his wyffe.

Aug. 18   Joh'nne Master bastard dowght' of Margerye Master synglewoma'.

This yeare Christened viii Children, whereof Mene Children iiij, Women Childre' iiij whereof Bastards one.

**1556. In the yeare, etc., as before.**

Nov.  8    Thomas ffelay sone of Rob^t ffelaye and M'garet his wyf.

Nov. 14   Margaret Walpule dowght' of Nycholes Walpule and Ameye his wyff.

Nov. 27   Agnes Hacon dowghter of Robart Hacon and Agnes his wyff.

Dec.  2    Olyff Skeitt dowghter of John Skeitt and Joh'nne his wyff.

Jan. 19   Susanne ffellay dowghter of John ffelay and Olyff his wyff.

Mar. 23   Anne Ameille dowght' of John Ameille and Dorythie his wyf.

Mar. 31   [blank] Starke sonne of Godfraye Starke and Agnes his wyf.

May  2    Margaret ffolkerd dowght' of W^m ffolkerd and Christyn his wyff.

May  6    Thomas Dowsyn bastard sone of Margaret Dowsyn synglewoman.

May 22   Rob't Wryght and John Wryght sones of Henry Wryght and Christyn his wyfe.

June 10   Thomas ffarro' sone of Nycholes ffarro' and Agnes his wyf.

Aug.  4    Margerye West dowghter of W^m West and Issabell his wyff.

Aug. 22   Rob't Joyn' sonne of John Joyn' and Joh'nne his wyff.

Aug. 27   Alice Rison dowght' of Ric' Ryson and Christyn his wyff.

Sep.  9    Henry Donet sone of Ric' Donet and Katheryn his wyff.

This yeare Christened xvi Children, whereof Mene Children viij whereof Bastards one, Womene Child'n viij.

**1557. In the yeare, etc., as before.**

Feb.  6    John ffelay sone of Thomas ffelay and Alice his wyff.

Feb. 14   Dorythie Brokett dowghter of Rob't Brokett and M'garet his wyff.

Mar.  2    Alice Veysie dowght' of Rob't Veysy and Anne his wyf.

Mar.  7    Thomas Clerke bastard sone of Brygytte Clerke synglewoman.

Mar. 26   John Gardyn sone of George Gardyn.

Aug. 20   Nycholes Dowsyn sone of Thomas Dowsyn and Alice his wyff.

This yeare Christened vj Children, whereof Mene Children iiij whereof Bastards one, Women Children ij.

**1558. In the yeare, etc., as before.**

Dec. 30   James Hacon sone of Robart Hacon and Agnes his wyff.

Jan. 11   Joh'es ffelay sone of Robart ffelay Jun' and Margaret his wyf.

Jan. 11   Marie Joyn' dowght' of John Joyn' and Joh'nne his wyff.

Mar.  9    Olyff Veysye dowght' of Robart Veysye and Anne his wyffe.

This yeare Christened iiij Children, whereof Mene Children ij, Women Children ij, Bastards none.

* Continued from p. 195.

*On the margin is written :*

The death of Quene Marie.
The Raign of our most noble Quene Elizabeth.

### 1558.

M^d. The xvii^th daye of November In the yeare of our lord god A Thousand ffyve hundreth ffiftie & eight dep'ted this present lyf oure moost vertuouse & noble Quene Marie And was Royallye buryed At Westm' the xxi^tie day of December in the same yeare whose soule god take to his Infynyte m'cye. Amen. And the xvij^th day of November was p'clamed & beganne hir gracyous Raygn our moost Noble & Sou'aign Ladye Quene Elizabeth whose gracyous Raign god grante long to Contenue. Amen.

1559. In the yeare of our lord god A Thousand ffyve hundreth ffyftie & ix And in the ffirst yeare of the Raigne of our most dread and Sou'aign Ladye Elizabeth by the grace of god of Ingland ffrance & Ireland Quene defend' of the faith, etc., was Christened At Bramefeild As here ensuyth, viz.

Dec. 10   [*blank*] Crispe dowght' of John Crispe and Anne his wyff.
Dec. 28   John Hacon sonne of Robart Hacon and Agnes his wyff.
Jan. 20   John ffelay sone of Robart ffelay and Margerye his wyffe.
Jan. 21   Thomas Richards sone of Richard Richards and Margaret his wyfe.
Sep. 29   Will'm Dowsyne sone of Thomas Dowsyne and Alys his wyf.
Feb. 13   John Skeeth sone of John Skeeth and Jane his wyf.
Mar. 17   John Scherwode sone of Thomas Scherwode and Annes his wyf littera d'm'calis F.

In the yeare of our lord god MCCCCLX And in the Seconde yeare of the Raygne of oure most godly Quene Elyzabet Quene of englond ffrannce and Irelond defender of the fayth and the churche of Inglond and Irelond Sup'me gou'nor in causys ecclesiasticall ase temp'all wasse Crystend att Bramfeld As here Insueth or folowyth :

Mar. 26   Harry farrar sonne of Thomas farrar andAnne hys wyffe littera d'm'calis F.
May 15    Raynald Clarke sonne of Robrt Clarke and Elyzabeth hys wyefe.
Sep.  7   Jone Dyannt' dowt' of Wat' Dyannt' and Vrsula hys wyeffe.
Oct.  6   Marget Ryckard dowt' of Rychard Ryckard and Marget hys wyeffe.
Dec.  9   Alys Storke dowt' of Godfraye Storke and Annes hys wyffe.
Dec. 13   Brygget Goodryche dowt' of M'get Goodryche stranger.
Dec. 19   Henry Grynlyng sonne of Henry Grynlyng.
Feb.  2   Han Calthorpe dowt' of Hantony Calthorpe gent. and Kateryn hys wyffe.

### 1560.

April 27  Grace Deye bastard dowt' of Besse Dey of Thoryngton.

### 1561.

June  1   Thomas Joyen' sonne of John Joyen' and Jone hys wyffe.
July 20   Raynald Donet sone of Rychard Donet and Cateryn hys wyffe.
July 27   Marye Garnar dowt' of John Garnar and Crysten hys wyffe.
Aug. 30   Artur Wannewrythe sone of John Wannewrythe and [*blank; on the margin is written* Olyff ] hys wyffe.
May 17    Anteny Leny sone of Anteny Leny [*interpolated in a different handwriting*].
Sep. 25   Jone Watlyng dowt' of Thom's Watlyng and Mary hys wyffe.
Oct. 25   Nyc'las Thyrlyng sonne of Nycolas Thyrlyng Vycar of Bramfeld and Cryste' hys wyfe.
Jan. 25   Mary Loggyn and Est Loggyn dowters of James Loggyn and Marget hys wyffe.
Feb.  1   Helyn Wrythe dowter of Thom's Wrythe and Wenefryde hys wyefe.

### 1562.

Aug. 28   Dauyd Oslore basterde.
Dec.  1   Jhon Agar sone to Jhon Agar and Alys hys wyefe.
Jan.  1   Jhon Weste sone to Wyllyam Weste and Margrete hys wyefe.
Jan.  1   Margery Gerlynge dowter to Hary Gerlynge and Margery hys wyefe.
Feb.  7   Jhon Haryson sone to Anys Haryson.

### 1563.

April 26  Hary sone to Johne Walpail the wyeffe nowe to Thomas Harvy.
May  9    Magaret Donnett dowght' of Will'm Donnett and Joone his wyff.
Aug. 15   Jhon Jaye sone to Rycharde Jaye, Wyker, and Margrete hys wyfe.
Nov.  8   Mary Wanwryte douter to Jhon Wanwryte and Margret hys wyfe.
Nov. 23   Samvell Lester bastarde.
Feb. 28   Henry Rabet sone to Ranolde Rabet gen^tel and Alys hys wyefe.
April 21  Ano p'dicto. John Rycard soon vnto Rychard Rycard and Margeret his wif [*interpolated in a different handwriting*].
Feb. 28   Jhon Donete sone to Rycharde Donete and Catryne hys wyefe.

### 1564.

May 21    Alys Clarcke dowter to Robarde Clarcke.
Aug.  8   Nycolas Raylton sonne to Wyllyam Raylton.
Nov. 10   Garge Chapman sonne to Rychard Chapman.
Dec. 28   Ranolde Wryte sonne to Thomas Wryte and Weny hys wyefe.
Jan.  1   Margrete Gerlynge dowter to Hary Gerlynge and Margrete hys wyefe.
Jan. 23   Paule Starke sone to Godfre and Annys hys wyfe.

### 1565.

July 19   Ane Rabete dowter to Ranovlde Rabete and Alys hys wyfe.

Nov. 25   Henry farrer sone to Henry farrer and faythe hys wyefe.

Dec. 23   Margret Clarcke and ffynet Clarcke dowters to Thomas Clarcke and Catryne hys wyeffe.

### 1566.

Aug. 17   Marye Rabete dowtere to Raynold Rabete and Alys hys wyfe.

Oct. 20   Edmund Donete sonne to Welyam Donite.

Sep. 1   Marrien Wesey davtere to Raynold Wesey and Margret his wyfe.

Feb. 9   Thomas Gyrlyng sone to Hary Gyrlyn' and Margret his wyfe.

Feb. 16   Alys Rychard dowter to Rychard Rycharde and Margrete hys wyefe.

### 1567.

April 6   Alys Sherwode dawghter to Thomas Sherwode and Rose hys wyfe.

April 20   Margaret Raignold Ragnolds dowghter unto John Raignolds and Anuys his wyf.

June 29   Roger Donyt sonne of Rychard Donyt and Katheryn his wyfe.

July 25   Margarett Clarcke dowght' of Robert Clarke and Elyzabeth his wyffe.

Oct. 8   John Byllny sonne vnto Elysebeth Byllny, basterd.

Nov. 23   George Veysey sonne of Reynould Vysey and Margeret his wyff.

Jan. 15   John Denny and Gone Denny sone and doughter of John Denny and Halles his wyffe. [*Both buried the same day, evidently twins; two more were baptized in October*.]

Mar. 12   Thommes Hedlyng sone to Wylli'm Hedlyng.

Mar. 21   Ryccharde Wrytt sone to Thommes Wrytte and Wynne hys wyfe.

### 1568.

April 4   Alles fellow dowghter to John fellow and Margere his wyffe.

April 11   Reynould Rebbett sone to Reynoulde Rebbett and Halles his wyffe.

July 25   Thommes Sherhod sone of Thomes Sherchode and Rosse his wyffe.

Aug. 1   Mageret farrer daughter of Hary farrer and fayth his wyfe.

Sep. 6   Wylli'm Hvehenes [Evens] sonne to Herter Hevhenes and Elysebeth his wyffe.

Oct. 31   Thommes Denny [*buried Nov.* 13] and Mageret Denny sonne and daughter to John Denny and Alles his wyfe. [*They had twins baptized on Jan.* 15 *last. John Denny was now vicar.*]

Jan. 6   Raynold Veysie sonne of Raynold Veysie Thelder and Margaret his wyff.

Jan. 16   Walter ffarro' sonne of Rob't ffarro'.

### 1569.

April 17   John Peres sonne of John Peres and Margeret his wyfe.

May 8   Thommes Broccket sonne vnto Robert Broccket gen' and Margeret his wyfe.

July 21   John Rabbet sonne of Raynould Rabbet and Alles his wyfe.

Aug. 7   Thommes More sonne vnto Robert More.

Sep. 25   John fallowe sonne vnto John fallow and Margery his wife.

### 1570.

Jan. 1   Luke Cox daughter vnto Thomes Cox and Marry his wif.

Jan. 9   Margeret Hawger davter to John Awger.

Feb. 2   Thomes Visye and franses Visi sones vnto Raynould Vise and Margaret his wife.

Mar. 16   Mari felltem daughter vnto Thommes feltem.

Mar. 24   Elyzabeth Denny daughter vnto John Denny Clerck and Alles his wif was baptysed y$^e$ xxiiij day of Marche & being borne on y$^e$ Monday which was y$^e$ xx day of Mar' betweyn v & vi of y$^e$ clock in y$^e$ mor'ing. *On the margin is written* y$^e$ Sone in Aris.

Sep. 28   Georg Rabbet sonne vnto Raynould Rabbet and Alles his wife.

Oct. 1   Roberd Sherhode sonne vnto Thomes Sherhod and Rose his wife.

Nov. 19   Anne Reue daughter vnto Thommes Reue and Ellener his wife.

Dec. 11   Jane Clarcke daughter vnto Roberd Clarck and Elyzabeth his wife.

### 1571.

Jan. 21   Dorrese Mills daughter vnto Roger Mills and Jone his wife.

Feb. 2   Elyzabeth Peres daughter vnto John Peres and Margeret his wif.

Aug. 12   Will'um fallow soon vnto Robard fallow and Margeret his wif.

Sep. 17   Mathew Stanard bastard sonne vnto Elyzabeth Stanard.

Oct. 7   Thommes Port sonn vnto Thommes Port and Elyzabeth his wife.

Oct. 14   John Broccket and Elyne Broccket sonne and daughter vnto Robert Broccket and Margeret his wif.

Nov. 4   John farrar soon vnto Roberd farrar and Grace his wif.

Nov. 6   John Denny soon vnto John Denny and Alls his wif.

Jan. 21   An'e Rabbet daughter vnto Raynould Rabbet Jentillman and Alles his wif.

Feb. 24   Jane Coott daughter vnto frances Coott and Mary his wif.

### 1572.

April 10   Will'um West soon vnto Will'um Weste and Ane his wif.

May 20   Ane farrer daughter vnto Harry farrer and faith his wif.

Nov. 9    Alise Reve dowght' of Thomas Reve and Elynore his wyff.

Jan. 13    Mary Bowe' dowghte' of Rob't Bowe' and Cristen his wyff.

#### 1573.

May 3    John Clerk sonne of Rob't Clerk and Elizabeth his wyf.

Sep. 6    Marye fellowe davghter of Will'm fellowe and Alys his wyff.

May 6    Thomas Gilden sonne of Thomas Gilden.

Aug. 9    Jone fallow dau'ter vnto John falow and Margeri his [blank].

Sep. 15    Margerye Baldwyn davghter of Arthur Baldwyn and Margaret his wyfe.

Aug. 12    Will'um Rabbet sone vnto Raynould Rabbet gen. and Alls his wif.

Feb. 15    Edmvnd Perse sonne of John Perse and Margaret his wif.

#### 1574.

April 28    Alls Man daughter vnto Raynould Man and Alls his wif.

May 16    Margeri Boolle daughter vnto frances Bolle and Marie his wif.

Sep. 11    Marye Mill daughter vnto Roger Mill ge' and Joh'ne hys wif.

Nov. 7    Alls Skeit daughter vnto Asten Sket and Seble his wif.

Nov. 14    Ellyzabeth Tood daughter vnto Will'um Tod and Margery his wif.

Feb. 2    John Gillden sone vnto Thomes Gillden and Jone his wif.

Mar. 13    Thommes Reue soon vnto Thomes Reue and Ellyny his wif.

Jan. 13    frances Rabbet sone vnto Raynould Rabbet ge' and Alls his wif.

#### 1575.

Mar. 27    Thomes falla sonne vnto Roberd falla and Margeret his wif.

June 12    John Payne and Rachell Payn sone and daughter vnto John Payne.

July 31    Marye Denny daughter vnto John Denny Vicar and Alls his wif.

Sep. 11    frances Knits daughter vnto John Knits and Ane his wif.

Oct. 3    Jon'as Visie daughter vnto Ravnould Visie and Margeret his wif.

Oct. 3    Harrye Mill sonne vnto Roger Myll and Jone his wif.

Dec. 4    Margeret Sket daughter vnto Asten Sket and Siblye his wif.

Feb. 12    Rose Brokket daughter vnto Roberd broccket ge' and Margeret his wif.

Feb. 19    Margeret Raynoulds daughter vnto John Raynoulds and Dorryfy his wif.

#### 1576.

April 8    John Bourges soon vnto John Bourges and Christen his wif.

Oct. 9    Elyzabeth Pers dawter vnto Roberd Pers and Marye his wif.

July 1    Alls Wryt daughter vnto Thomes Wryt and Esbell his wif.

July 5    Margeret Rabbet daughter vnto Raynould Rabet ge' and Alls his wif.

July 5    Raynould West sone vnto Will'm West and Ane his wif.

Aug. 19    Edm'nde Wappoll soon vnto Richard Wappoll and Alls his wif.

Aug. 26    John Todd soon vnto Will'm Tod and Margerye his wif.

Nov. 18    Dorryfi Gylldyn daughter vnto Thomes Gylldyn and Jone his wif.

Dec. 16    Alls Howers daughter vnto Will'm Houers and Margeret his wife.

Jan. 6    Gorge falla soon vnto Will'm ffalla and Alls his wif.

Jan. 27    Nicholas ffarro' sonne of Rob't ffarro' and Grace hys wiff.

#### 1577.

May 27    Joon Mills daughter vnto Will'm Mills and Margeret his wif.

July 14    Ane falla dawter vnto John falla and Margerye his wif.

Aug. 25    Thomes Bennet soon vnto Thomes Bennet and Ane his wif.

Sep. 1    Sissilye falla daughter vnto Necolas falla and Jonne his wif.

Mar. 2    Gane Mylls daughter vnto Roger Mylls and Jone his wif.

#### 1578.

April 13    Roberd Weaste sone vnto Robard Waste and Chrysten hys wif.

May 25    Marye Gillden daughter vnto Thomes Gillden and Jone his wife.

June 22    Alls Knits daute' vnto John Knits and Ane his wif.

Aug. 10    Margerye falla daughter vnto Necolas falla and Jone his wife.

Aug. 17    Marye Pers daughter vnto Roberd Pers and Marye his wif.

Sep. 27    Brigit Cvllum daughter vnto Will'm Cvllum and Annes his wif.

Nov. 9    Roberd Toode sonn vnto Will'm Tode and Margerye his wif.

Dec. 7    John Weste soon vnto Will'm West and An'e his wif.

Dec. 8    Gorg Vicie sone vnto Raynould Vici and Margerete his wife.

Dec. 21    Ane Brocket dawter vnto Roberd Brockkett ge' and [blank] his wif.

Dec. 21    Jane Knits dawter vnto Necolas Knits and Marye his wife.

Jan. 1    Dorrifi formman daughter vnto Thomes forman and Jone his wif.

#### 1579.

April 11    Simon Parcke sonne of Jonne Parcke.

June 9    Ales Tobe dawter of Roberd Tobe and Alls his wyfe.

Jan. 23    Sewessan Newman daughter vnto Will'm Newman.

Mar. 27    Grase Reue davghter vnto Thomes Reue and Ellynye his wif.

#### 1580.

July 8    Svesan fela dawter vnto John ffella.

July 10    Jone Mell dawter of Roger Mell and Jone his wyff.

Oct. 9    Elyzabeth Pers dawter vnto Roberd Pers and Marye his wif.

Jan. 1    Harrye Gildin sone vnto Thomes Gildin and Jonne his wif.

Jan. 15 Necolas Tallar sonne vnto Grigorie Tayller and Margery his wif.

Feb. 5 Grase Nollore dawter vnto John Nollor and Marye his wif.

1581.

Mar. 27 Ane Stevenson dawter vnto Jams Steuenson.

April 2 Robberd Knits soon vnto Necolas Knits and Marie his wife.

April 25 Tobbyas fall basteard sonn vnto Sisslye fall.

June 2 Necolas Vissy sonne vnto Raynovld Visye and Margerit his wif.

July 3 Phyllys Tood dawter vnto Will'm Tod and Margery his wif.

Oct. 1 Roberd Kerrison sone vnto John Kerrison of Pvllom and Ellini his wife.

Dec. 7 Richard Wappoll and Thomes Wappoll sonnes vnto Richard Wappoll.

Dec. 10 Antonye Skolforth sonne vnto Thomes Skolforth.

Jan. 6 Elizabeth Seppins davghter vnto Hammond Seppins and Jonne his wif.

Jan. 8 Marie ford dawter vnto John ford and Mari his wif.

Feb. 4 Margeri forman davghter vnto Thomes formman and Jone his wif.

(*To be continued.*)

# Upton.*

## EXTRACTS FROM PARISH REGISTERS.

### STOKE NEWINGTON, CO. MIDDLESEX.

#### *Married.*

1672 Dec. 26 Mr. Solomon Farrington and Mrs. Eliz[th] Upton. Licence.
1673 May 26 Mr. Thomas Upton, Minister, and Mrs. Dorothy Lambe. Licence.
167$\frac{4}{5}$ Feb. 11 Mr. John Sayer and Mrs. Mary Upton of this parish.
1680 Sep. 9 Mr. Thos. Uvedall and Mrs. Jane Upton. Licence.
1743 Nov. 1 Joseph Rotherford of St. John's, Hackney, bachelor, and Elizabeth Upton of same, spinster. Licence.

#### *Baptized.*

1662 April 19 Darchus dau. of Mr. Gillber and Mrs. Dorcose Upton.
1663 Oct. 10 Dorothy dau. of Gillbert and Mrs. Dorcas Upton; born 9th Oct.
1666 June 1 John 2[d] son of Gillbert Upton.
1667 Aug. 10 Gilbert 4th son of Gilbert Upton by Dorcas his wife.

#### *Buried.*

1665 April 5 Unbaptized Child of Mr. Gilbert Upton.
1672 Aug. 8 Mrs. Jane *ux.* John Upton, Esq.
1678 June 28 Mr. Nicholas Upton son of John Upton, Esq.
1689 Dec. 10 John Upton, Esq.
1692 Oct. 16 Anthony Upton.
169$\frac{3}{4}$ Mar. 6 Thomas Upton.
1694 June 25 John Upton.
169$\frac{4}{5}$ Mar. 7 Mary Upton.
1706 Dec. 12 Mr. John Upton, merchant; in his own vault.
1713 Oct. 4 Madam Upton of St. Margaret's, Westminster. Chancel.
1718 (between June 9 and July 6) Anthony Upton, Esq.
1723 April 21 Mrs. Mary Upton.
1743 Oct. 6 Susannah Upton.
1749 July 24 Anthony Upton.
1756 April 10 Joseph Upton.
1764 Oct. 10 William Upton.

### ALL HALLOWS BARKING, LONDON.

#### *Married.*

167$\frac{1}{2}$ Jan. 28 John Kinnard of this parish, widower, and Mary Upton of St. Leonard, East Cheap, virgin. Licence.

#### *Buried.*

16$\frac{19}{20}$ Feb. 21 George Upton, late of Feversham, Kent, gent.

* Continued from p. 202.

### ALL HALLOWS STAINING, LONDON.
*Married.*

1678  Oct.  10  John Upton of Stoke Newington and Mary Warren.  Licence.

*Baptized.*

1694  Aug. 28  Sarah dau. of Abraham and Mary Upton.

### CHRIST CHURCH, LONDON.
*Married.*

1770  Feb.   8  William Upton of this parish, bachelor, and Susanna Freeman of
                St. Botolph, Billingsgate, spinster.  Licence.
1770  June 19  Thos. Owen Upton of this parish, bachelor, and Margaret
                Hutchins of St. Faith's, spinster.  Licence.

*Baptized.*

16$\frac{88}{50}$  Jan.  17  Francis son of Francis and Sarah Upton.
1753  Nov. 21  John son of Thomas and Mary Upton ; born 7th.
1756  Aug. 26  Elizth dau. of Thomas and Mary Upton ; born 2d.
1758  Jan. 27  John son of Thomas and Mary Upton ; born 20th.
1759  April 23  Charles son of Thomas and Mary Upton ; born 22d.
1767  July   3  Thos. Owen son of Thomas and Martha Upton ; born 22d.

*Buried.*

1711  Sep.  11  Francis Upton, Dr of Physic ; in Chancel.
17$\frac{13}{14}$  Jan. 31  Dorothy Upton ; Middle Aisle.
1757  April  7  John Upton, Esq. ; Chancel.

### ST. BENNET, PAUL'S WHARF, LONDON.
*Married.*

1706  Mar. 30  John Upton of the Middle Temple, bachelor, and Ann Forster of
                St. Martin in the Fields, spinster.  Licence.

### ST. BRIDE'S, LONDON.
*Buried.*

1598  May 15  Elizabeth Upton, widow and householder.

### ST. GILES, CRIPPLEGATE, LONDON.
*Baptized.*

1640  Nov. 17  Nathan son of Nathan Upton, Chirurgeon.
1647  Oct.   7  Benjamin son of Nathaniel Upton, Chirurgeon.
16$\frac{78}{80}$  Jan.  4  Samuel son of Nathaniel Upton, Physician, and Katherine.

*Buried.*

1659  June  7  Benjn son of Nathl Upton, Master of the Pest House ; fever
                Chancel.
1666  May 29  Nathaniel Upton, Chirurgeon, Pest House.  Chancel.
1666  June  9  Ann Upton, widow, aged, Pest House.  Chancel.
1687  Aug. 10  Katherine ux. Nathl Upton, Physician ; consumption.  Tindall's.
1687  Sep. 23  Samuel son of Nathaniel Upton, Physician ; small pox.
1688  Sep.  1  Katherine dau. of Nathl Upton, Dr of Physic; fever.  Tindall's.

### ST. HELEN'S, BISHOPSGATE, LONDON.
*Married.*

1739  Nov. 13  John Kendrick, bachelor, and Sarah Upton, spinster, both of
                Islington, Midx.  Licence.

*Baptized.*

$\frac{1699}{1700}$  Feb.  2  William son of Mr. Arthur Upton, Merchant, and Cibilla ; buried
                2 March same year.

*Buried.*

167$\frac{3}{4}$  Jan.  9  Thomas Upton ; in Church.

## St. Lawrence, Jewry, London.
### *Married.*

1680 Sep. 28 John Archer, Merchant in Frogmorton (*sic*, ? Throgmorton) Street, and Mary Upton in St. James, Duke's Place. Licence.

1686 July 27 Richard Goodlad, widower, and Dorothy Upton, widow.

## St. Leonard's, East Cheap, London.
### *Baptized.*

1793 Oct. 6 Elizabeth dau. of Samuel and Martha Upton; born 25 Aug.

### *Buried.*

1796 May 3 Francis Upton, aged 3 years. Churchyard.

1796 May 22 Eliz$^{th}$ Upton, aged 5 years. Ch. y$^d$.

1797 April 27 Martha Upton, aged 29 years. Ch. y$^d$.

1797 Aug. 9 John Upton, aged a few months. Ch. y$^d$.

## St. Margaret's, Lothbury, London.
### *Married.*

1744 April 12 John Palmer, bachelor, and Susanna Upton, spinster, both of Stoke Newington.

1751 Nov. 19 Thos. Ludgate of Hornsey, Mid$^x$, bachelor, and Susanna Upton of Stoke Newington, spinster. Licence.

## St. Martin Outwich, London.
### *Baptized.*

169$\frac{4}{3}$ Jan. 18 Richard son of Ambrose and Jane Upton.

## St. Mary Abchurch, London.
### *Baptized.*

1635 Oct. 4 Sarah dau. of William and Dorothy Upton.

### *Buried.*

1636 July 21 William Upton.

1636 July 26 Dorothy Upton.

## St. Matthew, Friday Street, London.
### *Married.*

1589 June 29 Thomas Upton and Rose Adamms.

## St. Olave, Hart Street, London.
### *Baptized.*

1694 June 2 Anthony son of John and Mary Upton.

169$\frac{4}{6}$ Mar. 4 Lytcott son of Mr. John and Mary Upton; born 20 Feb.

### *Buried.*

169$\frac{3}{4}$ Mar. 6 Thomas son of Mr. Upton.

1706 Dec. 12 Mr. John Upton; bur$^d$ at St. Mary, Newington.

## St. Peter's, Paul's Wharf, London.
### *Buried.*

1610 April 9 Mr. John Upton was buried with consent of ye Parson: paying all dutys at St. Peter's, Paul's Wharf. He was buried at 12 at night at St. Mary Maddelins.

1610 April 25 Sir Carles Upton, late son to John Upton.

## St. Sepulchre's, London.

### Married.

1732   Sep.   3   William Upton and Jane Jenkins, both of St. Katherine's. Licence.

## Fleet Registers, London.

### Married.

1718   April   8   Timothy Hart of Cripplegate, Attorney, bachelor, and Mary Upton of Rumford, spinster.

## St. Anne (Soho), Westminster.

### Married.

1712   Sep.   18   Philip De la Place and Frances Upton.   Licence.

### Buried.

1696   May   13   Elizabeth Upton, child, at Mr. Marshalls.

## St. James, Westminster.

### Married.

1718   Aug.   30   Isaac De Robles and Ann Upton of this parish.   Licence.
1760   July   10   Morgan Vane, Esq., of this parish, and Anna Maria Magdalena Upton of St. Ann's, Westm$^r$.   Licence Canterbury.
1807   July   7   Hon. Fulk Greville Upton of Portland Place and Mary Howard of Grosvenor Square.   Special Licence.

### Baptized.

$17\frac{17}{18}$   Jan.   9   Elizabeth dau. of John Upton, Esq., and Elizabeth; born 1$^{st}$.
1766   Jan.   18   Sophia dau. of Clotworthy and Eliz$^{th}$ Upton; born 2$^d$.
1770   June   28   Augusta dau. of Clotworthy and Eliz$^{th}$ Upton; born 1$^{st}$.
1798   May   6   Katherine Elizabeth Upton dau. of R$^t$ Hon. John Henry and Mary, Lord and Lady Templetown of the kingdom of Ireland; born 5 April.   (The same child buried July 19, 1799.)

### Buried.

1812   May   30   Hon. Eleanor Upton, child.

## St. Margaret's, Westminster.

### Married.

1551   July   13   John Wenley and Agnes Upton.
1682   July   17   John Wiltshire and Dorothy Upton.
1689   Oct.   3   Richard Leng and Ellin Upton.
$17\frac{14}{5}$   Jan.   27   Thomas Upton and Frances Etherington.
1722   Oct.   20   Thomas Upton and Frances Edmonds.
$174\frac{7}{8}$   Mar.   2   John Upton and Ann Markwick.   Licence.
1750   Sep.   21   John Upton and Grace Goodlock.   Licence.
1821   Nov.   6   Charles Bridges, widower, and Isabella Upton, spinster, both of this parish.   Banns.

### Baptized.

1709   Oct.   22   Jane dau. of John and Mary Upton.

## Southwell, Nottinghamshire.

### Married.

$165\frac{5}{6}$   Feb.   18   William Upton of Southwell and Eliz$^{th}$ Horspoole of Upton. Pub$^n$.

### Buried.

1784   Oct.   1   Richard Upton, aged 85.

## Great Milton, Oxfordshire.

### Married.

1665   Sep.   4.   Mr. John Upton and Mrs. Ursula Clark.

### ALL SAINTS, CITY OF OXFORD.
#### Baptized.
1649 June 20 William son of William Upton.
1650 Aug. 14 William son of William Upton.
1652 Sep. 3 Thomas son of William Upton and Ursula.
#### Buried.
1649 Sep. 20 William son of William Upton.
1652 Sep. 3 Thomas son of William Upton.

### ST. GILES, CITY OF OXFORD.
#### Married.
1619 June 14 John Uppton and Dorothy Limes.
172⅚ Jan. 12 John Sanders and Mary Upton.
1730 Nov. 5 Matthew Prickett and Jane Upton.

### ST. MARY MAGDALEN, CITY OF OXFORD.
#### Married.
1632 Sep. 17 John Upton, tailor, and Anne Frame. Banns.
1705 Oct. 5 Thomas Upton and Elizabeth Sanders, both of Bloxham.
1708 Nov. 13 John Upton and Mary Nason, both of this parish.
#### Baptized.
1634 Aug. 31 Elizabeth dau. of John Upton, tailor.
#### Buried.
1644 Nov. 29 John Upton, tailor.
1644 Dec. 27 Widow Tillcockes and Upton's daughter.
167⅞ Jan. 3 Anne Upton, widow.
1699 Aug. 13 Thomas Upton of Cuddsdon; buried in ye Quakers' Meeting Place.

### ST. MICHAEL'S, CITY OF OXFORD.
#### Married.
1687 Nov. 17 Ambrose Upton, merchant, of London, and Jane Wright.

### ST. PETER'S IN THE EAST, CITY OF OXFORD.
#### Buried.
1678 Nov. 5 William Upton.
1755 May 23 Jane Upton.

### CLAPHAM, CO. SURREY.
#### Buried.
1661 Aug. 3 Dorothy Upton.

### RICHMOND, CO. SURREY.
#### Married.
1749 Aug. 13 Thomas Upton of St. James, Clerkenwell, bachelor, and Mary Mumpas of Xᵗ Ch., London, spinster.
#### Buried.
1699 June 3 George Upton, vintner.

### ST. OLAVE, SOUTHWARK, CO. SURREY.
#### Married.
1666 Aug. 8 Nathaniel Upton and Susan Varney.
1671 Oct. 22 Nathaniel Upton and Ann Thomas.
1720 July 19 Robert Upton and Elizabeth Shepard. Licence.
#### Baptized.
166⅞ Jan. 30 Nathaniel son of Nathaniel Upton, yeoman.

*Buried.*

| 1664 | June 21 | William son of Robert Upton. |
| 1665 | Sep. 16 | Jone *ux.* Nathaniel Upton. |
| 1671 | June 14 | Susan *ux.* Nathaniel Upton. |
| 1680 | Dec. 25 | Elizabeth Upton. |
| 1682 | Dec. 22 | Nathaniel Upton. |
| 168⅚ | Jan. 19 | Katherine *ux.* Thomas Upton. |
| 1702 | Mar. 26 | Anne Upton. |

CHUTE, WILTSHIRE.
*Married.*

1731   June   3   John Canteloe of Wherwell, Hants, and Joan Upton.

RATHRONAN, IRELAND.
*Baptized.*

1742   Jan.   14   Edward Upton of Ballinabearna, son of William and Mary Upton.

FIRST BOOK OF BIRTHS, MARRIAGES, AND DEATHS OF SALEM IN
NEW ENGLAND.

"John Upton, his son Wm. dyed Aprill '63 ; dau. Mary dyed 15th Aprill '63 ;
dau. Ellenor dyed 20th Aprill '63 ; their second son Wm. borne by Ellenor his wife
10th June '63 ; son James borne in Sept. 1660 ; son Samuell borne Oct. 1664 ; dau.
Issabell borne 3d 11 mo. '66 ; their son Ezekiell borne about ye middle of September
1668 ; their son Joseph borne the 9th of Aprill 1670 ; son Francis borne the first
July 1671."

NOTES FROM TABLETS IN BRIXHAM CHURCH, DEVONSHIRE.

[Anthony Upton born at Lupton 1571 ; died May 6, 1619, aged 48.]*
John Upton born April 7, 1590 [or 1591] ; died at Lupton Sep. 11, 1641.
Arthur Upton born in Dublin Feb. 14, and buried there in March 1666.
Anthony Upton buried at Lupton 1669.
Arthur Upton born at Lupton Jan. 6, 1667 ; died at Kingsbridge Nov. 28, 1680.
John Upton born at Lupton May 17, 1668 ; died and was buried at Oxford in
Dec. 1686.
Ursula Upton born at Lupton Jan. 13, 1671 ; died in London Aug. 21, 1687.
John Upton died at Salisbury Sep. 7, 1687, aged 49.
John Upton, Esq., died 1690.
Ursula Clarke, formerly wife of John Upton, died Dec. 16, 1709, aged 79.

* If such an inscription exists, it is unquestionably entirely erroneous, and is probably due to
a modern attempt to perpetuate the memory of Anthony Upton who died in 1669. The following
is furnished me as a translation from the Latin of this erroneous inscription :
    " Inscription to Anthony Upton who died on the 6th May 1619, at the age of 48.
    " Here lieth Anthony Upton third son of John Upton, Esquire, and of Dorothy his wife. Born
at Lupton in the County of Devon, 1571, he passed over early in life to Seville. There he lived
as a merchant for thirty years, and, by his integrity and skill, advanced in the good opinion of
his country as much as he increased in wealth, while he enhanced the fame of the most
celebrated of the marts in Spain. Firm in his constancy to God as to himself, by his
unchangedness in religion in the midst of a heterodox people, by the uprightness and justice of
his dealings among merchants, he made himself beloved by foreigners through whose means
he had been enriched. What remained of wealth after a life of generosity and munificence,
he bequeathed in legacies to his nephews and nieces, sixty in number. He left a numerous
family to mourn his loss, overwhelming them with benefits. His ashes, which were sent over from
Spain, were followed to the grave by five brothers and five sisters deploring his loss."
    Compare No. 64 of Abstracts of Wills, *ante.* Much of this is quite applicable to the real
Anthony, who was born about 1621 and died in 1669.

ARMS FROM BRASS OF ANTHONY SHUKBURGH, ESQ., 1594,
IN UPPER SHUCKBURGH CHURCH.

QUARTERLY OF SIX. 1 SHUCKBURGH, 2 CARBONELL, 3 NAPTON,
4 SYDENHALL, 5 DYSART, 6 LUNELL.

GENEALOGICAL MEMORANDA RELATING TO

# The Family of Shuckburgh.*

## Monumental Inscriptions.

*G on key plan.*

*On another slab, next and to north of last, with brass inscription immediately above figures of a man and his wife (the head of male figure only remaining).*

Above the inscription is placed a shield with the Shuckburgh arms, A chevron between three mullets pierced.†

𝕳ic jacet Tomas Shukburghe armiger & Elizabethe bror ei' quonda' d'us & patronus de Sup'iori Shukburghe qui obiit Anno d'ni millesimo qui'qe'tesimo ...‡... lx & pri'o die mensis Octobris Quoru' Animab' propitietur deus amen.

*H on key plan.*

*At the foot of the first, on a slab a shield of arms in brass above the figures of a man and his wife.*

Quarterly, 1 and 4, SHUCKBURGH, A chevron between three mullets pierced ; 2 and 3, NAPTON, On a fess three escallops.

(This shield belongs to the brass of Thomas Shuckburgh.)

*I on key plan.*

*Next to and to north of the last, on a slab this inscription on a brass plate.*

𝕳ere ly buried the Bodies of Anthony Shukburgh Esquire and Anne his wyffe the sayde Anthony Departed this lyfe the firste of Aprill in the yeare of our Lorde God 1594.

Mors Mortem Vincit et per mortem post mortem viuemus.

Above the inscription are two shields, each charged with two bars.

Under the inscription is the coat of arms represented in the illustration. Quarterly of six : 1, SHUCKBURGH ; 2, CARBONELL, Three swords in pale, two points downwards and one upwards ; 3, NAPTON, On a fess three escallops ; 4, SYDENHALL, A fess chequy ; 5, DYSART, Three dexter hands couped at the wrist, two and one ; 6, LUNELL, A fess between three crescents.

Under the last shield are, on the dexter side a group of three boys, and on the sinister side one of five girls.

There were originally four shields, one at each corner of the slab, two of them, each charged with the Shuckburgh arms, have been incorrectly placed above the brasses commemorating Margaret Cotes and Thomas Shukburghe. 1 and 4 shield, SHUCKBURGH ; 2 and 3 shield, Two bars, FOXLEY.

*J on key plan.*

*On a slab on floor of mortuary chapel over entrance of new vault.*

Sacred to the memory of

Sir Francis Shuckburgh 8th Baronet, born March 12th 1789, died Octr [29th 1876.

Sir George Thomas Francis Shuckburgh, 9th Baronet, born July 23rd [1829, died Jany 12th 1884.

Arms : Above the inscription, on dexter side, SHUCKBURGH, with Ulster badge on chevron, impaling DENYS ; on sinister, SHUCKBURGH, with Ulster badge as before, impaling ROBERTSON, Gules, three wolves' heads erased argent.

---

* Continued from p. 211.
† This shield belongs to the brass of Anthony Shuckburgh. The arms on the next slab ought to have been placed over the figures, viz., Quarterly, 1 and 4, SHUCKBURGH ; 2 and 3, NAPTON.
‡ Word punched out.

K *on key plan.*

*A large tomb in Shuckburgh mortuary chapel against the south wall.*

This tomb was originally on the north wall of the chancel.

*Inscription over the recumbent effigies of a man and his wife.*

HERE LYETH INTERRED THE BODY OF JOHN
SHVKBVRGH, LORD OF THIS MANNOVR, SON
OF ANTHONY SHVKBVRGH ESQVIRE WHO
DEPARTED THIS LYFE THE 20th DAY OF MARCH,
ANNO DOMINI 1631. BEING ABOVT THE AGE
OF 68 YEARS. AND MARGERY HIS WIFE
DAVGHTER OF RICHARD MIDLEMORE OF
EDGBASTON ESQVIRE. BY WHOM HE HAD
10 CHILDREN WHICH SAID MARGERY DE-
PARTED THIS LYFE THE 22d DAY OF MARCH,
ANNO DOMINI 1629.

Arms over inscription : SHUCKBURGH impaling MEDLEY ; and on either side of this centre shield two others, the dexter one bearing the arms of SHUCKBURGH, impaling, Argent, two bars gules, FOXLEY ;* the sinister, those of SHUCKBURGH, impaling, Argent, three bulls' heads erased sable, SKEFFINGTON.

At the top of the tomb there is a large shield in centre, with the arms of SHUCKBURGH quartering those of NAPTON, SYDENHALL, LUNELL, CARBONELL DYSART ;† and Shuckburgh crest above, the Moor dressed, but all painted black.  On either side of it a smaller shield, the dexter charged with the arms of SHUCKBURGH impaling NAPTON, and on the sinister SHUCK-BURGH, impaling, Gules, a chevron or between three mullets argent, FULWOOD.  Also two shields on the spandrils of the arch, the dexter one, SHUCKBURGH impaling SYDENHALL ; the sinister, SHUCKBURGH, impaling VAUX, Chequy or and gules, on a chevron azure three roses gules seeded proper.

At the base of the tomb are the following three shields :—

1st shield (dexter side), SHUCKBURGH, impaling MIDLEMORE, Per chevron argent and sable, in chief two moor-cocks proper.

2nd or central shield, SHUCKBURGH, impaling, Argent, two bars and in chief a cross pattée fitchée or, HOLT.‡

3rd shield (sinister side), SHUCKBURGH, impaling, Argent, three bulls' heads erased sable, SKEFFINGTON.

Besides these, there is a blank shield at either end of the base of the tomb.

---

L *on key plan.*

*Mural monument with bust in Shuckburgh mortuary chapel, against the east wall.*

Arms at top : SHUCKBURGH.

EPICEDIVM

RICHARDVS SHVKBVRGH EQUES ORDINE ⎫ DILEXIT DEVM ET ECCLÆSIAM
AD TEMPVS DORMIT HIC IN PULVERE. ⎪ REGEM PAVPEREM ATQUE PATRIAM
ECCE (LECTOR) VIRI IMAGINEM ⎬ IGNOVIT ILLI (CREDAS) OMNIA
RVS CVI VIDIT HOC VIX SIMILEM ⎭ QVI MVNDI CRVCE TVLIT CRIMINA
MORTVVS ⎫ EST LONDINI, 13°   JVNII ANNO    SALVTIS 1656
HVMATVS ⎭        HIC DOMI 25°              ÆTATIS 60.

Sculptor's name at base PET : BENNIER.

(*To be continued.*)

---

* This blazon is wrong, but is, however, so represented on the monument.
† These quarterings are in wrong order, but are thus marshalled in this one case.
‡ This blazon is wrong, but is, however, so represented on the monument.

# Genealogy of Browne.*

## Evidences.

### BRADELEY.

#### BRADELEY REGISTERS.

*Baptisms.*

1614　Julij 21ª.　Edwardus Browne filius Tho'æ Browne de Shradicott com. Staff⁴ gent. et
　　　　Appoloniæ uxoris ejus baptazatus fuit vicessimo primo die mensis Julij an'o s'p'icto.

1616　ffranciscus filius Thomæ Browne et Apolloniæ uxoris eius baptazatus fuit 17° Novembris 1616.

1636　George Browne of Shredicote gent. and Anne his wife had a child baptized named Appolina
　　　　the 29ᵗʰ of November.

1637-8　George Browne of Shredicott gent. & Anne his wife had a child baptized named Mar-
　　　　garet the 30ᵗʰ day of Januarye.

1641　George Browne and his wife of Shredicott had a child baptized named Elizabeth the 12ᵗʰ
　　　　daye of August.

1642-3　Mʳ George Browne of Shredicoate and Anne his wife had a child named Thomas [baptized]
　　　　the 23ʳᵈ of March.

1644　George Browne gent. and Anne his wife had a child baptized named Marye the 15ᵗʰ daie
　　　　of August.

1646　George Browne the sonne of George Browne of Shredicote gent. and Anne his wife gent.
　　　　was baptized the 4ᵗʰ of August 1646.

1669　Anne Browne the daughter of Thomas Browne gent. and Mary his wife gent. was baptized
　　　　the seventh day of October ann' s'p'dict.

1670　George Browne the sonne of Thomas Browne gent. and Mary his wife gent. was baptized
　　　　December the 29 anno s'p'dict.

1672　James Browne the son of Thomas Browne of Shredicote gent. and Mary his wife was
　　　　baptized the 27ᵗʰ of March anno s'p'dict.

1673　John Browne the sonn of Thomas Browne gent. and Mary his wife gen. of Shradacote was
　　　　baptized the 28ᵗʰ of August anno s'p'dict. test.† Sam B. John P. et m. Job.

1674-5　William son of Thomas Browne of Shreddicote gent. and Mary his wife gent. baptized
　　　　ffebruary the 11ᵗʰ.

1708　Gulielmus filius Johan'is Brown et Eleanoræ uxoⁱˢ bapᵗᵘˢ fuit 7ᵐᵒ die Augusti.

1712-3　Thomas filius Johan'is Browne et Eleanoræ uxoⁱˢ bapᵗᵘˢ fuit decimo die Martij.

1714　Elizabetha filia Johannis Browne et Eleanoræ uxoⁱˢ bapᵗᵃ fuit 7ᵐᵒ die 8bris [October].

1715-6　Eduardus filius Johan'is Browne et Eleanⁱᵃ uxoⁱˢ bapᵗᵘˢ fuit decimo quinto die Martij.

1717　Josephus filius Johan'is Browne et Eleanⁱᵃ uxoⁱˢ bapᵗᵘˢ fuit vicessimo sexto die 9bris
　　　　[November].

1719　Gualterus filius Johan'is Browne et Eleanⁱᵃ uxoⁱˢ bapᵗᵘˢ fuit vigessimo 2ⁿᵈᵒ die 8bris
　　　　[October].

1721　Petrus filius Johan'is Browne et Eleanoræ uxoⁱˢ bapᵗᵘˢ fuit vigessimo die Julij.

1723　Anna filia Johan'is Browne et Eleanoræ uxoⁱˢ bapᵗᵃ fuit undecimo die Julij.

*Marriages.*

1678　Ludovie Dickenson‡ de Acton Trussell gent. et Maria Brown De Shradacote gen. nupti
　　　　fuerunt Novembris vigessimo sexto die.

---

* Continued from p. 216.　　　† *Testes*—God-parents or witnesses.

‡ The following pedigree of Dickenson of Bradeley, co. Stafford, is compiled from Harl. MSS.
1173, fol. 100, and 1439, fol. 26, and from the Bradeley Register. The family bore as arms : Azure,
a fess erminois between two lions passant of the last. Crest: A demi-lion rampant per pale
erminois and azure.

William Dickenson.⊤.... d. and h. of .... Kinge of Penkridæe.

Richard Dickenson of Bradeley,⊤Eliza, d. of .... Bagnall (bur. [at Bradeley]
co. Stafford.　　　　　　　　　｜19 Aug. 1560).

Symon Dickenson⊤Catherine, d. of the Hon. Geoffrey Dudley, youngest son of Thomas,
of Bradeley.　　　｜Lord Dudley (mar. [at Bradeley] 21 Feb. 1583-4).

Edward Dickenson of Bradeley, now⊤Joyce, d. of Roger Fowke　Dudley Dickenson (b. 10 Feb.,
living 1614 (b. 24 Jan., bapt. [at ｜of Brewood, co. Stafford.　bapt. [at Bradeley] 13 Feb.
Bradeley] 28 Jan. 1584-5).　　　　　　　　　　　　　　　1585-6).

Walter Dickenson, "sonne and heire, ætat. 4 annoq. 1614."　　2. Fowke.　　Catherine.

1680   George Browne gent. and Mʳˢ Mary Wickstead were married at [*blank*] October 25ᵗʰ 1680.
1743   Thomas Ellits and Ann Brown May the twenty-fourth.

*Burials.*

1633   Thomas Browne de Shredicote Esquier was buried ann. supra d'cit.
1652   George Browne of Shredicoat gent. was buried Aprill 22ᵗʰ.
1653   Appolina Browne gent. vid. of Shredicoat was buried the 25 of May the year above written.
1675   William son of Thomas Brown of Shreddicote gent. and Mary gent. was buried Thursday
          May yᵉ 10ᵗʰ.
1689   Maria uxor Thomæ Brown de Shredicott generosi sepulta decimo nono die Decembⁱˢ.
1690-1 Domina An'a Brown et Domina Appalina Brown de Shredicott sepult vicessimo octavo
          die Jan.
1711   Georgius Browne genʳᵘˢ sepultus fuit 7ᵐᵒ die Junij.
1728   Thomas Brown genʳᵘˢ sepultus fuit decimo die Augusti.
1728   Maria Brown vidua sepulta fuit decimo tertio die Augusti.
1729-30 Elisabetha Brown vidua sepulta fuit vigessimo tertio die Januarie.

LICENCE TO EAT FLESH ON FISH DAYS.
(Parish Register of Bradeley, p. 82.)

20 Feb. 1619.   To all Christian people to whom these presents shall come, I Thomas fflecther [*sic*]
Clarke Bachelour of Arts and vicar of the parish of Bradeley in the County of Stafford send
greeting in our Lord God everlasting, whereas Thomas Browne of Shreddicote in the County afor-
said gent., being aged about fifty and eight yeares, for and during these three yeares last and more,
hath had and still hath of my certaine knowledge, A greefe and infirmitie in his ioynts and knees
soe that hee hath been and is weake in body and vnable to walke or goe any farther then About
his owne house, And hath been Advised by his physitians to obserue such kind of moderate diet
of fleshmeat as they haue vnder their hands præscribed him, and perceiving further, By the
opinions of the said physitians vnder their hands, And alsoe by the state of his Body which I
weekly behold, that hee shall be enforced for the recovery Off his health and strength, to eate flesh
for the time of his sickness and Infirmitie, Therefore know that I Thomas fflecther [*sic*] Vicar for
the causes Above menc'oned At the Earnest request of the said Thomas Browne (who hath paid toe
the poor mens Box where hee dwelleth for these six yeares and more and now still dwelleth in the
parish of Bradeley on the ffeasts of the Lady Mary last past bearing the date herof the sume of
viij shillings Eight pence) Haue given granted and bye these presents doe give and grant Accordinge to the tenure of the act in that case provided soe far forth license (As in me lyeth) to eate all
manner of fleshmeat fit and wholsome for the recovery of his strength and health duringe all the
time of the Continuance Of the said sickness and infirmity and noe longer vpon dajes usually
observed By the lawes of this realme as fish dajes (exceptinge as in the statute is excepted) In
Witness whereof I the said Thomas ffletcher have putt my hand & seale the twentieth day of
ffebruary 1619 in the yeare of our seu'agn [Sovereign] Lord Iames by the grace of God of England,
ffrance and Ireland the seaventeenth (And of Scotland fifty-third).

Vera Copia p'r
[a true copy by]
  me GULIEL. ROYSTON.

Sealed and deliv'd
        THOMAS FFLETCHER*
                  Vic.

"Bibles distributed to the Poor Inhabitants of the parish of Bradley 1772.  The gift of the
Reverend Dr. Peploe, Chancellor of Chester.

The great Importance of a religious Life.

| To | To |
|---|---|
| Thomas Baker. | Richard Tirer. |
| Robert Merrick. | Edward Stoker. |
| Joseph Leek. | Edward Winter. |
| Abel Benton. | John Tomlinson." |
| etc. | etc. |

The gift is also mentioned in the years 1755 and 1763.  The following note is appended to
the former date after the distribution of the Bibles and Prayer-books: "Which were left by the
Right Reverend Dr. Peploe, Lord Bishop of Chester."

* A Thomas Fletcher was instituted to the Rectory of Haughton, near Bradley, co. Stafford,
11 March 1619.

Copy of a Certificate (dated 1624) of exemption from payment of the second subsidy, granted to Thomas Browne, Esq., of Shredicote, co. Stafford, etc. (Harleian* MS. 6704, fol. 206.)

To the Righte Honourable the Lord Heigh Treasuror of England and Barons of His Ma^ties Exchequer and to all others to whome itt appertayneth. Whereas Thomas Browne of Shridicote in the County of Stafford gent. hath informed me that he is taxed and assessed in the Cunstablewick of Hungrie Bentley being w^thin the p'ish of Lanford and hundred of Apletree in the County of Derbie for towards the payment of the second subsidie granted to ou^r Seueragne Lord King James by the Temporalty by acte of p'liament in the xxj^th yeare of his heighnes Raigne : And that he is alsoe taxed and assessed for & towards the saide payment of the second subsidie aforesaid in the County of Stafford wheare his dwelling is, and hath lived many years: and hath prayed ou^r Certificate for his Discharge from doble payment towards the said subsidie according to the statute in that behalfe : Knowe ye theirfore that wee whose names are hearunder subscribed towe of the King's Mat^s Comissioners in the saide County of Stafford authorized & appoynted for the taxinge & assessinge of the saide payment of the saide second subsidie granted to his Ma^tie as aforesaide Doe certefy hearby that the said Tho. Browne was & is taxed & assessed in the saide County of Stafford fo^r & towards the payment of the saide second subsidie in the p'ishe of Bradley w^thin the hundred of Cutleston, where he & his ffamilie att & before the tyme of the assesm^t of the saide second subsidie haue lived manye years togeather resid'nt dwellinge & abyding and so are att this p'sent. In witness whearof wee haue hearunto subscribed ou^r names and sett ou^r seales this fyfte daye of October 1624 and in the xxij^th yeare of his mat^s Raigne of England, ffraunce &_Ireland, & of Scotland the fyfte & Eyghte.

WALTE^R CHETWOOD.<br>W.† BOWYER.

CHARITIES OF ANNE BROWNE AND APPOLINA BROWNE, 1690.

Copy of the tablet in Bradeley Church :—

" ANNO 1705.

Moneys given for y^e use of y^e Poor of the Parish of Bradley.

M^rs Ann Brown of Shreddicott wid. gave five pounds........ £5    0    0
M^rs Appaline Brown spinster gave ten pounds.............. £10    0    0
[Then follow other gifts.]

Extract from the Report of the Commissioners for Inquiring concerning Charities, 1824.
Report xiv., pp. 529–30.

BRADLEY.

POOR'S LAND—CHARITIES OF ANN BROWN, APPALINE BROWN, AND JOHN ALSOP.

By indentures of lease and release of 24^th and 25^th of March 1785, Major Dain, in consideration of £30 paid by the Rev. Sampson Wright, vicar, and Edward Brindley and John Turner, churchwardens and overseers of the poor of the parish of Bradley, being money by them received from sundry well-disposed persons, to be laid out in a purchase for the poor of the said parish, conveyed to the said Sampson Wright, Edward Brindley, and John Turner, and their heirs, three gardens, at Coton Clanford, the parish of Seighford, in the county of Stafford, in trust, that they and the survivors or survivor of them, and his heirs, should apply the rents and profits thereof, in bread or otherwise, to and amongst such of the poor of the parish of Bradley, as they the trustees, whilst any of them should be living, should think fit, and afterwards as the vicar and churchwardens of the parish of Bradley for the time being should direct and appoint.

At the beginning of an overseer's book for this parish is a list of gifts to the poor, in which it is mentioned that 16s., the interest of £20 in the Rev. Mr. Wright's hands, is distributed yearly, on the Sunday after Candlemas. From a note at the bottom of this page, and a subsequent entry in the book, it appears that this money, part of £30, was laid out in the above-mentioned purchase. In the list of parish charities, made by Mr. Wright, in 1787 the £20 appears to be made up of the following benefactions :—

Ann Browne 1690................. £5    0    0
Appaline Browne 1690............. £10    0    0
John Alsop 1783 ................ £5    0    0

And the rent being then £2 3s. 6d. is apportioned among them, as the produce of those benefactions. From whence the additional £10 of the purchase-money was derived does not appear.

---

* The book is endorsed "Entry book of the Wigley Family." The document there given is a copy of the original certificate which was probably given to the grantee.
† " Roger " erased.

The land consists of three small gardens, let to Thomas Wetton, as yearly tenant, at the high rent of £3 per annum.   He took them at this rent, wishing to have them in his possession, as they adjoin other land which he holds ; but he has intimated that he shall give them up, if the rent is not lowered.

The rent is given away upon New Year's Day to the settled poor, indiscriminately, whether they receive parish pay or not.

The land in 1885 was in the tenancy of Ephraim Owen at a yearly rent of £2.   A portion of the rent is given away in money (£1) on New Year's Day ; 10s. 6d. in bread on Candlemas Day ; and 10s. 6d. in bread on Easter Sunday, to the poor indiscriminately.

COPY OF MARRIAGE BOND BETWEEN THOMAS BROWNE OF SHREDICOTE AND MARY CARR
OF AQUALATE, CO. STAFFORD.

Extracted from the Diocesan Registry of the Lord Bishop of Lichfield.

Lichfield, July 13°, 1668°.
ffiat Licentia matrimonialis inter Thomam Browne de Shreddicoate Parochiæ de Bradley in comitatu Staffordiae ætatis 27° Annorum et Mariam Carr de acqualet Parochiae de fforton in comitatu Staffordiae praedicto ætatis 22° Annorum
Ministro de fforton
ob. dictus Thomas Browne de Shreddicoate praedicto generosus.
Jurat dictus Thomas Browne coram nobis

WA. LITTLETON.

Noverint universi per praesentes me Thomam Browne de Shreddicoate parochiae Bradeley in comitatu Staffordiae Generosum teneri et firmiter obligari Gualtero Littleton militi et Legum Doctori vicario in Spiritualibus generali Reverendi in Christo Patris et domini domini Johannis Providentia' Divina' Lichfeldensis et Coventrensis Episcopi in centum Libris bene et legalis Monete Angliae solvendum eidem Gualtero Littleton aut suo certo Attornato executori administratori vel assignis suis ad quam quidem solucionem bene et fideliter faciendum obligo me heredes executores et administratores meos formiter per praesentes sigillo meo sigillatum datum decimo tertio die Julij anno Regni Regis Domini nostri Caroli Secundi Dei Gratia' Anglie, etc., xx° Annoque Domini 1668°.

The condit'on of this obligac'on is such that if hereafter there shall not appear nor be found any lawful let or impediment by reason of any precontract consanguinity or affinity but that Thomas Browne and Mary Carr may lawfully solemnize mar'rimony together and afterwards in the same lawfully remaine like man and wife according to the Lawes in this case made and provided. And moreover if there be not at this present any action playnte suite Querele or demand made against either of the sᵈ partyes for any such matter or cause before any Judge Eccli'call or temporall.   And also if the said partyes doe not proceed to the solemnization of their sᵈ marriage without the consent of their parents or other Guv'nors nor in any other place then in the face of the Church of fforton nor at any other time then betwixt the houres of 8 & 12 of the clock in the aforenoon then this obligac'on to be voide or else to stand in full force and virtue.

(Signed)        THOMAS BROWNE.
Sigillat et Delibat. in praesentia' mei
MICH. EAST.

(*To be continued.*)

# Dalison Notes.*

Essonia capta apud Lincoln . . . . die Lune proxima post Festum Epiphanie Domini, anno regni Regis Edwardi tercii a conquestu, terciodecimo.

Alexander (querens) Blaunchard de Laughton versus Johannem Dalazon de Laughton, de placito assise nove disseisine—die Jovis proxima post Festum Sancti Jacobi Apostoli apud Lincoln.

Assize Roll, Divers Counties, N-2-18 5, m. 75, [10 January A.D. 1340].

Inquisicio capta die Martis proxima post Festum Ramispalmarum, anno regni Regis Ricardi secundi, quarto, post mortem Katerine que fuit uxor Willielmi de Blesseby, etc.

Juratores dicunt quod Dominus Rex ad firmam dimisit tam terciam portem manerii de Caylesthorp quam manerium de Blesseby per literas suas patentes cuidam

* Continued from p. 205.

MISCELLANEA GENEALOGICA ET HERALDICA.

Willielmo Dalason, ratione minoris etatis Willielmi filii Petri fratris Willielmi de Bleseby, etc.
    Inquisition post mortem, 4 Richard 2, No. 7, [9 April A.D. 1381].

---

Nomina generosiorum et validiorum hominum Comitatus Lincoln, necnon majorum, etc., ejusdem Comitatus, qui coram Anketillo Mallore, ac Vicecomite Lincoln sacramentum prestiterunt, virtute brevis Domini Regis eisdem Anketillo et Vicecomiti directi, juxta formam cujusdam cedule eidem brevi intercluse. [Inter alios.] Willielmus Dalyson.
    Close Roll, 11 Ric. 2, m. 23 d., 20 March 11 Ric. 2, [A.D. 1388].

---

Adhuc de placitis assisarum captis apud Lincoln . . . . die Jovis proximo post Festum Sancte Lucie Virginis, anno regni Regis Henrici quarti, septimo.
    Assisa venit recognitura si Walterus Anotte de Estbutterwyk et Willielmus Byndtre de Epworth injuste et sine judicio disseisiverunt Johannem filium Johannis Bussy, Chivaler, de libero tenemento suo in Estbutterwyk post primam, etc. Et predictus Willielmus in propria persona sua venit et predictus Walterus non venit set idem Willielmus respondit pro eo tanquam ejus ballivus. Et pro eo dicit quod ipse nullam injuriam seu disseisinam prefato Johanni inde fecit. Et de hoc ponit se super assisam, etc. Et predictus Johannes similiter, etc. Et predictus Willielmus dicit quod ipse tenet tenementa predicta in visu preposita cum pertinentiis cunjunctim cum Nicholao Tourney, Henrico Morley et Nicholao filio Willielmi Dalason per factum et feoffamentum Walteri Anot et Cecilie uxoris ejus et tenuit die impetracionis brevis predicti Johannis. Quiquidem Nicholaus Henricus et Nicholaus adhuc superstites sunt et non nominantur in brevi predicto: unde petit judicium, etc. Et profert hic in Curia quandam cartam sub nominibus predictorum Walteri Anot et Cecilie que predictam conjunctim tenenciam testatur in forma predicta cujus data est apud Estbutterwyk vicesimo octavo die Aprilis anno regni Regis Henrici quarti, quinto. Recognitores . . . . dicunt super sacramentum suum quod predictus Willielmus non est tenens tenementorum predictorum . . . . set dicunt quod predictus Walterus est tenens, etc. Ideo consideratum est quod predictus Johannes recuperet seisinam suam de tenementis predictis, etc.
    Assize Roll, Divers Counties, N-2-36 3, m. 93 d., [14 Dec. A.D. 1405].

---

Trinity, 1 Henry 5 [A.D. 1413].
    Abbas de Parco Lude per attornatum suum optulit se quarto die versus Willielmum Dalison et Johannem Swalowe de Croxby, etc. Et ipsi non venerunt, etc. Et vicecomes modo mandavit quod predictus Willielmus attachiatus est per Nicholaum Dalison, etc.
    De Banco Roll, Henry 5, No. 2, m. 80 d.

---

Feoda Honoris Lancastrie.
    Nicholaus Dalyson tenet dimidium feodi in Netelton et Olixby (sic) quod Willielmus Blaunchard quondam tenuit ibidem.
    Exchequer Q. R. Misc. Books, Vol. 4, fol. 195, [A.D. 1427-8].

---

Lincoln scilicet.
    Ricardus Spert et Katerina uxor ejus, administratores bonorum et catallorum que fuerunt Willielmi Dalyson, nuper de Stansby, qui obiit intestatus, etc., per attornatum suum optulerunt se iiij^{to} die versus Johannem Coppere, Abbatem de Tupholme, in Comitatu predicto, etc., executores testamenti Roberti Stykney nuper de Hemyngby, de placito quod reddant eis decem marcas quas eis injuste detinent, etc.
    De Banco Roll, Hil., 22 Edw. 4, m. 11 d., [A.D. 1483].

MONUMENTAL INSCRIPTIONS FROM THE BURIAL-GROUND OF
ST. GEORGE, HANOVER SQUARE, NEAR MARBLE ARCH.*

Henry, son of Henry & Sarah Eedes, of Pimlico, died 28 Jan. 1810, aged 2 years
& 3 weeks.
William, son of John & Mary Ann Eedes, of Pimlico, died 19 Aug. 1811, aged
exactly 2 years.
Joanna, daughter of the aforesaid John & Mary Ann Eedes, died 28 March 1814,
aged 2 years & 9 months.
Two more of their infant daughters are also interred in this ground. [Rest hidden
by a footstone. The inscription is continued on the other side of the stone.]
Mr John Eedes of Knight Rider Street, Doctors Commons, formerly of this parish,
died Feb. 2, 1847 in his 72nd year.
Mary Ann, the beloved wife of Stephen Boxall (and daughter of the above), died
July 18, 1847, aged 44.

———

Mr Thomas Hammond, late of Park Street, Grosvenor Square, Surveyor, died
Jan. 14, 1804, aged 63.

———

. . . . [daughter of] William & Ann Oliver, died 10 Jan. 1800 aged [5 ?] months.
Frances Olivia Oliver, sister of the above, died April 19, 1808, aged 15 months.
Also the above Ann Oliver, died 10 Aug. 1808, aged 30.
Mr George Day, died July 28, 1833, aged 55.
John James Day Esq. son [of the above] Mr George Day [. . . . 1836] in his 29th
year. [Rest hidden by a footstone.]

———

[William ?] son of Francis & Ann Engleheart of this parish, aged 9 years. [No
date inscribed, but on the footstone is 1801.]
Ann Elizabeth, wife of Francis Engleheart, died 19 June 1805, aged 64. [Rest of
inscription hidden by a footstone].

———

Mrs Mary Millin, died Oct. 6, 1808, aged 67.
Mrs Hannah Rogers, daughter of the above, died Nov. 12 1814, aged 32.
Also six of her children, who died in their infancy.

———

William Barnes, died 3 Dec. 1800, aged 80.

———

Mr John Barnes, late of Eaton Square, died March 2, 1837, aged 69.
Mrs Isabella Barnes, widow of the above [. . . .] 1842 . . . . [Part of the inscription
hidden by a footstone.]

———

Edward Mayhew, son of Edward & Sarah Mayhew, of this parish, died Dec. 3,
1804, aged 17.
Mr Edward Mayhew, father of the above, died 6 March 1814, aged 52.
Mrs Sarah Mayhew, wife of the above, died 7 April [. . . . aged 66 ?].

———

William Pickett, Artist, who died at Knightsbridge, 23 May 1821, aged 45.
In the same grave with the above lie the remains of James Henry Dyer, died 22
June 1822, aged 32.

———

Tabitha Barrett, died Sep. 18, 1808, aged 38.

———

Mrs Mary Barrett, wife of Mr John Barrett, died Jan. 24, 1802, aged 69.

———

Mr John Harvey, died 16 April 1802, aged 66.
Mrs Mary Beardsworth, died 20 January 1804, aged 74.
Likewise Mrs Jennet Jane Harvey, died 4 Nov. 1810, aged 77.

M<sup>rs</sup> Ann Williams, wife of M<sup>r</sup> John Williams, died Jan. 30, 1827, aged 47.

Sarah, wife of Edward Binns, of Mount Street, died 19 Nov. 1807, aged 33. Also the abovenamed M<sup>r</sup> Edward Binns, died March 25, 1835, aged 75.

M<sup>r</sup> John Frederic Cruse, died 9 April 1814, aged 33.

To the memory of the best of wives, M<sup>rs</sup> Elizabeth Gray [. . . . 1810].

M<sup>r</sup> Paul Valentine D'Iffenger, late of New Norfolk Street, in this parish, died March 5, 1803, aged 62.

(*To be continued.*)

---

## BROWNE. (See Vol. III., N.S., p. 42, etc.)

The will of William Browne of Etwall, co. Derby, was dated 31 July 1624, and proved at Lichfield 20 October 1625. His wife Anne was living 1624. Their son John Browne was buried at Etwall 8 Dec. 1666, and his will proved at Lichfield 1667 ; mentions his wife Mary (she was buried at Etwall 19 Dec.· 1671), his daughters Anne, Grace, and Elizabeth, and his son William Browne, who married 1699 (marriage licence at Lichfield 1699), and whose widow, Mary, took out letters of administration 6 Nov. 1674 at Lichfield. William Browne, who purchased property at Thurvaston in the parish of Sutton-on-the-Hill, co. Derby, had a son William Browne of Nether Thurvaston in parish of Longford, co. Derby, who was buried in Longford Churchyard 3 May 1686, aged 39 (will proved at Lichfield 1687), and who had by his wife Elizabeth daughters Ann, Mary (bapt. at Longford 27 March 1683 and buried there 28 March 1707), and Elizabeth (bapt. at Longford 30 April 1686), and a son William Browne of Nether Thurvaston (bapt. at Longford 2 October 1679 ; died 7 Jan. and buried at Longford 10 Jan. 1741; will proved at Lichfield 1742), who had by his wife Ann, daughter of Samuel Hurd (died 18 March 1734, aged 48), sons William Browne of Nether Thurvaston (bapt. at Longford 30 May 1714; died 23 March and buried at Longford 26 March 1767; will proved at Lichfield the same year), Thomas Browne, John Browne of Church Broughton (bapt. at Longford 20 Jan. 1719 ; died 16 Sept. 1754 ; will proved at Lichfield 1755), and daughters Elizabeth (bapt. at Longford 28 Sept. 1706 ; married . . . . Stone), Mary (bapt. at Longford 2 Feb. 1708 ; married . . . . Chawner), Ann (bapt. at Longford 24 July 1711 ; died 31 May 1769 ; will proved at Lichfield), and Sarah (bapt. at Longford 25 Feb. 1714). The Rev. William Browne, who married Ann, second daughter and coheiress of Isaac Hawkins, died 6 Jan. 1746. His son Isaac Hawkins Browne entered at Lincoln's Inn 5 June 1722, and was called to the Bar 27 June 1728; and his son Isaac Hawkins Browne of Hertford College, Oxford, took his M.A. degree 14 July 1767, and his D.C.L. 9 July 1773. I shall be very grateful for any additions as to this family of Browne. The Badger Hall Estate, mentioned on page 43 of the Third Volume, N.S., is now the property of Colonel Alfred Capel Cure, a nephew of Edward Cheney, named on that page.

REGINALD STEWART BODDINGTON.

*National Conservative Club,*
*9 Pall Mall, S.W.*

### WILLS.

William Browne of Etwall, co. Derby. Will dated 31 July 1624 ; pr. at Lichfield 20 Oct. 1625, by the executor. In the name of God Amen the last day of Julie A° D'm' 1624 I William Browne of Etwall being in p'fi'ct memorie God be praysed therefore doe constitute ordeane and make this my last will and testamente in maner and forme followinge firste I doe most faithfully and constantlie give comytt and bequethe my soule into the handes of Aulmity God my Creator and of Jasus [*sic*] Christe my Saviour

and Redeemer In and by whome I hope to be saved and my bodie to be buried in the
Church or Churchyard of Etwall afors'd.   For my temperall goods first I geve and
bequeth unto my sonne William Browne all my leace y[t] I have in the Great heigh
Field to enter at my deysese And allso I give and bequeth unto my s'd sonne William
Browne all my esteate feesimple or intrist that I have or may have of and in sartin
lands in Boylsonn bought of John Wilson and of his sonne Henrie Wilson as doth
appere by the conve'ances And also I give unto my s'd sonne William Browne
one hondered marks to bee paid him w[th]in one yeair after my dessease.   And also I
geve and bequeath unto my daughter Elizabeth Browne all the rev'c'one of my leace
of this tenem[t] in Etwall I had of John Orme to enter at my dessese And also I give
to my said doughter Elizabeth in the crop of corne of that grounde or in the barne
and money together to the value of therty pounds.   Also I geve and bequeath unto
my doughter Ellen Browne all that estate by leace or assig[t] I have or may have in
y[t] house in Darby w[ch] M[r] Thomas Walker holdeth in Sadlergate street which estate
cost me one hondered poundes as doth appere thereby.   Also I geve and bequeath
unto my doughter Margarett Browne foreschore pounds to be paid her w[th]in one
yeire after my desese.   Also I geve and bequeath unto my wiffe Anne Browne and to
my sonne John Browne my leace or leaces of the farme or tenement in Etwall I now
dwelle in that is to say the third p't thereof to my wiffe dureinge her liffe and also
her coffer free to her owne selfe And after her liffe all the whole liveinge to remane
wholy to my sonne John Browne.   Also I geve unto my sonne John Browne my whole
estate and feesimple of a little closse in Ashe called and knowne by the name of the
Pingle butts.   My will is that all my children unmarried shalbe kepte together w[th]
meate and drinke w[th] there mother and theire Brother for one yeire.   I geve to
Thomas Heacoke and my doughter Anne his wife either of them v[s].   Also I geve to
my Brother Charles Browne all my apparill but some of the worste to the pore and
doe forgeve him all debts.   I geve to my godsonne William Heycok x[s].   I geve to his
sister Grace v[s].   I geve to the pore of Etwall at the discrec'on of my Executor x[s].
All the rest of my goods and chatteles unbequised my debts and funeralls discharged
I geve to my sonne John Browne whom I make my sole and lawfull executor of this
my last Will and Testem[t].   In witnesse hereof I have putt my hand and seale the
day and yeire firste above written—bymee WILL'M BROWNE.
    Postscript.   I will also y[t] my Executor shall free the rest of my childeren from
all sutes condented or to bee condented agaynst any of them by John Orme.
    Sealed, signed, and published in the p[r]sentce of John Jennings,* Gerard Heath,
Thomas Heacock.

_____

    Summary of will of Mary Browne of Woodford, dated 15 March 1710; pr. at
Lichfield 4 Nov. 1715.   £5 to poor of Uttoxeter.   £1 10s. to y[e] poor of Uttoxeter
Woodlands.   £2 10s. to y[e] poor of Marchington.   20s. to y[e] poor of Marchington
Woodlands.   20s. to y[e] poor of Boylston.   "My son William Browne of Burton-
upon-Trent, Clarke.   My grandson Isaac Hawkins Browne.   My granddaughter
Anne Browne.   My daughter Mary Webb of Woodford, widow.   My grandson
Thomas Webb of Woodford.   My grandson William Webb of Woodford.   My
granddaughters Elizabeth and Katherine Webb of Woodford.   My son-in-law William
Blaydon of Handbury, Clarke.   My grandson William Blaydon Jun[r] and John and
James Blaydon.   My granddaughters Mary, Elizabeth, and Jane Blaydon of Hand-
bury.   Mary Malleber wife of Edward Malleber."   Executor, son Rev. William
Browne.   Witnesses, Arthur Onely and William Savage.   Codicil dated 28 Oct.
1714: "My grandson Edward Mallebur of Repleston.   My grandson John Savage."

_____

    6 Nov. 1674.   Adm'on of the goods, etc., of William Browne of Woodford,
parish of Uttoxeter, Yeoman, granted by Lichfield P. Court to relict "Marie."
Inventory dated 11 Aug. 1674, amount £522 5s., by Tho. Stubbinge, W[m] Challinor,
Tho. Hall, and Francis Spencer.   Children Elizabeth and William (minors).

* Vicar of Etwall.

# The Register Book of Bramfield, co. Suffolk.*

**1582.**

July 15  Thommes Stevenson sonne vnto Jams Stevenson and Alls his wif.

Jan. 6  Alls falla dawter vnto Harrye falla and Ellyzabeth his wif.

Jan. 13  Roberd Brockket sonne of Roberd Brockket ge' and Margerit his wif. Now allso $y^e$ soone of Will'm Dowtye who married the wif of $y^e$ forsayd Roberd Brocket after she was conceyuyd $w^t$ this child a v monthes as by this Register it doo apear both of the deth of $y^e$ forsayd Roberd Brockket & allso of $y^e$ marrige of the sayd Will'm Dowtye vnto $y^e$ wif of $y^e$ forsayd Will'm. [An evident lapsus calami for Roberd. There is no mention of this marriage in this Register. Robert Brocket was buried May 18, 1582.]

Mar. 24  Roberd Knyts sonn vnto Necolas Knits and Marye his wif.

Mar. 24  Alls Mylls dauter vnto Roger Myll and Jone his wif.

**1583.**

April 28  Will'm Tod sonn vnto Will'm Tod and Margerie his wif.

May 12  Alls Writ dauter vnto Edmvnd Writ and Ellyzabeth his wif.

Aug. 22  Samuell Visie soon vnto Raynovld Visi and Margerit his wif.

Aug. 28  Edmvnd Watlyng sonne vnto Thomes Watlyng and Esbill his wif.

Sep. 1  Jane falla dawter vnto John falla and Margeri his wif.

Oct. 13  Thomes Son'es sonne vnto Antonye Son'es and Alls his wif.

Jan. 12  Thomes Hacon sonne vnto Rychard Hacon and Rachell his wif.

Jan. 19  Alles Sherhod dawter vnto John Sherwood and Dorathe his wyff.

**1584.**

April 13  Ollise Reve davghter vnto Thomes Reue and Ellinye his wif.

May 24  Harrye Tood sone vnto Will'm Tode and Margeri his wif.

July 12  Thomes farrar and Alles farrar sonne and dawter vnto Roberd farrar and Grace his wife.

Oct. 18  Will'm Seppins sonne vnto Hammond and Jone his wif.

Nov. 1  Lidda Thorston davghter vnto John Thorston and Am'ye his wif.

Nov. 29  Thomes Smyth sonne vnto francis Smith and Marie his wif.

**1585.**

Feb. 15  francis Pavliner basterd sonne vnto Sara Pavliner.

Mar. 7  Marie Hacon davghter vnto Richerd Hackkon and Margerit his wif.

Mar. 25  Margerit Watlyng daghter of Thomes Watlyng and Eisbill his wif.

May 30  John Myll sonne vnto Roger Myll and Jonne his wif.

Aug. 1  Roberd Sones sovn vnto Antony Sone and Alls his wif.

Jan. 30  Necolas Knites sonne vnto Necolas Knites and Marrie his wife.

Jan. 30  Raynovld falla sonne vnto Harrye falla and Elyzabeth his wif.

Feb. 17  Alls forman dawter vnto Thomes forman and Marye his wif.

**1586.**

April 10  Thomas Dorrant sonne vnto Thomas Torrante and Amye his wif.

July 24  Roberd Man sonne vnto Roberd Mane and Marye his wife.

July 31  Edmvnd Visie sovne vnto Raynovld Visie and Margerit his wif.

Oct. 27  Raynovld Clarcke sonne vnto Raynovld Clarcke and Marye his wif.

Nov. 3  Jvdye ford davghter vnto John ford and Mari his wife.

Jan. 8  Thomes Watling sonne vnto Thomes Watlyn and Eisbill his wif.

**1587.**

Mar. 26  Alls Sonns davghter vnto Antonye Sonns and Alls his wif.

May 7  fransis Hackkon davghter vnto Rychard Hackon and Margerit his wif.

May 29  John Bravster sonne vnto John Brevster and Marie his wif.

June 1  Ellynie Reve davghter vnto Thomes Reve and Ellyny his wif.

June 25  Margerye Thorston davghter vnto John Thorston and Amye his wif.

Aug. 6  Alls forman davghter vnto Thomes forman and Jone his wif.

**1588.**

May 29  Elizabeth fforman daughter of Thomas fforman.

June 15  Rob't Vesey sonne of Reginald Vesey.

July 21  Henry Clarke sonne of Reginald Clarke.

Sep. 19  Reginald Man sonne of Rob't Man.

Nov. 1  Mary Calver daughter of Symon Calver.

Nov. 3  ffranncis Smyth daughter of ffranncis Smyth.

Nov. —  [blank] daughter of $W^m$ Todde.

Jan. 5  Henry Chickeringe sonne of Henry Chickeringe.

Jan. 29  Anne Ireland daughter of Samuell Ireland.

Mar. 9  Elizabeth Keble daughter of Humfrey Keble.

**1589.**

April 6  Grace Thurstone daughter of John Thurston.

April 10  John Watlinge sonne of Thomas Watlinge.

Jan. 22  Alys Reve daughter of Thomas Reve.

* Continued from p. 221.

Mar. 3  Mary ffellow daughter of Henry ffel-
        lowe.
Dec. 3  [*blank*] Man daughter of Thomas Man.

1590.

April 2  Thomas Neale sonne of John Neale.
April 20  Thomas Seppins sonne of Hamond
         Seppins.
April 12  Thomas Clarke sonne of George Clarke.
May 3    Margaret Hacon daughter of Richard
         Hacon.
Nov. 10  Thomas Man sonne of Thomas Man.
Nov. 22  Reginald fforman sonne of Thomas
         fforman.
Mar. 20  Thomas Reve sonne of Thomas Reve.

1591.

May 20  Mary Chickeringe daughter of Henry
        Chickering.
May 31  Lambert Noller sonne of John Noller.
Aug. 15  John Reve sonne of Thomas Reve.
Oct. 25  Alys Corker daughter of Gualter
         Corker.
April 13  William Brewster sonne of John
         Brewster.

1592.

May 15  Mary Nolloth daughter of John
        Nolloth.
June 19  Thomas Micklewood sonne of Thom's
         Micklewood.
July 16  Anne Harsamte daughter of Christo-
         pher Harsannte.
Nov. 19  Alys Clarke daughter of George
         Clarke.

1593.

April 1  Thomas Grene sonne of Henry Grene.

April 8  Marion Hakon daughter of Richard
         Hacon.
April 28  Ales Man daughter of Thom's Man.
Sep. 26  John Shildrake sonne of [*blank*] Shill-
         drake.
Dec. 28  John Chickeringe sonne of Henry
         Chickeringe.
Mar. 27  Rob't Hakon sonne of William Hakon.

1594.

April 14  Reginald Rabett sonne of Reginald
         Rabett, gent.
Sep. 8  Henry ffella sonne of Henry ffella.
Oct. 27  Thom's Brewst' sonne of John Brewster.
Feb. 28  Richard Martyn sonne of John Martyn.

1595.

Aug. 4  William fiske sonne of William fiske.
Sep. 11  Clemens Corker daughter of Gualter
         Corker.
Feb. 19  Ambrose Harsett sonne of [*blank*]
         Harsett, gent.
Sep. 12  Reginald Chickeringe sonne of Henry
         Chickeringe.
Nov. 23  Elizabeth Clark daughter of George
         Clarke.
Mar. 11  Mary Rabett daughter of Reginald
         Rabett.
Mar. 14  John Man sonne of Thom's Man.

1596.

May 23  Rob't Sparham sonne of Rob't Spar-
        ham.
Dec. 19  ffranno's Tokely daughter of John
         Tokely.
Jan. 30  Anne Barrowe daughter of Edm.
         Barrowe.

END OF THE FIRST BOOK OF BAPTISMS.

## The Second existing Book of Baptisms.

1693.

Feb. 14  Reginald s. of John Rabett, gent.,
        and Mary his wife.
Feb. 18  Elizabeth d. of John Winter and Eliza-
        beth his wife.

1694.

April 11  Margaret d. of Valentine Copping and
         Mary his wife.
May 4   Henry s. of Henry Hall and Rebeccah
        his wife.
July 1  Sarah d. of Francis Reeve and Mary
        his wife.
July 22  Mary d. of Roger Clark and Alice his
        wife.
July 26  Bridget d. of Lambert Nelson, gent.,
        and Mary his wife.
July 29  Owen s. of Robert Smith and Elizabeth
        his wife.
Aug. 23  Francis s. of Robert Mills and Eliza-
        beth his wife.
Dec. 31  Mary d. of Thomas Ellis and Emma
        his wife.
Feb. 24  Margaret d. of Thomas Edwards and
        Anne his wife.
Feb. 28  Sarah d. of Samuel White and Han-
        nah his wife.

Mar. 3  Mary d. of John Winter and Elizabeth
        his wife.

1695.

April 7  John s. of John Sparham and Eliza-
        beth his wife.
May 1   Mary d. of John Short and Mary his
        wife.
Oct. 4  John s. of Lambert Nelson, gent., and
        Mary his wife.
Dec. 6  Elizabeth d. of George Chapman and
        Mary his wife.
Dec. 16  John s. of John Chrispe and Margaret
        his wife.
Jan. —  George s. of John Rabett, gent., and
        Mary his wife.
Mar. 15  Thomas s. of Edmund Ellis and Mary
        his wife.
Mar. 15  Susan d. of Richard Poole and Mary
        his wife.
Mar. 19  Mary d. of Samuel French and Mary
        his wife.

1696.

April 5  Robert s. of Robert Smith and Eliza-
        beth his wife.
Aug. 2  Susan d. of James Steele and Sarah
        his wife.

Aug. 16   Mary d. of John Peck and Dorothy his wife.

Sep. 10   Robert s. of Samuel White and Hannah his wife.

Sep. 23   Margaret d. of John Winter and Elizabeth his wife.

Sep. 29   Lambert s. of Lambert Nelson, gent., and Mary his wife.

Feb. 22   Emme d. of Thomas Ellis and Emme his wife.

Mar. 7   Robert s. of Thomas Kempe and Elizabeth his wife.

Mar. 21   Thomas s. of Robert Mills and Elizabeth his wife.

Jo$^n$ Catchpool, Vic$^r$.

1697.

April 25   Thomas s. of Thomas Soane and Sarah his wife.

May 6   Frances d. of John Rabett, gent., and Mary his wife.

July 25   John s. of Roger Clarke and Alice his wife.

Sep. 26   John s. of Edmund Ellis and Mary his wife.

Oct. 7   Mary d. of Henry Hall and Rebeccah his wife.

Oct. 24   William s. of John Sparham and Elizabeth his wife.

Nov. 7   Susanna d. of Thomas Edwards and Anne his wife.

Dec. 17   George s. of George Chapman and Mary his wife.

Feb. 9   Anne d. of Lambert Nelson, gent., and Mary his wife.

Feb. 27   Susanna d. of Robert Smith and Elizabeth his wife.

Jo$^n$ Catchpool, Vic.
William Buckingham, ⎫ Church-
Thomas Browne,     ⎭ wardens.

1698.

April 9   Sarah d. of John Rabett, gent., and Mary his wife.

April 24   Mary d. of Matthew Sparham and Mary his wife.

Sep. 27   Daniel s. of John Short and Mary his wife.

June 16   Sarah d. of Samuel White and Hannah his wife.

Oct. 9   William s. of Thomas Soane and Sarah his wife.

Oct. 7   Lidia d. of John Winter and Elizabeth his wife.

Dec. 12   Joseph s. of Thomas Bishop and Anne his wife.

Jo$^n$ Catchpool, Vic.

1699.

June 23   John s. of William Browne and Sarah his wife.

Dec. 20   Mary d. of Samuel Harvey and Sarah his wife.

Dec. 27   Samuel s. of Henry Hall and Rebeccah his wife.

Jan. 24   Edward s. of Lambert Nelson, gent., and Mary his wife.

Mar. 10   Elizabeth d. of John Short and Mary his wife.

Mar. 24   Elizabeth d. of Thomas Ellis and Emme his wife.

Jo$^n$ Catchpool, Vic.

1700.

June 17   Martha d. of Thomas Pettiver and Elizabeth his wife.

Oct. 24   Elizabeth d. of John Rabett, gent., and Mary his wife.

Jan. 14   Joseph s. of John White and Elizabeth his wife.

Feb. 9   Elizabeth d. of Robert Smith and Elizabeth his wife.

July 17   Sarah d. of George Chapman and Mary his wife.

Mar. 21   Mary d. of Thomas Mills and Elizabeth his wife.

Jo$^n$ Catchpool, Vic.
Hen. Hall, Churchwarden.

1701.

April 11   Anne d. of Roger Clarke and Alice his wife.

April 24   Peter s. of Henry Hall and Rebeccah his wife.

June 1   Mary d. of Thomas Soane and Sarah his wife.

June 2   Thomas s. of Samuel Harvey and Sarah his wife.

June 2   Robert s. of Robert Mayhewe and Deborah his wife.

June 9   Thomas s. of Thomas Bishop and Anne his wife.

Nov. 3   Daniel s. of Daniel Howes and Mary his wife.

Feb. 20   Prudence d. of John Rabett, gent., and Mary his wife.

Feb. 25   Thomas s. of John Peck and Dorothy his wife.

Mar. 11   Mary d. of John Denny and Mary his wife.

Jo$^n$ Catchpool, Vic.
The mark of William Browne, Churchwarden.

1702.

April 19   Anne d. of Thomas Lawes and Elizabeth his wife.

May 21   Martha d. of John Short and Mary his wife.

July 15   Anne d. of Henry Hall and Rebeccah his wife.

Aug. 16   Samuel s. of Samuel Skoulding and Elizabeth his wife.

Sep. 17   William s. of George Chapman and Mary his wife.

Jo$^n$ Catchpool, Vic.
Sam$^{ll}$ White, Churchwarden.

1703.

Aug. 14   Bethiah d. of John Winter and Bethiah his wife.

Sep. 7   Samuel s. of Samuel Harvey and Sarah his wife.

Nov. 2   Christian d. of Henry Grint and Christian his wife.

Nov. 5   Mary d. of Thomas Matthews and Sarah his wife.
Nov. 20  Margaret d. of Robert Turrell and Mary his wife.
Jan. 9   John s. of Samuel Skoulding and Elizabeth his wife.
Feb. —   John s. of Thomas Sones and Sarah his wife.

Jon CATCHPOOL, Vic.
The mark of EDWARD FELLA, Churchwarden.

1704.

April 19  Mary d. of William Chrispe and Susan his wife.
April 23  Mary d. of Edmund Ellis and Mary his wife.
May 20   Elizabeth d. of James Steel and Sarah his wife.
June 16  Thomas s. of Thomas Lawes and Elizabeth his wife.
Sep. 26  James s. of James Skoulding and Mary his wife.
Jan. 5   Mary d. of Thomas Ellis and Emme his wife.
Feb. 14  Martha d. of John Winter and Bethiah his wife.
Mar. 4   Hannah d. of Samuel Skoulding and Elizabeth his wife.

Jon CATCHPOOL, Vic.
The mark of ROBERT COPPING, Churchwarden.

1705.

Mar. 26  Playford s. of Henry Grint and Christian his wife.
Mar. 28  Edward s. of Robert Smith and Elizabeth his wife.
April 1  John s. of John Peck and Dorothy his wife.
Aug. 25  Peter s. of Henry Hall and Rebeccah his wife.
Oct. 25  Sarah d. of James Steel and Sarah his wife.
Nov. 5   John s. of Joseph Poyntz and Mary his wife.
Mar. 17  Elizabeth d. of John Hurwood and Elizabeth his wife.

Jon CATCHPOOL, Vic.
JOHN FFELLA,      } Churchwardens.
JOHN HURWOOD,  }

1706.

July 26  John s. of William Chrispe and Susan his wife.
Aug. 8   John s. of John Baylie, gent., and Margaret his wife.
Sep. 7   Christian d. of Henry Grint and Christian his wife.
Nov. 6   Susan d. of John Winter and Bethiah his wife.
Jan. 9   Ezekiel s. of Ezekiel Smith and Susan his wife.
Feb. 26  Anne d. of Thomas Soanes and Sarah his wife.

Jon CATCHPOOL, Vic.

1707.

July 27  Robert s. of Robert Edwards and Mary his wife.

July 30  Dorothy d. of John Peck and Dorothy his wife.
Sep. 20  Thomas s. of Thomas Matthews and Sarah his wife.
Oct. 3   Edward s. of Edward Browne and Mary his wife.
Dec. 14  William s. of Edmund Ellis and Mary his wife.
Jan. 10  John s. of Thomas Copping and Elizabeth his wife.
Feb. 15  Robert s. of Thomas Ellis and Emme his wife.

Jon CATCHPOOL, Vic.

1708.

July 30  Hannah d. of John Winter and Bethuiah his wife.
Aug. 8   John s. of Samuel Harvey and Sarah his wife.
Aug. 19  Jane d. of Thomas Lawes and Elizabeth his wife.
Aug. 19  William s. of Roger Clark and Mary his wife.
Sep. 17  John s. of William Chrispe and Susan his wife.
Jan. 23  Mary d. of Ezekiel Smith and Susan his wife.
Feb. 24  Thomas s. of Thomas Matthews and Sarah his wife.
Feb. 24  Elizabeth d. of Henry Grint and Christian his wife.

Jon CATCHPOOL, Vic.
JAMES SKOULDING, } Churchwardens.
JOHN HOWARD,      }

1709.

June 12  William s. of Joseph Poyntz and Mary his wife.
Aug. 16  Thomas s. of Roger Clark and Mary his wife.
Aug. 19  Thomas s. of Thomas Copping and Elizabeth his wife.
Oct. 23  Jemima d. of John Winter and Bethuiah his wife.
Oct. 30  John s. of Thomas Edwards and Hannah his wife.
Oct. 30  Anne d. of Benjamin Gostling and Anne his wife.

Jon CATCHPOOL, Vic.
THO. MATHEW,       } Churchwardens.
JOHN BEDINGFIELD, }

1710.

April 2  Daniel s. of Ezekiel Smith and Susan his wife.
Oct. 15  Anne d. of Robert Smith and Susan his wife.
Jan. 10  Robert s. of Thomas Copping and Elizabeth his wife.
Jan. 20  Mary d. of Robert Tirrell and Mary his wife.
Jan. 30  Anne d. of William Newson and Anne his wife.
Mar. 18  Thomas s. of Roger Clarke and Mary his wife.

Jon CATCHPOOL, Vic.

### 1711.

April 18 Susan d. of William Chrispe and Susan his wife.

April 29 Elizabeth d. of James Skoulding and Mary his wife.

June 10 Elizabeth d. of Edward Bird and Elizabeth his wife.

June 27 Sarah d. of Thomas Matthew and Sarah his wife.

July 22 Jemima d. of John Winter and Bethuiah his wife.

Nov. 21 William s. of William Sheppard and Elizabeth his wife.

Mar. 23 Anne d. of Samuel Sheppard and Anne his wife.

Jon CATCHPOOL, Vic.

### 1712.

April 20 William s. of Ezekiel Smith and Susan his wife.

Sep. 11 Elizabeth d. of Thomas Copping and Elizabeth his wife.

Oct. 12 James s. of James Eade and Mary his wife.

Oct. 13 Mary d. of John Freeman, gent., and Mary his wife.

Jon CATCHPOOL, Vic.

### 1713.

April 5 Edward s. of Edward Bird and Elizabeth his wife.

April 12 Daniel s. of Samuel Amand and Mary his wife.

May 1 Sarah d. of William Crisp and Susan his wife.

May 31 Robert s. of Ezekiel Smith and Susan his wife.

June 7 Thomas s. of Thomas Saunders and Sarah his wife.

July 30 Philadelphia d. of John Winter and Bethuiah his wife.

Oct. 29 Hannah d. of Thomas Edwards and Hannah his wife.

Nov. 15 Sarah d. of Benjamin Gostling and Anne his wife.

Dec. 7 Marah d. of Thomas Matthew and Sarah his wife.

Nov. 29 Robert s. of Edmund Watling and Mary his wife.

Jan. 24 James s. of James Edwards and Anne his wife.

### 1714.

April 23 Valentine s. of Thomas Copping and Elizabeth his wife.

May 28 Elizabeth d. of James Eade and Mary his wife.

May 28 Sarah d. of John Peck and Dorothy his wife.

May 30 Samuel s. of Samuel Shepherd and Anne his wife.

July 11 Sarah d. of Henry Day and Sarah his wife.

Aug. 8 William s. of Ezekiel Smith and Susan his wife.

Aug. 15 Mary d. of William Crowfoot and Mary his wife.

Sep. 26 Sarah d. of Thomas Newson and Sarah his wife.

Nov. 26 George s. of George Browne and Elizabeth his wife.

Dec. 5 Mary d. of John Prue and Mary his wife.

Jan. 31 Thomas s. of Valentine Copping, Jun., and Elizabeth his wife.

Feb. 6 Sarah d. of Thomas Saunders and Sarah his wife.

Mar. 2 Edmund s. of Edmund Watling and Mary his wife.

### 1715.

Mar. 27 Anne d. of James Edwards and Anne his wife.

June 5 Mary d. of John Tibbald and Mary his wife.

July 22 Susanna Eade and Mary Eade twin dau'rs of James Eade and Mary his wife.

Sep. 11 Bridget d. of Ezekiel Smith and Susan his wife.

Nov. 21 John s. of Edward Bird and Elizabeth his wife.

Mar. 4 William s. of Thomas Copping and Elizabeth his wife.

Mar. 11 Mary d. of Henry Day and Sarah his wife.

### 1716.

Mar. 25 Lydia d. of Thomas Browne and Martha his wife.

July 1 Anne d. of John Prue and Mary his wife.

July 15 Benjamin s. of Benjamin Gostling and Anne his wife.

Aug. 2 John s. of John ffenn and Elizabeth his wife.

Aug. 2 Thomas s. of Thomas Ellis and Elizabeth his wife.

Aug. 24 Valentine s. of Valentine Copping, Jun., and Elizabeth his wife.

Dec. 25 Mary d. of Thomas Saunders and Sarah his wife.

Feb. 13 Susanna d. of James Eade and Mary his wife.

Mar. 8 Susan d. of Henry Grint and Christian his wife.

*(To be continued.)*

ORMSBY PEDIGREE.—Thomas Ormsby, the first name mentioned, Pedigree D, p. 221, Vol. II., Second Series, was grandfather and not father of Francis who married Mary Madden. There was an intervening Francis whose wife's name I have not discovered. Thomas had two other sons not mentioned, namely, Henry and Thomas, and may have had more. Rebecca Ormsby, on same page, set down as wife of Morris, had by him two sons, Theophilus and Frederick, and a daughter.

## GENEALOGICAL MEMORANDA RELATING TO THE FAMILY OF EVELYN.

### WILLS.

ROGER EVELYN of Stam'ar the More [Stanmore], co. Midd. Will dat. 28 July 1508 ; pr. 18 Aug. 1508 by Alice the relict and John Warnar. (4 Bennett.) To be bur^d in the Churchy^d of Our Lady of Stam'ar, and small bequests to that church, and also to that of Harrow on the Hill. To my wife Alice, horses, cattle, sheep, etc., and to the child she is with, a bullock and 20s. To my two da^s Agnes and Margaret two bullocks and 20s. each to their marriages. Residue of my cattle, etc., to my two sons John and Robert. My wife to deliver all the housyng and lands which she hath in Harrow to John our heir within a year and a day. To John Colyn a grey mare, and to John Warryn my servant a bay mare. To my brother Henry Evelyn a bay gelding, etc. Residue to Alice my wife, she and John Warnar to be ex'ors. Robert Waryn and Henry Evelyn, overseers. Wit., S^r Edw^d Thorp, p'son, John Warner, yeoman, Henry Evelyn, bandman, with others.

ROBERT EVELYN of Est Acton in the par. of Church Acton, Dioc. of Westminster. Will dat. 16 Oct. 1543 ; pr. 11 Jan. 1543-4 by Petronilla, relict and ex'ix. (1 Pynnyng.) To be buried in Acton Churchyard. Bequests to the Cathedral Church of Westminster and to Acton Church. To my brother John Evelyn 13s. 4d. To my cousin Lawrance Cannon my overseer 13s. 4d. To my son William, under age, £30 and three kine. To my da^s Johan and Margery, under age, each £13 6s. 8d. and three bullocks at their marriages. If my wife is with child at time of my decease, the said child to have £3 6s. 8d. and two kine. My wife to be sole ex'ix, to whom residue. Wit., Lawrance Can'on, Rob^t Todde, Philip Compaine, S^r Symonde Essex, curate.

WILLIAM EVELIN of Kingsburie, co. Midd., yeoman. Will dat. 27 Dec. 1599; proved 27 Sep. 1600 by Jon ffrancklin, power reserved. (Commissary of Lond., v. 19, fo. 173.) To be buried in Kingsburie Churchyard and to the poor 20s. Peter and Richard (the latter under age) sons of W^m ffrancklin late of Kingsburie dec^d. Rose da. of the s^d W^m ffrancklin and wife of John Winchester, and their da. Annes and son William Winchester (my godson) both under age. William ffrancklin son of Jon ffrancklin. My brother M^r George Needeler of London, gent. My sister Margerie ffrancklin, widow, and her son Jon ffrancklin, ex'ors. My brothers William Needeler of East Acton and John Needeler of Parva Perivall al's Little Grenford, co. Midd., yeoman, overseers. Wit., Tho^s Hanburie, John Walker.

GEORGE EVELYN of Wotton, co. Surrey, Esq. Will dat. 20 Jan. 40 Eliz. ; pr. 30 May 1603 by Tho^s Iles proctor for Joane the relict, power being reserved to Rich^d Eveline. (35 Bolein.) To be buried in Wotton Church. To 60 poor householders of Darkinge, 20 of Wotton, 30 of Abinger, and 40 of Sheere, 12^d each. To Thomas Bysshop and his wife dwelling at Clasgate £40. To Henry Tilte of Kingston 10s. To my da. Katherine Evelyn £500 at age of 18 to be paid by my son John Evelyn, and also £800 to be paid by my son Robert Evelin. To my son John Evelin lands at Kingston upon Thames which I purchased of Rich^d Hatton gent., and Tho^s Stamforde of Thissleworth, also my manor of Norlington Hall in Kingston, etc. Lands in Hooke and land called Surbiton field to my son Thomas Eveline. My manor and lands, etc., in Abinger, and my leasehold at East Clangdon, to my son Richard Eveline. To Mary wife of Richard Hatton, gent., and to his da. ffrances Hatton £100 each. Residue to my wife Joane and my son Richard Eveline, ex'ors. My cousin George Cole, and William Comber, gent., overseers. Wit., W^m Mathew, scr., Robert Rogers.

GEO. EVELIN, late of Wotton, co. Surrey, Esq^r, dec^d. (84 Stafford.) Sententiæ 4 Nov. 1606 to confirm will inter Joanne Evelin the relict of 1 part, and Thomas, John, and Robert Evelin the sons, and Mary Hatton and Katherine Stoughton the dau'rs of the afores^d Geo. Evelin, of the other part.

THOMAS EVELYN of Long Ditton, Surrey, Esq. Will dated 4 June 14 Jac. ;

pr. 17 Nov. 1617 by Frances Evelyn the relict. (111 Weldon.) To my eldest son Thomas Evelyn my bason and ewer of silver and two silver bowls having my arms engraven on them. By agreement between me and Thomas Reynell of the Strand, co. Midd., gent., my younger son Will^m Evelyn is to have £1000. The lease (26 years) of my house in Gardner's Lane, Westminster (now in the tenure of my son Worsley), to my two sons in law John Bodley and Thomas Keteley, in trust for my da. Mary Worsley during her life, rem^r to her children. Also to the s^d John Bodley and Tho^s Keteley £150 in trust for Thomas and John Worsley, two of my s^d da. Worsley's sons, and such child as she now goeth with or shall next have. There is a deed of conveyance of lands for my da^s portions amounting to £3500. To my sons George and William Evelyn my adventure of £200 in the East India Company. To the poor of Kingston, Thames Ditton, and Long Ditton, £4 each parish. Residue to my wife Frances, sole ex'ix. Wit., Richard Swayne, Ro. Talbott.

HENRY EVELING of Estclanden, Surrey, husbandman. Will dat. 9 May 1615 ; pr. 13 April 1620 by Marie the relict. (Archd^y of Surrey, Book Peter, 1616—1622, fo. 87.) To be buried in East Clandonne Churchyard. To my da. Marye wife of John Ellys of Chobham, Surrey, 10s. and a Linnen wheele, and to her son Henry Ellis 10s. To William Martynn's three sons 20s. Residue to my wife Mary Evelinge, sole ex'ix. M^r Tho^s Grever of Bagshott in the parish of Windelsham, co. Surrey, and John Jurden of Estclandonne afores^d, yeoman, overseers, and to each sixpence.

GEORGE EVELYN, Esq., late of West Deane, co. Wilts, dec^d. Adm'on 1 Feb. 1635-6 to his son Sir John Evelyn, Kn^t, with the consent of Elizabeth Evelyn relict of the defunct. (Adm'ons 1636, fo. 149.)

RICHARD EVELYN of Wotton, Surrey, Esq. Will dat. 27 Oct. 1640 ; pr. 9 Feb. 1640-1 by Geo. Evelyn. (1 Evelyn.) Leighe farm in Sussex after my death is settled upon my da. Jane Evelyn and her issue, and I give her £2000 in lieu of the legacy from her grandfather M^r John Stansfield, and other demands. To my son John Evelyn lands at South Maling and also £4000, and to my son Richard Evelyn £1000, in lieu of the legacies from their afs^d grandfather Stansfield. Residue to my son Geo. Evelyn, sole ex'or. My cousin Rob^t Hatton, Esq., and my brother in law George Duncombe the elder, overseers. To my servant Richard Higham an annuity of £10. Wit., Geo. Duncombe, Rob^t Rapley, Jerome Collins.

FRANCES EVELYN, widow, aged about 85 years, in Nov^r or Dec^r in Winter last was 12 months, and then sojourning at Hartingfordbury, co. Herts, but lately dec^d at Kingston upon Thames, Surrey, made her will nuncupative, in the presence of her son in law Thomas Keightley and her da. Rose his wife and in whose house she then lived, and gave all to her (the s^d Frances Evelyn's) eldest son George Evelyn. (143 Fairfax.) Adm'on Oct. 1, 1649, to George Evelyn son of testatrix.

FRANCES EVELYN, late of Kingston upon Thames, Surrey, widow, dec^d, on or about Feb. 1647 made her nuncupative will (as above). Sententiæ pro valore test. 26 Feb. 1649-50 inter W^m Evelyn and Eliz^th Constantine, widow, of 1 part, and Geo. Evelyn son of the defunct of the other part. (17 Pembroke.)

ELIZABETH EVELYNE of S^t Foster's, Foster Lane, London, spinster. Sententiæ pro valore test. 10 July 1652 inter John Buckeridge the ex'or of 1 part, and Sir John Evelyn, Knt. (brother of the defunct), Dame Jane Hart (sister of the def^t), Sir John Evelyn the younger, Kn^t., and Arthur Evelyne, sons of Geo. Evelyn, dec^d (brother of the def^t), and Elizabeth Foster, da. of . . . . Foster dec^d (sister of the def^t), of the other part. (209 Bowyer.)

GEORGE EVELIN of Huntercombe in the parish of Burneham, co. Bucks, Esq. Will dat. 20 April 1657 ; pr. 12 May 1658 by Dudly Evelin the relict. My manor of Huntercombe is settled upon Robert Leighe, Esq., and Thomas Balls, brother to my wife, in trust for her use during her life, remainder to my eld. son George Evelin. To my s^d son George Evelin all I bought of Sir Charles Lee, Jerveys Elweys, and Garrard Gore, and all household stuff after death of my wife. To my youngest son Thomas Evelin now in Ireland £1000, secured on the estate of Sir

John Henden of Biddenden, co. Kent, Kn$^t$, dec$^d$, M$^r$ Farmer of the Com'on Pleas and my nephew Wollaston being trustees for its payment. To my wife £300, she to be sole ex'ix. (229 Wotton.)

DAME ELIZABETH EVELYN, late of St. Paul, Covent Garden, Midd., dec$^d$. Adm'on 14 May 1658 to her husb$^d$ Sir John Evelyn, Kn$^t$. (Adm'ons 1658, fo. 116.)

Another grant 24 June 1658 to Arthur Evelyn, Esq., guardian of Elizabeth and Sarah Evelyn, minors, children of the s$^d$ Dame Eliz$^{th}$ Evelyn the defunct. (Adm'ons 1658, fo. 154.)

The last-named grant having expired, another was made May 28, 1661, to her husband Sir John Evelyn, Knt., her daughters Elizabeth Peirpoint *al's* Evelyn and Sara Evelyn first renouncing. (Adm'ons 1661, fo. 44.)

SIR THOMAS EVELYN of Long Ditton, co. Surrey, Knt. Will dat. 3 Oct. 1659; pr. 11 April 1660 by Dame Anne Evelyn the relict. To my wife Dame Anne Evelyn all my manors, lands, etc., upon the conditions of an agreement made with Mistress Mary Balam touching a marriage between her and my son Edward Evelyn, and to settle a jointure of £400 per ann. on the s$^d$ Mary Balam, and also £200 per ann. for increase of maintenance for my s$^d$ son Edward, and he to have the s$^d$ manors, etc., after my wife's death. My lands called Berry lands, etc., also to go to my son Edward on death of my wife. To my grandchild Sophia Evelyn £2000 at her age of 21 or marriage. To my sons Vincent Evelyn and Arthur Evelyn £1000 each. My wife Dame Anne Evelyn sole ex'ix. (36 Nabbs.)

GEORGE EVELYN, late of S$^t$ Martin's in the Fields, co. Midd., dec$^d$. Adm'on 24 Nov. 1660 to Thomas Worsley, guardian of Sophia Evelyn, a minor, granddau$^r$ (nepti ex filius) of the defunct, the relict Jane Evelyn having first renounced. (Adm'ons 1660, fo. 174.)

DUDLEY EVELYN.* Will dat. 28 Nov. 1660; pr. 4 Nov. 1661 by her son George Evelyn. To my brother Thomas Balls £40 and my diamond ring. My brother Edward Balls. To my son Thomas £50. To the poor widow Rylett £5, and her innocent child £10 to help to keep it. To poor of Burneham £5. Residue to my son George Evelyn, sole ex'or. In my other will I did remember many other of my near relations, but now your [her son George] losses have been so great, I will give no more from you, but only mourning rings to my sister Nan, and to Nan Balls and cousin George. (173 May.)

VINCENT EVELYN, late of Long Ditton, co. Surrey, bachelor, dec$^d$. Adm'on 24 June 1663 to his brother Edward Evelyn. (Adm'ons 1663, fo. 67.)

SIR JOHN EVELYN of Godstone, co. Surrey, Knt. Will dat. 20 April 1663; pr. 16 Jan. 1663-4 by Dame Thomazine Evelyn the relict. To be buried in the vault which I have erected and finished in the chancel of Godstone Church. My lands and tithes in Walkhamsted, Godstone, Tandridge, Bletchingly, and Caterham, co. Surrey (which were not settled on my eldest son John Evelyn in marriage), I give to my son George Evelyn. To my son in law Edward Hayles of Boughton Malherbe, Kent, Esq., £40 for mourning for himself and his wife. To my dau$^r$ Lady Leche £20 for mourning. To the poor of Godstone £6 yearly out of my farm called y$^e$ Blewe Anchor. To the poor of Godstone, Bletchingly, Tandridge, Caterham, and Woldingham £10 at my burial. My wife Thomazine sole ex'ix. My son George Evelyn to follow the study of the law. Wit., John Gainsford, Tho$^s$ Packenham, Rich$^d$ Alexander. (Archdeaconry of Surrey, 1660–1686.)

ARTHUR EVELIN, late of S$^t$ Margaret's, Westminster, Middx., dec$^d$. Adm'on 12 April 1666 to James Harrison, principal creditor, . . . . Evelin the relict having first renounced. (Adm'ons 1666, fo. 95.)

DAME ANN EVELYN, relict of Sir Thomas Evelyn, late of Long Ditton, co. Surrey, Knt., dec$^d$. Will dat. 16 June 1669; pr. 14 July 1669 by Edward Evelyn. To my eldest son Edward Evelyn, Esq., and his wife, my youngest son Arthur Evelyn and his wife, my dau. Naper and her husband, and Robert Naper, jun$^r$, Esq., husband of my grand-dau. Sophia Naper, £20 each for mourning. To my s$^d$ son

---

* She was widow of George Evelyn of Huntercombe, in Burnham, Bucks, and was buried at Burnham 6 Sept. 1661. (Par. Reg.)

ARMS OF LARDER QUARTERING PYNE, DENYS, ST. AUBYN, AND CHALLONS, AND IMPALING NICHOLLS.

NORTH WEALD CHURCH, ESSEX.

Arthur Evelyn £200. My cousin Richard Gardiner, sen$^r$. M$^r$ Robert Pococke. Poor of Long Ditton £10. Residue to my eldest son Edward Evelyn, sole ex'or. Wit., Eliz. Northage, Tho$^s$ Dickenson. (83 Coke.)

*(To be continued.)*

## Larder and Nicholls.

### Wills.

Walter Larder. Will dated 23 March 1531; proved 10 May 1532. To be buried in our Lady Chapel in the Church of St. Androw in Essex, called North Whele Bassett. My wife Katheryn sole ex'ix, to whom my lands in Dorsetshire in the p'ish of Axmowth (*sic*) and at North Wild Basset in Essex for 20 years, she to keep my four sons at school till of lawful age, and if she dies before the 20 years are expired, then my brother William to enter upon the said lands for the rest of the 20 years, and if he dies then to my brother Robert for the rest of the said term. My son William to have the aforesaid lands at the end of the said term of 20 years, and in default of issue, remainder to my sons George, Andrew, and Nicolas in succession. To my son Nicolas at his age of 21 all the "annbetes" which lieth in Dorsetshire, called brokes land, remainder in default to my sons Andrew, William, and George in succession, remainder to my brothers William and Robert in succession. To my son George at his age of 21 my lands and tenements in North Wild Basset, Essex, and also a close called Shepcot feld, remainder in default to my sons Androw, William, and Nicolas in succession, remainder to my brother William. Witnesses, S$^r$ Thomas Wanstanly, curate of North Wild Basset, William Larder, Androw Brodley, John Tanner. (Archdeaconry of Essex, Book Rypton, fo. 124.)

Andrewe Larder of Northwealde Bassett, Essex, gent. Will dated 20 April 1592; proved 1 July 1592 by Martha the relict, power reserved. To be buried in the chapel of the parish church of Northweald Bassett, near my late father Walter Larder. My lease of my farm where I now dwell called Weald Hall to my wife Martha till my son Walter Larder is 21, and then to him, as also certain marsh land in Westham, Essex. My brother Edward Bugg and his son Richard Bugg to be trustees for my wife and children. To my dau'rs Constance, Anne, Joyce, Elizabeth, and Martha Larder £100 each at ages of 18. My godda. Margaret Bugg 40s. Martha Bugg 20s. My godson Edward Aylett 40s. My godson Andrew Gybbin 20s. Poor of Northweald 40s. Bequests to divers servants. Residue to Martha my wife, she and my son Walter Larder ex'ors. The aforesaid Edward Bugg my brother, his son Richard Bugg, my friend Thomas Chevelly, gent., and my brother-in-law Henry Aylett, supervisors. Witnesses, my aforesaid supervisors, with Wm. Neale, clerk. (Archdeaconry of Essex, 1591–1603, Book Stephen, fo. 39$^b$.)

Walter Larder of Northweald Bassett, Essex, gent. Nuncupative will 25 Aug. 1606; proved 1 Oct. 1606 by Wm. Thwaites, Notary Pub., Proctor for Marie the relict. To his three children George, Martha, and Anne £100 each at ages of 21 or marriage, and if his wife be now with child the s$^d$ child also to have £100 at age of 21 or marriage. To his eldest son Walter Larder the six last years of his lease of Wealdhall and Wealde Parke. To Mr. Linch, Vicar of North Weald, £3. Residue to his wife Marie Larder, sole ex'trix. George Nicolls of Walden, gent., and Rob$^t$ Cooge of Mountnezinge, gent., overseers. Witnesses, Symon Linch, Samuell Searle, Richard Spranger. (Archdeaconry of Essex, 1603-8, Book Nevell, fo. 200.)

Walter Larder of Upminster, co. Essex, yeoman. Will dated 25 Feb. 1631; proved 15 May 1632 by his brother Richard Larder. To Mary Titmowse my servant, bedding, etc., and also £6. To Rabege Clerk my wife's son's da., bedding. To my grandchild Thomas Clerke, household stuff. To Rabedge Evans my servant,

40s. at age of 21. Residue to my brother Richard Larder, sole ex'or. My neighbours John Drywood and Thomas Sawkyns, overseers.

the mark of WALTER ✗ LARDER.

Witnesses, Wm. Lake, Francila (*sic*).

(Archdeaconry of Essex, 1632, filed will.)

John Nicolles the elder, of Walden [Essex], draper. Will dated 20 Nov. 1515; proved 19 Feb. 1515 (1515-16) by the ex'ors. To be buried in the Church of our Blessed Lady of Walden in the south aisle, between my wives Jane and Alys, and a stone of marble to be laid on my grave. Services, etc., in Walden Church, Walden Abbey, Priory of Roistone, Litilbury Church, etc. To my brother George £4, etc., he to be good friend to my wife and children. To my brother Richard Nicolles my best gown and 40s. and to his da. Elizabeth 10s. I forgive my brother John Nicolles of London what he owes me, and I give gowns to him and his wife, and to his children 3s. 4d. each. To my son Wm Halles of Ippiswich 20s. for a gown, my best cup silver gilt, etc., and to his wife my daughter six Apostle spoons and the best gown that was my wife's Jane Kersy's, and to his son Jamys Hall 10s. To my son in law Aleyn Osborn and his wife gowns, and to the said Aleyn £10. To my brother Richard Robkyn and his wife 23s. 4d. for black gowns, and 10s. among his children. To Robert Hanscom and his wife black gowns, and 10s. among his children. Bequests to the Church of Powlys in London, and to the Churches of Walden, Little Chesterford, Hadstokke, Wicken, Wenden Magna, Arkysden, Kyrsall, Heyden, Ansty, Hennome, and Depdens. To my wife Johane a gown of Sangwene that was my wife's sometime named Jane Kersye, and also £20 in plate, and to occupy my lands in Walden for one year. To my son John Nicolles £50 to be taken in cloth out of my shop. To my sons John and George household stuff between them, and to the said George 10 marks when he comes out of his apprenticeship. To my brother George Nicolles bedding, etc. To Xpofer Osborne and his brother, sons of Aleyn Osborne, 10 marks each at ages of 22. To John Boytun 40s. and his brother Thomas 20s. To Wm Boytun 5 marks at age of 20, and to Anable Boytun 5 marks at age of 16. To my da. Elizabeth, wife of Aleyn Osborne, bedding, etc. To John Smith and Agnes his wife gowns. Residue to my ex'ors, viz., John Nicolles my son, Geo. Nicolles my brother, and John Smyth, draper. Witnesses, Sr Olyvere Guddswane, priest, Thos Midylton, Thos Marteyne, Jamys Willyamson, Wm Cokke, John Boytun, etc. (P.C.C., 14 Holder.)

George Nicholles of Hinxton (co. Cambr.), Dioc. of Ely. Will dated 15 Dec. 1515; proved 14 Nov. 1516 by John Nicolles, ex'or. To be buried in the Chancel of St John's Church, Hinxton. Bequests to churches of Hinxton and Great Wenden. To my brother Richard Nicolles 40s. and my gold ring, and to his da. silver spoons, etc. To the children of my brother John Nicholles of London 3s. 4d. each. To John Nicholles, son of my brother John Nicholles of Walden, silver spoons. Prioress and Convent of Ikelton 20s. Priory of Barnwell £3 6s. 8d. Abbey of Walden £3. To John Clerke and Margaret his wife, my servants, my interest in the parsonages of Hinxton and Wenden. John Nicholles the younger of Walden, ex'or. (P.C.C., 24 Holder.)

John Nicolles of Walden [Essex], Dioc. of London, yeoman. Will dated 9 Sept. 1555; proved 12 Oct. 1555 by John Goodman, notary, Proctor for the ex'ors. Poor of Walden 10s. My freehold and copyhold in Walden, Littlebury, Wenden, and Newporte, co. Essex, to my wife Margery for life, and after to my son George Nicolles, remainder in default to my son Thomas Nicolles, remainder to my da. Annable Hallidance. A tenement in which Thomas Nicolles the butcher now lives. To my said da. Annable Hallidance £40, and a tenement in Walden in her husband's occupation. Two shops in the Market Place of Walden to John Nicolles son of Thomas Nicolles my son. Tenements in Walden to my son Thomas Nicolles. My wife Margery and my son Geo. Nicolles, ex'ors. My son in law Thomas Hallidance and my son Thomas Nicolles, overseers. Witnesses, John Corbett, gent., John Smyth, senr, Wm Strach the elder, Thos Birde the elder, Nicholas Prott. (P.C.C., 33 More.)

# Genealogy of Browne.*

## Evidences.

BRADELEY—continued.

NOTES OF BROWNE MARRIAGE BONDS AT LICHFIELD.

1666    Edward Browne, of Hillmorton, & Elizabeth Wilcox.
       Hugo        ,,    of Shrewsbury, & Anne Nevill.
       John        ,,    of Kingswinford, & Alice Hill.
       John        ,,    of Stretton, & Miriam Plant.
       Richard    ,,    of Condover, & Elizabeth Brasier.
       Seth        ,,    of Hansworth, & Eleanor Lathbury.
1667    Nil.
1668    John Browne, of Birmingham, & Elizabeth Smyth.
       Thomas    ,,    of Shredicote, & Mary Carr.
1669    William Browne, of Etwall, & Maria Jeffery.
1670    Robert Browne, of Tamworth, & Mary Albert.
       Samuel      ,,    of Crich, & Mary I . . . .
1677    Francis Browne, of Loppington, & Eleanor Carter.
1678    Nil.
1679    William Browne, of Lilburne, & Priscilla Brimington.
1680    Thomas Browne, of Manton, & Mary Taunton.
1721    Nathaniel Browne, of Mavesyn Redwaie, & Margaret Evans.
       Thomas        ,,    of Creek, Northampton, & Mary Spence.
       Joseph        ,,    of Derby, & Hannah Maddox.
       James        ,,    of Keel, & Elizabeth Beech.
       John        ,,    of Abbotts Bromley, & Mary Aston.
       Thomas        ,,    of Gaeton (?), & Grace Rankhorne.
       William        ,,    of Abbotts Bromley, & Dorothy Aston.
       Matthew      ,,    of Birmingham, & Sarah Lerner.
       John        ,,    of Fazeley, & Barbara Warner.
       Thomas        ,,    of Hanbury, & Mary Bradbury.
1722    John Browne, of Anniley, & Anne Sutton.
       John        ,,    of Coleshill, & Elizabeth Ashford.
       Anthony    ,,    of Hulland Ward, & Elizabeth Clown.
       John        ,,    of Alfreton, & Anne Gilbert.
       Richard    ,,    of Eccleshall, & Elizabeth Shaw.
       Stephen    ,,    of Compton, & Anne Page.
1723    John Brown, of Chilvers Coton, & Alice Shilton.
       James        ,,    of Handworth, & Mary Welch.
       Hannah        ,,    of Tamworth, & John Cox of Chilvers Coton.
       William Corbet, of Shrewsbury, & Ann Cooper.

---

## SHREDICOTE, CO. STAFFORD.

Shredicote is a hundred within the parish of Bradeley,† about three miles from the town of Stafford.

The Shredicote Estate must not be confused with another estate of a similar name, but known as the "Shredicote Hall" Estate, as the properties adjoin and both are situated in the parish of Bradeley. Shredicote Hall was never in the possession of the Browne family. For many generations it belonged to the Horton family, until it was sold by Mr. James Horton, by deed dated 3 May 1710, to the Rev. Samuel Peploe, M.A., then Vicar of Preston in Lancashire, afterwards Lord Bishop of Chester, who, as will be seen, also acquired the Shredicote Estate after his marriage with Anne, only daughter of Thomas Browne, Esq., of Shredicote.

The first of the Browne family‡ who resided at Shredicote, and probably acquired the estate, was Thomas Browne, a Proctor of the Arches Court of Canterbury. He was living there in 1614 with his wife Apollonia, daughter of George Southaicke of London, and widow of William

---

* Continued from p. 232.
† Haughton, on the L. and N.-W. Railway, is the nearest station to Bradeley.
‡ There can be little doubt that this Thomas Browne was the first owner of Shredicote, although the following MS. note in the handwriting of Mr. Samuel Pipe-Wolferstan, inserted at the foot of page 79 in vol. ii. of a copy of Shaw's 'Staffordshire' in the Library of the British

Fayrefax, goldsmith, of London. He died at Shredicote and was buried at Bradeley in 1633. By his will, dated 1630, he entailed Shredicote upon his eldest-surviving son, George Browne, who resided there, and married Anne, daughter of Sir Thomas Skrymshire, Kt., of Aqualate, co. Stafford. George Browne died intestate in 1652, when the estate descended to his eldest son Thomas Browne, who married first Mary Carr of Aqualate. Their eldest son George Browne, who died unmarried in the lifetime of his father, by will, dated 31 May 1711, in which his father joined, directed that the Shredicote Estate should be sold on a fair valuation to his brother-in-law the Rev. Samuel Peploe, M.A., who had married his sister Anne Browne, and who was then owner of Shredicote Hall. The proceeds of this sale were distributed in certain legacies : viz., £200 to each of the four children of the said Rev. Samuel Peploe, and the remainder was divided into equal portions between the children of James Browne (deceased) and of John Browne, brothers of George Browne.

With the Shredicote title-deeds are indentures, dated 19 and 20 March 1710, made between William Lee and Frances his wife, of the first part; Thomas Browne of "Shredicott" in the co. of Stafford, yeoman, and George Browne, son and heir-apparent of the said Thomas Browne, of the second part; and Simon Aston of the Priory in parish of Bradley, yeoman, of the third part. In consideration of £250, Thomas Browne and George Browne conveyed sixteen acres of land adjoining the Priory land unto the said Simon Aston in fee, etc.

By indentures, dated 29 and 30 Nov. 1727, the Right Rev. Samuel Peploe, B.D., Lord Bishop of Chester, settled Shredicote on the marriage of his son and heir, the Rev. Samuel Peploe, with Elizabeth Birch. They had issue a son John Peploe, who took the name of Birch, and, by will dated 20 July 1803, devised Shredicote to his son Samuel Peploe, Esq., who conveyed it, by deed dated 25 March 1807, to Thomas Blurton, Esq., of Longnor Hall, Bradeley, in consideration of the payment of the sum of £8000 by the said Thomas Blurton.

The latest transition of this property took place when Thomas Blurton, the last purchaser, by deed dated 29 Sept. 1859, conveyed the estate, consisting of the farmhouse and 208 acres of land to George Paddock, Esq., of Grove House, Hanley, co. Stafford, in whose possession it now remains.

The Shredicote Hall Estate also descended to the said Samuel Peploe, and was sold, by deed dated 24 June 1807, to John Blurton, Esq., for the sum of £8600. It was again sold in 1817, when Mr. Matthew Parkes became the owner. He died in 1848, and Shredicote Hall now belongs to his daughter, Miss M. E. Parkes of Severn Cliff, Bridgnorth, co. Stafford.

Shredicote is within a mile of Bradeley Church. The house appears to have been rebuilt and converted into a farmhouse, as, beyond an old wall of some thickness, there is nothing indicative of antiquity. It stands within a short distance of Shredicote Hall, which appears to be an ancient structure, likewise converted into a farmhouse.*

These estates being adjacent, considerable doubt has arisen regarding the identity of the property held by the Browne family. It was not until a careful search had been made through the title-deeds of the respective owners, Mr. G. Paddock, of the Shredicote Estate, and Mr. E. H. Wright, of Stafford, on behalf of Miss Parkes, of the Shredicote Hall Estate, that this could be definitely determined.

The title-deeds of the Shredicote Hall Estate plainly shew that it never was in the possession of the Browne family, while the title-deeds of the Shredicote Estate conclusively prove that Shredicote had formerly belonged to that family.†

---

Museum, seems to shew that Shredicote was first in the possession of Thomas Browne's cousin William, son of Ralph Browne of Caverswall :—

" By information of I[saac] H[awkins] B[rowne, Esq.] to S. P. W. [the writer] about 1791, his family was of Shredicote in Cuddleston hundred ; Plott's map gives the arms of Browne of that place nearly as in the text here. Carew, son & heir appa[t] of Walter Stury of Rossall, co. Salop, aged 22 at its Visitat[n] 1623, marries Mary dau[r] to Tho[s] Browne of Shredicote. And in T. Brailesford's Continuat[n] of Derb[re] Visit[n] 1569 MS. p. 110 stands 'Tho. Browne de Shredicote,' & under as if son 'Edmund' ma[d] to Dor[y] dau[r] of Sir Edw. Vernon of Sudbury with a son Thomas & 4 dau[s]. (But elsewhere, viz., in a Chetwy-Burt sheet, Edm. B. is called of Bentley, co. Derby.)

"A Whitehall pedigree found in Mr. Chetwynd's MS. Pyrehill volume from Ingestree (one of many loose sheets marked 'Burt. Coll.') has 'Willielm Browne de Shredicote son to Rad[s] Browne of Caverswall by Mary Whitehall (first marr[d] to Rob. Porter of Stallington) a dau[r] of Will[m] Wh[l] [Whitehall] of Bloxwich by Mary da[r] & coh[r] of J[n] Hardwick of Lindley; which latter named Mary died 1565.

"It adds somewhat to this authority that Burton's great-grandm[r] was own sister to Mary Hardwick."

It is quite certain that Ralph Browne of Caverswall married in 1563 Marie Porter, but I have been unable to obtain any further corroboration of the above statement. His fourth son William was baptized in 1574. He may have possessed Shredicote and sold it to his cousin Thomas Browne. He certainly did not reside there, as previous to the appearance of the baptisms of the children of Thomas Browne and his wife Apollonia in the Bradeley Registers no entries of the Browne family occur in those records, which date from 1538.

* My grateful thanks are due to the Rev R. Lomas Lowe, M.A., Vicar of Bradeley, who walked over to Shredicote with me in August 1884, and gave much kind assistance.

† This is of course assuming that the title-deeds of the two estates were kept separate while in the possession of one owner. There cannot, I think, be any doubt that such was the case.

There is no record of the purchase of this estate by Thomas Browne, nor does he allude to the manner in which it was acquired, as in the case of his other property, when bequeathing it in his will.

## LONGFORD.

### LONGFORD REGISTERS.

#### *Baptisms.*

1637 Mary dau. of Edmund Browne and Dorothy his wife christened 23<sup>th</sup> May.

1638 Edmund son of Edmund Browne christened the 14<sup>th</sup> June.

1639 William Browne son of Edmund Browne christened the 24 day October.

1640 Appolina Browne dau. of Edmund Browne christened y<sup>e</sup> 19<sup>th</sup> day November.

1641 Dorothy Browne daughter of Edmund Browne [bapt.] the 23 of December.

1644 Rupert Browne son of Edward [Edmund] Browne registred y<sup>e</sup> sixteenth July.

1645 George Browne son of Mr. Edmund Browne registred y<sup>e</sup> second October.

1651 Elizabeth Browne dau. of Will'm Browne baptiz. June 27<sup>th</sup>.

1652 Phillip Browne son of Edmund Browne baptized May y<sup>e</sup> 27<sup>th</sup>.

1656 Richard son of Edmund Browne gent. was baptiz. May y<sup>e</sup> 12<sup>th</sup>.

1671 Rupert the son of Tho. Browne and Grace his wife baptized January 9<sup>th</sup>.

1695 Grace daughter of Tho. Browne Jur. and Alice his wife bapt. March 5°.

1698 Rupert son of Tho. Browne Jun<sup>r</sup> and Alice his wife bapt. Dec<sup>r</sup> 5°.

1701 Penelope daughter of Thomas Brown Jun. and Alice his wife of Bentley bapt. June 9<sup>th</sup>.

1723 Thomas son of Rupert Brown Esq<sup>re</sup> of Bentley baptized Dec. 16.

1724-5 Eleanora daughter of Rup't Browne Esq. baptized 23 Jan.

1729 Edmund son of Rupert Browne Esq. of Bentley baptized 7 Oct.

1730-1 John son of Rupert Browne Esq. baptized Feb. 9.

1731-2 Elizabeth daughter of Rupert Browne Esq. baptized Mar. 9.

1733 James son of Rupert Browne Esq. baptized privately 11 May.

#### *Burials.*

1656 Richard the son of Edmund Browne gent. buried Septem. 7<sup>th</sup>.

1659 Dorothy Browne* buried January y<sup>e</sup> 16<sup>th</sup>.

1673 Eliza Crofts mother-in-law to Mr. Thomas Browne of Bentley buried April 19<sup>th</sup>.

1684 Grace dau. of Thomas Browne Esq<sup>r</sup> and Grace his wife buried April 15<sup>th</sup>.

1684 Edmund Browne Esq<sup>re</sup> of Bentley buried 29 June.

1690 Grace the wife of Thomas Browne of Bentley Esq<sup>re</sup> buried July 6<sup>th</sup> 1690.

1691 Old M<sup>rs</sup> Alice Crofts of Bentley buried June 18<sup>th</sup>.

1708 Thomas Browne Sen<sup>r</sup> of Bentley Esq<sup>re</sup> buryed July 17<sup>th</sup>.

1717 Thomas Brown of Bentley Esq<sup>re</sup> buryed Sept. 21.

1723 Mr. Walter Browne was buried Apr. 19.

1731-2 Alice relict of Thomas Browne of Bentley Esq. buried Jan. 24.

1733 Rupert Browne of Bentley Esq<sup>re</sup> buried 29 May.

1737 James son of y<sup>e</sup> late Rupert Browne Esq. of Bentley buried Sept. 20.

Previous to the restoration of Longford Church in 1826, the seat belonging to Bentley Hall was on the left-hand side of the centre aisle. It was then absorbed in the choir seats, and "a large seat was neatly fitted up at the expense of the parish and appropriated to Bentley Hall," which, however, is now in the parish of Alkmonton.

Inscription upon a black marble stone at the end of the middle aisle in Longford Church, co. Derby:—

"Hic jacet corpus EDMUNDI BROWNE de Bentley Armigeri qui obiit vicessimo septimo die Junii Anno Domini MDCLXXXIV Ætatis 73."

The above tablet was visible in Longford Church about 1820, when the above copy was made by the Rector for Lieut. John Browne. It seems to have been removed at the restoration of the church in 1826, as there is no such inscription there now.

*(To be continued.)*

---

* This entry, with some others, is in a miscellaneous portion of Longford Register, and was only discovered after diligent search.

# 𝕮𝖍𝖊 𝕱𝖆𝖒𝖎𝖑𝖞 𝖔𝖋 𝕾𝖍𝖚𝖈𝖐𝖇𝖚𝖗𝖌𝖍.*

## 𝔐onumental Inscriptions.

M on key plan.        *Mural monument, west side of mortuary chapel.*

Memoriæ Sacrum
CAROLI SHUCKBURGH Baronetti
Hujus Parochiæ Domini et Patroni,
Filii CAROLI SHUCKBURGH de Longborow
In Comitatu Glocestriæ Armigeri:
Vir, non minus Legum, quam Libertatis Vindex,
Spectatæ fidei, et verâ simplicitate bonus;
Fuit inter amicos hilaris et jucundus,
Inter alienos cautè tacitus:
Cecropiæ artibus Minervæ madidus Latiæque;
Nec non Anglas amavit Musas coluitque,
Sed apprimê Philosophiæ laudibus tollendus est,
ANNAM CAMPOBELLI PRICE relictam.  Uxorem duxit.
Nullâ tamen gaudebat fobole.
E vivis excedens anno 1773, Ætatis 52,
In Ecclesia Collegiali Stæ Mariæ Varvici humatus est.
Priori Anno, et in eodem loco cecidit et supultus fuit
Frater ejus Natu minor RICHARDUS, attamen
Virtute et humanioribus Animi dotibus non minor;
Per plures annos inter Satellites Regi'os præfectus meruit:
SARÆ filiæ JOHANNIS HAYWARD de Plumftead in Agro Kantiæ
Connubio felici junctus fuit; ex quo tres
GEORGIUM, RICHARDUM, et STEWKLEIUM filios suscepit;
Annos tantum quadraginta quatuor vixit!

No. 1 on key plan.        *Mural tablet at west end, north of tower arch.*

### 𝕾𝖆𝖈𝖗𝖊𝖉
TO THE MEMORY OF
GERTRUDE FRANCES ANNA MARIA SHUCKBURGH
YOUNGEST DAUGHTER OF SIR FRANCIS AND LADY SHUCKBURGH,
BORN 11th NOVEMBER 1833—
DIED 9th MARCH 1835 .
AGED 16 MONTHS.
AFFECTION WEEPS,
HEAVEN REJOICES!

E. H. BAILEY. R.A. SCULP. LONDON.

No. 2.        *On a tablet against the west wall of nave, north of tower arch.*

Arms at top : SHUCKBURGH ; impaling, Argent, a fess between three hearts gules, TYDD.

Near this sacred Place in the Vault of her Ancestors
are deposited the Remains of
CAROLINE, ANN, MATILDA SHUCKBURGH,
the beloved and eldest Daughter of Sir Stewkley
and Lady CHARLOTTE CATHARINE SHUCKBURGH,
who departed this Life
on Sunday Morning the 26th day of March, 1809 ;
in the 21st Year of her Age;
a bright Example of filial Love and Duty.
*This Tablet as a small Testimony of her Virtues,*
*is erected by her disconsolate Parent.*

* Continued from p. 228.

*No. 3.*            *Marble mural tablet on north wall, nave.*

SACRED TO THE MEMORY OF
SARAH ELIZABETH,
WIFE OF
CAPTAIN HENRY ADOLPHUS SHUCKBURGH,
*40ᵗʰ REGIMENT OF BENGAL NATIVE INFANTRY,*
AND ELDEST DAUGHTER OF WILLIAM DWARRIS, ESQUIRE,
*OF GOLDEN GROVE, JAMAICA,*
WHO DEPARTED THIS LIFE AT CHELTENHAM,
FEBRUARY 1ˢᵗ 1846, IN THE 53ʳᵈ YEAR OF HER AGE.
AFTER A LONG AND PAINFUL ILLNESS ENDURED WITH
CHRISTIAN FORTITUDE PATIENCE AND RESIGNATION
*THIS TABLET IS ERECTED BY HER AFFLICTED HUSBAND, AS A*
*TRIBUTE TO THE MANY CHRISTIAN VIRTUES THAT ADORNED*
*THE CHARACTER OF AN AMIABLE AND AFFECTIONATE WIFE.*

G. LEWIS, Sc.
CHELTENHAM.

*No. 4.*            *Brass on marble, north wall, under the last.*

Arms of Shuckburgh hanging on the initial I of In.

In
Affectionate Remembrance of a
Brother
Colonel Henry Adolphus Shuckburgh
This Tablet records His Death and Burial
at Weston super Mare,
January 10ᵗʰ
1861.

Arms at top : SHUCKBURGH.
Arms at base : SHUCKBURGH, impaling CLOETE, Argent, a Dutch boy holding in dexter hand
a hawk.

*No. 5.*

A Memorial over the door commemorating an old Servant of the Shuckburgh
family, Ann Jones, who died 26 September 1846, aged 85.

*No. 6.*            *White marble monument by Flaxman, north wall, nave.*

An equatorial on dexter side ; a celestial globe on sinister.

JUXTA
SUORUM CINERES
SUOS ETIAM PONENDOS
TESTAMENTO CURAVIT
GEORGIUS SHUCKBURGH EVELYN
RICARDI SHUCKBURGH FILIUS
VIR
QUI DIGNITATEM
QUAM HÆREDITARIUM HABUIT
SENATORIÂ CUMULAVIT
A
VARVICENSIBUS
QUINQUIES LECTUS

SE IN SENATU INCORRUPTUM
ET
QUOAD PER INFIRMAM VALETUDINEM LICERET
STRENUUM USQUE ET INDEFESSUM PRÆSTITIT
HUMANIORIBUS LITERIS
QUAS
RUGBÆÆ HAUSERAT
OXONII EXCOLUERAT
HAUD LEVITER IMBUTUS
IN PHYSICA RATIONE
DOMI FORISQUE PRÆCLARUS
IN ASTRONOMIÂ VERO PRÆCIPUE
EXCELLENS
IN VITÂ PARITER STUDIISQUE ET OFFICIIS
VERITATIS RIGIDUS SATELLES
DECESSIT
A.D. MDCCCIV.
ÆTAT. LIII.

FLAXMAN
SCULPTOR.

*(To be continued.)*

---

## FARR FAMILY.

NOTES ON FLY-LEAF OF FOLIO COPY OF STACKHOUSE'S 'HISTORY OF THE BIBLE.'

Esther Farr born the 23<sup>d</sup> Sept. 1729.
Richard Farr born the 22<sup>d</sup> April 1731.
Thomas Farr born the 22<sup>d</sup> July 1732.
John Farr born the 7<sup>th</sup> March 1733.
Paul Farr born the 18<sup>th</sup> Jan. 1735.
A son dead born the 15<sup>th</sup> Jan. 1737.
Stephen Farr born the 13<sup>th</sup> June 1739.
Samuel Farr born the 26 March 1741.
William Farr born the 17<sup>th</sup> March 1743-4.
Esther Joanna Farr born the 25<sup>th</sup> Octo<sup>r</sup> 1748.
Joanna Farr mother of the above children died 20<sup>th</sup> Feb. 1771 æt. 65.
Rich<sup>d</sup> Farr father of the above died        1782 æt. 74.
Tho<sup>s</sup> Farr died Oct. 1791 æt. 59, in London; married Miss Eliz<sup>th</sup> Creed daughter of M<sup>r</sup> J. S. Creed. No issue.
Esther Farr died 1731 æt. 2 years.
Rich<sup>d</sup> Farr died 1747 æt. 16.
Steph<sup>n</sup> Farr died 1753 æt. 14 in London.
Esther Joanna Farr (married to M<sup>r</sup> G. Gibbs) died at Combe House near Bristol, left 4 children, 2 sons, 2 daughters.
        [No date of death in MS.: she died 29 Oct. 1787.]
Paul Farr died 27<sup>th</sup> Dec. 1794 æt. 59.
Sam<sup>l</sup> Farr died 11<sup>th</sup> March 1795, in Taunton, æt. 54.
John Farr died 14<sup>th</sup> April 1797 æt. 64, at Redland, married Miss Diaper, daughter of the Rev<sup>d</sup> M<sup>r</sup> Diaper—no children.
Joanna wife of the above John Farr died 24<sup>th</sup> March 1805 æt. 70.

H. H. G.

SHUCKBURGH BOOK PLATES.

# The Family of Shuckburgh.*

## Monumental Inscriptions.

*No. 7.*                           *North wall, nave.*

Arms at top : SHUCKBURGH, impaling, Argent, on three mounds as many hop vines with their poles, all ppr., DARKER.

Heu ! quanto minus eſt cum *reliquis* verſari,
Quam *Tui* meminiſse !
Near to this Place repose the Remains of LADY SHUCKBURGH
Wife of Sir GEORGE SHUCKBURGH Bar$^t$ and Daughter of
JOHN DARKER of Gayton in the County of Northampton Esq$^r$ ;
whose unaffected Innocence and singular Sweetness of Manners
Were the delight of all who knew her ;
Her Piety and Purity of Heart
A bright Exception to the general Diſsipation of the Age :
In short, whose excellence of Character both
As a Christian and a Wife,
(If I knew how) I would describe,
That after Ages, who should see this, might reverence
And imitate her Example.
She died at Bristol April the 10$^{th}$ 1783
After an ineffectual trial for some Months
Of those Medicinal Waters and every other Aid
That Human Afsistance and the tendereſt Affection
Could beſtow ; closing a period of 28 Years
In a continued course of Duty and Affection
To her Parents, her Huſband and her God.

---

*No. 8.*           *Mural monument, north wall of nave, next to the last.*

Shuckburgh arms (Ulster badge on chevron) and crest.

NEAR THIS PLACE IS INTERRED THE BODY OF
SIR STEWKLEY SHUCKBURGH, BAR$^t$.
WHO DESCENDED FROM ANCESTORS AS ILLUSTRIOUS FOR
THEIR VIRTUES AS THEIR HONOURS
HELD FORTH IN HIS OWN SUCCESSION A CHARACTER IN
NOTHING DEGENERATE OR INCOMPLETE ;
A MAN OF PRINCIPLE, PROBITY AND BENEVOLENCE,
ONE ESPECIALLY DISPOSED TO FORGIVE INJURIES ;
AND IN THE TRUE SPIRIT OF THAT WISDOM AND LIBERALITY
WHICH DISTINGUISHES THE RELIGION HE PROFESSED .
TO RETURN THE UNKINDNESSES OF OTHERS WITH GOOD .
BELOVED AND ESTEEMED THROUGH LIFE BY THEM
WHO KNEW HIM MOST & BEST .
AN AFFECTIONATE FATHER, A TENDER HUSBAND,
AND A SINCERE FRIEND .
HE IS NOW LAMENTED WITH AN UNDISSEMBLED REGRET .
HE WAS TAKEN AWAY BY A FIT OF APOPLEXY,
ON THE 14$^{th}$ OF JULY 1809, IN THE 52$^d$ YEAR OF HIS AGE .

---

* Continued from p. 252.

*No.* 9.    *West end, south of tower arch.*

Above the medallion portrait are these words :—

NOW WE SEE THROUGH A GLASS DARKLY BUT THEN FACE TO FACE
NOW I KNOW IN PART BUT THEN SHALL I KNOW EVEN AS ALSO I AM KNOWN.

Below the medallion, inscription as follows :—

GEORGE THOMAS FRANCIS SHUCKBURGH 9th BARONET

MAJOR LATE SCOTS FVSILIER GVARDS
KNIGHT OF THE LEGION OF HONOVR & OF THE MEDJIDIE
BORN JVLY 23rd 1829 . DIED JANVARY 12th 1884.

THIS MONVMENT IS RAISED
TO HIS BELOVED MEMORY
BY HIS SORROWING WIFE.

H. H. ARMSTEAD. R.A.
1886.

Two shields of arms: the dexter one charged with arms of SHUCKBURGH, with Ulster badge on chevron ; the sinister, SHUCKBURGH impaling ROBERTSON.

---

*No.* 10.    *Mural tablet on south wall, nave.*

TO THE MEMORY
OF
THOMAS STEWKLEY SHUCKBURGH ;
(SECOND SON OF THE LATE SIR STEWKLEY SHUCKBURGH BARt)
FIRST LIEUTENANT OF HIS MAJESTY'S SHIP HELICON,
WHO DIED NEAR CROOKED ISLAND IN THE WEST INDIES
ON THE 25th DAY OF AUGUST 1824 ;
AGED 28 YEARS.
AND WAS BURIED AT SEA,
WITH ALL THE HONOURS DUE TO A BRITISH NAVAL OFFICER.
HIS BENEVOLENT DISPOSITION,        .
AND
AMIABLE MANNERS,
ATTACHED TO HIM THE PARTICULAR FRIENDSHIP
OF HIS BROTHER OFFICERS,
AND THE GENERAL REGARD OF ALL WHO KNEW HIM ;
WHILE HIS PROFESSIONAL CONDUCT AND BRAVERY,
MERITED AND RECEIVED THEIR HIGH ESTEEM.
THIS TABLET
IS INSCRIBED AS A MONUMENT OF A BROTHER'S AFFECTION,
BY
SIR FRANCIS SHUCKBURGH BARt.

---

*No.* 11.    *Mural tablet on south wall of nave, under the last.*

Sacred
to the Memory of
Dame Charlotte Catherine
Relict of the late
Sir Stewkley Shuckburgh Baronet
who died at her House in Bath
bijth ffebry MoV.CCC.XXX.VIII aged LXXII
and is interred in the ffamily Vault near

𝔱𝔥𝔦𝔰 𝔱𝔞𝔟𝔩𝔢𝔱 𝔴𝔥𝔦𝔠𝔥 𝔦𝔫 𝔡𝔲𝔱𝔦𝔣𝔲𝔩 𝔯𝔢𝔪𝔢𝔪𝔟𝔯𝔞𝔫𝔠𝔢 𝔬𝔣
𝔞 𝔱𝔢𝔫𝔡𝔢𝔯 𝔞𝔫𝔡 𝔞𝔣𝔣𝔢𝔠𝔱𝔦𝔬𝔫𝔞𝔱𝔢 𝔓𝔞𝔯𝔢𝔫𝔱 𝔦𝔰 𝔢𝔯𝔢𝔠𝔱𝔢𝔡
𝔟𝔶 𝔥𝔢𝔯 𝔢𝔩𝔡𝔢𝔰𝔱 𝔰𝔬𝔫 𝔖𝔦𝔯 𝔉𝔯𝔞𝔫𝔠𝔦𝔰 𝔖𝔥𝔲𝔠𝔨𝔟𝔲𝔯𝔤𝔥 𝔅𝔱
𝔄𝔩𝔰𝔬 𝔬𝔣 𝔥𝔦𝔰 𝔰𝔦𝔰𝔱𝔢𝔯
𝔖𝔞𝔯𝔞𝔥 𝔏𝔬𝔲𝔦𝔰𝔞 𝔖𝔥𝔲𝔠𝔨𝔟𝔲𝔯𝔤𝔥
𝔴𝔥𝔬 𝔡𝔦𝔢𝔡 𝔞𝔱 𝔅𝔞𝔱𝔥 𝔙𝔦𝔱𝔥 𝔍𝔞𝔫𝔯𝔶 𝔐𝔡𝔠𝔠𝔠.𝔵𝔵𝔵𝔳𝔦
𝔞𝔫𝔡 𝔴𝔞𝔰 𝔟𝔲𝔯𝔦𝔢𝔡 𝔦𝔫 𝔱𝔥𝔢 𝔄𝔟𝔟𝔢𝔶 𝔠𝔥𝔲𝔯𝔠𝔥
𝔬𝔣 𝔱𝔥𝔞𝔱 𝔠𝔦𝔱𝔶.

Arms : SHUCKBURGH, with Ulster badge on chevron ; impaling, Argent, a chevron between three hearts gules, TYDD.

(*To be continued.*)

# 𝕿𝖍𝖊 𝕽𝖊𝖌𝖎𝖘𝖙𝖊𝖗 𝕭𝖔𝖔𝖐 𝖔𝖋 𝕭𝖗𝖆𝖒𝖋𝖎𝖊𝖑𝖉, 𝖈𝖔. 𝕾𝖚𝖋𝖋𝖔𝖑𝖐.*

### 1717.

May 26  Samuel s. of Robert Tyrrell and Mary his wife.

Aug. 5  Mary d. of Edmund Watling and Mary his wife.

Oct. 6  Mary d. of Samuel Amand and Mary his wife.

Oct. 12  Richard s. of Thomas Copping and Elizabeth his wife.

Nov. 6  John s. of Matthew Fuller and Emme his wife.

Nov. 15  Mary d. of Valentine Copping, Jun., and Elizabeth his wife.

Nov. 15  Samuel s. of John Tibbald and Mary his wife.

Dec. 8  John s. of Benjamin Preston and Elizabeth his wife.

Dec. 8  Elizabeth d. of Samuel Ashley and Elizabeth his wife.

Dec. 18  John s. of Reginald Rabett, gent., and Elizabeth his wife.

Jan. 31  Mary d. of Thomas Newson and Sarah his wife.

PHILIP WILKINSON, Vic.

### 1718.

Mar. 30  Mary d. of James Smith and Elizabeth his wife.

May 23  Lydia d. of Samuel Shepherd and Anne his wife.

May 23  Robert s. of Edward Bird and Elizabeth his wife.

May 27  Elizabeth d. of Thomas Ellis and Elizabeth his wife.

Aug. 3  Thomas s. of Thomas Edwards, Jun., and Hannah his wife.

Aug. 15  Dorothy d. of Thomas Saunders and Sarah his wife.

Jan. 21  Reginald s. of Reginald Rabett, gent., and Elizabeth his wife.

Feb. 22  John s. of Benjamin Gostling and Anne his wife.

PHILIP WILKINSON, Vic.

### 1719.

May 3  John s. of James Bottom and Sarah his wife.

Nov. 25  Valentine s. of Valentine Copping, Jun., and Elizabeth his wife.

Mar. 6  Henry s. of Henry Grint and Christian his wife.

### 1720.

Oct. 29  Susanna d. of William and Mary Crisp.

Dec. 16  George s. of James and Mary Bottom.

Dec. 16  John s. of James and Elizabeth Smith.

### 1721.

April 9  Susanna d. of William and Elizabeth Woodward.

May 7  John s. of Henry and Sarah Day.

May 19  John s. of Edmund and Mary Watling.

Dec. 1  Hannah d. of Valentine and Elizabeth Copping.

Jan. 21  John s. of John and Mary Teball.

Jan. 21  Mary d. of William and Mary Crisp.

Feb. 11  Francis s. of Edward and Sarah Bird.

### 1722.

April 22  Stephen s. of Thomas and Sarah Saunders.

April 30  Elizabeth d. of Tho. and Hannah Mills.

May 6  Mary d. of Matthew and Emme Fuller.

May 14  Leddell base son of Mary Crawford.

June 20  Mary d. of Reginald Rabett, gent., and Elizabeth his wife.

June 26  William s. of Ezekiel and Sarah Smith.

July 1  Samuel s. of Henry Hall and Sarah his wife.

Jan. 30  Charles s. of Henry Grint and Christian his wife.

* Continued from p. 241.

Feb. 12   Mary d. of Thomas and Rachell Keble.
Mar. 17   Thomas s. of Ferebe and Sarah Browne.

### 1723.

April 7   Sarah d. of Edward and Sarah Bird.
May   5   Sarah d. of William and Mary Crisp.
July   5   Francis s. of Edmund and Mary Watling.
Aug.   4   James s. of James and Elizabeth Smith.
Nov. 29   Valentine s. of Tho. and Elizabeth Copping.
Dec. 11   Susanna d. of Henry and Sarah Day.
Jan.   3   Rachel d. of Thomas and Rachel Keeble.
Jan.   5   Robert s. of Samuel and Frances Bloss.
Jan.   8   Susan d. of John and Susan Scott.
Feb.   9   Mary d. of Thomas and Elizabeth Ellis.
Feb. 16   Robert s. of Nathanael and Sarah Estaugh.
Feb. 16   Mary d. of James and Mary Bottom.

### 1724.

Aug.   4   Mary d. of Valentine and Elizabeth Copping.
Nov.   5   John s. of Reginald Rabett, gent., and Elizabeth his wife ; born Oct. 17.
Aug. 15   Isaac base son of Sarah Gosling.
Jan. 13   William s. of William and Mary Crisp.
May 16   Mary d. of Nathan and Mary Kindred.
Feb.   7   Elizabeth d. of George and Elizabeth Long.
Feb. 14   Mary d. of William and Elizabeth Lerrodd.

### 1725.

Mar. 28   Mary d. of Samuel and Mary Sheppard.
April   3   William s. of William and Mary Field.
May 16   Maria d. of Edward and Sarah Bird.
June 27   John s. of Matthew and Emme Fuller.
Oct. 24   Edmund s. of Tho. and Elizabeth Ellis.
Nov.   7   John s. of George and Elizabeth Browne.
Nov. 28   John s. of William and Elizabeth Woodard.
Dec. 26   William s. of Ferrabe and Sarah Browne.
Jan. 21   Robert s. of Henry and Mary Briggs.
Mar. 13   Samuel s. of James and Elizabeth Smith.

### 1726.

May 15   Samuel s. of Samuel and Hannah Cullenford.
May 29   Thomas s. of James and Mary Bottom.
June 26   John s. of John and Sarah Thompson.
July 24   Mary d. of Samuel and Frances Bloss.
Oct.   2   William s. of Richard and Hannah Ransby.
Oct.   9   James s. of William and Mary Crisp.

Nov.   6   Thomas s. of George and Susan Bishop.
Nov.   6   Anne d. of John and Susan Scott.
Nov. 20   Anne d. of Edward and Sarah Bird.

### 1727.

Aug.   4   John s. of Francis and Ann Delph.
Aug. 14   Sarah d. of Henry and Sarah Hall.
Aug. 24   Henry s. of Henry and Mary Briggs.
Sep.   4   Robert s. of George and Elizabeth Long.
Oct.   3   Mary d. of John and Mary Chambers.
Dec.   8   Valentine s. of Valentine and Elizabeth Copping.
Feb.   4   Sarah d. of Pheribe and Sarah Browne.
Feb.   9   Hannah d. of James and Hannah Woolnow.
Feb. 11   Mary d. of Richard and Hannah Ransby.
Feb. 14   Thomas s. of John and Mary Tibbal.
Mar. 20   Jane d. of Edward and Sarah Bird.

### 1728.

April 21   Mary d. of John and Mary Poyntz.
May   8   Edward s. of William and Mary Crisp.
May 10   Elizabeth d. of Edmund and Mary Watling.
Dec. 16   Sarah d. of John and Susan Scott.
Feb. 11   Robert s. of Robert and Mary Turrell.
Mar.   6   Thomas s. of Henry and Mary Briggs.

### 1729.

Mar. 30   Francis s. of John and Sarah Tomson.
June 19   Mary d. of Samuel and Hannah Cullenford.
Oct.   5   Elizabeth d. of George and Susan Bishop.
Dec. 25   Elizabeth d. of Henry and Mary Tillett.
Feb. 12   Susanna d. of Robert and Susanna Newman.
Feb. 27   Mary d. of John and Mary Ead.
Mar.   5   Elizabeth d. of Edward and Sarah Bird.
Mar. 12   Stephen s. of Thomas and Hannah Lunniss.
Mar. 18   Mary d. of William and Mary Crisp.

J. HANCOCK, Cur.

### 1730.

Mar. 30   Hannah d. of Samuel and Frances Bloss.
April   1   Henry s. of James and Mary Bottom.
April 16   Mary d. of Henry and Sarah Hall.
May 10   Samuel s. of Richard and Hannah Ransby.
July 29   Joseph s. of Joseph and Ann Smith.
Oct. 20   Lydia d. of Thomas and Ruth Hayward.
Nov. 16   Thomas s. of Robert and Susanna Ellis.
Jan.   7   William s. of Edmund and Mary Watling.
Feb. 12   Samuel s. of Henry and Mary Briggs.
Feb. 26   Mark s. of John and Mary Savage.

**1731.**

| | |
|---|---|
| May 24 | Sarah d. of John and Sarah Tomson. |
| May 24 | Mary d. of Cornelius and Sarah Wallis. |
| May 25 | Elisha and Jehu sons of Samuel and Hannah Cullingford. |
| June 6 | Mary d. of Pheribe and Sarah Brown. |
| July 11 | Henry s. of Henry and Sarah Hall. |
| July 13 | Ann d. of John and Mary Ead. |
| July 21 | Thomas s. of Thomas and Hannah Lunnis. |
| July 26 | Samuel s. of Charles and Christian Spendlove. |
| Aug. 15 | Rose d. of Rob't and Mary Tyrrel. |
| Oct. 11 | Elizabeth d. of Will^m and Mary Crisp. |
| Oct. 17 | Robert s. of John and Susan Scot. |
| Nov. 27 | Anne d. of Valentine and Elizabeth Copping. |
| Dec. 5 | Mary d. of John and Mary Read. |
| Dec. 26 | Mary d. of Henry and Mary Tillet. |
| Feb. 2 | Elizabeth d. of Sarah Dambrook a base child. |
| Feb. 15 | Thomas s. of Robert and Susanna Ellis. |

**1732.**

| | |
|---|---|
| April 2 | Mary d. of Thomas and Anne Kent. |
| April 23 | John s. of John and Sarah Pointz. |
| April 30 | Thomas s. of Thomas and Mary Reynolds. |
| June 3 | James s. of James and Mary Crisp. |
| June 18 | John s. of Samuel and Frances Bloice. |
| Sep. 24 | Mary d. of John and Mary Savage. |
| Nov. 12 | Will^m s. of Rich^d and Hannah Ransby. |
| Nov. 19 | James s. of Joseph and Anne Smith. |
| Nov. 25 | Margaret d. of James and Mary Crisp. |

**1733.**

| | |
|---|---|
| April 1 | Hannah d. of Thomas and Hannah Lunnis. |
| April 8 | Cornelius s. of Cornelius and Sarah Wallage. |
| April 13 | Samuel s. of Samuel and Mary Barker. |
| April 29 | Henry s. of Henry and Mary Blois. |
| June 17 | William s. of Mary Crawford. |
| July 18 | Mary d. of Henry and Mary Briggs. |
| Aug. 28 | Thomas s. of Thomas and Ruth Haward. |
| Sep. 24 | Rob^t s. of Rob^t and Susanna Ellis. |
| Dec. 28 | Mary d. of James and Mary Crisp. |
| Jan. 9 | Thomas s. of John and Susan Scot. |
| Jan. 9 | Thomas s. of Rob^t and Mary Turrel. |
| Feb. 11 | John s. of John and Catharine Smith. |
| Feb. 17 | Edm^d s. of Oliver and Elizabeth Waters. |
| Feb. 27 | Martha d. of Martha Hitchman. |

**1734.**

| | |
|---|---|
| April 18 | Mary d. of Thomas and Anne Kent. |
| May 5 | James s. of Joseph and Sarah Smith. |
| July 3 | Elizabeth d. of Will^m and Eliz. Miller. |
| Sep. 1 | Will^m s. of John and Mary Read. |
| Sep. 15 | Samuel s. of Samuel and Eliz. Ellis. |
| Oct. 26 | Stephen s. of Thomas and Mary Reynolds. |
| Oct. 27 | William s. of John and Sarah Pointz. |
| Oct. 31 | Elizabeth d. of Rob^t and Susanna Ellis. |

| | |
|---|---|
| Nov. 5 | Mary d. of Thomas and Mary Lunnis. |
| Nov. 17 | Nathaniel d. of Thomas and Eliz. Copping. |
| Dec. 31 | Mary d. of Thomas and Ruth Haward. |
| Jan. 5 | Hannah and Everard d. and s. of Sam. and Hannah Cullenford. |
| Feb. 14 | John s. of William and Mary Crisp. |
| Feb. 14 | Sarah d. of Henry and Mary Tillet. |

**1735.**

| | |
|---|---|
| April 15 | Mary d. of Rob't and Susanna Newman. |
| April 20 | Will^m s. of John and Mary Tomson. |
| April 27 | Cornelius s. of Cornelius and Sarah Wallage. |
| June 24 | Thomas s. of Isaac and Martha Block. |
| June 24 | Will^m s. of Will^m and Elizabeth Miller. |
| June 20 | John s. of John and Susan Scot. |
| Aug. 18 | Will^m s. of Hugh and Margaret Jakes. |
| Sep. 7 | Benjamin s. of Jonathan and Mary Chamberlain. |
| Sep. 14 | Hannah d. of Rich^d and Hannah Ransby. |
| Sep. 21 | John s. of Pheribe and Sarah Brown. |
| Jan. 10 | Will^m s. of James and Mary Crisp. |
| Jan. 16 | Mary d. of Thomas and Eliz. Copping. |

**1736.**

| | |
|---|---|
| April 27 | Will^m s. of Tho. and Mary Lunnis. |
| May 23 | Edw^d Shepherd a base child. |
| May 25 | Thomas s. of Rob^t and Susanna Ellis. |
| June 13 | Thomas s. of Joseph and Sarah Smith. |
| June 20 | Mary d. of Thomas and Mary Talent. |
| June 30 | Sarah d. of Henry and Mary Briggs. |
| Aug. 8 | Samuel s. of Samuel and Mary Almand. |
| Sep. 19 | Thomas s. of Oliver and Elizabeth Walters. |
| Jan. 3 | John s. of Richard and Alethea Savage. |
| Jan. 10 | Benjamin s. of John and Mary Chamberlain. |
| Jan. 23 | Susanna d. of James and Mary Bottom. |
| Mar. 16 | James s. of James and Eliz. Smith. |

**1737.**

| | |
|---|---|
| Aug. 27 | Susannah d. of Rob^t and Susannah Ellis ; born July 28. |
| May 13 | Will^m s. of Hugh and Margaret Jakes. |
| May 13 | Richard s. of Rich^d and Hannah Ransby. |
| June 16 | Rob^t and John sons of Henry and Mary Tillett. |
| Mar. 1 | John s. of James and Mary Crispe. |

**1738.**

| | |
|---|---|
| April 1 | James s. of John and Sarah Thompson. |
| April 11 | Elizabeth d. of James and Elizabeth Smith. |
| April 17 | Robert s. of Robert and Susannah Newman. |

CH. MABOURN, Vic.

| | |
|---|---|
| Sep. 7 | Robert s. of William and Mary Crisp ; born May 13, 1737. |
| Dec. 3 | Hannah d. of Richard and Hannah Ramsby. |
| Nov. 11 | Hannah d. of Thomas and Mary Talent. |
| Dec. 31 | Martha d. of John Scrocold, a stranger. |

Jan. 5 John s. of Henry and Mary Briggs.
Jan. 7 James s. of James and Anne Scoulding.
Jan. 28 Christina d. of Cornelius and Sarah Wallage.
Feb. 16 Mary d. of John and Sarah Bedingfield.
Feb. 18 Everard s. of Samuel and Hannah Cullingford.
Feb. 18 James s. of William and Mary Garwood.

### 1739.

June 3 Elizabeth d. of Isaac and Martha Block.
Oct. 14 Eastaugh Sallows a bastard child.
Oct. 15 Susannah d. of John and Susannah Freeman.
Dec. 25 Sarah d. of Henry and Mary Tillett.
Jan. 10 Benjamin s. of John and Mary Chamberlain.
Jan. 21 John s. of Zephaniah and Mary Tillett of Walpole.
Jan. 25 John s. of John and Susannah Scot.
Jan. 10 Mary d. of John and Mary Chamberlain.
Jan. 13 John s. of Daniel and Sarah Short.
Feb. 17 Sarah d. of John and Sarah Poyntz.

### 1740.

April 27 John s. of John and Ann Day.
June 1 Bridget d. of Phereby and Sarah Brown.
Aug. 16 James s. of James and Ann Andrews.
Sep. 4 Benjamin s. of Thomas and Ruth Haward.
Sep. 28 Daniel s. of Richard and Ann Ramsby.
Feb. 6 James s. of James and Elizabeth Smith.
Mar. 22 Charles s. of James and Mary Crispe.

### 1741.

May 9 Nathaniel s. of Henry and Mary Briggs.
June 3 Edward s. of John and Susannah Freeman.
Oct. 11 Sarah d. of Samuel and Mary Amand.
Dec. 1 John s. of Robert and Susannah Newman.
Jan. 15 Thomas s. of Tho. and Hannah Sallows.
Jan. 16 Sarah d. of John and Mary Chamberlain.
Jan. 29 John s. of John and Sarah Bedingfield.
Feb. 16 Richard s. of Richard and Hannah Ramsby.

### 1742.

May 9 Cornelius s. of Cornelius and Sarah Wallage.
June 20 Mary d. of John and Sarah Poyntz.
July 23 Daniel s. of Daniel and Sarah Short.
Aug. 29 William s. of William and Mary Nunn.
Sep. 21 Thomas s. of Thomas and Mary Edwards.
Oct. 27 James s. of John and Susannah Freeman.
Dec. 31 John s. of Thomas and Ruth Howard.
Feb. 27 Mary d. of John and Mary Aldred.

### 1743.

April 20 Susannah d. of William and Elizabeth Miller.
Nov. 7 Vincent s. of John and Margaret Woolnough.
Oct. 31 Thomas s. of Thomas and Elizabeth Randall.

### 1744.

Mar. 26 Edward s. of James and Mary Crisp.
April 8 Edmund s. of Edmund and Sarah Chambers.
April 8 Sarah d. of James and Ann Scoulding.
April 11 Ann d. of William and Elizabeth Millar.
May 6 William s. of John and Susannah Freeman.
Aug. 8 John s. of James and Elizabeth Smith.
Aug. 10 Robert s. of John and Mary Chamberlain.
Oct. 4 Thomas s. of John and Margaret Woolnough.
Oct. 7 John s. of Thomas and Mary Edwards.
Oct. 14 William s. of Cornelius and Sarah Wallage.
Nov. 11 Mary d. of Stephen and Elizabeth Mayhew.
Dec. 20 Deborah d. of Thomas and Hannah Sallows.
Nov. 26 Richard s. of Richard and Susanna Nunn.
Dec. 28 Sarah d. of John and Mary Aldred.
Feb. 27 Mary d. of William and Mary Nunn.
Mar. 21 Elizabeth d. of Thomas and Elizabeth Randal.
Mar. 21 James s. of John and Sarah Bedingfield.

### 1745.

April 27 Jonathan Rodwell a base child.
June 23 Hannah d. of John and Sarah Poyntz.
Aug. 11 Benjamin s. of William and Elizabeth Millar.
Aug. 25 Thomas s. of Henry and Mary Pinkney.
Nov. 1 Sarah d. and Thomas s. of Thomas and Sarah Wade.
Dec. 6 Joseph s. of Thomas and Ruth Hayward.
Dec. 27 Sarah d. of Samuel and Ann Theobald.
Mar. 3 Hannah d. of John and Margaret Woolnough.
Mar. 19 George s. of George and Susannah Greenard.
Mar. 22 William s. of Thomas and Mary Roberts.

### 1746.

May 18 James s. of Thomas and Mary Edwards.
June 1 Marianne d. of Samuel and Mary Heigham.
Oct. 25 William s. of Richard and Ann Clarke.
Nov. 2 William s. of Cornelius and Sarah Wallage.
Nov. 6 John s. of James and Ann Scolding.

Dec. 21   Thomas base son of Elizabeth Cheston.
Feb. 2   Sarah d. of Stephen and Elizabeth Mayhew.
Mar. 6   Susannah d. of James and Mary Crisp.
Mar. 8   Hannah d. of John and Mary Aldred.
Mar. 9   Robert s. of James and Elizabeth Smith.

### 1747.

April 22   Mary d. of William and Elizabeth Millar.
June 8   Samuel s. of Samuel and Susannah Amand.
July 25   Susannah d. of Thomas and Susannah Wade.
Aug. 9   Katherine d. of James and Ann Smith.
Nov. 23   Richard s. of Richard and Elizabeth Clark.
Nov. 25   John s. of William and Mary Nunn.
Jan. 11   Sarah d. of Samuel and Mary Higham.
Jan. 21   John Richards s. and Susannah d. of Thomas and Elizabeth Randal.
Mar. 12   Noah daughter (sic) of James and Ann Scolding.
Mar. 20   Susannah d. of George and Susannah Greenerd.
Mar. 24   Ann d. of Samuel and Ann Theobald.

### 1748.

April 17   Rebecca d. of Thomas and Mary Edwards.
May 30   Margarett d. of James and Martha Colthorp.
Jan. 9   Hannah d. of Edmund and Sarah Chambers.
Jan. 30   John s. of John and Bridget Prime.
Mar. 10   Elizabeth d. of John and Mary Aldred.

### 1749.

April 30   John s. of John and Elizabeth Fuller.
July 22   James s. of James and Ann Smith.
Oct. 23   Mary Bell base daughter of Mary Freeman.
Oct. 31   John s. of James and Martha Colthorp.
Oct. 31   Jane d. of Samuel and Susannah Amand.
Jan. 15   John s. of Samuel and Mary Higham.
Mar. 17   Anne d. of George and Susannah Greenerd.

### 1750.

June 18   Eunice d. of John and Elizabeth Warn.
Aug. 16   Mary d. of Stephen and Elizabeth Mayhew.
Aug. 31   John s. of John and Sarah Pearson.
Sep. 1   Elizabeth d. of George and Mary Long.
Sep. 13   Thomas s. of James and Ann Scolding.
Sep. 16   Sarah d. of James and Elizabeth Smith.
Sep. 18   Ann d. of Samuel and Susannah White.
Oct. 21   Sarah d. of Noah and Sarah Hamblin.

Nov. 25   James s. of James and Martha Colthorp.
Dec. 10   John s. of Thomas and Elizabeth Copping.
Jan. 10   Robert s. of William and Mary Nunn.
Jan. 13   Cornelius s. of Thomas and Mary Roberts.
Feb. 14   Philip s. of John and Bridget Prime.

### 1751.

Mar. 30   James s. of George and Susannah Greenerd.
June 28   William s. of John and Margaret Woolnough.
Sep. 15   Sarah d. of John and Sarah Pearson.
Sep. 15   Margaret d. of Edmund and Sarah Chambers.
Dec. 14   John s. of John and Mary Aldred.

### 1752.

Jan. 7   Sarah d. of James and Frances Crisp.
Jan. 25   Ann and Katherine dau'rs of James and Ann Smith.
April 5   Elizabeth Hanner base child.
April 20   Sarah d. of John and Sarah Puttock.
May 17   Sarah d. of Thomas and Mary Edwards.
June 5   Mary d. of George and Susannah Greneerd.
July 3   John s. of John and Elizabeth Gillman.
July 29   William s. of John and Elizabeth Fuller.
Oct. 6   Lydia base dau'r of Mary Wright.
Oct. 25   Margaret d. of John and Sarah Pearson.
Oct. 31   Judith d. of Samuel and Mary Higham.
Nov. 27   John s. of John and Katherine Thompson.

### 1753.

Feb. 12   William s. of John and Elizabeth Warn.
Feb. 15   Elizabeth base dau'r of Elizabeth Elliott.
Feb. 27   Samuel s. of Samuel and Elizabeth Smith.
Mar. 2   Susannah d. of James and Ann Scolding.
Mar. 6   Samuel s. of Samuel and Susannah White.
May 15   Robert s. of James and Martha Colthorp.
June 17   Robert s. of Thomas and Mary Edwards.
Oct. 26   Stephen s. of Stephen and Elizabeth Mayhew.
Nov. 26   Thomas s. of Thomas and Elizabeth Randal.

### 1754.

Feb. 6   Susannah d. of Samuel and Susannah Amand.
Mar. 26   Robert s. of Robert and Martha Higham.
May 9   James s. of James and Frances Crisp.
June 2   Sarah d. of Thomas and Mary Roberts.

(*To be continued.*)

# Hopkins of Llanfihangel Ystern Llewern, Monmouthshire.*

\* at Llanfihangel Ystern Llewern, co. Monmouth.     † at Newland, co. Gloucester.     ‡ at St. Faith the Virgin under St. Paul's, London.

Howell Hopkin of Llanfihangel Ystern Llewern.=Cybell.=....1st husband. Will not dated, but endorsed 1600.

William Howell. Mentioned in Howell Hopkin's will as "son of Cybell my wife."

John Howell.=....

Hopkyn Howell.

Catherine.=Hopkin Richards.

William Hopkyn Richards.

Howell John Howell.

.... Hopkins of Llanfihangel Ystern Llewern.=....

William Probyn of Newland,=Elizabeth, da. of Edmund Bond co. Gloucester, Gent. Ob. 11 of Walford, co. Hereford, Gent., Feb. 1702. Bur. at Newland. and relict of William Hopton of M.I. Huntley, co. Glouc. Ob. 19 Dec. 1714, æt. 70. Bur. †. M.I.

John Hopkins of Llanfihangel Ystern Llewern, Gent. Will dated 5 June 1684; proved at Llandaff 16 Oct. 1684.=Elizabeth .... Will dated 12 Feb, 1698; proved 12 Jan. 1698. Described as of Llangattock Vibon Avel. Bur. * 9 Feb. 1697.

Henry Hopkins. Mentioned in the will of his brother John.

Sir Edmund Probyn=Elizabeth, da. of Kt., bap. † 16 July Sir John Blen- 1678, Chief Baron cowe, Kt., Justice of the Exchequer. of Common Pleas. Ob. 17 May 1742. Ob. 22, bur. † 28 Bur. †. M.I. Oct. 1749. M.I. S.p.

William Probyn, bap. † 9 Nov. 1686.

Mary.

Hannah, bap. † 5 Jan. 1674. Bur. †. . Feb. 1741. M.I.

Frances, ob. † 27 Oct. 1786. M.I.

Blanch, ob. † 10 Aug. 1741. M.I.

Elizabeth, mar. ..... Williams.

James=Rachel. Powell of Llan- gattock Vibon Avel.

William Hopkins, Clerk,=Sarah, bap. † Rector of Llanfihangel 27 May 1672. Ystern Llewern. Born* Mar.* 9 Sep. 7 June 1659. Will dated 1692. Bur.* 17 Oct. 1708; pr. 4 Oct. 7 Sep. 1710. 1709, "of Llangattock Vibon Avel." Bur. * 4 Nov. 1708.

A     B

\* Compiled by J. A. BRADNEY, Esq., B.A., from title-deeds, parish registers, and wills.

For much relating to the Probyns the compiler is indebted to the pedigree of that family published by Sir John Maclean in the 'Transactions of the Bristol and Gloucestershire Archæological Society.' It will be observed that he has been able to correct several mistakes which had crept into the pedigree as published.

Arms borne by the family and are to be seen on the monument in Llanfihangel Church, 1749 : Sable, on a chevron between three pistols argent as many roses gules. In 1734 a grant was made to John Hopkins (afterwards Probyn) : Ermine, on a fesse gules a lion passant-guardant argent, a canton of the second charged with a rose or.

Tho.ˢ Hopkins Esq.ʳ

Newland, Gloucester-shire.

Chris.ʳ Taddy

B

A

Mary, bap.* 9 Feb. 1697.

Elizabeth, bap. * 13 Feb. 1693. Ob. unm.

Sarah, bap.* 12 Feb. 1699.

Bur. † 9 March 1759. M.I.

Edmund Hopkins, bap.* 29 Nov. 1706.

Sarah, da. of WalterWilliams of Dingestow, co. Mon., Esq. Ob. † 14 Feb. 1749, æt. 48. M.I. 1st wife.

Elizabeth=William Hopkins of London, Merchant. Bap. * 25 Jan. 1704. Ob. † 12 April 1763, æt. 59. M.I. Will pr. 10 May 1763.

....= Married 1753. 2nd wife.

Adam Thomas= of Llanfihangel YsternLlewern, Gent. Will dat. 16 Dec. 1698; pr. 26 April 1699.

....= (Anne)

Thomas Hopkins of Newland, Esq.,=Amelia, da. of Sir John Hopkins. Ob. s.p. only child, born 28 Nov. 1739.

John Hopkins of Newland and of Lincoln's Inn,=Ann, da. and sole heir of John Howell of Lincoln's Inn, Esq. Ob.† 18 Nov. 1784, æt. 72. M.I.
Esq., nephew and heir to Sir Edmund Probyn, in compliance with whose will he assumed the name of Probyn. Bap. * 3 Feb. 1708. Bur. † 25 March 1773. M.I. In 1734 he had a grant of arms: Ermine, on a fesse gules a lion passant-guardant argent, a canton of the second charged with a rose or.

William Hopkins, bap. * 11 Feb. 1695. Bur.* 30 Aug. 1698. M.I.

James Hopkins. Mentioned in his mother's will as "beyond the seas."

Elizabeth, of Llantilio Crossenny, spinster. Will dated 13 April 1713; pr. 19 May 1713. Bur. * 20 April 1713.

Jane, ob. 18 May 1722, Bur. † M.I.

Samuel Lewis.=Anne. Bur. * 20 Feb. 1709.

Anne, bap.* 29 Dec. 1695. Bur.* 5 Sep. 1709.

Elizabeth, born * 3 Jan. 1689. Bur. * 20 April 1713.

David Hopkins of Llangattock Llingoed, Gent. Born * 26 Dec. 1692. Bur. at Llangattock Llingoed 29 Nov. 1771.

Charles Simkins=.... of Avebury, co. Wilts, Esq.

Elizabeth, bap. * 16 Nov. 1726.

D

Edmund Probyn of Newland, Esq., Sheriff of co. Gloucester 1747. Bur. † 26 April 1819, æt. 82.=Sophia, da. of Richard Dalton.

Elizabeth Anne.

Elizabeth Anne.

For the descendants of this marriage, vide vol. vi, part i., of the 'Transactions of the Bristol and Gloucestershire Archæological Society.' The present representative of the family is Edmund Probyn of Huntley, co. Gloucester, Esq.

Onias Hopkins of Llanfihangel Ystern Llewern, Gent. Executed a deed settling his land on his children 2 Dec. 1720. Bur. * 15 March 1722.=Anne. ....

John Hopkins of Llanfihangel Roggiet, Gent. Will dated 14 May 1680; pr. 2 June 1680.=Anne ....

Nicholas Hopkins of Llantilio Pertholy, Yeoman. Born * 3 Jan. 1688. Will dat. 21 April 1764; pr. 9 May 1764.=Anne ....

John Hopkins of Llanfihangel Ystern Llewern, Gent., born * 18 Oct. 1685. Ob. * 9 Nov. 1749. M.I. Made a post-nuptial settlement 3 May 1722.=Mary, da. of Wm. Prichard of the Graig, Gent. Bur. * 23 Jan. 1726.

David Hopkins, bap. * 4 Dec. 1730.

Nicholas Hopkins, bap. * 17 Dec. 1727.

....=Mary, bap. * 11 Oct. 1720.

Taylor.=Mary, bap. *

Philip Price, Clerk, Vicar of Walterston, co. Hereford. Ob. 6 April 1786, æt. 51. M.I.=Anne, bap. * 28 Oct. 1722. M.I.

C

C |

D |

William Hopkins of=Elizabeth Llanfihangel Ystern ..... Ob. Llewern, Gent. 26 April Bap. * 9 July 1714. 1812, æt. Killed by a fall from 90. Bur.* his horse 18 April M.I. S.p. 1751. Bur. *. M.I. Adm'on granted to his brother John 16 May 1751.

James Hopkins, bap. * 2 June 1717.

Thomas Hopkins, bap. * 6 Dec.1722. — 16 July Both bur. * 1724.

Richard Hopkins, bap. * 27 Oct. 1723.

David Hopkins, bap. * 27 Nov. 1724.

Sir John Hopkins,=Anne, eventual Kt., bap. * 21 July sole heir. 1715. Lord Mayor Died 5 Sep. of London 1791-92. 1806, æt. 78. Ob. 14 Oct. 1796. Bur. at Wan- Bur. at Wanstead, stead. M.I. co. Essex. M.I.

Sir John William=Dorothy, coheiress, Anderson, Bart., Ob. s.p. 9 Dec.1817. Lord Mayor of Bur. at Hendon. London 1797-98. M.I. Ob. 21 May 1813, aged 77. Bur. at Hendon, co. Middx. M.I.

Charles Hopkins, born 24 April, bap. ‡ 17 May 1761. Died at Strafford, Essex, 20 Feb. 1834. Bur. at Wanstead 27 Feb. 1834. M.I. S.p.

William Hopkins of Llanfihangel Ystern Llewern,=Mary, da. of Philip Wyatt Crowther, and of Paternoster Row, Esq. Bap. ‡ 13 Nov. Esq. Bur. 16 Feb. 1836 at Trinity 1751. Buried 29 March 1833 at Trinity Church, Church, Cheltenham. 2nd wife. Cheltenham. S.p.

=Mary, da. of Richard Lewis of Lawrence Lane, Cheapside, Merchant. Mar. at St. Mary, Stoke Newington, 10 July 1777. 1st wife.

Christopher Taddy of London,=Mary Anne, born Merchant. Mar. at St. Augus- 22 Sep, bap. ‡ 2 tine's and St. Faith's, London, Oct. 1753. Died 21 Sep.1771. Bur. at Croydon 24 March 1801. 30 Jan. 1824. Buried 31 March 1801 at Wanstead.

Joseph Bradney of Bradney,=Elizabeth, born 24 Aug, bap. ‡ co. Somerset, and of Ham, 11 Sep.1755. Mar. at Wanstead co. Surrey, Esq., Buried 22 19 June 1793. Bur. at Trinity July 1817, æt. 79, at Kings- Church, Cheltenham, 27 April ton-on-Thames. M.I. 1830.

Thomas Hopkins=Amelia, born 9 Dec, of Newland, Esq. bap. ‡ 28 Dec. 1757. Bur. 14 March 1835 at Ottery St. Mary, co. Devon. S.p.

John William Hopkins of=Hannah, da. of Llanfihangel Ystern William Heard. Llewern, Esq., Barrister- Mar. at Padding- at-Law. Bap. at St. An- ton 27 Sep. 1843. drew's, Holborn, 29 Oct. S.p. Still living. 1782. Bur. at Padding- Remarried ..... ton Church 17 Feb. 1852. McCoan.

Richard Lewis Hopkins, bur. at the Church of St. Peter and St. Paul, Bath, 18 July 1825, aged 23 years.

David Hopkins, Clerk,=Ann Cockell, Vicar of Bucknell, co. mar. at West- Salop. Bur. at Trinity bury, co. Wilts, Church, Cheltenham, 14 Dec. 1824. 3 Feb. 1842.

Elizabeth, bap. 27 May 1778 at St. Andrew's, Holborn. Bur. at St. John's Church, Clifton, 10 June 1863, æt. 85.

Mary Anne, bap. 5 June 1779 at St. Andrew's, Holborn. Bur. 2 March 1859 at St. John's, Clifton.

Sarah, bap. 25 Jan. 1781 at St. Andrew's, Holborn. Bur. 22 April 1857 at St. John's, Clifton.

William Vaughan Hopkins, bap. at Bucknell 18 July 1829. Buried there 1 Feb. 1830.

MONUMENTAL INSCRIPTIONS FROM THE BURIAL-GROUND OF ST. GEORGE, HANOVER SQUARE, NEAR MARBLE ARCH.*

M<sup>rs</sup> Ann Broad, wife of James Broad, of Drury Lane, died 22 Aug. 1804, aged 45.
Catherine Broad, grand daughter of the above, born 12 May 1811, died Oct. 16, 1811, aged 5 months, 4 days.
M<sup>r</sup> James Broad, died 16 May 1826 in his [68<sup>th</sup>?] year. [*Rest of inscription hidden by a footstone.*]

Sarah [Maycock?] . . . . . . . .

M<sup>rs</sup> Elizabeth Streeting, widow of the late M<sup>r</sup> George Streeting, of Windsor Castle, died Feb. 6 1823, aged 70.
Emma Mary Willson, niece of the above, & daughter of John & Elizabeth Willson of South Molton Street, died Dec. 4 1808, aged 3 years and 2 months.
John Frederick Hastings Willson son [of the above John & Elizabeth Willson?] . . . . 1829. [*Rest of inscription hidden by a footstone.*]

Mary Dickinson, wife of William Dickinson, of the parish of S<sup>t</sup> Mary-le-bone, died Dec. 9 1800, aged 39.
Miss Hannah Dickinson, daughter of the above, died June 24, 1823, in her 31<sup>st</sup> year.
M<sup>r</sup> William Dickinson, died Oct. 1, 1824, aged 62.
M<sup>rs</sup> Mary Law, died Aug. 13, 1851, aged 61.

Joseph Lomax Esq. Lieutenant of her Majesty's 16<sup>th</sup> Foot, died 3 Dec. 1838 aged [. .] years. [*Age hidden by footstone.*]

Mary Savage, of this parish. [*Rest hidden by a footstone.*]

M<sup>r</sup> John Ollivier, died 10 Sep. [1810], aged 80.
M<sup>rs</sup> Elizabeth Ollivier, widow of the above, died 17 Aug. 1816, aged 74.
Ann, wife of Claude Ollivier, son of the above John & Elizabeth [...] 1819. [...]. [*Part of inscription hidden by footstone.*]

M<sup>r</sup> Michael Dunn, died Aug. 23, 1814, aged 40.
George Dunn, son of the above, died Sep. [. . 1819], aged 18 years.

Matthew Cook, of Norfolk Street, Grosvenor Square, died Dec. 28, 1810, aged 72.
All three of his children died in their infancy.

George, son of John & Ann Lane, died Jan. 25 1823, aged 11 months.
Lucy Lane, died 19 Jan. 1830, aged 9 years & 6 months ; daughter of the above.
Charles Lane, son of the above, died Dec. 10, 1851, in his 23<sup>rd</sup> year.

The family grave of James & Emma Green, of Great Portland Street.
Eliza Mary, died March 7, 1845, aged 6 years & 7 months.
Caroline, died Feb. 7, 1848, aged 18 days.
Helena Emelie, died March 20, 1853, aged 2.

M<sup>r</sup> Isaac Talboys, died June 26, 1801, aged 59.
M<sup>rs</sup> Abigail Talboys, wife of the above, died Dec. 22, 1819, aged 89.
M<sup>r</sup> George Peisley, son-in-law of the above, late of the General Post Office, died May 17 1820, aged 56.
M<sup>rs</sup> [. . . . Peisley] [wife of the above] [. . . . 1830]. [*Part of inscription hidden by a footstone.*]

* Continued from p. 235.

Mary Ann Tadloo, died 9 May 1825, aged 16.
James Tadloo, brother of the above, died 11 Aug. 1827, aged 22.
George Tadloo, brother of the above, died 22 Jan. 1830, aged 22.

Mary, wife of M<sup>r</sup> William Smale, died Jan. 28 1843, aged 48.
Mary Ann Taylor, a dear and respected friend of the above, died 9 Dec. 1846, in
    her 68<sup>th</sup> year.
William, husband of the above Mary Smale, died Jan. 4, 1852, in his 71<sup>st</sup> year.

. . . . Georgiana, daughter of the above, aged 3 weeks.

M<sup>r</sup> William May (formerly of Ramsholt, in the county of Suffolk), died Sep. 12,
    1847, aged 50.

M<sup>r</sup> William Davison, died March 21, 1844, in his 39<sup>th</sup> year.
Also near this place lie the remains of M<sup>rs</sup> Margaret Davison, mother of the above,
    died Dec<sup>r</sup> 11, 1839, aged 62.
M<sup>r</sup> Robert Davison, died June 16, 1847, aged 74.

Mary, wife of Geo<sup>e</sup> Maynard, died Dec. 10, 1825, aged 44.

Thomas Fenton Esq. late of Davies Street, Berkeley Square, & Brook Green
    Terrace, died Jan. 8, 1847, aged 44.
Four of his children died in their infancy.

Mary Latham, Spinster, died May 27, 1827, aged 68.

Six infant children of William & Susannah Chalmers, who died under the age of
    3 years & 6 months.
William James, and William (twins) Alexander and Cornelius, interred near this
    spot.
And Emma Ellen, interred at Hampton.
Susannah, wife of M<sup>r</sup> William Chalmers, of her Majesty's Household, died Dec. 4,
    1844, aged 46.
Ann Sophia Adams, niece of M<sup>rs</sup> Chalmers, died 27 July 1845, in her 17<sup>th</sup> year ;
    interred near this spot.
Also her sister Jane Ann, died 20 Sep. 1846 in her [26<sup>th</sup> ?] year.

M<sup>r</sup> John [Whitehead ?] . . . . . . .

Anna, daughter of William & Anna Stevenson, died Dec. 11, 1822, aged 2.
Frederick Stevenson, son of the above, died Feb. 3, 1834, aged 7 months.
Eliza, wife of Edward Hundley & daughter of the above, died July 16, 1850,
    aged 27.

Grace, wife of Jn<sup>o</sup> Sansbury, of Edgware Row, died 13 Dec. 1777, aged 76.
M<sup>r</sup> Jn<sup>o</sup> Sansbury [husband] of the above Grace Sansbury, died 17 [Feb. ?] 1791,
    aged 76.

M<sup>r</sup> Edmund Woods, late of Queen Street, Grosvenor Square, died Dec. 21, 1836,
    in his 74<sup>th</sup> year.
M<sup>rs</sup> Sarah Woods, wife of the above fifty years, died March 29, 1839, in her 78<sup>th</sup>
    year.

M<sup>rs</sup> Mary Hibbert, died July 27, 1812, aged 60.
*(To be continued.)*

# 𝔅𝔯𝔬𝔴𝔫𝔢.*

*Baptisms.*

| | | | |
|---|---|---|---|
| 1662 | Sep. | 2 | Charles son of William Browne. |
| 1664 | May | 6 | Jana daughter of William Browne. |
| 1665 | Nov. | 5 | Thomas son of William Browne. |
| 1668 | Sep. | 26 | Henricus son of William Browne. |
| 1694 | June | 17 | Maria daughter of Thomas and Hester Browne. |

*Marriage.*

| | | | |
|---|---|---|---|
| 1710 | Feb. | 9 | Richard Brown of Weston on Trent and Maria Ford of Burnaston. |

*Burials.*

| | | | |
|---|---|---|---|
| 1666 | Dec. | 8 | Johannis Browne. |
| 1671 | Dec. | 19 | Maria relicta Johannis Browne. |
| 1678 | May | 25 | Henricus son of William Browne. |
| 1702 | April | 20 | Maria Browne. |
| 1713 | Sep. | 24 | Anna Browne. |
| 1714 | Dec. | 20 | Thomas Browne. |

INSCRIPTIONS ON TOMB-STONES IN LONGFORD CHURCHYARD, CO. DERBY, EVIDENT IN 1885.

On the south side of the chancel of Longford Church in the churchyard two altar-tombs built of stone.

*No. 1 altar-tomb.*—*Two copper-plates missing from panels, one of which is preserved in the church with the following inscription in incised letters :*

Here lieth the Body of
WILLIAM BROWN
OF
NETHER THURVASTON
𝔴𝔥𝔬 𝔡𝔢𝔭𝔞𝔯𝔱𝔢𝔡 𝔱𝔥𝔦𝔰 𝔏𝔦𝔣𝔢
March 23ᵈ j767
In the 53ᵈ Year of his Age.†

*Round the top of tomb.*

HERE LIETH THE BODY OF
WILLIAM BROWN OF NETHER THVRVASTON WHO DYED
THE .... DAY‡ OF MAY IN
THE YEAR OF OVRE LORD j686 AND OF HIS AGE 39.

*No. 2 altar-tomb.*—*Two panels filled with copper-plates with incised letters.*

[i]

Here
Lyeth the Body of Ann
the wife of *WILLIAM BROWN*
of Nether THURVASTON
Daughter of Samuel
and Elizabeth Hurd of
OSMASTON next ASHBURN
Deceased March§ yᵉ j8ᵗʰ
j734 Aged 48.

---

\* Continued from p. 236.
† Bapt. at Longford 30 May 1714 ; buried there 26 March 1767.
‡ Buried at Longford 3 May 1686.
§ Buried at Longford 25 February [*sic*] 1734.

[ii]

HERE lieth the Body
of William Brown
of Nether Thurvaston
who departed this life
January the 7<sup>th</sup> j74j,
in the 62<sup>d</sup> year of his Age.*

The altar-tomb [i] is in a decayed condition.

---

*Two head-stones of blue slate, in good preservation, with the following inscriptions :*

𝕳ere
lieth the Body of
John Brown† Son of
WILLIAM and ANN Brown
of Nether Thurvaston.
He died
September the j6<sup>th</sup> j754
**aged 34 Years.**

---

𝕳ere
lieth the Body of
Ann Brown Daughter
of William and Ann Brown
of Nether Thurvaston
She died May 31<sup>st</sup> j769 Aged 57
Years.‡

---

TRINITY COLLEGE, CAMBRIDGE, CHAPEL.

M.S.
Isaac Hawkins Browne A.M.
Gulielmo Browne Nati
Hujusæ Collegii
Cujus Et Pater Socius Fuerat
Alumni
Portae
Venusti Sublimis
Senatoris
Spectati, Gravis,
Viri
Excellenti Animo,
Ac Virtuti Præditi,
Immortalitate,
Quam Christianus Praesenserat
Vates Illustraverat
Frui Corpit
A. S. MDCCLX.
Aet. LV.
Ut Aedes
Quas Vivos Colebat
Defunctum Ne Silerent
Hoc Marmor
Patri Optimo
Filius Unicus
T. H. Browne
P. C.

---

* Bapt. at Longford 2 Oct. 1679; buried there 10 Jan. 1741.
† Of "*Church Broughton*." Bapt. at Longford 20 Jan. 1719; buried there 19 Sept. 1754.
‡ Bapt. at Longford 24 July 1711; buried (brought from Derby) 3 June 1769.

## GENEALOGICAL MEMORANDA RELATING TO THE FAMILY OF EVELYN.

### WILLS.*

RICHARD EVELYN of Woodcott in the par. of Ebisham *al's* Epsham, Surrey, Esq. Will dat. 5 Feb. 1669 ; proved 17 June 1670 by Elizabeth Evelin the relict. To be buried in the Chancel of Ebisham Church, belonging to Woodcott house, and for my funeral £250. To poor of Ebisham £15, of Wootton 50s., and of Ewhurst 50s. Manors and lands in Pevensey, Mankesey, and Hoo, co. Sussex, and in Horley, Horne, and Sheire, co. Surrey, were by deed conveyed to Sir Edward Thurland, Knt., and Christopher Buckle, Esq., in trust for the advancement of my dau. Anne in marriage, and my Ex'ix is to pay my s$^d$ da. Anne £1000. To my brothers George and John Evelyn and my brother in law William Glanville, Esq., £20 each for rings. To my nephew and godson William Glanville £100. To my friends Sir Edward Thurland, Knt., and Christopher Buckle the elder, Esq., £10 each, they to be guardians of my dau. Anne if my wife dies before she is of age. To my s$^d$ wife a messuage and farm, etc., in Longhurst Hill, Cranley, co. Surrey. By my marriage settlement, dat. 20 May 1648, the manor house of Baynards and other lands, and the manor of Somersbury in Ewhurst and Ockley, were settled on me and my wife for our lives, remainder in default to my brother George Evelyn, he to pay my brother John Evelyn £1000, and my nephew and godson William Glanville £500. My wife Elizabeth sole ex'ix, and to have the custody of my dau. Anne Evelyn during her minority. My s$^d$ brothers George Evelyn and John Evelyn, overseers. Wit., Edw$^d$ Thurland, Tho$^s$ Hollier, and James Martin. (68 Penn.)

SIR JOHN EVELYN of Godstone, co. Surrey, Bart. Will dat. 20 April 1671 ; pr. 14 Nov. 1671 by Mary Gittings. My capital messuage or farm called Marden or Merdyn farm of 1000 acres in the parishes of Walkhamsted otherwise Godstone, Caterham, and Tandridge, co. Surrey, with other lands in the said parishes, to my dear friend Mary Gittings, my sole ex'ix. To my dau. Frances Evelyn £500 at age of 18 or marriage, and the s$^d$ Mary Gittings to be her guardian. Poor of Godstone £5. To the minister who buries me 40s. To my friend M$^r$ Francis Fuller of Tandridge Court £20. Wit., Fra. Fuller, Tho$^s$ Pakenham, Ralph Drake, Tho$^s$ Smith, John Earle, John Gunner. Codicil June 5, 1671. Revokes the legacy of £500 to his dau. Frances Evelyn. (127 Duke.)

ANNE EVELYN of S$^t$ Paul's, Covent Garden, co. Midd., widow. Will dat. . . Nov. 1674 ; pr. 3 Feb. 1676-7 by Frances Bagshaw. My cousin Mary Ledbetter of Aldermarston, co. Berks. My brother James Harrington, Esq. To my sister Ashton at Westminster my pearl necklace. My sister Billingham. My sister Frances Bagshaw sole ex'ix. My brother Bagshaw overseer. The three daughters of my brother W$^m$ Harrington, dec$^d$, viz., Angell, Elizabeth, and Mary Harrington. The two children of my sister Bagshaw, viz., Elizabeth and Harrington Bagshaw. Wit., Hester Rose, Eliz. Antrobus, John Gethin, Rich$^d$ Eustis. (16 Hale.)

WILLIAM EVELIN, late of Stepney al's Stebonheath, co. Midd., dec$^d$. Adm'on 22 Oct. 1683 to his relict, Martha Evelin. (Adm'ons 1683, fo. 45.)

SIR JOHN EVELYN of West Deane, co. Wilts. Will dat. 13 May 1676 ; signed 15 May 1676 ; codicil 2 March 1684 (1684-5) ; proved 24 Nov. 1685 by his da. Elizabeth Pierrepont, widow. To be buried in my vault in West Deane Church. My dau. Elizabeth Pierrepont, widow, sole ex'trix, to whom all my manors, lands, and tenem$^{ts}$ in England, and if her youngest son Evelyn Pierrepont shall be a dutiful son to her, then she no doubt will settle the said lands on him. To my dau. Dame Sarah, Viscountess Castleton, five shillings for her legacy. To my kinswoman M$^{rs}$ Frances Kelsey £40 yearly for life. To the poor of West Deane and East Grimstead, Wilts, £30, of Broughton £10, of Ashton Keynes £10, and of Whiteparish £10. Wit., Gabriel Thistlethwaite, Rich$^d$ Carpenter, Alexander Thayne, Francis Wither, etc. By the codicil the bequests made to the poor are revoked, and a yearly payment substituted as follows :—To the poor of West Deane

* Continued from p. 245.

£8, of East Grimsted in West Deane £4, of Broughton, co. Southamp., £4, Ashton Keynes, Wilts, £4, and of Whiteparish, Wilts, £40. To Geo. S$^t$ Barbe, gent., an annuity of £10. Wit., Fra. Wither, Mich. Trimnell, Giles Ingram, Geo. Osborne the elder, and Geo. Osborne the younger. (133 Cann.)

*(To be continued.)*

# Genealogy of Browne.*

## Evidences.

### LONGFORD—*continued.*

### BENTLEY HALL.

The ancient residence of Bentley Hall faces the high-road from Longford to Cubley in Derbyshire, at a distance of three miles from Longford and ten from the town of Derby. The Hall stands upon the manor of Hungry Bentley, which is of considerable antiquity, being mentioned in 'Doomsday Book.' Through the kindness of its present proprietor, S. W. Clowes, Esq., enhanced by the courtesy of his Solicitors, Messrs. Taylor, Kirkman, and Colley, of Manchester, I have obtained full information from the title-deeds with respect to the acquisition and possession by the Browne family of this property.

An epitome of title with the deeds recites as follows :—" 20 April 1613. By deed enrolled Lord Windsor in consideration of £2600 Grants The Manner of Hungrie Bentley etc. to Thomas Brown and his heirs."

Thomas Browne, the purchaser, was a Proctor of the Arches Court of Canterbury, and was born at Caverswall in 1561. He died at Shredicote (another and the chief family property) in 1633, and was buried in Bradeley Church, where his kneeling effigy is still to be seen. By will dated 27 Oct. 1631, he entailed the Hungry Bentley Estate upon his third-surviving son Edmund Browne, who it is known resided there, and married Dorothy, daughter of Sir Edward Vernon. Edmund was buried in Longford Church in 1684, having executed a deed, dated 25 Feb. 1663, which limited the estate as to part for 99 years to himself if he so long lived, with residue and remainder to his eldest son Thomas Browne, subject to a term vested in him the said Edmund Browne for securing the payment to him by his son of £1200 by instalments. The deed being practically a conveyance of the estate (on sale) to his son. Thomas Browne resided at Bentley, and married Grace, daughter of Anthony Crofts, Esq. He died there in 1708, having entailed Bentley, by will dated 22 May 1708 (of which probate does not seem to have been granted), upon his eldest son, also Thomas Browne. This Thomas married Alice, daughter of Richard Simpson, Esq., and died at Bentley in 1717, having entailed the estate by will, dated 12 Sept. 1717 (which document at his death could not be found, and an affidavit and draft will were filed), upon his eldest son Rupert Browne. It is believed that this Rupert restored and enlarged Bentley Hall, adding the "Queen Anne" portion. He married Eleanora, daughter of Roger Corbet, Esq., and died at Bentley in 1733, at the age of 35. By will dated 3 April 1733, his eldest son Thomas Browne succeeded to the property. He married in 1748 Catherina, daughter of Charles Yonge of Shrewsbury, and within one year after his marriage, by deeds dated 21 Feb. 1749, and in which his mother joined, he conveyed the whole of the estate for £12,000 to Edward Wilmot, Esq., M.D., of Jermyn Street, London (created a Baronet in 1759). The property thus alienated by Thomas Browne remained in the Wilmot family for four generations, when it was conveyed by Sir Henry Sacheverel Wilmot, Bart., by deed dated 27 March 1860, to the Trustees of Lord Vernon ; and it was finally conveyed by the present Lord Vernon, by deed dated 15 April 1878, to S. W. Clowes, Esq., of Norbury, Ashbourne, co. Derby, in whose possession it now remains.

In 1878 the estate consisted of 1040 acres, at a rental of about £2000 per annum.

The principal portion of the house is brick quoined with stone and stone mullioned windows. The Hall proper was built in the earlier part of the seventeenth century, most probably by the purchaser, Thomas Browne; and the "Queen Anne" addition was made to it probably by Rupert Browne in the earlier part of the eighteenth century. It is now used as a farmhouse, and at the time of my visit in August 1884 was tenanted by the late John Massey, whose grandfather and uncle had held the farm in the same way. The fireplace in the hall, partly bricked up in 1848, measures 10 feet across and 4 feet in recess. There is a very massively carved-oak staircase in the old portion of the house about 5 feet wide. The staircase in the later portion is about 8 feet in width, built of plain oak with oaken balustrade and balusters of curiously twisted wrought-iron. The entrance-door to this later hall is 12 feet high. Inside this hall there still hang several large old allegorical paintings in oil and in distemper. One of them I ascertained represented "Joan of Arc." These relics of former grandeur, in their tarnished gilt frames, have a very melancholy appearance in the old house, which is now fast going to decay. I could not learn anything of their history beyond the fact that they had "always been there."

---

* Continued from p. 249.

# To All and Singvler

vnto whom these Presents shall come J Sr Edward Bysshe Esqr Clarenceux Principall Herald and King of Armes of all the South East and West Parts of the Realme of England from the River of Trent Southward, send Greeting Whereas John Blackmore of London Esquire hath Desired mee to Assigne vnto him such Armes and Crest as he and his ~~~ Posterity may Lawfully beare Know yee therefore that I have thought fitt to Assigne vnto him the Armes hereafter menconed, viz: Or, a fesse Sable betweene three Moores heads erased Proper, And for a Crest, On a Helmet and Wreath of his Colours an armed ~~ Arme Proper supporting a Standard Or~Mantled Gules Doubled Argent, As in the Margent more lively is Depicted. Which Armes and Crest as before expressed I the said Clarenceux King of Armes by the Power and Authority to my Office annexed by Vertue of my Letters Patents to mee granted under the Greate Seale of England Doe by these Presents Assigne Give and Grant vnto the said John Blackmore and to the Heires of his Body Lawfully to be begotten, To hee by them and every of them borne with their due Differences according to the Lawes of Armes for ever, In Witnesse whereof I have hereunto affixed the Seale of my Office and subscribed my Name. Dated this Five and Twentyth day of Aprill in the Thirteenth year of the Reigne of our Soveraigne Lord Charles the Second by the Grace of God of England Scotland Fraunce and Ireland King Defendr of the Faith &c And in the yeare of our Lord One Thousand Six Hundred Sixty and One.

Edward Bysshe Clarenceux
King of Armes /

GENEALOGICAL MEMORANDA RELATING TO

# The Family of Evelyn.

## WILLS.*

DAME ANNE EVELYN of London, widow. Will dat. 14 June 1681 ; proved 20 April 1691 by W<sup>m</sup> Campion, Esq., the other ex'or Sir W<sup>m</sup> Glynn, Bar<sup>t</sup>, being dead. To be buried in S<sup>t</sup> Margaret's, Westminster, near my only dau. Frances. To my brother Sir W<sup>m</sup> Glynn £500, and to his eight children £100 each. To my brother in law William Campion, Esq., and my sister Frances, his wife, £500, and to her five children, viz., Elizabeth, William, Anne, Barbara, and Philadelphia, £100 each. To my brother Thomas Glynn £100. To my nieces Frances Campion and Katherine Campion £50 each. To my nephew Henry Campion my purse and all the broad gold in it. To my niece Anne Anderson my best diamond ring. If my sister Campion dies, her £500 to go to her son Henry Campion. My brother Sir William Glynn and my brother in law William Campion to be ex'ors. Wit., Norton Curteis, Norton Curteis, jun<sup>r</sup>, Fran. Griffith, Scr., Edm. Goldgay. (66 Vere.)

JOHN EVELYN, late of Wotton, Surrey, Esq<sup>r</sup>, dec<sup>d</sup>. Adm'on 22 July 1691 to his relict Catherine Evelyn. (Adm'ons 1691, fo. 120.)

SIR EDWARD EVELYN of Long Ditton, co. Surrey, Kn<sup>t</sup> and Bar<sup>t</sup>. Will dat. 12 Oct. 1691 ; proved 1 July 1692 by the relict Dame Mary Evelyn. To be buried in the church or chancel of Long Ditton. My copyhold lands in the manor of Maldon, and an annuity of £30 to my brother Arthur Evelyn. All my manors, lands, etc., to my wife Dame Mary Evelyn for life, and at her death to be disposed as under : Ruxley farm in Thames Ditton, now in the occupation of Dame Eliz<sup>th</sup> Blake, with other lands, etc., in Thames Ditton afores<sup>d</sup>, to my brother Arthur Evelyn. The manors of Ditton al's Long Ditton, etc., late the inheritance of my grandfather Thomas Evelyn, dec<sup>d</sup>, the manor of Long Ditton, heretofore the inheritance of Thomas Nott, Esq., with the advowson of the Rectory of Long Ditton, and divers other lands in Long Ditton, Talworth, Maldon, etc., to my da. Dame Penelope Alston, as also my mansion or manor house of Long Ditton, in which I now dwell. By Indenture, 4 July 4 Jac. II., I have mortgaged certain premises to my brother in law Sir William Glynn, Bar<sup>t</sup>, for payment of £2500, parcel of the marriage portion of my eld. da. Dame Mary Glynn, now wife of Sir William Glynn, Bar<sup>t</sup>, eldest son of the s<sup>d</sup> Sir W<sup>m</sup> Glynn, dec<sup>d</sup>. The manor of Talworth al's Talworth Court, Surrey, and lands in Talworth and Ewell to my said da. Dame Mary Glynn. The manor of Thames Ditton, Cleygate al's Claygate, co. Surrey, to my da. Sophia Evelyn, now under age. My aforesaid three da<sup>s</sup> are to pay an annuity of £10 each to Thomas Evelyn eldest son of my brother Arthur Evelyn. To my two sons in law, Sir William Glynn and Sir Joseph Alston, £20 each for mourning, and also £10 to Robert Pocock, Clerk. My wife Dame Mary, sole ex'ix. Wit., Brocas Gardiner, Tho<sup>s</sup> Hamersley, Rawlins Brownjohn. (143 Fane.)

ELIZABETH EVELYN of Woodcott, in the parish of Ebisham, co. Surrey, widow of Richard Evelyn of Woodcott, Esq. Will dat. 22 Jan. 1691 ; proved 3 Aug. 1692 by the ex'ors. To be buried in my chancel in Epsom Church. My lands and tenements in Ashted, Headly, and Walton on the Hill, co. Surrey, and at Hertingfordbury, Herts, to be sold. To the augmentation of the Vicarage of Ebisham £20 yearly. To my godda<sup>r</sup> Tomasin Terrick £500. My manors, lands, and tenements in Ebisham and Ewell, etc., to my ex'ors, in trust for my sister Dame Anne Morley (now wife of Sir William Morley of Halnaker, co. Sussex, K.B.), and my nephew John Lewknor (only son of my said sister by her former husband Sir John Lewknor late of West Dean, co. Sussex, dec<sup>d</sup>) for their use, and after the death of my s<sup>d</sup> sister, the said lands to go to the said John Lewknor and his heirs male, and in default of issue male, my mansion house of Woodcott and my manor

* Continued from p. 268.

of Horton, etc. (late the inheritance of my father George Mynn, Esq[r], dec[d]), to go to the R[t] Hon. Charles Calvert, Baron of Baltimore in Ireland, rem[r] to his son and heir apparent Benedict Calvert, rem[r] in default to John Parkhurst of Catesby, co. Northamp., Esq., rem[r] to his son and heir Nathaniel Parkhurst, rem[r] to Dormer Parkhurst, 2nd son of the afores[d] John Parkhurst, and as to the manor of Ebisham al's Epsom, with the presentation to the Church of Epsom, and lands in Epsom and Ewell which were bought by my mother Ann Mynn, widow, dec[d], I give the same to the afores[d] John Parkhurst of Catesby, with rem[r] in succession to his sons (as above), rem[r] to the said Charles, Lord Baltimore and his son Benedict Calvert. My friends Sir Christopher Buckle of Burrough in the par. of Banstead, co. Surrey, Knt., and his eldest son Christopher Buckle, Esq., to be ex'ors and trustees. To Master Sarjeant Mountague, late Lord Chief Baron of the Exchequer, all those pictures in my house at Woodcott relating to his family, viz., one of the old Lord Mountague of Boughton, one of the old Earl of Lindsey, one of the afores[d] Master Sarjeant Mountague when Lord Chief Baron, three pictures of his now Lady, two of his sons William and Christopher Mountague, dec[d], one of Master Freeman of Absden [? Aspeden], Herts, and one of his dau. M[rs] Margaret Freeman, and also the furniture in the room at Woodcott which was my dau. Mountague's room. Poor of Epsom £20. John Moorhouse, Vicar of Epsom. M[rs] Jane Lane, sister of Sir Christopher Buckle. Lewis Buckle, 2nd son of Sir Christopher. M[r] Terrick the Elder. M[rs] Jane, wife of Master Tho[s] Moreton. Residue to the afores[d] Sir Christopher Buckle. Wit., Fra. Fuller, Sam[l] Mason, W[m] Rant, Ro. Podmore. (150 Fane.)

ELIZABETH DYOT al's EVELIN, late of S[t] Giles in the Fields, co. Midd., dec[d]. Adm'on 20 May 1695 to her husband Richard Dyot. (Adm'ons 1695, fo. 89.)

RALPH AVELYN, late of Reading, co. Berks, Bachelor, dec[d]. Adm'on 7 May 1697 to his father Ralph Avelyn of Reading afores[d]. (Archdeaconry of Berks, Act Book iii., fo. 4.)

DAME MARY EVELYN, widow of Sir Edward Evelyn of Long Ditton, co. Surrey, Kn[t] and Bar[t]. Will dat. 30 June 1696 ; proved 18 Nov. 1696 by Sophia Glynne. My friend M[r] Shem Bridges to be guard[n] of my two grandchildren Mary Hill and Edw[d] Hill, and to the said Mary my silver salver with my own arms on it. My dau. Dame Penelope Alston and her son (my grandchild and godson) Evelyn Alston, under age. My grandchildren Penelope Alston and Sophia Glynne. Sir James Clark of Moulsey, Surrey. My sister the Lady Walden. My sister M[rs] Colton. My sister M[rs] Sandys. M[r] Robert Pocock, Rector of Long Ditton. Poor of Long Ditton. Residue to my da. Sophia Glynne, sole ex'trix. No witnesses, Dame Mary Evelyn having died before the will should have been sealed. (221 Bond.)

JOHN EVELYN, late of S[t] Martin's in the Fields, co. Midd., Esq[r], dec[d]. Adm'on 4 July 1699 to John Evelyn, Esq[r], grandfather and guardian of John Evelyn and Elizabeth Evelyn, minors, children of the defunct, the relict Martha Evelyn having first renounced. (Adm'ons 1699, fo. 120.)

The above grant expired, and another made 6 Sep. 1705 to the son John Evelyn, Esq[r], now of full age. (Adm'ons 1705, fo. 183.)

GEORGE EVELYN, of Wootton, co. Surrey, Esq. Will dat. 22 July 1699; codicil 15 Sep. 1699; proved 3 Feb. 1699-1700 by Dame Mary Wych, power reserved to W[m] Glanvill. To be buried in my vault near adjoining Wootton Church next my late dearest wife Dame Mary Cotton. Poor of Wootton, Abinger, and Dorking, £10 each parish. To my brother in law William Glanvill £100. To my brother John Evelyn, Esq., my library of books, my gilt bowl of plate, and three pictures of my father, mother, and sister Darcy. My grandchildren M[rs] Katherine Fulham and M[rs] Mary Evelyn. My great grandchild Jane Dyett. Sir Cyrill Wych. My nephew John Evelyn. My nephew William Glanvill £200. Indenture 23 June 1699 between me and my brother John Evelyn of one p[t], Stephen Hervey, Esq., of the second p[t], and Francis Stratford, Esq[r], and W[m] Draper, Esq., of the third part, to pay the said Steph. Hervey and Fran. Stratford £6500 upon certain trusts. Residue of my goods, etc., my rent charge of £38 16s. out of the manor of

Sommersbury and other lands, etc., in Ewhurst and Cranley, co. Surrey, and all rents which have come to me by the death of my brother Richard Evelyn, Esq., I give to my dau. Dame Mary Wych, sole ex'trix. Codicil (15 Sep. 1699) : To my nephew William Glanvill £300 more, and to be joint ex'or with my dau. Dame Mary, wife of Sir Cyrill Wych. Wit. (to will and codicil), Rob<sup>t</sup> Wye, William Morley, James Marten. (22 Noel.)

GEORGE EVELYN of Nutfield, co. Surrey, Esq. Will dat. 19 June 1699 ; proved 21 Feb. 1700-1 by his son John Evelyn. By agreement with my son John Evelyn, I have charged my manor of Wolhamsted al's Godstone, etc., with £6000 for portions for my children. To my two da<sup>s</sup> Thomazin Evelyn and Mary Evelyn £1500 each at ages of 21 or marriage. To my son Richard Evelyn £1000, and my son William Evelyn £500, at ages of 21. My copyhold lands and tenements to my son John Evelyn, he to pay my son William Evelyn £500. To my wife all my plate which hath her and my arms upon it. My son John Evelyn sole ex'or. Wit., Dan. Cox, John Woodward, Robert Gay, Sam. Woodcock, Edw. Haberfeild. (20 Dyer.)

*(To be continued.)*

---

# The Register Book of Bramfield, co. Suffolk.*

### 1754.

June 18  Matthew s. of Matthew and Deborah Todd.
July 9  Susannah d. of William and Mary Nunn.
Aug. 26  Benjamin s. of John and Elizabeth Warn.
Oct. 28  John s. of John and Sarah Puttock.
Dec. 4  Mary d. of James and Ann Smith.

### 1755.

Jan. 10  Robert s. of John and Elizabeth Gillman.
Jan. 25  Sarah base dau'r of Sarah Smith.
Feb. 1  John s. of John and Martha Smith.
May 19  John s. of Robert and Martha Higham.
May 23  William s. of John and Mary Aldred.
June 15  James s. of Samuel and Elizabeth Smith.
Aug. 16  Daniel s. of Daniel and Mary Harman.
Sep. 28  Robert s. of Richard and Elizabeth Cooper.
Dec. 14  Robert s. of Robert and Elizabeth Cornish.

### 1756.

Jan. 2  Leonard s. of John and Sarah Peirson.
Feb. 3  William s. of James and Frances Crisp.
Feb. 16  Sarah d. of Joseph and Sarah Bunn.
Feb. 27  Susannah d. of Samuel and Susannah Amand.
April 28  Deborah d. of Matthew and Deborah Todd.

May 23  Thomas s. of Edmund and Elizabeth Freeman.
July 10  Elizabeth d. of John and Elizabeth Gillman.
Aug. 2  George s. of William and Mary Nunn.
Aug. 8  Mary d. of Daniel and Mary Harman.
Nov. 28  John s. of John and Sarah Sevidge.

### 1757.

Mar. 15  Mary d. of Jonathan and Mary Laughter.
May 30  Elizabeth d. of Thomas and Mary Edwards.
May 30  Sarah d. of Richard and Elizabeth Cooper.
June 20  Arabella d. of John and Sarah Peirson.
July 13  Thomas s. of Robert and Martha Higham.
July 13  Alice d. of John and Sarah Puttock.
July 14  Mary d. of James and Martha Colthorp.
Aug. 8  Henry s. of James and Ann Smith.
Oct. 11  Elizabeth d. of Joseph and Sarah Bunn.

### 1758.

Mar. 14  Alice d. of John and Sarah Puttock.
Mar. 21  Hannah d. of Samuel and Mary Smith.
May 15  Edmund s. of Edmund and Elizabeth Freeman.
Nov. 19  George s. of John and Elizabeth Gillman.
Dec. 31  Thomas s. of John and Martha Smith.

---

* Continued from p. 259.

### 1759.

Jan. 26  Joshua s. of William and Mary Nunn.
Mar. 12  Samuel s. of Robert and Martha Higham.
April 1  Elizabeth d. of John and Elizabeth Fuller.
April 15  Elizabeth d. of Daniel and Mary Harman.
April 25  Mary d. of Thomas and Mary Roberts.
May 13  Joseph s. of Joseph and Sarah Bunn.
May 20  Christopher s. of John and Ann Wright.
July 1  William s. of John and Sarah Pearson.
Aug. 26  Jeremiah s. of Richard and Elizabeth Cooper.
Sep. 2  Ann d. of Samuel and Elizabeth Smith.
Nov. 29  James s. of Edmund and Elizabeth Freeman.
Dec. 9  William base son of John Adams and Deborah Mash.
Dec. 30  Elizabeth d. of James and Ann Smith.

### 1760.

Jan. 5  James s. of James and Sarah Green.
Jan. 16  Sarah d. of John and Martha Smith.
Feb. 3  Mary d. of John and Sarah Puttock.
Feb. 10  Martha d. of William and Alice Haws.
Feb. 10  John s. of John and Margaret Bedingfield.
Feb. 10  John s. of James and Frances Crisp.
Mar. 25  William s. of Joseph and Sarah Bunn.
May 25  John base son supposed of John Blowers and Susan Howard.
July 16  Mary d. of John and Sarah Savage.
Sep. 7  Richard s. of Richard and Mary Gaifer.
Sep. 29  Isabella d. of Robt and Martha Higham.

### 1761.

Mar. 2  Linah d. of Daniel and Mary Almond.
July 19  Hannah d. of Joseph and Sarah Bunn.
July 26  Elisabeth d. of William and Mary Nunn.
Aug. 30  Robert s. of John and Sarah Peirsons.
Oct. 29  Elisabeth d. of Richard and Elisa: Cooper.
Oct. 30  Henry s. of John and Ann Wright.
Nov. 2  William s. of John and Mary Aldred.
Nov. 2  Susan d. of the same.
Dec. 24  John s. of Edward and Elisabeth Freeman.

### 1762.

Feb. 14  Daniel Mash a base child.
April 18  John Driver a base child.
May 9  John s. of James and Sarah Green.
May 19  Susan d. of John and Susan Thompson.
Nov. 14  Saml s. of Willm and Mary Dew.
Nov. 28  Thos s. of Thos and Elisabth Howard,

### 1763.

Jan. 7  Saml s. of John and Ann Baldry.
Feb. 3  Ann d. of James and Martha Caltrup.
May 23  Thos s. of Thos and Ann Dunnett.
May 23  Martha d. of Robert and Martha Higham.
May 29  Frances d. of Willm and Mary Nun.
May 29  Mary d. of John and Deborah Adams.
June 5  John s. of Ricd and Elisabeth Cooper.
July 17  Hester d. of Willm and Mary Alps.
July 20  Nathaniel s. of Daniel and Mary Harman.
July 30  Daniel s. of John and Sarah Peirson.
Sep. 7  Richard s. of John and Sarah Puttuck.
Sep. 21  Robert s. of Henry and Frances Tillett.
Oct. 5  Sarah d. of James and Frances Crisp.

### 1764.

Feb. 9  William s. of John and Elisabeth Baldry.
Mar. 11  Henry s. of Thos and Mary Edwards.
Mar. 24  Frances d. of Willm and Mary Nunn.
June 9  Mary Ann d. of Matthew and Deborah Todd.
July 22  Elisabeth d. of James and Susan Thompson.
July 22  Ann d. of James and Mary Skoulding.
Aug. 12  Jemima d. of Joseph and Sarah Bunn.
Aug. 19  Richard s. of Thomas and Mary Dunnett.
Sep. 16  Thomas s. of Robert and Martha Higham.
Dec. 7  Thomas s. of Robert and Lydia Eastaugh.

### 1765.

Jan. 6  Mary d. of Robert and Elisabeth Berry.
Jan. 20  Edmund s. of Edmund and Mary Hurren.
Jan. 27  Elisabeth d. of Thos and Elisabeth Howard.
Mar. 29  Robert s. of Matthew and Deborah Todd.
April 7  Richard s. of Richard and Elisabeth Cooper.
June 30  Maray d. of John and Deborah Adams.
June 30  Robert s. of Willm and Alice Hawes.
July 14  Sarah d. of James and Mary Green.
Sep. 23  James s. of James and Elisth Crisp.
Sep. 29  Thos s. of John and Sarah Peirson.
Oct. 6  Edward s. of James and Frances Crisp.

### 1766.

Jan. 6  Mary d. of Richd and Mary Gaifer.
Jan. 19  James s. of Joseph and Sarah Bunn.
Feb. 15  John s. of Thos and Mary Dunnet.
May 29  William Puttock of John and Sarah.
June 24  Sarah Reeve of Henry and Mary.
June 28  Lydia Eastoe of Saml and Lydia.
July 2  Mary Reynolds of Roger and Mary.
Oct. 1  Mary Noller of Charles and Mary.

Nov. 2 Sarah Chamberlain of Christopher and Susan.
Nov. 2 Robert Berry of Robert and Elisabeth.
Nov. 24 Henry Wade of Henry and Sarah.

## 1767.

Mar. 8 Mary Cooper of Richard and Elisabeth.
Mar. 22 Simon Baldry of John and Mary.
April 24 Sam¹ Harvey of John and Sarah.
May 29 Leonard Peirson of John and Sarah.

T. WISTON.

June 14 Mary Bunn of Joseph and Sarah.
July 26 Sarah Hawes of William and Alice.
Oct. 4 John Adams of John and Deborah.
Oct. 25 Thomas Elner of John and Rachael.
Nov. 29 John Crisp of James and Elisabeth.

## 1768.

Mar. 20 Sarah Grise d. of Elisabeth Grise.
Mar. 29 Ann Crisp of John and Ann.
June 5 Luther Grise of Margaret Grise.
Oct. 2 Fanny Gaifer of Ric⁴ and Mary.
Oct. 16 Thomas Smith of John and Martha.
Nov. 4 Frances Tillett of Henry and Frances.

## 1769.

Jan. 12 Elisabeth Reynolds of Stephen and Martha.
April 16 Elisabeth Peirson of John and Sarah.
April 30 Mary Wall of Sam¹ and Mary.
June 11 William Higham of Sarah Higham.
June 12 Ann Bunn of Joseph and Sarah.
July 2 Ann Crisp of James and Frances.
July 17 Judith Higham of Robert and Martha.
Aug. 27 Sarah Harvey of John and Sarah.
Sep. 24 Rachael Elnough'of John and Rachael.
Oct. 1 Hannah Howell of Thomas and Hannah.
Dec. 10 Elisabeth Kerridge of William and Elisabeth.

## 1770.

Jan. 7 William Phillips of William and Mary.
Jan. 24 Ann Emerson of Ezekiel and Lydia.
April 1 Robert Eastoe of Samuel and Lydia.
April 1 James Berry of Robert and Elisabeth.
April 10 Harriot Berney of William and Sarah.
May 27 Robert Reynor of Jonathan and Ann.
Aug. 27 Robert Adams of Francis and Elisabeth.
Aug. 27 Reuben Adams of the same.
Aug. 27 Ann Adams of the same.
Sep. 30 Diana Edwards of John and Mary.
Nov. 11 William Gayfer of Richard and Barbara.
Dec. 2 James Garrod of James and Sophia.
Dec. 2 Sarah Smith of William and Susan.

## 1771.

Jan. 6 Jonathan Roddle of Jonathan and Sarah.
Feb. 3 John Harvey of John and Sarah.
Feb. 17 Henry Niker of Henry and Hannah.
Mar. 10 Ann Gayfer of Ric⁴ and Mary.
Mar. 24 Reginald Rabet of Reginald and Mary.

Mar. 30 Charles Noller of Charles and Mary.
Mar. 30 William Skoulding a base child.
April 21 John Elner of John and Rachel.
June 9 Rachel Bunn of Joseph and Sarah.
June 16 Benjamin Balls of Benjamin and Susan.
June 23 John Phillips of William and Mary.
Aug. 20 Thomas Kerrich of William and Elisabeth.
Sep. 1 William Crisp of James and Elisabeth.
Sep. 21 Mary Reynolds of Stephen and Martha.
Sep. 29 Rachel Moyse of Mary a base child.
Nov. 22 John Beley of Robert and Elisabeth.

## 1772.

Jan. 10 Samuel King of Thomas and Bridget.
Mar. 22 Richard Cooper of Richard and Elisabeth.
Mar. 22 Mary Garrod of James and Sophia.
Mar. 29 Mary Phillips of William and Mary.
April 12 Edward Harvey of John and Sarah.
April 19 Elisabeth Rabbett of Reginald and Mary.
April 20 Henry Wright of John and Ann.
April 20 Joseph Wright of the same.
April 20 Ann Wright of the same.
April 20 Sarah Wright of the same.
June 7 Tho⁸ Rodwell of Jonathan and Sarah.
June 14 Samuel Smith of John and Martha.
June 28 John Edwards of Samuel and Elisabeth.
Aug. 16 William Howell of Thomas and Hannah.
Sep. 27 Elisabeth Hill of Robert and Elisabeth.
Oct. 14 Elisabeth Reeve of Henry and Mary.
Oct. 25 Martha Balls of James and Susan.
Nov. 1 Rebecca Lusher of Tho⁸ and Sarah.
Dec. 20 Elisabeth Palmer a base child.
Dec. 20 John Crisp of John and Ann.
Dec. 25 Hannah Reynolds of Roger and Hannah.

## 1773.

Jan. 3 Thomas Nicor of Henry and Hannah.
Jan. 17 Thomas Reeve of Tho⁸ and Elisabeth.
Feb. 28 Mary Smith of William and Susan.
Mar. 13 George Ellnour of John and Rachael.
April 4 John Rabett of Mary and Reginald Rabett, Esq.
June 7 William Kerrich of William and Elisabeth.
July 4 Marg⁴ Smith of William and Elisabeth.
July 4 John Harvey of John and Sarah.
Aug. 8 William Berry of Robert and Elisabeth
Aug. 21 Sam¹ Phillips of William and Mary.
Sep. 26 John Bunn of Joseph and Sarah.
Sep. 28 James Strovger a natural child of Sarah.

## 1774.

Jan. 30 Roger Benstead of Roger and Sarah.
Feb. 18 Elisabeth Brown of Simon and Mary.
Feb. 20 William King of Tho⁸ and Bridgett.
Mar. 6 Elisabeth Ellner of John and Rachael.
Mar. 6 Samuel Edwards of Sam¹ and Elisabeth.

Mar. 13    John Reeve of Tho⁸ and Elisabeth.
Mar. 27    John Aldred of John and Elisabeth.
Mar. 27    Mary Gaifer of Ric^d and Barbara.
May   1    Stephen Balls of Sam^l and Sarah.
May   1    Will^m Garrod of James and Sophia.
June 12    Hannah Hill of Robert and Elisabeth.
June 19    Elisabeth Rabbett of Reginald and Mary.
July 16    Samuel Howard of Sam^l and Mary.
Aug.  7    Will^m Todd of William and Esther.
Aug. 28    Judith Cooper of Ric^d and Elisabeth.
Aug. 28    Elisabeth Phillips of Will^m and Mary.
Sep.  4    Elisabeth Higham of Sam^l and Elisebeth.
Oct. 23    James Balls of James and Susan.
Oct. 30    James Andrews of James and Susan.
Dec. 13    Sarah Kerrich of Will^m and Elisabeth.
Dec. 18    Elisabeth Crisp of James and Martha.

### 1775.

Feb. 19    Tho⁸ Harvey of John and Sarah.
Mar.  5    Tho⁸ Luniss a natural child of Elisabeth.
Mar.  5    Elisabeth Berry of Robert and Elisabeth.
April 9    Thomas Lusher of Thomas and Sarah.
April 23   Elisabeth Reeve of Thomas and Elisabeth.
June  4    Elisabeth Smith of John and Susan.
June 11    George Elnor of John and Rachael.
June 18    Tho⁸ Gaifer of Ric^d and Mary.
June 25    Will^m Rabett of Reginald and Mary.
July 16    Elisabeth Sparrow of Tho⁸ and Elisabeth.
July 16    Mary Howell of Tho⁸ and Hannah.
Aug.  6    Will^m Smith of Will^m and Susan.
Aug.  7    Will^m Knights of Will^m and Sarah.
Aug. 13    Jeremiah Wright of John and Ann.
Aug. 13    Sarah Wright of the same.
Aug. 22    Will^m Alpe of William and Mary.
Nov. 12    John Phillips of William and Mary.
Dec. 24    Richard Rumsby a natural child of Ann Rumsby.
Dec. 24    James Aldred of John and Elisabeth.
Dec. 25    Sam^l Higham of Sam^l and Elisabeth.

### 1776.

Jan. 10    Elisabeth Noller of Charles and Mary.
Jan. 21    James Crisp of James and Martha.
Feb. 21    Ann Rose of Nathaniel and Elisabeth.
Feb. 22    Robert Benstead of Roger and Sarah.
Feb. 24    Phillip Kerridge of Will^m and Elisabeth.
Mar. 17    James Smith natural child of Ann Smith.
April 7    Will^m Fuller of William and Mary.
April 7    Jemima Smith a natural child of Jemima.
April 8    Hannah Collins of Will^m and Hannah.
May 19     Robert Hill of Robert and Elisabeth.
May 19     Elisabeth Harwood of Sam^l and Mary.
May 19     Sarah Rodwell of Jonathan and Sarah.
May 26     Sarah Gaifer of Ric^d and Barbara.
June  9    Frances Hatcher of Will^m and Frances.
June 23    George Rabett of Reginald and Mary.
Sep.  8    Noah Skoulding of Tho⁸ and Mary.

Sep.  8    Rachael Harvey of John and Sarah.
Sep. 15    Robert Swan of Matthew and Elisabeth.
Oct. 13    Hannah Edwards of Sam^l and Elisabeth.
Oct. 13    Elisabeth Bird a natural child of Elisabeth.
Oct. 20    James Crisp of James and Elisabeth.
Nov. 10    John Andrews of James and Sarah.
Nov. 17    Lydia Cooper of Ric^d and Elisabeth.

### 1777.

Feb.  2    Hannah Balls of Benjamin and Susan.
Mar. 12    Will^m Kerrich of Will^m and Elisabeth.
Mar. 16    George Lusher of Tho⁸ and Sarah.
Mar. 23    Wil^m Aldred of John and Elisabeth.
April 20   Tho⁸ Phillips of Wil^m and Mary.
April 20   Robert Alpe of Wil^m and Mary.
April 27   James Smith of Wil^m and Mary.
May   2    Ric^d Gaifer of Ric^d and Mary.
June  1    Robert Strowger a base child of Sarah.
July 27    Mary Todd of William and Esther.
July 27    Hannah Berry of Robert and Elisabeth.
July 27    Lydia Hatcher of William and Frances.
Aug. 10    Edward Rabbett of Reginald and Mary.
Sep. 21    Sarah Sparrow of Tho⁸ and Elisabeth.
Sep. 21    Ann Sparrow of the same.
Oct. 12    Mary Higham of Sam^l and Elisabeth.
Oct. 19    Robert Higham of John and Mary.
Nov. 16    Sarah Smith of James and Elisabeth.

### 1778.

Feb. 15    Robert Moss Fuller of Will^m and Sarah.
April 12   Will^m Brown of Simon and Mary.
May 10     Sarah Garrd of James and Sarah.
May 31     Will. Andrus of James and Sarah.
June 28    Ann Ellnor of John and Rachael.
June 28    Francis Wall a natural child of Mary.
July 12    Sarah Noller of Charles and Mary.
Aug. 16    Elisabeth Swan of Matthew and Elisabeth.
Aug. 30    Mary Reeve of Henry and Mary.
Sep. 22    Robert Hill of Rob^t and Elisabeth.
Oct. 18    John Gillman of Robert and Sarah.
Oct. 25    John Todd of Will^m and Esther.
Nov.  1    Elisabeth Crisp of W^m and Elisabeth.
Nov.  1    Mary Higham of John and Mary.
Nov.  1    John Wright of John and Sarah.
Nov. 29    John Hatcher of Will^m and Frances.
Dec. 25    Will^m Harvey of John and Sarah.

### 1779.

Jan. 10    Ann Gooday of Morris and Elizabeth.
Jan. 10    Hannah Gaifer of Ric^d and Barbara.
Jan. 24    Rob^t Aldred of John and Elisabeth.
Jan. 24    John Rodwell of Jonathan and Sarah.
Feb. 14    Susan Cooper of Ric^d and Elisabeth.
Mar. 21    John Alpe of Wil^m and Mary.
April 4    Tho⁸ Edwards of Sam^l and Elisabeth.

| April | 4 | Philip Philipps of Will[m] and Mary. |
|---|---|---|
| April | 11 | Mary Rabett of Reginald and Mary. |
| April | 18 | John Smith of Will[m] and Susan. |
| July | 25 | Ann Kerrison base born child of Hannah. |
| Aug. | 8 | Mary Nunn of Wil[m] and Sarah. |
| Sep. | 5 | James Smith of Lazarus and Ann. |
| Sep. | 26 | Robert Gilman of Robert and Sarah. |
| Oct. | 3 | Joseph Godfrey of Joseph and Mary. |
| Oct. | 10 | Robert Hill of Robert and Mary. |
| Oct. | 24 | Mary Crisp of Wil[m] and Elisabeth. |
| Oct. | 31 | Robert Cooper of Robert and Elisabeth. |
| Dec. | 12 | Mathu Swain of Mathew and Elisabeth. |
| Dec. | 19 | James Benstead of Roger and Sarah. |
| Dec. | 26 | Sarah Higham of Sam[l] and Elisabeth. |

1780.

| Jan. | 30 | Levi Todd of Wil[m] and Esther. |
|---|---|---|
| Jan. | 30 | John Hatcher of Wil[m] and Frances. |
| Mar. | 5 | Ann Godfrey of Morris and Elisabeth. |
| Mar. | 5 | John Knights of W[m] and Sarah. |
| April | 5 | James Skoulding a natural child of Ann Skoulding. |
| April | 9 | James Reeve of Tho[s] and Elisabeth. |
| May | 4 | Elisabeth Sarah Welton a natural child of Ann Welton. |
| July | 9 | Ann Howard of Sam[l] and Mary. |
| Aug. | 13 | James Fuller of Will[m] and Mary. |
| Sep. | 24 | Anna Kerridge of Will[m] and Mary. |
| Oct. | 15 | Charlotte Cooper of Robert and Elisabeth. |
| Nov. | 12 | Mathew Swan of Mathew and Elisabeth. |
| Nov. | 12 | Mary Wright of Tho[s] and Ann. |
| Dec. | 24 | John Garrod of James and Mary. |

1781.

| Jan. | 11 | Elisabeth Aldred of John and Elisabeth. |
|---|---|---|
| Jan. | 14 | Elisabeth Crisp of James and Elisabeth. |
| Feb. | 4 | Samuel Alpe of Will[m] and Mary. |
| Mar. | 11 | Susan Gooda of Morris and Elisabeth. |
| Mar. | 15 | Susan Gaifer of Richard and Barbara. |
| April | 25 | Sarah Puttock a natural child of Alice. |
| April | 29 | Elisabeth Avis a natural child of Elisabeth. |
| May | 20 | Amy Sarter of John and Mary. |
| May | 27 | Christopher Andrews of James and Sarah. |
| May | 27 | Mary Edwards of Sam[l] and Elisabeth. |
| June | 3 | Will[m] and Edward Rabett of Reginald and Mary. |
| June | 27 | Henry Briggs of Wil[m] and Ann. |
| Aug. | 13 | Martha Crisp of James and Martha. |
| Aug. | 13 | Ann Crisp of the same. |
| Sep. | 16 | Sarah Rodwell of Jonathan and Sarah. |
| Nov. | 18 | Charlotte Higham of Sam[l] and Elisabeth. |
| Dec. | 2 | Mary Bunn a natural child of Jemima Bunn. |

1782.

| Feb. | 3 | Elisabeth Garrod of James and Mary. |
|---|---|---|
| April | 4 | Elisabeth Gilman of Rob[t] and Sarah. |
| April | 21 | Mary Swain of Martha [Mathew, see Dec. 12, 1779, and Nov. 12, 1780] and Elisabeth. |
| May | 5 | Hannah Howard of Robert and Elisabeth. |
| May | 19 | Elizabeth Crisp of William and Eliz[th]. |
| June | 23 | John Howord of Sam[l] and Mary. |
| Aug. | 14 | Phillip Kerrich of William and Elizabeth. |
| Aug. | 18 | Sarah Francis of John and Susan. |
| Aug. | 18 | Eliz[th] Francis of the same. |
| Aug. | 23 | Sarah Elvin of John and Agnes. |
| Sep. | 1 | Eliz[th] Wright of Thomas and Ann. |
| Oct. | 20 | Robert Rabbit of Reginald and Mary. |
| Nov. | 15 | Lydia Eastaugh of Samuel and Martha. |
| Nov. | 26 | Ann Smith of James and Elizb[th]. |
| Dec. | 15 | Christopher Self of Christopher and Mary. |
| Dec. | 24 | Eliz[th] Nun of William and Sarah. |

1783.

| Jan. | 12 | Sarah Reeve of Thomas and Elisabeth. |
|---|---|---|
| Feb. | 2 | Lucy Self of Christopher and Mary. |
| Mar. | 29 | Thomas Fuller of William and Mary. |
| April | 6 | Jeremiah Cooper of Jeremiah and Hannah. |
| April | 13 | Sarah Long d. of Lucy Long, base born child. |
| June | 15 | Elizabeth d. of Henry and Mary Smith; born Feb. 19. |
| June | 15 | William s. of John and Elizabeth Hill. |
| June | 22 | Sarah natural dau'r of Jemima Smith. |
| June | 22 | William s. of Matthew and Eliz[th] Swain. |
| July | 3 | William s. of William and Ann Briggs. |
| Aug. | 3 | John s. of William and Eliz[th] Aldous. |
| Aug. | 10 | Benjamin s. of John and Eliz[th] Aldred. |
| Sep. | 7 | George s. of John and Agnes Elvin. |
| Aug. | 17 | William s. of John and Mary Goose. |
| Sep. | 28 | Rebecca Spalding natural dau'r of Mary Birch. |
| Sep. | 28 | Robert s. of Robert and Rebecca Smith. |

October 1, 1783. M[r] Mease was this day Licenc'd to enter Christenings, Burials, and Marriages in the several Register Books of the Parish of Bramfield without Stamps.

M. D. MEASE.

[*In the Marriage Register Mr Mease signs himself as off[s] min[r], but so frequently that he was probably curate of the parish.*]

| Oct. | 5 | George s. of William Burton and Anne his wife (late Skoulding, spinster); born Sep. 25. Privately. |
|---|---|---|
| Nov. | 2 | John s. of Henry Nicker and Hannah his wife (late Cooper, spinster); born Aug. 1. |

Nov. 2 John s. of James Garrod and Mary his wife (late Rouse, spinster) ; born same day. Privately. (A Pauper. No Tax paid.)

Dec. 7 Nathanael Harmond natural s. of Diana Harmond rec⁴ into the Church. Privately baptized at Wrentham, Dec. 18, 1782.

Dec. 21 Lydia d. of John Smith and Mary his wife (late Berry, spinster) ; born Nov. 20.

Dec. 30 Anne d. of James and Martha Crisp (late Mayhew, spinster) ; born Dec. 23.

1784.

Feb. 8 Mary d. of William Woodyet and Ann his wife (late Cone, spinster) ; born Feb. 3.

Feb. 22 Mary d. of Rob^t Goddard and Marg^t his wife (late Knights, spinster).

Mar. 7 John s. of Joseph Godfrey and Mary his wife (late Harman, spinster) ; born Feb. 25.

Mar. 7 Mary d. of Charles Scrivener and Isabella his wife (late Higham, spinster) ; born Feb. 23. Privately.

(*To be continued.*)

## Armorial Bookplate.

### RACHEL, DUTCHESS OF BEAUFORT, 1706.

Rachel, da. and coheiress of Wriothesley Baptist Noel, Earl of Gainsborough, married 26 Feb. 1706 Henry, second Duke of Beaufort, K.G., by whom she had Henry, Marquis of Worcester, born 26 March 1707 ; John, born and died in 1708 ; and Charles Noel, born 12 Sept. 1709. The Dutchess died 13 Sept. 1709, and was buried at Badminton. Adm'on granted to her husband 20 Oct. 1709. (P.C.C. Adm'ons, 1709, fo. 211.)

### WILL OF HENRY, SECOND DUKE OF BEAUFORT.

Henry Somerset, Duke of Beaufort. Will dated 19 Aug. 1712 ; proved 17 Sept. 1714 by Mary, Duchess of Beaufort. To be buried at Badminton, and not more than £200 to be expended on my funeral. To my wife Mary, Duchess of Beaufort, wearing apparel, jewels, necklaces, etc., the furniture in my houses in London and Middlesex, one of my coaches and six of my coach horses, and £1000 in money. To my eldest son Henry, Marquess of Worcester, the furniture in my houses in the counties of Gloucester and Monmouth and all my plate. All my manors, lands, tenements, etc., in the counties of Middlesex, South'ton, Devon, and Dorset, and my proprietorship, etc., of and in the province of Carolina and the Bahama Islands, to the Hon. James Bertie of Stanwell, Middx., Esq., the Hon. Doddington Greville, Esq., now or late Fellow of All Souls' Coll., Oxford, and Francis Clerk of Weston, co. Oxon, Esq., in trust, to sell the same, and with the proceeds to perform the agreement made on my marriage with my now wife, and to pay my debts, including what I shall at my death owe to my sister the Lady Henrietta Somersett. My estate settled on my eldest son the Marquess of Worcester is charged with the sum of £15,000 as portion for my younger son the Lord Charles Noell Somersett. A monument to be erected at Badminton to me at a cost of £400. Residue of my personal estate to my wife, sole ex'ix. My aforenamed trustees to be guardians of my eldest son the Marquess of Worcester till his age of 21, they to be from time to time advised in his education, etc., by James, Duke of Ormond. My sister the Lady Henrietta Somersett to be guardian of my said younger son the Lord Charles Noell Somersett till his age of 21. If I have any children by Mary, Duchess of Beaufort, my present wife, she to be guardian of the same, and I give such children £5000 each.

BEAUFORT.

Wit., John Busby, Thos. Stephens, Emanuel Lee. (P.C.C., 171 Aston.)

MUTARE VEL TIMERE SPERNO

The Most Noble Rachel Dutchess of Beaufort 1706

# 𝕲𝖊𝖓𝖊𝖆𝖑𝖔𝖌𝖞 𝖔𝖋 𝕭𝖗𝖔𝖜𝖓𝖊.*

## 𝕰𝖛𝖎𝖉𝖊𝖓𝖈𝖊𝖘.

### LONDON.

REGISTERS OF ST. GREGORY BY ST. PAUL'S, LONDON.

*Baptisms.*

1674  Doroythy the daughter of George Browne and of his wife baptized 23 August.
1675  Humfrey the son of Rupert Browne and of Sibill his wife baptized 31 July.
1677-8  Mark the son of Rupert Browne and of Sibill his wife baptized 5 January.
1680  Anne the daughter of George Browne and of Elizabeth his wife baptized 18 August.
1680  Knightly the daughter of Rupart [*sic*] Browne and of Sibyll his wife borne the 30 November, baptized 5 December.
1685  Sibyll the daughter of Rupart Browne and of Sibyell his wife borne the 30 and baptized the 31 May.
1687  Charles the son of Rupart Browne and of Sibyll his wife borne the 27 and baptized 30 March.

*Marriage.*

1664  George Musgrave and Dorothy Browne by a Licence from yͨ Vicar Generall married 24ᵗʰ May 1664.

*Burials.*

1674  Sebell the daughter of Rupert Browne buryed 18 July.
1678  Rupart the son of Rupart Browne buryed 28 October.
1679  Humphery the son of Rupart Browne buryed 2 June.
1679-80  Elizabeth the daughter of Rupart Browne buryed 21 March.
1681  Mark the son of Rupart Browne buryed 4 Jaune [June].
1683  Knightley the daughter of Rupart Browne buryed 19 September.
1686  Mary Tomkinson Mʳ Ruparts [*sic*] browne [*sic*] made [maid] buryed 2 September.
1688  Margaret Knight Mr. Rupart Browne made [maid] buryed 21 July.
1689  Katherin Sherman from Ruperte Browne buryed 25 December.
1690  Luke Allet Mr. Rubart [*sic*] Brones [*sic*] man buryed 23 July.
1691  Frances Stanton Mr. Rupart Browne made [maid] buryed 17 May.
1715  Rupert Barnsley (a Proctor) buryed 19 April.

### VESTRY BOOKS.

At a vestrie held in the parish of St Gregories the 8ᵗʰ day of June Anno Dom. 1683.

It was then ordered and agreed by a full Vestrie That the parishoners of St. Gregories are purposed & doe resolve to remove the Tabernacle of the vnited parishes into St. Gregories Churchyard vntill such tyme as the parish Church shall be rebuilt and for that end that the said parishoners or such p'sons as shalbe by them chosen be hereby impowred to wait upon & [supplio H .... *here erased*] intercede with Sʳ X'opher [Christopher] Wren & such other p'sons as are therein concerned by petition or letter, or otherwise and that the concurrence of the parishoners of St. Mary Magdelens be desired for the removing of the said Tabernacle in St. Gregories Churchyard as above menc'oned.

Ordered alsoe at the same tyme that Sʳ Wᵐ Dodson Knᵗ Mich'o Charlton Esq. Mr. Thomas Bedford Mʳ Robᵗ Bedingfield Capt. John Clark Mʳ Thomas Warren together with the two churchwardens for the tyme being be and they are hereby appointed to take and to pursue the precedent order for the [rebuild *here erased*] removing the Tabernacle in to St. Gregories Churchyard, etc.

[Then follow thirty-four signatures, of which the seventh is :—]

At a vestry held in the Parish of St. Gregories the 13ᵗʰ day of December 1692 for the Choice of ward officers for to serve the year ensuing vizᵗ.

[Here follows list of officers.]

Ordered the same tyme that Cussins the Translator has his Rent paid vntill Easter next not exceeding Tenn shillings or till further order.

[Then follow thirty-one signatures, of which the thirtieth is :—]

[Vestry Book 1702—1730, p. 26.]

September 17th 1708.

At a Vestry held in the united parish Church for the choice of a Parish Clerk in the Roome or Stead of Mr Robert Potter lately deceased, and the Two Candidates being Mr Valentine Acton and Mr Matthew Beardmore and upon a first poll each of them appeared to have 76 hands, the Churchwardens Mr Territt and Mr Joseph Grimstead decided the matter by the addition of their own hands, for and in the behalfe of Mr Beardmore.

Wm Perritt } Ch'wardens.
Joseph Grinstead }

[Signed] *Rupt Browne*

[followed by sixteen signatures].

---

## GREENFORD.

### REGISTERS OF GREENFORD MAGNA.

*Baptisms.*

1711-2   Sibyll daughter of Mr. Rupert & Mrs. Sibyll Browne baptized Mar : 21.

1713   Henrietta Dorothea daughter of Mr. Rupert & Mrs. Sibyll Browne bapt. Mar : 27.

1713-4   Rupert son of Mr. Rupert & Mrs. Sibyll Browne bapt. Mar : 18.

1715   William Frederick son of Rupert Browne Esqr & Mrs. Sibyll Browne bapt. May 20.

1720-1   Knightly daughter of Rupert Browne Esqr & Mrs. Sibyll Browne bapt. Janu : 28.

1722   Crofts son of Rupert Browne Esqr & Mrs. Sibyll Browne bapt. May 25.

*Burials.*

1710   Mrs. Sibyll Browne Decemb. 26 bur. wife of Mr. Rupert Browne was buried.   Affidavit brought Dec : 30.

1711   Mr. Rupert Browne bur. June 6.   Affidavit brought June 6.

1713   Sibyll Browne daughter of Rupert Browne Esqr was bur. April 30.   Affidavit brought May 6.

1713   Henrietta Dorothea an infant bur. June 4.   Affidavit brought June 10.

1739-40   Browne (Rupert Esqr) of . . . . was buried Jan. 24.

12 June 1716.

The Burialls* for the Two years last past were seen & allowed by us his Maties Justices of the Peace for the sd County of Middlesex.

Will : Buttereck [?].

[Signed] } *Rupt Browne*

Inscription upon a tablet to the right of the east window above the communion table in Greenford Magna Church, co. Middlesex.

HERE LYES
THE BODY OF SIBYLL, WIFE
OF RUPERT BROWNE OF THIS PARISH
ESQr; ELDEST DAUGHTER OF HUMPHREY WYRLEY
OF HAMSTEAD-HALL IN Ye COUNTY OF STAFFORD
ESQr, BY SIBYLL HIS WIFE, DAUGHr OF . . . .† MASTERS
IN Ye COUNTY OF KENT ESQr, WHO DEPARTED THIS LIFE
THE 21st OF DECEMBr 1710.   IN Ye 59th
YEAR OF HER AGE.

HERE ALSO LYES Ye BODY OF RUPERT HUSBAND TO Ye
sd SIBYLL, & FOURTH SON OF EDMUND BROWNE OF
BENTLEY HALL IN Ye COUNTY OF DERBY ESQr, BY HIS WIFE
DOROTHY ELDEST‡ DAUGHTER OF Sr EDWARD VERNON OF
SUDBURY IN Ye sd COUNTY WHO DEPARTED THIS LIFE Ye 29th
MAY 1711.   IN Ye 66th YEAR OF HIS AGE.

* Referring to burials in woollen.
† The name here omitted in the inscription was "Christopher."
‡ *Mary* was the *eldest* daughter of Sir Edward Vernon, *Dorothy* was the *second* daughter. *Vide* Visitation of Derbyshire 1661, Coll. of Arms MS., C. 34, fol. xxix, and Browne pedigrees entered at Coll. of Arms.

They left behind them One only Daughter by whom this Monument was Erected thinking nothing could be more lasting to perpetuate y$^e$ memory of them who were y$^e$ best Husband & Wife, best Parents & best Friends, And as they Excell'd in those Quality's soe they did in Charity & Piety.

[And on a black marble gravestone :—]*

" Underneath this Stone lie the Bodies of RUPERT BROWNE, and SIBYLL his wife, which are the same Persons mention'd in the opposite Monument."

The tablet, which is carved in white marble of a very ornate design, is surmounted by a large marble urn, under which are carved and emblazoned in marble the Browne Arms and Crest with a martlet for difference (signifying the fourth son), impaling, Argent, three bugle-horns sable, stringed vert, for WYRLEY. The mantling, with an emblazoned gold fringe, descends from the arms in graceful folds, forming the background of the inscription. The whole is in excellent preservation.

(*To be continued.*)

# The Family of Shuckburgh.†

## Monumental Inscriptions.

*No.* 12.

*Mural monument by Flaxman on south wall, nave, a bas-relief representing death of Lady Shuckburgh-Evelyn, her husband and only daughter weeping.*

On the plinth : FLAXMAN, SCULPTOR.

Arms : SHUCKBURGH-EVELYN, Quarterly of eight : 1 and 8, Quarterly, 1 and 4, SHUCK-BURGH, 2 and 3, EVELYN ; 2, CARBONEL ; 3, NAPTON ; 4, SALCETO ; 5, SYDENHALL ; 6, DYSART ; 7, LUNELL ; impaling EVELYN, Quarterly of six : 1, EVELYN ; 2, AYLARD ; 3, STEVENS ; 4, MEDLEY ; 5, PARTRIDGE ; 6, REYNES.

Shuckburgh crest on dexter side ; Evelyn crest on sinister side.

TO THE REVERED MEMORY
OF A BELOVED WIFE,
JULIA ANNABELLA LADY SHUCKBURGH-EVELYN,
THE ONLY SURVIVING DAUGHTER OF JAMES EVELYN
OF FELBRIDGE IN THE COUNTY OF SURRY ESQ$^r$
AND OF ANNABELLA DAUGHTER OF THO$^s$ MEDLEY
OF BUXTED IN THE COUNTY OF SUSSEX ESQ$^r$
TWO FAMILIES OF APPROVED WORTH
AND MOST RESPECTABLE LINEAGE :—
BUT WHATEVER IS ILLUSTRIOUS IN A LONG LINE OF VIRTUOUS ANCESTRY
WAS FAR OUTSHONE BY HER OWN PRIVATE VIRTUES :
SHE WAS OF THE MOST ENGAGING MANNERS,
OF THE MOST EXTENSIVE BENEVOLENCE,
IN PIETY MOST SINCERE ;
AFFECTIONATE TO ALL HER RELATIONS ; BENEVOLENT TO ALL THE POOR.
IN 1785 SHE BECAME THE ADORED WIFE OF S$^r$ GEORGE SHUCKBURGH BAR$^t$
BY WHOM SHE HAS LEFT ONE ONLY DAUGHTER JULIA.—
BUT IT PLEASED GOD, THAT THIS BOND OF CONJUGAL HAPPINESS,
WHICH HAD NEVER BEEN INTERRUPTED BEFORE,
SHOULD AT LENGTH BE DISSOLVED BY—DEATH !
WHICH, TO THE SINCEREST REGRET OF HER SURROUNDING FAMILY & FRIENDS,
AND THE UNUTTERABLE GRIEF OF HIM,
WHO BEARS THIS TESTIMONY TO HER DISTINGUISH'D WORTH,
TOOK PLACE ON THE 14$^{th}$ OF SEPTEMBER 1797,
AT THE AGE OF 40 YEARS.

* This inscription is given in Le Neve's 'Monumenta Anglicana.' The gravestone, which is at the S.E. corner of the church, is not now visible, as a (moveable) raised floor of chancel has been placed over it.

† Continued from p. 255.

*No. 13.*

*A brass on the south wall of nave immediately under the preceding monument.*

JULIA EVELYN MEDLEY SHUCKBURGH-EVELYN only dau[r] and heir of the above SIR GEO : AUG : W[m] and LADY SHUCKBURGH-EVELYN, married 19 July 1810 the HON : C. C. C. |
JENKINSON of Pitchford Hall Salop. aft[ds] 3[d] and last EARL OF LIVERPOOL. She died 8 April 1814 aged 23 leaving 3 dau[rs] and coheirs, of whom the 2[d] (but eldest to leave |
issue) was SELINA CHARLOTTE VISCOUNTESS MILTON who died 24 Sept : 1883 aged 71 whose eldest son CECIL G. S. FOLJAMBE erects this brass Aug : 1888.

This brass has a border of oak-leaves, on which are six shields : that at the top in the middle, FOLJAMBE, with quarterings—Quarterly of eight, viz., 1, FOLJAMBE ; 2, THORNHAGH ; 3, SAVILE ; 4, JENKINSON, EARL OF LIVERPOOL ; 5, OTTLEY ; 6, SHUCKBURGH ; 7, EVELYN ; 8, MEDLEY—impaling on the dexter side HOWARD, and on sinister side CAVENDISH. The middle shield at the base is SHUCKBURGH, quarterly of nine : 1, SHUCKBURGH ; 2, CARBONELL ; 3, NAPTON ; 4, SALCETO ; 5, SYDENHALL ; 6, DYSART ; 7, LUNELL ; 8, HAYWARD ; 9, Quarterly —1 and 4, EVELYN ; 2 and 3, MEDLEY. On the dexter side at the top is HOWARD, Quarterly of six : 1, HOWARD ; 2, BROTHERTON ; 3, WARREN ; 4, MOWBRAY ; 5, DACRE ; 6, GREYSTOKE (Mr. FOLJAMBE'S first wife) ; and below, HOWARD impaling CAVENDISH (for her father and mother) ; on the sinister side at top is CAVENDISH, Quarterly of six : 1, CAVENDISH ; 2, HARD-WICK ; 3, BOYLE ; 4, CLIFFORD ; 5, SAVILE ; 6, COMPTON (for Mr. FOLJAMBE'S second wife) ; and below, CAVENDISH impaling LAMBTON (for her father and mother).

---

*No. 14.*      *Mural monument on south wall, nave.*

This is in memory of y[e]
Lady GRACE SHUCKBURGH
who was Daughter to S[r] THOMAS HOLT of Afton
neer Bermingham in this County K[t] & Barr[t] &
wife to S[r] RICHARD SHUCKBURGH late Lord of this
Mannor by whome ſhee had Iſſue 6 ſon'es &
3 Daughters & after his deceaſe Viz[t] 27th of Octob[r]
1659. TOOKE to huſband JOHN KEATINGE second
ſon of EDMUND KEATINGE of Norraghmore in y[e]
County of Kildare Eſq[r] then a ſtudent att
Lincolns inn & afterwards Lord Cheife Juſtice of
y[e] Courte of Common Pleas in Ireland, ſhee
departed this life att his houſe in Dublin y[e]
12th of Aprill 1677. and was buryed in y[e]
Chappell of Palmerſton 3 miles diſtant from
that Citty in a new Vault by him there made for
y[t] purpoſe, who alſoe in memory of her singular
Vertue hath Cauſed this ſmall monument to be
ſett vp.

Arms : SHUCKBURGH, impaling, Azure, two bars and in chief a cross patée fitchée or, HOLT.

---

The corbels supporting the roof of the nave have the following shields on them : North side, beginning at west end : 1, England, with a bordure argent ; 2, Gules, a cross moline argent ; 3, SHUCKBURGH, with Ulster badge. South side, beginning at east end : 1, England, with a bordure argent ; 2, Argent, a cross gules ; 3, SHUCKBURGH, with Ulster badge.

At the porch is a slab as you enter, which is about 6 feet 4 inches long and 3 feet wide, with matrices of brasses ; two shields at the top, then an inscription, then a larger shield, and below three sons on the dexter side and five daughters on the sinister side. So this probably was the original slab with brasses to Anthony Shuckburgh and Anne his wife, now fixed on a slab in chancel—I on key plan.

There are two carved stones built into the wall of the south gable of the mortuary chapel, outside, one above and one below the blocked two-light window. They have skull and cross-bones, hour-glass, etc., on them, and are said to have formed part of Shuckburgh monuments.

In the churchyard, north of the church, are three stone coffin lids with crosses on them, one a large one, and two smaller ones, besides portions of a fourth. These are said to belong to the early Shuckburghs, and to have been formerly inside the church.

To the west of the church in the churchyard is the tomb of Captain and Mrs. Laugharne, with the following inscription :—

> In
> affectionate
> and
> pious memory of
>
> *{ At end of tomb.}*

> Mary Amelia
> Wife of Thomas Lamb Polden Laugharne Cap<sup>t</sup> R.N.
> and Daughter of Sir Stewkley Shuckburgh Bar<sup>t</sup>
> Born xvii April mdccxciii called hence xx Feb. mdccclviii
> she sleeps deeply loved, dearly remembered.
>
> *{ South side of tomb.}*

> Thomas Lamb Polden Laugharne
> of Laugharne, Carmarthenshire; Esq.
> Senior Captain, Royal Navy & Greenwich Hospital:
> Born in June mdcclxxxvi, Departed xxx Sep, mdccclxiij.
> Loved, Respected, Regretted.
>
> *{ North side.}*

> I Believe in the Resurrection
> of the Dead
> and the Life everlasting. Amen.
>
> *{ Round tomb.}*

Lower Shuckburgh Church was rebuilt in 1862, and has no memorial in it.
(*To be continued.*)

---

## MONUMENTAL INSCRIPTIONS FROM THE BURIAL-GROUND OF ST. GEORGE, HANOVER SQUARE, NEAR MARBLE ARCH.*

Elizabeth, wife of Edward Bailey, of Mount Street, in this parish, died June 14, 1849, in her 66<sup>th</sup> year.
Edward Bailey, husband of the above, died Sep. 14, 1853, in his 70<sup>th</sup> year.

. . . . [Barclay] Surgeon . . . . S<sup>t</sup> George, Hanover Square . . . . October [1817 ?]
. . . .
John Barclay, Jun<sup>r</sup>, his son, born Aug. 1800, died Jan. 1801.
[Grissee?] Barclay, 3<sup>rd</sup> daughter of the Rev. Patrick Barclay, late of [Zetland or Zealand ?], and niece of the above named D<sup>r</sup> Barclay, born 8 Feb. 1788, died [. . . .] 1807.

M<sup>r</sup> John Henderson, late of Liverpool, merchant, died Dec. 30, 1803, aged 41. His remains were removed from this burial ground to the Cemetery at Kensall Green, 16 April 1849, and placed in the same tomb with those of Mary, his widow, died June 23, 1848.

Rev. John Griffith, Clerk, Rector of Landawke and Pendine in the county of Caermarthen, died Dec. 8, 1805, aged 62.

Charlotte, wife of M<sup>r</sup> William Adams, of North Audley Street, died 10 April 1825, aged 35.

* Continued from p. 264.

[M<sup>r</sup> or M<sup>rs</sup>?] Spencer West, died Nov. 23, 1831, aged 27.

M<sup>r</sup> Thomas Archall, died April 2, 1814, aged 72.

Robert Johnson, died Oct. 21, 1802, aged 71.

M<sup>r</sup> Thomas Wake, late of the Queen's Palace, died March 28, 1801, aged 65.
[A . . . .] Wake [wife of the above] . . . . May 1827. *[Part of inscription hidden by a footstone.]*

M<sup>rs</sup> Maria Dupasquier, late of Pimlico, died Sep. 26, 1802, aged 37.

Michael Woollett, late of Pimlico, died April 5, 1806, in his 37<sup>th</sup> year.

M<sup>r</sup> Charles Peregrine, late of Milford, in the county of Pembroke, died July 7, 1816, in his 16<sup>th</sup> year.

M<sup>rs</sup> Johanna Halse, Relict of John Halse, Esquire, late of Truro, in Cornwall, died 15 June 1807, aged 77.

John Nixon, son of John & Mary Nixon, of Pimlico, died Aug. 16, 1809, aged 12 years & 8 months.

M<sup>rs</sup> Ann Cushing, wife of James Cushing, of Down Street, Piccadilly, died June 19, 1827, aged 46.

Mary, wife of William Dean, died Jan. 21, 1815, aged 53.
James, son of the above, who died in his infancy.
Sarah, wife of W. J. S<sup>t</sup> Leger, & daughter of the above, who died in childbed, Aug. 28, 1830, aged 22.
James Eccott, son in law of the above, died Oct. 3, 1831. *[Rest of inscription hidden by a footstone.]*

M<sup>rs</sup> Hannah Davies, wife of M<sup>r</sup> Herbert Davies of Pimlico, died Aug. 16 1817, aged 56.
The above named M<sup>r</sup> Herbert Davies, died May 31, 1833, aged 71.
Their son Herbert Davies, died July 12, 1829, aged 31.

M<sup>r</sup> John Clark, died Nov. 10, 1807, aged 48.

In memory of the children of James & Elizabeth Linton, of New Norfolk Street.
Ann, died April 29, 1815, aged 10 months & 8 days.
Thomas, died Dec. 7, 1826, aged 2 years & 10 days.
Also the above named M<sup>rs</sup> Elizabeth Linton, born Sep. 11, 1786, died Jan. 1, 1831.

Mary, wife of James Nicholas, of Knightsbridge, died 24 Jan. 1809 . . . *[Part of inscription hidden by a footstone.]*

M<sup>rs</sup> Frances Ann Weightman, died 31 Oct. 1803, aged 32.
[This stone was placed by her affectionate] [sister ?] Mary [Breckley ?].

Miss Caroline Goodchild, daughter of the late James Goodchild, of this parish. She died March 22, 1809, aged 26.
Henry, son of John & Rebeckah Goodchild, & nephew of the above Caroline Goodchild, died June 13, 1824, aged 7 months, 14 days.
Elizabeth Goodchild, died June 12, 1826, aged 11 months, 5 days.
M<sup>r</sup> John Goodchild, surgeon, father of the above named children, born Jan. 18, 1779, died Dec. 24, 1843.

*(To be continued.)*

# Hopkins of Llanfihangel Ystern Llewern.*

[It may be noted that the regular list of entries commences with the year 1695, and that the entries prior to that date were evidently then (in 1695) put in by the Rector, the Rev. William Hopkins. The rest of the page was left blank, and the succeeding births of his own and his brother Onias's children were placed there as they occurred instead of with the entries of the other parishioners.]

Jo. filius Oniæ Hopkins natus 18° Octor an'o 1685.

Nicholas filius Oniæ Hopkins natus 3° Junij an'o 1688.

Eliza. filia Oniæ Hopkins nata 3° Januarij 1689.

David filius Oniæ Hopkins natus 25° Decembr an'o 1692.

Anna filia Oniæ Hopkins nata 27 10bris 1695.

Gul. Hopkins filius Jo. Hopkins rector de Langell natus die Martis vic° 7mo die junij [sic] an'o Domnl 1659.
    [This refers to the birth of the rector, William Hopkins.]

Sarah Probyn filia Gul. Probyn de Newland uxor ejusdem Gul. Hopkins nata 27° Maij vid. die dominica in albis an'o 1672.

[Sarah, the wife of Wm. Hopkins, the rector, was not born here, though her husband entered the date of her birth in his book. She was born at Newland in the county of Gloucester, and in the Newland Register her birth is given as 26th May, and her baptism as 27th, 1672.]

Gul. Hopkins cler. et Sarah Probyn conjuncti matrimonio 9° 7bris 1692.

Eliz. filia Gul. Hopkins cler. baptizat. 13° februar. nata 2do ejusdem mensis an'o 1693.

Gul. filius Gul. Hopkins natus 2do baptizat. 11 februar. an'o 1695.

Maria filia Gul. Hopkins cler. nata 2do baptizat. 9° februar. 1697.

Gul. filius Gul. Hopkins cler. sepultus 3° August. an'o 1698.

Sarah filia Gul. Hopkins cler. nata 12° 7bris 1699.

Jo. filius Gul. Hopkins cler. baptizat. 3° 7bris an'o 1702.

Gul. filius Gul. Hopkins cler. baptizat. 25° Januar. an'o 1704.

Edmundus filius Gul. Hopkins cler. natus necnon baptizat. 29°      1706.

1695   Anna filia Oniæ Hopkins nata fuit 27° die Decembris an'o sup'dicto baptizata fuit 29° die ejusdem mensis. [This entry occurs also above, but without the date of baptism.]

1697   Elizabetha Hopkins vidua parochia de Langattock vibon avell sepulta fuit 9° die februar. an'o sup'dicto.

Anna Hopkins vid. sepulta fuit 15° Maij anno supr'dicto.

1708   Gulielmus Hopkins cler. sepultus fuit 4to die Novembris anno pr'dict.

1709   Anna filia Oniæ Hopkins sepulta fuit 5to die Septembris anno prædicto.

1709   [Here occurs the signature " Jno Hopkins churchwarden for the year 1709."]

1710   Sarah Hopkins vidua sepulta est decimo sexto die septembris An'o Prædicto.

1713   Elizabetha Hopkins Parochiâ de Lantilio Gressonny spinstr sepulta fuit vicessimo die Aprilis An'o Prædicto.

1714   Gulielmus filius Johannis Hopkins baptizatus est nono die Julij Anno supradicto.

1715   Johannes filius Johannis Hopkins baptizatus est vicessimo primo die Julij An'o supradicto.

1717   Jacobus filius Johannis Hopkins baptizatus est secundo die Junij Anno Prædicto.

1720   Maria filia Nicholai Hopkins baptizata fuit undecimo die Octobris Anno supradicto.

1722   Onias Hopkins sepultus est decimo quinto die Martij anno 17 2/2 .

Thomas filius Johannis Hopkins baptizatus est sexto die septembris Anno Prædicto.

Anna filia Nicholai Hopkins Baptizata fuit vicessimo octavo die octobris Anno Prædicto.

* Continued from p. 262.

1723   Richardus filius Johannis Hopkins baptizatus est vicessimo septimo die
       Octobris Anno Prædicto.
1724   Thomas nec non Richardus filij Johannis Hopkins sepulti fuere decimo sexto
       die Julij Anno Prædicto.
       David filius Johannis Hopkins baptizatus est vicessimo septimo die Novem-
       bris An'o supradicto.
1726   Maria uxor Joh. Hopkins sepulta fuit decimo tertio die Januarij Anno supra-
       dicto.
       Elizabetha filia Nicolai Hopkins Baptizata fuit decimo sexto die Novembris.
       Elizabetha filia Nicolai Hopkins sepulta fuit decimo tertio die decembris
       An'o Prædicto.
1727   Anna Hopkins vidua Parochiâ de Langattock vibon avell, nec non nuper de
       hac Parochia, sepulta fuit tertio die Octobris An'o Prædicto.
       Nicholaus filius Nicholai Hopkins Baptizatus est decimo septimo die decem-
       bris Anno supradicto (vid.) 1727.
1730   David filius Nicholai Hopkins Baptizatus est quarto die decembris Anno
       prædicto vid. 1730.
1812   April 30ᵗʰ   Mʳˢ Elizabeth Hopkins was buried 91 yʳˢ.

FROM THE PARISH REGISTERS OF LLANGATTOCK LLINGOED, MONMOUTHSHIRE.
1771   Burᵈ David Hopkins, Nov. 29.

---

FROM A RENT ROLL OF SIR WILLIAM HERBERT, 1ST EARL OF PEMBROKE, of
his Manors of " St. Michael " [Llanfihangel] and " Styrnllewyrn " [Ystern
Llewyrn], and other manors in the parish of Llantilio Crossenny in the county
of Monmouth, for the year 1459.

---

Watkin ap David ap Rune tenet unam parcellam terre continentem dimidium ⎫
acris quondam Nicholi ap Hopkyn jacentem super ripam rivuli de Blaen ⎬ ijᵈ
Llymon in uno crofto ibidem vocato Crofte Roppert ad finem borealem ⎭
dicti crofti et reddit per ann. ad eosd. term.

The brook here mentioned is still known as the Llyman, which means *naked*,
but there is no place now called Croft Robert. Blaen Llyman would mean properly
the source of the Llyman.
This MS. was copied verbatim by the late Mr. Thos. Wakeman of the Graig,
and it is from his copy that this extract has been made.

---

MONUMENTS IN THE CHURCH OF LLANFIHANGEL YSTERN LLEWERN TO THE
HOPKINS FAMILY.

*A handsome monument, formerly in the south-west corner of the chancel, now on the
north wall of the nave.*

GVL' FIL' GVL' HOPKINS RECTOR'
HVJVS PAR' SEPVLTVS 3'MO DIE
AVG'STI A' D' 1698 ÆTAT' 3'TIO.

Above are a skull and cross-bones carved, and the motto : QUOD TIBI HOC ALTERI.

---

*On the south wall of the nave.*

Sacred to the Memory of John Hopkins, Gent. late
of this Parish who died Novʳ yᵉ 12ᵗʰ 1749 aged 64.
Also of Wᵐ Hopkins Gent. Son of yᵉ above who
died April yᵉ 18ᵗʰ 1751 aged 36.
Also of Elizabeth Relict of Wᵐ Hopkins who died
April the 26ᵗʰ 1812 Aged 90.

Above are the arms : Sable, on a chevron between three pistols argent as many roses gules.
Crest : A castle argent.

(*To be continued.*)

# The Register Book of Bramfield, co. Suffolk.*

### 1784.

April 25   Robert s. of James Andrews and Sarah his wife (late Pattison, spinster); born March 11.

April 25   Marianne natural d. of Sarah Smith; born Nov. 12, 1783.

May 18   Richard s. of Christopher and Mary Self (late Harpur, spinster).

May 21   Thomas s. of Thomas and Ann Wright (late Balls, spinster); born same day. Privately.

May 30   Sarah d. of William Crisp and Elizabeth his wife (late Adkins, spinster); born March 30. Publickly.

May 30   George s. of William Nunn and Sarah his wife (late Easter, spinster); born Feb. 21.

May 30   George s. of William and Elizabeth Kerridge (late Kerridge, spinster); born March 2.

June 6   William s. of Henry Briggs and Sarah his wife, of Blythburgh (late Goulby, spinster); born Dec. 24, 1782.

June 13   Robert s. of Robert Gillman and Sarah his wife (late Savage, spinster); born May 23. Privately.

July 11   Mary d. of John Hill and Elizabeth his wife (late Fuller, spinster); born June 28.

Aug. 8   Robert s. of John Harvey and Sarah his wife (late Catchpole, spinster); born Ap. 17.

Nov. 21   Samuel s. of Samuel and Alice Armant (late Puttock, spinster); born Oct. 1.

Nov. 7   Robert s. of Matthew Swain and Elizabeth his wife (late Clarke, spinster).

Nov. 17   Elizabeth d. of John Elvin and Agnes his wife (late Pearl, spinster).

Dec. 26   John s. of Lionel Harmant and Diana his wife (late Watts, spinster); born Dec. 2.

Dec. 26   Daniel s. of Daniel Spalding and Mary his wife (late Birch, spinster); born Nov. 19.

### 1785.

Jan. 23   Robert s. of Robert Churchyard and Mary his wife (late Dowsing, spinster).

Mar. 1   Mary d. of William Burton and Ann his wife (late Skoulding, spinster); born Feb. 15.

April 17   Susanna Crisp natural d. of Mary Snelling; born March 20.

April 17   James s. of William Fuller and Mary his wife (late Amys, spinster).

April 24   John Read s. of Daniel Borrett and Alice his wife (late Read, spinster); born March 2.

May 3   James s. of James Smith and Elizabeth his wife (late Jacob, spinster).

May 18   Susan d. of Robert Smith and Rebecca his wife (late Redhead, spinster); born May 12.

May 15   Susan d. of Ann Baker, spinster; born same day.

June 20   Marianne d. of Joseph Goose and Mary his wife (late Mountain, spinster); born Oct. 6, 1784.

June 26   William s. of John Crisp and Ann his wife (late Reynolds, spinster); born June 22.

July 31   William s. of Samuel Barnby and Hannah his wife (late Gayfer, spinster); born July 22.

Aug. 7   William Henry s. of Reginald Rabbett, Esq., and Mary his wife (late Newson, spinster); born July 18.

Aug. 14   Lucy d. of John Sarter and Mary his wife (late Stammers, spinster); born Aug. 11.

Oct. 9   Thomas s. of John Elvin and Agnes his wife (late Pearle, spinster); born Sep. 27.

Oct. 12   John s. of John Hill and Eliz$^{th}$ his wife (late Fuller, spinster); born Sep. 12. Privately.

Dec. 11   Martha d. of William and Ann Woodyard (late Cone, spinster); born Dec. 7. Privately. [*Woodyet, Feb.* 18, 1784.]

### 1786.

Jan. 1   Elizabeth d. of Samuel Edwards and Eliz$^{th}$ his wife (late Grice, spinster); born Sep. 2, 1784.

Mar. 12   Hannah d. of William Girling and Hannah his wife (late Alexander, spinster); born Jan. 20.

Mar. 12   Elizabeth natural d. of Phœbe Branch; born Feb. 6.

Mar. 12   Charlotte d. of Thomas and Ann Wright (late Balls, spinster); born Feb. 27.

April 2   Elizabeth Freeman natural d. of Mary Barney; born March 24. Privately.

May 14   Thomas s. of John and Elizabeth Aldred (late List, spinster). Privately.

May 21   Rachel d. of Daniel Spalding and Mary his wife (late Burch, spinster); born Ap. 22.

July 3   Mary d. of Robert Briggs and Mary his wife (late Briggs, spinster); born July 1. Privately.

July 26   John s. of Robert Smith and Rebecca his wife (late Reddit, spinster); born May 28.

Oct. 22   Thomas s. of John Elvin and Agnes his wife (late Pearle, spinster); born same day. Privately.

Nov. 5   Mary d. of John Gosling and Eliz$^{th}$ his wife (late Cooper, spinster); born Oct. 24.

Nov. 19   William s. of Samuel Edwards and Elizabeth his wife (late Grice, spinster); born Sep. 24. Privately.

Dec. 10   Sarah d. of James Skoulding and Sarah his wife (late Wright, spinster); born Dec. 7. Privately.

* Continued from p. 276.

1787.

Jan. 14 James s. of John Eades and Sarah his wife (late Crisp, spinster) ; born Oct. 27, 1786. Privately.

Feb. 4 Daniel s. of Lionel Harman and Diana his wife (late Watts, spinster) ; born Nov. 18, 1786.

Feb. 8 Mary d. of James Mills and Lucy his wife (late Long, spinster) ; born same day.

Feb. 11 James s. of Samuel Higham and Mary his wife (late Stegall, spinster) ; born same day. Privately.

Feb. 11 Thomas s. of Samuel Armant and Alice his wife (late Puttock, spinster) ; born Feb. 2.

Feb. 18 Samuel s. of James Garrod and Mary his wife (late Roos, spinster) ; born June 21, 1786.

April 8 James s. of Samuel Barnby and Hannah his wife (late Gayfer, spinster) ; born Jan. 2.

May 2 Hannah d. of Thomas Lane and Sarah his wife (late Trip, spinster) ; born Ap. 8. Privately.

May 13 Elizabeth d. of James Smith and Elizabeth his wife (late Danbroke, spinster).

June 10 William s. of William and Priscilla Denney (late Self, spinster) ; born May 29. Privately.

June 24 Richard s. of Mary Clarke, spinster ; born May 25, 1786.

July 8 Ziporah Godfrey d. of James Crisp and Martha his wife (late Mayhew, spinster) ; born June 26. Privately.

July 22 Edward s. of John Crisp and Mary his wife (late Snelling, spinster) ; born June 24.

Aug. 5 Henry s. of John Aldred and Elizabeth his wife (late List, spinster) ; born June 19.

Aug. 5 Mary d. of Ann Skoulding, widow ; born July 25.

Aug. 19 Henry s. of Robert Briggs and Mary his wife (late Briggs, spinster) ; born Aug. 13. Privately.

Sep. 2 Ann d. of Robert Smith and Rebecca his wife (late Reddit, spinster) ; born Aug. 29. Privately. Publickly Sep. 30, 1789.

Oct. 23 John s. of John Elvin and Agnes his wife (late Pearle, spinster) ; born Oct. 1.

Nov. 25 Martha d. of Robert Fieldbank and Martha his wife (late Amiss, spinster) ; born Nov. 16. Privately. Publickly May 31, 1789.

Dec. 16 Elizabeth d. of William Hawes and Elizabeth his wife (late Dutt, spinster) ; born Dec. 13. Privately.

Dec. 30 William s. of William Chaseton and Ann his wife (late Wade, spinster) ; born Dec. 20. Privately.

1788.

Feb. 3 Eve d. of Thomas Wright and Ann his wife (late Balls, spinster) ; born Dec. 24, 1787.

Feb. 10 James s. of James Aldred and Elizabeth his wife (late Borrett, spinster) ; born Feb. 3. Privately.

Feb. 26 Mary d. of John Sarter and Mary his wife (late Stammers, spinster) ; born Feb. 17. Privately.

Mar. 16 Lydia d. of John Eades and Sarah his wife (late Crisp, spinster); born Mar 1.

Mar. 30 James s. of Robert Churchyard and Mary his wife (late Dowsing, spinster) ; born March 26. Privately.

Mar. 30 William s. of Robert Peck and Elizabeth his wife (late Beaumont, spinster) ; born Nov. 27, 1787.

Mar. 30 Lydia d. of William Woodyard and Ann his wife (late Cone, spinster) ; born March 28. Privately.

April 6 Sarah d. of William Fuller and Mary his wife (late Amoss, spinster) ; born March 17.

Nov. 13 Elizabeth d. of David Borrett and Alice his wife (late Read, spinster) ; born Sep. 16.

Oct. 12 Susannah d. of Wm Balls and Mary his wife (late Cooper, spinster) ; born Oct. 10. Privately.

Oct. 12 Mary d. of Samuel Harvey and Fanny his wife (late Gayfer, spinster) ; born Oct. 11. Privately.

Nov. 23 John s. of Wm Peirson and Elizabeth his wife (late Reynolds, spinster) ; born Nov. 17. Privately.

1789.

Jan. 3 William s. of Wm Aldiss and Elizabeth his wife (late Taylor, spinster) ; born Dec. 23, 1788. Privately.

Jan. 4 John natural son of Ann Baker ; born Oct 20, 1787.

Feb. 1 Bridget d. of Lionel Harman and Diana his wife (late Watts, spinster) ; born Dec. 6, 1788. Privately. Publickly Ap. 12, 1789.

Feb. 15 John Aldis natural son of Elizabeth Frances ; born Feb. 10. Privately.

Feb. 15 Henry s. of Henry Wright and Mary his wife (late Adams, spinster) ; born Aug. 12, 1788.

Mar. 15 Hannah d. of James Smith and Elizabeth his wife (late Jacob, spinster) ; born Feb. 18. Privately. Publickly Ap. 18, 1790.

April 12 Maria Lyddy d. of John Easter and Anne his wife (late Crisp, spinster) ; born Ap. 9. Privately. Publickly Jan. 10, 1790.

April 12 James s. of James Adams and Mary his wife (late Ward, spinster) ; born March 28. Privately.

April 19 Sarah d. of Robert Smith and Rebecca his wife (late Reddit, spinster) ; born Ap. 14. Privately. Publickly Sep. 30, 1789.

April 19 John s. of Henry Tillet and Jane his wife (late Almond, spinster) ; born May 15, 1788.

May 31 Mary d. of James Aldrid and Elizabeth his wife (late Borrett, spinster) ; born Sep. 27, 1788.

June 14  Henry s. of Henry Smith and Mary his wife (late Savage, spinster) ; born Jan. 23.

July  5  Mary d. of Robert Fieldbank and Martha his wife (late Amos, spinster) ; born June [blank].

Sep. 27  Maria Anne d. of Robert Cooper and Elizabeth his wife (late Burnham, spinster) ; born Sep. 24. Privately. Publickly Dec. 27.

Oct.  4  Mary d. of Samuel Harber and Frances his wife (late Gayfer, spinster) ; born Oct. 4, 1788.

Nov. 15  Mary d. of William Greenard and Mary his wife (late Manning, spinster) ; born Nov. 13. Privately. Publickly May 23, 1790.

Jan.  2  William s. of William Aldis and Elizabeth his wife (late Taylor) ; born Dec. 23, 1788. Privately. Publickly Jan. 15, 1790.

1790.

Jan.  3  Mary Anne natural d. of Elizabeth Kerridge ; born May 25, 1789.

Jan. 10  John natural s. of Hannah Harwood ; born Dec. 23, 1789, Privately.

Jan. 17  Henry s. of William Haws and Elizabeth his wife (late Dut, spinster) ; born Jan. 14. Privately.

Feb.  8  Agnes d. of John Elwin and Agnes his wife (late Pearle, spinster) ; born Jan. 8.

Feb. 28  Edmund s. of Daniel Spalding and Mary his wife (late Birch, spinster) ; born Feb. 1. Privately. Publickly July 24, 1791.

Feb. 28  Stephen s. of William Denny and Priscilla his wife (late Self) ; born Feb. 2. Privately.

Mar.  7  John s. of Samuel Barnaby and Hannah his wife (late Gayfer, spinster) ; born Feb. 26, 1789.

Mar. 21  John s. of Samuel Armant and Alice his wife (late Puttock, spinster) ; born Feb. 10.

Mar. 28  Susan d. of Thomas Wright and Ann his wife (late Balls, spinster) ; born Mar. 7. Privately. Publickly Dec. 25, 1792.

April  4  Esau and Bela sons of James Crisp and Martha his wife (late Mayhew, spinster) ; born March 28. Privately. Publickly Ap. 17, 1791.

April 11  Charlotte d. of James Garrod and Mary his wife (late Roos, spinster) ; born April 6. Privately. Rec^d into the Church Aug. 25, 1793.

April 18  Mary d. of Elizabeth Gosling ; born Feb. 15.

May  2  Richard s. of John Aldred and Elizabeth his wife (late List, spinster) ; born Dec. 11, 1789.

May 23  Matthew s. of Thomas Reeve and Elizabeth his wife (late Goodwin, spinster) ; born April 26, 1788.

July  4  James s. of James Aldred and Elizabeth his wife (late Borrett, spinster) ; born June 30. Privately.

July 21  Lucy d. of Samuel Philpot and Elizabeth his wife (late Blandon, spinster); born Aug. 29, 1788.

July 26  William s. of William Peirson and Elizabeth his wife (late Reynolds, spinster) ; born July 21. Privately. Publickly Aug. 8.

Aug.  1  Anne d. of William Cheston and Anne his wife (late Wade, spinster) ; born July 26. Privately. Publickly Sep. 19.

Aug.  1  Mary d. of Henry Wright and Mary his wife (late Adams, spinster) ; born same day. Privately. Publickly Jan. 19, 1794.

Aug. 12  Anne d. of Robert Briggs and Mary his wife (late Briggs, spinster) ; born Aug. 11. Privately. Publickly Dec. 30, 1792.

Sep. 19  Charles s. of William Cheston and Ann his wife (late Wade, spinster) ; born July 20.

Oct.  3  Hannah d. of John Eades and Sarah his wife (late Crisp, spinster) ; born Sep. 27. Privately.

Oct.  3  Henry s. of William Balls and Mary his wife (late Cooper, spinster); born Dec. 27, 1789. Privately.

Oct.  7  Mary Anne d. of Samuel Higham and Mary his wife (late Stegall, spinster); born Sep, 27. Privately.

Dec. 28  Elizabeth Sparrow natural d. of Rachael Wright ; born Dec. 7. Privately.

1791.

Feb.  6  Leonard natural s. of Lydia Bickers; born Feb. 1. Privately.

Mar.  6  Elizabeth d. of John Elwin and Agnes his wife (late Pearle, spinster) ; born Feb. 21.

Mar.  6  Elizabeth d. of Samuel Barnby and Hannah his wife (late Gayfer, spinster) ; born Feb. 21.

Mar. 13  Robert s. of Joseph Amis and Mary his wife (late Roberts, spinster) ; born Feb. 2. Privately.

Mar. 20  William s. of Lionel Harman and Diana his wife (late Watts, spinster) ; born Dec. 18, 1790.

Mar. 27  William natural s. of Deborah Marshall ; born March 17.

Oct.  1  James s. of Robert Churchyard and Mary his wife (late Dowsing, spinster) ; born March 26, 1788.

Oct.  2  James natural s. of Rachael Bunn ; born Oct. 1. Privately.

Oct.  2  [blank] of James Aldred and Elizabeth his wife (late Borrett, spinster) ; born Aug. 7.

Nov. 27  William s. of William Greenard and Mary his wife (late Maynard, spinster) ; born Nov. 4. Privately. Publickly July 13, 1794.

Dec. 31  John s. of Robert Cornish and Mary his wife (late Elmy, spinster) ; born Dec. 23. Privately. Publickly March 18, 1792.

T 2

1792.

Jan. 8 Ann d. of John Wright and Ann his wife (late Pearl, spinster) ; born Dec. 11, 1791.

Jan. 29 George s. of Daniel Spalding and Mary his wife (late Birch, spinster) ; born Dec. 25, 1791. Privately.

Jan. 8 Elizabeth natural d. of Mary Berney ; born March 24, 1786.

Feb. 6 William natural s. of Hannah Harwood ; born Jan. 10.

Feb. 19 Sarah d. of William Puttock and Rebecca his wife (late Reeve, spinster) ; born Feb. 6 [see 1793-1796].

Mar. 11 Martha d. of Robert Smith and Rebecca his wife (late Redhead, spinster) ; born Feb. 27. Privately.

Mar. 11 Samuel s. of Samuel Harber and Frances his wife (late Gayfer, spinster) ; born March 1. Privately.

Mar. 18 John natural s. of Ann Bunn ; born Feb. 15. Privately.

Mar. 18 Harriet natural d. of Mary Cooper ; born March 9.

April 29 William s. of John Smith and Jane his wife (late Hall, spinster) ; born Ap. 17. Privately.

July 15 John s. of William Peirson and Elizabeth his wife (late Reynolds, spinster) ; born July 9. Privately. Publickly June 30, 1794.

July 22 Mary d. of William Hawes and Elizabeth his wife (late Dutt, spinster) ; born June 21.

Oct. 20 Sarah d. of James Mayhew and Mary his wife (late Ling, spinster) ; born Oct. 8. Privately.

Oct. 20 Benjamin s. of William Balls and Mary his wife (late Cooper, spinster) ; born Oct. 6. Privately. Publickly Nov. 11.

Dec. 30 Stephen s. of Thomas Wright and Ann his wife (late Balls, spinster) ; born Nov. 19. Privately.

Dec. 30 Sophia d. of Robert Briggs and Mary his wife (late Briggs, spinster) ; born Nov. 20.

1793.

Jan. 27 Thomas s. of Lionel Harmant and Diana his wife (late Watts, spinster) ; born Dec. 30, 1792.

Feb. 3 Sarah d. of Samuel Barnaby and Hannah his wife (late Capper, spinster) ; born Jan. 7. Privately.

Jan. 3 John s. of John Elvin and Agnes his wife (late Pearle, spinster) ; born Nov. 24, 1792.

Feb. 10 James s. of James Gorble and Mary his wife (late Aldred, spinster) ; born Jan. 14. Privately.

Feb. 10 Mary d. of William Kerrich and Elizabeth his wife (late Kerrich, spinster) ; born Jan. 26.

April 14 Sarah Ann d. of Henry Wright and Mary his wife (late Adams, spinster) ; born Dec. 23, 1792. Privately. Publickly Jan. 19, 1794.

May 5 Samuel Steggal s. of Samuel Higham and Mary his wife (late Steggal, spinster) ; born Ap. 24. Privately. Recd into Church Sep. 29.

May 5 James s. of James Smith and Elizabeth his wife (late Jacobs, spinster) ; born Ap. 20. Privately.

May 12 Mary Ann d. of William Winter and Mary his wife (late Wilson, spinster) ; born May 7. Privately.

May 19 Daniel s. of George Smith and Susanna his wife (late Chambers, spinster) ; born Ap. 15.

June 23 Sarah d. of Samuel Barnaby and Hannah his wife (late Gayfer, spinster) ; born May 17.

June 23 James s. of Samuel Armant and Alice his wife (late Puttock, spinster) ; born June 18. Privately. Recd into the Church Aug. 4.

July 21 Isaac s. of John Aldred and Elizabeth his wife (late List, spinster) ; born June 10.

Aug. 11 David s. of James Garrod and Lydia his wife (late Roos, spinster) ; born July 28. Privately. Recd into the Church Aug. 25.

Aug. 18 Robert s. of Thomas Hyem and Charlotte his wife (late Alldiss, spinster) ; born Aug. 15. Privately.

Aug. 25 Elizabeth d. of James Garrod and Mary his wife (late Roos, spinster) ; born 1789.

Aug. 25 Esther d. of the same ; born 1791.

Aug. 25 Thomas s. of William Balls and Mary his wife (late Cooper, spinster) ; born Aug. 16. Privately. Recd into the Church Sep. 15.

Sep. 15 William s. of William Mantle and Mary his wife (late Buxton, spinster) ; born Ap. 12, 1792.

Sep. 15 Lydia d. of John Eastaugh and Ann his wife (late Crisp, spinster) ; born Sep. 13. Privately. Recd into the Church Oct. 6.

Oct. 6 Ann d. of John Smith and Jane his wife (late Hall, spinster) ; born Sep. 30. Privately.

Oct. 27 Hannah d. of John Ellis and Rachel his wife (late Bunn, spinster) ; born Oct. 25. Privately.

Nov. 24 Katharine d. of Robert Smith and Rebecca his wife (late Reddit, spinster) ; born Nov. 19. Privately.

Nov. 24 Richard s. of Richard Puttock and Rebecca his wife (late Reeve, spinster) ; born Nov. 22. Privately. Publickly Jan. 19, 1794. [His name is given as William Feb. 19, 1792.]

Dec. 1 Harriet Manning d. of William Greenwood and Mary his wife (late Manning, spinster) ; born Nov 15. Privately.

Dec. 1 John s. of John Feltham and Ann his wife (late Reeve, spinster) ; born Nov. 15. Privately.

(*To be continued.*)

# Genealogy of Browne.*

## Evidences.

### ST. STEPHEN'S, HERTFORD.

REGISTERS OF ST. STEPHEN'S, CO. HERTFORD.

[*Baptisms deficient* 1656—1717. *Burials deficient* 1691—1724.]

CHURCHWARDENS' ACCOUNTS.

Nou: 16, 1690.   Collected for New-Alresford in Ham'psh: .......... £0  13  8
[Then follows in Edmund Browne's handwriting.]

Rec^d x^s & xiiij^d & a Suspicious halfe Crown together xiijs. & viij 23^d ffeb^ry 1690-1 Edm : Browne R^egr.

1704.   Collected for the Protestants of the Principality of Orange & Paid to M^r Edmund Brown Register the sum'e of three pounds nineteen shillings May 17^th 1704.

Collected for the widows and Orphans of the Seaman Cast away in the storm & paid to M^r Edmund Brown Register the sum'e of one pound one shilling & nine pence November 5^th 1704.

Inscription upon a large blue slab of slate in pavement of the chancel of St. Stephen's Church, co. Hertford, opposite the Communion rails.

Here lyes the Body of EDMOND BROWNE Gent: Third son of EDMOND BROWNE of HUNGARY BENTLEY in y^e County of Derby Esq^r by his wife Dorothy Eldest† Daughter of S^r Edward Vernon of Sudbury Hall in y^e Said County Kn^t He departed this Life July 27, 1716, Aged 78 years.

Here also lyes Interr'd Elizabeth wife of y^e Said EDMOND BROWNE who departed this Life May 20, 1711, aged 85 years.

Above the inscription are the following arms and crest :—BROWNE, impaling .... a fess between three talbots' heads erased .... for ....

This slab, which is very little defaced by wear, is at present entirely covered with matting.

---

## INSCRIPTIONS AT WITHINGTON.

The following copies of inscriptions are taken from tablets now fixed upon the north and south walls of the interior of Withington Church tower, having previously stood in the chancel, from whence they were removed at the recent restoration of the church.‡

[South wall, marble tablet.]

Elizabeth the Daughter of the Rev^nd CORBET BROWNE Rector was buried May 14^th 1788 in the 19^th year of her age.

The Rev^d CORBET BROWNE, Rector of Upton Magna and Withington was buried Nov. 6^th 1807 in the 80^th year of his age ; and JANE wife of the above Rev^d CORBET BROWNE died October 18^th 1822 aged 89 years.   " The memory of the just is blessed "—Proverbs 10, 7.

[North wall, stone tablet.]

This Memorial is erected in affectionate remembrance of SARAH the beloved wife of the Reverend CORBET BROWNE Rector of Upton Magna cum Withington also to the above Rev^d CORBET BROWNE who departed this life April 17^th 1854, aged 77 years.

[In the Churchyard.   Flat stone with raised and fluted cross.]

I. In memory of SUSANNAH, wife of RUPERT BROWNE, of Onslow, (3^rd Son of the Rev. CORBET BROWNE of Upton Magna cum Withington,) who died January 27^th 1854, aged 50 years. Also RUPERT BROWNE, Husband of the above who died June 13^th 1869 aged 64 years.

In memory of JOHN, Son of M^r RUPERT BROWNE, of Onslow who died January 3^rd 1837 aged 2 months.

[Flat stone, raised cross.]

II. In memory of CORBET SPENCER BROWNE, late of Withington, Died 1^st March 1869, aged 68 years.  Also of ANNE, widow of CORBET SPENCER BROWNE.  Died October 2^nd 1874 aged 77 years.

[Upright head stone, formed at top as a cross with crown.]

III. In affectionate remembrance of CHARLES FLEMYNG BROWNE Son of the late Rev^d CORBET BROWNE Rector of Upton Magna cum Withington Died October 1^st 1860, aged 45 years.  " Thy Brother shall rise again."

---

* Continued from p. 279.        † *Vide* note, p. 278.
‡ The earlier generations of this branch of the family are interred beneath pavement of the chancel; the later generations are buried in the churchyard.

## Wills.

Copy of the Will of RALPH BROWNE of Caverswall, co. Stafford.    Dated 1669 ; proved 1670.

[Lichfield.]

IN THE NAME OF GOD AMEN The nineth day of October in the one and twentieth yeare of the Raigne of our Soveraigne Lord Charles the second by the Grace of God of England &c. Annoq. D'm' 1669 I Raphe Browne of Cookeshill in the parish of Careswell in County of Stafford Gent : beinge weake in body but of sound and p'fecte memory (praised be God) doe make this my last Will and Testament in manner and forme followinge Impr'is I bequeath my soule into the handes of Almighty God my Maker hopeinge by the onely merritts of Jesus Christ my Savio' to obtaine life everlastinge and my bodye to the earth to be buried in the parish Church of Careswell And as to the disposinge of my worldly estate I give and devise the same as followeth viz' : I give and bequeath unto my son in law William Langley Clearke five shillings and to my son in law Henery Smith five shillings and to my son in law Thomas Launder five shillings which I give to every of my said son in lawes in full of any childes parte or other claime they or any of them cann or may make or p'tend to my goods or personall estate. It'm I give unto my daughter Jane Langley wife of the said William Langley fifty poundes to be paid to her owne handes for her owne use and benifitt. It'm I give unto my daughter Marie Clowes one shillinge and to her two daughters Marie and Sarah the sume of fifty poundes to be equally divided betweene them. It'm I give unto my daughter Abigall Smith wife of the said Henery Smith tenn poundes to be paid to her owne handes for her owne use and benifitt. It'm I give unto my daughter Sarah Launder wife of the said Thomas Launder fifty poundes to be paide to her owne handes for her owne proper use and benifitt. It'm I give unto my grandchildren Allexander Joyce Ellin and Sarah Howe children of my son in law Allexander Howe deceased twenty poundes to be equally divided amongst them. It'm I give unto Katherin Abraham Three poundes which my will is shall be paid to her att such time or times and in such manner as to my executor shall seeme fittest. It'm I give and bequeath unto these my tenants and servants followinge (that is to saie) Marie Meare Widowe Thomas Asburye John Walker the younger Richard Swinnerton Thomas Ansell Mary Spooner Widowe Lawrance Wheywall Thomas Fallowes twenty shillinges apeece. It'm I give unto my loveinge friend M' Thomas Bagnall of Newcastle fifty shillinges and to my lovinge friend George Boulton of Forsbrooke fifty shillings. It'm I give and devise unto my grandchilde Raphe Browne and his heires and assignes for ever all that messuage cottage or tenem' scituate in Meare which I lately purchased of and from one Raphe Haslam togeather with the Backsides and Garden and appurten'nces thereunto appertaineinge. It'm I give unto my said Grandchilde Raphe Browne one silver watch one silver Boule one silver gilded salt six silver spoones one clocke one Jacke and all my bedsteds and bedinge linen and wollen tables trunkes formes chests coffers and arkes and allsoe all my brasse and pewter and all my cartes geares plowes loose boardes and all other my husbandry waire whatsoever which my Will is shall be delivered to him within one moneth next after hee shall accomplish the age of one and twenty yeares. It'm my will is that the severall legacyes before herein by mee bequeathed for payment whereof no time or other order is p'ticularly appoynted shall bee paid within one yeare next after my decease and that if any of the said legatees bee not att such age that my executor upon paym' thereof to them cannot be lawfully discharged that then my said executor shall pay the severall legacyes of such of the said legatees to whom paym' to them will not be a good discharge to him to the parent or parents guardian or guardians of such legatee or legatees which shall be a sufficient paym' of the said legacye or legacies given to such legatee or legatees by this my last Will and the said parent or parents guardian or guardians to be accountable to the said legatee or legatees for the same. It'm my debts legacies and funerall expences being paid and discharged I give all the rest and residue of my goods cattles and chattles whatsoever to me in my owne right belonginge to my grandchilde John Clowes and I doe hereby nom'ate ordaine and appoynt the said John Clowes sole Executor of this my last Will and testam' and my Will is and charge to my said executor that he take care that the severall sumes of money and legacies given by my deceased sonne John Browne which are secured to bee paid by a lease made to mee for one thousand yeares of Hartwell Farme by my said son in law William Langley be truly paid and discharged and the trust thereby and by my said sonne in me reposed be in all thinges faithfully p'formed and executed And I doe hereby desire and appoynt the said Thomas Bagnall and George Boulton overseers of this my last Will and testam' and give assistance to my said executor in the p'formance thereof. In witnes whereof to this my last Will and testam' I the said Raphe Browne have putt my hand and seale the day and yeare first above written.

*Ralph Browne*

Sealed signed & delivered in p'sence of Thom. Porter Rob' Austin George Boulton John Lomax.

MEM' The Testator Ralph Browne beinge in p'fecte minde and memorye having a desire to make a Codicill or addiconall Will did on Thersday the seaventh day of Aprill last past declare these words following or the like in effect I would have (if my executor John Clows please) my daughter Langley to have tenne poundes my daughter Launder tenne pounds and my two grandchildren Mary and Sarah Clowes tenne poundes to be equally devided betwixt them and to every other grandchilde ten shillings apiece w'ch words he declared in the p'sence & hearinge of George Boulton.

Proved 13th May 1670 by John Clowes the sole Executor.  Amount of Inventory £446 19s. 7d.

*(To be continued.)*

## MONUMENTAL INSCRIPTIONS FROM THE BURIAL-GROUND OF ST. GEORGE, HANOVER SQUARE, NEAR MARBLE ARCH.*

Miss Louisa Vion, died 30 Jan. 1809, aged 21.
Mrs Mary Louisa Le Grand, died 24 Sep. 1815, aged 56.

William Elvin, died May 3, 1811, in his 17th year.

Mrs Sarah Tibson, Widow : who was cut off in the full possession of her faculties by a sudden, but not unexpected death, 31st March 1808, at the age of 88 years, above forty of which were spent in the same family.

Mr Charles Callcott, died 20 March 1834, aged 47.
Mrs Eleanor Callcott, wife of the above, died 7 March 1852, in her 72nd year.

Mr Charles Alabaster, died Feb. 22, 1820, aged 44.
Mr Henry Alabaster, son of the above, died June 16, 1834, aged 23.
Mary Ann Alabaster, his infant daughter.
Mary, wife of Charles & mother of Henry Alabaster, died June 12, 1838, aged 52.

Evelina, daughter of Charles & Mary Alabaster, Piccadilly ; died Jan. 7, 1815, aged 5 years & 2 months.
Charles Alabaster, brother of the above, aged 1 year & 8 months.
Mary, daughter of James Chaloner & Harriet Alabaster, & grand daughter of the above, ob. Oct. 1832, ætat. 1 year & 1 month.

Mr Francis Elsbee, died April 2, 1814, aged 29.
Mrs Elizabeth Anstey, wife of Mr Thomas Anstey and mother of the above, died Aug. 26, 1815, aged 52.

Mr William Walker, of Old Bond Street, died Jan. 19, 1803, aged 40.

Mrs Ann Farrow, of Park Village, Regents Park, died Sep. 18, 1847, aged 57.
Mr Thomas Aguther Howe, nephew of the above, died July 26, 1847, aged 19.

Mrs Mary Perrin, died Feb. 14, 1834, aged 55.

Mrs Mary Smithson, died 30 Aug. [1826] in her 40th year.

John Milliner, died Feb. 16, 1823, aged 38.
Henry John, son of the above, died April 11, 1823, aged 14 months.
Eliza Mary, daughter of the above, died Jan. 19, 1838, aged 20.
David Marshall [. . . . 20th] 1848.  [*Rest of inscription hidden by a footstone.*]

William Enoch, of St Georges Parack (*sic*), in this parish, died May 25, 1825, aged 45.

* Continued from p. 282.

Elizabeth Barnett, late of Berkley Square, died Oct. 12, 1800, aged 62.
M$^r$ Richard Barnett, died April 6, 1804, aged 68.

———

M$^{rs}$ Elizabeth Revell, wife of M$^r$ Thomas Revell, of Farm Street Mews, Berkeley
    Square, died 12 March 1826, in her 30$^{th}$ year.
John Revell, son of the above, died March 2, 1833, in his 13$^{th}$ year.

———

M$^{rs}$ Mary Wootten, died 30 Dec. [1821 ?] aged 76.

———

Robert Seller, late of Peterhead, in Scotland, merchant, who died in this parish 14
    Feb. 1800, in his 28$^{th}$ year.

———

M$^r$ Philip Hales, died 4 June 1800, aged 35.

———

M$^{rs}$ Frances Milley, died Nov. 10 1816, aged 59.
Edward Milley, husband of the above, died June 24 1826, in his 84$^{th}$ year.

———

M$^r$ Edward Bramah, of Pimlico, in this parish, died July 13, 1806, in his 55$^{th}$ year.
Also Robert [Bramah ?] .... of the above .... 1807.   [*Rest of inscription hidden
    by a footstone.*]

———

Edward son of Richard & Mary Peachey, Hanover Square, died Dec. [26 ?] 1798,
    aged 5 years & [6 ?] months.
M$^{rs}$ Ann Nicholas, grandmother of the above, died Jan. 19, 1811, aged 75.

———

M$^r$ John Newman, late of this parish, died June 4 1805, aged 50.
Elizabeth Shayle, died June 10 1808, aged 32.

———

M$^r$ Thomas Rice, late of Pimlico, died Sep. 10 1808, aged 45.

———

M$^{rs}$ Elizabeth Churton, wife of M$^r$ [W ? ....] of Oxford Street . . . . . . . .

———

M$^r$ John Rastall, died Dec. 31, 1826, aged 74.
Elizabeth, relict of the above, died Jan. 26, 1847, aged 86.

———

M$^{rs}$ Ann Watts, died Nov. 14, 1807, aged 62.
M$^r$ James Watts, died Dec. 4, 1821, aged 73.
Mary Watts, daughter of the above named James & Ann Watts, died 15 Aug.
    1828, aged 46.

———

Near this place are interred the remains of Samuel French, and Peace French, wife
    of the above.
Also beneath this, (*sic*) their daughter Catherine French, died 11 Nov. 1830, aged 38.
M$^{rs}$ Frances Rattenbury, died Jan. 24, 1837, aged 71.

———

M$^r$ Thomas Chapman, died Dec. 23, 1827, aged 74.
M$^r$ Thomas Chapman, son of the above, died March 2, 1825, aged [. .] years.
Also M$^{rs}$ Mary [ . . . . . . . . 1839].

———

M$^{rs}$ Sarah Hamilton, late of S$^t$ James's Street, died June 5, 1802, aged 61.
M$^{rs}$ Ann Hamilton, died April 3, 1794, aged 80.

———

Lieutenant Colonel Commandant William Troughton, died 27 April 1799, aged 32.

(*To be continued.*)

SEMPER PARATUS

## CONFIRMATION OF ARMS BY ROBERT COOKE, CLARENCEUX, TO WILLIAM RODES OF SKYRKET, CO. YORK, 1585.

To all and singular as well nobles and gentles as others to whom theys presents shall come Robert Cooke esquyer alias Clarenceux king of Armes sendeth greytyng in o' lord god everlasting. That Wheras W'l<sup>m</sup> Rodes of Skyrket in the County of Yorke gentleman is descendyd of an auncient howse beryng Armes hath therefore required me the sayd Clarencieulx to set forth under my hand & seale of office the Arms of his ancestors as he may lawfully bayer them w'out preiudice of any other of the name or family In consideracon ther of I have thought good to set forth the said Armes as they appear in the Registers & Records of my offis that is to say the fylde silver on a crosse engreled betwyn iiij lyones rampant gules fyve bessants and for the Creasts on the helme on a wreath silver and gules a ounce seant sables besante w' a collar silver manteled gules dobeled silver as more pleanly appereth depictyd in the margint w' armes and crest and every part and parcel therof I the sayd Clarencieulx kyng of Armes do ratifye and confirme unto the sayd Wil' Rodes gentleman & his posterity & he and they the same to use bayr and shew forth accordyng to the laws of Armes at al tymes hereafter at his and their libertye and pleasure. In witnesse whereof I the sayd Clarenceulx &c.

Datyd the xxi<sup>th</sup> of August a° 1585.

I hereby certify that the above is a true extract from the Records of Her Majesty's College of Arms, London. Witness my hand this twenty-third day of July 1885.

(Signed) H. MURRAY LANE, Chester Herald, Registrar.

## GRANT OF ARMS BY SIR ISAAC HEARD, GARTER, TO JAMES ROYDS OF MOUNT FALINGE, CO. LANCASTER, 1820.

To all and singular to whom these Presents shall come Sir Isaac Heard Kn<sup>t</sup> Garter Principal King of Arms and Ralph Bigland Esquire Norroy King of Arms of the North Parts of England from the River Trent Northwards send Greeting: Whereas James Royds of Mount Falinge in the Parish of Rochdale in the County Palatine of Lancaster, Esquire, One of the Deputy Lieutenants of the said County, second son of John Royds late of Falinge in the said Parish, Merchant, deceased, hath represented unto Henry-Thomas Howard-Molyneux-Howard, Esquire, commonly called the Right Honourable Lord Henry-Thomas Howard-Molyneux-Howard, Deputy (with the Royal approbation) to his Brother the Most Noble Bernard-Edward, Duke of Norfolk, Earl Marshal and Hereditary Marshal of England, that his Ancestors for several Generations resided in the neighbourhood of Halifax in the County of York and have borne Armorial Ensigns which upon enquiry he finds were granted in the year 1585 to William Rodes then of Skircoates near Halifax, but being unable at this distance of time to prove his Descent from the said William Rodes and unwilling to continue the use of the said Armorial Ensigns without unquestionable Authority, he therefore requested the favour of His Lordship's Warrant for our granting and confirming the same with such variations as may be necessary to be borne by him and his Descendants and by the other Descendants of his said late Father, according to the Laws of Arms. And forasmuch as His Lordship did by Warrant under his Hand and Seal bearing date the Twentieth day of September last Authorize and direct Us to grant and confirm such Armorial Ensigns accordingly. Know Ye therefore that We the said Garter and Norroy in pursuance of His Lordship's Warrant and by virtue of the Letters Patent of our several Offices to each of Us respectively granted have devised and do by these Presents grant and confirm unto the said James Royds the Arms following that is to say Ermine on a cross engrailed between four Lions rampant Gules a tilting Spear erect Or and four Bezants, And for the Crest on a Wreath of the Colours a Leopard sejant Sable bezantée gorged with a Collar Argent the dexter fore-paw resting on a Pheon Or as the same are in the margin hereof more plainly depicted to be borne and used for ever hereafter by him the said James Royds and his descendants and by the other descendants of his said late Father with due and proper differences according to the Laws of Arms. In Witness whereof We the said Garter and Norroy Kings of Arms have to these Presents subscribed our Names and affixed the Seals of our several Offices this Sixth day of October in the first Year of the Reign of Our Sovereign Lord George the Fourth by the Grace of God of the United Kingdom of Great Britain and Ireland King Defender of the Faith, &c. and in the Year of our Lord one thousand eight hundred and twenty.

> I hereby certify the above to be faithfully extracted from the Records of the Heralds' College, London, this fourth day of January 1889.
>
> H. FARNHAM BURKE, Somerset Herald.

# Hopkins of Llanfihangel Ystern Llewern.*

FROM SIR JOHN MACLEAN'S MSS.

Bigland's 'Gloucestershire'—Newland.

*On a neat marble monument in the chancel.*

John Howell, Esq. | On the 24th of August 1778 | in the 91st year of his age, | drew his last breath without a groan | and crowned a long and well-spent life | by a death of peace | To whose Memory this was erected | by his grandson | Edmund Probyn Esq. | of this Place.

Arms : Sable, a lion rampant-reguardant argent.

*On flat stone in chancel.*

Edmund Probyn, Esq. | died 21st Sept. 1793 aged 34.

*On flat stone in middle aisle.*

Hic jacet quod mortale Gulielmi Probyn | Hujusæ Villæ, Newland, gen. | obiit undecimo die Februarii | Anno Dom. 1702, anno ætatis 85.

Here lyeth the body of | Edward Probyn, Gent. | second son of Mr William Probyn | and Sarah his wife ; he died the | 23rd day of Jan : 1732 aged 27 years.

Anne, the wife of William Probyn | died May 12, 1740, aged 35.
Also the body of | Mr Wm Probyn, | who departed this life the 27th day of | Sept. 1761, aged 58 years.

Frances, daughter of William and | Elizabeth Probyn, and sister to the | Right Hon. Chief Baron Probyn, | died June 22, 1766, aged 90.

Here lyeth the body of | Mary Probyn, widow, | late wife of William Probyn, | who died 7 day of March 1673.
Also the bodies of | Thomas and Anne | their children.

Here lyeth the body of | William Probyn, Gent. | who departed this life the 2d day of | December 1724.

Here lyeth the body of | John Probyn, A.M. son of William | Probyn of Newland, Gent. | died 10 March 1736 aged 27.

Mrs Sarah Williams | died 12th July 1777, aged 76.

* Continued from p. 284.

In Memory of | William Probyn, Gent. | of Newland who died the 7<sup>th</sup> Nov. | 1756 aged 82.

M<sup>rs</sup> Frances Probyn | died Oct. 27, 1786 aged 81.

To the pious memory of | M<sup>rs</sup> Hannah Probyn, of this place, | who died the 10<sup>th</sup> day of Feb. 1711 | aged 67 years.

To the pious memory of | M<sup>rs</sup> Blanch Probyn, of this Place | who died the 10<sup>th</sup> of August, 1741 | aged 60 years.

The remains of | M<sup>rs</sup> Elizabeth Hopkins, spinster | lie interred near this place, | She died the 9<sup>th</sup> day of March 1759 | Aged 62 years.

Here lyeth the body of | Jane Hopkins of the Parish of | Llanvihangle, Gent. who departed | this life the 18<sup>th</sup> day of May, 1722.

Here lyeth the body of | Anne relict of Abraham Casson, | Rector of Sutton, near Hereford, | who departed this life 21<sup>st</sup> day of Nov. | 1683.
Also in memory of | Edith wife of William Probyn gent. | of Newland who departed this life | 2<sup>d</sup> day of Nov. 1729, aged 80.

*In Probyn's Chapel, on a large neat mural monument with the bust of Lord Chief Baron Probyn.*

Arms : Ermine, on a fesse gules a lion passant-guardant argent, on a canton of the second a rose or.

Sacred to the Memory of | Sir Edmund Probyn, Knt. | Lord Chief Baron of his Majesty's | Court of Exchequer, who died the 17th | day of May 1742 | Dame Elizabeth Probyn, | the widow and relict of Sir Edmund | Probyn, the daughter of Sir John Blen | cowe, Knt. one of the Justices of | Common Pleas, at Westminster | died the 22d day of October 1749 | and at her particular desire was buried | in this Chancel near the remains of her | deceased husband.

John Probyn Esq. nephew and heir | of Sir Edmund Probyn died March 22 | 1773 aged 70. | Anne his wife daughter of John | Howell Esqre died the 18 Nov. | 1784 aged 72 | They left one son and one daughter | Edmund Probyn Esq. of this place | and Elizabeth Anne, his sister.

*On another monument.*

Arms as before.

In memory of William Probyn | of Newland, Gent. and Elizabeth | his wife. He was son and heir of | Edmund Probyn of Newland Gent. | by Mary his wife the daughter of | Thomas Symonds of Clewerwal, Gent. | and grandson & heir of John Probyn | of Newland Gent. by Mary his wife | one of the daughters of Christopher | Hall of High Meadow Esq. He died | 11 day of Feb. 1702 aged 85 and lies | buried in the middle aisle of this church. | She was the eldest daughter of Ed | mund Bond of Walford in the County | of Hereford Gent. and had issue by her | said husband, five daughters Mary, | Sarah, Hannah, Frances, and Blanch | and two sons Edmund Probyn now of | the Middle Temple, Barrister at Law, | and William Probyn a captain of one | of his Majesty's Ships of Warr. She died | the 19<sup>th</sup> day of Dec. 1714 aged 70 | and lies buried in this chancel.

*On a monument in the south aisle.*

Arms : Quarterly, 1 and 4, Sable, on a chevron between three pistols or three roses gules ; 2 and 3, Ermine, on a fesse gules a lion passant-guardant argent, on a canton gules a mullet or.

In memory of William Hopkins | of London Merchant who died the | 12th April 1763 aged 59 | And of Sarah his wife daughter of | Walter Williams of Dingestow in the | County of Monmouth Esqʳ who died | the 14 day of February 1749 aged 48.

---

*In the church porch.*

Richard youngest son of Edmund | Probyn Esqʳ and Sophia his wife | died the 3ʳᵈ day of Jan. 1794, in the | 9ᵗʰ year of his age after a year's | tiresome illness, which he bore with | uncommon fortitude.

---

*In the churchyard on flat and head stones.*

John Watkins died 1 Aug. 1723 also his daughter Mary wife of
James Howell of Redbrook died 27 Oct. 1722.
James Howell died 20 Sep. 1772 aged 68.
James Howell died 8 March 1788 aged 49.
John Howell of Clowerwall died 6 Feb. 1753 aged 55.
Sarah wife of John Howell of Clowerwall 7 Nov. 1768 aged 59.

(*To be continued.*)

---

# The Family of Shuckburgh.*

## Monumental Inscriptions.

### FARTHINGHOE CHURCH.

*On a slab.*

Elizabeth Shuckburgh, daughter of Richard Shuckburgh, gent., and Anne ; born 1 May, buried 7 May 1677.

---

H.S.E.
ANTONIVS SHUKBVRGH†
de Farthinghoe
Filius
JOHANNIS SHUKBURGH
de Shukburgh
in Agro Warwiceni
Armigeri
Qui mortalitatis Exuvias
Decembris xv MDCLXXVIII.
Annoq' Ætatis LXXX.
deposuit.
Una cum Conjuge sua
Elizabetha
Quæ decimo partu laborans
octavo die Novembris
MDCLIII.
& ætatis xxxv.
expiravit.

---

\* Continued from p. 281.
† Anthony Shuckburgh was third son (but second surviving) of John Shuckburgh of Shuckburgh by Margery Midlemore.

## LONGBOROUGH CHURCH, GLOUCESTERSHIRE.

*Blue slab, 40 inches by 33 inches, on floor of south side of nave, next to reading desk and pulpit, and close to chancel arch.*

| | |
|---|---|
| Here Lyeth y<sup>e</sup> Body of Cha: Shuckburgh* Eldest Son of Cha: Shuckburgh Esq<sup>r</sup> Who Dy'd Dec<sup>b</sup> 28<sup>th</sup> 1719 Aged one Month | and Also the Body of Cha : Shuckburgh second Son of C: Shuckburg<sup>h</sup> Esq<sup>r</sup> Who Dy'd Mar: y<sup>e</sup> 18<sup>th</sup> 172¼ Aged 3 Months 2 Weeks & 3<sup>d</sup>. |

Serius aut citius sedem properamus ad Unam.

| | |
|---|---|
| Arabella 2<sup>d</sup> Daugh<sup>t</sup> & Sarah his Wife Ætatis 7° Months | of Cha: Shuckburg<sup>h</sup> Dy'd July 22<sup>d</sup> 1730 and 1 Day. |

---

## NAPTON CHURCH.

*Brass, north wall, chancel, under figure of a man in civilian costume, kneeling at a desk, on which is an open Bible.*

HERE LYETH ALSO INTERRED IN THIS TOMBE BE-
NEÁTH Y<sup>e</sup> BODY OF JOHN SHVKBVRGH GENT.
ELDEST SONE OF JOHN SHVKBVRGH OF OVER-
SHVKBVRGH IN Y<sup>e</sup> COUNTY OF WARR. ESQ<sup>r</sup>
WHO DEP'TED THIS LIFE VNMARRIED Y<sup>e</sup> 16 DAY
OF OCT<sup>r</sup> IN Y<sup>e</sup> 37 YEARE OF HIS AGE
AN'O D'NI 1625.
HOMO QVASI BVLLA.

On a brass shield inserted in north wall, below the last, are the arms of SHUCKBURGH quartered with those of NAPTON.

The north transept of Napton Church (the mortuary chapel of the Napton family) belongs to the Shuckburghs, and there are two recessed tombs on the north side, and an old slab at the east side. The north window, three-light, is filled with modern stained glass, the arms of John of Gaunt, Duke of Lancaster, at the top, with his name and title on a scroll under, and date 1342, and in the centre a shield quarterly of eight : 1, SHUCKBURGH ; 2, CARBONELL ; 3, NAPTON ; 4, SALCETO ; 5, SYDENHALL ; 6, DYSART ; 7, LUNELL ; 8, SHUCKBURGH. The names of quarterings on a scroll under, and dates 1156 and 1412.

Below, in centre light, is a shield : SHUCKBURGH impaling NAPTON, with names under on a scroll, and date 1328.

In left-hand light : Arms of Napton, and on a scroll, Adam de Napton, and date 1156.

In right-hand light a shield : NAPTON impaling BEAUCHAMP, EARL OF WARWICK. Scroll with names and date 1307.

A lancet on west side of this transept has stained glass in it, a geometrical pattern.

A three-light east window of the same transept has a representation of St. Lawrence in it, and next to it a lancet with a small piece of old stained glass with these words on it :—

SHVCKBVRGH
AND
MEDLEY
1573.

---

* Charles Shuckburgh, according to this inscription, died 28 Dec. 1719, and, according to the Register, was buried 27 Dec. 1719.

## ST. MARY'S CHURCH, WARWICK.

*North transept, on a flat marble slab.*

Here lie the remains of Sir Charles Shuckburgh Bart
Late of Upper Shuckburgh in the County of Warwick
He died Aug^t 10^th 1773, in the 52^nd year of his age.
And also of his Brother Richard Shuckburgh Esq^r
Lieut: Col^l in the 1^st Regiment of Foot Guards
He died Sept 3^rd 1772, aged 45.
Lady Shuckburgh died Oct: 8^th 1776.

---

## HARROW CHURCH.

*Mural, south transept.*

Here lyeth y^e Body
of
S^r Edward Waldo Knight.
A kind and faithful Husband,
A tender and provident Father,
A constant and hearty Friend,
A regular and sincere Christian :
Eminently distinguished
by an uninterrupted course
of
Charity & Humility
and not less so,
by an inviolable fidelity,
in keeping sacred his Word.
universally esteem'd when alive
and lamented when dead
to his pious Memory
Elizabeth
Daugh^r of S^r R^d Shuckburgh of Shuckburgh
in
Warwickshire,
His third Wife,
out of a dutyful affection
erected this marble Table
He died the 4^th of Feb. MDCCVII Aged LXXVI.

*(To be continued.)*

---

## GENEALOGICAL MEMORANDA RELATING TO

# The Family of Evelyn.

---

### WILLS.*

Rebecca Evelyn al's Rollenson, late of S^t Paul, Covent Garden, Midd^x, dec^d. Adm'on 14 May 1703 to her husband George Evelyn, Esq. (Adm'ons 1703, fo. 101.)

* Continued from p. 271.

JOHN EVELYN of Wotton, co. Surrey, Esq.   Will dat. 25 Feb. 1705; proved 18 March 1705 (1705-6) by his grandson John Evelyn, Esq.   To be buried at Wotton.   My late son John Evelyn, dec<sup>d</sup>.   To my wife Mary certain plate, jewels, my coach and horses, and the lease of my dwelling house in Dover Street, S<sup>t</sup> Martin's in the Fields, with the furniture, etc., except the furniture belonging to the apartments of my dau. in law Evelyn which my s<sup>d</sup> dau. in law is to have.   To my granddau. Elizabeth Evelyn an annuity of £14 for life out of H.M. Exchequer. All my books at Wotton and Dover Street to my grandson John Evelyn, Esq., he to be sole ex'or and residuary legatee.   Wit., Jos. Sherwood, John Strickland, Thomas Bedingfeld.   (60 Eedes.)

MARY EVELYN, widow of John Evelyn (Sylva Evelyn), late of Wotton, co. Surrey, Esq.   Will dat. 9 Feb. 1708; proved 26 Feb. 1708 (1708-9) by her grandson John Evelyn.   "My body to be deposited in the parish church of Wotton aforesaid in a stone coffin and sett near that of my dear Husband whose love and freindshipp I was happy in fifty-eight yeares nine months but by God's providence left a desconsolate widow the seaven and twentyeth day of ffebruary 1705 in the 71<sup>st</sup> year of my age."   Poor of Wotton £5, and of Deptford £5.   The lease and furniture of my house in Dover Street to my dau<sup>r</sup> Martha Evelyn for life, rem<sup>r</sup> to my grandson John Evelyn.   To my s<sup>d</sup> dau<sup>r</sup> Martha the ring given me by Lady Stonehouse.   To my son William Draper 20 guineas for a ring or piece of plate, and to my dau<sup>r</sup> Susanna Draper a purse with 22 pieces of gold, etc.   To my grandson Draper a purse with six dozen counters, French coin; to Susan Draper a bracelet of Moucca stones, etc.   To my goddau<sup>r</sup> Evelyn Draper a Moucca stone bracelet, etc., and to Sarah Draper ten half guineas for a ring.   To my grandson John Evelyn a cup and salver, a purse with 51 gold coins, a purse with 129 silver coins, a tortoiseshell box with a gold medal of Andrea Doria, also my wedding ring, a seal with my arms only, and an onyx seal with both coats engraved.   To my grandda<sup>r</sup> Ann Evelyn old china, cabinets, etc., etc.   To my grandda<sup>r</sup> Elizabeth Evelyn a silver chased box with coins, etc.   To my godda<sup>r</sup> Frances Glanville, a purse with ten gold pieces.   Bequests to M<sup>rs</sup> Mary Fowler, my godda<sup>r</sup> Ann Sherwood, M<sup>rs</sup> Thyer, M<sup>r</sup> Sherwood, M<sup>r</sup> Strickland, and M<sup>r</sup> Bedingfeild.   Residue to my grandson John Evelyn, sole ex'or.   Wit., Ann Strickland, Mary Fownes. (32 Lane.)

ARTHUR EVELYN, late of London, widower, dec<sup>d</sup> at Amersden, co. Oxon. Adm'on 15 Jan. 1712-13 to his son Thomas Evelyn.   (Adm'ons 1713, fo. 14.)

WILLIAM EVELYN of Martyr Worthy, co. Southampton, Esq.   Will dat. Aug. 6, 1722; proved 4 Feb. 1723-4 by Edward Hooker.   My house and land at Worthy, and my farm at Steventon, Hants, to M<sup>r</sup> Edward Hooker, sen<sup>r</sup>, of Winchester, my ex'or, rem<sup>r</sup> to his son Edward Hooker.   My South Sea Stock to my afs<sup>d</sup> ex'or, he to pay my sister Elizabeth Somner an annuity of £200.   To my friend Major Richard Mullins £1000 Stock in Million Bank.   To my cousin George Evelyn of Rookesnest, co. Surrey, £500.   To Paul Burrand, Esq., late Commissioner of Leather, £500.   To Peter Hussey of Surrey, Esq., £20.   James Crosse of Winchester, Esq., £20.   M<sup>rs</sup> Susanna Bignell, sen<sup>r</sup>, of Suffolk Street, London, £20, and to her children £5 each.   My houses in the Minories and Gray's Inn Lane to my niece Elizabeth Everard.   To poor Seamen of Greenwich Hospital £2000.   Wit., Thomas Godwin, Thomas Hussell, Nicholas Purdue.   Affidavit 4 Feb. 1723-4 by John Paltock of S<sup>t</sup> Clement Danes, Midd., Goldsmith, and Bernard Bolen of S<sup>t</sup> Peter's, Cornhill, London, Merch<sup>t</sup>, to verify the afores<sup>d</sup> will.   Sententiæ "pro valore test."  6 May 1724.   (8 Bolton.)

GEORGE EVELYN, late of Godstone, co. Surrey, Esq., dec<sup>d</sup>.   Adm'on 1 Dec. 1724 to his relict Mary Evelyn.   (Adm'ons 1724, fo. 236.)

Another grant 17 Feb. 1734-5 to Elizabeth Garth, widow, grandmother and guardian of Ann, Elizabeth, and Mary Evelyn, minors, da<sup>s</sup> and only issue of the afs<sup>d</sup> Geo. Evelyn, of goods unadm<sup>d</sup> by Mary Evelyn (afterwards Boone) relict of the s<sup>d</sup> Geo. Evelyn, and now also dec<sup>d</sup>.   (Adm'ons 1735.)

A further grant 9 Dec. 1754 to Anne, da. of the abovesaid George Evelyn, and wife of Daniel Boone, Esq.   (Adm'ons Dec. 1754.)

ANNE EVELYN *al's* PASTON of Rooksnest, co. Surrey, dec<sup>d</sup>, late wife of George Evelyn, Esq<sup>r</sup>, dec<sup>d</sup>.  Adm'on 27 May 1725 to her mother the Hon. Anne Paston, widow, George Evelyn, Esq<sup>r</sup>, husband of the said defunct having died before taking adm'on.  (Adm'ons 1725, fo. 95.)

MARTHA EVELYN, late of S<sup>t</sup> Margaret's, Westminster, co. Midd., widow, dec<sup>d</sup> at Wotton, Surrey.  Adm'on 22 Dec. 1726 to her son Sir John Evelyn, Bar<sup>t</sup>.  (Adm'ons Dec. 1726.)

ELIZABETH EVELYN of S<sup>t</sup> Andrew, Holborn, Midd., spinster.  Will dat. 9 Dec. 1739 ; proved 15 Dec. 1739 by Mathew Cutter.  To be buried in the parish where I shall die, but not in the church or in a vault.  To Major Humphrey Grey £50. My kinswomen Elizabeth Chase and M<sup>rs</sup> Sophia Glynn.  M<sup>rs</sup> Margaret Page.  To M<sup>rs</sup> Alice Miller my ring and silver teapot.  Residue to my friend M<sup>r</sup> Mathew Cutter of Fetter Lane, Merch<sup>t</sup>, sole ex'or.  Wit., F. Warden, Tho<sup>s</sup> London.  (256 Henchman.)

THOMASINE EVELYN, late of Hammersmith, parish of Fulham, co. Midd., spinster, dec<sup>d</sup>.  Adm'on 28 March 1743 to her brother Edward Evelyn, Esq. (Adm'ons March 1743.)

SUSANNA, wife of Charles Evelyn, Esq., late of S<sup>t</sup> James's, Westminster, Midd., but now of Yerlington, co. Som.  Will dat. 29 July 1741 ; proved 14 July 1747 by Charles Evelyn, Esq.  If I die at Exeter, to be buried at Newton S<sup>t</sup> Cyres, but if in London, then to be bur<sup>d</sup> near, but not in London.  Settlement 18 Nov. 1732 (previous to my marriage with Charles Evelyn) between me, by my then name of Susanna Prideaux of one part, my s<sup>d</sup> husband of the 2<sup>nd</sup> part, and Phineus Cheeke and Henry Cruwys of the 3<sup>rd</sup> part.  My late father Peter Prideaux, Esq.  The s<sup>d</sup> Phineas Cheeke and Henry Cruwys trustees of £6000 for my children.  My eldest son Charles Evelyn and my son John Evelyn, both under age.  My repeating watch and chain to my son John.  Residue to my husband Charles Evelyn, sole ex'or. Wit., George Case, Mary Case, John Fraine, jun<sup>r</sup>.  (175 Potter.)

CHARLES EVELYN of Yerlington, co. Som., Esq.  Will dat. 13 Jan. 1748 ; proved 7 Feb. 1748 (1748-9) by Sir John Evelyn, Bar<sup>t</sup>.  By will of my late wife Susanna dated 29 July 1741, I am entitled to the reversion of a third part of the Manors or Lordships of Paington *al's* Penington, Goodrington *al's* Godrington, Ludbrooke *al's* South Ludbrooke, Ingleborne Prior, Hearnford, etc., co. Devon, as set forth in my Marriage Settlement dated 18 Nov. 1732.  I give the said estate to Francis Newman of North Cadbury, Somerset, Esq., and John Fullerton of Shaston, Dorset, Esq., in trust to the use of my brother William Evelyn and the heirs male of his body, rem<sup>r</sup> to my brother John Evelyn, rem<sup>r</sup> to my brother Sydney Evelyn, rem<sup>r</sup> to my right heirs.  If my sons Charles and John Evelyn die under age or unmarried, I am, by my s<sup>d</sup> wife's will, entitled to the sum of £6000 settled on them, and I direct it to be disposed as follows, to my sisters Anne and Mary Evelyn and my brother Sydney Evelyn £1000 each, and the remainder to my brother W<sup>m</sup> Evelyn.  I desire to be buried with my wife in the vault in Yarlington Churchyard.  Residue to my father Sir John Evelyn, Bar<sup>t</sup> (sole ex'or), in trust for my son John Evelyn at age of 21.  My said father and my brother John Evelyn, Esq., to be guardians of my sons Charles and John Evelyn during minority.  Wit., Sam. Foot, Josiah White, James Davidge.  (38 Lisle.)

EDWARD EVELYN of Felbridgwater, in parish of Godstone, Surrey, Esq.  Will dat. 26 Oct. 1737 ; proved 21 Feb. 1752 by his relict Julia Evelyn.  To be buried in the family vault in Godstone Church and some small monument to be erected in the little Chapel where my grandfather's monument is, and the following sentence inscribed on it " Ens Entium Miserere Mei."  To my son James Evelyn my farm at Felbridgwater and two cottages called the Fashalls, and the common of Felbridge which I purchased of my brother Glanville, with other lands and tenements in Godstone and Tandridge, co. Surrey.  By virtue of a power vested in me by my marriage settlem<sup>t</sup>, I give my da. Julia Evelyn £2000, which sum is secured on the estate of the Earl of Arran in Ireland.  I also give her a further sum of £1000. My wife Julia sole ex'ix.  Wit., W<sup>m</sup> Radcliff, Tho<sup>s</sup> Davis, Edw<sup>d</sup> Halliday. (34 Bettesworth.)

*(To be continued.)*

# The Register Book of Bramfield, co. Suffolk.*

1794.

Jan. 5    Marianne d. of William Aldis and Elizabeth his wife (late Taylor, spinster); born Jan. 26, 1792.

Feb. 16    Mary d. of Reginald Rabett, Esq., and Mary his wife (late Kerrison, spinster); born Feb. 14. Privately.

April 27    William s. of Mary Cooper; born March 31. Privately. Rec⁴ into the Church May 26, 1806.

June 5    Elizabeth d. of Willᵐ Pearson and Elizabeth his wife (late Reynolds, spinster); born June 2. Privately. Publickly June 30.

Sep. 7    Thomas s. of Samuel Barnaby and Hannah his wife (late Gayforth, spinster); born Sep. 4. Privately. Publickly Nov. 5, 1797.

Sep. 14    Hannah d. of Samuel Harbor and Hannah his wife (late Gayforth, spinster); born Sep. 10.

Sep. 15    Joseph s. of William Fuller and Mary his wife (late Amis, spinster); born Sep. 14. Privately.

Oct. 26    Samuel s. of John Edwards and Mary his wife (late Cross, spinster); born Oct. 14. Privately.

1795.

Jan. 18    Reginald s. of Reginald Rabett, Esq., and Mary his wife (late Kerrison, spinster); born Jan. 11. Privately.

Jan. 25    John s. of Thomas Elner and Anne his wife (late Bullard, spinster); born Jan 20. Privately.

Jan. 25    Maria Press Dalton d. of Harriet Berney; born Jan. 23. Privately.

Feb. 14    Thomas s. of Thomas Higham and Charlotte his wife (late Aldis, spinster); born Feb. 11. Privately. Rec⁴ into the Church Aug. 18, 1796.

Feb. 14    Harriet natural d. of Deborah Marshall; born Feb. 2. Privately. Publickly Jan. 19, 1806.

Mar. 7    Hannah d. of Robert Smith and Rebecca his wife (late Reddit, spinster); born March 1. Privately.

Mar. 30    Lionel s. of Lionel Harmant and Diana his wife (late Watts, spinster); born Feb. 1.

April 5    Thomas s. of John Smith and Jane his wife (late Hall, spinster); born March 9. Privately.

April 5    John Hunt natural s. of Frances Hatcher; born Feb. 1.

April 5    William Tutthill natural s. of Sarah Harvey; born Feb. 1.

April 12    John s. of John Edwards and Mary his wife (late Cross, spinster); born Oct. 19, 1794.

June 28    John s. of Thomas Elner and Anne his wife (late Bullard, spinster); born Dec. 26, 1794.

June 14    Hannah d. of John Aldrich and Elizabeth his wife (late Last, spinster); born July 25, 1794.

July 5    Sarah d. of Robert Cooper and Elizabeth his wife (late Burnham, spinster); born June 28.

Aug. 2    Lucy d. of Thomas Wright and Anne his wife (late Balls, spinster); born July 31. Privately. Rec⁴ into the Church Jan. 2, 1800.

Sep. 27    Robert s. of Robert Rowe and Susan his wife (late Girling, spinster); born Sep. 19. Privately.

Sep. 27    Mary d. of George Smith and Susanna his wife (late Chambers, spinster); born Sep. 23. Privately.

Oct. 11    Mary d. of George Smith. Publickly.

Oct. 11    Samuel s. of William Balls and Mary his wife; born Sep. 27. Privately. Rec⁴ into the Church Feb. 9, 1800.

Oct. 19    Lionel s. of James Mayhew and Mary his wife (late Ling); born Oct. 15. Privately. Publickly Dec. 8.

Dec. 26    George William s. of Reginald Rabett, Esq., and Mary his wife (late Kerrison, spinster); born Dec. 22. Privately.

1796.

Jan. 17    James s. of James Smith and Elizabeth his wife (late Jacob); born Ap. 20, 1793.

Jan. 10    Sarah d. of Richard Puttock and Rebeccah his wife (late Reeve, spinster); born Jan. 2. Privately. Rec⁴ into the Church July 3. [His name is given as William Feb. 19, 1792.]

Feb. 7    Jane d. of William Winter and Mary his wife (late Wilson); born Jan. [blank]. Privately. Rec⁴ into the Church May 27.

Feb. 7    Susanna d. of Samuel Hammond and Eliah [? Alice, see Oct. 20, 1799] his wife (late Puttock); born Dec. 30, 1795. Privately. Publickly Jan. 19, 1806.

Mar. 6    Elizabeth d. of John Smith and Jane his wife (late Hall, spinster); born March 3. Privately.

Mar. 29    Elizabeth d. of William Wollard and Elizabeth his wife (late Scrutten); born March 15. Privately. Rec⁴ into the Church May 12, 1799.

May 1    Robert Reynolds s. of William Peirson and Elizabeth his wife (late Reynolds, spinster); born Ap. 26. Privately.

June 12    Deborah d. of Henry Wright and Mary his wife (late Adams); born Ap. 7. Privately.

July 3    John Crisp s. of John Eastaugh and Anna his wife (late Crisp, spinster); Privately.

* Continued from p. 288.

Aug. 14  Thomas s. of Tho⁸ Briggs and Ann Wright, spinster; born Aug. 26, 1792.

Aug. 14  Mary natural d. of the same; born Aug. 21, 1793.

Dec. 11  William s. of John Wincop and Elizabeth; born Dec. 5. Privately. Publickly June 25, 1797.

1797.

Feb. 5  Rachel d. of Isaac and Elizabeth Watling (late Elner, spinster).

Feb. 5  Catherine d. of Thomas and Sarah Lame (late Trip, spinster).

Feb. 26  Amas s. of William and Mary Fuller (late Amas, spinster); born Feb. 24.

Mar. 8  Edward s. of John and Jane Smith (late Hall); born March 6.

May 28  Elizabeth d. of Joseph and Keziah Clements (late Calver, spinster).

June 4  John s. of John and Mary Edwards (late Cross, spinster).

June 4  Mary d. of Lionel and Dinah Hammond (late Watts, spinster).

July 2  William Aldous s. of Thomas and Charlotte Higham (late Aldous, spinster).

July 9  Sophia d. of William and Hannah Taylor (late Martin, spinster).

Aug. 6  Sarah d. of William and Ann Smith (late Crisp, widow); born July 21.

Aug. 13  John s. of William and Lydia Phillips (late Leggett, spinster); born Jan. 26, 1793.

Sep. 10  William s. of Robert and Susan Rowe (late Girling, spinster); born Aug. 26.

Nov. 5  Benjamin s. of Samuel and Hannah Barnaby (late Gayforth, spinster); born Sep. 4, 1796.

Nov. 13  Patty d. of Robert and Rebecca Smith (late Reddit, spinster).

Oct. 29  Robert s. of Robert and Lucy Cairn (late Tyler, spinster). Privately.

Oct. 29  Ann d. of Thomas and Ann Elner (late Bullard, spinster). Privately.

1798.

Feb. 11  Charlotte d. of George and Susan Smith (late Chambers, spinster); born Jan. 29. Privately.

Feb. 4  Robert s. of Samuel and Hannah Barnaby (late Gayforth, spinster); born Jan. 8. Privately. Recᵈ into the Church with Ann and George his sister and brother March 19, 1803.

CHARLES NEWTON, Curate.

Feb. 11  Mary son [? daughter] of Benjamin and Ann Jordan (late Phillips, spinster); born Feb. 10. Privately.

Feb. 13  William s. of Samuel and Hannah Harbor (late Gayforth, spinster); born Feb. 13.

Mar. 25  George Ling s. of James and Mary Mayhew (late Ling, spinster); born March 21. Privately.

April 15  Matilda d. of William and Mary Winter (late Wilson); born Ap. 9. Privately. Publickly Jan. 2, 1799.

April 29  Susan d. of Henry and Mary Wright (late Adams, spinster); born Ap. 15. Privately.

May 4  Elizabeth d. of Robert and Mary Augur, aged 20 years, was received into the Church.

May 4  Robert aged 7 years s. of Mary Augur, Base Born, was received into the Church.

May 4  Joseph aged 5 years s. of the same, B. B., was received into the Church.

May 6  Mary Ann d. of William and Mary Balls (late Cooper, spinster); born May 1. Privately. Recᵈ into the Church Feb. 9, 1800.

May 27  Eliza d. of Daniel and Sarah Nursey (late Stock, spinster); born May 20. Privately.

June 10  James s. of James and Elizabeth Aldred (late Borrett, spinster); born Oct. 11, 1797.

June 17  Susan and Sarah, Twins, dau'rs of John and Mary Edwards; born Ap. 6.

July 15  Arthur s. of Harriott Barney; born Nov. 9.

July 29  George s. of James and Mary Gorble (late Aldred, spinster); born July 28. Privately.

Aug. 26  Mary Ann d. of Rachel Ellis. Privately.

Sep. 23  Robert s. of Robert and Sarah Moore (late Knights, spinster); born Sep. 19. Privately. Publickly Jan. 19, 1806.

Sep. 30  Mary d. of William and Elizabeth Peirson (late Reynolds, spinster); born Sep. 25. Privately.

Oct. 7  Mary d. of Isaac and Elizabeth Watling (late Elner, spinster); born Oct. 6. Recᵈ into the congregation Sep. 27, 1801. Quod vide.

Dec. 16  Phœbe d. of Simon and Sarah Leney (late Hurring, spinster); born June 21.

1799.

Jan. 6  Mary d. of Richard and Rebeccah Puttock (late Reeve); born Dec. 25. Privately. Recᵈ into the Church Jan. 5, 1800.

Jan. 6  William s. of Thomas and Ann Wright (late Balls); born Dec. 23. Privately. Recᵈ into the Church Jan. 2, 1800.

Feb. 17  Sarah d. of William and Elizabeth Woolward (late Scrutten); born Feb. 3. Recᵈ into the Church May 12.

Mar. 25  George Ling s. of James and Mary Mayhew (late Ling, spinster); born March 21. Privately. Recᵈ into the Church Ap. 19.

April 28  Sarah d. of John and Sarah Helling (late Reeve).

June 9  William s. of William and Elizabeth Haws (late Dutton).

June 9 Joshua s. of William and Mary Bowls (late Cooper). [*Balls, Dec.* 1801.]
Aug. 25 James s. of Thomas and Sarah Lame.
Oct. 27 Elizabeth d. of Mary Cooper, base born. Privately. Rec⁰ into the Church May 25, 1806.
Interpolated. Ann d. of Samuel Barnaby and Hannah his wife (late Gayforth, spinster) was born Oct. 29, 1799. Publickly baptised March 19, 1803.
Oct. 20 Mary d. of Samuel and Alice Armant (late Puttock). Privately. Publickly Jan. 19, 1806.
April 28 Christopher s. of Thoˢ and Ann Edwards (late Wright).
Nov. 3 Elizabeth d. of Thoˢ and Charlotte Higham (late Aldous).
Nov. 3 Lucy d. of Lionel and Diana Harmant. Privately. Rec⁰ into the Church May 18, 1800.
Nov. 10 Hannah d. of John and Mary Edwards (late Cross).
Nov. 17 Samuel s. of Robert and Sarah Gilman; aged 13 years.
Nov. 17 Sarah d. of the same; aged 12 years.
Nov. 17 Sophia d. of James Mayhew and Mary his wife (late Ling). Privately.
Nov. 24 Catherine d. of Thomas and Sarah Lame (late Trip) was received into the Church; aged 3 years.
Nov. 24 George son of the same was received into the Church; aged 10 years.
Nov. 25 Richard s. of Daniel and Sarah Nursey (late Stock, spinster); born same day.
Dec. 1 Thoˢ son and Ann dau'r of Thoˢ and Sarah Lame (late Trip) rec⁰ into the Church.
Dec. 1 Henry s. of [*blank*] Tillet, widow, was rec⁰ into the Church; aged, according to yᵉ mother, 7 years.
Dec. 1 Ann natural dau'r of the same was publicly baptized; aged 2 years.
Dec. 1 Thoˢ natural s. of Mary Andrews. Privately.
Dec. 15 William s. of Samuel and Fanny Waters (late Keebal). Privately. Rec⁰ into the Church Oct. 31, 1802.
Dec. 15 Anne d. of Robert and Susan Rowe.
Dec. 20 Japhet and Jephtha Twin sons of John Smith and Hall his wife. Privately. Rec⁰ into the Church March 7, 1800.

1800.
Mar. 10 Elizabeth d. of Thoˢ and Ann Elner (late Bollard). Privately. Publicly Jan. 19, 1806.
Mar. 11 Elizabeth d. of Harmon and Sarah Garrett (late Fisher). Privately. Rec⁰ into the Church Ap. 20.
April 1 John s. of Thoˢ and Mary Kerridge (late Jackson). Privately. Rec⁰ into the Church Ap. 13.
April 20 Susan d. of Wᵐ and Ann Smith (late Crisp).
May 20 Wᵐ s. of John and Edna Banks (late Eastaugh). Privately. Publicly Jan. 19, 1806.
June 1 Mary Ann d. of George and Sarah Borrett; aged 2 years.
June 27 Sarah d. of Samˡ and Sarah Cross. Privately. Rec⁰ into the Church Mar. 2, 1801, by Mʳ Badely, Rector of Ubeston.
June 29 Wᵐ s. of Sarah Gayfer, natural child.
Aug. 14 Wᵐ Hayward s. of Robert and Sarah Hinsby (late Hayward). Privately.
Sep. 3 Louisa d. of Thoˢ and Ann Wright. Privately. Publicly Jan. 9, 1806.
Nov. 2 Elizabeth d. of John and Lydia Crisp (late Eastaugh). Privately.
Nov. 18 Mary d. of Edward and Mary Ife (late Cole, spinster). Privately.
Dec. 18 Wᵐ s. of James and Mary Mayhew. Privately. Rec⁰ into the Church Nov. 19, 1801.
Dec. [*blank*] Mary Ann d. of Thoˢ and Sarah Lame (late Trip).

1801.
Jan. 21 Mary Ann d. of Thoˢ and Mary Kerridge. Privately. Rec⁰ into Church Dec. 12, 1802.
Feb. 20 Mary d. of Jonathan and Eliz. Rayner (late Adams).
June 14 Mary d. of Joseph and Elizᵗʰ Kemp (late Newson).
July 12 Thomas natural s. of Deborah Marsh. Privately.
Aug. 30 Mary d. of John and Esther Fiske (late Burgess).
Aug. 31 Robert s. of Robert and Susan Savage.
Nov. 19 Sophia d. of James and Mary Mayhew (late Ling).

(*To be continued.*)

# Hopkins of Llanfihangel Ystern Llewern.*

WANSTEAD CHURCH, ESSEX.

*On an oval tablet of white marble at the west end of the church.*

In a vault near this place are deposited the remains of Sir John Hopkins, Knt., late Alderman of the City of London, who departed this life October 14ᵗʰ 1796, aged 81 years.
And of Ann his widow, who died the 5ᵗʰ September 1806, aged 78 years.

* Continued from p. 296.

U 2

Also of their eldest daughter Mary Anne, wife of Christopher Taddy, Esq., of Croydon, who died the 24th March 1801, aged 47 years.

And of Mary Ann, daughter of the said Christopher and Mary Ann Taddy, who died the 24th February 1809, aged 23 years.

And of Charles Hopkins, youngest son of Sir John Hopkins, Knt., who died at Stratford the 20th of February 1834, aged 73 years.

Arms : Sable, on a chevron between three pistols or as many roses gules. barbed vert, seeded or ; impaling, Argent. a fesse sable, charged with two fleurs-de-lis or and a white rose between three lions passant-guardant gules.

Crest : A turreted castle argent in flames ppr.

---

## HENDON, MIDDLESEX.

*In the north-eastern extremity of the churchyard, near the entrance, is an altar-tomb with the following inscription on the top :—*

Sacred
to the memory of
Sir John Wm Anderson Bart.
who departed this life
the 21st of May 1813
Aged 77 years.
Also of
Charles Simkins Esqre
of Devizes, Wilts,
who died the 11th of June 1792
Aged 49 years.

---

NEWLAND.—Edmund Probyn, Esq., has a seat and estates. They derive these from Lord Chief Baron Probyn, who dying in 1742 devised his estates to his nephew John Hopkins, Esq., whose descendants bear the name and arms of Probyn. Another Edmund Probyn, Esq., of a distinct family, had also a house and estates which has (*sic*) descended by inheritance to William Perry, Esq., of Bristol [Bigland, vol. ii., p. 257].

---

### PEDIGREE OF PROBYN FROM HERALDS' COLLEGE RECORDS.

(Communicated by Sir John Maclean, F.S.A.)

John Probyn of Newland in com. Gloucester.=Mary, da. of Christopher Hall of Highmeadow.
Ob. circ. 1626, æt. circ. 70.           Ob. circ. 1627.

Anne, wife of Henry Worgan of Clewerwall.     Susan, wife of . . . . Cecill of Monmouth, after to Wm. Catchmay of same place.

Christopher, died young. | Thomas Probin=Mary, da. of Newland. Ob. circ. 1646. of . . . . of . . . . in Wales. | Edmund Probyn=Mary, da. of of Newland. Ob. circ. 1623, æt. 45. Thos. Symonds of Clowerwall. Ob. circ. 1638. | William Probin of Dean Magna. Ob. s.p.

Elizabeth, da. of Edmund Bond of=William Probin of=Elizabeth, da. and heir of James Newland, and widow of William | Newland, now | Woodruff of Wollaston, co. Glouc. Hopton of Huntley, by whom she | living 1682. Born Ob. circ. 1658, s.p. had one daughter. | 1621.

Elizabeth Hopton, aged circ. 16 years. | Edm. Probin, only son, aged . . year 1682. | Mary, aged 11 years. | Sarah, aged 9 years. | Hannah, aged 7 years. | Frances, aged 2 years.

## PROBYN.

### FROM THE PARISH REGISTERS OF NEWLAND, CO. GLOUCESTER.

(From Sir John Maclean's MSS.)

1584　Marcij 27 die, bap. fuit Maria filia Joh'is Probyn de Churchend.
1594　Nov. 17 die bap. fuit Thomas Probyn filius Joh'is Probyn, Churchend.
1630　Mar.　18　Sep. fuit Maria Probin de Newland vidua.
1650　Jun.　2　Will'us filius Will'mi Probyn de Newland (bap.).
1654　Thomas son of Thomas Probyn & Jane his wife of Newland was born Feb. 10.
1656　Arthur son of William Probyn & Mary his wife of Newland born Jan. 28 bap. 4 Feb.
1656　Arthur son of William Probyn & Mary his wife buried May 18.
1658　Anne dau. of William Probyn of Newland born 4 Nov. bap. 1 Dec.
1671　April.　6　Sepult. Gulielmus Probyn Coriarius (tanner).
1672　Maij　26　Nata fuit Sarah filia Gulielmi et Elizabethæ Probyn et bap. 27 die Maij of Newland.
1674　Jan.　5　Bap. Gulielmus filius Gulielmi et Idith Probyn de Newland.
1674　Oct.　7　Bap. Hannah filia Gulielmi et Elizabethæ Probin de Newland.
1675　Mar.　15　Bap. Elizabetha filia Will'i et Eadij (?) Probyn de Newland.
1678　July　16　Bap. Edmundus fil. Gulielmi et Elizab. Probyn gent. de Newland.
167-　Feb.　16　Sepult. Philipus Probyn de Newland House.
1679　July　—　Sepult. Thomas filius Will'i et Edithæ Probyn de Newland.
1680　Jan.　20　Bap. Blanch fil. Will'i et Elizab. Probyn de Newland.
1681　Maij　9　Bap. Joh'es fil. Will'i et Edith. Probyn de Newland.
168⅔　Mar.　—　Bap. Joh'es fil. Joh'is et Annæ Probyn.
1683　Mar.　20　Sep. Maria Probyn vidua.
1684　Sep.　12　Bap. Abraham fil. Gul. et Edithæ Probyn bur. 21.
1686　Ap.　17　Thoˢ fil. Joh'is et Annæ Probyn.
1686　Nov.　9　Bap. Gul. fil. Gul'mi et Elizab. Probyn de Newland.
1688　Oct.　4　Sep. Edward son of John Probyn.
1707　June　18　Bap. Tho. fil. Gul. et Saræ Probyn gen. de Newland.
1708　Maij　23　Tho. fil. Gulielmi et Saræ Probyn gen. de Newland.
1708　Nov.　24　Bap. Francis fil. Gulielmi et Saræ Probyn gen. de Newland.
1712　Thos. fil. Gulielmi et Saræ Probyn de Newland.
1714　Decʳ　—　Margareta fil. Gulielmi et Saræ Probyn de Newland.
1729　Dec.　4　Sep. Editha Probyn gen. de Newland.
1732　Dec.　13　Bap. Anna fil. Gull'i et Annæ Probyn gen. de Newland.
1732　Jan.　25　Sep. Edwardus Probyn gent. de Newland.
173¾　Feb.　6　Bap. Sarah fil. Guil. et Annæ Probyn gent. de Newland.
1736　April　6　Bap. Catherina fil. Gul. et Annæ Probyn gen. de Newland.
173⁶⁄₉　Martij 14　Sep. Joh'es Probyn A.M. fil. Will'ᵐⁱ Probyn gen. de Newland.
1737　Oct.　26　Bap. Elizabeth dau. of Wᵐ & Ann Probyn gent. de Newland.
1738　Jan.　9　Bap. William son of William & Ann Probyn gent. Newland.
1738　Feb.　7　Bur. William　　　,,　　　　　,,　　　　　,,
1740　May　15　Bur. Ann wife of William Probyn gent. Newland. ,,
1741　Sep.　—　Bur. Mʳˢ Blanch Probyn, Newland.
1741　Feb.　2　Bur. Mʳˢ Hannah Probyn, Newland.
1742　June　—　Bur. Sʳ Edmund Probyn Kᵗ Lord Chief Baron of Excheq.
1749　Oct.　28　Bur. Lady Probyn.
1753　Sep.　20　Marr. at Bream Chapel Mʳ Nicholas Perry of Bristol & Mʳˢ Anne Probyn of Newland.
1756　Nov.　12　Bur. William Probyn gent. Newland.
1758　Oct.　27　Bap. Ann dau. of Edmund Probyn Esq. & Sophia, Newland.
1760　June　2　Bap. Edmund son of　　　,,　　　　　　,,
1761　Feb.　27　Bap. John son of　　　,,　　　　　　,,

1761 Sep.   29  Bur. William Probyn Esq. Newland.
1762 June    2  Bap. William son of Edmund Probyn Esq. & Sophia, Newland.
1762 June   29  Bur. Mʳˢ Ann Probyn, Newland.
1763 June   14  Bap. Thomas son of Edmund Probyn Esq. & Sophia, Newland.
1766 July    3  Bur. Mʳˢ Frances Probyn, Newland.
1766 Oct.    7  Bap. Henry son of Edmund Probyn Esq. & Sophia, Newland.
1768 Feb.    2  Bap. Sophia dau. of          „
1770 April   6  Bap. Elizabeth dau. of Edmund & Sophia Probyn, Newland.
1771 Sep.   14  Bap. Decima dau. of Edmund Probyn Esq. & Sophia, Newland.
1773 March  25  Bur. John Probyn Esq. Newland.
1775 May    17  Bap. Richard son of Edm. Probyn Esq. & Sophia, Newland.
1778 Aug.   27  Bur. John Howell Esq. Newland.
1784 Jan.    5  Bur. Richard son of Edm. Probyn & Sophia, Newland.
1787 June   20  Bur. Mʳˢ Margaret Probyn, Newland.
1788 Sep.    8  Bap. John & Edmund sons of Rev. John Probyn & Anne.
1790 Sep.   30  Bap. Sophia Cholmondley dau. of Rev. John Probyn & Anne, Newland.
1791 Oct.   15  Bap. Caroline dau. of Rev. John Probyn & Anne, Newland.
1792 Nov.    6  Bap. Mary Anne dau. of Rev. John Probyn & Anne, Newland.
1793 Sep.   27  Bur. Edmund Probyn Junʳ Esq. Newland.
1799 Jan.    2  Bap. Maria dau. of Rev. John Probyn & Thoˢ his son by Anne, Newland.
1802 Dec.   31  Bur. Sophia wife of Edmund Probyn Esq., Newland.
1819         Bur. Edmund Probyn Esq. aged 82, Newland.

*Marriages from 1754.*

1756 Oct.   25  Thomas Jukes of Bromley Kent Esq. & Sarah Probyn mar.
1770 Oct.    1  John Rumsey of Trelleck co. Monm. Esq. & Miss Frances Probyn of this parish mar. by licence.
1791 Aug.   25  Thomas Lloyd of Coedmore in p'ish Llangoedmore co. Cardigan Bach. & Miss Elizabeth Probyn of this Parish by lic.

## WHITE AND BALL.

The following are extracts from the wills of two Bishops of the name of White. FRANCIS WHITE, now Lord Bishop of Ely. Will dat. 4 March 1636 ; proved 27 Feb. 1637-8 by his relict Joane White. To my nephew and grandchild (*sic*) Francis White £1500 at his age of 21, and to have for his maintenance £60 yearly till age of 18, and £70 yearly from 18 to 21. To my grandchild John White £500 at age of 21, and till then £30 yearly. To my grandchild William White £300 at age of 21, and till then £20 yearly. To my grandchild Daniel White £300 at age of 21, and till then £20 yearly. To the children of my da. Martha Goodherd £300 amongst them, to the sons at ages of 21, and the das. at ages of 21 or marriage, and until then the money to be in the hands of their father Thomas Goodherd. To my grandchild Francis Wickham £100 at his age of 21, to be paid to his father Mica Wickham during minority. To my da. in law Elizabeth White £100. To my poor kindred £60 amongst them. To my servants £60 amongst them. To the poor of Ely £20. Poor of Downeham in the Isle of Ely £20. To my da. Elizabeth Nicholls £40. To my da. Hester Manby £40. To my da. in law Margaret Gately £60. To my wife Dame Joane White £500, and also the residue of my goods and chattels, she to be sole ex'ix. FRA. ELIENSIS. Witnesses, John Peake, Anthony Holmes, notʸ pub., Francis Allsupp. (P.C.C., 10 Lee.)

[Francis White, Dean of Carlisle, consecr. Bp. of Carlisle 3 Dec. 1626. Translated to Norwich 22 Jan. 1629. Translated to Ely 8 Dec. 1631 (or 15 Nov. 1631). Died Feb. 1638. (Nicolas's ' Synopsis.')]

THOMAS WHITE, D<sup>r</sup> of Div., late Bishop of Peterburgh.  Will dat. (no month) 169- (date incomplete) ; proved 19 July 1698 by George Baxter.  To be buried in the parish where I shall die, without any funeral pomp or expense above £10, without any monument or inscription saving this upon a little stone if it may be allowed "The body of Thomas White, D.D., late Bishopp of Peterborough, deprived of that Bishopprick for not taking the Oathes of Allegiance and Supremacy establisht one thousand six hundred eighty-nine, is buryed here in hope of a happy resurrection."  To the poor of the parish where I shall die £10.   To the poor of Aldington in Kent, where I was born, £240.    Poor of Newark, co. Notts, £240, of Bottesford, co. Leic., £240, of Peterburgh £240, and of Castor, co. Northamp., £240, all which sums to be laid out in lands for the poor, and £10 yearly to be distributed in each of the said places, to certain of the poor of the parishes, upon condition that those who receive shall correctly repeat the Lord's Prayer, Apostles' Creed, and Ten Commandments.    To the poor among the deprived Clergy for not taking the Oath 1689, £200, to be distributed by Francis Turner, late Bishop of Ely.  To my cousin M<sup>r</sup> Thomas Blechynden £50.  My cousin Theophylas Blechynden 30s.   To my cousins M<sup>rs</sup> Anne Blechynden, M<sup>rs</sup> Mary Bilkes, M<sup>rs</sup> Margaret Blechynden, and M<sup>rs</sup> Dorothy Blechynden 50s. each.  To my cousin M<sup>r</sup> Peirson Blechynden £50, and my cousin M<sup>r</sup> Rich<sup>d</sup> Blechynden £30.  To my friend D<sup>r</sup> Walter Needham, Rob<sup>t</sup> Marris of Newark, and M<sup>r</sup> William Whatton of Belvoire, £10 each.  My cousin M<sup>r</sup> James White living near Deane, co. Kent, £5.  My cousin M<sup>rs</sup> Mary Rowsewell, wife of M<sup>r</sup> Rowsewell, now or late minister of Riselip, near Uxbridge, co. Buck. (sic), £10.   My old good friend Major John Pownell of Borton, near Wye, co. Kent, £20.   To my godson M<sup>r</sup> Rich<sup>d</sup> Blechynden (son of the above Thomas Blechynden) £30 towards the expense of taking of Bach<sup>r</sup> of Laws at Oxford.   To Gratian Blechynden (son of Thomas Blechynden of Symnels in Aldington, Kent, late dec<sup>d</sup>) £10 to his apprenticeship, provided his brother John Blechynden pays the arrears of his rent for Giggers Green, etc.    To M<sup>rs</sup> Lucy Brockman of Canterbury my watch, clock, and alarme, which I formerly received from her.  I bequeath Gigger's Green and Copherst to my heir at law, being I think the grandson of my uncle M<sup>r</sup> Paul White.   My faithful servant M<sup>r</sup> George Baxter to be my sole ex'or.   My friends William Thursby of the Middle Temple, Esq., and Edward Jennings of Lincoln's Inn Fields, Midd., Esq., overseers, and to each £10.   Rings of 20s. each to D<sup>r</sup> W<sup>m</sup> Sancroft, late Archbishop of Canterbury, D<sup>r</sup> Rob<sup>t</sup> Frampton, late Bishop of Gloucester, D<sup>r</sup> W<sup>m</sup> Lloyd, late Bishop of Norwich, D<sup>r</sup> Francis Turner, late Bishop of Ely, and D<sup>r</sup> Tho<sup>s</sup> Ken, late Bishop of Bath and Wells.  Rings of 15s. each to D<sup>r</sup> Zachary Cradock and M<sup>r</sup> John Newborough, both of Eaton, D<sup>r</sup> W<sup>m</sup> Sherlock of the Temple, D<sup>r</sup> W<sup>m</sup> Cane of Windsor, D<sup>r</sup> John Scott of S<sup>t</sup> Peter's Poor, D<sup>r</sup> Robert Grove of S<sup>t</sup> Andrew Undershaft, D<sup>r</sup> Henry Dove of S<sup>t</sup> Bridgett's, London, Sir Tho<sup>s</sup> Pinfold, Chancellor of Peterburgh, D<sup>r</sup> Henry Watkinkon (sic), Chancellor of York, D<sup>r</sup> Samuel Crobrow, late Archdeacon of Nottingham, M<sup>rs</sup> Owham of Westminster, and the afores<sup>d</sup> M<sup>rs</sup> Lucy Brockman. All my papers, sermons, prayers, etc., to be burnt.   All my printed books to the Town of Newark upon Trent to form a library or beginning of a library for that town.  No witnesses named. (P.C.C., 172 Lort.)

Thoresby's ' History of Leeds ' gives the pedigree of the above Bishop of Ely, who was born, I gather, at S<sup>t</sup> Neot's, Hunts, and his arms are stated as, " Gules, a chevron between three boars' heads coupè argent."   Who represent these two Bishops, and can any one give their pedigrees down to the present time ?  Mary, daughter of William White of Newport, Rhode Island, United States of America, married 1727 or 1728 William Ball of Philadelphia, and it is believed that she belonged to the same family as one of these Bishops, and as to this information is very much desired.

REGINALD STEWART BODDINGTON.

*National Conservative Club,*
  *9 Pall Mall, S.W.*

### GRANT OF ARMS TO JOHN HOPKINS OF LINCOLN'S INN, AND NEWLAND, CO. GLOUCESTER, 1734.

To all and singular to whom these presents shall come John Anstis Esq. Garter Prin[ll] King of Arms and Knox Ward Esq. Clarenceux King of Arms send Greeting Whereas John Hopkins Barrister at Law of Lincoln's Inn and of Newland in the County of Gloucester Esq. hath represented unto the Right Hon[ble] ffrancis Earl of Effingham, Deputy (with the Royal approbation) To the most Noble Edward Duke of Norfolk Earl Marshal and Hereditary Marshal of England, That thro' the Neglect of his Ancestors by Their not makeing due entries in the College of Arms He cannot prove a Right to Coat Arms and being unwilling to bear any without an unquestionable Authority ; hath therefore prayed his Lordship's Warrant for our devising and Granting to him & to the Descendants of William Hopkins deceased and Sarah his wife one of the Daughters of William Probyn of Newland in the said County of Gloucester and Elizabeth his wife both deceased, the Father and Mother of the said John Hopkins such Arms and Crest as he and they may lawfully bear. And for as much as his Lordship having duely considered the Request of the said John Hopkins and being satisfied that he is well Qualified to support the condition of a Gentleman did by Warrant under his Lordship's Hand and Seal bearing Date the Twenty-ninth Day of August last past, Order and Direct Us to devise Grant and Assign unto the said John Hopkins and the other Persons above mentioned such Arms and Crest accordingly, Now know ye that we the said Garter and Clarenceux in Pursuance of the Consent of the said Earl of Effingham and by Virtue of the Letters Patent of our offices to each of Us respectively granted under the Great Seal of great Britain have devised and Do by these presents Grant and Assign unto the said John Hopkins the Arms and Crest hereafter mentioned Viz[t] Ermin on a Fess Gules a Lyon Passant Guardant Argent, a Canton of the Second charged w[th] a Rose Or, and for his Crest an Ostrich's Head coup'd Ermin, holding in the Beak a Key Azure, as the same in the Margin hereof are more plainly depicted, to be borne and used for ever hereafter by him the said John Hopkins and his Descendants, and also by the Descend[ts] of the said W[m] Hopkins deceased and Sarah his Wife one of the Daughters of W[m] Probyn of Newland in the said County by Elizabeth his Wife, both deceased, with their due Differences according to the Law and Usage of Arms without the Let Interruption of any Person or Persons whatsoever. In Witness wherof We the said Garter and Clarenceux Kings of Arms have to these presents Subscribed our Names and affixed the Seals of Our Severall Offices the Sixteenth day of Septem[r] In the Eighth Year of the Reign of our Sovereign Lord George the Second by the Grace of God King of Great Britain France and Ireland Defender of the ffaith etc. Annoq' Domini 1734.

JOHN ANSTIS Garter  
Principal King of Arms.

KNOX WARD Clarenceux  
King of Arms.

---

### INSCRIPTIONS RELATING TO THE YORKE FAMILY IN THE CHURCH OF ST. JAMES, DOVER.

*Slab placed against wall.*

Here lyes the Body of the said
Symon Yorke who dyed the 3[d]
day of Febrvary An° 1682 Aged
76 yeares 11 Moneths
In Spe Beatæ Resurrectionis
Here lieth the Body of Alice
the wife of Simon Yorke by
whom he had issve 5 sons
and one davghter.   She died
y[e] 4th of X[br] Ann° Salut. 1663
Ætat. 52.

ARMS, YORKE; IMPALING GIBBON.

ARMS, JONES; IMPALING YORKE.

ARMS FROM LEDGER STONES, ST. JAMES' CHURCH, DOVER.

Simon Yorke Esq[r] was the eldest
son of Barthemew Yorke of Calne
in Wilts : He was born in March
1605, and was a branch of the ancient
family of that name long settled in
North Wiltshire, now extinct ; They
suffered much on account of their
Loyalty during the Great Rebellion
At that period M[r] Simon Yorke
left his Native County, and resided
at Dover many years.
The Lord Chancellor Hardwicke
was his Grand-son and Heir at Law.

*Ledger stone, middle aisle.*

Arms : YORKE, impaling GIBBON.

Here lieth the Body of Philip Yorke
Gent ; who married Elizabeth y[e] only Child
of Richard Gibbon Gent ; & had Issue three
Sons & six Daughters of whom one Son
& two Daughters are surviving, the other
six lye interr'd near this place.   He died
June 18, 1721, in the 70 Year of his Age
Here lieth alsoe the Body of the said
Elizabeth Wife of y[e] above mentioned
Phillip Yorke who died October 17th
1727 in the 69 Year of her Age.
Quos Amor in vitâ conjunxit, non
ipsa mors divisit.

*Ledger stone in porch.*

Arms : JONES, impaling YORKE.

Here Lieth the Body of
Charles Vaience Jones Esq[r]
who married Mary, one of the Daughters
of Philip Yorke Gentleman, and by her
had Issue three Sons, and two Daughters
of whom one Son, and two Daughters are
surviving, the other two Sons lie interred
near this place, he died July 1st 1737 : in
the Thirty Eighth Year of his Age
Here Lieth also, the Body of the
said Mary, Wife of the above mentioned
Charles Vaience Jones, who
died October 6th 1762 : in the
Sixty Seventh Year of her Age.
In the same Grave with his Father and Mother
are deposited the Remains of their only surviving son
Hugh Valence (*sic*) Jones Esq[r]
who was born at Dover December 27, 1722
and died at London, January 9th 1800
From 1756 to 1759, he had the Honour of sitting
as one of the Representatives in Parliament
for the place of his birth, and during a long course of years
discharged the Duties of different and respectable offices
in a manner at once useful to his friends,
and faithful to his Trusts.

## 𝕿𝖍𝖊 𝕱𝖆𝖒𝖎𝖑𝖞 𝖔𝖋 𝕾𝖍𝖚𝖈𝖐𝖇𝖚𝖗𝖌𝖍.*

### 𝔓𝔞𝔯𝔦𝔰𝔥 𝔑𝔢𝔤𝔦𝔰𝔱𝔢𝔯𝔰.

UPPER SHUCKBURGH.

*Baptisms.*

1805 April 7    Julia Isabella, daughter of Sir Stewkley and Lady Charlotte Catharine Shuckburgh, baptized April 7th.

1806 May 24    Saliza Sophia, daughter of Sir Stewkley and Lady Charlotte Catharine Shuckburgh, baptized May 24th.

1808 Nov. 6    Emily Almeria, daughter of Sir Stewkley Shuckburgh, Baronet, and Lady Charlotte Catharine Shuckburgh, was baptized Novr 6th.

1880 Aug. 8    Stewkley Frederick Draycott, son of Sir George Thomas Francis Shuckburgh, Baronet, and Ida Florence Geraldine, Upper Shuckburgh ; born 20 June 1880. No. 44.

1882 April 16    Gerald Francis Stewkley, son of Sir George Thomas Francis Shuckburgh, Baronet, and Ida Florence Geraldine, Upper Shuckburgh ; born 28 Feb. 1882. No. 51.

*Burials.*

1783 April 18    Lady Shuckburgh, wife of Sir George Shuckburgh, Bart, was bur.

1797 Sep. 23    Julia Annabella Lady Shuckburgh, wife of Sr George Shuckburgh: Evelyn, Bart, was buried Sepr 23d 1797.

1804 Aug. 20    Sir George Augustus William Shuckburgh-Evelyn, Bart, buried August 20th.

1809 April 3    Caroline Ann Matilda, daughter of Sir Stewkley Shuckburgh, Bart, and Lady Charlotte Catherine Shuckburgh, was buried on the 3d of April.

1809 July 23    Sir Stewkley Shuckburgh, Baronet, was buried in the church of Upper Shuckburgh in the county of Warwick on the twenty-third day of July 1809.

1815 Dec. 21    Elizabeth Tydd, relict of Coll Tydd, residence Northampton, aged 79 years. No. 5.

1837 Feb. 18    Dame Charlotte Catherine, relict of Sir Stewkley Shuckburgh, Baronet, residence Bath, aged 72 years. No. 16.

1846 Nov. 17    Anna Maria Draycott Shuckburgh, wife of Sir F. Shuckburgh, Bart, Upper Shuckburgh, aged 54. No. 24.

1858 Feb. 27    Mary Amelia Laugharne, Royal Hospital, Greenwich, aged 65 years. No. 28.

1863 Oct. 7    Thomas Lamb Polden Laugharne, Royal Hospital, Greenwich, aged 77 years. No. 29.

1876 Nov. 4    Francis Shuckburgh, 8th Baronet, Upper Shuckburgh, aged 88 years. No. 36.

1884 Jan. 18    George Thomas Francis Shuckburgh, 9th Baronet, Upper Shuckburgh, aged 54. No. 38.

LONGBOROUGH, GLOUCESTERSHIRE.

*Baptism.*

1721 Mar. 17    Charles the (second) third sone of Charles Shuckberg, Efqr, was baptized ye 17th of March 1721.

*Burials.*

1719 Dec. 27    Charles ye sone of Charles Shuckberg, Efqr, buried 27th Decemb. 1719.

1721 Mar. 21    Charles ye second sone of Charles Shuckberg, Efqr, was buried ye 21th of March 1721.

1730 July 27    Arrabella Shugburgh was buried July ye 27, 1730.

* Continued from p. 298.

HERE LYETH BVRIED THE BODIE OF WILLIAM GOMSALL LATE CITTIZEN AND IREMONGER OF LONDON WHOE CHANGED THIS MORTALL LYFE THE FIRST DAY OF IVLIE IN THE YERE OF OVR LORD GOD 1597 IN FVLL AND FRECT HOPE OF A IOYFVLL RESVRRECTION. AND LEFT BEHINDE HIM ONE SONNE AND TWO DAVGHTERS.

BRASS. HILLINGDON CHURCH. MIDDLESEX.

## WILL OF WILLIAM GOMERSALL OF HILLINGDON, 1597.

William Gomersall of Hillington, Middx., Gent. Will dated 22 May 1597 ; proved 4 July 1597 by John Burrough, notary pub., proctor for Rob^t Gomersall the ex'or. All my lands and tenem^ts in Uxbridge and Edmonton to my son Robert Gomersall for life, and at his death to his son William Gomersall, and his heirs, my s^d son to pay to my wife Anne Gomersall £20 yearly for her life, and also to pay to my wife within a month after my decease the sum of £20 at my son George Lee's house in Westminster. To Mary Lee, da. of George Lee, Esq., my house at Debtford Strande now in the tenure of the Lord High Admirall of England, rem^r in default of issue to her brother Thomas Lee, rem^r to my son Robert Gomersall, and whoever possesses the fee simple of the said house is to pay to Thomas Nune, clerk, late of Debtford, the sum of £10 yearly. To Margaret More, wife of John More, £10, to be paid by Christofer Aclye of Cowly. To Annys Aclye, da. of Lawrence Aclye of Uxbridge, £10, to be paid by Christofer Aclye of Cowly, her uncle. To John Aclye, now my servant, 5 marks. Debts owing to me by James Mathewe of Iver, William Roberts of Feltham, Thomas Lawrence of Bray, William Redinge and Richard Redinge, Henry Ponde and John Clarke, and George Gibe and W^m Weden. To my da. Elizabeth 300 marks to be paid by my son Robert Gomersall out of the above debts owing to me. Poor of Hillington £5. To Christofer Aclye and his wife a silver gilt spoon each, weighing 2 ounces. To Margaret Moore, wife of John Moore, and Annys Aclye, bedding, etc. John Heaver of Harvill to be paid £120 which I owe him. If my son Robert Gomersall puts in sureties to the Chamber of London to pay to W^m Gomersall his son £500 at his age of 24, then my s^d son may sell and take to his use all such lands, etc., as I have given him by my will. My said son Robert Gomersall, sole ex'or, to whom residue. Christofer Aclye to be overseer. WILLIAM GOMERSALL.

Wit., Richard Gomersall, Jonas Arnold, and others. (P.C.C., 66 Cobham.)

## Genealogy of Browne.*

### Wills.

Copy of the Will of JOHN BROWNE of Caverswall, co. Stafford. Dated 1665 ; proved 1666.

[Lichfield.]

IN THE NAME OF GOD AMEN The four and twentyth day of November in the seaventeenth year of the Raigne of our Soveraign Lord Charles the second by the grace of God of England Scotland France and Ireland King Defender of the Faith &c. Annoq. D'm'i 1665 I John Browne of Cooks-hill in the parish of Carswall and county of Stafford Gent. being of perfect health and memory but knowing that all men must dy but the time of death being uncertain do make publish and ordaine this my last Will and testament in wryting And first I give and bequeath my soul unto the hands of Almighty God my Maker and Creator hopeing to be saved by the onely merritts and passion of my blessed Saviour and Redeemer Jhesus Christ his onely begotten sonne and my body to be buried at the discretion of my executors hereafter named And for y^t worldly estate which God of his mercy hath bestowed upon me I give and devise the same in manner and forme following First I give and devise all y^t messuage or tenement called Hartwell Farme and all the lands tenem^ts and hereditam^ts thereunto belonging lying in the parish of Barlaston and Stone or one of them in the said county of Staff^d to be sould by my Execut^rs hereafter named for the paym^t of my debts and funerall expences and such legacies as are hereafter in and by this my last Will and Testam^t expressed limited and appoynted And I further devise and bequeath unto my executors hereafter named all my personall estate Bills Bonds & debts whatsoever to be imployed for the uses aforesaid And first I desire that my debts and funeralls may be satisfied and discharged and after those are satisfied I will and devise that untill the lands are sould there may be paid out of the rents and profitts thereof the sume of five pounds a year to my sister Abigail Browne and after the said lands are sould then I will and devise that out of the money which shalbe received for the same there shalbe the sume of one hundred pounds paid unto her for a legacy by me given unto her And I will and devise that Katherine Abraham al's Browne shall have paid unto her out of the profitts of the said land twenty shillings a year during her life by five shillings a quarter. Item I will and devise that forth of the issues and profits of the same lands untill itt be sould there

* Continued from p. 291.

should be five pounds a year raised whereof three pounds to be yearly paid to the poor of the said parish of Carswall to be disposed of in such manner and forme as my execut$^{rs}$ hereafter named during their or eyther of their lives shall think fitt and after the decease of the survivor of them then as the Minister Churchwardens and Overseers of the poor of the said parish of Carswall for the tyme being or the greater part of them shall appoynt and that the other fourty shillings thereof shalbe yearly paid the Minister of the said parish of Carswall to preach two sermons yearly the one of them yearly upon the day that it shall please God I shalbe buried and the other yearly upon St. John's Day the Baptist and in case there be no Minister at Carswall then to be preached by the Minist$^r$ of Dilhorn and the Legacy for that tyme given to him And that the residue of the rents and profitts of the said lands untill it shalbe sould I doe hereby give and bequeath to and amongst all my sisters children being in number nineteene share and share alike And to the intent that the said yearly some of three pounds a year to the poor of the said parish and fourty shillings a year to the Minister of the said parish may continue for ever I will and devise that upon sale of the said lands out of the money for which the said land shalbe sould there shalbe three pounds a year in lands purchased in the name of the Churchwardens and overseers of the poor of the said parish of Carswall and their successors for ever to be paid yearly to the poor of the said p'ish of Carswall for ever And lands of the value of Fourty shillings a year shall be likewise purchased of the same money for the payment of the said fourty shillings a year to the minister of the said parish and his successors for ever And I desire that a table may be made and these legacies to the poor and minister may be written in the same and the same to be affixed in the church that the poor and minister may not in tyme to come be defrauded of the said legacies And after my debts funeralls and these other legacies to my sister Abigail the poor and minister and the twenty shillings a year secured to the said Katherine Abraham al's Browne for her life I do give and bequeath all the residue of the money that shalbe raised by sale of the said lands to and amongst all my said sisters children being in number nineteene to have every one an equal share of it And if any one of them be not at age to give a sufficient discharge Then I will and devise the same to be paid to the Father or Mother of such child and to be paid to such child when it comes to age without any allowance for it And the acquittance of the said Father or mother shalbe a sufficient discharge to my Execut$^r$ for the paym$^t$ of it And if any of my said sisters children dy before their legacies be paid then I will and devise that his or her part shalbe equally divided between the Brothers and sisters of such child and if such child have neyther Brother nor sister then living then the same to be equally divided amongst all my said sisters children share and share alike. Item I give and devise to my nephew Ralph Browne sonne of my Brother Ralph Browne deceased the sume of fifty pounds to be paid unto him after he shall attayn his age of one and twenty yeares if he shall so long live and if he dy before he attayn the said age of one and twenty yeares then the same to be equally divided to and amongst my said sisters children share and share alike Provoided that if any of my said sisters children shall sue molest or trouble my Execut$^{rs}$ or eyther of them or their or eyther of their Execut$^{rs}$ or administrators or any of them for or by reason of any legacy hereby given to them then such person and persons soe sueing molesting or troubling them shall loose their legacy and the same shall go to and amongst the rest of my said sisters children And I doe hereby nominate my dear Father Ralph Browne Gent. and my good brother in law Alexander Howe Gent. Executors of this my last Will who are to have their reasonable charges born out of my whole estate And I nominate my two brother in laws William Langley, Clarke, and Thomas Launder to be overseers of this my will. WITNESSE my hand and seale the day and year above written.

*John Browne*

Signed sealed and published by the said John Browne as his last Will and Testament in the presence of us John Burtinshaw Vicar de Carswall William Cookes John Lomax William Fisher.
Proved 31$^{st}$ May 1666 by Ralph Browne the Father and Alexander How the Executors. Personal estate £85 9s. 6d.

---

Copy of the Will of WILLIAM BROWNE of Caverswall, co. Stafford. Dated 1602; proved 1603.
[Lichfield.]

IN THE NAME OF GOD AMEN The xxx$^{th}$ day of December in the yeare of our Lord god a thousand sixe hundred and two I William Browne of Cookshill in the parish of Careswell w$^{th}$in the countie of Stafford Yoman beinge of good and p'fect remembrance (thanks be to God therefore) doe ordayne and make this my last Will and testament in maner and forme followinge first I bequeath my soule to Almightie God the redeemer therof and my body to be buryed in the parish Church of Careswall. Item I gyve and bequeath to my welbeloved daughter Ann Whittrance and to her chilldren of currant English money fyve pownds to be payd to my sayde daughter Ann w$^{th}$in one moneth after my decease. Item I gyve and bequeath to my sonne in law Thomas Heelie and to his two chilldren w$^{ch}$ he had by my daughter Alice two shillings. Item I gyve to my brother James Browne yf he survive or overlyve me xl<sup>s</sup> in money. Item I gyve unto ev'y godchilde I have that shalbe lyvinge at the daye of my decease iiij<sup>d</sup>. Item I gyve unto my sonne in lawe William Browne xl<sup>s</sup> for and in full payment & satisfacc'on of all such legacies w<sup>ch</sup> he might have or clayme from me w<sup>ch</sup> weare gyven unto his wyfe by my brother Richard Browne. Item I gyve unto ev'y one of my sonne in lawe John Bridgwood his chilldren xx<sup>s</sup>. Item I gyve to my daughter Margery ij<sup>s</sup> vi<sup>d</sup>. Item I gyve to my godsonne Rauffe Browne my cozen Rauffe Browne's little boye one ewe and a lambe. Item I gyve to the poore people in Careswell p'ishe x<sup>s</sup> to be distributed amongst them. Item I gyve unto my sonne Thomas Browne xl<sup>s</sup>. Item I gyve unto Issabell Leeke one payre of sheetes. Item I gyve unto my sayde daughter Anne Whitterins v<sup>£</sup> w<sup>ch</sup> w<sup>th</sup> the foresayde v<sup>£</sup> before gyven maketh x<sup>£</sup>. Item my mynde and Will is that my executors shall bringe me well and honestly home accordinge to their discretions. Item I gyve unto my sonne in lawe William Lees two daughters w<sup>ch</sup> he had by my daughter Elizabeth xij<sup>d</sup> a peece. Item I gyve unto Thomas Warner my parte of that daye worke of corne w<sup>ch</sup> he sowed on my grownde to the partes. Item I gyve unto Elizabeth Rawlins daughter to William Rawlins one ewe and a lambe The residue of my goods not before gyven nor bequeathed my funerall expences dischardged and my debts and legacies first payde I gyve to my executors to be bestowed accordinge to their discretions And I doe ordayne and make my sonne in law John Bridgewood and my cozen Rauffe Browne my executors whome I desyre to see this my Will p'formed accordinge to my intent and meaninge hearin expressed. Item I gyve unto my daughter Ann Whittrens children all my part or parts of the corne nowe growinge in my grounds called the newe close and Dodle (except my parte of that daye worke form'ly gyven to Thomas Warner Also it is my wyll and meaninge that Thomas Warner shall have all my parte of the corne growinge in Dodle before gyven to my daughter Anns children payinge such reasonable price for y<sup>t</sup> as my executors shall sett downe. Item it is my further mynde and will that yf my executors shall want or not have sufficient to p'forme this my Will that then my executors shall have all the corne before gyven to my daughter Anns children for the better p'formance of the same.

Signed and acknowledged in the p'sence of Margaret Malpas Catherine Grindie.

Proved 18<sup>th</sup> July 1603 by John Bridgwood and Ralph Browne. Amount of Inventory £42 8s. 9d.

(*To be continued.*)

## MONUMENTAL INSCRIPTIONS FROM THE BURIAL-GROUND OF ST. GEORGE, HANOVER SQUARE, NEAR MARBLE ARCH.*

Frances Daller, daughter of Samuel Henry & Fanny Daller, died June 30 1793, aged 1 year & 10 months.
William Hugh Walker, died Dec. 20, 1806, aged 1 year & 6 months.
Samuel Henry Daller, died June 14, 1821, aged 75.

———

Margaret [Rochat] .... Oct. .... aged 1 year & 4 months.
Sophia [Rochat] died June [. . . .] aged 2 years & 6 months.
Margaret Rochat, mother of the above two children, died Nov. 29, 1805, aged 55. [*Rest illegible.*]

———

Stuart Cummine Esq. late Captain of Artillery in Bengal, died April 16<sup>th</sup> 1791, aged 45. He was the 4<sup>th</sup> son of Charles Cummine Esq. of [Keinimonth?] in Aberdeenshire, by Sophia, eldest daughter of James, the 16<sup>th</sup> Lord Forbes of Scotland.

———

Susanna Yeats, wife of M<sup>r</sup> Yeats, Bookseller, of Pimlico, died 16 May 1786, aged 44. Also the above named M<sup>r</sup> Alexander Yeats died Jan [31<sup>st</sup>?] 1814, aged 82. Sophia Yeats [daughter?] of the above M<sup>r</sup> Yeats, died Nov. 16, 1791, aged 18.

———

M<sup>r</sup> William Mitchell, died April 22, 1809, aged 77. He lived with the Duke of Queensbery, as Servant more than thirty years. By his Will he settled the Interest of Two hundred Pounds for ever upon the Poor of the Parish of S<sup>t</sup> Fergus, where he was born.

———

M<sup>rs</sup> Elizabeth, wife of M<sup>r</sup> John Sheild, of Park Street, in this parish, died 8 March 1788 [. . . .]. [*Rest hidden by a footstone.*]

* Continued from p. 292.

Hannah Todd, beloved wife of Thomas Todd, died Jan. 5, 1827, aged 45.
Also near this spot are interred Thomas and Harriet, son & daughter of the above,
who died infants.
George Todd, son of the above, died Sep. 2, 1842, aged 35.
William Todd, son of the above, died Nov. 15, 1847, aged 34.
Thomas Todd, husband of the above named Hannah Todd, died Nov. 16, 1853,
aged 78.

---

M$^r$ Frederick Plincke, third son of the late M$^r$ Frederick Plincke, of this parish, died
April 4 1838, aged 54.

---

M$^r$ Samuel [Yaxley] died March [. .] 1804, aged 28.
M$^{rs}$ Elizabeth Dibbs, sister of the above & wife of M$^r$ William Dibbs, died Dec.
12, 1824, aged 50.

---

[Fanny] Hounso . . . . Dec. . . in her 62$^{nd}$ year.

---

Master Henry Robert Jones, died 13 March 1827, aged 3 years & 6 months.

---

M$^r$ Thomas Walkden, died June 20, 1829, aged 56.

---

M$^{rs}$ Sarah Goodwin, wife of T. B. Goodwin, of George Street, Portman Square, died
Dec. 12, 1831, aged 31.

---

M$^{rs}$ Reid, of Little Maddox Street, in this parish, died 1 January 1825, aged 41.
Also two of her children, who died in their infancy.
George Reid, husband of the above, died June 20, 1833, aged 64. Requisecat in pace.

---

M$^{rs}$ Catherine Thomson, died 8 Nov. 1835, aged 73.
M$^r$ Donald M$^c$Leod, son in law of the above, died 7 June 1853, aged 49.

---

M$^{rs}$ Mary Fortescue, died Jan. 30, 1834, aged 56.
M$^{rs}$ Elizabeth Fortescue, died March 3, 1838, aged 35.

---

In memory of two sons of Owen & Mary Macdonagh.
George, died 10 May 179[6 ?], aged 2 years and 6 months.
Thomas, died 21 Aug. 1801, aged 3 years & [. .] months.

---

M$^r$ Thomas Brown, died Feb. 9. 1802, aged 39.
Miss Sophia Augusta Brown, his daughter, died Dec. 13, 1800, aged 4.
M$^{rs}$ Sophia Quatermass, died March 29, 1848, aged 85.
M$^{rs}$ Elizabeth Hales, died Feb. 22, 1803, aged 61.
Also two daughters of Charles James & Mary Brown : Mary Sophia, died March 1,
1840, aged 6 years & 3 months ; Emily died May 19, 1843, aged 5 years &
7 months.
And of their son Thomas Albert, died Jan. 18, 1844, aged [. .] years.

---

M$^{rs}$ Jane Stokes, died 29 Nov. [1831] aged 38.
Charles Stokes, died Feb. 17, 1836, aged 5.
M$^r$ Richard Stokes, died Aug. 21 1844, in his 51$^{st}$ year.

---

Maria Louisa Ainge, daughter of Joseph and Clarissa Ainge, died June 17 1848,
aged 24.
Also eight children of the above J & C Ainge, died infants.

Robert Cottam, died March 20 1829, aged 37.
Also two of his daughters : Emma, aged 6 years and 6 months ; Catherine, aged 2 years and 6 months.
Also two infant children.

Elizabeth Gertckex, died March 7, 1807, in her 22nd year.

.... Gertckex ........ 1795 .... 1798.

Sally Gregory, died Aug. 18 1831, aged 30.

Mr [Robert ?] Lewis ........ 1824.

William Jones, died Nov. 5 [1857 or 1837 ?] in his 30th year.
Likewise William Edward, son of the above, died March 24 1830, aged 3.

Charlotte Russell, daughter of Henry & Mary Ann Russell, died June 19 1836, aged 3.

In memory of the children of James and Mary Ann Russell, of this parish :
Frederick, died Dec. 17 1809.
Edward, died May 29 1812.
Louisa, died Jan. 13 1817.
Elizabeth Jane died Feb. 21 1824.
Also the above mentioned Mrs Mary Ann Russell, died March 13 1824, aged 40.
Also the above named Mr James Russell, born 2 Aug. 1777, died at [. . . .] Dec. 1847.

*(To be continued.)*

# Cullum.

## ST. CLEMENT'S, IPSWICH.

1654 John Cullum and Abigaell Taylor married the 2d day of January.
1655 Abigael ye wife of John Cullum buried 6 of ffebruary.
1658 John Cullum and Mary Low were maried the 24th of October.
1660 John Cullum son'e of John and Mary was baptized the 22th of July.
1661 Mary Cullham daughter of John and Mary was baptized the 22th September.
1664 Robert ye son'e of John Cullam and of Mary his wife was baptized ye 26th of October.
1667 Mr Cullam's child was buried August the 22.
1669 Abigail the daughter of John Cullum and Mary his wife was baptised October 25th.
1673 Maria daughter of John Cullum was buried October the 18.
1677 Abigail daugh: of Joh Cullum (buried) Dec. 19.
1685 Mary Daugh: of John Cullum and Mary (bap.) July 21.
1688 William son of John Cullome and (blank) his wife (bap.) Nov. 4.
1692 Robt : son of Robt : Cullum and Margt his wife (bap.) Sept. 11.
1693 Abigail daughter of John Cullum (buried) Sept. 3.
1694 Mary daughter of Robt : Cullum and Margt his wife (bap.) May 14.
1694 Thomas son of John Cullum and Mary his wife (bap.) Sep: 9.
1695 John son of Robt: Cullum and Marg: his wife (bap.) Dec. 8.

1696   Elizabeth daughtʳ of John Cullum and Mary his wife (bap.) March 18.
1698   Edwᵈ son of Robᵗ Cullum and Margᵗ his wife (bap.) June 15.
1698   Edward sonn of Robt : Cullum (bur.) June 23.
1699   John Callam (bur.) June 25.
1702   Samˡ sonn of John Cullum and Mary his wife (bap.) Oct. 4.
1702   Richᵈ sonn of Robt. Cullum and Margᵗ his wife (bap.) Oct : 18.
1704   Edward sonn of Robt. Cullum and Margᵗ his wife (bap.) Aug : 17.
1706   Mary Cullum Widdᵒ (bur.) May 31.
1707   Mary Cullum (bur.) June 24.
1716   Thomas Cole to Mary Cullum Sept : 23.
1723   John Cullum (bur.) June 10.
1740   Margett Cullam, widow (bur.) Nov : 5.
1741   Mary Collom (bur.) August 29.
1748   Elizᵗʰ dau : of Robart and Elizᵗʰ Collom (bap.) April 3.
1752   Elizbeth Daughter of Edward Cullom (bur.) June 9.
1762   Elizb : Culham (bur.) July 1.

### St. Stephen's, Ipswich.

1688   John Cullham vid : and Mary Bowle vid : both of St : Clement's Parish married November 21.

### St. Mary le Tower, Ipswich.

1688   Samuel son of Samuel Cullam and Jane was baptized Octobˢ 7º.
1688   Samuel son of Samuel Cullum was buried Octobˢ 7º.
1690   Samuel son of Samuel Cullum and Jane was baptized Aprilˢ 8º.
1690   Joseph Scowen and Sarah Cullum both single w. marᵈ Julij : 3º.
1696   Jane yᵉ wife of Samuel Cullum was buryed Septembˢ 22º.
1719   Mary the wife of Samuel Cullum was Buried April : 3.
1726   Samuel Cullam of this parish widower and Ann Marchant of Sᵗ Mathew's Parish widow were married Jan : 16.
1731   Mʳ Samuel Cullum was Buried Jan : 16.
1732   William Strauchan of this parish single man and Hannah Cullum of the same widow were married Jul : 3.
1747   William Forsdick of Helmingham singleman and Elizabeth Cullum of Framsden single woman were mᵈ Augˢᵗ 29.

### St. Mathew's Church, Ipswich.

1633   Sara daughter of John Cullom and Rose his wife was baptized the 12 daie of Januarie.
1749   Samuel Cullom was buried September 12ᵗʰ.

### St. Mary Quay Church, Ipswich.

1635   William the sonne of John Cullum and Rose his wife was baptized Nov. 1.
1636   Stephen the sonne of John Cullom and Rose his wife was baptized Marche 22.

From the Great Court Book of Ipswich. 17 May, 18 Chas. II.

"Agreed that Mʳ Wᵐ Cullam shalbe admitted A ffree Burgesse of this towne & to take his oath att some pettie Court & to be discharged of all offices except Portman & those offices belonginge to Portmen."

From the Ipswich Assembly Book. 13 August, 18 Chas. II.

"Att this Assembly Mʳ Thomas Reeve, Mʳ Edward Keene & Mʳ William Cullam was elected to be three of the Portmen of this Towne in the places & Roomes of John Smythier gen' John Robinson gen' & Thomas Burrough gen' deceased & to take their oathes att some petty Court."

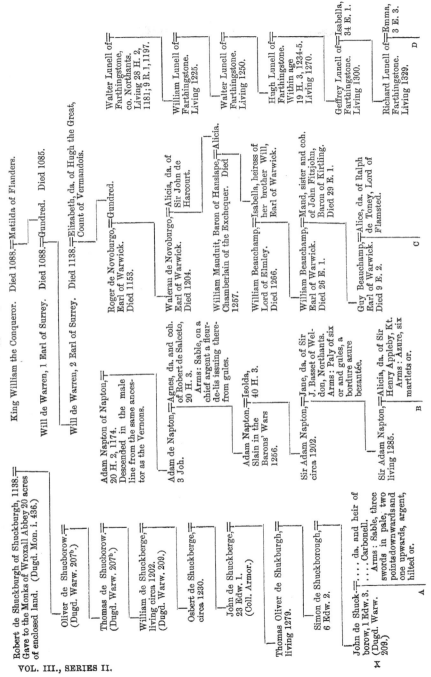

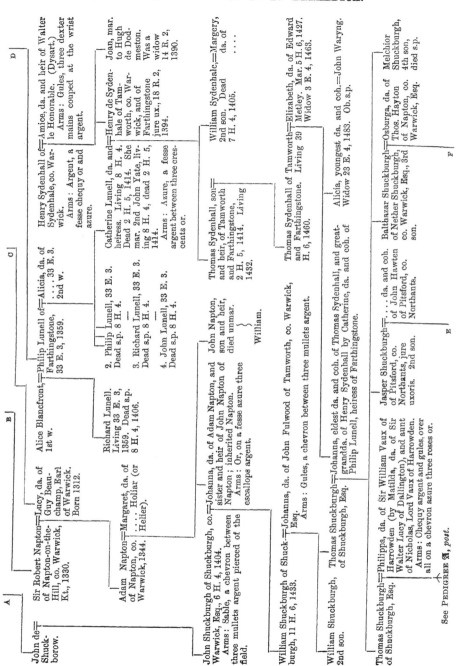

F |

E |

Thomas Shuckburgh, 2nd son.

Anthony Shuckburgh of Nether Shuckburgh, and of Harrowden, co. Northants, Esq. = Anne, da. of Henry Gage of Burton Latimer, co. Northants, gent. 1st wife.

Isabel, relict of John Pharro of Little Harrowden, 2nd wife.

Alice, da. of .... Marley of Cheshire, gent., and relict of Thos. Barnewell. 3rd wife.

John Shuckburgh of Naseby, co. Northants, and of Pitsford, 6, E. 6. = Anne, da. of .... Acton of Warwick, gent.

John Shuckburgh.

William Shuckburgh.

Margery, mar. John Reade of Hardwick.

Margaret, mar. Fras. Alderman of Harrowden, co. Northants.

Elizabeth, mar. William Hawford of Clipston, co. Northants.

Thomas Shuckburgh of Little Harrowden, 1618. = Bridget, da. of Gilbert Wheeler of Rowbright, co. Oxon.

Margaret, mar. Thomas Pickering of Isham, co. Northants.

1. Alice, mar. Geo. Dillingham of Deane, Northants.

3. Susannah.

5. Anne, mar. William Harrison of Wellingborough, Northants.

Jasper Shuckburgh.

Anthony Shuckburgh, da. of John Bent. = Elizabeth, eldest son. Died s.p.

Thomas Shuckburgh of Little Harrowden, 2nd son, but at length heir 1618. = Eleanor, da. of Thos. Foukes of Twywell, co. Northants.

2. Mary, mar. Tho. Alderman of Pytchley, Northants.

4. Bridget.

6. Dionysia, mar. Robert Meddowes of Kettering, Northants.

John Shuckburgh.

Margaret, mar. John Congleton of Flower, co. Northants, gent.

Dorothy, da. of .... Dicons of Welford, co. Northants. 2nd wife.

John Shuckburgh.

George Shuckburgh of Pitsford, co. Northants, 14 Eliz. Had lands in Great Billing, co. Northants, 14 Eliz. = Cassandra, da. of .... Burton.

John Shuckburgh of Naseby, co. Northants. Died 25 Sept. 1576. Bur. at Naseby. = Joan, da. of Roger Knolles of Cold Ashby, co. Northants. M.I.

Edward Shuckburgh of Naseby, Esq. High Sheriff of Northants 1624, M.P. 22 Jas. 1. Died 25 April 1658, æt. 86. Bur. Naseby. M.I.

Henry Shuckburgh.

Dorothy, mar. Edward Hanbury of Kelmarsh Hall, Esq., and had two children, John Hanbury, son and heir, and Dorothy, mar. George Fant of Easton, co. Leicester, Esq. (Edward Hanbury mar. 2ndly Lucy Martin, and left by her four sons and three dau'rs. He died 1656.)

John Shuckburgh = Anne, da. of of West Haddon, co. Northants, æt. 3 14 Eliz. Died s.p. = Richard Knolles of Cold Ashby, co. Northants.

Mary, da. of Tho. Andrewes of Charwelton; born 5 May 1576 at Winwick. 1st wife. = Edward Shuckburgh, 3rd son.

Elizabeth, mar. Tho. Cotton of Laughton, co. Leicester.

Knightleya.

Agnes or Anne.

Sarah.

Eusebius Shuckburgh of Naseby, Esq. = Mary Shuckburgh, only da. and heir.

George Ashby of Quenby, co. Leic., Esq. 1st husb. = George Hewet of Gray's Inn, Esq., and of Rotherby, co. Leicester. 2nd husb.

Whence Ashby of Naseby and Quenby.

1. Frances, eldest da., mar. Lawrence Saunders of Sibbertoft, co. Northants.

2. Elizabeth, mar. 1st, Peter Coles of Preston; 2nd, Tho. Knightley of Brough Hall, co. Staff, and Preston Capes.

3. Margaret, m. William Harcourt of Dadlington, co. Leicester.

4. Anne, mar. 1st, John Hopkins of Northampton; 2nd, .... Tiringham of Weston.

5. Judeth, mar. Sir Thos. Brooke of Oakeley, co. Northants, Kt.

6. Mary, mar. Valentine Acton, Esq.

7. Avice, mar. Thomas Love of Sulby.

8. Maud.

9. Jane.

10. Dorothy.

11. Anne.

12. Elizabeth.

13. Frances.

Died young.

x 2

(To be continued.)

# The Register Book of Bramfield, co. Suffolk.*

### 1801.

Nov. 19  William s. of the same [James and Mary Mayhew] received into the Church at the same time.

[blank]  James s. of James Crisp, jun., and Ann (Sholders) his wife.

Aug. 16  John s. of James and Elizabeth Aldred (late Borret).

Sep. 27  Mary d. of Isaac and Elizab: Watling (late Eleanor) was rec^d into Church.

Sep. 27  Anne d. of the same Persons; born Sep. 27, baptized the same day.

FRAN. J. WARING, A.M., Curate.

Oct. 4  John s. of Richard and Rebecca Puttock (late Reeve).

Dec. 19  Mary d. of William and Mary Balls (late Cooper) rec^d into the Church June 4, 1806. [Bowls, June 1799.]

Dec. 28  James s. of Robert and Susan Row (late Girling) rec^d into Church Mar. 21, 1802.

### 1802.

Jan. 10  Hannah d. of Margaret Holmes. Spurious.

Jan. 31  Isaac s. of Isaac and Elizabeth Watling (late Elenor). Publicly Jan. 9, 1806.

Feb. 22  Daniel s. of William and Elizabeth Pearson (late Reynolds). Privately.

Feb. 28  John s. of John and Betty Hillin (late Reeve).

Feb. 28  Isaac s. of Harmon and Sarah Garret (late Fisher).

Feb. 28  Mary d. of Thomas and Anne Ellener (late Bullard). Privately. Rec^d into the Church Jan. 19, 1806.

April 1  Thomas s. of Joseph Bellamy and Marianne Estaugh his wife. Privately.

May 13  Joseph Charles s. of Joseph and Elizabeth Badeley (late Smith). Privately; born May 2.

July 11  Amelia Estaugh d. of John and Lydia Crispe (late Estaugh).

June 18  Obadiah s. of William and Lydia Pitches. Privately.

Aug. 15  Marianne d. of William and Eliz. Woollard (late Scrutton).

Oct. 17  Israel s. of old William Hawes, aged 75, and Elizabeth (Dutt) his wife.

Nov. 7  Edna d. of Elizabeth Crispe. Spurious. Privately.

Dec. 4  Marianne d. of Sam^l and Sarah Cross (late Pead). Privately.

Dec. 12  Maria d. of Tho^s and Mary Kerridge (late Jackson).

Nov. 11  Omitted. Anne d. of John and Anne Hart (late Calver, spinster). Privately.

### 1803.

Feb. 20  Louisa d. of Samuel and Elizabeth Leggett (late Wright, spinster); born Feb. 5. Privately. Rec^d into the Church Feb. 9, 1806.

Feb. 27  Sarah d. of Thomas Lame and Sarah his wife (late Tripp, spinster); born Feb. 12.

Mar. 9  Maria d. of James Mayhew and Mary his wife (late Ling, spinster); born March 2. Privately.

Mar. 19  George s. of Samuel Barneby and Hannah his wife (late Gayfer, spinster); born Feb. 10.

Mar. 20  James s. of William Watling and Esther his wife; born Feb. 5. Privately.

Mar. 23  John s. of Thomas Edwards and Ann his wife; born March 21. Privately. Died an infant.

April 10  Joseph s. of Joseph Kemp and Elizabeth his wife (late Newson, spinster); born Jan. 29.

July 17  James s. of Sam^l and Frances Harber; born July 2.

Aug. 14  Hannah, Bastard dau'r of Sarah Gayfer. Publicly Jan. 19, 1806.

Aug. 21  Robert s. of John and Rebecca Gilman; born Aug. 17.

Sep. 14  William s. of Edward and Sarah Thrower; born Aug. 8.

Sep. 21  William s. of John and Mary Steggal; born Sep. 14. Publicly Feb. 21, 1806.

Oct. 4  Isaac and Rebeccah Twin children of Richard Puttock and Rebeccah his wife; born Aug. 25. Privately. Publicly Jan. 10, 1806.

Dec. 18  Jane d. of William and Elizabeth Haws.

### 1804.

Jan. 19  Maria, Bastard of Ann Burn. Rec^d into the Church June 9, 1808.

Mar. 11  Mary d. of Robert Savage and Mary his wife (late Pipe, spinster); born Feb. 29. Privately. Rec^d into the Church Jan. 19, 1806.

Mar. 18  Mary d. of John Banks and Mary his wife (late Maggs, spinster); born March 12. Privately.

April 1  William s. of William Hatcher and Ann his wife (late Skeet). Privately.

C. NEWTON, Curate from Sunday Feb. 26, 1804.

April 28  Louisa d. of Joseph Badeley and Elizabeth his wife (late Smith, spinster); born Ap. 20. Privately.

Aug. 5  William s. of William Woolard and Elizabeth his wife (late Scrutton, spinster); born Aug. 4. Privately. Publicly Jan. 19, 1806.

* Continued from p. 303.

Sep. 2 Lydia d. of Lionel Hammond and Diana his wife ; born March 2. Privately.

Aug. 26 John s. of John Hart and Anne his wife (late Calver, spinster) ; born Aug. 12, 1801. Privately.

Oct. 14 Sarah d. of Thomas Edwards and Anne his wife (late Wright, spinster) ; born Feb. 6, 1801. Privately. Being 3 years old six weeks after X'mas Day, 1804.

Dec. 30 John s. of Isaac Watling and Elizabeth his wife (late Ellenor) ; born Dec. 20. Privately.

1805.

Feb. 17 James s. of Robert Savage and Sarah his wife (late Pipe, spinster) ; born Feb. 16. Privately.

Feb. 18 Louisa d. of John Crisp and Lydia his wife (late Estaugh, spinster) ; born Feb. 16. Privately.

Mar. 3 Susan d. of W<sup>m</sup> Watling and Esther his wife (late Flowers, spinster) ; born March 2. Privately. Rec<sup>d</sup> into the Church Jan. 31, 1808.

Feb. 24 William s. of Henry Waight and Mary his wife (late Adams, spinster). Privately. Publicly Feb. 19, 1806.

Mar. 24 John s. of John Banks and Mary his wife (late Maggs, spinster) ; born March 22. Privately. Publicly Jan. 19, 1806.

April 7 Eliza d. of Samuel Leggatt and Elizabeth his wife (late Wright, spinster); born March 31. Privately. Publicly Feb. 9, 1806.

April 28 Stephen s. of Joseph Kemp and Elizabeth his wife (late Newson, spinster) ; born Ap. 18. Privately. Publicly Feb. 9, 1806.

May 26 Thomas s. of Thomas Ellener and Anne his wife (late Bullard, spinster) ; born May 19. Privately. Publicly Jan. 19, 1806.

May 26 Ezra s. of Ezra Edwards and Mary his wife (late Clack, spinster) ; born May 20. Privately. Publicly Feb. 23, 1806.

June 25 James s. of Thomas Lame and Sarah his wife (late Tripp). Privately. Publicly Jan 19, 1806.

July 14 James Bastard s. of Jemima Smith ; born July 7. Privately. Publicly Jan. 19, 1806.

Aug. 4 John s. of John Alp and Maria his wife (late Cady, spinster) ; born Aug. 2. Privately. Publicly Jan. 12, 1806.

Oct. 6 Sam<sup>l</sup> s. of John and Eliz: Gilman; born Oct. 1.

Nov. 2 John s. of the widow of the late John Steggal and Mary his wife ; born same day. Publicly Feb. 26, 1806.

Nov. 2 Margaretta d. of W<sup>m</sup> and Eliz: Pierson; born Nov. 1.

Nov. 5 Harriott bastard d. of Sarah Danford; born Oct. 29. Publicly Jan. 19, 1806.

Nov. 17 William s. of Richard and Rebeccah Puttock ; born same day.

1806.

Jan. 19 Mary d. of John and Eliz: Hellen (late Reeve); born Ap. 6, 1805.

Jan. 19 Rob<sup>t</sup> s. of Lionel and Diana Hammond (late Wats); born Nov. 1801.

Jan. 26 James s. of John and Mary Thurlow (late Katspool) ; born Aug. 12, 1803.

Feb. 9 Mary Ann d. of W<sup>m</sup> and Ann Hatcher (late Skeet) ; born Nov. 28, 1805.

Feb. 9 Elizabeth d. of Isaac and Eliz: Watling (late Ellener, spinster) ; born Dec. 4, 1803.

CHRIST<sup>r</sup> MASON.

Mar. 31 Charlotte d. of Tho<sup>s</sup> and Charlotte Higham (late Aldis) ; born July 20, 1803.

Mar. 31 Martha d. of the same ; born Jan. 24.

April 20 Mille d. of Jonathan and Mary Reyner (late Reyner, spinster) ; born Ap. 16. Privately. Rec<sup>d</sup> into the Church June 11.

May 11 Charlotte d. of John and Mary Thurlow (late Katspool, spinster) ; born May 3. Privately. Rec<sup>d</sup> into the Church Aug. 10.

July 20 Sarah d. of Rob<sup>t</sup> and Sarah Savage (late Pipe, spinster) ; born July 10. Privately. Rec<sup>d</sup> into the Church Nov. 30.

Aug. 3 John s. of Samuel and Francis Harber (late Gayfer) ; born July 17.

July 27 John s. of Isaac and Elizabeth Watling (late Ellins, spinster) ; born July 12. Privately.

Aug. 24 Noah s. of John and Ann Newson (late Annal, spinster) ; born June 14. Privately.

Sep. 21 James s. of Mary Malter ; born Sep. 3.

Sep. 28 Philip s. of W<sup>m</sup> Kerridge and Elizabeth his wife (late Ward) ; born Sep. 11. Privately.

Nov. 30 Tho<sup>s</sup> s. of John and Mary Banks (late Maggs, spinster) ; born Nov. 4.

Dec. 15 Francis s. of Rob<sup>t</sup> and Susan Raw (late Girling, spinster) ; born Dec. 5. Privately. Rec<sup>d</sup> in the Church Jan. 18, 1807.

1807.

Feb. 14 Mary d. of John and Hanah Balls (late Riches, spinster) ; born Feb. 10. Privately. Rec<sup>d</sup> in the Church June 8, 1808.

Mar. 9 Mary d. of George and Elizabeth Watson (late Harrison) ; born March 6. Rec<sup>d</sup> in the Church Nov. 1.

C. MASON.

April 21 Elizabeth d. of Thomas and Sarah Lame (late Trip, spinster) ; born Ap. 11. Privately. Rec<sup>d</sup> in the Church May 10.

June 5 Sophia d. of W<sup>m</sup> and Elizabeth Hawes (late Dutt, spinster) ; born June 1. Privately. Rec<sup>d</sup> in the Church July 12.

June 8   Clarissa d. of Hanah Hand; born illegitimate May 28. Privately.

June 30   Harriet d. of Samuel and Lydia Ward (late Stern, spinster); born Feb. 27, 1794.

June 30   Harbert s. of the same; born Nov. 15, 1796.

July 12   Phillis d. of Thoˢ Elner and Ann his wife (late Bullard, spinster); born Feb. 15.

July 24   John Ashford s. of Deborah Mash; born illegitimate Ap. 15. Privately.

Sep. 11   James s. of Samˡ and Elizabeth Leggat (late Wright, spinster); born Sep. 5. Privately. Recᵈ in the Church Sep. 1, 1811.

Sep. 13   Susan d. of Edwᵈ and Elizabeth Ashford (late Cudde, spinster); born Aug. 7.

Sep. 7   John s. of Wᵐ and Elizabeth Woollard (late Skaiton, spinster) [*Scrutton*, 1802, 1804]; born Sep. 1. Privately.

Oct. 12   Sarah Ann d. of Isaac Watling and Elizabeth his wife (late Elner, spinster); born Sep. 5. Privately. Recᵈ in the Church Ap. 10, 1808.

Oct. 25   Edna d. of Elizabeth Crisp was recᵈ in the Church.

Nov. 1   Danˡ s. of George and Elizabeth Watson (late Harrison, spinster) was recᵈ in the Church.

Nov. 30   Lettice d. of Wᵐ and Esther Watling (late Flowers, spinster); born Nov. 27. Privately. Recᵈ in the Church Jan. 31, 1808.

Dec. 22   James s. of Robᵗ and Sarah Savage (late Pipe, spinster); born Dec. 20. Privately. Recᵈ in the Church Jan. 31, 1808.

### 1808.

Feb. 4   Joseph s. of Thoˢ and Elizabeth Mills (late Watson, spinster); born Jan. 31. Privately.

July 13   Maria d. of Wᵐ and Ann Scarlet (late Colthrop, spinster); born July 7. Privately. Recᵈ in the Church, Oct. 16 [*as Mary Ann, see Oct.* 16].

Oct. 4   George s. of John and Mary Thallow (late Catchpole, spinster); born Oct. 2. Privately. [*Thurlow and Katspool, see Jan.* 26, 1806.]

Oct. 16   Louisa d. of Sarah Hawes; born illegitimate Sep. 9.

Oct. 16   Mary Ann d. of Wᵐ and Ann Scarlet (late Colthrop, spinster) was recᵈ in the Church. [*She was baptized as Maria, see July* 13.]

Nov. 21   James s. of James and Mary Gorbould (late Aldred, spinster); born Nov. 19. Privately. Recᵈ in the Church Feb. 16, 1811.

### 1809.

Jan. 26   Kezia d. of Robᵗ and Mary Gooden (late Carver, spinster); born Aug. 15, 1807. Privately.

Jan. 26   James s. of the same; born Dec. 14, 1808.

Feb. 12   Harriot d. of Isaac and Elizabeth Watling (late Elner, spinster); born Aug. 12, 1808.

Feb. 12   Thomas Francis s. of Sarah Martin; born illegitimate same day. Privately.

May 25   Charles s. of Jonathan and Mary Reyner (late Reyner, spinster); born May 8. Privately. Recᵈ in the Church Ap. 8, 1810.

July 16   Lucy d. of Robert Row and Susannah his wife, an Infant. Recᵈ in the Church Ap. 12, 1810.

Aug. 3   Sarah d. of Samuel Hommet and Catherine his wife.

Aug. 20   Mary Ann d. of Samuel and Elizabeth Legget; born June 27. Recᵈ in the Church Sep. 1, 1811.

Aug. 25   John s. of Henry and Mary Wright; born Aug. 21. Privately.

Sep. 13   William s. of Thomas and Sarah Lame (late Trip, spinster); born Sep. 11. Privately.

Sep. 28   John s. of Robert and Sarah Savage (late Pipe, spinster); born Sep. 21. Privately.

Oct. 6   Amelia d. of Willᵐ and Esther Watling (late Flowers, spinster); born Sep. 11. Privately.

Oct. 15   Mary Ann d. of James and Elizabeth Wright (late Aldred, spinster); born March 16.

Oct. 22   Lydia d. of Thomas and Charlotte Higham (late Aldis, spinster); born Sep. 15.

Nov. 5   Charlotte Ablett illegitimate d. of Susan Smith; born Oct. 12.

Dec. 17   Ann d. of Robert Eastaugh and Isabella his wife (late Forcroft, spinster); born Nov. 19.

Dec. 24   Rebecca d. of Richard and Rebecca Puttock (late Reeve, spinster); born May 29.

Dec. 31   Peter Took s. of Wᵐ Lidemy and Mary his wife (late Took, spinster); born Dec. 30. Privately. [*Lizzamore, Ap.* 19, 1812.]

### 1810.

Mar. 11   James s. of Wᵐ and Elizabeth Woollard (late Skaiton, spinster) [*see* 1807]; born March 7. Privately.

June 17   Mary d. of Edward and Elizabeth Ashford (late Catton, spinster); born June 11. Privately.

Aug. 13   Samuel s. of Samuel and Elizabeth Leggat (late Wright, spinster); born Aug. 5. Privately. Recᵈ in the Church Sep. 1, 1811.

Aug. 20   Maria d. of Wᵐ and Elizabeth Hawes (late Dutt, spinster); born Aug. 5. Privately.

Dec. 1   Thomas s. of John and Mary Thurlow (late Catchpole) [*see Oct.* 1808]; born Nov. 28. Privately.

Dec. 8, 1811.   David s. of Robert Row and Susannah his wife; born Nov. 28. Privately. Recᵈ in the Church Ap. 12, 1812. [*The entry of this baptism is in a different handwriting from that before* and after it, and is an interpolation. It has evidently been entered in the wrong year. In the baptism of Dec. 15, 1806, the name is spelt Raw.]

Dec. 30    John s. of Amos Aldis and Rachael his wife (late Harvey, spinster); born Dec. 29. Privately. Recᵈ in the Church Feb. 3, 1811.

1811.

Jan. 13    Jemima d. of Thoˢ Mills and Elizabeth his wife (late Watson, spinster); born Jan. 11. Privately.

Jan. 13    Samuel s. of Wᵐ Scarlet and Ann his wife (late Colthrop, spinster); born Dec. 13, 1810.

Feb. 3    Louisa d. of Thoˢ Elner and Ann his wife (late Bullard, spinster); born Jan. 12.

Feb. 3    John s. of Nathaniel Smith and Elizabeth his wife (late Cross, spinster); born Feb. 1. Privately. Recᵈ in the Church June 2.

April 21    Edward Philip s. of George and Elizabeth Watson (late Harrison, spinster); born March 26.

April 28    Charlotte d. of James Wright and Elizabeth his wife (late Aldred); born Ap. 7.

April 28    George s. of Robert and Sarah Savage (late Pipe, spinster); born same day. Privately. Recᵈ in the Church June 9.

June 23    Louisa d. of Thomas and Elizabeth Crawford (late Cushion); born June 20. Privately. Recᵈ in the Church Ap. 12, 1812.

Aug. 11    Caroline d. of Jacob Stainton and Sarah his wife (late Ashford); born July 25. Privately.

Nov. 24    Charlotte d. of Thomas Eade and Mary his wife (late Elliot); born Aug. 31.

1812.

April 19    Elizabeth d. of William Lizzamore and Mary his wife (late Took); born Ap. 16. Privately. [Lidemy, Dec. 31, 1809.]

April 19    Reeve s. of Richard Puttock and Rebecca his wife (late Reeve); born Ap. 7. Privately.

May 31    Lydia d. of James Archer and Maria his wife (late Webb); born May 30. Privately.

June 21    Stephen s. of Amos Aldis and Rachael his wife (late Harvey); born June 14. Privately.

June 28    Sarah d. of William Watling and Esther his wife (late Flowers); born June 26. Privately.

June 28    John s. of Samuel Leggat and Elizabeth his wife (late Wright); born June 24. Privately.

June 28    Thomas s. of Joshua Flatt and Sarah his wife (late Godfrey); born June 14. Privately.

Oct. 4    Isaac s. of Sarah Aldred, a bastard.

Oct. 11    Ann d. of Wᵐ Stewart and Ann his wife (late Cane); born Oct. 4. Privately.

Nov. 12    Mary d. of Nathaniel Smith and Elizabeth his wife (late Cross). Privately.

END OF THE SECOND EXISTING BOOK OF BAPTISMS.

(*To be continued.*)

# Sydenham of Brympton.*

In a chapel on the north side of the parish church of Brympton d'Evercy, in the county of Somerset, is a stately marble monument, erected by John Sydenham to the memory of his father, Sir John Sydenham, Kt., who died in 1625, and his ancestors. A Corinthian column at each corner supports the fine canopy, and the whole is adorned with many coats of arms, which, commencing on the north side, illustrate, as it were, the pedigree of the family. On either side the canopy is surmounted by the arms of Sir John Sydenham, on the north impaling those of his first wife, and on the south the arms of his second; each coat is flanked by a small shield supported by a ram. Round the edge of the canopy are thirteen shields, on which are impaled the arms brought in by various matches. On each side of the tomb itself are three large shields: those on the north side bearing the arms of Sydenham, impaling those of Audley, Bruges, and Godolphin, with their various quarterings; on the south are the arms of John Sydenham, who erected the monument, his sister impaled with those of her husband Edward Paston, and another coat in which the sinister side is not filled in. Probably it was meant to await the marriage of Sir Ralph Sydenham, a younger brother of the founder. At the west-end base is the large quartered coat of Sir John Sydenham, impaling the arms of

* Communicated by H. STANLEY HEAD, Esq.

Buckland with its nine quarterings.  At the head of the tomb, surmounted by the helmet, crest, and lambrequin, is the Sydenham coat of twelve quarterings, beneath which is the following inscription :—

> "My foundir Sydenham, match'd with Hobye's Heyr,
> Badde me inform thee (gentle Passenger)
> That what hee hath donne in mee is onlie meant
> To memorize his father and s discent
> Without vayne glorye but he doth intreat
> That if thou comst his legende to repeate
> Thou speak him truly as he was and than
> Report it so, hee dyed an honest mane—
> 10 November 1626."

In the accompanying sketches I have tricked the arms as they exactly appear on the monument, while in the pedigree I have given the arms according to the authority of the Heralds' College.  There are several errors of the carver and painter, such as substituting choughs for martlets in the Guilford coat ; and a field vert for azure in that of Fitz-James.  Many of the quarterings seem to have been brought in without any reason, and contrary to the laws of arms.  The coat borne by the family of Delingrige seems to have properly belonged to Hertley, whose heir married Thomas Delalynde, and the descendants continued to bear the arms until the heiress married Robert de Delingrige, whose daughter brought them into the Sydenham family.  In the shield of Sydenham, impaling Godolphin (c), there appears as a quartering a coat which is ascribed to the name of Donmare, but no trace can I find of a connection with such a family, or mention of such a coat in any pedigree of Sydenham.  I have also been unable to find the match which brought in the arms of Balune to the Godolphin coat, though the name occurs in other Cornish pedigrees.  Nor am I able to trace any other alliance with the family of Bonython than that of Thomas Godolphin, a brother of William Godolphin, which of course would not bring in the coat to the Sydenhams.  There seems to be but little record of the Buckland family, though the nine quarterings represented on the tomb are given in a collection of Somersetshire pedigrees at the Heralds' College, with the slight difference that the three escallops in the arms of Clevedon are *within a bordure sable*.  Most of the quarterings must, I think, have been brought in by the marriage of James Fitz-James with the heiress of Draycot of Redlinch, co. Somerset—a very ancient family, but of which I have been able to find but little.  That there was doubt about the identity of some of the early quarterings seems clear by a letter which is preserved among the Egerton MSS. at the British Museum, in which Mr. Prince, writing in 1712 to Philip Sydenham, says, " I am sorry, Sir, I can't give you the satisfaction you desire, in adjusting the matches of your family.  And I must declare I am altogether as unsatisfied at your disowning Sydenham of Somerset, his marrying the daughter and heir of Sydenham of Devon, when the first of those matches, in your most curiously engraved Atchievement (for which I humbly thank you) gave the coat belonging to your name in this county, viz., The Bend fusilee, according to the unanimous Testimony of all our Antiquaries.  Nor do I anywhere find it ever did belong to Kitsford, nor indeed so much as the name to any Book of Heraldry I have yet met with.  As to the 3rd Coat which you say belongs to Dallingrig, though I meet with yͤ name in Fuller, yet I cannot find this coat there as belonging to it.  But this I do in the 49ᵗʰ page of his Worthys, that it did belong to Green of Drayton.  The account I lately sent you agrees very well with 5 of the matches in your Atchievement ; only my Author puts Godolphin before Sturton.  How he comes to differ in that, & the 3 later coates, I cannot tell ; but tis possible the Heralds may be able to adjust the matter."

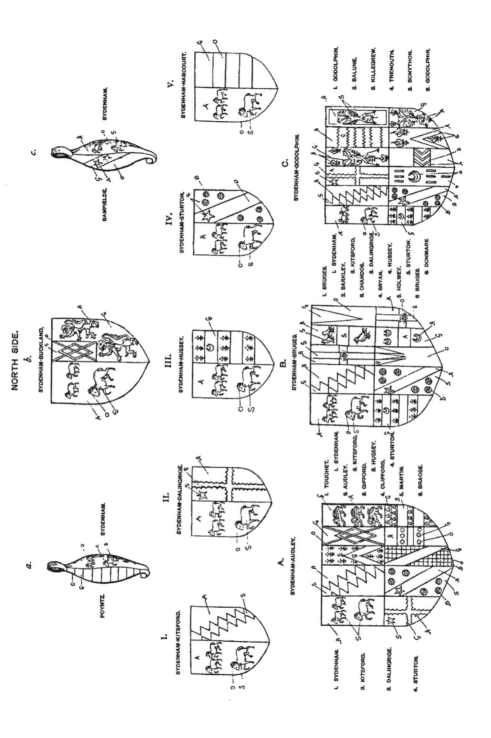

NORTH SIDE.

*a.* POYNTZ

*b.* SYDENHAM-BUCKLAND.

*c.* BAMPFIELDE. SYDENHAM.

SYDENHAM.

I. SYDENHAM-KITSFORD.

II. SYDENHAM-DALINGRIGE.

III. SYDENHAM-HUSSEY.

IV. SYDENHAM-STURTON.

V. SYDENHAM-HARCOURT.

A. SYDENHAM-AUDLEY.

1. SYDENHAM.
2. KITSFORD.
3. DALINGRIGE.
4. STURTON.

1. TOUCHET.
2. AUDLEY.
3. GIFFORD.
4. CLIFFORD.
5. MARTIN.
6. BRAOSE.

1. SYDENHAM.
2. KITSFORD,
3. HUSSEY.
4. STURTON.

B. SYDENHAM-BRUGES.

1. BRUGES.
2. BARKLEY.
3. CHANDOS.
4. BRYAN.
5. HOLWEY.
6. BRUGES.

1. SYDENHAM.
2. KITSFORD.
3. DALINGRIGE.
4. HUSSEY.
5. STURTON.
6. DONMARE.

C. SYDENHAM-GODOLPHIN.

1. GODOLPHIN.
2. BALUNE.
3. KILLEGREW.
4. TRENOUTH.
5. BONYTHON.
6. GODOLPHIN.

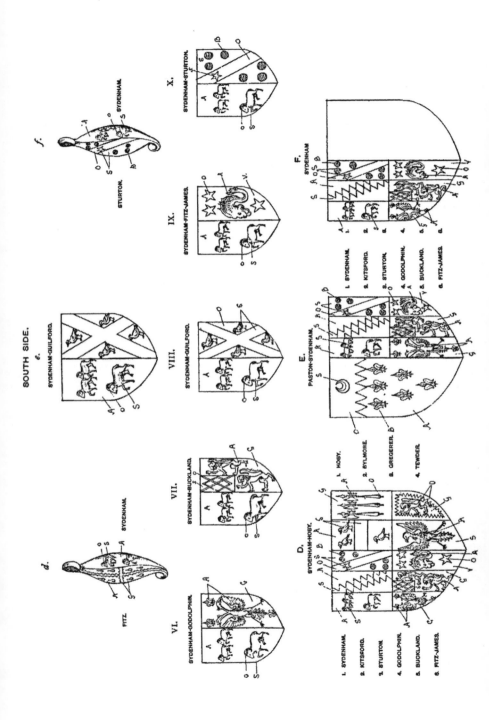

SOUTH SIDE.

*d.* FITZ. SYDENHAM.

*e.* SYDENHAM-GUILFORD.

*f.* SYDENHAM. STURTON.

VI. SYDENHAM-GODOLPHIN.

VII. SYDENHAM-BUCKLAND.

VIII. SYDENHAM-GUILFORD.

IX. SYDENHAM-FITZ-JAMES.

X. SYDENHAM-STURTON.

D. SYDENHAM-HOBY.

1. SYDENHAM.
2. KITSFORD.
3. STURTON.
4. GODOLPHIN.
5. BUCKLAND.
6. FITZ-JAMES.

1. HOBY.
2. BYLMORE.
3. GREGERER.
4. TEWDER.

E. PASTON-SYDENHAM.

1. SYDENHAM.
2. KITSFORD.
3. STURTON.
4. GODOLPHIN.
5. BUCKLAND.
6. FITZ-JAMES.

F. SYDENHAM

1. SYDENHAM.
2. 
3. 
4. 
5. 
6.

# WEST END.

**XI.**
SYDENHAM-AUDLEY.

1. TOUCHET.

2. AUDLEY.

**XII.**
SYDENHAM-ARUNDEL.

**XIII.**
SYDENHAM—BRUGES.

SYDENHAM    **G.**    BUCKLAND.

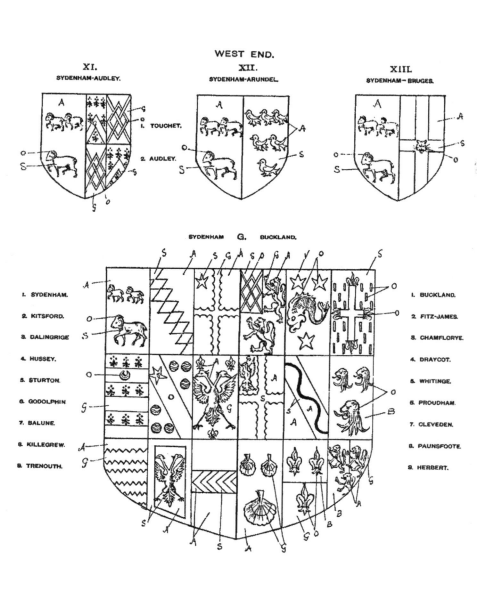

1. SYDENHAM.
2. KITSFORD.
3. DALINGRIGE.
4. HUSSEY.
5. STURTON.
6. GODOLPHIN
7. BALUNE.
8. KILLEGREW.
9. TRENOUTH.

1. BUCKLAND.
2. FITZ-JAMES.
3. CHAMFLORYE.
4. DRAYCOT.
5. WHITINGE.
6. PROUDHAM.
7. CLEVEDEN.
8. PAUNSFOOTE.
9. HERBERT.

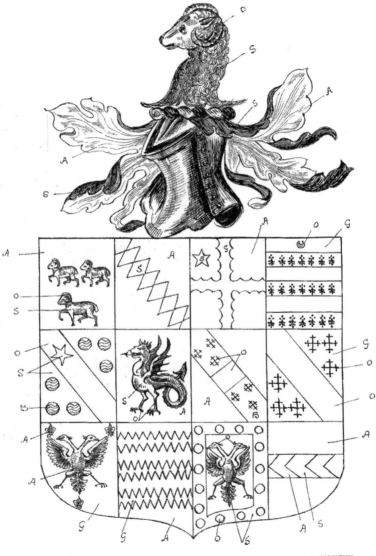

1. SYDENHAM.

2. KITSFORD.

3. DALINGRIGE.

4. HUSSEY.

5. STURTON.

6. LANGLAND.

7. BEAUPRÉ.

8. FURNEUX.

9. GODOLPHIN.

10. BALUNE.

11. KILLEGREW.

12. TRENOUTH.

# The Family of Sydenham of Brimpton, co. Somerset.

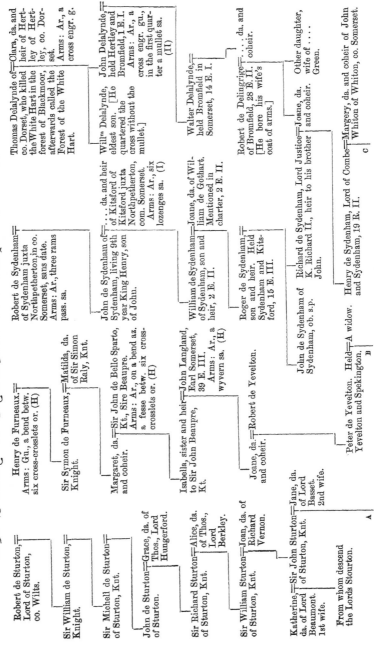

Thomas Delalynde of=Clara, da. and co. Dorset, who killed heir of Hert-
the White Hart in the ley of Hert-
forest of Blackmoor, ley, co. Dor-
afterwards called the set.
Forest of the White Arms: Ar., a
Hart. cross engr. g.

Robert de Sydenham=
of Sydenham juxta
Northpetherton, in co.
Somerset, sans date.
Arms: Ar., three rams
pass. sa.

John Delalynde of=... da. and
held Hertley and coheir of John
Bromfield, 1 E.I. Whiton, co. Somerset.
Arms: Ar., a
cross engr. gu.,
in the first quar-
ter a mullet sa.
(II)

Will^m Delalynde,
eldest son. [He
quartered the
cross without the
mullet.]

John de Sydenham of=... da. and heir
Sydenham, living 9th of Kitsford of
year King Henry, son Kitsford juxta
of John. Northpetherton,
com. Somerset.
Arms: Ar., six
lozenges sa. (I)

Walter Delalynde,
held Bromfield in
Somerset, 14 E. I.

William de Sydenham=Joane, da. of Wil-
of Sydenham, son and liam de Gothart.
heir, 2 E. II. Mentioned in
charter, 2 E. II.

Robert de Delingrige=... da. and
of Bromfield, 28 E.II. coheir.
[He bore his wife's
coat of arms.]

Roger de Sydenham,
son and heir. Held
Sydenham and Kits-
ford, 15 E.III.

Richard de Sydenham, Lord Justice=Joane, da.
K. Richard II., heir to his brother and coheir.
John.

Other daughter,
wife of ....
Green.

Henry de Sydenham, Lord of Combe=Margery, da. and coheir of John
and Sydenham, 19 R.II. Whiton of Whiton, co. Somerset.

John de Sydenham of
Sydenham, ob. s.p.

c

Henry de Furneaux.
Arms: Gu., a bend betw.
six cross-crosslets or. (H)

Robert de Sturton,=
Lord of Sturton,
co. Wilts.

Sir William de Sturton,
Knight.

Sir Symon de Furneaux,=Matilda, da.
Knight. of Sir Simon
Raly, Knt.

Sir Michell de Sturton
of Sturton, Knt.

Margaret, da.=Sir John de Bello Sparto,
and coheir. Kt, Sire Beaupre.
Arms: Ar., on a bend az.
a fesse betw. six cross-
crosslets or. (H)

John de Sturton=Grace, da. of
of Sturton. Thos., Lord
Hungerford.

Isabella, sister and heir=John Langland,
to Sir John Beaupre, Earl Somerset,
Kt. 39 E. III.
Arms: Ar., a
wyvern sa. (H)

Sir Richard Sturton=Alice, da.
of Sturton, Knt. of Thos.,
Lord
Berkley.

Joane, dn.=Robert de Yevelton.
and coheir.

Sir William Sturton=Ioan, da. of
of Sturton, Knt. Richard
Vernon.

Peter de Yevelton. Held=A widow.
Yevelton and Spekington.

B

Katherine,=Sir John Sturton=Jane, da.
da. of Lord of Sturton, Knt. of Lord
Beaumont. Basset.
1st wife. 2nd wife.

A

From whom descend
the Lords Stourton.

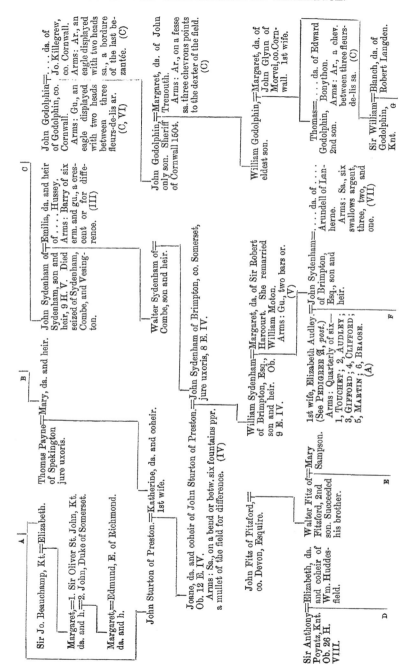

Sir Jo. Beauchamp, Kt.=Elizabeth.

Margaret, da. and h.=1. Sir Oliver St. John, Kt.
=2. John, Duke of Somerset.

Margaret, da. and h.=Edmund, E. of Richmond.

Thomas Payne=Mary, da. and heir. of Spekington jure uxoris.

John Sydenham of Sydenham, son and heir, 9 H. V. Died seized of Sydenham, Combe, and Vesington.=Emilia, da. and heir of .... Hussey. Arms: Barry of six erm. and gu., a crescent or for difference. (III)

John Godolphin of Godolphin, co. Cornwall. Arms: Gu, an eagle displayed with two heads between three fleurs-de-lis ar. (C, VI)=... da. of Jo. Killegrew, co. Cornwall. Arms: Ar, an eagle displayed with two heads sa., a bordure of the last bezantée. (C)

John Godolphin, only son. Sheriff of Cornwall 1504.=Margaret, da. of John Trenouth. Arms: Ar, on a fesse sa. three chevrons points to the dexter of the field. (C)

William Godolphin, eldest son.=Margaret, da. of John Glynn of Morvel, co. Cornwall. 1st wife.

Thomas Godolphin, 2nd son. Arms: Ar, a chev. between three fleurs-de-lis sa. (C)=... da. of Edward Bonython.

Sir William Godolphin, Knt.=Blanch, da. of Robert Langden. (C)

Walter Sydenham of Combe, son and heir.

John Sturton of Preston.=Katherine, da. and coheir. 1st wife.

Joane, da. and coheir of John Sturton of Preston. Ob. 12 E. IV. Arms: Sa, on a bend or betw. six fountains ppr. a mullet of the field for difference. (IV)=John Sydenham of Brimpton, co. Somerset, jure uxoris, 8 E. IV.

William Sydenham of Brimpton, Esq., son and heir. Ob. 9 E. IV.=Margaret, da. of Sir Robert Harcourt. She remarried William Moton. Arms: Gu, two bars or. (V)

John Fitz of Fitzford, co. Devon, Esquire.

1st wife, Elizabeth Audley (See Pedigree A, post.) Arms: Quarterly of six—1, Touchet; 2, Audley; 3, Gifford; 4, Clifford; 5, Martin; 6, Braose. (A)=John Sydenham of Brimpton, Esq., son and heir.=... da. of .... Arundell of Lanherne. Arms: Sa, six swallows argent, three, two, and one. (VII)

Sir Anthony Poyntz, Knt. Ob. 26 H. VIII.=Elizabeth, da. and coheir of Wm. Huddasfield.

Walter Fitz of Fitzford, 2nd son. Succeeded his brother.=Mary Sampson.

A  B  C

D  E  F  G

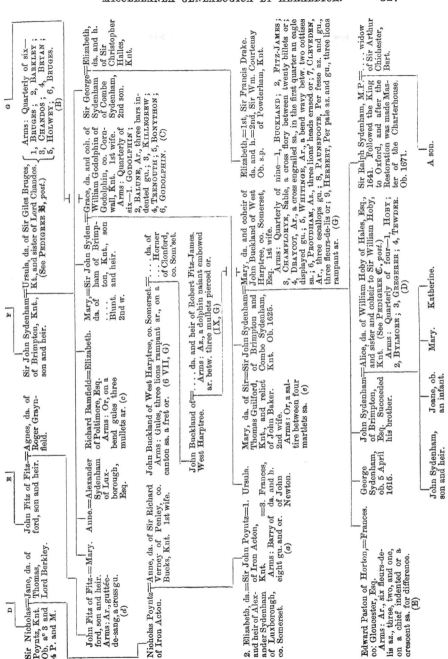

D     B     F     G

Sir Nicholas=Jane, da. of
Poyntz, Knt. | Thomas,
Ob. a° 3 and | Lord Berkley.
4 P. and M.

John Fitz of Fitz-=Agnes, da. of
ford, son and heir. | Roger Grayn-
field.

Sir John Sydenham=Ursula, da. of Sir Giles Bruges,
of Brimpton, Knt. | Knt., and sister of Lord Chandos.
son and heir. | (See Pedigree B, post.)

Arms: Quarterly of six—
1, Bruges; 2, Barkley;
3, Chandos; 4, Bryan;
5, Holwey; 6, Bruges.
(B)

John Fitz of Fitz.=Mary.
ford, son and heir.
Arms: Ar., guttée-
de-sang, a cross gu. (d)

Anne.=Alexander
Sydenham
of Lux-
borough,
Esq.

Richard Bamfield=Elizabeth.
of Poltimore, Esq.
Arms: Or, on a
bend gules three
mullets ar. (c)

Mary,=Sir John Syden-
da. of | ham of Brimp-
...... | ton, Knt., son
Blunt. | and heir.
2nd w.

Grace, da. and coh. of=Sir George=Elizabeth,
William Godolphin | Sydenham | da. and h.
Godolphin, co. Corn- | of Combe | of Sir
wall, Knt. 1st wife. | Sydenham, | Christopher
Arms: Quarterly of | 2nd son. | Halles,
six—1. Godolphin; | | Knt.
2, Balune, Ar., three bars indented gu.; 3, Killgrarw;
4, Trenouth; 5, Bonython;
6, Godolphin. (C)

Nicholas Poyntz=Anne, da. of Sir Richard
of Iron Acton. | Verney of Penley, co.
Bucks, Knt. 1st wife.

John Buckland of West Harptree, co. Somerset.=...da. and heir of Robert Fitz-James.
Arms: Gules, three lions rampant ar., on a | ...da. of
canton sa. a fret or. (6 VII, G) | Horner
| of Clonford,
| co. Son'set.

Arms: Az., a dolphin naiant embowed
ar. betw. three mullets pierced or.
(IX, G)

John Buckland of=......da. and heir
West Harptree.

2. Elizabeth, da.=Sir John Poyntz=1. Ursula.
and heir of Alex- | of Iron Acton,
ander Sydenham | Knt. =3. Frances,
of Luxborough, | Arms: Barry of da. and h.
co. Somerset. | eight gu. and or. of John
| (a) Newton.

Mary, da. of Sir=Sir John Sydenham=Mary, da. and coheir of
Thomas Guilford, | of Brimpton and | John Buckland of West
Knt., and relict | Combe Sydenham, | Harptree, co. Somerset,
of John Baker. | Knt. Ob. 1625. | Esq. 1st wife.
2nd wife. | |
Arms: Or, a sal- | | Arms: Quarterly of nine—1, Buckland; 2, Fitz-James;
tire between four | | 3, Champfloure, Sable, a cross flory between twenty billets or;
martlets sa. (e) | | 4, Draycot, Ar., a cross engrailed sa., in the first quarter an eagle
| | displayed gu.; 5, Whitinge, Ar., a bend wavy betw. two cottises
| | sn.; 6, Proudham, Az., three lions' heads erased or; 7, Claveden,
| | Ar., three escallops gu.; 8, Paunsfoote, Per fesse az. and gu.,
| | three fleurs-de-lis or; 9, Herbert, Per pale az. and gu., three lions
| | rampant ar. (G)

Elizabeth,=1st, Sir Francis Drake.
da. and h.=2nd, Sir Wm. Courtenay
Ob. s.p. of Powderham, Knt.

Edward Paston of Horton,=Frances.
co. Gloucester, Esq.
Arms: Ar., six fleurs-de-
lis az., three, two, and one,
on a chief indented or a
crescent sa. for difference.
(E)

George
Sydenham,
ob. 5 April
1615.

John Sydenham,=Alice, da. of William Hoby of Hales, Esq.,
of Brimpton, | and sister and coheir to Sir William Hoby,
Esq. Succeeded | Knt. (See Pedigree C, post.)
his brother. | Arms: Quarterly of four—1, Hoby;
| 2, Bylmore; 3, Gregerer; 4, Tewder. (D)

Sir Ralph Sydenham, M.P.=...widow
1641. Followed the King | of Sir Arthur
to Oxford, and after the | Chichester,
Restoration was made Mas- | Bart.
ter of the Charterhouse.
Ob. 1671.

John Sydenham,
son and heir.

Joane, ob.
an infant.

Mary.

Katherine.

A son.

# Cullum.

## GREAT DUNMOW REGISTERS.

*Burials.*

| | | | |
|---|---|---|---|
| 1656 | May | 5 | Thomas the sonne of Thomas Cullom gent. and sitizen of London buried the 5 daye. |
| 1662 | Sep. | 4 | M<sup>rs</sup> Mary Cullom y<sup>e</sup> wife of Thomas Cullum of London Buried. |
| 1676 | Aug. | 14 | John Cullum Gent. |
| 1677 | Jan. | 3 | Thomas Cullum Gent. |
| 1689 | Oct. | 15 | M<sup>r</sup> Charles Cullum. |
| 1697 | Aug. | 10 | Tho. Cullum (y<sup>e</sup> Broth<sup>r</sup> of M<sup>r</sup> Charles deceased) a Londoner. |

## SLANY, BRADGATE, AND WELD.

Of the numerous printed pedigrees of the Weld family, that given in Harl. Soc. Publ., xviii., 244 ('Visitation of Cheshire'), is the only one that notices the fact that Sir Humphrey Weld, Lord Mayor of London in 1608, was twice married. From his first wife Anne, daughter of Nicholas Wheler, Esq., descend the Welds of Lulworth. His second wife was Mary, daughter of Sir Stephen Slany, Lord Mayor in 1595, and widow of Richard Bradgate, citizen and skinner of London. The omission is strange, inasmuch as this second marriage is mentioned both in the monumental inscription to Sir Humphrey, given in Strype's 'Stow,' book iii., 56, and in that to Sir Stephen Slany at book ii., 191, of the same work. These inscriptions no longer exist, but they are confirmed by the will of Sir Stephen Slany, dated 2 Aug. 1598, and proved in the P.C.C. 3 Jan. 1628-9 (5 Dorset), of which his three sons-in-law, of whom Sir Humphrey Weld was one, were overseers.

Richard Bradgate's will was dated 15 Oct. 1589, and proved in the P.C.C. 3 Dec. following. He mentions no children, but makes bequests to his wife's father and mother, and to several of their children. Among his own relatives is named his brother Robert Bradgate.

Robert Bradgate of London, merchant taylor, made his will 15 June 1593, and it was proved in the P.C.C. 3 Sept. following. Amongst many other relatives he mentions two whom he describes as his brother and sister-in-law Humfrey and Mary Weld, and he also makes a bequest to their daughter Joane.

It may be remarked that from the way in which this Joane is here mentioned it seems doubtful whether she was identical with Sir Humphrey's eldest daughter by his first wife, who bore the same name, and became the wife of Sir Robert Brooke of Cockfield, Suffolk.

From the evidences referred to, therefore, it appears that Mary Slany, the daughter of Sir Stephen, had for her first husband Richard Bradgate, who died in 1589, apparently without issue ; and for her second, Sir Humphrey Weld, to whom she was married between 1589 and 1593, and whom she survived ; and that it is at least possible that this latter union was a fruitful one. The will of Sir Humphrey, which has not been examined in this connection, would probably throw further light upon the matter.       E. H. H.

## JONES—HAVARD. (See Vol. II., N.S., p. 216.)

I have recently made out that Evan Jones, Surgeon, of Oakham, co. Rutland, was the only son and heir of Evan Jones of Forddfawr, in the parish of Llanddew, near Brecon, by Jane, daughter of Joshua Havard of the parish of Llanvillo, also near Brecon. The Registers at Llanddew only go back to the beginning of this century. The Registers at Llanvillo give " Jane filia Josua " (*sic*) " Havard de Pen-y-giffordd baptizata fuit nono die Februarij 1696," and, " Gulielmus filius Joshua Havard de Pen-y-giffordd baptizatus erat se'do die Aprilis 1699."

I shall be greatly indebted for any information as to Evan Jones of Forddfawr, Llanddew, and as to his wife Jane, daughter of Joshua Havard of Llanvillo.

# Genealogy of the Family of Harvey,

OF FOLKESTONE, CO. KENT; LONDON; HACKNEY AND TWICKENHAM, CO. MIDDLESEX; CROYDON, PUTNEY, AND KINGSTON, CO. SURREY; HEMPSTEAD, CHIGWELL, AND BARKING, CO. ESSEX; CLIFTON AND WIKE, CO. DORSET, ETC.*

ARMS (Ancient): Argent, two bars nebulée sable, on a chief of the last three crosses pattée fitchée.
(Modern) exemplified by Sir William Segar, Garter (1).: Or, on a chief indented sable three crescents argent.
CREST: A dexter-hand appaumée proper, over it a crescent inverted argent.

Juliana (or Julian), eld. da. of William Jenkin (or Jenkine) of Folkestone, Esq., and Mary Juliana, da. of .... Haute (? Hawke) his wife; b. 1554 (P); mar. 1575 (P); d. (probably in childbed of da. Julian) 1576 (P?), bur. at Folkestone (P) (1A). 1st wife.
ARMS: Argent, a lion rampant-reguardant sable.

Thomas Harvey (2) of Folkestone, co. Kent, Yeoman; of Hackney, co. Middx., gent.; b. 1549; Jurat (or Alderman) of Folkestone; elected Mayor of same 1600; d. 12 June, bur. at Hackney 17 June 1623. Will dated 12 June 1623; proved 16 July following. (P.C.C., Swann 77.) Apparently descended from, or of the same branch of the family as, Sir Walter Harvey, "Pepperer" (3), Warden (or Mayor) of London 1272 and 1273, who bore the like arms.

Joane, da. of Thomas Halke (Haulke, or Hawke) (4) of Hastingleigh, co. Kent; b. 1555; mar. 21 Jan. 1576-7; d. 8 Nov. 1605, bur. at Folkestone (5). M.I. 2nd wife.
ARMS: Gules, a fesse between three hawks belled or.

Thomas Cullen of Dover, co. Kent, gent.; b. 1573 (P); d. 1636 (P).
ARMS: Or, an eagle displayed sa., armed gules.

Juliana (Juliana or Gillian) Harvey; b. 1576 (P?); mar. 1597 (P); living 12 June 1628; d. 1639 (P).

1. William Harvey of St. Martin, Ludgate, and Broad Street in St. Peter-le-Poor, London; "Coome, near Croydon," and Lambeth, co. Surrey; b. at Folkestone 1 April 1578; educated at the King's School, Canterbury, co. Kent, 1588-93; admitted Gonville and Caius Coll., Camb., 31 May 1593; B.A. 1597; M.D. Padua 25 April 1602; F.R.C.P. London 5 June 1607; discovered the circulation of the blood; Physician Extraordinary to James I. c. 1615; admitted Gray's Inn, London (6), 6 March 1624-5; Physician in Ordinary to Charles I. 1630; M.D. Oxon 7 Dec. 1642; Warden of Merton Coll. 1645; elected President R.C.P. London 1654; d. at his brother Eliab's house at Roehampton 3 June, s.p.; bur. in "outer" vault beneath Harvey Chapel in Hempstead Church (7), co. Essex, 26 June 1657. M.I. (8); re-interred in sarcophagus provided by R.C.P. London in Harvey Chapel 18 Oct. 1883 (9). Will and codicil dated 28 Dec. 1656 (10), proved 2 May 1659, and confirmed by sentence. (P.C.C., Pell 270.)
ARMS: Quarterly—1 and 4, modern coat; 2 and 3, ancient coat, as above (11).

Elizabeth, da. of Lancelot Browne of St. Sepulchre, London, M.D., F.R.C.P. London, first Physician to Q. Eliz., and Ja. I., and Joane his wife (12); b. 1580; mar. at St. Sepulchre's (P) (13) Nov. 1604 (Lic. Bp. London 24 Nov. 1604); d. before her husband, and prob. in or near London c. 1646.
ARMS: Argent, on a chevron between three demi-griffins erased gules, as many towers triple-towered of the first.

2. John Harvey, Senr, of London, and of Westminster, co. Middx., Esq.; b. at Folkestone 12 Nov. 1582; Footservt. in ordinary ("Footman") (14) to Ja. I.; "Castleman" at Sandgate, co. Kent; admitted Gray's Inn (6) 14 March 1624-5; King's Receiver for Lincolnshire with his brother Daniel (grant, with survivorship, 15 March 1625-6); M.P. for Hythe, co. Kent, 1640; d. unmar. 20 July 1645. Will dated 26 June 1645, proved 28 July following. (P.C.C., Rivers 93.)

A

(11A)

W. H. Harvey.

Numbers within parentheses refer to Notes which will appear at end of Pedigrees.

* Compiled from original sources by WILLIAM J. HARVEY, ESQ., F.S.A. Scot.

Elizabeth, da. of Nicholas Exton of London, Merchant; born 1595 (?); mar. c. 1618; d. in childbed of son Henry 1 Jan., bur. at St. Peter-le-Poor 4 Jan. 1618-19. M.I.

Arms: Azure, a cross argent between twelve crosses-crosslet fitchée or.

=3. Thomas Harvey of St. Laurence Pountney, London, Turkey (?) Merchant, of Grocers' Co., London (?); b. at Folkestone 17 Jan. 1584-5; d. 2 Feb., bur. at St. Peter-le-Poor 13 Feb. 1622-3. M.I. Will dated 31 Jan. 1622-3, adm'on 10 Feb., and proved 9 April following; further adm'on 21 Nov. 1633. (P.C.C., Swann 27.)

=Elizabeth, da. of Sir Robert Parkhurst, Kt. (15), of Clothworkers' Co., Alderman and Lord Mayor of London (1634), and Ellen his wife; b. 1603 (?); renmar. E. S. at St. Leonard's, Shoreditch, co. Middx. 14 July 1624; bur. at St. Andrew Undershaft 19 Aug. 1624. Adm'ons P.C.C. 15 Oct. 1624 and 19 Nov. 1625.

Arms: Argent, a cross ermine between four bucks trippant proper, on a chief gules three crescents or.

=Sir Edmund Sawyer of Dunston, co. Norfolk; St. Andrew Undershaft; and Heywood, co. Berks; one of the seven Auditors of the Exchequer; b. 1579; knighted at Chesterford Park 24 Feb. 1624-5; purchased Manor of Heywood 1627; M.P. for Berwick-on-Tweed 3 March 1627-8; expelled the House c. Sept. following; d. 14 June 1676; bur. at White Waltham, co. Berks. Will dated 24 Feb. 1671; codicil pr. 7 Nov. 1676. (P.C.C., Bence 117.) Confirmed by sentence 11 Dec. 1676.

Arms (granted to him by Wm. Camden, Clarenceux): Azure, a fess chequy or and sable between three sea-pies ar.

=Anne, sole da. of Sir William Whitmore of Apley, co. Salop, Kt., and Margaret, da. of Rowland Mosely of Hough, co. Lancashire, his first wife; b. c. 1608; mar. c. 1625; d. 1651, bur. at White Waltham. 2nd wife.

Arms: Vert, fretty or.

2. John Harvey, Junior, of London and Antwerp, Turkey Merchant, of Grocers' Co., only surviving son; bap. at St. Peter-le-Poor 7 April 1616; M.P. for Hythe 1661 (Long Parliament); King's Receiver for Lincolnshire; living 28 March 1665; d. (unmar. 1679?) (19).

3. Henry Harvey; b. 1 (?) Jan., bur. at St. Peter-le-Poor 8 Jan. 1618-19.

Thomas Harvey, posthumous son, b. 1623; living 19 Nov. 1625; probably d. in infancy.

1. Thomas Harvey; bap. at St. Peter-le-Poor 14 Dec., bur. there 20 Dec. 1614.

4. Daniel Harvey of Folkestone; Laurence Pountney Hill, London; Combe, in Croydon, and Lambeth, co. Surrey, Esq., Turkey Merchant, of Grocers' Co.; b. at Folkestone 31 May 1587; Churchwarden of St. Laurence Pountney 1624-5; King's Receiver for Lincolnshire with his brother John (vide antea); fined for Sheriff of London before 1640; d. 10 Sep. 1649, bur. at St. Laurence Pountney (8). Will dated 21 April 1647, proved 21 Oct. 1649. (P.C.C., Fairfax 144.)

=Elizabeth Kynnersley (or Kinnarsley), da. of Henry Kynnersley of London, Merchant; b. 1601 (?); mar. c. 1619; d. at Lambeth, co. Surrey, bur. at St. Laurence Pountney 7 May 1655.

Arms: Argent, a chevron engrailed between three mullets sable.

5. Eliab Harvey of Laurence Pountney Hill; Broad Street; in St. Peter-le-Poor; Roehampton in Putney, co. Surrey; and Chigwell, co. Essex, Esq., Turkey Merchant, of Grocers' Co.; b. at Folkestone 26 Feb. 1589-90; built the Harvey Mortuary Chapel with "outer" vault beneath in Hempstead Church c. May 1655; d. 27 May 1661, bur. at Hempstead. M.I. Will dated 10 March 1658-9, proved 18 June 1661. (P.C.C., May 91.) Confirmed by sentence 26 same month. (P.C.C., May 86.)

=Mary, da. of Francis West of London, gent.; b. 1607(?); mar. at St. Laurence Pountney 15 Feb. 1624-5; d. 30 Dec. 1678, bur. at Hempstead 18 Jan. 1673-4 (17). M.I. Will dated 20 June 1670, proved 7 Feb. 1673-4. (P.C.C., Bunce 20.)

Arms: Argent, a fesse dancettée between three leopards' faces sable.

*Eliab Harvey* [signature]

See PEDIGREE A, post.

B

**Mary**, da. of William Baker of London, "Draper," b. 1612 (?); mar. at St. Laurence Pountney 29 April 1630 (Lic. Abp. Cant.); d. s.p. 1631 (?).

Arms; Azure, on a fesse between three swans' heads erased or and ducally gorged gules, as many cinquefoils of the last.

**=6. Michael Harvey of St.** Laurence Pountney, and "Merchant Taylor," of London, gent.; Turkey (?) Merchant; of Grocers' Co. (P); twin brother with Matthew; b. at Folkestone 25 Sept. 1593; d. 22 Jan. 1644 (P); bur. in Chancel (North Quire?) of St. Helen's 27 Jan. 1642-3.

**=Mary**, third and youngest da. of John Mellish of London, and "Merchant Taylor," and Elizabeth, da. of John Dade of London, his wife; b. c. 1611; mar. c. 1635; remarried, and second wife of W. S. (18) 1644 (P); d. c. Feb. 1691-2. Will dated 3 Sept. 1689; proved 16 March 1691-2. (P.C.C., Fane 45.)

Arms: Azure, two swans in pale argent between as many flaunches ermine.

**=William Steele** (eld. son of Richard Steele of Sandbacke, co. Chester, and Finchley, co. Middx., and Laetitia his wife) of Hatton Garden, co. Middlesex; born c. 1616; admitted Gray's Inn 13 June 1616; called to the Bar 23 June 1637; Recorder of London (per resig. Serjeant Glynne) 25 Aug. 1649; Serjeant-at-Law 25 Jan. 1654; M.P. for City of London 1654; Chief Baron of Exchequer 28 May 1655; Lord Chancellor of Ireland 26 Aug. 1656; nom. one of Cromwell's "Lords" 10 Dec. 1657; d. at his house in Hatton Garden c. Sept. 1680; bur. in St. Werburgh's Churchyard, Dublin. Will dated 17 Sept., Codicil 18 Sept. 1680; proved 19 Oct. following. (P.C.C., Bath 134.) His first wife was Elizabeth, da. of Richard Godfrey of Wye, co. Kent, Esq., M.P. for New Romney, and Mary, da. of John Moyle; born 1620; mar. at Elmstead, co. Kent, 15 May 1638; died 1643 (P), leaving a son Richard.

Arms: Argent, a fesse componé ermine and azure between two lions' heads erased, on a chevron azure three billets or.

*See PEDIGREE B, post.*

---

**7. Matthew Harvey of London,** "Merchant"; of Grocers' Co. (P); twin brother with Michael; b. at Folkestone 25 Sept. 1593; d. 21 Dec., bur. at Croydon 30 Dec. 1642. Will dated 18 Aug. 1642; pr. 4 Jan. 1642-3. (P.C.C., Crane 7.)

**=Mary**, da. of Robert Hatley, of Barford, co. Bedford, and London, Esq., and Dorothy, da. of Griffith Hampden, of Great Hampden, co. Bucks, Esq., his wife; b. 1610 (?); mar. at St. Helen's, Bishopsgate, 15 Dec. 1628; d. 16.. , prob.

Arms: Azure, a sword in bend argent, hilt and pommel or (the hilt to the dexter chief point), between two mullets of six points pierced of the third.

*See PEDIGREE C, post.*

**1. Daniel Harvey,** bapt. at St. Laurence Pountney 14 June, bur. there 19 June 1620.

**2. Thomas Harvey,** bapt. at St. Laurence Pountney 30 Aug., bur. there 3 Sept. 1621.

**3. John Harvey,** bapt. at St. Laurence Pountney 19 March, bur. there 29 March 1625.

---

C

**1. Sarah Harvey;** b. at Folkestone 5 May 1580; d. 18 June 1591; prob. buried at Folkestone (1 A).

**George Fowke** (Fouke, Foulke, or Foulkes) of St. Michel-le-Quern, London, "Citizen and Merchant Taylor"; b. 1593 (P); d. c. Nov. 1623. Will dated 16 Nov. 1623; proved 3 Dec. following. (P.C.C., Swann 130.)

Arms: Vert, a fleur-de-lis argent.

**=2. Amye** (Amey or Amy) Harvey; b. at Folkestone 26 Dec. 1596; mar. shortly after 4 April 1615; living 18 Aug. 1645; d. before her husband (?).

---

**4. Sir Daniel Harvey of Combe Nevel** a's Combe Nevel (16) in Kingston, co. Surrey; bapt. at St. Laurence Pountney 10 Nov. 1631; educated at Croydon under Mr. Webb 5 years (1639-43); adm. Pembroke Coll., Oxford, 3 March 1643-4, and prob. there until adm. Fellow Commoner Gonv. and Caius Coll., Camb., 12 Nov. 1646; knighted at Canterbury 26 May 1660 (20); Keeper (or Ranger) of Richmond Park (Grant in reversion Aug. 1660), and of Harbleton Lodge and Walk in same Park (Grant 19 July 1661); J.P. county Surrey; Ambassador at the Port of Constantinople (21) (Commission dated 22 Feb. 1667-8); d. there .. Aug. 1672; embalmed, brought to England, and buried at Hempstead 1 Oct. 1674 (8). Will dated 26 March 1666; adm'on 14 Nov. 1672, and proved 4 May 1677. (P.C.C., Eure 186.)

**=Elizabeth,** only da. of Edward (Montagu), 2nd Lord Montagu of Boughton, co. Northampton, and Anne, da. and eventual heir of Sir Ralph Winwood, of Ditton Park, co. Surrey, Kt., his wife; b. c. 1639; mar. c. 1657; d... July, bur. in vault of Sir R. Winwood at St. Bartholomew-the-Less, London, 16 July 1702. Will dat. 19 Nov. 1700 (22); proved 12 Aug. 1702. (P.C.C., Herne 136.)

Arms: Argent, three lozenges conjoined in fesse gules within a bordure sable.

*See PEDIGREE D, post.*

D

5. William Harvey; bapt. at Croydon 13 Aug. 1687; prob. died in infancy.

Heneage (Finch), 1st Earl of Nottingham, of Ravenstone, co. Bucks, and of Gt. Queen Street, Covent Garden, co. Middx., son of Sir Heneage F., of Kensington, co. Middx., Kt., Recorder of London, and Speaker of House of Commons, and Frances, da. of Sir Edw. Bell of Beaupré Hall, co. Norfolk, his first wife; b. 1621; educated at St. Peter's Coll. (Westminster School) and at Christ Church, Oxford, 1635—8; of the Inner Temple, London; Solicitor-General 6 June 1660; Bart. 7 June n.s. 1660; M.P. University Oxford 1661—73; D.C.L. Oxon. 1665; Attorney-General 10 May 1670; Lord Keeper 9 June 1673; P.C. 12 Nov. 1673; Baron Finch of Daventry, co. Northampton, 10 Jan. 1673-4; Lord Chancellor 15 Nov. 1675; Earl of Nott. 12 May 1681; died at his house in Covent Garden 18 Dec. bur. at Ravenstone 28 Dec. 1682. M.I. Will dated 31 March 1682; proved 5 Jan. 1682-3, confirmed by sentence 13 same month. (P.C.C., Drax 145.)
Arms: Argent, a chevron between three griffins passant wings endorsed sable.

1. Elizabeth Harvey; bapt. at St. Laurence Pountney 19 April 1627; mar. at All Hallows-in-the-wall, London, 30 July 1646; d. c. 1675; bur. in chancel at Ravenstone.

Sir Edward Dering of Surrenden Dering in Pluckley, co. Kent, and of Gerard Street, Soho, co. Middx., (2nd) Bart.; only son of Sir Edw. D., 1st Bart., and Anne, 3rd da. of Sir John Ashburnham of Ashburnham, co. Sussex, Kt., his 2nd wife; b. at Pluckley 8 Nov. 1625; M.P. for co. Kent 1640 (Long Parliament); Com. of the Treasury; d. 24 June, bur. in chancel at Pluckley 28 June 1684. M.I. Will dated 24 Feb. 1682-3; proved 4 July 1684. (P.C.C., Hare 88.)
Arms: Quarterly—1 and 4, Argent, a fesse azure, in chief three torteaux (in augmentation); 2 and 3, Or, a saltire sable.

2. Mary Harvey; bapt. at St. Laurence Pountney 3 Sept. 1629; mar. at St. Bartholomew-the-Less 5 April 1648 (24); d. 7 Feb., bur. in chancel at Pluckley 12 Feb. 1703-4. M.I. Said to have clandestinely mar. (c. 1646) her father's apprentice, her second-cousin, William, son of Richard Halke, but which marriage was (c. 1647) declared null and void. (25)

A quo the Earls of Winchelsea and Aylesford. (23)

3. Sarah Harvey; bapt. at St. Laurence Pountney 6 March, bur. there 8 March 1682-3.

Robert (Bulkley), 2nd Viscount Bulkley of Cashells in Ireland, eldest surviving son and heir of Thomas, 1st Viscount, and Blanch, da. of Robert Coytmore of Coytmore, co. Carnarvon, Esq., his 1st wife; b. 16 ..; died 18 Oct. 1688; bur. in the Fam. Chapel, Beaumaris Church, co. Anglesey. Will dated 14 Sept. 1688, codicil 2 Oct. following; proved 20 Nov. 1689. (P.C.C., Ent 150.)
Arms: Sable, a chevron between three bulls' heads cabossed argent.

4. Sarah Harvey; bapt. at Croydon 8 Sept. 1636; mar. c. 1657; survived her husband and living 20 Nov. 1689; d. 1699 (?).

5. Anye Harvey; bapt. at St Laurence Pountney 16 Nov. 1638; probably died in infancy.

6. Hannah Harvey; b. c. 1639; bur. at Croydon 26 Dec. 1642.

(To be continued.)

# Genealogy of the Family of Harbey, etc.*

## Pedigree A. (Vide p. 330.)

Eliab Harvey of Laurence Pountney Hill.=Mary, da. of Francis West.

1. Sir Eliab Harvey, of St. Peter-le-Poor, and Chigwell; bapt. at St. Laurence Pountney 3 June 1635; admitted Merchant Taylors' School, London, 11 March 1642-3; knighted at Canterbury 26 May 1660 (20); J.P., D.L. for co. Essex; founded Folkestone Grammar School 1674; admitted to Freedom of City of Salisbury, Wilts, with his son Eliab, 31 Jan. 1678-9; M.P. for co. Essex, 1678-9; for Old Sarum, Wilts, 1679, 1680-1; "carried away" from that Church 2 March to Hempstead, and bur. there 14 March 1698-9. Will dated 5 June 1695; proved 10 March 1698-9. (P.C.C., Pett 42.)

=Dorothy, da. of Sir Thomas Whitmore of St. Giles-in-the-Fields, and Apley, co. Salop (1st) Bart.; b. 1638 (?); mar. at St. Giles-in-the-Fields 7 Dec. 1658; d. 1 Feb., bur. at Hempstead 17 Feb. 1725-6.
Arms: Vert, fretty or.

2. Thomas Harvey; bapt. at Croydon 9 Sept. 1636; prob. d. in infancy.

3. Mathew Harvey of Twickenham, co. Middx., Esq.; bapt. at St. Laurence Pountney 9 April 1689; d.s.p. 14 Jan., bur. at Twickenham 19 Jan. 1693-4. M.I. Will dated 1 Nov. 1693; proved 15 Jan. 1693-4. (P.C.C., Box 11.)

=Dame Frances Whitmore (26), da. of Sir William Brooke al's Cobham, and relict of Sir Thos. Whitmore of Bridgnorth and Buddwas (or Buildwas), co. Salop, Kt. (who d. 1653); b. 1638 (?); mar. 1660 (?); d. ...May, bur. at Twickenham 15 May 1690. M.I.
Arms: Gules, on a chevron argent a lion rampant ducally crowned or.

4. William Harvey, of Roehampton, Esq.; bapt. at Putney, co. Surrey, 30 June 1640; d. s.p. 13 Aug., bur. at Hempstead 25 Aug. 1719. M.I. (27) Will dat. 24 July 1713; proved 3 Sept. 1719. (P.C.C., Browning 168.)

=Bridget, da. of Sir Richard Browne (al's Moses) and Depden, co. Essex, Bart. (Ald. of Lond.; Ld. Mayor 1661), and Bridget, da. of Robt. Brian (or Bryan) of Henley-on-Thames, co. Oxon., his wife; b. c. 1643; mar. c. April 1664 (Lic. Fac. Off. Abp. Cant. 18 April 1664), died 13 Nov. "carried away" from Church of St. Giles-in-the-Fields 28 Nov. to Hempstead and bur. there 29 Nov. 1701. (28) M.I.
Arms: Argent, on a chevron between three griffins' heads erased gules as many castles of the first.

Sir William Whitmore of Apley, co. Salop (2nd and last) Bart., eldest son of Sir Thos. W., first Bart.; b. 8 April 1637; died s.p. 1699, when baronetcy expired; bur. in vault, Stockton Church, co. Salop. Will dat. 12 Nov. 1695; proved 11 Nov. 1700. (P.C.C., Noel 169.)
Arms: Vert, fretty or.

=Mary Harvey; bapt. at St. Laurence Pountney 15 Nov. 1637; mar. c. Aug. 1658 (29); died 30 Jan, bur. at Hempstead 15 Feb. 1710-11. M.I. Will and codicil dat. 1 May 1710; pr. 21 Feb. 1710-11. (P.C.C., Young 41.)

2. Sarah Harvey; bapt. at St. Laurence Pountney 11 Nov. 1642; died 17 May 1665; bur. in "outer" vault beneath Harvey Chapel in Hempstead Church. (30) M.I.

3. Elizabeth Harvey; bapt. at Putney 10 Jan. 1643-4; buried there 9 Sept. 1645.

4. Elizabeth Harvey; bapt. at Putney 2 June 1647; died 5 July 1656; bur. at Hempstead. M.I.

*Chas Harvey* [signature]

* Continued from p. 332.

1. Eliab. Harvey of Chigwell, Esq.; bapt. at St. Peter-le-Poor 2 Nov. 1659; mat. Ch. Ch. Oxon. 18 Feb. 1675-6; adm. to Freedom of City of Salisbury, with his father, 31 Jan. 1678-9; died s.p. 3 June, bur. at Hempstead 10 June 1681. M.I.

=Dorothy, sole da. and h. of Sir Robert Dyoer (or Dioer) of Wrentham, co. Suff., Uphall in Braughing, co. Hertf., and Hackney, co. Middx. (2nd Bart., and Judith, youngest da. of Richard Gulston of Widdial, co. Hertford, his wife; bapt. at Braughing 11 May 1668; mar. at St. Peter-le-Poor 23 Nov. 1680 (31); survived her husband Eliab, and remar. his next bro. William at St. Martin Outwich, London, 1 Sept. 1681 (Lic. Bp. Lond. 14 July 1681); died 28 June, buried at Hempstead 10 July 1711. M.I. (33)

Arms: Gules, on a chevron between three eagles displayed or as many torteaux.

2. William Harvey of Chigwell, and Gt. Greys, co. Essex, Esq. (34); bapt. at St. Peter-le-Poor 18 Dec. 1663; M.P. for Old Sarum, Wilts, in the six Parliaments 1689-90—1702 and 1708, Appleby, co. Westmoreland, 1705, Weymouth and Melcombe Regis 1711 and 1713, co. Essex 1715 (not duly elected) and 1722; died 31 Oct., bur. at Hempstead 7 Nov. 1731. M.I. Will dated 1 Feb. 1726-7; lim. adm'on 17 May 1739. (P.C.C., Henchman 104.)

3. Mathew Harvey, Esq.; b. c. 1670; first Page of Honour to Will. III.; served his Mat. at Battle of the Boyne, in Ireland, and in three succeeding campaigns in Flanders; died 23 Jan., bur. at Hempstead 30 Jan. 1692-3. M.I.

4. Eliab Harvey; b. 5 Nov. 1690; bapt. in St. Giles-in-the-Fields same day; prob. died in infancy.

Edward Harvey. (Vide postea.) = 1. Elizabeth Harvey. (Vide postea.)

2. Mary Harvey; bapt. at St. Peter-le-Poor 19 Nov. 1661; died 4 Feb. 1664-5; bur. at Hempstead.

3. Dorothy Harvey; bapt. at All Hallows Staining, London, 27 Nov. 1671; died 9 Nov., buried at Hempstead 15 Nov. 1686.

4. Mary Harvey; bapt. All Hallows Staining 25 Mar. 1673; d. 23 (?) Nov., buried at Hempstead 29 Nov. 1677.

2. Eliab Harvey; b. 1690; mat. Ch. Ch. Oxon. 2 Dec. 1706; died of small-pox unmar. 21 March 1709-10; buried at Hempstead 29 March 1710. M.I.

3. Matthew Harvey; b. c. 1691; died 1692 (?); bur. at Hempstead. (37) M.I.

(See Pedigree ℭ, post.)

1. William Harvey of Winchlow Hall in Hempstead, and Chigwell, Esq.; b. 20 April, bapt. at St. Giles-in-the-Fields 30 April 1689; mat. Ch. Ch. Oxon. 13 Oct. 1705; M.P. for Old Sarum 1710; Verderer of Epping Forest 1738 (35); died at Chigwell 24 Dec. (36) 1742; bur. at Hempstead 8 Jan. 1742-3. M.I. Adm'on P.C.C. 25 Feb. 1742-3.

=Mary, da. and h. (? co-h.) of Ralph Williamson of Berwick (or Berwick), co. Northumb., Esq.; b. c. 1686; mar. c. 1714; died 21 April, bur. at Hempstead 25 April 1761. M.I. Will dated 20 Feb. 1742-3; codicils 9 and 10 May 1755, 16 Jan. 1756-7, 6 Oct. 1758, and 9 April 1760; proved 27 April 1761. (P.C.C., Cheslyn 133.)

Arms: Argent, on a chevron azure between three trefoils slipped sable as many crescents or.

B

B |

1. William Harvey of Rolls, Chigwell, Esq.; b. 9 June 1714; created D.C.L. Oxon. 8 July 1756; Colonel of Western Battalion Essex Militia; M.P. for co. Essex in three Parliaments, 1747, 1754, and 1761; d. 11 June (40), bur. at Hempstead 18 June 1763. M.I. Adm'ons P.C.C. 22 Aug. 1763, 21 Nov. 1776, and Oct. 1780.

=Emma, eldest da. and co-heiress of Stephen Skynner of Walthamstow, co. Essex, Esq., and Mary, da. and h. of Samuel Remington of Low Layton, same co., Esq., his w.; b. c. 1732; mar. 13 Aug. (41) 1750 (Settlement dated 11 Aug. 1750); d. 14 March, bur. at Hempstead 21 March 1767. Will dated 9 April 1766; proved 4 April 1767. (P.C.C., Legard 136.)
Arms: Sable, a chevron or between three griffins' heads erased ar.

2. Eliab Harvey (46A) of Claybury Hall at Woodford Bridge in Barking, co. Essex, and Lincoln's Inn Fields, co. Middx., Esq.; b. 23 May 1716; educated at St. Peter's College (Westminster School) 1730-4; elected thence to Trinity College, Cambridge, 1734; B.A. 1787; M.A. 1741; admitted Inner Temple 5 May 1733; called to Bar 12 June 1741; Bencher 2 June 1768; Reader 1766; K.C. 1763; M.P. for Dunwich, co. Suffolk, 1761; built the "inner" vault beneath Harvey Chapel at Hempstead 1766 (47); d. at Woodford Bridge 23 Oct., bur. at Hempstead 6 Nov. 1769. M.I. Will dated 3 Jan. 1764; codicil 29 Oct. 1768; proved 11 Nov. 1769. (P.C.C., Bogg 882.)

=Mary, da. of Richard Benyon of Gidea (or Geddy) Hall, near Rumford, co. Essex, Esq., Governor of Bengal; b. c. 1725; mar. at St. George's, Hanover Square, co. Middx., 20 Nov. 1756; d. 6 Sept. (48), bur. at Hempstead 14 Sept. 1765.
Arms: Vert, on a chief argent three mullets pierced gules.

Montagu Burgoyne of Mark Hall, Harlow, co. Essex, Esq., second and youngest son of Sir Roger Burgoyne of Sutton, co. Bedford, sixth Bart., and Frances Montagu, eldest da. of George, Earl of Halifax (who died 24 July 1788); b. 19 July 1750; ed. at Trinity Hall, Cambridge; cr. M.A. 1774; one of the two Chamberlains of the Exchequer 17 July 1772; Verderer of Epping Forest; d. at East Sheen, co. Surrey, 6 March 1886.
Arms: Gules, a chevron or between three talbots argent, on a chief crenelle of the last as many martlets azure.

=2. Elizabeth Harvey; only surviving d. and h.; b. 30 Sept., bapt. at St. Giles-in-the-Fields 28 Oct. 1761; mar. at St. George's, Hanover Square, 30 Oct. 1780 (51); surv. her husband and d. 1842 (?).

1. Eliab Harvey; b. c. 1757; d. 29 Oct. 1768, bur. at Hempstead. (49)

2. Richard Harvey; b. c. 1759; d. 11 April, bur. at Hempstead 16 April 1767.

3. Edward Harvey, Esq.; bapt. at St. Giles-in-the-Fields 26 Feb. 1765; d. 15 April, bur. at Hempstead 2 Oct. 1784. (50)

1. Mary Harvey; bapt. at St. Giles-in-the-Fields 10 Jan. 1760; died 9 March, buried at Hempstead 19 March 1778.

1. Mary Harvey; b.1715; d. . . May, bur. at Hempstead 1715. M.I.

=...; da. of ...; married 17 ..; d. prob. in childbed of s. Edward ....17 ..

2. Philadelphia Harvey; born 1717; d. . . June, bur. at Hempstead 28 June 1723. M.I.

3. Edward Harvey, of Cleveland Court, St. James's, Westminster, Esq.; b. 1 Aug., bapt. at Chigwell 17 Aug. 1718; Adjt.-General of the Forces 13 Dec. 1763; Lt.-General 26 May 1772; Col. of Inniskilling Dragoons; Governor of Portsmouth; M.P. for Gatton, co. Surrey, 1761; for Harwich, co. Essex, in two Parliaments 1768 and 1774; d. 27 March 1778, bur. at Hempstead. (49) Will dat. 5 March 1778, codicils 23 and 25 same month; pr. 1 April following. (P.C.C., Hay 155.)

Edward Harvey, of Twickenham, Esq., only s.; b.1773 (?); d. 18..

=...; da. of ...; married 17..; d.18..

=2. ...; da. of Thomas Harben of Lewes, co. Sussex, Esq.; b. 1776 (?); mar. at Lewes 1 Feb. 1794; d. 18 ..
Arms: Azure, a saltire voided between four cronells or.

Y 2

c

c

1. William Harvey of Rolls Park, Esq.; b. 10 Sept., bapt. at Chigwell 30 Sept. 1754; M.P. for co. Essex 1775(?); d. unmar. at Chigwell 24 April (42), bur. at Hempstead 3 May 1779. Will and codicil dated 22 April 1779; proved 7 May following. (P.C.C., Warburton 204.)

2. Edward Harvey; b. 17 Aug., bapt. at Chigwell 11 Sept. 1756; d. 17 Oct., bur. at Hempstead 21 Oct. 1760.

3. Stephen Harvey, Esq.; of Saratoga, N. America, Lieut. H.M. 2nd Regiment of Foot; bapt. at Chigwell 26 Nov. 1757; killed in America Sept. 1779; probably buried there; unmar. Adm'on P.C.C. 24 Dec. 1782.

4. Sir Eliab Harvey of Rolls Park; b. 5 Dec., bapt. at Chigwell 26 Dec. 1758; Admiral of the Blue (42A); G.C.B. 17 Jan. 1825; M.P. for Maldon, co. Essex, in the two Parliaments 1780; for co. Essex in the five Parliaments 1802–7, 1820–6; d. at Rolls 20 Feb., bur. at Hempstead 27 Feb. 1880. (42B) M.I.

Arms and Crest: HARVEY (*ut supra*), with Motto over, "Téméraire."

Supporters (granted to him): Dexter, a Triton, holding over the dexter shoulder a trident, laurel entwining it, all proper; Sinister, a horse argent gorged with a naval crown or, on the rim the word "Trafalgar" sable hanging to it by a white ribbon with two blue stripes the Trafalgar medal or.

Motto: Redoubtable et fougueux.

Louisa, youngest da. and coheiress of Robert (Nugent), first Earl Nugent, of St. Martin's-in-the-Fields, and Eliz., relict of Augustus, fourth Earl of Berkeley, his wife; b. c. 1758; mar. at St. George's, Hanover Square (Special Licence Abp. Canterbury), 15 May (42C) 1784; d. at Skreens in Roxwell, co. Essex, 4 Dec. 1841, bur. at Roxwell. M.I. at Hempstead.

Arms: Ermine, two bars gules.

(See Pedigree ff, *post.*)

5. Thomas Harvey; b. 8 Dec. (43), bapt. at St. Anne (Soho), Westminster, 31 Dec. 1759; d. 14 Nov., bur. at Hempstead 18 Nov. 1760.

1. Mary Harvey; b. 2 Aug. (44), bapt. at St. Anne (Soho), Westminster, 27 Aug. 1752; d. 23 June, bur. at Hempstead 26 June 1755.

William Chaloner of Guisborough, co. York, Esq., eldest s. and h. of William C. of same, Esq., and Mary, da. and h. of Jas. Finny of Finny Lane, co. Staff., and late of Durham, Esq., his w.; b. 1750 (?); d. 1813 (?).

Arms: Sable, a chevron between three cherubims' heads or.

2. Emma Harvey; b. 29 Aug. 1753; mar. 8 Aug. 1771; d. 1835.

3. Maria Harvey (45); b. 20 Sept., bapt. at Chigwell 13 Oct. 1755; mar. 13 Oct. 1774; died at her house in Chigwell Row 11 Sept. 1822. (45A)

4. Henrietta ("Harriott") Harvey of Grange, near Middlewich, co. Chester; b. 13 Jan., bapt. at St. Anne (Soho), Westminster, 11 Feb. 1762; died unmar., . . . June, bur. at Hempstead 3 July 1782 (46). Adm'on P.C.C. 24 Dec. 1782.

George Wilbraham of Townsend, in Nantwich, and Delamere Lodge, in Cuddington, co. Chester, Esq., eld. s. and h. of Roger W. of Nantwich, Esq., and Mary, eld. da. of Thos. Hunt of Mollington, same co., his 2nd w.; b. 4 April 1741; Sheriff of Cheshire 1791; d. at Delamere Lodge 4 (? 9) Dec. 1813, bur. at Nantwich.

Arms (Ancient): Argent, three bends wavy azure.

(Modern): Azure, two bars argent; on a canton of the first, a wolf's head erased argent.

Both coats generally borne quarterly.

(*To be continued.*)

# The Register Book of Bramfield, co. Suffolk.*

## The Third Book of Baptisms.

### 1813.

Mar. 17 Charles Reed, Bastard of Ann Mattie, late Serv^t to M^r Badeley.

May 9 Harriott of Samuel and Hannah Barnaby, Laborer.

May 13 John of John and Martha Howlet, Farmer.

May 20 Robert s. of Amos and Rach^l Aldis, Laborer.

June 14 Jonathan s. of the late Jonathan and Mary his widow, Reyner, Farmer.

June 21 Elizabeth d. of James and Eliz. Wright, Laborer.

July 4 Sarah d. of Nathaniel and Hannah Osburn, Laborer.

July 25 John of John and Mary Jacob, Laborer.

Aug. 2 Jeremia of Robert and Sarah Savage, Laborer.

Aug. 15 Lazarus s. of John and Mary Smith, Laborer.

Nov. 22 John s. of Caroline Boatman, late a Serv^t.

Dec. 12 Robert Buxton s. of John and Margaret Howe, Farmer.

Dec. 13 Charles s. of William and Elizabeth Woollard, Malster.

Dec. 19 William s. of William and Ann Scarlett, Laborer.

### 1814.

Jan. 16 Elizabeth d. of Thomas and Elizabeth Crawfoot, Laborer.

Mar. 13 Matilda d. of Jacob and Sarah Stainton, Miller.

April 19 Mary d. of James and Mary Hurren, Laborer.

June 19 Isabella d. of Thomas and Charlotte Higham, Butcher.

July 3 Mary d. of William and Catharine Lines, Laborer.

July 10 Maria d. of Thomas and Mary Eade, Laborer.

Aug. 21 James s. of James and Maria Archer, Tailor.

Aug. 28 Philip s. of George and Frances Kerridge, Laborer.

Sep. 4 Parmella d. of John and Martha Howlett, Farmer.

Sep. 11 Richard s. of Robert and Sarah Sevidge, Laborer.

Oct. 2 Ann d. of John and Sarah Hammant, Cordwainer.

Oct. 2 Samuel s. of Robert and Mary Gilman, Laborer.

Nov. 7 Charlotte d. of William and Hannah Witmore, Laborer.

### 1815.

Jan. 15 William s. of Samuel and Elizabeth Leggat, Laborer.

Feb. 24 Robert s. of William and Hannah Sparrow, Laborer.

Feb. 25 James Stephen s. of Stephen and Mary Capon, Farmer.

Mar. 19 James s. of Robert and Lydia Borrett, Laborer.

April 16 Sarah d. of Samuel and Hannah Barnaby, Laborer.

April 30 James s. of Joseph and Sarah Kemp, Laborer.

June 4 Charlotte d. of Nathaniel and Hannah Osburn, Laborer.

June 4 Amy d. of Amos and Rachael Aldis, Laborer.

June 25 Charles s. of James and Bridget Burrows, Laborer.

July 16 Eliza d. of William and Mary Lizzamoore, Laborer.

July 16 Harriot d. of Isaac and Elizabeth Watling, Laborer.

July 16 Charlotte d. of the same.

Aug. 6 Henry s. of John and Lydia Briggs, Laborer.

Sep. 24 James s. of Robert and Ann Ransby, Laborer.

Oct. 22 William s. of Mial and Mary Newson, Laborer.

Oct. 24 John s. of John and Margaret Howe, Farmer.

Nov. 5 William s. of Thomas and Eleanor Fleet, Laborer.

Nov. 5 Sophia d. of William and Rebecca Ship, Laborer.

Dec. 10 Robert s. of James and Mary Hurren, Laborer.

Dec. 17 Mary d. of Sarah Smith, late a Serv^t.

Dec. 24 Honor d. of Samuel and Catharine Hammant, Laborer.

Dec. 31 Mary d. of William and Mary Hansey, Laborer.

### 1816.

Jan. 14 Mary d. of Thomas and Elizabeth Crawfoot, Laborer.

Jan. 14 Robert s. of Elizabeth Turner, late a Serv^t.

Feb. 25 Emily d. of John and Martha Howlett, Farmer.

Mar. 10 Rebecca d. of William and Hannah Witmore, Laborer.

April 12 George s. of Sarah Mane, late a Serv^t.

April 28 Frederic s. of Elijah and Elizabeth Clarke, Innkeeper.

May 19 Mary Ann d. of Abraham and Elizabeth Sadd, Laborer.

June 2 Mary Ann d. of Arthur and Sarah Copper, Shoemaker.

June 23 Maria d. of Robert and Ann Cornish, Laborer.

July 14 Stephen Hanton s. of Stephen and Mary Capon, Farmer.

* Continued from p. 323.

July 21  George s. of Jacob and Sarah Stanton, Miller.

Aug. 7  Deborah d. of William and Debora Peake, Wheelwright.

Sep. 15  Charlotte d. of Samuel and Elizabeth Leggatt, Laborer.

Oct. 6  Ann d. of Thomas and Catharine Chapman, Laborer.

### 1817.

Jan. 12  Mary d. of John and Lætitia Cooper, Laborer.

Feb. 16  Charles s. of Joseph and Sarah Kemp, Laborer.

Feb. 23  Mary d. of Robert and Lydia Borrett, Laborer.

Mar. 16  James s. of James and Mary Hurren, Laborer.

Mar. 23  Sarah d. of William and Ann Scarlett, Laborer.

April 20  Thomas s. of Sarah Smith, late a Serv$^t$.

May 4  Henry s. of Mary Ann Cooper, late a Serv$^t$.

June 1  Stephen s. of Robert and Sarah Sevidge, Laborer.

July 27  Martha d. of James and Maria Archer, Tailor.

Nov. 9  Sarah Ann d. of Mial and Mary Newson, Laborer.

Nov. 16  George Barns s. of George and Mary Osborne, Farmer.

Nov. 30  Mary Ann d. of John and Rachel Cullingford, Laborer.

### 1818.

Jan. 11  Louisa d. of Robert and Mary Gilman, Laborer.

Jan. 18  Mary Ann d. of John and Letitia Cooper, Laborer.

Feb. 1  Thomas s. of Thomas and Sarah Haward, Yeoman.

Mar. 1  John s. of Mary Cross, late a Serv$^t$.

Mar. 15  Maria d. of Samuel and Elizabeth Smith, Cordwainer.

Mar. 15  Thomas s. of William and Catharine Lines, Laborer.

Mar. 20  James s. of John and Sarah Hammont, Cordwainer.

Mar. 22  William s. of John and Lydia Briggs, Laborer.

Mar. 29  Charles s. of Robert and Ann Cornish, Laborer.

April 19  Sarah d. of Thomas and Elizabeth Crawfoot, Laborer.

May 3  Sarah d. of Arthur and Sarah Copper, Shoemaker.

May 17  James s. of William and Rebecca Ship, Laborer.

June 7  James s. of Samuel and Catharine Hammant, Laborer.

June 21  Mary Ann d. of John and Maria Randal, Laborer.

July 5  Sarah d. of Amos and Rachel Aldis, Laborer.

July 5  Sampson s. of Mary Hawes, late a Serv$^t$.

July 26  Ann d. of James and Hannah Farthers, Laborer.

Aug. 9  Mary d. of Stephen and Mary Capon, Farmer.

Aug. 23  Hannah d. of William and Hannah Witmore, Laborer.

Sep. 20  George Lame s. of Thomas and Catharine Chapman, Laborer.

Sep. 27  Sarah d. of James and Mary Reid, Laborer.

Oct. 4  Lydia d. of Joseph and Sarah Kemp, Laborer.

### 1819.

Jan. 3  Ann d. of Thomas and Mary Lame, Laborer.

Feb. 7  James s. of William and Ann Bartram, Laborer.

Feb. 14  Joseph s. of Joseph and Hannah Pooley, Carpenter.

Mar. 4  Sarah d. of James and Elizabeth Wright, Laborer.

Mar. 28  Henry s. of Samuel and Elizabeth Leggat, Laborer.

April 4  Charlotte d. of James and Rebecca Porter, Laborer.

June 20  William s. of Benj$^n$ and Mary Balls, Farmer.

June 27  Mary Ann d. of Stephen and Sarah Candler, Laborer.

June 27  Samuel Wright s. of Henry and Louisa Lock, Tailor.

Aug. 1  Henry Balls s. of Henry and Mary Drake, Groom.

Aug. 29  Susan d. of Robert and Susan Appleton, House Carpenter.

Oct. 24  Maria d. of James and Mary Hurren, Laborer.

Nov. 21  William s. of Arthur and Sarah Copper, Shoemaker.

Dec. 25  Charlotte d. of William and Esther Watling, Laborer.

### 1820.

Mar. 22  Mary Ann d. of Emily Cullum, Spinster.

Mar. 27  Mary d. of Thomas and Elizabeth Squire, Laborer.

April 3  George s. of William and Hannah Barnaby, Laborer.

April 12  Samuel s. of Samuel and Lydia Smith, Laborer.

April 30  Henry s. of John and Honor Todd, Laborer.

May 7  Mary Ann d. of Mial and Mary Newson, Laborer.

June 20  William s. of Mary Hammant, Spinster.

July 30  Jemima d. of Joshua and Jemima Newman, Joiner.

July 30  Samuel s. of the same.

Aug. 4  Jacob s. of Jacob and Sarah Stanton, Miller.

Aug. 20  Mary d. of Robert and Ann Cornish, Laborer.

Aug. 20  Mary Ann d. of Elizabeth Elner, Spinster.

Sep. 17  Susan d. of William and Ann Scarlett, Laborer.

Oct. 31  Mary d. of Robert and Ann Weavers, Laborer.

Nov. 1  Sophia d. of Sarah Crane, Spinster.

Nov. 14 Charlotte d. of Thomas and Elizabeth Crawfoot, Laborer.

Dec. 4 Mary Ann d. of Henry and Mary Drake, Groom.

### 1821.

Jan. 4 William s. of Benjamin and Mary Balls, Farmer.

Feb. 28 Henry Debney s. of Henry and Louisa Lock, Tailor.

Mar. 2 Caroline Davy d. of William and Catharine Lines, Laborer.

Mar. 11 Harriet d. of Richard and Susan Haking, Laborer.

Mar. 15 Henry Jakes s. of Henry Jakes and Maria Tuthill, Millwright.

April 1 Thomas Wright s. of Samuel and Elizabeth Leggatt, Laborer.

April 8 William s. of Daniel and Sally Smith, Laborer.

April 23 Maria d. of John and Maria Randal, Laborer.

May 1 Susan d. of Samuel and Catharine Hammant, Laborer.

May 14 Thomas s. of Thomas and Mary Lame, Laborer.

May 17 John s. of John and Letitia Cooper, Laborer.

May 24 Charlotte d. of Joseph and Ann Borton, Laborer.

July 8 Harriet d. of James and Rebecca Porter, Laborer.

Aug. 5 Charlotte d. of William and Rebecca Ship, Laborer.

Aug. 30 Harriet d. of Philip and Eliza Prime, Shoemaker.

Sep. 4 William s. of Jonas and Caroline Tibenham, Butcher.

Sep. 12 Thomas s. of Thomas and Catharine Chapman, Laborer.

Sep. 29 Mary Ann d. of Elizabeth Barnaby, Spinster.

Oct. 26 Thomas s. of Robert and Mary Ann Scarlett, Coachman.

Nov. 11 Charlotte d. of John and Honor Todd, Laborer.

Dec. 10 Arthur s. of Arthur and Sarah Copper, Shoemaker.

### 1822.

Mar. 30 Mary Ann d. of William and Hannah Witmore, Laborer.

April 8 Barnaby s. of James and Ann Reade, Laborer.

May 20 Robert s. of Samuel and Sarah Edwards, Laborer.

June 1 Charles Cross s. of Hannah Squire, Spinster.

July 19 Eliza d. of John and Elizabeth Broome, Laborer.

July 28 John s. of John and Elizabeth Holmes, Laborer.

Oct. 23 Henry s. of Benjamin and Mary Balls, Farmer.

Nov. 13 John s. of John and Sarah Hatcher, Blacksmith.

Dec. 27 Mary Ann d. of John and Lydia Briggs, Laborer.

### 1823.

Jan. 4 Mary Ann d. of Thomas and Mary Lame, Laborer.

Jan. 6 Lydia d. of William and Ann Scarlett, Laborer.

Jan. 20 Thomas s. of Thomas and Elizabeth Crawfoot, Laborer.

Jan. 29 John s. of James and Maria Button, Laborer.

Feb. 16 Sarah d. of Robert and Lydia Borrett, Laborer.

Mar. 17 Elizabeth d. of John and Mary Doddington, Butler.

Mar. 20 Samuel s. of Keziah Clemments, Spinster.

Mar. 30 Sophia d. of Daniel and Sarah Smith, Laborer.

April 28 James s. of Joseph and Ann Bolton, Laborer.

May 25 Lydia d. of Samuel and Elizabeth Leggat, Laborer.

July 6 Robert s. of George Manby and Phebe Smith, Laborer.

July 24 Sarah Ann d. of Mary Mann, Spinster.

Sep. 17 William s. of Robert and Mary Ann Scarlett, Coachman.

Sep. 28 Naomi d. of James and Mary Hurren, Laborer.

Oct. 19 Betsy d. of John and Honor Todd, Wheelwright.

Nov. 23 Mary Ann d. of Joseph and Sarah Gilbert, Laborer.

### 1824.

Jan. 25 David s. of John and Ann Spindler, Laborer.

Feb. 1 Robert s. of Arthur and Sarah Copper, Shoemaker.

Mar. 18 Maria d. of Samuel and Catharine Amant, Laborer.

May 3 William Joseph s. of Robert Curtis and Abigail Andrews, Miller.

May 29 Hannah d. of Susannah Edwards, Spinster.

June 16 Sarah d. of Benjamin and Mary Balls, Farmer.

July 10 Mary d. of Richard and Susan Haking, Laborer.

July 19 Caroline d. of Thomas and Catharine Chapman, Laborer.

July 29 George s. of George and Elizabeth Bertram, Laborer.

Oct. 28 William s. of William and Hannah Witmore, Laborer.

Nov. 7 Robert s. of Mary Marsh, Spinster.

Nov. 10 Mary d. of John and Amy Ammant, Laborer.

Nov. 29 Andrew Sherlock s. of Andrew and Marianne Lawson of Aldboro', Yorkshire, Gentleman.

### 1825.

Feb. 13 Mary Ann d. of Robert and Lydia Borret, Laborer.

Feb. 18 Lucy d. of Joseph and Mary Chapman, Laborer.

Mar. 6 Emma d. of William and Ann Scarlett, Laborer.

Mar.   6   George s. of Samuel and Sarah Edwards, Laborer.
Mar. 27   Mary d. of James and Rebecca Porter, Laborer.
April   3   Samuel s. of George Manby and Phebe Smith, Laborer.
April 13   Maria d. of William and Emily Wright, Blacksmith.
April 17   Sarah d. of John and Sophia Thurlow, Laborer.
April 21   Mary Ann d. of Mary Randal, Spinster.
May    1   Robert s. of Joseph and Ann Bolton, Laborer.
May  22   Susanna d. of Robert and Sarah Rawlinson, Laborer.
June 30   Sarah d. of Thomas and Mary Lame, Laborer.
Aug.  21   Eliza d. of Robert and Mary Ann Scarlett, Coachman.
Aug.  25   Hannah Hunt d. of John Hunt and Sarah Hatcher, Blacksmith.
Sep.  29   Maria d. of Henry and Theresa Browne, Laborer.
Oct.  23   Charlotte d. of Daniel and Sally Smith, Laborer.
Nov.  12   Elizabeth Bridget d. of Robert Curtis and Abigail Andrews, Miller.
Dec.  28   Mary Ann d. of Benjamin and Mary Balls, Farmer.

### 1826.

Jan.   6   Joseph s. of Joseph and Sarah Gilbert, Laborer.
Jan.  27   Charlotte d. of James and Maria Button, Laborer.
Feb.  26   Caroline d. of Joseph and Tabitha Redgrave, Laborer.
Mar.   6   William s. of James and Mary Hurren, Laborer.
Mar.  24   John s. of John and Elizabeth Broome, Laborer.
Mar.  24   Elizabeth d. of the same.
April   8   James s. of James and Ann Reade, Laborer.
April 15   William s. of James and Sophia Watling, Laborer.
April 26   James of Arthur and Sarah Copper, Shoemaker.
April 30   Betsy d. of John and Ann Spindler, Laborer.
May  20   William s. of William and Elizabeth Ling, Farmer.
May  23   William s. of James and Harriet Clarke, Laborer.
June   2   William s. of William Aldis and Elizabeth Higham, Farmer.
June   2   Mary d. of the same.
July  19   Amy d. of Robert and Susan Appleton, Farmer.
July  19   Edward s. of the same.
July  20   William s. of Edward and Sarah Jones, Butler.
July  31   William s. of William and Hannah Witmore, Laborer.
Nov.   1   Edward s. of Stephen and Mary Self, Laborer.
Nov.  18   Mary Ann d. of Robert and Mary Ann Westgate, Laborer.

### 1827.

Feb.   4   Sophia d. of Samuel and Catharine Amant, Laborer.
Feb.   8   Robert Clarke s. of Jonas and Caroline Tibenham, Butcher.
Feb.  17   Isaac Bellamy s. of Isaac and Elizabeth Eastaugh, Laborer.
Feb.  19   George Valentine s. of Henry and Louisa Locke, Tailor.
April   1   James s. of John and Amy Amant, Laborer.
April   6   James s. of Thomas and Catharine Chapman, Laborer.
June   3   Robert William s. of Samuel and Sarah Edwards, Laborer.
June   8   Mary Ann d. of Sarah Leggatt, Spinster.
July  29   Maria d. of Daniel and Sarah Smith, Laborer.
Aug.   7   Elizabeth Augusta d. of William and Elizabeth Ling, Farmer.
Sep.  13   Mary d. of Benjamin and Mary Balls Farmer.
Sep.  16   Sophia d. of John and Sophia Thurlow, Laborer.
Sep.  16   James s. of George and Elizabeth Bartram, Laborer.
Nov.  22   Elizabeth d. of Arthur and Sarah Copper, Shoemaker.
Nov.  25   William s. of James and Sophia Watling, Laborer.
Nov.  27   William s. of Edward and Susannah Crisp, Laborer.
Dec.   5   James Forman s. of Susan Aldred, Widow.
Dec.  17   Nicey d. of Joseph and Sarah Gilbert, Laborer.
Dec.  23   Sarah d. of Richard and Susan Haking, Laborer.
Dec.  29   Mary d. of Joseph and Ann Bolton, Laborer.
Dec.  31   Thomas s. of William Aldis and Elizabeth Higham, Farmer.

### 1828.

Jan.   9   Rachel d. of Joseph and Mary Chapman, Laborer.
Feb.  14   William s. of John Hunt and Sarah Hatcher, Blacksmith.
Feb.  20   Emily d. of James and Mary Hurren, Laborer.
Mar.  23   Eliza d. of William and Hannah Barnaby, Laborer.
April   6   James s. of George Manby and Phebe Smith, Laborer.
April 20   Mary Ann d. of Samuel and Jane Vincent, Laborer.
May  14   William s. of Hannah Edwards, Spinster.
June   4   Charles s. of Thomas and Elizabeth Crawfoot, Laborer.
June   9   Salome d. of Stephen and Mary Self, Laborer.
June   9   Frederic William s. of James and Margaret Ann King, Farmer.
July  12   Maria d. of James and Maria Button, Laborer.

July 17   Thomas Gooch s. of Robert and Susan Appleton, Farmer.

July 28   Sarah d. of Daniel and Sophia Watson, Laborer.

Aug. 3   William s. of Robert and Lydia Borrett, Laborer.

Aug. 3   Samuel s. of Joseph and Tabitha Redgrave, Laborer.

Sep. 5   Samuel Augustus s. of Samuel and Ann Tipple, Draper.

Sep. 14   James s. of James and Ann Read, Laborer.

Sep. 21   Eliza d. of William and Susan Lock, Laborer.

Oct. 5   George s. of John and Ann Spindler, Laborer.

Oct. 17   Betsy d. of Robert and Mary Ann Westgate, Laborer.

Oct. 19   David s. of William and Catharine Lines, Laborer.

Oct. 27   Edward Ashford s. of Joseph and Susannah Youngman, Butcher.

Oct. 28   Emma d. of Abraham and Rachel Smith, Laborer.

Oct. 31   Josiah Frederick s. of John and Sarah Smith, Miller.

Dec. 28   Hepzibah of William and Hannah Witmore, Laborer.

1829.

Jan. 9   Robert s. of William Aldis and Elizabeth Higham, Farmer.

Feb. 29   William s. of William and Lucy Land, Cordwainer.

Mar. 9   Mary Girling d. of William and Elizabeth Ling, Farmer.

Mar. 17   Isabel d. of James and Hannah Cross, Farmer.

July 23   Henry s. of Arthur and Sarah Copper, Shoemaker.

Aug. 2   Eliza d. of Elizabeth Waters, Spinster.

Aug. 17   Sophia d. of John and Amy Amant, Laborer.

*(To be continued.)*

---

# Genealogy of Browne.*

## Wills.

Copy of the Will of THOMAS BROWNE, Esq., of Shredicot, co. Stafford.† Dated 1631; proved 1633.

[50 Russell, P.C.C.]

IN THE NAME OF GOD AMEN The seaven and twentieth daie of October Anno Domini One thousand six hundred thirty and one and in the seaventh yeare of the Raigne of our Soveraigne Lord Charles by the grace of God of England Scotland France and Ireland defender of the faith &c. I Thomas Browne one of the Procurators of th'arches London calling to minde the ever changing course of all flesh in this world doe therefore in my health (before sicknes the messenger of death approach) make and declare this my last will and Testament in maner and forme following First I commend my Soule to the everlasting mercy of my most gracious God promised in my Redeemer Christ Jesus his onely sonne the worlds onely Saviour with assured confidence that by and through his onely meritts death and passion I have and shall have free remission and pardon of all my sinnes and be reconciled to my most glorious God and be accepted iust and righteous before him through the righteousnes of my most blessed Saviour who being most cleare from sinne was made sinne for me by imputac'on of my sinnes vnto him that I might be made righteous before God in him by imputac'on of his righteousnes vnto me being full of all sinne and corruption And I most stedfastly beleeve that after this life my soule shall have an inheritance among them wᶜʰ are sanctified by faith in Christ Jesus by the power of whose resurrec'on my bodie shalbe raised vpp at the last daie vnto the resurrection of life and both bodie and soule be revnited and enioy for ever the beatitude and glorie which noe tongue can expresse even the fruition of ioyes eternall and vnspeakable among the sonnes of God My bodie whose mother is earth I leave to be interred in its mothers bowells where it shall please God to appoint there to reste and sleepe vntill the resurrection. Touching the goods God hath lent mee First I give to the poore people in the parish of Careswall where I was borne five pounds And to the poore people of the parish of Dillorne next adioyninge forty shillings And to the poore of the parish of Bradeley where I now dwell fortie shillings And to the poore of the parish of Langford in the County of Daʳby fortie shillings to be distributed respectively by the Vicars Churchwardens and Overseers of the poore of each parish for the tyme being. Item I give and bequeath vnto my loving sisters Joyce Browne Anne Beech Marie Bridgwood and Margerie Goodanter vnto every of them fortie shillings apeece And to every of my sister Joyce her children fortie shillings apeece and to Joyce Withering & Mary Withering my sister Beech her daughters by her first husband to either of them fortie shillings apeece And to my neece Marie Rodes forty shillings And I give and bequeath vnto every of the children of my sister Goodanter fortie shillings apeece And to every of the children of my sister Ley [? Lee] and my sister Hely deceased fortie shillings to every of them apeece being fower in all And I will that if any of my said sisters children die before they receave theire said legacies being then due then the brothers and sisters of such child soe dying to have the legacie

---

* Continued from p. 313.

† A copy of this Will is filed at Somerset House. A note, in Latin, states that the original document was returned to the executrix.

and porc'on of him and her soe dying equally to be devided among them. Item I give vnto my approved good Cosin and friend John Browne of Stafford gentleman fortie shillings And to Mr. Fletcher parson of Haughton twentie shillings and my two bookes of St Augustins workes wch I lent him And where there were and are small legacies bequeathed to divers of my children by sundry mine and theire friends part of which legacies some of my children have themselves received and have given theire acquittances for receipt and part thereof I have received for their vse and have given my acquitances and bonds for saveing harmlesse the Executors of the said Testaments from and against my said children Therefore I doe will that if any of my children to whom any such legacies were given which I have receaved shall in any sort sue molest goe about or attempt to trouble any of the said Executors or any other for any such legacies That then he she or they who shall soe attempt or goe about such legacie shall forfeite and loose the benefitt of all and every legacie gift and disposic'on given or bequeathed to him her or them in and by this my last will And for that I am perswaded my loving wife out of her motherly love and affecc'on ever shewed towards our children will out of such good meanes which (if it please God) I shall leave her augment and encrease the porc'ons and livelihood of such our children as shall stand in most neede especially them who she shall finde of best desert And also give them such educac'on and maintenance with all necessaries as are and shalbe fitt for them wch that she maie be the better enabled to doe and to paie my debts and performe the legacies and disposic'ons in this my will Therefore I doe give devise and bequeath vnto my said wife Apolyne Browne (vnder the condic'ons and provisoes hereafter in this my will expressed) All and singular my lands messuages tenements rents reverc'ons services and hereditaments lying and being in Shredicote Barton and Bradeley in the Countie of Stafford together with all houses and other edifices there and also all that Parke or impaled ground comonly called or knowne by the name of Middleton Parke al's Barton old Parke which I lately purchased of the then Lord Stanhoppe and of Mr. Awdley and Mr. Willis lying in the Countie of Darby together with all rents reverc'ons and remainders therevnto belonging To have hold occupy and enioy all and singular the premises severally given to her as aforesaid with theire appurten'nc' to her the said Apolyne my wife and her assignes from the daie of my death for and during the terme of her naturall life And I also give vnto my said wife Apoline Browne all my estate interest lease and terme of yeares which are yet to come in the said Parke and impaled ground by vertue of assignment made to me at the tyme of the said purchase from the said Mr. Audley Mr. Willis by theire deed dated the first of July in the nineteenth yeare of the raigne of or late Soveraigne Lord King James Provided alwaies neverthelesse and vpon condic'on and my will and minde is that she my said wife shall at any tyme during her life grant bargaine assigne sell or make awaie her said estate interest and term of years in the said Parke or any part or parcell thereof to any person or persons but only to such person or persons to whom I shall by my deed or by my last will and Testament in writing give and devise the inheritance of the said Parke And after her decease I will give and bequeath all the said estate interest and terme of yeares of and in said Parke to such person and persons to whom I shall by my deed or last will in writing give and devise the inheritance of the said Parke Furthermore for the reasons aforesaid my minde and will is that my said wife Apoline Browne shall have take occupie and enioy the rents issues revennues and profitts of all and singuler my lands tenements and hereditaments lying and being in Hungrie Benteley in the said Countie of Darbie together with the mansion house messuage and tenemt and other edifices there and of two closes and pastures therevnto adioyning the one called the Spittle Hinckle and th'other called the pale slate All which I purchased of the Lord Windsor for and during the terme and space of seaven yeares next and imediately ensuing the date of my death if she live soe longe sole and vnmarried And I will that my said wife during the said term shall not make any spoile or waste either of or in any of the timber trees Runt trees or woods or of or in any okes ashes elmes maples withies or ollers there growing or of or in any the timber trees runt trees and woods oakes ashes maples withies or ollers growinge in the said Parke or in the pale rowe of the said Parke nor shall cause to be cutt or felled any of the said tymber trees or other trees except it be for the necessarie reparac'ons of the houses and buildings vpon the premisses and for the necessary paling and railing about the said Parke and for fenceing and fewell to be spent in and about the same premisses.

Item I doe give and bequeath vnto my daughter Apoline Browne five hundred pounds of lawfull money of England to be paid vnto her at the daie of her marriage or within one yeare next after my decease Provided allwaies and my will is that if she doe marry with the consent and good likeing of her mother and of my sonne living then my will and minde is that the said five hundred pounds shalbe made vp full eight hundred pounds to be paid vnto her within one yeare after her said marriage soe to be had and done with consent and good likeing as aforesaid and not otherwise And I will that if my said daughter Apoline Browne depart this life before she be married and before she receive her said legacie then I will and bequeath the said legacie of five hundred pounds given to her as aforesaid vnto the rest of my children vizt vnto George Browne Mary Stury William Browne Edmond Browne and Edward Browne or to soe many of them as shalbe then living to be equallie devided among them And I give vnto my said daughter Apoline my ringe sett with five litle diamonds. Item I doe give and bequeath vnto my three sonnes George Browne William Browne and Edward Browne (over and besides the lands annuities rent charges exhibic'on and mainten'nce which I have in and by this my will severally and respectively given and appointed vnto them) to each of them fortie pounds apeece to be paid vnto every of them at the end of two yeares next after my decease with purpose that my Executrix maie see and try wch of them will best imploy the same and soe to respect them accordingly. Item I doe give vnto my loving daughter in law M<sup>rs</sup> Elizabeth Leving five pounds and to her sonne Thomas Leving my god sonne five pounds to be paid to his father for his vse. Item I doe give and bequeath vnto my daughter Mary Stury five pounds And to Elizabeth Stury her daughter five pounds And vnto Apoline Stury her other daughter twentie pounds w<sup>ch</sup> said five pounds and twentie pounds soe given to the said two daughters I will shalbe paid vnto theire father Carew Stury for theire vse within one yeare next after my decease soe as he become bound by himselfe in the some of fortie pounds of lawfull money of England to my Executrix and overseer hereunder named or to one of them to paie the said severall legacies to his said two daughters at their severall ages of eighteene yeares or daies of marriage which first shall happen. Item I give vnto every man servant and maid servant servinge me at my decease twentie shillings apeece over and above theire wages then due. All the rest and residue of all and singuler my goods chattells cattells jewells plate ready money and debts (after my debts paid and funeralls and legacies discharged) I doe wholy give and bequeath vnto my said wife Apoline Browne And doe constitute and ordaine her Executrix of this my last will and Testament and doe name and appoint my sonne in lawe Timothy Levinge Esqr. to be Overseer of the same desiring him to be aydinge and assistinge vnto my said Executrix and to my children with his best counsell and direction when they stand in neede and for his paines therein to be taken I give him five pounds. Item I will my sonne Edmond Browne shall have my written bookes of D<sup>r</sup> Androwes his Catechisinge preface to the lawe and of his sermons made vpon the first commandem<sup>t</sup>. Item I will that all my other bookes and papers printed and manuscripts shalbe given and bestowed by my wife to and amongst all my children as by and with the advice of my said sonne Levinge shalbe thought most fitting to theire severall qualities and disposic'ons. Item I will that if all my said goods chattells cattells jewells plate household stuffe ready money and debts will not suffice to pay my debts which I shall owe the legacies w<sup>ch</sup> I have given in this my will & to discharge my funerall (which I desire maie be performed without excesse) then I will that my said wife Apoline Browne out of all the rents issues and proffitts of all my said lands tenem<sup>ts</sup> and other revenues given and bequeathed vnto her in this my will for life or for yeares shall well and truly satisfie and pay all and every my said debts legacies and funerall expences And if she depart this life before the same be paid then I will that the said debts legacies & funeralls then remayning vnpaid shalbe truly paid and discharged out of all such goods chattells cattells jewells plate household stuffe ready money and debts w<sup>ch</sup> shall remayne vnadministred by my said wife at her death and out of all the rents issues and profitts of all the lands tenem<sup>ts</sup> and hereditaments hereafter in this my last will and Testament given and devised unto my son Edmond Browne And where at the tyme of my marriage with my said wife or shortly after I became bounden in one obligac'on vnto my wives Father George Southaike since deceased in the some of two thousand pounds with condic'on to give bequeath or suffer to come vnto the right or possession of my said wife after my decease in lands tenements ready money goods chattells cattells or debts the some and value of Two thousand m<sup>ks</sup> [marks] as by the said obligac'on and condic'on maie appeare Now for that I hold her fullie advanced to that some and value and to much more when I depart this life by the severall gifts and disposic'ons in this my will Therefore my will and minde is that if either my said wife or any other person or persons to whom the said obligac'on is made belongeth or shall come or hath any right of app'on or title or interest to put the said bond in suite of law doe or shall endeavo<sup>r</sup> or goe about to take any benefitt or advantage of the said bond or put the same in suite either for my wives vse or otherwise molest or trouble my heires executo<sup>rs</sup> or administrato<sup>rs</sup> or shall thereby hinder the true performance of this my will Or if my said wife after my decease doe clayme challenge sue for or endeavo<sup>r</sup> to have or obtaine any dower or claime title of dower or thirds in any my said lands tenements and hereditaments over and besides the disposic'ons gifts and devices made given and devised vnto her in this my will Or if such person whom my said wife shall marry after my decease (if she happen to marry) doe not within one moneth next before the said marriage enter into bond and become bound with two good and sufficient suerties in the some of Two thousand pounds of lawfull money of England vnto the Judge of the Prerogative Court of Canterbury for the tyme being vpon and with condic'on for the true and sure payment of the severall legacies and bequests given and disposed in this my will and also for the true performance of this my last will and Testament Or if my said wife doe not prove my said will and Testament and take vpon her the execuc'on thereof within six moneths next after my decease (there being noe lawfull impediment to hinder her to the contrary) Then my will and minde is that the severall disposic'ons legacies giftes and devises made and given vnto her of all or of any part of my land tenements and hereditamt<sup>ts</sup> or other things in this my present last will and Testament and alsoe the disposic'on and gift of the residue of all my goods chattells cattells jewels plate readie money and debts given to her in this my will and the nameing of her my Executrix and all other benefitts w<sup>ch</sup> she might take enioy or have in or by my said will shall cease and be vtterly voide frustrate and of none effect as if she had never been named in this my will and testament anythinge therein contayned to the contrary not w<sup>th</sup>standing And then I doe will and bequeath the residue of all and singuler my said goods chattells cattells jewells plate household stuffe ready money and debts vnto George Browne William Browne Edmond Browne and Edward Browne my sonnes and vnto Marie Stury and Apoline Browne my daughters to be equallie devided among them six And then I make and ordaine my said sonne Edmond Browne the sole Executor of this my last will and Testament.

(*To be continued.*)

# Delpratt Pedigree.*

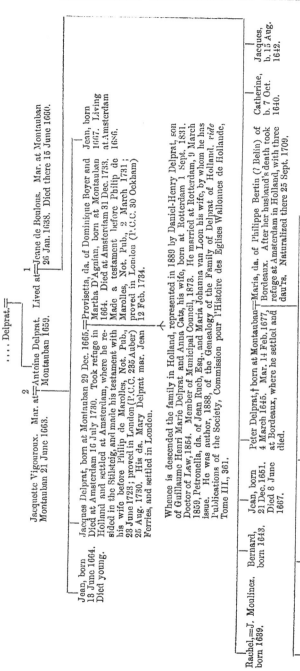

.... Delprat.=

Jacquette Vigouroux.  Mar. at Montauban 21 June 1663. | 2 Antoine Delprat. Montauban 1659. | 1 Lived at — Jeane de Boulous.  Mar. at Montauban 26 Jan. 1638.  Died there 15 June 1660.

Jean, born 18 June 1664. Died young.

Jacques Delprat, born at Montauban 29 Dec. 1665.= Took refuge in Holland and settled at Amsterdam, where he resided in the Stilsteig, and made his testament with his wife before Philip de Marolles, Not. Pub., 23 June 1723; proved in London (P.C.C. 235 Auber) 25 Aug. 1730. His da. Mary Delprat mar. Jean Ferries, and settled in London.

Provisetta, da. of Dominique Boyer and Martha D'Agnian, born at Montauban 1664.  Died at Amsterdam 31 Dec. 1733.  Made a testament before Philip de Marolles, Not. Pub., 2 March 1731; proved in London (P.C.C. 30 Ockham) 12 Feb. 1734.

Jean, born 1667.  Living at Amsterdam 1686.

Whence is descended the family in Holland, represented in 1889 by Daniel-Henry Delprat, son of Guillaume Henri Marie Delprat and Anna Cats, his wife, born at Rotterdam 1 Sept. 1831. Doctor of Law, 1854. Member of Municipal Council, 1873. He married at Rotterdam, 9 March 1859, Petronella, da. of Jean Rueb, Esq., and Maria Johanna van Loon his wife, by whom he has issue. He was author, 1888, of the Genealogy of the Family of Delprat of Holland, vide Publications of the Society, Commission pour l'Histoire des Eglises Wallonnes de Hollande, Tome III., 361.

Peter Delprat,† born at Montauban 4 March 1645.  Mar. 14 Feb. 1677, at Bordeaux, where he settled and died.= Maria, da. of Philippe Bertin (? Belin) of Bordeaux.  After her husband's death took refuge at Amsterdam in Holland, with three dau'rs.  Naturalized there 25 Sept. 1709.

Madeleine, born at Bordeaux 3 April 1681.  Bur. at Amsterdam 15 Oct. 1765.  Testament dated 26 Sept. 1762.  Her heir John King, her great-nephew, of London, son of Jean Roy, who was son of Jean Roy and Susanne Delprat, sister of Madeleine.

Catherine, b. 7 Oct. 1640.

Jacques, b. 15 Aug. 1642.

Rachel,=J. Moulinez, born 1689.

Bernard, born 1643.

Jean, born 21 Dec. 1651. Died 8 June 1667.

Philippe Delprat, born at Bordeaux 1684.

Peter Delprat, born at Bordeaux 17 July 1685.

Judith, born at Bordeaux 23 May 1683.  Buried at Amsterdam 28 May 1763.

Marie, born at Bordeaux 23 March 1682.  Mar. at Amsterdam, Feb. 1709, Jean Pierre Hoigelles.

* Compiled by W. J. C. MOENS, Esq., F.S.A.

† Peter Delprat had also another daughter named Susanne, living in London, and married to Jean Roy.  Their son, John Roy alias King, had a son John, who was heir to the estate of his great-aunt Madeleine by her testament made at Amsterdam 26 Sept. 1763.  It may be that Peter Delprat had this daughter Susanne by a first wife Susanne, and that she came to England on the Revocation of the Edict of Nantes with Daniel Duprat or Delprat, who was naturalized 12 William III.

Peter Duprat.* Lived at Nerac in France.=Susanna....

William Field, born ... 1690.=Judith ...., born 1698. Died 21 June 1764, æt. 74. | Died 9 Sept. 1752, æt. 54.

Seven children, died before their parents.

1. William. 2. Christopher. 3. Pitman. 1. Scandrett, a da.

Daniel Duprat, born at Nerac. Naturalized in England by Act of Parliament 12 William III. (1700).

Samuel Delpratt, of the firm of Messrs. Foord and Delpratt of Bristol, died at sea, circa 8 July 1783, returning from Jamaica, where he was owner of Mount Sinai, Coldstream, and other plantations. Testament made in Jamaica. Went there 24 Dec. 1779.=Martha, da. of Michael Foord of Bristol, born c. 1760? Died in Jamaica 27 Aug. 1782.

Elizabeth Fry,† da. of ... Married 28 Oct. 1750 at St. Michael's Church, Bristol, by lic. 1st wife. Died between 1758 and 1769. Aged 21 and above 27 Oct. 1750.

William Delpratt,=Mary Field, mar. 14 Dec. 1769. of the parish of St. James, Bristol, a West Indian Merchant. Died between 30 May and 3 Nov. 1784. Aged 21 and above 27 Oct. 1750.

Daniel Delpratt.

Diana Delprat, born circa 1700. Died May 1790, æt. 90. Bur. 6 May 1790.

...=... Price.

Vide Mrs. Turner's papers.

Judith Marie=Stephen Turner. Delprat, born 21 Mar. 1775. Bapt. St. John's Ch., Bristol. Died circa 1853, s.p. —Stephen Turner of Bath. Died Aug. 1835.

Judith Delpratt, born 4 Jan. 1771. Died July 1774.

Joseph Delpratt, born 5 Feb. 1768. Died in Jamaica 18 May 1835. Will dat. 25 Feb. 1828. Unmar.

William Delpratt, born 2 April 1752. Bapt. St. James Church. Died in his house, Berkeley St., Bristol, 20 July 1826. Bur. in Chancel of St. Stephen's Church, Bristol, unmar. Will dat. 10 July 1826.

Samuel Delpratt, Surgeon H.E.I.C.S. Born 1 Nov. 1828. Died at Worthing 17 Feb. 1876.=Lydia Eliza, da. of ... Baker. Died 1886 at Weston-super-Mare. Bur. at Worthing. S.p.

Mary Ann=John William Harris, son of John Harris and Elizabeth (Delpratt). A Surgeon at Exeter. Delpratt, born 18 Feb. 1827.

John Delpratt Harris. Minnie Harris.

Second son.

Edward Delpratt,=Eliza, 2nd da. of John Robertson, Esq., of Kingston, Jamaica. Mar. 19 March 1794. married 20 March 1819. Died Jan. 1888, in Jamaica.

Thomas, born 26 Jan. 1756. Bapt. at St. Michael's Church, Bristol. Died 24 July 1756.

Elizabeth, born 19 July 1753. Bapt. at St. James Ch., Bristol. Died 22 Sept. 1763.

William Delpratt, born 19 July 1822 at Jamaica. Surgeon in Hon. E.I. Co.'s Service. Living 1889 at Heatherside, Moorland Road, Bournemouth, S.A.

Edward Delpratt, born 5 March 1825 at Jamaica. Lieut. H.E.I.C. Navy. Died 30 Jan. 1857. Bur. St. Thomas Church, Charlton, co. Kent.

Isabella Helen Delpratt, born 15 April 1820 at Jamaica. Died .. Aug. 1885. Bur. in Widcombe Churchyard, near Bath.

A.

* Query this Peter married 1st Susanna; 2nd, Maria Bertin or Belin.
† Daniel Fry of Bristol, by will (6 Plymouth), proved 4 Jan. 1725-6, names the children of "my daughter Ann Delpratt" (probably the mother of William Delpratt).

A    Eldest son.

Samuel Delpratt, died at Kingston, Jamaica, 26 Aug. 1821. He was of Bath, co. Somerset, and of the parish of St. David, Jamaica. His will dat. 30 Oct. 1814; codicil 16 Nov. same year, was proved = Agnes Ross, da. of William Ross,* Esq., of Richmond Plantation, Jamaica. (He lived at Kingston, and was born in Scotland (? Aberdeen) 28 April 1753.) Mar. 28 Oct. 1796, at Bathwick, co. Somerset. Died in Jamaica 10 July 1815. M.I.

William Delpratt, living in Jamaica in 1819, unmar.

Martha Delpratt, mar. at Kingston, Jamaica, circa 6 May 1783. Living in London 1819. = James Mitchell, born circa 1750. A merchant of Kingston, Jamaica. Died before 1804.

Elizabeth Delpratt, mar. before 1819, when she was living at Exeter. = John, son of . . . Harris, Surgeon at Exeter. Died 30 June 1855.

Agnes Delpratt, born 25 July 1797 at Greenwich, Mar. 1823. = Charles Basil Bacon of Moor Park, and of Culverlands, near Farnham, co. Surrey.

Elizabeth Martha Delpratt, born 2 Jan. 1799 at Kingston, Jamaica. Married 11 Sept. 1827 at St. Martin's, London. Died 5 Nov. 1880. s.p. = Edmund Finucane Morris (son of Samuel Morris and his wife Rachel, da. of J. Samuels, Esq., of Jamaica), Col. of 49th Regt., K.C.B. Born 26 April 1792 in Jamaica. Died 16 Dec. 1871.

Robert Delpratt, born 14 June 1802 at Exmouth, co. Devon. Bapt. there. Accidentally drowned at Mundsley, co. Norf., 18 Sept. 1819. Buried in chancel of that church.

Mary Herring Delpratt, born 5 Aug. 1800 at Mount Sinai Estate, Jamaica. Died 1876, unmar.

Isabella Delpratt, born at Widcombe House, near Bath, 7 May 1804. Mar. Feb. 1831. Died 23 Jan. 1886 at Freshwater, Isle of Wight. = Noel Thomas Smith, son of Noel Thomas Smith, M.D., of Newcastle, by Anne Mitchell his wife, da. of Abraham Dunkley of Clarendon, Jamaica.

Charlotte Helen Delpratt, born 13 Sept. 1805 at Lyde House, Sion Hill, Bath. Bapt. at Queen Street Chapel. Mar. Jan. 1838. = Robert Taylor, Capt. in 65th Regt, Bengal N.I.

Joseph Delpratt, born 30 July 1808. Bapt. at Widcombe House. Died at Freshwater, Isle of Wight, 23 Jan. 1884. Bur. in family vault in St. Thomas Churchyard, Charlton, co. Kent.
Arms granted 17 Dec. 1867, to Joseph Delpratt of Queen's Gardens, co. Middlesex, gent, only surviving son of Samuel Delpratt, late of the Island of Jamaica, gentleman, and grandson of Samuel Delpratt, late of Bristol, merchant, both deceased : Per fesse, gules and ermine, in chief a cross couped or, and in base a bull passant sable.
Crest: Upon a mount vert, between two wings ermine, a cross couped or.
Motto: TASCHE SANS TACHE. = Sarah Elinor, da. of Henry Boldero Barnard of Cave Castle, co. York, by Sarah Eliz., elder da. and coh. of Roger Gee of Bishop Burton. Born 11 Aug. 1810. Mar. at Christ Church, St. Marylebone, co. Middlesex, 10 Oct. 1832. Died 7 Jan. 1852. Bur. at St. Thomas's, Charlton, co. Kent.

B

William Delpratt, born 13 Jan. 1811. Died Feb. 1813.

Samuel William Delpratt, born 20 Dec. 1813. Died Feb. 1814. Both buried in family vault at St. Augustine's Church, Bristol.

* His brothers were Robert Ross; Sir John Ross, Governor of Guernsey; General Alexander Ross, A.D.C. to Lord Cornwallis, and married to Miss (better known as) Bella Gunning, da. of Sir Robert Gunning.

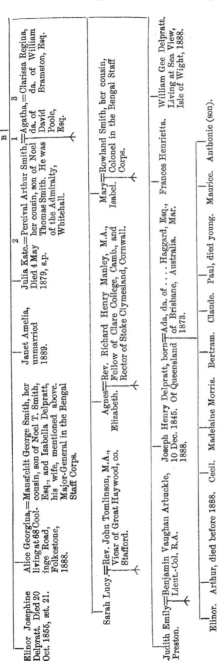

## GREY OF GROBY AND PIRGO.

Sir Bernard Burke in his Peerage books states that Lord John Grey of Pirgo, fourth son of Thomas Grey, Lord Ferrers of Groby and Marquis of Dorset in 1511–1530, had an only son, Sir Henry, created Lord Grey of Groby, ancestor of the Earls of Stamford. But in the last Calendar of Irish State Papers, edited by H. C. Hamilton, Esq., F.S.A., Assistant-Keeper of the Records, is the following, dated 12 May 1589 :—"The answer of Sir Edward Denny to her Majesty's articles touching the proceedings of the undertakers. He has assigned 1000 acres to Mr. Edward Gray, son to Lord John Gray, and is to allot unto farmers, copyholders, etc., according to her Majesty's plot as followeth."

In the same volume Mr. Hamilton calendars a letter, dated May 15, 1590, Youghal, from Edward Gray, suggesting the propriety of placing a band of soldiers at Tralee or Dingle. He seems to have held his lands in Kerry until 1596 or 1600, when he may have died ; but in 1640 Daniel Gray, evidently his son, was a householder in Tralee. The name is not mentioned in the depositions of 1642-9, but it reappears in and around Dingle in the seventeenth and eighteenth and present centuries among the respectable middle-class Roman Catholic inhabitants of that district. Can any one versed in east of England genealogies give me some information respecting the Edward Gray of 1588–1600, who has evidently slipped out of the old family history and peerage books, although he was the uncle of Lady Jane Grey and the brother-in-law of the Queen Dowager of France ? An Englishman of the sixteenth century, who went to reside permanently in the wild west of Ireland, unless he had a title or a high official position, was probably as much lost to his family as one who went to the Antipodes. When the former married amongst the Irish native Roman Catholics he was often forgotten even by the Anglo-Irish Protestants around him. Edward Gray of 1592 seems to have married an Irishwoman.

HIBERNIS.

## Boddington Pedigree.

George Boddington, born 28 Jan. 1706-7. British Cancellier at Smyrna.=.... dau. of ....
(A fire at Consulate on 15 March 1797 destroyed all the Church or | Glicofridi, mar.
Chapel Registers.) Died probably before this fire. See Vol. II., New | 19 May 1756.
Series, p. 187.

Marianna, born 5 June 1757.

Sarah, born 14 May 1758.

Margaret, born 24 Feb. 1760.

Elizabeth, born 28 Oct. 1761.

George Boddington,=Henrietta Armayo of the parish of
born 9 Oct. 1763. St. Nicolo in the Island of Pino.
British Cancellier at *Mar. 18 Oct. 1809 at Smyrna by
Smyrna. *Bur. 31 Francis Werry, Consul, in absence
Dec. 1829. of a Protestant Minister.

Frances, born 30 April 1765.

Anastassa Rosalina=Benjamin Boddington, born 28 Sept.=Anthula Chinopulo,
Alexander, *mar. at 1770; *died 26 Aug. 1854 at the *mar. 27 April 1814
Smyrna 17 March Austrian Hospital; *bur. 27 Aug. at Bonjah, near
1802 (1st wife). 1854. Smyrna (2nd wife).

Catherina, born 4 March and bapt. 13 March 1803.*

Henrietta, born 11 and bapt. 16 Feb. 1806.*

George Boddington, born 15 and bapt. 23 March 1807.*

Helena, born 20 and bapt. 27 Feb. 1808.*

Joseph John Bod-
dington, *born 2
Jan. and bapt. 22
Feb. 1815; *bur.
3 Sept. 1833.

Elizabeth, *born=George Thow-
11 and bapt. 24 burn, son of
Sep. 1816; *mar. George Thow-
28 Sep. 1839. burn.

John Boddington, *born
1 and bapt. 18 Feb. 1818;
*bur. 21 July 1821 at
Smyrna, aged 3½ years.

Caroline,
*bapt. 25
March
1820.

Edward Thowburn, living at
Smyrna 12 May 1871.

Eliza.=Stephen Watkins.

William Thowburn.

Valentine Boddington,=Argyré
born 4 Aug. 1772; | Alexanderson,
*buried 6 Aug. 1825 | *married 12
(Merchant). | March 1804.

Henrietta, born=Atkin
14 Sep. 1774 Wilkin.
(query Susan
Henriette) and
query *mar. 7
Nov. 1803.

Joseph William Boddington,
born 10 Oct. 1778; died 12
Jan. 1838; buried in West
Hackney Churchyard. See
Vol. II., New Series, p. 187;
and 'The Gentleman's Magazine.'

Henry Perigal=Amelia, *born 23 and
Borrell of Lon- | bapt. 28 Dec. 1804
don. | (query *Emily at mar-
 | riage 9 June 1820).

Charlotte, birth not
recorded at Smyrna;
*buried at Smyrna
24 Sep. 1823, aged 16.

Sophia Josephina,=Jules Antoine
*born 3 and bapt. Charles de Co-
13 Nov. 1813; dalvere.
*married 25 Feb.
1832.

Octavius Borrell.    Frederick Anthony Borrell.

Any additions to the above, with the descendants to the present time of any of
those named, and with as many dates as possible, and any corrections, will be much
valued by

                          REGINALD STEWART BODDINGTON.

*National Conservative Club,*
  *9 Pall Mall, S.W.*

    * Denotes an entry in the Registers of the Anglican Church at Smyrna in the diocese of
Gibraltar.

# Sydenham of Brympton.*

PEDIGREE A (*vide* p. 326).

Walter de Clifford.⊤
Arms : Chequy or and az., a bend gu.
(A)

---

Maude de Clifford,⊤John Gifford of Brimfield,
da. and heir.   co. Gloucester.
    Arms : Gu., three lions
    passant in pale ar. (A)

William, Lord Braose of⊤Eva, da. of William
Brecknoc, son and heir | and sister and co-
of Reginald, murdered | heir to Anselm Mar-
temp. H. III. | shall, Earl of Pem-
Arms : Vairé erm. and | broke.
gu., two bars az. (A)

Catherine Gifford,⊤Nicholas de Aldithly or
da. and coheir.   Audley. Summoned to
    Parliament 26 Jan. 1297.
    Ob. 1299.

Maude, 2nd da. and⊤Roger Mortimer,
coheir.   Earl of March.

Nicholas de Audley,⊤Joane, sister and coheir to
2nd son. Summoned | William, Baron Martin.
to Parliament 8 Jan. | Arms : Ar., two bars gu.,
1313. Ob. 1319. | each charged with three
Arms : Gu., a fret or. | bezants. (A)
(A, XI)

Sir Robert Touchet,⊤Elizabeth, da. and co-
Knt.   heir of Sir Jo. Kine,
  Knt.

Sir James de Audley, K.G.⊤Joane, 1st wife.
Ob. at Heleigh 1 April 1386.

Sir Thomas Touchet, Knt.⊤
Ob. 1349.

Nicholas, Lord Audley.=Elizabeth, da. of
Summoned to Parlia-  Adelice de Beau-
ment 17 Dec. 1387.  mont.
Ob. s.p. July 1392.

Joane, eldest da. and⊤Sir John Touchet, Knt.,
coheir to her brother | only son and heir, Lord
Nicholas, Lord Aud- | of Merton, co. Derby.
ley.

John Touchet, son and heir.⊤
Arms : Erm., a chev. gu.
(A, XI)

Sir Phillip Courtenay.⊤Elizabeth, da. of Sir
Ob. 29 July 1406.  Thomas Wake of Bris-
 worth, co. Northants,
 Knt.

Sir John Touchet,⊤Isabel.
Knt., son and heir.
Succeeded his great-
uncle as Baron Aud-
ley.

Sir John Courtenay.⊤Margaret, da.
Ob. before 1415.  of Sir Phillip
 Champernoune
 of Beer Ferrers.

Edmond Holland,⊤Constance,
Earl of Kent.  da. of Lang-
 ley, Duke of
 York.

James Touchet, Lord Audley.⊤Eleanor (nat. da.).
Slain at battle of Blore Heath.

Sir Phillip Courtenay.⊤Katherine, da. of
Ob. 16 Dec. 1463.  Walter, Lord
 Hungerford.

Sir Humphrey Audley. Killed at Tewkesbury.⊤Elizabeth.
Assumed the name of Audley.

Elizabeth.⊤John Sydenham.
See *ante*, p. 326.

---

* Continued from p. 327.

Sydenham.—PEDIGREE 13 (*vide* p. 327).

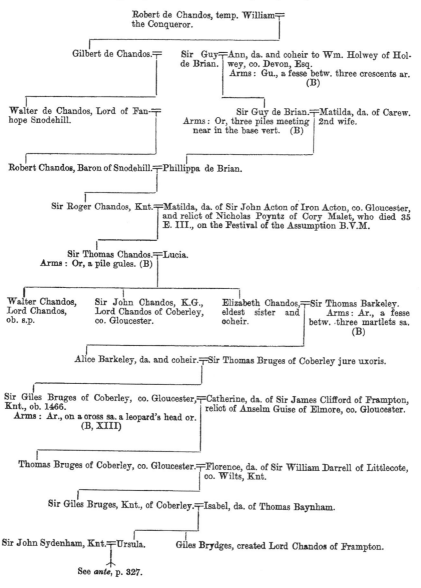

Robert de Chandos, temp. William⹋
the Conqueror.

Gilbert de Chandos.⹋

Sir Guy⹋Ann, da. and coheir to Wm. Holwey of Hol-
de Brian. | wey, co. Devon, Esq.
Arms: Gu., a fesse betw. three crescents ar.
(B)

Walter de Chandos, Lord of Fan-⹋
hope Snodehill.

Sir Guy de Brian.⹋Matilda, da. of Carew.
Arms: Or, three piles meeting | 2nd wife.
near in the base vert.  (B)

Robert Chandos, Baron of Snodehill.⹋Phillippa de Brian.

Sir Roger Chandos, Knt.⹋Matilda, da. of Sir John Acton of Iron Acton, co. Gloucester,
and relict of Nicholas Poyntz of Cory Malet, who died 35
E. III., on the Festival of the Assumption B.V.M.

Sir Thomas Chandos.⹋Lucia.
Arms: Or, a pile gules. (B)

Walter Chandos,   Sir John Chandos, K.G.,   Elizabeth Chandos,⹋Sir Thomas Barkeley.
Lord Chandos,      Lord Chandos of Coberley,   eldest sister and      Arms: Ar., a fesse
ob. s.p.           co. Gloucester.            coheir.            betw. three martlets sa.
                                                                  (B)

Alice Barkeley, da. and coheir.⹋Sir Thomas Bruges of Coberley jure uxoris.

Sir Giles Bruges of Coberley, co. Gloucester,⹋Catherine, da. of Sir James Clifford of Frampton,
Knt., ob. 1466.                      relict of Anselm Guise of Elmore, co. Gloucester.
Arms: Ar., on a cross sa. a leopard's head or.
(B, XIII)

Thomas Bruges of Coberley, co. Gloucester.⹋Florence, da. of Sir William Darrell of Littlecote,
co. Wilts, Knt.

Sir Giles Bruges, Knt., of Coberley.⹋Isabel, da. of Thomas Baynham.

Sir John Sydenham, Knt.⹋Ursula.      Giles Brydges, created Lord Chandos of Frampton.

See *ante*, p. 327.

## Sydenham.—Pedigree ℭ (*vide* p. 327).

Rice ap Tewder, Lord of Caermarden, and one of the Princes of Wales.
Arms : Gu., a lion rampant within a bordure indented or.
(D)

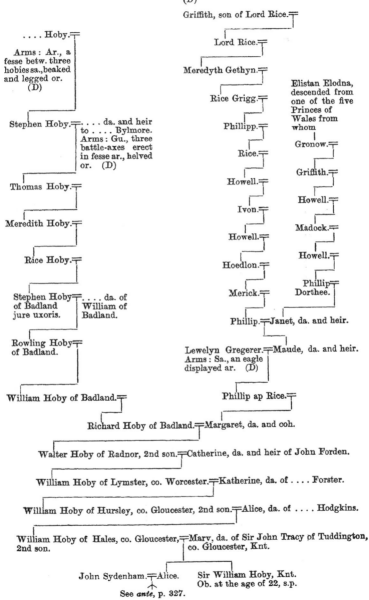

See *ante*, p. 327.

# Shuckburgh Pedigree.*

### PEDIGREE A. (*Vide* p. 318.)

Thomas Shuckburgh=Philippa, da. of Sir William Vaux, Esq.

Thomas Shuckburgh of Shuckburgh,=Isabella, da. of Benedict Medley of Whitnash, co. Warwick, Clerk of the Signet to Henry VII, Esq. Arms: Sable, two pairs of bars-gemmelles argent, and on a chief of the last three mullets of the first.

Thomas Shuckburgh of Shuck-=Elizabeth, da. of George Smith, a younger son of John burgh, Esq. Died 1 Oct. 1560. Smith of Sherford, co. Warwick. Buried at Upper Shuckburgh, Arms: Argent, semée of crosses formée fitchée sable, where is a brass to his memory. three greyhounds courant in pale of the last collared or, a crescent gules for difference.

2. William Shuckburgh, died inf.
3. William Shuckburgh, died inf.
4. Jasper Shuckburgh.
5. Melchor Shuckburgh. Both died inf.
6. Balthazar Shuckburgh.

Benet Shuckburgh=.... of Cubington, co. Warwick, 3rd son. Living 1681.

William=....da. of Auditor Shuck-Rigge of Straggle-burgh, thorpe, co. Linc. 4th son.

Thomas Shuckburgh,=Ursula, da. of 5th son, of Clifton, Anthony co. Warwick. Living Andrewes. 1576.

6. Francis.
7. Matthew.
8. George.
9. Thomas.

Margaret, mar. John Cotes of Honingham, co. Warwick, Esq. Buried at Upper Shuckburgh. Brass in chancel.

Thomas Greswold of Clayhall,=Elizabeth, sole da. and h, born 1568. Died Nov. 1645, æt. 77.=William Lisle of Evenley, co. Warwick, Esq. 1st husb. Buried at Evenley, co. Northants. co. Northants. 2nd husb.

Anthony Shuckburgh of Shuck-=Anne, da. of William Skeffington of burgh, Esq., Northants, Esq. Skeffington, co. Leic., Esq., 2nd wife. Died 1 April 1694. Sheriff 27 Eliz. Arms: Argent, three bulls' heads Buried at sable. Shuckburgh. (The brass says 1694, the stained-glass 1693.)

John Shuckburgh of=Elizabeth, da. of Bourton, co. Warw., Richard Coombe 2nd son, Clerk in of Hemel Hemp-Chancery. Died 42 stead, Herts, Esq. Eliz., 1600.

1. Frances. 3. Anne. 5. Mary.
2. Rebecca. 4. Joice.

Anne, da. of Thomas Foxley=Anthony Shuckburgh of Shuck-of Foxley, co. Northants, Esq. burgh, Esq. Mar. 1660. 1st wife. Arms: Gules, two bars argent.

Thomas, Died s.p.

Henry Shuckburgh of Bourton, Esq.=Christian, da. of .... Young, Esq.

John Shuckburgh of Bourton, Esq. Died 1647.=Anne, da. of .... Yorke.

2. Thomas. 4. John.
3. Henry. 5. George. All died s.p.

Richard Shuckburgh of Bourton, Esq.,=Grace, da. of Sir Robert Doyen, born 1639. Living 1688. Lord Chief Justice of Ireland. Died 29 Jan. 1707, aged 70. M.I. at Bourton on Dunsmore.

B

* Continued from p. 319.

B |

Henry Shuckburgh, M.A.=Judith, da. of .... Thynne.
Rector of Bourton.

Thynne and Charles, both died unmar.

John Shuckburgh of Bourton, co. Warwick, Esq.=Frances, da. and sole h. of Alexander Jermyn of Lordington in co. Sussex, Esq. Called Frances, Lady More, on her son's monument at Bourton.
Died 23 April 1740, æt. 77. M.I. at Bourton.

John Shuckburgh=Mary, da. of of Winwick, co. .... Ward. Northants.

Catherine, died=Richard Shuckburgh of Bourton, 22 March 1764, Esq., Lieut.-Col. of the 3rd Regi-æt. 48. M.I. at ment of Horse. Died 14 May 1762, Bourton. æt. 67, s.p. M.I. at Bourton.

Eleanor, died unmar. 12 March 1788, æt. 42. M.I. at Bourton.

Frances, mar. ....Wheeler. Died s.p.

Julia, mar. ....Slowe.

Catherine, mar. Joseph Bird.

Elizabeth, da. of ....=John Slowe, called himself Shuckburgh.=Jane, da. of .... Craven.
Biker. Died 11 March 1767, æt. 26. | Died 11 Jan. 1770, æt. 46. M.I. Bourton.
M.I. at Bourton.

John Shuckburgh.　Mary.

John Shuckburgh, born 1767. Died s.p. 12 May 1837 in the 71st year of his age. M.I. Bourton. Left Bourton to his widow for life,=Sophia Venour. and afterwards to Rev. Charles Blencowe, who took the name of Shuckburgh; he married, but died s.p. 1875, leaving Bourton to Died 18 Jan. 1848 Richard, the second son of his sister Elizabeth, wife of Richard Wood, who, on succeeding, also took the name of Shuckburgh, though in 79th year. M.I. they do not inherit the blood of that family. at Bourton.

Elizabeth, mar. Reginald Staunton of Smewens, Bucks. ? of Stockgrove, co. Bucks.

Three other daurs. Ob. v.p.

Thomas Shuckburgh, eldest son and heir. Died s.p. 1619.

John Shuckburgh of Shuck-=Margery, eldest da. of Richard burgh, 2nd son, but eventual Middlemore of Edgbaston, co. heir. Sheriff 15 Jas. I. Died Warwick. Died 22 March 1629. 20 March 1631, æt. 68. M.I. Arms: Per chevron argent at Upper Shuckburgh. and sable, in chief two black hens, beaked, wattled, and legged gules.

Simon Shuck-=Elizabeth, da. of burgh of Edward Arden Napton. of Park Hall, co. Warwick, Esq.

Mary, mar. .... Symons.

Seven other children, died young.

3. Anthony Shuckburgh of Farthinghoe, 3rd son. Living 1634.=Elizabeth. Died 18 Nov. 1653, æt. 35.
Died 15 Oct. 1678, æt. 80.

Richard Shuckburgh.=Anne.　　Charles Shuckburgh.
Elizabeth.

John Shuckburgh, ....=Mary, da. of Ralph Sneyd=Elizabeth, da. of Sir Robert=Sir Richard Shuckburgh,=Grace, da. of Sir Thomas Holte of Aston, eldest son and h. Crompton, of Keyle, co. Stafford. Lee of Billeslee, co. Warwick. aged 30 Esc. 8 Car. M.P. Bart. Mar. 1634. 3rd wife. She sur-Died s.p. v.p. 16 1st husb. Mar. 30 Nov. 1627. Died Mar. 10 Dec. 1630. Died s.p. for co. Warwick 1640-54. vived him, and mar. 2ndly John Keating, Oct. 1625, æt. 37. s.p. 5 Sept. 1629. 1st wife. 1633-4. 2nd wife. Knighted by K. Chas. I. Chief Justice Common Pleas in Ireland. Bur. at Napton. Arms: Argent, a scythe Arms: Argent, a fesse at Edgecot 22 Oct. 1642. She died at Dublin 12 April 1677, and M.I. and fleur-de-lis sable. between two ogresses and a Died in London 13 June, was bur. in the Keating vault in Palmer-martlet sable. buried at Shuckburgh 25 ston Chapel, three miles from Dublin. June 1656, æt. 60. M.I. Arms: Azure, two bars or, and in chief at Upper Shuckburgh. a cross formée fitchée of the last.

c

c

I.—**Sir John Shuckburgh** of Shuckburgh, co. Warwick. Created a Baronet 26 June 1660. Died 1661, æt. 26.

Catherine, da. of Sir Hatton Fermor of Easton=Neston, co. Northants, Kt. Mar. at All Saints, Northampton, on 18 Dec. 1666. Died 19 May 1681. Arms: Argent, a fesse between three wolves' heads erased sable.

Richard Shuckburgh, 2nd son, born 1639. Died s.p. Of Farthingstone, Married Anne, da. of Mich. Woodhull, Esq., of Thenford, Northants.

=Sir Roger Norwich of Brampton, co. Northants, 2nd Bart. Died 1691. 2nd husb.

George Shuckburgh, 3rd son.

---

Charles Shuckburgh, 4th son. The Shuckburghs of Downton, co. Wilts, claim to descend from him, but their arms have the chevron engrailed.

Edward and another son, died in Italy, v.p.

1. Anne, mar. Henry Edmunds, Esq., of Preston Deanery, Died 28 Feb. 1701, æt. 76.

2. Elizabeth, born 1636. Died 1643.

3. Grace, born in Kenilworth Castle 1643. Mar. Sir John Barnard of Brampton, Hunts, 2nd Bart., as his 2nd wife, who died 1679. She died s.p. 1677.

4. Elizabeth, born in Kenilworth Castle. Mar. Sir Edward Waldo, Kt., of Pinner, co. Middx., as his 3rd wife. He died 4 Feb. 1707, æt. 76.

---

Catherine, eldest da. of Sir Hugh Stewkeley of Hinton Ampnor, co. Hants, Bart., by his 1st wife Catherine, da. and h. of Sir John Trott, Bart. Mar. 1679. She died 17 Aug. 1688. Bur. at Upper Shuckburgh. M.I. 1st wife. Arms: Chequy argent and sable, a fesse and bordure gules.

II.—**Sir Charles Shuckburgh**, 2nd Bart, born Nov. 1659. Sheriff 1687. M.P. for co. Warwick in five Parliaments, 1698–1705. Master of the Buck and Stag Hounds to Queen Anne. Died at Winchester 2 Sept., bur. at Shuckburgh 8 Sept. 1705.

=Diana, da. of Richard Verney, Lord Willoughby de Broke, by his 2nd wife Frances, da. and coh. of Thos. Dove of Upton, near Peterborough. Mar. 1684. She had Farthingstone in dower. Died at Highwood Hill, co. Middx. Bur. at Shuckburgh 5 Oct. 1725. 2nd wife. Arms: Gules, three crosses recercellé or, a chief vair sable and ermine.

Catherine, died inf. 1602.

Richard Shuckburgh, born 1680. Of Bedford Street, Covent Garden, London. Ob. circa 1740.

=Elizabeth, da. of John Tooley of St. Mary, Somerset. Mar. at St. Martin's in the Fields 27 Jan. 1704. Aged 21, 1704.

---

III.—**Sir John Shuckburgh**, born 18 Aug. 1683. Died at Yelvertoft 8 June 1724, æt. 41. Bur. at Upper Shuckburgh. M.I.

=Abigail, da. of John Goodwin of Latchford, near Thame, co. Oxon, Esq. Mar. 1704. She died March 1755.

Catherine, born 1681. Mar. 1699 Sir William Boughton of Lawford, Bart. Died 1725.

Saliza or Sarah, born 1682. Mar. Edward Bentley of Kineton, co. Warwick. Died 1726.

John Shuckburgh, ob. 1761.

=Anne, da. of .... Salt, Esq.

Honora, mar. 1740 John Hasker of Laverstoke, Gent.

Johanna, mar. Thomas Plaumpin, Esq., of Yelvertoft. Died 1770, æt. 54.

---

IV.—**Sir Stewkeley Shuckburgh**, 4th Bart, born 9 March 1711-12. Died unmar. at Bath 6 March 1759, aged 47. Bur. at Upper Shuckburgh. M.I.

Grace, mar. 1st Sir Edw. Boughton of Lawford, 5th Bart. He died Feb. 1721-2. 2nd, Matthew Lister, of Burwell, co. Leic, Esq. Died 1779.

Catherine, died unm. 30 June 1730.

Elizabeth, mar. Charles Jefferson of Dullingham, co. Cambridge, Esq. She died 1773.

Sarah, mar. 1st William Fielding of Shilton, co. Warwick, Esq.; 2nd, Henry St. Nicholas; 3rd, Francis Tatum of Lutterworth, co. Leicester.

Margaret, mar. 1753 Rev. Thomas Hall. Died 1774, s.p.

Jane, mar. 1744 Rev. Gilbert Jackson, D.D. Died 1754, aged 46. He died May 1779.

Penelope, mar. 1st, .... Plastow, Esq.; 2nd, .... Hitch, Gent.; 3rd, Robert. Clerke of Daventry. Died s.p. 1780. She was buried at Dunston Basset, co. Leic.

Rachel, mar. 1st, Altham Parkhurst, Esq., of Catesby; 2nd, Rev. Slaughter Clerke of Theddingworth, co. Leicester. Died s.p. 1771. He died 1765.

B

D

E

D | E

F

Charles Shuckburgh of Longborough, co. Glouc., and of Farthingstone, co. Northants, Esq., eldest son by the 2nd marriage. Born 1694. Died 1752. = Sarah, da. and heir eventually of Col. Henry Hunt of Blockley, co. Worcester, Esq. Mar. 1718-19. Died 1732-3.
Arms: Azure, on a bend between six leopards' faces or three water-bougets sable.

Richard Shuckburgh, Captain in the Army. Born 1695. Died unmar. 1724.

Edward Shuckburgh, Fellow of All Souls, Oxon., Rector of Bromsall, co. Stafford. Born 1702. Died unmar. Feb. 1729-30.

1, Frances, eldest da., born 1686.

2, Grace, born 1691. Mar. Rev. ..... Crabbe of Brimore, co. Hants.

3, Diana, born 1692. Died inf.

4. Sophia, born 1697. Mar. Francis Loggin of the Temple, Gent. Died at Kensington 1739, s.p.

5. Diana, born 1698. Died inf.

6. Mariana, born 1700.

7, Diana, born 1701. Mar. 17— Rev. Nicholas Webb, for fifty years Vicar of Downton, co. Wilts. He died 1776, æt. 83. = Rev. Thos. Read, D.D., 2nd husb. Mar. 1785.
She died 1753.

8. Penelope, born 1703. Died inf.

Sarah, mar. Dec. 1747 John Cleveland of Tapeley, co. Devon, Esq., Secretary to the Admiralty. Died Nov. 1764.

Arabella, 2nd da., died at Longborough 22 July 1780, aged 7 months and 1 day, and was bur. 27 July 1780 at Longborough.

John Shuckburgh of Downton, born 1744. Died 1782. 1st husb. = Henrietta, da. of John Blake of Salisbury, Esq.

Rev. Charles William Shuckburgh of The Moot, Downton, Wilts. Born 1772. Died 29 Aug. 1833. = Diana Webb, died 1788.

V.—**Sir Charles Shuckburgh**, 5th Bart, 3rd but eldest surviving son, born 1722. Succeeded his cousin in title and estates 1759. Sheriff 1769. Died s.p. 10 Aug., 1773 in 52nd year. Bur. at Warwick. M.I. there and at Upper Shuckburgh. = Anne, da. of ..... Robinson of Covent Garden, and relict of Campbell Price of Westbury, co. Bucks, Esq. Mar. 5 May 1749. Died 8 Oct. 1776, æt. 57. Bur. at Upper Shuckburgh.

Richard Shuckburgh, 4th son, born 6 March 1728. Mar. 6 Feb. 1760. Died 3 Sept. 1772, in 45th year. Bur. at Warwick. M.I. there and at Upper Shuckburgh. = Sarah, da. and h. of John Hayward of Plumstead, near Woolwich, co. Kent, Capt. R.N. (by ...da. of the Hon. Ch. Finch), and relict of Edw. Bate, Esq. Died at Oakingham, Berks, 1762. = Edward Bate, 1st husb.
Arms: Argent, three torteaux in bend cotised gules within a bordure of the last.

Charles Shuckburgh, eldest son. Died at Longborough in infancy 28 Dec. (M.I.), buried there 27 (sic) Dec. 1719 (Reg.).

Charles Shuckburgh, 2nd son, bapt. at Longborough 17 March 1721. Died 18 March, and buried at Longborough 21 March 1721.

Sarah Bate, only issue by 1st husb. Mar. Rev. Humphrey Willyams, who was born Feb. 1755, 3rd but 2nd surviving son of James Willyams, Esq., of Carnanton, Cornwall. Died s.p.

See PEDIGREE **, post.

F

Henrietta, mar. W. W. Collins, Esq., 1828.

William Pigott Shuckburgh, Captain Wilts Militia.==2nd wife, Joanna, da. of Admiral Tomlinson
Of The Moot. Died 29 Sept. 1860, aged 59.    of Middleton House, Sussex.

1st wife, . . . .

1. Diana, mar. 6 July 1861 Rev. William John Swayne, Vicar of Chilterne, Wilts, and has 4 sons and 1 da.

2. Henrietta Shuckburgh, unmar.

Charles Stukeley Shuckburgh,==Elizabeth, da. of Capt. born Oct. 1840, Lieut. R.N., J.Ward Tomlinson, R.N., Served in Crimea and in China of Babicombe, Devon. Wars, and in the Congo Expe- Mar. 26 Sept. 1867. dition 1865,

William Coles Shuckburgh,==Maria Petronella, Capt. R.N., retired. Born   da. of Christoffe 23 Dec. 1840.   François Albertyn.

Diana Clare.

Walter Shuckburgh, born 1814. Drowned at Berck 31 Aug. 1833.

Mariana, married Richard Brouncker, Esq., of Boveridge, co. Dorset, 1827.

Diana Christian, mar. 1830 Rev. W. P. Hop- ton, Vicar of Bishops Frome, co. Norfolk.

Rev. Robert Shuck-==Elizabeth, da. of burgh, Rector of   Giles King Lyford, Aldborough, Norf.   Esq., Mar. 7 July Died 8 April 1860.   1834. Died 18 May 1876,

Charles Verney Shuck-==Elizabeth, da. of burgh, Clerk in Holy   John Loard, Esq. Orders, Rector of Long-   Married 23 May ford, Essex. Died s.p.   1837. 11 May 1872.

7. Margaret Louisa, mar. 15 Jan. 1876 Christopher George Croft of Richmond, and has 2 sons and 3 dau'rs.

6. Adelaide Martha, mar. 19 Oct. 1882 D'Arcy Bedingfield Collyer, 3rd son of the late John Collyer of Hackford Hall, Esq.

5. Mariana Augusta, mar. 19 Oct. 1882 Thomas, youngest son of late Robert Copeman, Esq., of Aylsham, Norfolk.

4. Gundrada Christian.

3. Emily, mar. 23 Dec. 1873 Edward Philip Ash, a Master at Hailey- bury College, and has 2 dau'rs.

2. Grace Agnes, mar. 14 July 1870 Tertius Galton Molliiet, Esq., and has issue.

1. Elizabeth.

Evelyn Shirley Shuck-==Frances Mary, da. of burgh, M.A., late a   Rev. Joseph Pullen Master at Eton Coll.,   of Cambridge. Mar. late a Fellow Emanuel   11 Aug. 1874. Coll., Camb. Born 12 July 1848.

3. Dorothy Frances, born 9 June 1880.

2. Florence Amy, born 18 Dec. 1878.

1. May.

2. Robert Shirley Shuckburgh, born 6 April 1882.

1. John Evelyn Shuckburgh, born 18 March 1877.

*(To be continued.)*

# Shuckburgh Pedigree.*

## PEDIGREE B. (*Vide* p. 355.)

Richard Shuckburgh.=Sarah, da. and h. of John Hayward.

VI.—Sir George Augustus William Shuckburgh-Evelyn, 6th Bart., born 23 Aug. 1751. Succeeded his uncle in the title and estates 1773. Was M.P. for the County of Warwick in five Parliaments, 1780-1804. Took the additional name and arms of Evelyn in 1794. Died s.p. at Shuckburgh 11 Aug. 1804. Bur. at Shuckburgh 20 Aug. 1804. M.I.

1st wife, Sarah Johanna, youngest da. and coh. of John Darker of Gayton, co. Northants, Esq., M.P. for Leicester, by Mary his wife, da., of John Parker of Retford, co. Notts, Esq. She was born 1755. Mar. 3 July 1782. Died s.p. at Bristol 10 April 1782, aged 28. Bur. at Upper Shuckburgh 18 April 1783. M.I.
Arms: Argent, three hop-poles with hop-vines proper.

2nd wife, Julia Annabella, da. and sole heir of James Evelyn of Felbridge in the parish of Godstone, co. Surrey, Esq., by Annabella his wife, sister and in her issue sole h. of George Medley, Esq., of Buxted, Friston, and Coney-burrows, all co. Sussex. Born 7 Jan. 1767. Mar. at St. Margaret's, Westminster, 6 Oct. 1785. Died 14 Sept. 1797, aged 40. Bur. at Shuckburgh 23 Sept. 1797. M.I.
Arms: Azure, a griffin passant and a chief or.

Richard Shuckburgh, born 1766. Lieut. R.N. Died unmar. 16 Oct. 1784, aged 28. Buried at St. Erths, Cornwall.

Julia Evelyn Medley Shuckburgh-Evelyn, only da. and heiress, born 5 Oct. 1790 in Park Street, Westminster, her father's London house. Mar. at St. George, Hanover Square, 19 July 1810. Died at 10 (now 13) Portman Square, London, 8 April 1814. Bur. at Pitchford, co. Salop, in the family vault 24 April 1814.

Charles Cecil Cope, 3rd and last Earl of Liverpool, G.C.B. Was of Pitchford, co. Salop, which he inherited from the Ottley family. Born 29 May 1784. Succeeded his half-brother the Prime Minister 4 Dec. 1828. Was M.P. for Sandwich 1807-12; for Bridgnorth 1812-18; and for East Grinstead 1818-28. Was Under-Secretary of State for the Colonial and War Departments. Lord Steward 1841-46. Died at Buxted 3 Oct. 1851. Bur. in the family vault at Buxted 10 Oct. 1851.

John Cotes of Woodcote, co. Salop, Esq., born 17 July 1799. M.P. for N. Shropshire 1832-34. Died at Woodcote 10 Jan. 1874. Buried there.

Lady Louisa Harriet, 3rd da. and coh., born at 10 (now 13) Portman Square, London, 28 March 1814. Mar. at the Chapel Royal, Whitehall, 5 Sept. 1839. She had Pitchford. Died at Pitchford 5 Feb. 1887. Bur. at Woodcote 10 Feb. 1887.

George Savile Foljambe of Osberton, co. Notts, and of Aldwarke, co. York, Esq. Born at Aldwarke 4 June 1800. Mar. 1st Harriet Emily Mary, eldest da. of Sir William M. S. Milner, Bart., by his 2nd wife Elizabeth, da. of Lord Edward Bentinck. She died 1830. He died 18 Dec. 1869. Bur. at Scofton 23 Dec. 1869, in the family vault.

Lady Selina Charlotte, Viscountess Milton, born at 10 (now 13) Portman Square, London, 3 July 1812. 2nd da. and coh., but eldest to leave issue. She had Felbridge, co. Surrey, which she sold, and bought Haselbech, co. Northants. Mar. 1st at St. George's, Hanover Square, 15 Aug. 1833; 2ndly, at Wentworth-Woodhouse 28 Aug. 1846. Died at 2 Carlton House Terrace, London, 24 Sept. 1883. Buried at Scofton 2 Oct. 1883, in the family vault.

William Charles, Viscount Milton, eldest son and heir of Charles William, 5th Earl FitzWilliam, K.G., born 18 Jan. 1812. Died at Wentworth-Woodhouse 8 Nov. 1835. Bur. at Wentworth in the family vault.

Lady Catherine Julia, born in Grosvenor Square, London, 23 July 1811. Lady in Waiting to the Duchess of Kent. Mar. at St. James's, Piccadilly, 20 Nov. 1837. Died s.p. 5 Dec. 1877 at Buxted. Bur. in family vault at Buxted 12 Dec. 1877. Left Buxted to her niece Mrs. Portman.

Colonel Francis Vernon-Harcourt, 9th son of the Archbishop of York, born 7 Jan. 1801. Died s.p. at Buxted 23 April 1880, in his 80th year. Bur. in the family vault at Buxted 29 April 1880.

1. Victoria Alexandrina, mar. 1st, Thomas Owen of Condover, co. Salop, Esq.; 2nd, Col. Robert Grand, R.E.

2. Charles Cecil, born 1846. Unmar.

3. Charles James, born 1847. Unmar.

3. Elizabeth Evelyn, mar. John M. Mordaunt, Esq., brother of Sir Charles Mordaunt, Bart.

4. Selina Charlotte.

5. Louisa Harriet.

1. John, died young.

2. Charles Cecil, born 1846. Unmar.

3. Charles James, born 1847. Unmar.

Mary Selina Charlotte, only da. by 1st marriage, born at Fife House, London, 9 Jan. 1836. Mar. at Chapel Royal, Whitehall, 21 June 1855, the Hon. William Henry Berkeley Portman, eldest son and heir of Lord, afterwards Viscount Portman, and has issue. She has Buxted under her aunt's will.

Son, stillborn 14 Nov. 1834. Bur. at Wentworth.

* Concluded from p. 356.

B

A

3. Caroline Frederica, mar. at St. Margaret's, Westminster, 4 Aug. 1881 Arthur Francis Gresham Leveson Gower, Esq., Secretary of Legation at Berne.

4. Evelyn, born at Fife House 31 Dec. 1852. Died at Filey 3 Sept. 1853. Bur. at Scofton, Notts, in the family vault.

5. Constance Blanche Alethea Mary.

1. Elizabeth Anne, mar. at St. Mary's, BryanstonSquare, 31 Jan. 1888 Rev. William Bury, Rector of Harlestone, co. Northants.

2. Frances Mary, mar, at Haddington 10 Oct. 1876 Rev. Savile Rich^d William L'Estrange-Malone of Pallas Park, King's Co., Rector of Dalton Holme, co. York.

4. Margaret Susan Louisa Mary, born at Osberton 14 Jan. 1884. Died there 16 Jan. 1884. Bur. at Scofton 19 Jan. 1884.

Henry Savile Foljambe, born at Osberton 14 Oct. 1849.

George Foljambe, born at Osberton 29 Dec. 1851. Died 30 Dec. 1851. Buried at Scofton in the family vault.

1. Edith Margaret Emily Mary.

2. Alice Etheldreda Georgiana Mary.

3. Mabel Evelyn Selina Mary.

Robert Anthony Edward St. Andrew Savile Foljambe, born at Cockglode 3 April 1887. Bapt. at Carburton, Notts, 1 May 1887.

Cecil George Savile Foljambe, Esq., of Cockglode, Notts; and Kirkham Abbey, York; and Haselbech Hall, co. Northants. Born at Osberton 7 Nov. 1846. Served in R.N. 1860; in New Zealand War, with Naval Brigade, 1863-4. Lieut. 1867. Retired 1870. J.P. and D.L. for Notts, Yorkshire, Northants, and Leicestershire. M.P. for North Notts 1880-85, and for Mansfield Division of Notts since 1886.

= 2nd wife, Susan Louisa, eldest da. of Lieut.-Col. William Henry Frederick Cavendish of West Stoke, Sussex, by Lady Emily Augusta, 2nd surviving da. of John George, 1st Earl of Durham, by Lady Louisa Elizabeth, eldest da. of Charles, 2nd Earl Grey, K.G. Married at Chapel Royal, Whitehall, 21 July 1877.

1st wife, Louisa Blanche, eldest da. of Frederick John Howard, Esq., of Compton Place, Sussex, only sister of William, 7th Duke of Devonshire, K.G. Mar. at St. James's Place 22 July 1869. Died at Compton Place, Sussex, 7 Oct. 1871. Bur. at Scofton, Notts, 14 Oct. 1871, in the family vault.

Josceline Charles William Savile Foljambe, born at 2 Carlton House Terrace, London, 16 Oct. 1882. Bapt. at the Chapel Royal, Whitehall, 28 Nov. 1882.

Gerald William Frederick Savile Foljambe, born at 2 Carlton House Terrace, London, 12 May 1878. Bapt. at St. Martin's in the Fields 24 June 1878.

Frederick Savile Foljambe, 2nd son, born at Compton Place 20 Aug. 1871. Died 21 Aug. 1871. Bur. at Scofton 25 Aug. in the family vault.

Arthur William de Brito Savile Foljambe, son and heir, born at Compton Place, Sussex, 27 May 1870. Bapt. at Haselbech 15 July 1870.

D

VII.—Sir Stewkley Shuckburgh, 7th Bart., born 31 Aug. 1757. Died at Shuckburgh 14 July 1809 in his 52nd year. Bur. at Upper Shuckburgh 28 July 1809. M.I.

= Charlotte Catherine, da. of Thomas Tydd, Esq., of Bridalk 6 Sept. 1786. Died Upper Shuckburgh 18 Feb. 1837. M.I. Tydd, bur. at Upper Shuckburgh 21 Dec. 1815, aged 79. N.B.—Most of their elder children were born at Chester.

Died at her house at Bath 7 Feb. 1837, aged 72. Her mother Elizabeth, relict of Colonel

Charles. Caroline. Augusta. All three died inf.

C

1st wife, Sarah Elizabeth, da. of William Dwarris, Esq., of Golden Grove, Jamaica. Mar. 16 Nov. 1843. Died s.p. at Cheltenham 1 Feb. 1846, in her 53rd year. M.I. at Upper Shuckburgh.

= Colonel Henry Adolphus Shuckburgh, 4th son, Col. 40th Bengal Native Inf. Born at Chester 25 Nov. 1800. Died at Weston super Mare 10 Jan. 1861, and buried there.

= 2nd wife, Catherine, eld. da. of Daniel J. Cloete, Esq., High Sheriff of Capetown. Mar. 5 May 1854. Died 17 April 1866.

1. Caroline Anne Matilda, born 1788. Died 26 March 1809 in her 21st year. Bur. at Upper Shuckburgh 3 April 1809. M.I.

2. Mary Amelia, 2nd da., born 17 April 1793. Mar. in 1820 Thomas Lamb Polden Laugharne of Laugharne, Carmarthenshire, Esq., Senior Captain R.N., and of Greenwich Hospital. He was born in June 1786. Died 30 Sept. 1863. Bur. in Upper Shuckburgh Churchyard 7 Oct. 1863. She had died 20 Feb. 1858. Bur. in Upper Shuckburgh Churchyard 27 Feb. 1858. M.I.

3. Penelope Augusta (or Augusta Penelope), 3rd da. Died unmar. at Bath 2 Jan. 1863.

4. Sarah Louisa, 4th da., died at Bath 6 Jan. 1836. Buried in Bath Abbey Church. M.I.

5. Charlotte Catherine, 5th da., died unmar. at Bath 1885. Bur. at Bath 17 Dec. 1885.

6. Julia Isabella, 6th da., bapt. at Upper Shuckburgh 7 April 1805. Died unm. at Bath 22 April 1879.

7. Saliza Sophia, 7th da., bapt. at Upper Shuckburgh 24 May 1806. Living at Bath unmar. 1888.

8. Emily Almeria, 8th and youngest da., bapt. at Upper Shuckburgh 6 Nov. 1808. Mar. as his 2nd wife at Bath 5 June 1867 to the Rev. Samuel Sampson of Colyton Grove, Axminster, co. Devon, Incumbent of St. Timothy's, Liverpool. He died s.p. 22 Feb. 1875.

D

C

VIII.—Sir Francis Shuckburgh, 8th Bart, F.R.S., born 12 March 1789. Was in the Army. High Sheriff co. Warwick 1844. Died at Shuckburgh 29 Oct. 1876, æt. 87. Bur. at Upper Shuckburgh 4 Nov. 1876. M.I.

=Anna Maria Draycott, only da. of Peter Denys, Esq., and Lady Charlotte his wife, da. of George, 2nd Earl of Pomfret. Mar. at Chelsea 27 Oct. 1826. Died 8 Nov. 1846 at Shuckburgh. Bur. at Upper Shuckburgh 17 Nov. 1846. M.I.

Thomas Stewkley Shuckburgh, Lieut. R.N., 2nd son, born 1796. First Lieut. of H.M.S. Helicon. Died near Crooked Island in the West Indies 25 Aug. 1824, aged 28. Bur. at sea. M.I. at Upper Shuckburgh.

1st wife,=Lieut.-Col. Charles=2nd wife, Mary Anne, eldest da. of James Conway Travers, K.H., Major in the Rifle Brigade. Mar. Oct. 1842. She died at Wendover 1 Aug. 1881.

Emma Biggs, 2nd da. of James Butler, Esq, Died 1883.

Robert Shuckburgh, 3rd son. Died 17 Jan. 1873.

George Stewkeley Shuckburgh, 2nd son, born 5 Aug. 1860 at Weston super Mare. Entered the Royal Navy; became a Lieutenant in 1883.

Caroline Emma, living 1888.

IX.—Sir George Thomas Francis Shuckburgh, 9th Bart., born 23 July 1829. Major in Scots Fusilier Guards. Served in the Crimea. Wounded severely at Inkerman. Died at Shuckburgh, Saturday evening, 12 Jan. 1884. Bur. at Upper Shuckburgh, Friday, 18 Jan. 1884. M.I.

=Ida Florence Geraldine, only da. of the late Rev. Frederick W. Robertson of Brighton (see Denys, Bart.), her mother being Helen, 4th da. of Sir George Denys, Bart., eldest son of the before-mentioned Peter Denys, Esq. Mar. at St. Luke's, Chelsea, Tuesday, 24 June 1879; 2ndly, by special licence at St. John the Baptist Church, Lower Shuckburgh, by Rev. A. D. Cope, Vicar, 25 Nov. 1886.

Major Henry James Shuckburgh, eldest son, born 25 Feb. 1855 at Dinapore, India. Major in the 2nd Battalion Norfolk Regiment. Served in the Jowaki Campaign, 1877-8, medal and clasp; also in the Affghan Campaign, 1879-80, medal with clasp.

Charlotte Georgiana Amelia, mar. 24 April 1860 Rev. John Richard Errington, M.A., Vicar of Ashbourne, afterwards Rector of Ladbroke, Hon. Canon of Worcester. He died 4 Oct. 1882 at Ladbroke Rectory, aged 74, having had four sons, Fredreick Francis, born 30 July 1861; Wilfred John, born 10 Aug. 1865, died 1 May 1883; Walter Alfred, born 24 Feb. 1868; and Arthur Edmund, born 17 Sept. 1869, died 31 Jan. 1878; and a da. Eliza Margaret.

Gertrude Frances Anna Maria, born 11 Nov. 1833. Died 9 March 1835 at the Pavilion, Hans Place, London. M.I. at Upper Shuckburgh.

X.—Sir Stewkeley Frederick Draycott Shuckburgh, 10th Bart., born at Shuckburgh Park 20 June 1880, bapt. at Upper Shuckburgh 8 Aug. 1880. Succeeded his father Jan. 1884.

Gerald Francis Stewkeley Shuckburgh, born at Shuckburgh Park 28 Feb. 1882. Bapt. at Upper Shuckburgh 16 April 1882.

# Genealogy of Browne.

## Wills.

Copy of the Will of THOMAS BROWNE, Esq., of Shredicot, continued from p. 343.

And whereas by my Deed of Feoffem$^t$ vnder my hande and seale dated the sixteenth daie of June in the first yeare of the raigne of our Soveraigne Lord Charles [1625] by the grace of God of England Scotland Fraunce and Ireland Kinge I have given graunted and confirmed vnto my said sonne in lawe Timothy Levinge Esq$^r$ Recorder of the Towne of Darby Thomas Moorton of Brockton Grange in the Countie of Stafford Esq$^r$ William Prince the elder of Marston woodhowses in the said Countie of Darby yeoman and John Stanley the younger of Alston al's Awson in the said Countie of Stafford yem$^n$ theire heires and assignes all the aforesaid capitall messuage in Shredicote in the Countie of Stafford and all the said Manor or Lordshipp of Hungery Bentley with the said two parcells of ground therevnto adioyninge And all the said Parke called Middleton Parke al's Barton old Parke and a pasture and feedinge ground called Pitford owle and a close and pasture called the broome close in the said Countie of Darbie (which said pasture and feeding ground called Pitford owle and close and pasture called the Broome close I have since sold vnto Edward Villiars of Hanbury in the said Countie of Stafford Gent. and to his heires and assignes for ever and all other the messuage land tenements and hereditaments of me the said Thomas Browne in Shredicote Barton & Bradeley in the said Countie of Stafford and alsoe in Hungerie Benteley Barton Langford Marston and Scropton neere the River of Dove or elsewhere within the said Countie of Darbie To have and to hold all and singuler the premises with theire appurten'nce (except the said two pastures since sold as aforesaid) to the said Timothy Leving Thomas Moorton William Prince and John Stanley theire heires and assignes to the vse and behoofe of me the said Thomas Browne for and during my naturall life and after my decease to the vse and behoofe of Apoline Browne my wife for and during such terme and termes of life or for yeares as I the said Thomas by my Deed of Feoffem$^t$ have given devised limitted and appointed and after her decease and determinac'on of such yeares to such vses intents and purposes and to the vse and behoofe of such person and p'sons heir and heires and of such estate and estates and w$^{th}$ such provisoes remainders and limitac'ons as I by my Deed or last will and Testament in writinge shall lymitt declare and appoint Therefore according to the power which I have by the said Deed and for the settling of the inheritance of all my said lands tenements and hereditaments according to my minde and purpose in that behalfe I doe first give devise and bequeath lymitt declare and appoint vnto my eldest sonne George Browne all and singuler my said messuages lands tenements and other hereditaments scituate and being in Shredicote Barton and Bradeley with theire and every of theire appurtenances in the said Countie of Stafford To have and to hold the same lands tenements and hereditamt$^s$ with theire appurten'nce vnto my said sonne George Browne after the decease of me and the said Apoline Browne my wife for the terme of his life and after his decease to such wife or wives as he shall happen to marry for the terme of the life and lives of every such wife and after the decease of every such wife and wives to the vse and behoofe of the first sonne of the body of the said George Browne my sonne lawfullie begotten and to the heires of the bodie of such first sonne lawfullie begotten And for default of such issue to the vse and behoofe of the second sonne of the bodie of my said sonne George Browne lawfullie begotten and to the heires of the bodie of such second sonne lawfullie begotten And for default of such issue to the vse and behoofe of the third sonne of the body of my said sonne George Browne lawfully begotten and to the heires of the body of such third sonne lawfully begotten And for default of such issue to the vse and behoofe of the fourth sonne of the body of my said sonne George Browne lawfullie begotten and to the heires of the bodie of such fourth sonne lawfullie begotten And for default of such issue to the vse and behoofe of the first sonne of the body of my said sonne George Browne lawfullie begotten and to the heires of the bodie of such fifth sonne lawfullie begotten And for default of such issue to the vse and behoofe of the sixt sonne of the body of my said sonne George Browne lawfullie begotten and to the heires of the bodie of such sixt sonne lawfullie begotten And for default of such issue to the vse and behoofe of every other sonne of the body of my said sonne George Browne lawfullie begotten successively one after another as they shalbe in seniority of birth and to the heires of the bodie of every such sonne lawfullie begotten successively And for default of such issue to every daughter and daughters of the body of my said sonne George Browne lawfullie begotten and to the heires of theire bodies lawfullie begotten and for default of such issue to my youngest sonne Edward Browne during his life and after his decease to the vse and behoofe of the first sonne of the body of my said sonne Edward Browne lawfullie begotten and to the heires of the bodie of such first sonne lawfullie begotten And for default of such issue to the vse and behoofe of the second sonne of the bodie of my said sonne Edward Browne lawfullie begotten and to the heires of the body of such second sonne lawfullie begotten And for default of such issue to the vse and behoofe of the third sonne of the bodie of my said sonne Edward Browne lawfullie begotten and to the heires of the bodie of such third sonne lawfullie begotten And for default of such issue to the vse and behoofe of every other sonne of the bodie of my said sonne Edward Browne lawfullie begotten successively one after another as they shalbe in senioritie of birth and to the heires of the bodie of every such sonne lawfully begotten respectively And for default of such issue to my sonne William Browne during his life and after his decease to the vse and behoofe of the first sonne of the body of my said sonne William Browne lawfullie begotten and to the heires of the bodie of such first sonne lawfullie begotten And for default of such issue to the vse and behoofe of the second sonne of the bodie of my said sonne William Browne lawfully begotten and to the heires of the bodie of such second sonne lawfullie begotten And for default of such issue to the vse and behoofe of the third sonne of the bodie of my said son William Browne lawfullie begotten and to the heires of the bodie of such third son lawfullie begotten And for default of such issue to the vse and behoofe of every other sonne of the body of my said sonne William Browne lawfully begotten successively one after another as they shalbe in seniority of age and to the heires of the body of every such sonne lawfullie begotten respectively And for default of such issue to my sonne Edmond Browne during his life and after his decease to the vse and behoofe of the first sonne of the bodie of my said sonne Edmond Browne lawfullie begotten and to the heires of the bodie of such first sonne lawfullie begotten And for default of such issue to the vse and behoofe of the second sonne of the bodie of my said sonne Edmond Browne lawfullie begotten and to the heires of the bodie of such second sonne lawfullie begotten And for default of such issue to the vse and behoofe of the third sonne of the bodie of my said sonne Edmond Browne lawfullie begotten and to the heires of the body of such third son lawfullie begotten And for default of such issue to the vse and behoof of every other sonne of the body of my said sonne Edmond Browne lawfullie begotten successively one after another as they shalbe in seniority of birth and to the heires of the body of every such sonne lawfully begotten respectively And for default of such issue to my two daughters Mary Stury and Apoline Browne her sister and to theire heires and assignes for ever. Item according to the power I have by my Deed of Feoffement above recited I doe give devise and bequeath limitt declare and appoint vnto my said sonne Edmond Browne beinge my third sonne now living All that my Manno$^r$ or Lordshippe called Hungerie Bentleley with all messuages lands tenements and hereditaments therevnto belonging together with the said two closes or parcells of ground therevnto belonging the one called the Spittle Hinckle the other paleflatt in the said Countie of Darby together w$^{th}$ all woods vnderwoods hedgrowes and other comodities growinge and beinge in vpon the premisses with theire appurtenances.

*(To be continued.)*

## VAVASOUR.

William Vavasour paid subsidy at Kippax 1597.
Widow Vavasour paid 1665.
Thomas Vavasour paid 1674.

### KIPPAX REGISTERS.

1566  John, son of Raphe Vavasour, baptized.
1568  John Vavasour buried.
1568  Elisabeth Vavasour buried.
1569  William Vavasour baptized.
1633  Peter, son of Thomas Vavasour, buried.
1634  Isabella Vavasour baptized and buried.
1640  Sara, daughter of Thomas Vavasour, baptized and buried.
1641  *Margaret, daughter of Thomas Vavasour, baptized.
1661  Sarah Vavasour buried.
1676  Johannis Vavasour, filius Papisti Thomæ Vavasour, baptized mori Romæ June 22.
1678  Thomas Vavasour buried Aug. 17.

The last named Thomas Vavasour would be the Thomas who paid subsidy 1674, and son of the first named Thomas. His sister *Margaret married 1st, Watson; 2nd, Nicholson. Thomas Vavasour married Elisabeth, daughter of Richard Harwood of Welburn. Marriage settlement dated 1665. His son John married Ann Milner 1696. I should be grateful for any information shewing the connection of these Vavasours with the Vavasours of Haslewood.

*Boston Lodge, near Tadcaster.* WILLIAM CLARKE VINCENT.

# Genealogy of the Family of Harvey, etc.

## PEDIGREE B. (*Vide* p. 331.)

Michael Harvey of St. Laurence Pountney.=Mary, da. of John Mellish of London.

Susan (or Susanna), da. of William Underwood (53) of Bucklersbury in St. Stephen Walbrook, London, Turkey Merchant, of Grocers' Co., Sheriff (1652), and Alderman of London, and Alice his wife; b. 1644 (?); mar. c. 1662; d. s.p. 19 Aug., bur. in chancel at Bradford Abbas 22 Aug. 1663. M.I. 1st wife.
Arms: Gules, on a fess ermine between three annulets or a lion passant-guardant azure, in chief a cross-crosslet fitchée between the annulets argent.

=1. Michael Harvey of Clyfton Mabanke (or Clifton) (52), co. Dorset, Esq.; b. c. 1638; admitted Gray's Inn 21 Oct. 1650; J.P. co. Dorset; M.P. for Weymouth and Melcombe Regis, co. Dorset, in eight Parliaments 1678-9—1680-1 and 1688-9—1700-1; d. 19 Feb., bur. in Chancel at Bradford Abbas, co. Dorset, 29 Feb. 1711-12. M.I. Will dated 15 Aug. 1709; proved 4 March 1711-12. (P.C.C., Barnes 61.)

=Agnes, da. of Thomas (?) Yeoman (Yeoman or Yemans); b. c. 1648; mar. at St. Foster's (?), London, Sept. 1664 (Lic. Fac. Off. Abp. Cant. 1 Sept. 1664); d. s.p. 12 March 1716-17, bur. in Chancel at Bradford Abbas 26 March 1717. M.I. (54) Will dated 21 Aug. 1716; codicils 27 Jan. and 18 Feb. 1716-17; proved 8 April following. (P.C.C., Whitfield 79.) 2nd wife.
Arms: Gules, a chevron between three spearheads argent.

2. William Harvey (55) of Wyke (or Wike), co. Dorset, gent.; bapt. at St. Peter-le-Poor 18 Oct. 1638; d. of wounds received in service of James II. at Bridport, co. Dorset, 2 July 1685. M.I. at Bradford Abbas. Will dated 24 Nov. 1680; proved 18 July 1685. (P.C.C., Cann 88.)

=Margaret, da. of ... Gascoyne (of Cardington, co. Bedford, Esq. ?); b. c. 1641; mar. 1659 (?); d. 4 Dec. 1704; proved 20 Dec. following. (P.C.C., Ash 253.) Codicil dated 22 Oct. 1704; proved 7 June 1709. (P.C.C., Lane 144.)
Arms: On a pale sable a demi-lucy (or conger's head) erect coupled or.

... Hunt, of ... co. Somerset; b. 1657 (?); d. 17 .. =Margaret (?) Harvey; b. 1660 (?); mar. 1678 (?); d. 17 ..
Arms: Azure, two chevronels between three martlets argent.

Richard Steele,=Mary Harvey, sole da.; bapt. b. 1638 (?); liv- at St. Helen's, Bishopsgate, ing 3 Sept. 1689; 25 Feb. 1640-1; married d. 1701 (?). 1659 (?); living 3 Sept. 1689; d. 1704 (?).
Arms: STEELE (*ut supra*).

## PEDIGREE C. (*Vide* p. 334.)

William Harvey of Chigwell, and Great Greys, co. Essex.=Dorothy, sole da. and h. of Sir Robert Dycer (or Dicer) of Wrentham, co. Suffolk.

Sir Phillip Monoux of Wotton (or Wooton), co. Bedford, third Bart., eldest surviving son of Sir Humphrey M. (who d. July 1685), son of Sir Thomas Cotton of Connington, co. Hunt., Bart.; b. c. 1679; d. 25 Dec. 1707, bur. in chancel at Wotton. M.I. Will dated 6 Nov. 1707; proved 19 Jan. 1707-8. (P.C.C., Barrett 15.)

=1. Dorothy Harvey; b. 12 March 1683-4, bapt. in St. Giles-in-the-Fields same day; mar. 1 May 1701; d. c. May 1758, bur. in chancel at Wotton near her husband. Will dated 20 May 1758; proved 7 June following. (P.C.C., Hutton 193.)
Arms: Argent, on a chevron sable three bezants between as many oak-leaves vert.

Sir Edmund Anderson of Kildwick Percy (or Kilnwick Piercy), East Riding, co. York, fifth Baronet, son of Sir Edmund A. of Broughton, co. Lincoln, Bart., and Eliz., da. of Sir Anthony Deane of London, Kt., his second wife; b. 1682 (?); remar. Frances, da. ... Batty of Tadcaster, co. York, Esq., by whom issue; d. 3 May 1765. Will dated 25 April 1763; proved 19 Oct. 1765. (P.C.C., Rushworth 359.)

=2. Mary Harvey (38); b. 30 April, bapt. at St. Giles-in-the-Fields 1 May 1685; mar. 11 March 1712; d. before her husband 1748 (?).
Arms: Argent, a chevron between three crosses flory sable.

Pulter Forester of Broadfield (or Bradfield), co. Hertford, Esq., eldest son of James F. and Martha, third da. of Sir Henry Chauncy of Yardley Bury, Kt., his wife; b. at Cottered, co. Hertford, 30 March 1690; Sheriff of Herts 1717; d. at Bradfield 3 Dec., bur. at Cottered 6 Dec. 1753. Will dated 10 Nov. 1758; proved 21 Jan. 1762. (P.C.C., Pinfold 11.)

=3. Agnes Harvey; b. c. 1686; mar. 29 June 1713; d. c. Dec. 1761, bur. at Cottered 8 Jan. 1762. Will (with codicil) dated 21 Sept. 1759 (39); proved 24 Jan. following; admons 9 Aug. 1809 and 29 Jan. 1819. (P.C.C., St. Eloy 11.)
Arms: Argent, a chevron sable between three hunting-horns of the last stringed and garnished gules.

PEDIGREE C. (*Vide* p. 331.)

Matthew Harvey of London.=Mary, da. of Robert Hatley.

Mary Harvey; bapt. at St. Nicholas Acons, London, 16 July 1632; bur. there following day.

PEDIGREE E. (*Vide* p. 331.)

...niel Harvey of Combe, co. Surrey.=Elizabeth, da. of Edward, 2nd ord Montagu.

---

Elizabeth, eldest da. of Sir Eliab Harvey of St. Peter-le-Poor, Lond. and Chigwell; b. c. 1661; mar. at St. Peter-le-Poor 8 May 1679; died in childbed of da. Dorothy 15 Jan., bur. at Hempstead 30 Jan. 1695-6. M.I. She was cousin to her husband. 1st wife.
Arms: Or, on a chief indented sable three crescents argent.

=1. Edward Harvey, Sen. (56) of Combe; b. 30 March, bapt. in St. Giles-in-the-Fields 31 March 1658; High Steward of Kingston-on-Thames 29 Sept. 1707; M.P. for Bletchingley, co. Surrey, 1678-9; for Clitheroe, co. Lancashire, 1705, and in four Parliaments 1705—14-15; died at Dunkirk in France ("Fr. Flanders") 24 Oct. 1736; bur. at Hempstead (37). Will dated 20 Jan. 1731-2; codicils 19 March 1733 N.S., and 31 May N.S. 1735; pr. 19 Oct. 1736. (P.C.C., Derby 221.)

=Elizabeth, da. of Francis (Newport) Earl of Bradford, and Diana, da. of Francis, Earl of Bedford, his wife; relict of Sir Henry Littleton of Frankley, co. Worc., Bart. (who d. c. 1699) (57); b. c. 1670; mar. (at St. Martin's-in-the-Fields?) July 1702 (Lic. Bp. London 21 March 1699-1700); died s.p. 7 March, bur. at Kingston-on-Thames 19 March 1723-4. Adm'on P.C.C. 30 March 1724. 2nd wife.

=Mary, da. of Edward (?) Carteret (Esq., M.P. for Beerlaston, co. Devon?); b. c. 1707; mar. at St. Dionis Backchurch, London, 6 July 1726; survived her husband and died s.p. 17 . . 3rd wife.
Arms: Gules, four fusils in fess argent.

Arms: Argent, a chevron gules between three leopards' faces sable.

---

2. Daniel Harvey of Mitcham, co. Surrey, Esq.; b. c. 1664; mat. at Ch. Ch., Oxon, 16 Oct. 1677; B.A. 8 Dec. 1681; M.P. for Clitheroe, co. Lancaster 1706; Dunwich, co. Suffolk, 1708; Weymouth and Melcombe Regis, co. Dorset, 1713 (not duly elected), 1714-15; Lieut.-General of the Forces 22 April 1708; General 1 Jan. 1709; Lieut.-Governor of Guernsey 21 Dec. 1714; died s.p. 6 Sept., bur. in Chancel at Mitcham 15 Sept. 1732. M.I. Will dat. 19 March 1730-31; proved 18 Sept. 1732. (P.C.C., Bedford 229.)

=Anne, only da. of Ralph (Montagu), 1st Duke of Montagu, of Boughton, co. Northampton, and Elizabeth, da. of Thomas Wriothesley, Earl of Southampton, his 1st. wife; relict of Alexander Popham of Littlecott, co. Wilts, Esq. (who died 15 June 1705) (58); b. 1674; mar. 6 May 1707; died 2 Jan., bur. in Chancel at Mitcham 9 Jan. 1741-2. Will dated 11 Nov. 1737 (59); codicil 16 Nov. 1739; proved 16 Jan. 1741-2. (P.C.C., Trenley 17.)
Arms: Argent, three lozenges conjoined in fess gules within a bordure sable.

---

Thomas (Grey), 2nd Earl of Stamford, co. Lincoln, of St. Paul, Covent Garden, co. Middlesex; only son of Henry (1st Earl) and Anne Cecil, youngest da. and coh. of Wm., 2nd Earl of Exeter, his wife; b. c. 1653; P.C. 1694; Lord Lieut. and Cust. Rot., co. Derby, 24 April 1696; Chancellor Duchy of Lanc.; Lord Lieut. and Cust. Rot., co. Leic., 28 April 1697; survived his 1st wife Elizabeth, and remarried Mary, da. and coh. of Joseph Maynard of Gunnersbury, co. Middlesex, Esq., who survived him and died s.p. 9 Nov. 1722; died 31 Jan. 1719-20; bur. at Bradgate, co. York. Will dated 10 Sept. 1719; pr. 11 Feb. 1719-20; adm'on .. Jan. 1730-31. (P.C.C., Shaller 49.)
Arms: Barry of six argent and azure.

=1. Elizabeth Harvey; b. 1660 (?); mar. 1678 (?); died before her husb. 17 .. 1st wife

2. Ann Harvey; b. at Combe Nevel 19 June 1661; living 26 March 1666; probably died young.

1. Edward Harvey, Junior, of Tilton-on-the-Hill, co. Leicester, Esq.; bapt. at St. Bartholomew-by-the-Exchange, London, 4 Dec. 1680; admitted Inner Temple, London, 24 Dec. 1695; d. in St. James, Westminster, 9 Feb., bur. at Hempstead 17 Feb. 1707-8. Will dated 2 Feb. 1707-8; proved 9 March following. (P.C.C., Barrett 63.)

= Frances, da. of Col. Francis Lutterell (or Luttrell) of Dunster Castle, co. Somerset, M.P. for Minehead 1660—90, and Jane (60), only da. and h. of John Tregonwell of Milton Abbey, co. Dorset, Esq., his wife; b. c. 1675; mar. c. 1705; remar. B.A. at St. Giles-in-the-Fields 17 Aug. (Settlement dated 2 Aug.) 1710; d. 30 March 1748, bur. at Heytesbury. M.I. Arms: Or, a bend between six martlets sable.

= Edward Ashe of Heytesbury, co. Wilts, Esq.; son of William A. of same, Esq., and Anne, da. of Alexander Popham of Littlecot, his first wife; b. c. 1673; M.P. for Heytesbury; d. s.p. 22 May 1748, bur. at Heytesbury. M.I. Will dated 25 Jan. 1743-4; codicils 22 May following and 20 March 1746-7; proved 23 June 1748. (P.C.C., Strahan 169.) Arms: Argent, two chevrons sable.

2. Daniel Harvey, Esq.; bapt. at Kingston-on-Thames 12 May 1683; d. in Turkey from the kick of a horse, and probably bur. there before April 1715; unmar. (61)

1. Elizabeth Harvey; bapt. at Kingston-on-Thames 20 Feb. 1681-2; bur. at Hempstead 22 Nov. 1686.

2. Dorothy (or Dorothea) Harvey; b. 6 Nov., bapt. at Kingston-on-Thames 13 Nov. 1684; d. 1 Jan., bur. at Hempstead 5 Jan. 1691-2. (62)

Edward (?) Harvey; b. c. 1706; probably d. in infancy.

Frances (?) Harvey; b. c. 1707; probably d. in infancy.

3. Michael Harvey (61A) of Combe Nevel, Clyfton Mabanke, and St. Ann, Soho, co. Middx., Esq.; b. 10 May, bapt. at Kingston-on-Thames 18 May 1694; mar. for Milborne Port, co. Somerset 1722, 1734, 1741-2, 1747 (not duly elected); d. of apoplexy, intest. and s.p. 3 Oct. 1748. Adm'on P.C.C. 2 Nov. 1748.

= Rebecca, da. of Sir John Wolstenholme of Edmonton, co. Middx., Bart, M.P. for co. Middx. in three Parliaments 1695—1703, and Mary his first wife; b. 1686; mar. c. April 1715 (Settlement dated 23 April 1715); d. . . Nov., bur. at Hempstead 26 Nov. 1747. Arms: Azure, a lion passant-guardant between three pheons or.

*Michael Harvey*

4. Frances Harvey, of Great Poland Street, Westminster; b. 1690; died unmar. 11 July, bur. at Hempstead 21 July 1761. Will dated 18 Aug. 1759; proved 29 July 1761. (P.C.C., Cheslyn 253.)

5. Martha Harvey; b. 20 April, bapt. at Kingston-on-Thames 2 May 1691; bur. there 8 April 1695.

6. Elizabeth Harvey; b. 24 Nov., bapt. at Kingston-on-Thames 4 Dec. 1692; died unmar. 31 May, buried at Hempstead 10 June 1729.

7. Ann Harvey, of St. Ann, Westminster; b. 1693; d. unmar. 6 July, bur. at Hempstead 18 July 1745. Will dated 19 Jan. 1736-7; proved 17 July 1745. (P.C.C., Seymer 196.)

8. Dorothy (or Dorothea) Harvey; b. 5 Jan, bapt. at Kingston-on-Thames 12 Jan. 1695-6; bur. there 10 Dec. 1696.

Nicholas Breton of Norton, co. Northampton, Esq., only son of Robert B. of same, Esq., and Elizabeth his wife; bapt. at Norton 25 April 1682; died (15?) Sept., bur. at Norton 30 Nov. 1709; proved 15 Nov. 1716. (P.C.C., Fox 201.) Arms: Azure, a bend between six mullets pierced or.

= 3. Mary Harvey; born 26 May, bapt. at Kingston-on-Thames 9 June 1686; mar. at St. Mary Aldermanbury, London, 23 Jan. 1706-7; died 20 (?) May, bur. at Norton 27 May 1764. Will dated 6 April 1758 (63); proved 11 July 1764. (P.C.C., Simpson 250.)

*Michael Harvey*

PEDIGREE ℱ. (*Vide* p. 336.)

Sir Eliab Harvey of Rolls Park.=Louisa, da. of Robert, 1st Earl Nugent.

1. William Harvey; b. 25 March, bapt. at Chigwell 2 April 1786; d. 20 March, bur. at Hempstead 25 March 1794.

2. Edward Harvey, Esq.; b. 11 June, bapt. at Chigwell 17 July 1788; Capt. Coldstream Guards; killed in the lines of Burgos, Spain, 18 Oct. 1812, and probably bur. there; unmar. M.I. at Hempstead (65).

3. William Harvey of Rolls Park, Esq., Esq.; b. 24 Dec. 1801 (66), bapt. at Chigwell 22 March 1802; matriculated at Brasenose College, Oxon., 14 Jan. 1819; B.A. 5 Dec. 1822; d. unmar. at Rolls 3 March, bur. at Hempstead 11 March 1823. M.I.

William Lloyd of Aston Hall, Oswestry, co. Salop,=1. Louisa Harvey (67); b. and bapt. at St. Marylebone, co. Middx, 1785; married at St. George's, Hanover Square (Special Licence), 8 Oct. 1804; d. at Aston Hall 7 March 1866.
Robert L. of Aston, and Martha, 4th da. of John Shakespeare of London, Esq., his wife; b. 21 Dec. 1779; J.P., D.L., High Sheriff co. Salop 1810; d. at Aston Hall 29 April 1843.
Arms: Per fess sable and argent, a lion rampant counterchanged armed and langued gules.

Rev. William Tower, Clerk in Holy=3. Maria Harvey; b. 6 April, bapt. at Chigwell 23 May 1791; mar. 13 June 1825; d.
Orders, 6th and youngest son of Christopher T. of Huntsmoor Park, co. Buck., and Weald Hall, co. Essex, Esq., and Elizabeth, only da. of George Baker of Elemore Hall, co. Durham, Esq., his wife; b. 1789; of St. John's Coll., Camb., B.A. 1812; died at How Hatch, South Weald, co. Essex, 2 Aug. 1847.
Arms: Sable, a tower or.

John Drummond, Junior, of Fulham, co. Middx, Esq., only son of John Drummond of Stanmore, and Charing Cross, co. Middx., Banker, and Hester, eldest da. of Thos. Cholmondeley, Esq., and sister of Thos., 1st Lord Delamere, his wife; b. 1791; d.
Arms: Quarterly—1 and 4, Or, three bars wavy gules; 2 and 3, Or, a lion's head erased within a double tressure flory counter-flory gules.

4. Georgiana (or Georgianna Augusta) (68) Harvey; b. 7 Dec. 1795; bapt. at Chigwell 2 Jan. 1796; mar. 22 April 1816; d.

Sir William Cornwallis Eus-=2. Emma Harvey; b. 14 April, bapt. at Chigwell 10 May 1787; mar. at Rolls Park 16 Feb. 1830 (Spec. Lic. Cant.); d.
tace of Sampford Hall, co. Essex; K.C.H., C.B., Lieut.-Genl. in the Army; 4th son of Lieut.-Genl. Chas. E. of Robertstown, co. Kildare, and Corbally, Queen's co., Ireland, and Alice, da. of Oliver McCausland of Stronorland, Esq., his wife; b. 1778 (?); d. 9 Feb. 1855.
Arms: Or, a saltire gules.

Thomas William Bramston of=5. Eliza (or Elizabeth) Harvey; b. 25 June, bapt. at Chigwell 21 July 1798; mar. at St. George's, Hanover Sq., 12 Aug. 1880; d.
Skreens, in Roxwell, co. Essex, Esq., eld. son of Thos. Gardiner B. of same, Esq., and Maria Anne, da. of Wm. Blaauw of Queen Anne Street, London, Esq., his wife; b. 30 Oct. 1796; d.
Arms: Or, on a fess sable three plates argent.

Robert George Cecil Fane, Esq., youngest son of Hon. Henry Fane of Ful-=6. Isabella Mary Harvey; bapt. at Chigwell 25 Dec. 1806; mar. at St. George's, Hanover Square, 24 June 1835; d. at Rolls Park 15 Dec. 1838 s.p. 1st wife.
beck, co. Lincoln, and Anne, da. of Edw. Buckley Batson, Esq., his wife; b. 8 May 1796; educated at the Charterhouse, London, 1808-13; matric. Balliol Coll., Oxon., 22 May 1813; Demy and Fellow of Magdalen Coll., Oxon., 1824-35; B.A. 1817; M.A. 1819; called to the Bar, Lincoln's Inn, 1 June 1821; Bankruptcy Commissioner 2 Dec. 1831; remar. 7 Sept. 1841, Harriet Anne, only da. of Admiral the Hon. Sir Henry Blackwood, Bart., and by her (who died 31 Dec. 1869) had issue; d. at Weymouth 4 Oct. 1864.
Arms: Azure, three dexter gauntlets backs affrontée or.

For Notes to Pedigrees *vide post.*

# The Register Book of Bramfield, co. Suffolk.*

### 1829.

Aug. 17 — Sarah d. of John and Mary Sucker, Laborer.

Aug. 27 — Sarah d. of Joseph and Ann Bolton, Laborer.

Sep. 13 — William s. of James and Mary Hurren, Laborer.

Oct. 12 — Eliza d. of Samuel and Catharine Amant, Laborer.

Nov. 24 — Jemima d. of James and Ann Gorred, Laborer.

Dec. 6 — Eliza d. of James and Ann Reade, Laborer.

Dec. 17 — George s. of Daniel and Mary Berry, Shoemaker.

Dec. 21 — Elizabeth d. of Stephen and Mary Self, Laborer.

### 1830.

Feb. 14 — Charlotte d. of Robert and Lydia Shade, Laborer.

Feb. 17 — Gater William s. of Francis and Frances Balls, Farmer.

Feb. 20 — William s. of Mary Ann Moore, Spinster.

Mar. 3 — Elizabeth d. of James and Louisa Bird, Laborer.

Mar. 17 — Mary Ann d. of James and Harriet Clarke, Laborer.

Mar. 29 — Mary Ann d. of Jane Freeman, Spinster; by C. Mason, Curate.

April 22 — Louisa d. of Robert and Mary Ann Westgate, Laborer; by C. Mason, Vicar.

April 23 — Louisa Maria d. of Henry and Louisa Loch, Tailor.

April 26 — William s. of Daniel and Sophia Watson, Laborer.

May 8 — John s. of Sarah Aldred, Spinster.

May 22 — Samuel s. of John and Sophia Thurlow, Laborer.

June 6 — James s. of John and Charlotte Moore, Laborer.

June 27 — Thomas s. of Daniel and Sarah Smith, Laborer.

June 27 — Harriet d. of Abraham and Rachel Smith, Laborer.

June 27 — William s. of Samuel and Mary Clarke, Laborer.

July 19 — James s. of Richard and Susanna Haking, Laborer.

July 19 — Henry s. of the same.

July 26 — John Gallan s. of William and Elizabeth Ling, Farmer.

Aug. 30 — Emma d. of Jonas and Caroline Tibenham, Butcher.

Sep. 12 — James s. of Joseph and Sarah Gilbert, Laborer.

Sep. 21 — Elizabeth Adelaide d. of William Aldis and Elizabeth Higham, Farmer.

Sep. 26 — Lucy d. of George Manby and Phebe Smith, Laborer.

Oct. 14 — Caroline d. of Charles and Charity Gorrod, Blacksmith.

Nov. 14 — William s. of James and Ann Reade, Laborer.

Nov. 21 — Robert Davy s. of Samuel and Sarah Edwards, Laborer.

Nov. 21 — Letitia d. of James and Sophia Watling, Laborer.

### 1831.

Jan. 9 — William s. of William and Hannah Tuthill, Laborer.

Jan. 16 — Robert Sciorett s. of Sarah Leggat, Spinster.

Jan. 25 — Mary d. of James and Mary Nicholson of Sᵗ Mary, Ipswich, Sailor.

Feb. 13 — Robert s. of James and Maria Button, Laborer.

Mar. 14 — John S. of Arthur and Sarah Copper, Shoemaker.

Mar. 20 — Hannah d. of Robert and Lydia Borrett, Laborer.

Mar. 31 — Emma d. of Robert and Susan Appleton, Farmer.

April 14 — Mary Ann d. of John and Sarah Flegg, Laborer.

April 24 — Liddy of Samuel and Catharine Amant, Laborer.

April 25 — Joseph s. of Joseph and Ann Bolton, Laborer.

May 17 — Charles s. of Joseph and Mary Chapman, Laborer.

May 17 — Robert s. of John Hunt and Sarah Hatcher, Blacksmith.

May 29 — William s. of Robert and Lydia Shade, Laborer.

June 16 — Mary Ann d. of John and Ann Spindler, Laborer.

June 20 — Matilda d. of James and Hannah Cross, Farmer.

July 3 — John s. of Samuel and Phillis Philpot, Laborer.

July 31 — William s. of Benjamin and Mary Ann Hubbard, Butcher.

Aug. 15 — John s. of William and Hannah Witmore, Laborer.

Sep. 4 — Isaac s. of Isaac and Ann Smith, Shoemaker.

Nov. 17 — Mary Ann d. of James and Louisa Bird, Labourer.

Nov. 20 — Charlotte Amelia d. of John and Maria Stigall, Schoolmaster.

Nov. 21 — Emma d. of William Aldis and Elizabeth Higham, Farmer.

Dec. 9 — Arthur Dix s. of Robert and Mary Ann Westgate, Laborer .

Dec. 9 — William Last s. of the same.

Dec. 13 — Harriet d. of Stephen and Mary Self, Laborer.

Dec. 19 — William s. of Mary Nunn, Spinster.

Dec. 19 — Mary d. of Harriet Soanes, Spinster.

Dec. 21 — Francis Girling s. of William and Elizabeth Ling, Farmer.

* Continued from p. 341.

### 1832.

Feb. 10 Isabel d. of James and Ann Gorred, Laborer.

Feb. 29 Frederick s. of Isaac and Elizabeth Eastaugh, Laborer.

Mar. 22 George s. of James and Ann Reade, Laborer.

May 29 William s. of Robert and Susan Appleton, Farmer.

July 27 Eliza d. of John and Amy Amant, Laborer.

July 29 Emily d. of Daniel and Sarah Smith, Laborer.

Aug. 8 Emma Clarke d. of Simon and Sophia Lenny, Laborer.

Aug. 8 Charlotte d. of Abraham and Rachel Smith, Laborer.

Aug. 24 John Eli s. of Henry and Elizabeth Wright, Farmer.

Sep. 27 Thomas s. of William and Hannah Tuthill, Laborer.

Nov. 12 Sarah Ann d. of Samuel and Mary Clarke, Labourer.

### 1833.

Feb. 7 James s. of Benjamin and Mary Ann Hubbard, Butcher.

Feb. 13 Emma d. of Robert Curtis and Abigail Andrews, Miller.

Mar. 10 Eliza d. of John and Mary Waters, Laborer.

Mar. 30 William s. of Sarah Leggatt, Spinster.

April 15 John s. of Joseph and Sarah Gilbert, Laborer.

April 15 Thomas s. of Edward and Mary Ludbrooke, Labourer.

April 25 Mary d. of James and Maria Button, Laborer.

May 5 Edgar d. of Harriet Amant, Spinster.

May 15 Jane Maria d. of Robert and Mary Ann Westgate, Laborer.

June 4 Sarah d. of Robert and Sarah Clow, House Carpenter.

June 5 Anne d. of Robert and Susan Appleton, Farmer.

June 19 Francis s. of Arthur and Sarah Copper, Shoemaker.

July 1 Lucy Ann d. of William and Emily Wright, Blacksmith.

Aug. 27 Edwin George s. of John and Maria Stigall, Schoolmaster.

Sep. 7 Betsy d. of Jonas and Caroline Tibbenham, Butcher.

Sep. 29 Robert s. of Robert and Lydia Borrett, Laborer.

Nov. 18 Maria d. of John and Ann Spindler, Laborer.

Nov. 30 Maria d. of James and Harriet Clarke, Laborer.

Dec. 15 John s. of James and Sophia Watling, Laborer.

Dec. 25 William s. of James and Ann Reade, Laborer.

### 1834.

Jan. 5 Eliza d. of Simon and Sophia Lenny, Laborer.

Jan. 13 William s. of John and Charlotte Moore, Laborer.

Mar. 3 John s. of William Aldis and Elizabeth Higham, Farmer.

Mar. 17 William George s. of James and Ann Gorred, Labourer.

Mar. 25 James s. of William and Hannah Tuthill, Laborer.

April 9 Mary Ann d. of George Catchpole and Mary Ann English, Shoemaker.

June 28 Charlotte d. of Joseph and Mary Chapman, Laborer.

July 7 Maria d. of William and Susan Whitman, Laborer.

July 13 James s. of Isaac and Ann Smith, Laborer.

Aug. 3 James s. of Daniel and Phebe Dale, Laborer.

Aug. 24 Robert s. of Daniel and Sarah Smith, Laborer.

Sep. 4 Frederica Ellin d. of William and Mary Heffer, Butcher.

Sep. 14 Emma d. of Robert and Maria Haddingham, Farmer.

Sep. 26 Anna d. of Henry and Elizabeth Wright, Farmer.

Dec. 5 Maria d. of William and Jane Reynolds, Exciseman.

Dec. 28 James s. of Stephen and Maria Kemp, Laborer.

### 1835.

Jan. 19 Emma Maria d. of John and Maria Stigall, Schoolmaster.

Mar. 6 Emma d. of James and Harriet Clarke, Laborer.

Mar. 12 Eliza d. of Samuel and Mary Clarke, Laborer.

Mar. 17 Louisa d. of Sarah Barnaby, Spinster.

May 10 William s. of Joseph and Sarah Gilbert, Laborer.

May 13 James s. of Stephen and Mary Self, Laborer.

June 1 Joseph s. of Joseph and Rebekah Hilling, Wheelwright.

July 6 Elizabeth Sarah Ann d. of John and Lucy Brown, Laborer.

July 10 Lydia Theresa d. of Joseph and Charlotte Sillett, Innkeeper.

Oct. 13 Edward s. of William Aldis and Elizabeth Higham, Farmer.

Oct. 17 Charles s. of Edward and Mary Ludbrooke, Laborer.

Nov. 6 Margaret d. of Robert and Susan Appleton, Farmer.

Nov. 11 Ann d. of Maria Edwards, Spinster.

Nov. 28 Elizabeth d. of Arthur and Sarah Copper, Shoemaker.

Dec. 26 Robert s. of Maria Smith, Spinster.

Dec. 31 John s. of James and Hannah Cross, Farmer.

Dec. 31 Elizabeth d. of the same.

### 1836.

Jan. 18 Harriet d. of Daniel and Sarah Smith, Laborer.

Jan. 31 Eliza d. of Samuel and Catharine Amant, Laborer.

Mar. 6   Alfred s. of Robert and Maria Haddingham, Farmer.
Mar. 17  John s. of John and Mary Waters, Laborer.
April 24 Charles s. of Richard and Susannah Haking, Laborer.
May 21   Robert s. of James and Charlotte Row, Shoemaker.
May 22   Isabella d. of Mary Ann Waters, Spinster.
May 22   Susan d. of William and Hannah Tuthill, Laborer.
June 18  Mary Ann d. of James and Ann Reade, Laborer.
Aug. 14  Ann d. of Daniel and Phebe Dale, Laborer.
Sep. 3   John George s. of Samuel and Anne Eastaugh, Harnessmaker.
Nov. 15  Joseph s. of Joseph and Charlotte Sillett, Innkeeper.

1837.

Jan. 2   John s. of Robert and Elizabeth Chapman, Laborer.
Jan. 10  Isaac s. of John and Mary Butcher, Laborer.
Jan. 31  Sarah Ann Collier d. of Lucy Leggatt, Spinster.
Feb. 5   James s. of James and Harriet Reeve, Laborer.
Mar. 1   Charlotte d. of Jonas and Caroline Tibenham, Butcher.
Mar. 19  James Almony s. of Sarah Barnaby, Spinster.
Mar. 29  Samuel s. of William Aldis and Elizabeth Higham, Farmer.
April 10 James Reeve s. of Sarah Porter, Spinster.
June 1   Daniel s. of Daniel and Sarah Smith, Laborer.
June 4   Elizabeth d. of Robert and Sarah Clow, Carpenter.
June 5   Jane d. of Honor Amant, Spinster.
June 6   Mary d. of James and Maria Button, Laborer.
June 9   John s. of Stephen and Mary Self, Laborer.
June 18  Maria d. of Mary Hurren, Spinster.
June 28  Alfred John s. of John and Maria Stygall, Land Surveyor.
July 2   Robert s. of Samuel and Jane Vincent, Laborer.
July 2   John s. of William and Susan Whitman, Laborer.
July 2   Charles s. of Henry and Ann Reade, Laborer.
July 30  Ellin d. of John and Anne Spindler, Laborer.
July 30  Ellin d. of Simon and Sophia Lenny, Laborer.
Aug. 20  Edward s. of Samuel and Mary Clarke, Laborer.
Aug. 27  James s. of James and Eliza Sarter, Laborer.
Oct. 8   John s. of James and Harriet Clarke, Laborer.
Nov. 3   John s. of James and Hannah Cross, Farmer.

1838.

Mar. 12  John s. of Abidia Howard, Spinster.
Mar. 23  Charlotte d. of Robert and Elizabeth Chapman, Laborer.
April 8  William s. of John and Lucy Browne, Laborer.
June 6   Sarah d. of William Aldis and Elizabeth Higham, Farmer.
July 5   John s. of William and Hannah Tuthill, Laborer.
Aug. 5   James s. of Joseph and Mary Chapman, Laborer.
Aug. 26  Sarah d. of James and Mary Haselup, Laborer.
Oct. 21  Daniel s. of Daniel and Phebe Dale, Laborer.
Nov. 4   Robert Cooper s. of Sarah Johnson, Spinster.
Dec. 9   Edward s. of Simon and Sophia Lenny, Laborer.
Dec. 23  Mary Anne of Alderman and Hannah Fellgate of Laxfield, Smith.
Dec. 24  Martha d. of John and Ann Spindler, Laborer.
Dec. 26  Eliza d. of Mary Ann Waters, Spinster.

1839.

Feb. 23  Caroline d. of Henry and Elizabeth Wright, Farmer.
Mar. 9   George s. of Samuel and Lucy Collier, Laborer.
Mar. 9   Hannah d. of the same.
April 7  Elizabeth d. of Joseph and Charlotte Sillett, Innkeeper.
April 25 John Chilver s. of Samuel and Anne Eastaugh, Harnessmaker.
May 3    Harriet d. of James and Harriet Reeve, Laborer.
May 5    Sarah d. of Samuel and Sarah Smith, Laborer.
May 18   James s. of James and Hannah Mayhew, Laborer.
May 18   Eliza d. of the same.
June 16  Elizabeth d. of Sarah Aldis, Spinster.
June 23  Alfred s. of Charlotte Tuthill, Spinster.
July 21  Helen d. of Robert Curtis and Abigail Andrews, Miller.
July 29  Betsy d. of James and Anne Reade, Laborer.
Aug. 4   William s. of William and Maria Aldis, Laborer.
Aug. 5   George s. of William and Lucy Lines, Laborer.
Sep. 15  Elizabeth d. of Robert and Esther Blumfield, Farmer.
Oct. 26  William s. of Robert and Mary Anne Dale, Farmer.
Oct. 27  Angelina d. of Benjamin and Naomi Cattermull, Shopkeeper.
Nov. 3   Alfred s. of John and Lucy Brown, Miller.
Nov. 12  Emma d. of Thomas and Sarah Smith, Laborer.
Nov. 15  Mary d. of Elizabeth Bartram, Married Woman.

1840.

Mar. 2   Emma d. of Stephen and Mary Self, Laborer.

April 22 William s. of William and Mary Anne Haking, Laborer.
April 24 Mary Anne d. of Robert and Elizabeth Chapman, Laborer.
April 27 Sarah d. of James and Harriet Clarke, Laborer.
July 10 Phœbe d. of Jonas and Caroline Tibbenham, Butcher.
July 19 John s. of Sarah Barnaby, Spinster.
Aug. 17 John s. of William and Lucy Lines, Laborer.
Sep. 18 Martha d. of Harriet Clarke, Spinster.
Sep. 27 James s. of James and Sarah Croft, Miller; by Reginald Rabett, Vicar of Thornton, Leicestershire.
Oct. 18 Anna d. of Daniel and Sarah Smith, Laborer.
Oct. 25 George s. of Robert and Charlotte Hurren, Laborer.
Nov. 15 William s. of John and Anne Becket, Laborer.
Nov. 16 James s. of Richard and Susan Haken, Laborer.
Dec. 7 Elizabeth d. of William and Hannah Tuthill, Laborer.
Dec. 8 Thomas s. of Thomas and Sarah Smith, Laborer.
Dec. 31 Arthur s. of William and Harriet Cupper, Shoemaker.

1841.

Jan. 24 Elizabeth d. of Robert and Maria Shade, Laborer.

Jan. 24 Mary Ann d. of the same.
Jan. 24 William s. of James and Harriet Reeve, Laborer.
Feb. 14 James s. of James and Rebecca Mills, Laborer.
Feb. 21 John s. of Daniel and Phœbe Dale, Laborer.
Feb. 24 George s. of James and Ann Reade, Laborer.
Mar. 7 Albert s. of John and Lucy Brown, Miller.
Mar. 21 Samuel s. of William and Susan Whitman, Laborer.
May 7 Jane d. of Caroline Clarke, Spinster.
May 28 Emma d. of John and Harriet Oaks, Laborer.
June 29 Mary Arabella d. of John and Maria Stagoll, Land Surveyor.
July 17 Elizabeth Mary d. of Mary Ann Elner, Spinster.
Aug. 8 John s. of Samuel and Lucy Collier, Laborer.
Aug. 18 Herbert William s. of William and Mary Heffer, Butcher.
Aug. 22 James s. of Robert and Charlotte Hurren, Laborer.
Sep. 26 Albert s. of Simon and Sophia Lenny, Laborer.
Nov. 21 Charles s. of William and Mary Ann Button, Laborer.
Dec. 12 Robert s. of Robert and Ann Eliza Edments, Husbandman.
Dec. 19 Charles s. of Charles and Elizabeth Kemp, Laborer.

(*To be continued.*)

# Pedigree of the Family of Hamilton,[*]

FORMERLY OF THE COUNTY OF TYRONE, AFTERWARDS OF DONAGHADEE IN THE COUNTY OF DOWN, AND THEN OF DUBLIN, ETC.

William Hamilton, born circa tempore Jac. I., was seised in demesne of the quarter of land of Termegan, being four townlands called Knockro, Lissnetinny, Terremenagh, and Ballemullarty, with a house, garden, and orchard in the town of Strabane, all in the barony of Strabane and county of Tyrone, all of which (in 1641) formed part of the estate of the Earl of Abercorn; also of the town and land of Brackagh in the barony of Omagh in said county, which (in 1641) formed part of the estate of Sir Wm. Usher; also of the quarter of land of Loghimuck with the mill thereof, being four townlands, Fferreagh, Cornemucklagh, Lonegoe, and Cammy, in the barony of Omagh and said county, which (in 1641) formed part of the estate of Sir Audley Mervyn. He mortgaged the latter lands by deed of 18 Sept. 1640. Settled all his lands on the marriage of his son John Hamilton by deed of 6 Jan. 1658.

* Communicated by JAMES FRANKLIN FULLER, Esq., F.S.A., Dublin.

# Hamilton Pedigree.

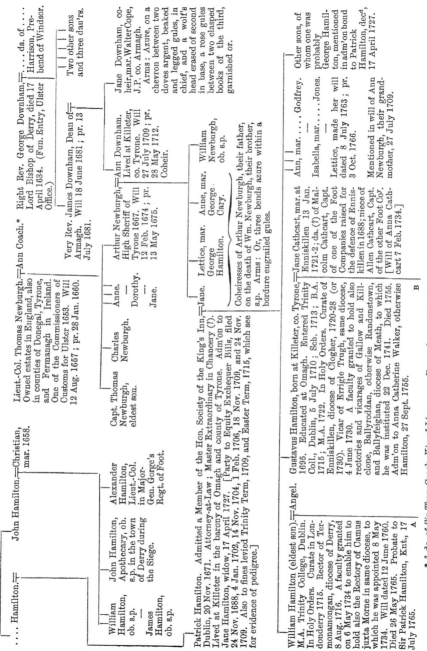

William Hamilton.=

....=Hamilton.=

John Hamilton.=Christian, mar. 1658.

Lieut.-Col. Thomas Newburgh.=Ann Coach.* Owned estates in England, also in counties of Donegal, Tyrone, and Fermanagh in Ireland. One of the Commissioners of Customs for Ulster 1653. Will 12 Aug. 1667; pr. 28 Jan. 1660.

Right Rev. George Downham, Lord Bishop of Derry, died 17 April 1634. (Fun. Entry, Ulster Office.)

....da. of .... Harrison, Prebend of Windsor.

Two other sons and three dau'rs.

Very Rev. James Downham, Dean of Armagh. Will 18 June 1681; pr. 13 July 1681.

Jane Downham, co-heir, mar. Walter Cope, J.P. co. Armagh. Arms: Azure, on a chevron between two doves argent, beaked and legged gules, in chief, and a wolf's head erased of second in base, a rose gules between two clasped books of the third, garnished or.

John Hamilton, Apothecary, ob. s.p. in the town of Derry during the Siege.

Alexander Hamilton, Lieut.-Col. in Major-Gen. George's Regt. of Foot.

Capt. Thomas Newburgh, eldest son.

Charles Newburgh.

Anne. — Dorothy. — Jane.

Ann Downham, Lived at Killeter, co. Tyrone. Will 27 July 1709; pr. 28 May 1712. Coheir.

Arthur Newburgh, High Sheriff of Tyrone 1667. Will 12 Feb. 1674; pr. 13 May 1675.

William Hamilton, ob. s.p. — James Hamilton, ob. s.p.

Patrick Hamilton. Admitted a Member of the Hon. Society of the King's Inn, Dublin, 20 Nov. 1671. Attorney-at-Law; Master Extraordinary in Chancery (?). Lived at Killeter in the barony of Omagh and county of Tyrone. [Party to Equity Exchequer Bills, filed 24 Nov. 1688, 4 Jan. 1702, 14 Nov. 1704, 1 Feb. 1706, 18 Nov. 1709, and 24 Nov. 1709. Also to fines levied Trinity Term, 1709, and Easter Term, 1715, which see for evidence of pedigree.] =Jane Hamilton, widow, 17 April 1727.

Jane. — Lettice, mar. George Hamilton. — Anne, mar. George Cary. — William Newburgh, ob. s.p.

Coheiresses of Arthur Newburgh, their father, on the death of Wm. Newburgh, their brother, s.p. Arms: Or, three bends azure within a bordure engrailed gules.

William Hamilton (eldest son).=Angel. M.A. Trinity College, Dublin. In Holy Orders. Curate in Londonderry 1715. Rector of Termonamongan, diocese of Derry, 8 Aug. 1716. A faculty granted on 6 May 1734 to enable him to hold also the Rectory of Camus juxta Morne in same diocese, to which he was appointed 8 May 1734. Will dated 12 June 1760. Died 26 May 1765. Probate to Sir Patrick Hamilton, Knt., 17 July 1765.
A

Gustavus Hamilton, born at Killeter, co. Tyrone, 1695. Educated at Omagh. Entered Trinity Coll., Dublin, 5 July 1710; Sch. 1713; B.A. 1715; M.A. 1722. In Holy Orders. Curate of Enniskillen, diocese of Clogher, 1720-28 (or 1730). Vicar of Errigle Trugh, same diocese, 4 June 1730. A faculty granted to hold also rectories and vicarages of Gallow and Killclone, Ballyroddan, otherwise Randonstown, and Ballyfeighan, diocese of Meath, to which he was instituted 22 Dec. 1741. Died 1755. Adm'on to Anna Catherine Walker, otherwise Hamilton, 27 Sept. 1755. =Jane Cathcart, mar. at Enniskillen 13 Jan. 1721-2; da. (?) of Malcolm Cathcart, Capt. of one of the Foot Companies raised for the defence of Enniskillen in 1688; niece of Allen Cathcart, Capt. of the other Foot Co[l]. [Will of Anna Cathcart 7 Feb. 1734.]

Ann, mar. .... Godfrey. — Isabella, mar. .... Jones. — Lettice, made her will dated 8 July 1763; pr. 3 Oct. 1766.

Mentioned in will of Ann Newburgh, their grandmother, 27 July 1709.

Other sons, of whom one was probably George Hamilton, mentioned in adm'on bond to Patrick Hamilton, dec'd, 17 April 1727.

B

* ? da. of Sir Thos. Coach, Kt., of Lismongan, Donegal, one of the Undertakers mentioned by Nic' Prynnar 1618-19.

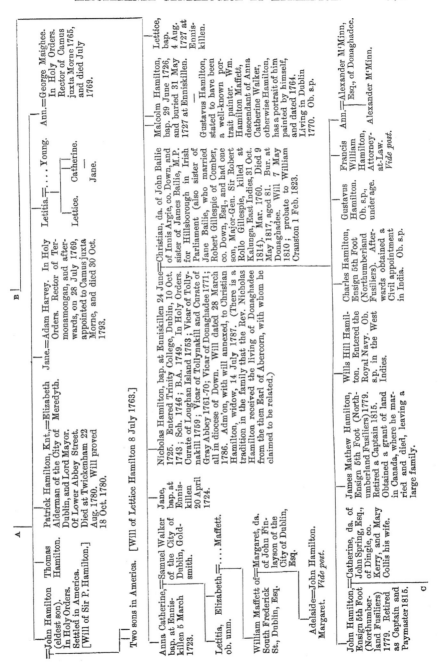

c |

Nicholas Hamilton, Entered 5th Foot (Northumberland Fusiliers). Served in Peninsular War. Was present at Siege of Badajos. Lost a leg in the Walcheren Expedition, 1809. Inspecting Field Officer, Northern Recruiting District in Ireland, 1814-52. Knight of the Royal Hanoverian Guelphic Order (K.H.), Major-General 11 Nov. 1851. Colonel of 82nd Foot (Prince of Wales's Volunteers). Died in Dublin 12 Dec. 1859. Adm'on to William Hamilton 14 Jan. 1860. = Frances, da. of Rev. Samuel Beamish of Mount Beamish, co. Cork.

John Spring Hamilton, Ensign 6th Foot (Northumberland Fusiliers). Served in Peninsular War. Was present at Salamanca. Retired a Major. = Eliza, da. of James Pratt, Esq., co. Cork, and niece of Gen. Sir Charles Pratt, K.C.B.

Charles Pratt Hamilton. Served in 35th Regt, and was on Recruiting Staff in Dublin. Retired with Hon. Rank of Major. = Louisa Butler.

John Butler Hamilton, Brigade Surgeon, A.M.D. = Annie McPherson. Married in the Bahamas.

Charles James Hamilton. Served in 3rd Buffs. Retired with Hon. Rank of Colonel. Resides at Folkstone. Served in = Isabel, da. of Charles Taddy, Esq.

Bernard Champion Hamilton.

Leonie. = John Clibborn, Capt. Indian Staff Corps.

Louisabel.

Hilda. Pauline Rose. Kathleen Norah.

William Hamilton, Capt. 37th Regt. Ob. s.p. 1878. = Harriette Beamish, his cousin. Resides in Dublin (1889).

Meredith. .... Marianne, da. of Rev..... Resides at Bedford (1889).

Walter Gustavus Hamilton, Lieut. in the German Army (1889). = Frances Harriett.

Marianne.

Samuel Beamish Hamilton, Lieut.-Col. 26th Regt. King's Own Borderers 1857. Died 1870.

Alexander Beamish Hamilton, Lieut. 26th (King's Own Scottish Borderers) Regt. (1889).

Archibald Samuel Hamilton, Lieut. 45th Regt. (Sherwood Foresters) (1889).

William George Hamilton, Staff Officer Allahabad, Captain 30th (East Lancashire) Regt. (1889).

Richard Hamilton, Sch., B.A. Trinity Coll., Dub. In Holy Orders. Vicar of Kilmersden, Somersetshire. = Charlotte, 5th da. of William Cooper, Esq., of Cooper Hill, Queen's Co.

Elizabeth. = Major Bullivant, 5th Foot.

Catherine, ob. s.p.

J. Bullivant. In Holy Orders. Rector of Pytchley, Northamptonshire. = Elizabeth Laughlin. Vide post.

One son. Alice.

William Hamilton, Ensign 5th Foot (Northumberland Fusiliers). Killed at Siege of Flushing 1809. S.p.

James Bunbury Hamilton, Ensign 12th Regt. Served in Peninsular War. Wounded at Salamanca. Adjutant Bristol Recruiting District. Retired with Hon. Rank of Major. Died s.p. at Clevedon, Somersetshire, Oct. 1869. = Margaret Fetherston Haugh of co. Westmeath,

Elizabeth Dorothea. = W. Grimshaw, Esq. Ob. 1878.

Catherine Jane.

Walter Hamilton Grimshaw. Edmund Usher Grimshaw.

Hamilton Pedigree—*continued.*

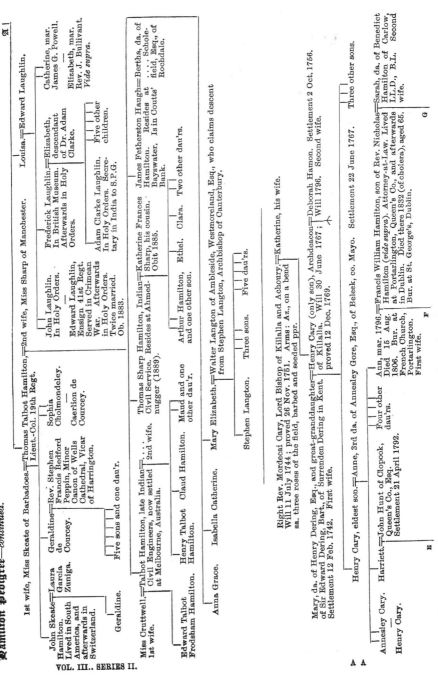

E       F       G

Anne.=Maurice Mahon, 3rd son of Thomas Mahon, Esq., of Ballinafad, co. Roscommon. Younger brother of Maurice, 1st Baron Hartland.

Mary Grant.=Gustavus Hamilton,=Catherine Laughlin. Ob. Jan. 1837. Attorney-at-Law, Ob. s.p. Buried at St. Solicitor in Chancery. Second wife. Anne's, Dublin. Born 1800. Ob. 15 First wife. March 1868. Bur. at Mount Jerome, Dublin.

Catherine, mar. George Strong, Esq. Settled in Sydney, N.S.W., in 1834.

Anne, mar. John Egan, Esq., M.D.

Harriett, mar. George Turpin, Esq.

Sarah Jane, ob. s.p.

Oliva Anna, mar. Henry Bolton of co. Wexford, Esq. Ob. s.p.

Benedict Gillespie Hamilton. Settled in Canada, and died there.

James Hamilton. Settled in Philadelphia, U.S.A., and died there.

William Cranston Hamilton, died at Acapula, U.S.A., in 1853.

Henry Forster=Eliza Freeman Hamilton, of Leamington, Land Agent, Warwickshire. Dublin.

Charles Frederick Hamilton,=Mary Garvey, bapt. 19 Dec. 1825, St. Mary's, who mar. 2ndly Dublin. Newspaper Proprie- Stephen Gash- tor. Died at San Francisco, wiler of San U.S.A. Francisco, Esq.

Richard Gustavus Hamilton, born 24 Nov. 1833; bap. St.Anne's,Dublin. Ob. s.p.

Hans Hamilton. Ob. s.p. in Australia.

Ernest C. Hamilton. Ob. s.p.

Henry Egerton Hamilton. Ob. s.p.

Frances, — Ambrosia.

Beatrice=James Cordelia. Wilson, Esq.

Florence Margaret.

Catherine.

Gustavus Hamilton, bap. 8 Dec. 1822 at St. Thomas,=Emily Pauline Dublin. Attorney-at-Law; Solicitor in Chancery. Alday, mar. Settled in Brisbane, Queensland. Died there 4 Nov. 1884. 1846.

Francis Hamilton, Solicitor.=Matilda, da. of . . . Rodd, Settled in New York, U.S.A. Librarian to the Duke of Died there 22 April 1874. Sussex.

John Edward Hamilton, Land Surveyor, Queensland.

Charles W. Hamilton, Crown Solicitor, Bowen, Queensland.

Frederick G. Hamilton, Solicitor, Toowoomba, Queensland.

George Hamilton, Richard Hamilton, Land Surveyors, Queensland.

Francis Alexander Hamilton.

William Alfred Hamilton.

Adelaide Margaret (first wife),=John Hamilton, born 28 June=Sara Elizabeth (second da. of William Maffett, Esq. 1828. Bap. St. Thomas, Dub- wife), da. of James (vide supra). Born 30 Jan. lin, 6 July 1828. Attorney-at- Groves, Esq., of Armagh. 1835. Bap. St. Anne's, Dublin. Law; Solicitor in Chancery. Mar. 25 April 1867 at St. Mar. 18 May Died 25 Nov. 1879. Bur. at Anne's, Belfast. 1853 at St. Mount Jerome, Dublin. Pro- Anne's, Dublin. bate to Sara E. Hamilton and Died 31 Jan. 1862. Buried at Everard Hamilton 23 Dec. Mount Jerome, Dublin. 1879.

Alexander Hamilton, Barrister-at-=Anita Ellen Mary, da. of Law, J.P. Co. Dublin. Assistant- Wm. Hamilton, Esq., M.D., Secretary to the Lord Chancellor of Urlar House, co. Sligo. of Ireland. Mar. at Christ Ch., Taney, co. Dublin, 14 Aug. 1883.

Mildred Anita.

Muriel Maud.

Sara Adelaide Olivia.

Villiers Sidney Hamilton, born 12 Feb. 1854. Bap. at St. Peter's, Dublin. Died 8 Aug. 1861. Bur. at Mount Jerome, Dublin.

Everard Hamilton, born 30 June 1855.=Elinor Anna, da. of Andrew Nolan, Esq., Baptism registered at St. Peter's, Dub- M.D., of Wicklow, and Emma Lyster, da. lin, 7 Nov. 1855. B.A. Trinity Coll., of Chaworth Lyster, Esq., of Grenan, Dublin, 1876. Attorney-at-Law. Queen's Co. Mar. 21 April 1881 at Christ Solicitor in Chancery 1877. Church, Taney, co. Dublin.

Florence Aubré.

Maud Caroline. Died 27 July 1866.

Helen Mary Adelaide.

Sylvia Grace Victoria.

Gustavus Everard Hamilton, born 14 March 1882. Bap. at Christ Church, Taney, 7 May 1882.

## HAMILTON NOTES.

Michaelmas Term, 1671.—Memorandum that on y<sup>e</sup> 20<sup>th</sup> of November 1671 Patrick Hamilton, Gent., was admitted a Member of this Society, and hath paid for his admission the sum of 13<sup>s</sup> 4<sup>d</sup>. (Records of Society of King's Inn, Dublin.)

24 Nov. 1709.—Equity Exchequer Bill,* filed by Alexander Hamilton, Esq., Lieut.-Colonel in the Hon. Major-General Gorge's Regiment of Foot, against Patrick Hamilton, attorney, of the county of Tyrone and others, states that William Hamilton, the petitioner's grandfather, was seized in demesne of two towns and lands, viz., the quarter of land of Termegan, being four towns and lands commonly called Knockro, Lissnetinny, Terremenagh, and Ballemullarty, together with a house, garden, and orchard in town of Strabane, all in the barony of Strabane and county of Tyrone. Also the town and land of Brackagh, the quarter of land of Loghimuck with the mill thereof, the said quarter containing four towns, Fferreagh, Cornemucklagh, Lonegoe, and Cammy, all in the barony of Omagh and county of Tyrone, and being so seized had executed a settlement, dated 6th January 1658, on marriage of petitioner's father and mother, John and Christian Hamilton ; that there were four sons of the marriage, namely, William, James, John, and the petitioner (Alexander) ; that William, James, and John had died without issue ; that John (the younger) had died in Derry during the late siege.

2 May 1710.—Answer* of Patrick Hamilton to the above bill states that William Hamilton had mortgaged the lands of Feaghreagh, Cornamucklea, Lanygea, and Cammy on y<sup>e</sup> 18 Sept. 1640 ; that he, Patrick Hamilton, had purchased the interest in these lands from John Hamilton, the petitioner's father, who was his uncle.

12 Feb. 1674.—Will* of Arthur Newburgh. Executrix his wife Ann Newburgh, to whom he left all his property, and directs her "to take to her assistance some of our neer relations to wit the Right Rev. Mr. James Downham, Dean of Ardmagh, her loveing ffather, to compute what my estate may be worth," and after computation to consider what "she may be able to give a portion unto Lettice, Ann, and Jean Newburgh my daughters, and thereof to make a cleer estate for my son William." Proved by Ann Newburgh, widow, 15 May 1675.

18 June 1681.—Will* of James Downame (or Downham), Dean of Armagh. Imprimis, I give to my daughter Jane Cope all my ready money and plate. Item, after payment of debts and funeral expenses, I leave the remainder of my estate to my said daughter Jane Cope and my daughter Ann Newburgh to be equally divided between them. Proved by Jane Cope, 13 July 1681.

18 Nov. 1709.—Equity Exchequer Bill.* Patrick Hamilton, Esq., and Jane his wife, George Hamilton and Lettice his wife, Anne Cary, widow and relict of George Cary, against Sir James Caldwell, Bart. States that Lieut.-Colonel Thomas Newburgh was seized of the manor of Banaghmore, co. Fermanagh, in the plantation of Ulster, and had made his will, dated 27 August 1657, devising same to his son Arthur Newburgh ; that Arthur Newburgh had died, leaving one son William, who had since died without issue, and three daughters, Jane, who had married Patrick Hamilton ; Lettice, who had married George Hamilton ; and Ann, who had married George Cary ; and that the three daughters claimed the lands as coheiresses of their father on the death of their brother without issue.

Trinity Term, 1709.—Fine* levied by George Hamilton, Esq., Patrick Hamilton, Esq., and Jane his wife, William Hamilton, clerk, and Anne Newburgh, affecting the lands of Omagh, Blyths Park, Barley Park, Loghamuck *alias* Lannegye, Cornamucklo, Fferreagh, Camy et Crevangan in Barony de Omagh et com. Tyrone.

27 July 1709.—Will* of Ann Newburgh of Killeter, co. Tyrone, widow. Mentions her second daughter Ann Cary, the younger sons of her daughter Jane Hamilton ; Ann Hamilton, eldest daughter of her daughter Jane ; Isabella and Lettice Hamilton, sisters of Ann ; grandson Brockwell Perrott and Ann Hamilton

* Public Record Office, Dublin.

A A 2

his sister ; William Hamilton, eldest son of daughter Jane ; son-in-law Patrick Hamilton. She directs payment of the expense of levying a fine and of the conveyance of lands by her daughter Jane, and Patrick and their son William, to George Hamilton of Coleraine. Mentions her daughter Lettice. Proved 28 May 1712.

Easter Term, 1715. Fine* levied. George Stewart against Patrick Hamilton of Killeter, in the county of Tyrone, Esq., and Jane his wife ; William Hamilton of Londonderry, clerk, the eldest son and heir apparent, and Angel his wife, affecting the lands of Ferreagh, Cornamuckla, Loghamuck, Camy, and Crevanagh in the barony of Omagh and county of Tyrone.

5 July 1710.—Gustavus Hamilton Filius Patricii Hamilton generosi ætat. 15 an. Nat. Killeter com. Tyrone Doc. Omagh. (Matriculation entry, Trinity College, Dublin.)

4 June 1730.—Re'ndus Gustavus Hamilton collatis fuit ad Vicariam de Errigle Trugh in com. Monaghan Dioces. predicti quarto die mens. Junii Anno Dom'i 1730 vacant per mortem na'lem Re'ndi Johannis Crawford ult. idem Incumbentis. (First Fruits Returns Diocese of Clogher.*)

22 Dec. 1741.—Hamilton, Gustavus, rectories and vicarages of Gallow and Kilclone and Ballyrodan *alias* Randonstown and Ballyfeighan and Drumlorgan, diocese of Meath. (Presentation to living by the Crown, Liber Munerum Publicorum Hiberniæ, vol. ii., part v., p. 12.)

21 January 174½.—Petition* of Gustavus Hamilton, clerk, Master of Arts, to the Lord Primate for a faculty to hold the livings of Errigle Trugh and Gallow Union together, whereupon the Primate sent requests to the Bishops of Clogher and Meath to certify the value of the livings, whether the cures could be served together, and whether they would recommend the faculty to be granted. The Bishop of Clogher certified that Errigle Trugh was of the yearly value of £100 and had forty acres of glebe, that he did not know what the distance was between the two parishes, and that " the petitioner is a very worthy clergyman, and both deserves and, considering his numerous family, needs " (the two livings). The Bishop of Meath certified that Gallow Union was of the yearly value of £150 ; that as to the distance, " I am pretty much a stranger." " Mr. Hamilton is a gentleman of a very worthy character and has a very numerous family, and therefore if your Grace thinks fit may be a proper object of the favour." (Books of Faculty Petitions, Prerogative Court.*)

10 October 1743.—Nicholas Hamilton filius Re'ndi Gustavi Hamilton ætat. 16 Nat. Enniskillen. (Matriculation Book, Trinity College, Dublin.)

27 Sept. 1755.—Administration* of the goods, etc., of the Rev. Gustavus Hamilton, late deceased, granted to Anna Catherine Walker otherwise Hamilton (wife of Samuel Walker of the city of Dublin, goldsmith), the natural and lawful daughter and next of kin of deceased, Jane Hamilton, the widow and relict, having first renounced and consented to the grant.

12 June 1760.—Will* of Rev. William Hamilton of Strabane. Mentions sister Letitia Hamilton ; sons, Rev. John Hamilton, Thomas Hamilton, Sir Patrick Hamilton, Knt., Alderman of the city of Dublin ; daughters, Jane Hamilton, married to Adam Harvey, Letitia Hamilton, married to . . . . Young, and Ann Hamilton, married to . . . . Macghee ; grandson, John Hamilton ; and granddaughter, Catherine Young. Proved by Sir Patrick Hamilton of the city of Dublin, Knt., 17 July 1765.

8 July 1763.—Will* of Lettice Hamilton of Strabane. Mentions niece Lettice Caulfield, sisters Jones and Ann Godfrey, nephew John Hamilton and his two younger sons " now in America," nieces Catharine, Lettice, and Jane Young, and niece Macghee. Proved 3 Oct. 1766.

24 April 1771.—Will* of Sir Patrick Hamilton, Knt. Mentions his wife Elizabeth Meredyth ; sisters Lettice Young, Jane Harvey, and Ann McGee ; brothers,

* Public Record Office, Dublin,

Rev. John Hamilton of America and Thomas Hamilton; nephew, Rev. William Hamilton; and grand-niece Lettice Lendrum. Will proved 18 Oct. 1780.

28 March 1786.—Will of Rev. Nicholas Hamilton. In the name of God amen. I Nicholas Hamilton, Cl$^{ke}$ Vicar of Donaghadee, in the coy. of Down, being in health and of sound and disposing mind and memory, Blessed be God, do make publish and declare this to be my last will and testament hereby revoking all wills by me heretofore made. I give devise and bequeath unto my dearly beloved wife Christian Hamilton, John Forde of the city of Dublin, James Forde of the town of Dundalk Esq., and to the survivor and survivors of them, and to the heirs of such survivor, all my real and personal estate of what nature and kind soever which I shall die possessed of or entitled unto, to hold unto them my said trustees upon the special trusts and confidence hereinafter mentioned and none other. I order and appoint that my said trustees shall as soon after my death as can be done conveniently and with prudence and advantage to my wife and children sell and convert into ready money all my real estate with such part of my chattels as my wife may not have occasion for, and that the moneys arising from the sale thereof after paying all my just debts and most moderate funeral expenses shall be by my said trustees lent out at legal interest on the best security or securetys that can be had for the same and that interest thereof shall yearly and every year be paid to my wife during her life for her support and the support of such of my children as may not be in a way of supporting themselves at the discretion of my said wife and with a full power to my said wife to dispose of the principal or any part thereof during her life or by her will among my children as she shall think their wants or merits may require, reposing the firmest confidence in her goodness sence and prudence as she has ever been to me the best of wives and to our children the best of mothers. In witness whereof and every part thereof I have hereunto affixed my hand and seal, the whole being in my own handwriting, this 28$^{th}$ day of March in the year of our Lord one thousand seven hundred and eighty-six.—NICHOLAS HAMILTON. (L.S.)

Signed published and declared to be the last will and testament of the Rev$^d$ Nicholas Hamilton in the presence of us who have witnessed the same in his presence and in the presence of each other.—Will. Chapman, Will$^m$ Hull, Will. Brown.

14 July 1787.—Administration* with the will annexed of Rev$^d$ Nicholas Hamilton, Vicar of Donaghadee, co. Down, granted to Christian Hamilton, his widow and principal legatee.

7 May 1810.—Will* of Christian Hamilton of Donaghadee, co. Down, widow. Mentions her daughter Ann MacMinn otherwise Hamilton, sons John, James, Francis, and Charles, her great-grandson William Charles Cranston, and Charlotte Cranston and Anna Christian Cranston his sisters. Probate to William Cranston, Attorney, 1st Feb. 1823. Assets under £910.

---

# Genealogy of Browne.

## Wills.

Copy of the Will of THOMAS BROWNE, Esq., of Shredicot, continued from p. 361.

Alsoe according to the said power I have by my said Deed of Feoffement I doe further give devise and bequeath lymitt declare and appoint vnto my said sonne Edmond Browne being my third sonne now living All that my Manno$^r$ or Lordshippe called Hungery Benteley with all messuages lands tenements and hereditaments therevnto belonginge together with the said two closes or parcell of ground therevnto adioyning the one called the Spittle Hinckle the other paleflatt in the said Countie of Derby together with all woods vnderwoods hedgrowes and other comodities growinge and being in and vpon the premisses with theire appurten'nces Alsoe according

---

* Public Record Office, Dublin.

to the said power I have by the said Deed of Feoffem^t I doe further give devise and bequeath lymitt declare and appoint vnto my said sonne Edmond Browne all that my said Parke and impaled ground called Middleton Park al's Barton old Parke in the said Countie of Darbie together with all woods vnderwoods palerowes hedgrowes houses cottage buildings and other comodities growinge and beinge in and vpon the same premisses To have and to hold the said Mano^r Lo:shipp messuages lands tenements Parke and impaled ground and all other the premisses with all and singular theire appurten'nce to him the said Edmond Browne my sonne from and after my decease and from and after the expirac'on and determinac'on of such terme and terms for life or for yeares w^ch I have formerly in this my will given devised lymitted and appointed vnto my said wife for the terme of his life and after his decease to such wife or wives as he the said Edmond Browne shall happen to marry for the terme of the life and lives of every such wife and after ye decease of every such wife and wives To the vse and behoofe of the first sonne of the body of the said Edmond Browne my sonne lawfullie begotten and to the heires of the bodie of such first sonne lawfullie begotten And for default of such issue to the vse and behoof of the second sonne of the bodie of my said sonne Edmond Browne lawfullie begotten and to the heires of the bodie of such second sonne lawfullie begotten And for default of such issue to the vse and behoofe of the third sonne of the bodie of my said sonne Edmond Browne lawfullie begotten and to ye heires of the bodie of such third sonne lawfullie begotten And for default of such issue to the vse and behoofe of the fourth sonne of the bodie of my said sonne Edmond Browne lawfullie begotten and to the heires of the bodie of such fourth sonne lawfullie begotten And for default of such issue to the vse and behoofe of the fyft sonne of the bodie of my said sonne Edmond Browne lawfullie begotten and to the heires of the bodie of such fift sonne lawfullie begotten And for default of such issue to the vse and behoofe of the sixt sonne of the bodie of my said sonne Edmond Browne lawfullie begotten and to the heires of the bodie of such sixt sonne lawfullie begotten And for default of such issue to the vse and behoofe of every other sonne of the bodie of my said sonne Edmond Browne lawfullie begotten successively one after another as they shalbe in seniority of birth and to the heires of the body of every such sonne lawfully begotten respectively And for default of such issue to my sonne William Browne during his life and after his decease to the vse and behoofe of the first sonne of the bodie of my said sonne William Browne lawfullie begotten and to the heires of the bodie of such first sonne lawfullie begotten And for default of such issue to the vse and behoofe of the second sonne of the bodie of my said sonne William Browne lawfullie begotten and to the heires of the body of such second sonne lawfullie begotten And for default of such issue to the vse and behoofe of the third sonne of the body of my said sonne William Browne lawfullie begotten and to the heires of the bodie of such third sonne lawfully begotten And for default of such issue to the vse and behoofe of every other sonne of the bodie of my said sonne William Browne lawfullie begotten successively one after another as they shalbe in senioritie of birth and to the heires of the bodie of every such sonne lawfullie begotten respectively And for default of such issue to my youngest sonne Edward Browne during his life and after his decease to the vse and behoofe of the first sonne of the bodie of my said sonne Edward Browne lawfullie begotten and to the heires of the bodie of such first sonne lawfullie begotten and for default of such issue to the vse and behoofe of the second sonne of the bodie of my said sonne Edward Browne lawfully begotten and to the heires of the bodie of such second sonne lawfullie begotten And for default of such issue to the vse and behoofe of the third sonne of the bodie of my said sonne Edward Browne lawfullie begotten and to the heires of the body of such third sonne lawfullie begotten And for default of such issue to the vse and behoofe of every other sonne of the bodie of my said sonne Edward Browne lawfullie begotten successively one after another as they shalbe in seniority of birth and to the heires of the bodie of every such sonne lawfullie begotten respectively And for default of such issue to my said sonne George Browne during his life and after his decease to the vse and behoofe of the first sonne of the bodie of my said sonne George lawfullie begotten and to the heires of the bodie of such first sonne lawfully begotten And for default of such issue to the vse and behoofe of the second sonne of the bodie of my said sonne George Browne lawfullie begotten and to the heires of the bodie of such second sonne lawfullie begotten And for default of such issue to the vse and behoofe of the third sonne of the bodie of my said sonne George Browne lawfullie begotten and to the heires of the bodie of such third sonne lawfullie begotten And for default of such issue to the vse and behoofe of every other sonne of my said sonne George Browne lawfullie begotten successively one after another as they shalbe in seniority of birth and to the heires of the bodie of every such sonne lawfullie begotten respectively And for default of such issue to my said two daughters Mary Stury and Apoline Browne her sister and to their heires and assignes for ever And whereas by my said Deed of Feoffement vnder my hand and seale bearing date as aforesaid I have among other things therein contained given granted and confirmed vnto the said Timothy Leving Thomas Moorton William Prince and John Stanley their heires and assignes all that my said Manno^r or Lordshipp of Hungerie Benteley and the two closes adioyninge therein menc'oned and all the said Parke called Middleton Parke al's Barton old Parke in the Countie of Darby To the vse intent and purpose That my said sonnes Edmond Browne and Edward Browne shall and maie yearly during theire lives severallie have and take either of them an annuitie or yearely rent charge of fiftie pound a yeare out of the premisses in Hungrie Bently Barton and Langford aforesaid to be paid yearely at such tyme and tymes and to such further vse intent and purpose and with such severall clauses of distresse and distresses as in and by the said Deed of Feoffem^t more fullie appeareth And where further by the said Deed of Feoffem^t I have power and it is provided thereby that it shall and maie be lawfull to and for me the said Thomas Browne at any tyme or tymes by my deed or last will and Testament in writing to graunt lymitt or appoint any rent charge or rent charges to every or any or as many of my children for the term or terms of their severall lives or yeares respectively out of all or any of the p$^r$misses as to me the said Thomas Browne shall seeme good as in and by the said deed of Feoffement it doth appeare Now therefore accordinge to the power I have by the said deed and provisoe aforesaid I doe by this my last will and Testament give will and devise graunt lymitt and appoint vnto my said sonne William Browne one annuity or rent charge of fiftie pounds of lawfull money of England yearely duringe the term of his naturall life to be by him receaved and taken out of the premisses in Hungary Bentley Langford and Barton aforesaid or in any part or parcell thereof to be paid yearely at the Feast daies of S$^t$ Michaell tharchangell and the annunciac'on of our blessed Virgin Marie by even and equall porcon's the first payment thereof to begin at the first of the said feast daies w$^{ch}$ shall next happen after my decease And I doe hereby will give graunt lymitt and appoint that if the said annuity or yearly rent charge of fiftie pounds or any part thereof to be behinde and vnpaid in part or in all after any of the said Feasts at w$^{ch}$ it ought to be paid as aforesaid that then and from thenceforth it shall and maie be lawfull to and for the said William Browne and his assignes into all and singuler the premisses in Hungrie Benteley Langford and Barton aforesaid to enter and distrayne and the distresse and distresses then and there found to leade drive carry awaie and impound and inpound to keepe till aft the said annuitie or yearly rent charge and of the arrerage thereof they shalbe well and trulie contented and paid And my will and mind is that as well my said sonne William Browne as alsoe my said sonne Edward Browne maie either of them have receave take and enioy theire said severall annuitie or yearely charge of fiftie poundes apeece as aforesaid respectively lymitted and appointed to either of them according to the tenor and effect of the said deed and of this my present last will and Testament Provided nevertheless and vpon condic'on that if the said William Browne and Edward Browne my sonnes or either of them shall graunt sett lett or assigne theire said severall annuities or yearly rent charge of fiftie pounds apeece as aforesaid lymitted and appointed to either of them or any part thereof to any person or persons whatsoever for any terme or termes whatsoever or that the said annuities or rent charge of either of them or any part thereof shalbe at any time hereafter by the negligence or default of them or either of them extended Or that my said sonnes Will'm Browne and Edward Browne or either of them shall doe suffer or consent vnto any act or thing whereby the annuities of them or either of them or any part of them shalbe forfeited That then the said graunt and disposic'on of the said annuities contayned either in the said Feoffement or in this my last will & Testament and every clause and article concerning the same shalbe void frustrate and of none effect to or for either of them my sonnes by whom and by and through whose neglect or default any such act or acts thinge or things shalbe done or suffered to be done whereby the said annuities or rent charge of them or either of them or any part thereof shalbe graunted sett lett assigned be extended or forfeited as aforesaid And I will that if any my above named children in this my will sonnes or daughters goe about or endeavo$^r$ to impugne or make void this my last Will and Testament or hinder the due execuc'on thereof Then such child or children shalbe barred from takeinge any benefitt thereby anythinge therein contained to the contrary notw$^{th}$standing.

*(To be continued.)*

---

## REGISTER EXTRACTS FROM THE GIBSON FAMILY BIBLE.*

Anne, D$^r$ of W$^m$ & Mary Kent, born y$^e$ 10$^{th}$ Sept$^r$ 1690. Married 14$^{th}$ Sept$^r$ 170$\frac{8}{9}$.

Anne, Daughter of John & Anne Haynes, born y$^e$ 22$^d$ Sept$^r$ 1710, between 10 & 11 in y$^e$ forenoon ; and Baptized y$^e$ 5$^{th}$ of October 1710. W$^m$ Turton of Cliffords Inn, Gent$^n$; Godfather. M$^{rs}$ Rebekah Hussey of Chelsea, Wid. ; M$^{rs}$ Anne Bateman of Whitehall, Godmothers. Dyed at Chelsea 20$^{th}$ July 1717 at near 11 at night, aged 6 years & 10 months. Dear Child !

Mary, Daughter of John & Anne Haynes, born y$^e$ 16 Sept$^r$ 1713, near 1 in the afternoon, was Baptized Octob$^r$ y$^e$ 6$^{th}$ 1713. Edw$^d$ Tenison, Esq$^r$, Godfather. Lady Keat, Wid., & M$^{rs}$ Vincent in ffleet St., Godmothers.

Thomas, Son of John Haynes & Anne his Wife, born y$^e$ 26$^{th}$ of Apr$^l$ 1715, abo$^t$ 12 in the night, was Baptized May y$^e$ 11$^{th}$ 1715 by the Rev$^d$ M$^r$ Benjamin Ibbot, Chapl$^n$ to y$^e$ Abp. of Canterbury, as were also Anne & Mary. Dyed at Chelsea 24$^{th}$ Dec$^r$. Buried 27$^{th}$ Dec$^r$ 1728, aged 13 y$^{rs}$, 7 mo., 26 days. Rob$^t$ Clavering, Clk., Dean of Bocking ; Thomas Bateman, Gent$^n$, Godfathers. Susana Faulkener, Wid., Godmother.

The three foregoing children were born at Lambeth.

* Communicated by CHARLES DALTON, Esq., F.R.G.S.

Elizabeth, Daughter of John & Anne Haynes, born in Lawrence St. in Chelsea y^e 26^th of February 1717, being Ash Wedn'sday,. abo^t 12 at noon, was Baptized March y^e 7^th 1717 by the Rev^d D^r John King, Rector of Chelsea in Middx. afores'd. Dyed y^e 22^d of Apr^l 1718, after 6 at night. The Rev^d D^r Edw^d Tenison, God-father. M^rs Anne Culliford; M^rs Constance Bishop, Godmothers.

Mary, Second Daughter of John & Anne Haynes, was marry'd to Thomas Gibson Jan^y 7^th 173⅘. He dyed Apr^l 15, 1742, aged 31. She Dec. 6^th 1763, aged 50. Their Issue:—

Margaret, born Oct^r 12^th 1735. Baptized Nov^r 4^th 1735. M^r Haynes & M^rs Gibson (Bishop's lady) & Miss Gibson, Sponsors. Died May 31^st 1744, Bury'd at Chelsea June 2^nd.

Elizabeth, Born Jan^y 25^th 1737. Bap. Feb. 16^th 1737. Bishop, his Lady, & M^rs Bettesworth, Sponsors. Died March 14^th 1766, Bury'd at Fulham March 22^nd.

Mary, born March 19^th 173⅘. Baptized Apr^l 13^th 1739. M^r Haynes, M^rs Tyrwhitt, & Miss J. Gibson, Sponsors. Died Jan^y 25^th & was bury'd at Chelsea Jan^y 28, 173₄₆⁹.

Edmund, Born April 3^rd 1740. Bap. May 1^st. Bishop, his Lady, & D^r Bettes-worth, Sponsors. Marry'd to Miss Mary Ann Gastine Feb^y 5^th 1765.

Jane, born Feb. 20^th 174⁰. Bap. March 20^th 174₁⁰. D^r Tyrwhitt, Miss Gibson, & Miss J. Gibson, Sp^rs. Marry'd M^r Joseph Nicholson Dec. 14^th 1768. Died July 24 & and was bury'd in Hackney Church July 29, 1777.

Ann, born Sept^r 8^th 1742. Bap. Oct^r 1^st 1742. M^r E. Gibson, Miss Gibson, & Miss J. Gibson, Sp^rs. Marry'd to Mr. J. Dorville Ap^l 14^th 1763.

Edmund, the only son of Thomas & Mary Gibson, was marry'd to Miss Mary Ann Gastine Feb^y 5, 1765. She was born Feb^y 21^st 1744. Their issue:—

Mary-Ann, Born Ap^l 20^th & Bap. May 12^th 1766. M^r G. Gibson, M^rs Gastine, & Sister Dorville, Sponsors. Dy'd Jan^y 29^th & was bury'd at Marybone Jan^y 31^st 1767. (N.B. born in Jermyn St., St. James's.)

Jane, Born Aug^st 6^th. Bap. Aug^st 27^th 1767. M^r Gastine, M^rs Wilson, & Sister J. Gibson, Sponsors. Dyed May 9^th & was bury'd at Bishop's Stortford May 13^th 1769. (N.B. born in Dufours Court, Broad St., St. James's.)

Frances, Born March 5^th. Bap. March 25^th 1769. M^r Dorville, M^rs Scott, & M^rs G. Gibson, Sponsors. (N.B. born in James Street, Golden Square, St. James's.) Marry'd to Rev^d N. I. Hill March 16^th 1790.

Elizabeth, Born March 25^th. Bap. Ap^l 15^th 1772. D^r Wilson, M^rs Gastine, & Sister Dorville, Sponsors. (N.B. Born in Rathbone Place, St. Mary-le-Bon.) Marry'd to Rev^d Jonathan Lipyeatt, Jun^r, Sept^r 17, 1793.

Maria, Born in Rathbone Place Nov^r 25^th. Bap. Dec. 15^th 1773. M^r R. Gibson, M^rs Gastine, & Sister Dorville, Sponsors. Marry'd to Rev^d James Dalton Dec. 4, 1794.

Rebecca, Born in Rathbone Place Feb^y 27^th. Bap. March 19^th 1776. M^r T. Tyrwhitt, M^rs Gastine, & Sister Dorville, Sponsors. Died Ap^l 29^th & was bury'd at Mary-bone May 3^rd 1779.

Mary Ann Gibson, the excellent mother of the above children, died May 27 & was bury'd at Mary-Bone June 4^th 1779. "An Unspotted Life is Old Age."

The said Edm^d married to his second Wife Miss Ann Savage Sep^r 19^th 1780. Their issue :—

Edmund, Born in Marlboro' St., St. James's, June 1. Bap. June 26^th 1782. M^r Dorville, M^r J. Lipyeatt, Sen^r, & M^rs Savage, Sponsors. Died April 30^th & was bury'd at Mary-bone May 3, 1783.

The Rev^d Edmund Gibson died Feb^y 3^d 1798, aged 57. He was buried in the family vault of his grand-father Bishop Gibson at Fulham. "The souls of the righteous are in the hand of God." Wis. Ch. 3.

His second wife Ann Gibson died at Swindon in the County of Wiltshire 29 May 1837, aged 86, & was buried at Purton in the same county.

DR. THOMAS GIBSON'S COMMISSION AS PHYSICIAN GENERAL OF THE ARMY.

(From a copy in the Public Record Office.)

GEORGE R.

George, &c.   To Our Trusty & well beloved D[r] Thomas Gibson greeting.   We reposing especial trust in your experience, prudence, & ability do by these presents constitute & appoint you to be Physician General of Our Land Forces raised, & to be raised, for Our Service.   You are therefore carefully & diligently to discharge the duty of Physician General by doing & performing all, & all manner of things, thereunto belonging.   And you are to observe & follow such orders & directions from time to time as you shall receive from Us, or any other your superior officer, according to the rules & discipline of war.   Given at Our Court at St. James's the twenty-third day of January 171⅜ in the fifth year of Our Reign.   By His Majesty's commands.

J. CRAGGS.

# Genealogy of the Family of Harvey, etc.*

## NOTES.

(1) Said to have been *granted* by Segar to *Sir Daniel Harvey*, but which could not have been the case, inasmuch as the former died when the latter was only about two years of age; the misstatement probably arising from an entry of the blazon *as belonging to Sir* (?) *Daniel* being among the dockets of Segar's Grants at the College of Arms, which does not necessarily shew more than that he had some title to such arms.   Moreover, the family previously bore the same quarterly with their ancient coat.   So that, if by Segar, the grant must have been in confirmation only, and to some earlier member of the family.

(1A) The Parish Register not commencing until 1635, the dates of earlier burials at Folkestone cannot be ascertained therefrom.

(2) He had three sisters and a brother, all married and had issue.   The brother's children were Thomas, Joane, and Elizabeth Harvey, all living 12 June 1623.

(3) The Pepperers' was the original of the Grocers' Company of London.

(4) So pronounced, and which would account for the *hawks* in the Family Arms.

(5) There, in the parish church, the inscription on the memorial brass quaintly describes her as a " godly harmles Woman, a chast loveing Wife, a charitable qviet Neighbovr, a cofortable frendly Matron, a prvident diligent Hvswyfe, a carefvll t'ederharted Mother, deere to her Hvsband, reverensed of her Children, beloved of her neighbovrs, elected of God."   This inscription many suppose to have been the veritable production of her son, the great physician himself, and that the brass was erected at his instance; but there is far more reason for believing that the same owe their origin to her husband, who was then living.

(6) As a mark of honour, and not for the study of the law.   Brady (*Visitor's Guide to Knole*, 1839, p. 23), in referring to Thomas, 1st Lord Buckhurst's admission to the Inner Temple (*temp.* Eliz.), states that it was " then fashionable for every young man of fortune, before he began his travels, or was admitted into Parliament, to be initiated in the study of the law."   The latter part of the statement is, however, incorrect.   It was certainly customary in those days for elder sons of our gentle families to obtain formal admission to an Inn of Court, but if they went there it was more frequently only for social and residential purposes, to form acquaintances and friendships which might lead to their future advancement, and for an introduction to the world of London life: these Inns having apparently then occupied in a great measure the place of the modern West-End Clubs.   And until recently comparatively few of those admitted to our Inns of Courts were called to the Bar.

(7) All burials named herein as "at Hempstead" were in the Family Vault beneath Harvey Chapel; those prior to 1766 being in the "outer," and subsequently in the "inner" chamber. Several of the coffins have, however, since been misplaced.

(8) It would appear from Payne-Fisher's *Cat. of Tombs in London Churches*, 1666, that there was a M.I. to Dr. Harvey "the [most] famous Physician of his time," and to his brother Daniel " of Folkston " in one of our City churches—probably St. Laurence Pountney—before the Great Fire.   He also mentions another (in this, as in all instances, without naming the church) to "M[ris] Mary Harvie, wife of the late Eliab H., Esq.; and both father and mother of the now Sir Eliab H., Knight-B[art.];" but which could not have been at St. Laurence Pountney, inasmuch as she not die until 1673, being buried with M.I. at Hempstead, and when the church in question was not extant.   The reference, however, shews that the book was partly compiled, and issued, long after the date it bears.

* Continued from p. 365.

(9) The compiler was among the select few present in the small Harvey Chapel on this memorable occasion, but took no part in the ceremony. And during his sojourn in the neighbourhood carefully copied, under great difficulties, the numerous coffin inscriptions in the family vault, as well as the monumental inscriptions and arms in the Chapel above, and (by kind permission of the Rev. Mr. Eustace, a relative of the family) the Harvey entries in the Parish Register, communicating the results, with copious notes, to the *Miscellanea Genealogica et Heraldica* (2nd Series, Vol. I., pp. 357—62 and 384—88). It may be here mentioned that, where differing from such previous notes, this genealogy should be taken as the most correct.

(10) It was, however (with the exception of the Codicil), evidently made some time previously, *i.e.* between 10 July 1651 and May 1655, when his brother Daniel's wife died—probably shortly after the former date. And was drawn by his "coosin" (nephew) Heneage Finch, afterwards Earl of Nottingham, and Lord Chancellor, to whom he therein bequeaths £100 " for his paines counsell and advice about the contriving" of it. It should be noted that nephews and nieces were at that time frequently also termed cousins—a fact the knowledge of which will prove alike interesting and valuable to Antiquaries, and clear up many a doubt, but which it is believed has never previously been mentioned in print.

(11) So borne on his monument at Hempstead.

(11A) The doctor's autograph is of extreme rarity, as the following note by a well-known authority in such matters, inserted in the *Album Amicorum* of Phillip de Glarges 1636-41, now in the Brit. Mus. (Add. MS. 23,105), and from which the Latin specimen facsimiled below, dated 8 May 1641, is copied, will testify: " No. 521 of the Sypistien Sale, where I bought it, principally because it contains the autograph of one of the most illustrious men that ever existed—Harvey, who discovered the Circulation of the Blood; and I never could find that his handwriting is to be seen anywhere else tho' I have inquired in all directions. D. T. [Dawson-Turner]." The volume, which formed lot 657 at the latter's sale, 10 June 1859, also contains another note, apparently by the same hand: " It has been commonly supposed that much of Harvey's autograph

is to be found in the College of Physicians, or in Caius College, Cambridge, or in St. Bartholomew's Hospital; but I believe there is no authentic specimen of it in any of these; and the late Sir Henry Halford told me, not long before his death, that, as far as he had been able to find, this is the only undoubted one in existence. Where is Dr. Paget's Letter to me about Harvey ? " These authorities were, however, to a great extent in error, for not only is his signature to be found among the Rupert Correspondence in Brit. Mus. Add. MS. 18,980, fo. 125, dated 17 Oct. 1643, and from which our other specimen is copied, but his MS. on the circulation of the blood, now in the Sloane Collection, is holograph, as are undoubtedly also three of the four pages and the signatures of his will and codicil in P.C.C., for we have his own evidence therein to that effect; and the compiler, during many years spent in collecting literary rarities, has met with two other specimens of his signature.

(12) Her will was proved in Commissary Court of London 1608.

(13) The Parish Register of this date not being extant, it cannot unfortunately be ascertained whether the marriage took place at " St. Sepulchre's " *as named in the Licence.* Probably it did (although marriage licences were formerly comparatively seldom complied with in such respect), as both parties resided in the immediate neighbourhood, where, it should be remembered, the College of Physicians then stood. There is no record of the union in the Register of the adjoining Parish Church of St. Martin, Ludgate.

(14) There was a grant to him of a pension of £50 per annum on resigning his place of King's Footman to Toby Johnson, 6 July 1620.

(15) His will, dated 28 June 1636, was proved 22 Feb. following (P.C.C., Goare 14).

(16) Otherwise variously written *Coom, Coomb, Comb, Combe Nevill, Combe Neville, Combe Neovill,* and *Comb Park.* This manor, which was purchased by Sir Daniel of Charles, Viscount Cullen, eld. s. of Sir Wm. Cokaine, *c.* 1652, and sold by the Harveys in 1753 to the Trustees of John Spencer, Esq. (then a minor, and afterwards 1st Earl Spencer), has been frequently confounded with Combe in Croydon, with which the family were also at one period connected.

(17) The earliest Harvey burial entered in Hempstead Burial Register, the same not commencing until April 1665.

(18) Their children at date of his will were Richard (? by his first wife), William, and Benjamin Steele.

(19) He was a Merchant as early as 6 Jan. 1638-9 (Lewes Roberts' *Merchants Mappe of Commerce* 1638), if not in 1637, and is probably identical with the John Harvey of London, Merchant, who was of parish of St. Andrew Undershaft, and buried at St. Helen's in the North Quire 24 Oct. 1701, leaving a wife Mary surviving—will dated 10 Oct. 1701, proved 10 Nov. following (P.C.C., Dyer 154). There was a John Harvey, Merchant, in Bishopsgate Ward 1640 (see the compiler's *List of the Principal Inhabitants of the City of London,* 1640, in *Miscellanea Genealogica*

*et Heraldica*, 2nd Series, Vol. II., p. 37). And a John Harvey, Merchant, of Beerbinder Lane, appears in the first London Directory 1677.

(20) Sir Daniel and Sir Eliab Harvey were knighted same day by Charles II., on his first coming over. They, and Edward Harvey of Combe (who was not even knighted), have frequently been described in error as Baronets.

(21) Said by some English Historians to have been "sent" there as Ambassador, 13 Aug. 1668, which was probably the date of his departure from England. There is a copy of his commission in British Museum (Add. MS. 28,937, fo. 120).

(22) Then described as "of Parish of St. James's, Westminster." Below is a facsimile of her signature, 3 Aug. 1699, from Brit. Mus. Add. MS. 22,910, fo. 485.

(23) The Earldom of Nottingham has been united with that of Winchelsea since 1729, when, upon the death of John, 5th Earl of Winchelsea, unmarried, that title devolved on Daniel, 2nd Earl of Nottingham. This Daniel's next younger brother, Heneage, was created Earl of Aylesford 19 Oct 1714.

(24) She appears to have received from her father-in-law a marriage portion of £3000.

(25) The "anecdote" has been narrated by Hasted (*History of Kent*) and his copyists, but very incorrectly as to date and circumstances, and without the name of the husband. The secret marriage, which doubtless took place, appears to have been *illegally* dissolved.

(26) A lady of great personal beauty. Her monumental epitaph was written by Dryden. She had three daughters by her 1st husband, Sir Thomas Whitmore.

(27) By his will he directed a monument to be erected for him in Hempstead Church (then called a "Chapel"), after the model of that in Putney Church for Sir Tho. Dawes, at a cost not exceeding £100, and which monument was subsequently placed on the East wall of the Harvey Chapel, in compliance therewith.

(28) Entered in Parish Register of St. Giles as buried *there* 28 Nov. 1701.

(29) The marriage portion was £10,000, according to a letter of 20 July 1658, from Rachell, Lady Newport, to her brother Sir R. Leveson, in possession of the Duke of Sutherland. She resided in the house of her nephew, Nicholas Breton, at Norton, near Daventry, co. Northampton, after her husband's death.

(30) The earliest burial in the Harvey vault at Hempstead.

(31) She had licence (Fac. Off. Abp. Cant.) 5 July 1676 to marry Ralph Freeman (of Aspeden, co. Hertford), Bachelor, "*aged about* 10" (!), she herself being then but *little over 8 years* (! !). Doubtless the marriage never took place, and probably he died before her union with Eliab Harvey in 1680, when she was but 12½ years of age. And it appears from the entry in the Vicar-General's Book at Somerset House (fo. 410) as to her having been on examination 13 July 1681 found to be *a virgin*, and obtained licence to marry William Harvey, that such first marriage was not consummated. Her parentage, age, and marriage have hitherto been involved in much doubt and mystery.

(32) M.I. states in error "2 September."

(33) M.I. states "aged 48," but her coffin inscription "æt. 43," which is correct.

(34) By death of his elder brother Eliab he became eldest son and heir.

(35) In the room of Sir Henry Maynard, deceased.

(36) Died 25 Dec. (*Gent. Mag.*)

(37) The burial carelessly omitted in the parish register.

(38) She appears to have been his "pretty cozin Mistress Mary Harvey," his "wife's goddaughter," mentioned in will of Sir William Whitmore 12 Nov. 1695.

(39) She is described therein as "of Hamels in parish of Braughing, co. Hertford."

(40) Died 10 June. (*Gent. Mag.*)

(41) Berry (*Essex Pedigrees*) states 14 Aug.

(42) Died 25 April. (*Gent. Mag.*)

(42A) Entered R.N. 1769, and was in constant and active service in America, the West Indies, and the Channel for forty years. Particularly distinguished at the Battle of Trafalgar, where he commanded the *Téméraire* of 98 guns, Nelson's supporting ship. Dismissed the service, May 1809, but restored by an Order in Council, March the following year. With his death the family became extinct in the male line.

(42B) The latest burial in the Harvey vault.

(42C) Married 14 May. (*Gent. Mag.*)

(43) Born 8 Nov. (*Gent. Mag.*)

(44) Born 11 Aug. (*Gent. Mag.*)

(45) Niece of Thomas Grosvenor of Walthamstow, co. Essex, and Cavendish Square, co. Middx., Esq., M.P. for co. Chester.

(45A) In consequence of a fall from her carriage in Hainault Forest.

(46) Entered in Hempstead Burial Register as "Harriott" Harvey.

(46A) Horace Walpole describes him as "bred a Tory," but "very sensible."

(47) His will orders this to be done by his executors at a cost not exceeding £200. It was, however, carried out in his lifetime, two years subsequently.

(48) Died 10 Sept. (*Gent. Mag.*)

(49) Not entered in the parish register.

(50) Said to have died abroad, which would account for the delay in burial.

(51) They were a pattern of conjugal affection, and it is stated were entitled to, if they did not actually receive, the Dunmow flitch of bacon. (*Gent. Mag.*, 1836, p. 550.)

(52) The manors of Clyfton Mabanke, Bradford, and Wyke were purchased by Eliab Harvey, of London, Esq., 3 Dec. 1649. The deed of feoffment, dated 26 Feb. 1649-50, from Henry Rogers of Canington, co. Somerset, Esq., and Edward Phillipps of Mountague, same county, Esq., granting the same with other lands adjoining, in consideration of £21,300, is in the compiler's possession. Hutchins' *Dorset*, however, gives the date of purchase of the first-named estate as "about *1660*"—"from . . . . Hungerford, by *Michael* Harvey." From the above-mentioned deed the facsimile of this Eliab Harvey's signature is taken.

(53) His will (an extremely long one), dated 5 Dec. 1657, was proved 29 April 1658 (P.C.C., Wotton 147).

(54) M.I. states in error "ob. æt. 50," whereas she is described in marriage licence (1664) as "aged 16." Her age at death was 69 or 70.

(55) He was godson to Dr. William Harvey, after whom he was named.

(56) "A weak man, strongly attached to the interest of the Stuart family." (Manning and Bray, *Surrey*, i., 402.) In a note to an entry of 20 May 1705 in Evelyn's 'Diary,' ed. Bray, he is termed "a violent Tory."

(57) His arms were: Argent, a chevron between three escallops sable.

(58) His arms were: Argent, on a chief gules two bucks' heads cabossed or.

(59) Then described as "of parish of St. Anne, Westminster." She mentions in codicil her "daughter Lady Hinchingbrooke," then living.

(60) Burke (*Landed Gentry*, 1886) gives her name as "Mary," in error.

(61) Intended to have been married to Rebecca Wolstenholme (afterwards his brother Michael's wife) had not death prevented.

(61A) He bore the ancient and modern family arms quarterly (as did Dr. Harvey), according to an impression of his armorial seal, impaling his wife's arms, on a deed, dated 25 March 1718, in the compiler's possession; and from which deed his facsimile signature is taken.

(62) The parish register states "buried 5 Dec. 1691," and the coffin inscription "deceased 1 Jan. 1691 [1692]." The date of burial having doubtless been entered in error for 5 Jan.

(63) Then described as "of Broad Street in the parish of St. James, Westminster, co. Middx."

(64) Coffin inscription gives her age incorrectly as "47."

(65) Died in his twenty-fifth year. M.I. states in error "aged 22 years." Not buried at Hempstead.

(66) Born 23 Dec. (Coffin and Mon. Ins.)

(67) She and her five sisters were coheiresses of their father.

(68) Not "Georgina," as sometimes stated.

---

HARVEY (or HERVEY) FAMILY.—The undersigned, Compiler of the above communication, having, as a labour of love, long been engaged in collecting materials, chiefly from original sources, for (*inter alia*) a History of the *various* important families of the name, will be glad to hear direct from any one interested therein, or who may be able and willing to afford information for the purpose of such undertaking, either by the loan of any deeds, documents, papers, or otherwise. And also to hear from members of the same families, and their connections by marriage, and others, both in this country and America, who may be desirous of joining, or of otherwise promoting the objects of a Society (similar to those in the United States) about to be formed for collecting and printing everything of interest relating to the family history—for forming a bond of fellowship between the members, and for their periodical meeting together, etc.

*Heathell, Melbourne Grove, Champion Hill, S.E.*        W. J. HARVEY, F.S.A. Scot.

---

# The Register Book of Bramfield, co. Suffolk.*

### 1842.

Jan. 7    James Wells s. of Robert and Maria Hadingham, Farmer.

Jan. 9    Anna d. of Robert and Mariann Saker, Laborer.

Jan. 11    Thomas s. of Robert and Maria Hadingham, Farmer.

Jan. 16    Denniss s. of Samuel and Sarah Smith, Laborer.

Jan. 30    Emma d. of Stephen and Maria Kemp, Laborer.

Mar. 13    Alfred s. of John and Charlotte Bezant, Cordwainer.

Mar. 29    Edward Albert s. of Mary Ann Barnaby, Spinster.

* Continued from p. 369.

| | |
|---|---|
| April 17 | Mary Charlotte d. of Joseph and Charlotte Sillett, Innkeeper. |
| May 15 | John s. of John & Jemima Gold, Shoemaker. |
| May 15 | Julia d. of John and Lucy Browne, Miller. |
| May 15 | Esau s. of Esau and Harriet Howard, Laborer. |
| Oct. 9 | Sarah d. of William and Lucy Lines, Laborer. |
| Oct. 23 | Hannah d. of Robert and Mary Gilman, Laborer. |
| Nov. 24 | George s. of Stephen and Mary Self, Laborer. |
| Dec. 9 | Eunice d. of Mary Ann Gilbert, Spinster. |
| Dec. 18 | William s. of John and Mary Ann Tennant, Dealer. |

### 1843.

| | |
|---|---|
| Jan. 4 | James s. of Robert and Maria Hadingham, Farmer. |
| Feb. 24 | Robert s. of Robert and Mary Anne Dale, Farmer. |
| Feb. 25 | Elizabeth d. of James and Harriet Clarke, Laborer. |
| Feb. 26 | Sarah Ann d. of Charles and Elizabeth Kemp, Laborer. |
| Mar. 5 | Elizabeth d. of William and Harriet Cupper, Shoemaker. |
| Mar. 8 | Hannah d. of William and Hannah Tuthill, Laborer. |
| Mar. 29 | Alfred William s. of Maria Hurren, Spinster. |
| April 23 | William s. of Robert and Charlotte Hurren, Laborer. |
| June 11 | Maria Anne d. of William and Elizabeth Winter, Farmer. |
| July 9 | Isabel d. of William Aldis and Elizabeth Higham, Farmer. |
| July 27 | Elizabeth d. of James and Charlotte Powells, Laborer. |
| Aug. 13 | Edna d. of Robert and Maria Shade, Laborer. |
| Sep. 10 | Jehoshaphat s. of William and Susan Whitman, Laborer. |
| Sep. 12 | Frederick Charles s. of George and Hannah Whiting, Farmer. |
| Oct. 8 | William s. of William and Mary Ann Haken, Laborer. |
| Oct. 29 | Mary d. of Samuel and Lucy Coolier, Laborer. |
| Nov. 15 | Elizabeth d. of John and Sarah Markham, Laborer. |
| Dec. 17 | Thomas Porter Webster s. of Charlotte Porter, Spinster. |
| Dec. 18 | Mary Ann d. of Elizabeth Becket, Spinster. |

### 1844.

| | |
|---|---|
| Jan. 15 | Maria d. of James and Mary Kemp, Laborer. |
| Feb. 11 | Mary Ann d. of John and Harriet Johnson, Laborer. |
| Feb. 11 | William s. of Mary Ann Lame, Spinster. |
| Mar. 17 | Charlotte d. of William and Mary Ann Button, Laborer. |

| | |
|---|---|
| April 21 | Elizabeth d. of William and Mary Debney, Grocer. |
| May 11 | Samuel s. of George and Mary Ann Lines, Laborer. |
| June 16 | Ellin d. of Isaac and Martha Aldred, Laborer. |
| June 16 | Mary Ann d. of the same. |
| June 16 | Ellin d. of Simon and Sophia Lenny, Laborer. |
| July 10 | Sarah Lucy d. of James and Sarah Croft, Miller. |
| Aug. 9 | Eliza d. of Charles and Charlotte Masterson, Laborer. |
| Aug. 25 | Charles s. of John and Mary Wyatt, Laborer. |
| Sep. 29 | Samuel s. of Charles and Sarah Catling, Shoemaker. |

### 1845.

| | |
|---|---|
| Jan. 17 | William s. of Joshua and Jemima Newman, Carpenter. |
| Jan. 17 | Samuel s. of James and Hannah Cross, Farmer. |
| Mar. 9 | Maria d. of William and Mary Ann Kerridge, Laborer. |
| Mar. 14 | Martha d. of Samuel and Caroline Mills, Laborer. |
| Mar. 18 | Ephraim s. of Esau and Harriet Haward, Laborer. |
| June 29 | Sarah d. of William and Harriet Cupper, Shoemaker. |
| June 29 | Alfred s. of Ephraim and Zipporah Hillen, Laborer. |
| June 29 | James s. of Zipporah Lenny, Spinster. |
| July 26 | Mariann d. of Marianne Borrett, Spinster. |
| Aug. 3 | George s. of William and Elizabeth Dugdell, Shoemaker. |
| Aug. 11 | William s. of Stephen and Mary Self, Laborer. |
| Aug. 17 | Robert s. of George and Emily Flatt, Laborer. |
| Sep. 15 | Alice d. of Elizabeth Beckett, Spinster. |
| Sep. 21 | Benjamin s. of Benjamin and Eliza Goodchild, Laborer. |
| Oct. 19 | Mariann d. of Septime Lenny, Spinster. |
| Oct. 19 | Harriett Ann d. of John and Septime Finch, Laborer. |
| Oct. 30 | Alfred s. of Daniel and Sarah Smith, Laborer. |
| Nov. 14 | William s. of John and Ann Spindler, Laborer. |
| Nov. 16 | Maria d. of William and Mariann Button, Laborer. |
| Nov. 23 | Martha d. of James and Harriet Reeve, Laborer. |
| Dec. 16 | George s. of George and Mary Ann Lines, Laborer. |

### 1846.

| | |
|---|---|
| Jan. 14 | William Joseph s. of Charles and Elizabeth Kemp, Laborer. |
| Jan. 16 | Charles William s. of Emily Browne, Spinster. |
| Feb. 6 | William s. of Mary Hurren, Spinster. |
| Feb. 15 | Albert George s. of Mary Ann Smith, Spinster. |
| Feb. 22 | Harriet d. of William and Lucy Lines, Laborer. |

Mar. 19 Albert s. of Isaac and Martha Aldred, Laborer.
April 12 George s. of William and Mariann Haken, Laborer.
April 19 Elizabeth d. of James and Sarah Croft, Miller.
May 3 George William s. of George Thomas Grayston and Sophia Kitson, Gardener.
May 10 William s. of Samuel and Lucy Coolier, Laborer.
May 10 Albert s. of George and Rachael Grey, Joiner.
May 31 Samuel s. of Robert and Mary Gilman, Laborer.
June 7 William s. of Samuel and Mary Anne Smith, Laborer.
June 14 Betsy d. of Robert and Maria Shade, Laborer.
June 28 Eliza d. of Stephen and Maria Kemp, Laborer.
July 5 Isabella d. of Daniel and Phœbe Dale, Laborer.
Sep. 30 George s. of Charles and Elizabeth Kemp, Laborer. Privately.
Oct. 4 Jemima d. of James and Hannah Cross, Farmer.
Oct. 11 Samuel s. of George and Hannah Kerridge, Laborer.
Nov. 1 Frederick of William and Susan Whitman, Laborer; by N. Simons, Vicar.
Nov. 8 Ellen of Henry and Susan Balls, Laborer.
Nov. 8 Betsy of the same.
Nov. 8 Mary of the same.
Dec. 6 Frederick William and Alice Mary of William and Mary Ann Andrews, Farmer.

1847.

Feb. 9 Simon of Simon and Sophia Lenny, Laborer.
Feb. 14 Sophia of the same.
June 6 Elizabeth of Esau and Harriet Haward, Laborer.
June 13 Maria of William and Lucy Lines, Laborer.
June 20 Sarah Ann of Isaac and Martha Aldred, Laborer.
July 4 William of Henry and Susan Balls, Laborer.
Aug. 1 Matilda of William and Mary Ann Andrews, Farmer.
Dec. 5 Maria of Frederick and Mary Ling, Farmer.
Dec. 12 Sarah Ann of Septima Lenny now Finch.
Dec. 12 Louisa of John and Septima Finch, Laborer.

1848.

May 7 Charlotte of James and Mary Ann Howling, Blacksmith.
June 4 Harriet of Stephen and Maria Kemp, Laborer.
July 21 John of George and Emily Flatt, Laborer.
July 30 Ann of James and Harriet Reeve, Laborer.

Aug. 20 Louisa Caroline of Charles and Caroline Haddingham, Miller.
Oct. 8 Richard of William & Mary Newson, Laborer.
Oct. 29 George Haddingham of William and Mary Ann Andrews, Farmer.
Nov. 12 Mary of Samuel and Lucy Collier, Laborer.
Nov. 19 William of Thomas and Emma Crowfoot, Laborer.
Nov. 19 Harriet Amelia of Jonathan and Louisa Rayner, Farmer.
Nov. 19 Jonathan of the same.
Nov. 19 Mary Louisa of the same.
Nov. 26 James of Charles and Charlotte Masterson, Laborer.
Nov. 26 William of the same.

1849.

Jan. 7 Henry of George and Hannah Kerridge, Laborer.
Mar. 4 Eliza of John and Harriet Johnson, Laborer.
May 2 James Cupper of Emma Tibbenham.
May 20 Ellen Eliza of James and Sarah Croft, Miller.
May 27 Esther of Esau and Harriet Haward, Laborer.
May 27 Emma Jane of George and Sarah Savage, Laborer.
July 15 Frederick of Frederick and Mary Ling, Farmer.
July 22 Thomas of William and Lucy Lynes, Laborer.
July 22 Eglon Fiske of William and Mary Newson, Laborer.
July 22 Matilda of John & Mary Ann Lynes, Laborer.
Aug. 5 George of Samuel and Mary Smith, Laborer.
Sep. 23 Martha of Rachel Chapman.
Sep. 23 Henry of Charles and Rachel Nunn, Laborer.
Nov. 4 Mary Eliza of George and Sarah Flatt, Laborer.
Nov. 4 Elizabeth Angelina of Rufus Marmaduke and Angelina Marsden, Carpenter.
Dec. 2 Thomas of Charles and Elizabeth Kemp, Laborer.
Dec. 2 Edgar of the same.
Dec. 4 Henry Samuel of George and Rachel Gray, Carpenter.
Dec. 30 Sarah Ann Turner, aged 11 years, of John and Hannah Reeder, of Walpole, Farmer.
Dec. 30 Ellen Clementia of Charles and Sarah Catling, Farmer.

1850.

Jan. 21 Ann Maria of John and Septima Finch, Laborer.
Feb. 3 Maria of Isaac and Martha Aldred, Laborer.
Feb. 10 James Manby of Samuel and Maria Smith, Laborer.
Feb. 24 Sarah Ann of Robert and Sarah Smith, Laborer.

June 9  Emma of William and Harriet Cupper, Cordwainer.
June 9  Harriet of the same.
June 23  Harriet of James and Harriet Reeve, Laborer.
June 28  James of William and Lucy Lynes, Laborer.
July 7  William George of George and Sarah Savage, Laborer.
July 7  Sarah Elizabeth of John and Betsy Savage, Laborer.
Sep. 20  Louisa of Samuel and Sarah Clarke, Laborer.
Nov. 10  Charles of Daniel and Phœbe Dale, Laborer.
Nov. 28  Ann of Ann Ling, singlewoman.
Dec. 2  Sarah Frances of Rufus Marmaduke and Angelina Marsden, Carpenter.
Dec. 15  Anna Maria of Jonathan and Louisa Rayner, Farmer.

### 1851.

Jan. 18  William of Sarah Bolton.
Feb. 16  Walter of Simon and Sophia Lenny, Laborer.
Feb. 16  Louisa of the same.
Feb. 16  Mary of John and Charlotte Moore, Laborer.
Feb. 16  George of the same.
Feb. 23  Hannah of George and Hannah Kerridge, Laborer.
Mar. 9  Harriet Ann of William and Mary Eades, Laborer.
Mar. 16  Samuel of Samuel and Lucy Collier, Laborer.
July 13  John of Thomas and Emma Crowfoot, Laborer.
July 27  George of William and Lucy Lynes, Laborer.
Aug. 3  Henry of Charles and Sarah Catling, Farmer.
Sep. 7  Margaret of James and Sarah Croft, Miller.
Sep. 2  William George of Hephziba Johnson.
Dec. 14  William of James and Elizabeth Kemp, Laborer.
Dec. 14  Maria of the same.

### 1852.

Jan. 11  William of John and Mary Ann Lynes, Laborer.
Jan. 11  Emma of George and Mary Ann Lynes, Laborer.
Jan. 11  William of Sophia Hammont.
Feb. 1  Harry of William and Emma Philpott, Laborer.
Mar. 7  James of Samuel and Mary Ann Smith, Laborer.
Mar. 21  John of Thomas and Sophia Lynes, Laborer.
April 11  James Alfred of William and Mary Ann Eade, Laborer.
April 18  William of Esau and Harriet Haward, Laborer.
May 2  George Edward of George and Sarah Flatt, Laborer.
May 10  Elizabeth of Robert and Sarah Agers, Innkeeper.
May 30  Emma of Letitia Watling.

May 30  Charlotte of the same.
June 6  Edwin Rufus of Rufus Marmaduke and Angelina Marsden, Carpenter.
Sep. 19  Mary Ann of Samuel and Maria Smith, Laborer.
Sep. 19  William Robert of Mary Ann Brown.
Dec. 5  Elizabeth Clementia of William and Mary Newson, Laborer.

### 1853.

Mar. 6  William of George and Hannah Kerridge, Laborer.
Mar. 13  James of William and Mary Ann Clark, Laborer.
Mar. 30  Henry of Betsy Winter of Beccles, widow.
April 16  Harry Wright of George and Lucy Ann Bezant, Blacksmith.
May 8  Mary Ann of Samuel and Susan Tuthill, Laborer.
May 8  Emma Matilda of Robert and Maria Tibbenham, Laborer.
May 15  Jane Ann of Jonathan and Louisa Rayner, Farmer.
June 26  Georgiana of James and Sarah Croft, Miller.
July 3  William of William and Harriet Cupper, Cordwainer.
July 3  Sarah of Samuel and Lucy Collier, Laborer.
July 12  Charles of Charles and Martha Harvey, Gardener.
Aug. 7  Elizabeth of Isaac and Martha Aldred, Laborer.
Aug. 7  Louisa of Mary Ludbrook, widow.
Aug. 13  Henry of Henry and Maria Larkings, Laborer.
Sep. 9  Frederick of John and Charlotte Bezant, Shoemaker.
Sep. 25  Betsy of John and Hannah Reader, Farmer.
Sep. 25  Emma of the same.
Sep. 25  Mary Ann of the same.
Oct. 23  Robert of Sarah Bolton, singlewoman.
Oct. 23  Joseph of the same.

### 1854.

April 2  Samuel Edward of Robert and Sarah Smith, Laborer.
July 23  Mary Elizabeth of George and Mary Winn, of London, Custom House Officer.
Aug. 13  Harriet of William and Mary Ann Clark, Laborer.
Aug. 20  Harriet of Eliza Smith, singlewoman.
Aug. 20  Amelia Wright of George and Lucy Ann Bezant, Blacksmith.
Sep. 10  Francis Samuel of John and Betsy Savage, Laborer.
Sep. 10  James of the same.
Sep. 10  Sarah Maria of George and Sarah Savage, Laborer.
Sep. 17  Susannah of Thomas and Emma Crowfoot, Laborer.
Oct. 15  Ellen Kate of Samuel and Katharine Burrell, Innkeeper.

## 1855.

May 27   Elizabeth Martha of George and Hannah Kerridge, Laborer.
July   8   Ellen of William and Harriet Cupper, Cordwainer.
July   8   Eleanor of Esau and Harriet Haward, Laborer.
July 12   William of David and Betsy Spindler, Laborer.
Aug. 26   Arthur of James and Sarah Kemp, Innkeeper.
Sep.   2   Charlotte of Thomas and Sophia Lynes, Laborer.
Sep.   8   Henry of Henry and Maria Larkins, Laborer.
Oct. 14   Ellen Maria of William and Ellen Ludbrook, Laborer.
Oct. 14   Edward Charles of the same.
Oct. 14   William of William and Lucy Lynes, Laborer.

## 1856.

Jan. 13   John of William and Elizabeth Watling, Laborer.
Feb.   3   Susan of Robert and Thyrza Peck, Laborer.
Feb. 24   Sarah Elizabeth of George and Sarah Flatt, Laborer.
April 13   Elizabeth of James and Elizabeth Kemp, Laborer.
April 13   Charles of the same.
April 13   Francis Ann of Henry and Ann Haward, Laborer.
April 13   Charles of the same.
April 20   Samuel of James and Jane Bolton, Laborer.
May 25   Frederick of Charles and Rachel Nunn, Laborer.
June   8   Sarah Annie Esther of Samuel and Catharine Burrell, Innkeeper.
June 22   Samuel of Samuel and Lucy Collier, Laborer.
June 29   Sarah Ann of William and Mary Ann Clarke, Laborer.
July 27   Amelia Martha of William and Mary Newson, Laborer.
July 27   Isaac Richard of the same.
July 27   William Garrod of Edward and Susannah Barker, Miller.
Oct.   5   Sarah of Thomas and Emma Crowfoot, of Beccles, Miller.
Oct. 22   Charles James of John and Mary Ann Lawes, Cordwainer.
Oct. 28   Frederick of William and Susannah Sawer, Engineer.
Oct. 28   George of the same.
Nov.   9   Henry William of William and Jesse Higham, Brewer and Malster.
Dec. 11   Jane of Henry and Maria Larkins, Laborer.
Dec. 14   Charles of William and Emily Philpot, Laborer.
Dec. 21   Harry of Harry and Joanna Canham, Farmer.
Dec. 21   Annie of the same.

## 1857.

Jan.   4   Emily of George and Hannah Kerridge, Laborer.
Jan. 11   Elizabeth of John and Mary Ann Aldred, Servant.
Feb.   1   George of Henry and Ann Haward, Laborer.
Mar.   1   Sarah of Charles and Mary Coleman, Railway Laborer.
Mar. 15   Sarah of William and Elizabeth Watling, Laborer.
Mar. 22   Henry Louis of Henry and Charlotte Barstead, Servant.
April 12   Charles of George and Sarah Savage, Laborer.
April 12   Mary Maria of William and Maria Nunn, Laborer.
May   3   Edward Youngman of William and Maria Prior, of London, Shopkeeper.
May   3   Amelia Maria of the same.
June 21   William David of Thomas and Melville Denley, Bricklayer.
July 12   Maria Wright of George and Lucy Ann Bezant, Blacksmith.
Aug.   2   Harry of David and Betsey Spindler, Laborer.
Aug. 30   Emma of James and Jane Bolton, Laborer.
Aug. 30   Ellen Walker of Mary Bolton.
Oct.   4   James of Harriet Parr now Nunn.
Oct.   4   David of George and Harriet Nunn, Laborer.
Oct. 11   John Frederick of Samuel and Catharine Burrell, Innkeeper.
Nov. 15   Henry Reid of Charles and Martha Harvey, Gardener.
Nov. 15   Sarah of James and Sophia Byles, Laborer.
Dec. 27   Ann Elizabeth of William and Ellen Ludbrook, Laborer.

## 1858.

Jan.   3   John Frederick of James and Elizabeth Kemp, Laborer.
Mar.   2   Frederick of William and Jesse Higham, Brewer and Malster.
April   4   Charles of Thomas and Sophia Ludbrook, Laborer.
April 11   Robert of William and Mary Ann Clarke, Laborer.
April 11   William Edward of Maria Smith.
April 28   Sarah of Henry and Ann Haward, Laborer.
May   9   Caroline of William and Lucy Lynes, Laborer.
May 23   Emma Amelia of George and Anna Hurley, Railway Laborer.
Sep. 19   Edward of Esau and Harriet Haward, Laborer.

## 1859.

Jan. 16   William of Charles and Sarah Ludbrook, Laborer.
Jan. 23   Hannah Charlotte of George and Harriet Nunn, Laborer.
Feb. 27   William Thomas of Thomas and Hephziba Haward, Laborer.

# To All and Singular

Unto whom these presents shall com Edward Bysshe Knight
Clarenceulx, principall Herald and King of Armes, of all the South
East, and West parts of the Realme of England from the River
of Trent Southward, sendeth greeting, Whereas William Kempe of
South Malling in the County of Sussex gent. hath desired me to Assigne unto
him such Armes & Crest as he and his posterity may lawfully beare, Know
ye therfore that I have thought fitt to grant unto him the Armes hereafter
following (that is to say) gules, a fess ermins, betwene three garbes Or,
within a border of the second, And for his Crest, on a helmet, and
wreathe of his cullers, a Falcon volant ermyns standing on a garbe Or, Mantled gules
doubled argent, as in the margent hereof is more lively depicted, All which Armes, & Crest,
I the said Clarenceulx King of Armes by power and authority of my Office to me granted un-
the great Seale of England doe assigne give & grant unto the said William Kempe, and to
his heires lawfully begotten, observing their due differences according to the lawe of
Armes for ever. In Witnes wherof I have unto these presents fixed the Seale of my Office, and
subscribed my name, Dated the first day of December An: Dom 1662 And in the 4th yeare of
the Raigne of our Dread Soveraigne Lord Charles the 2d by the grace of GOD King of England
Scotland, France, & Ireland Defender of the Faith &c /

Edward Bysshe Clarenceulx

# Genealogy of Browne.

## Wills.

Copy of the Will of THOMAS BROWNE, Esq., of Shredicot, concluded from p. 379.

Furthermore I will that my said wife Apoline Browne of the issues revenues and profitts of the said lands ten'ts and hereditaments and out of all my goods which I have by this my will given devised & bequeathed vnto her shall finde and allow vnto my said sonne George Browne vnto my said daughter Apoline Browne and to my said two sonnes Edmond Browne and Edward Browne such convenient exhibic'on meate drinke apparell and other necessaries as shalbe fitting and necessary for them and every of them vntill it please God to enable them to live of themselves not doubting of her motherly affec'on and care (as I have before remembered) to augment theire severall porc'ons and to help to preferre them especially such of them as she shall finde to be of best desert and to stand in most need And further my will and minde is that if my said wife depart this life before my said sonne Edward Browne accomplish his full age of twentie and one yeares Then my said Feoffees and the survivor or survivors of them shall receive and take into theire hands & detaine the said annuity or rent charge of fiftie pounds given to the said Edward by the said Deed of Feoffent and menc'oned in this my will vntill the said Edward accomplish his full age of one and twentie yeares and shall therewth keep and maintaine him in such sort as they shall thinke fitt and shall imploy the said annuity to and for his best profitt And when he hath accomplished his full age of one and twentie yeares Then I will my said Feoffees shalbe accomptable to my said sonne Edward Browne of and for the said annuity and shall pay and allow vnto him the said Edward such monies and profitts as shalbe raised and made of the said annuity of fiftie pounds per annu' duringe his minoritie deducting allowing and retayning to themselves all such charges and costs wch they or any of them shalbe put vnto and shall necessarily pay and distribute in and about the educac'on and maintenance of the said Edward and in and about the imploying of his annuity aforesaid And I doe give and bequeath vnto the said Timothy Leving Thomas Moorton William Prince and John Stanley my Feoffees aforesaid to every of them fortie shillings apeece for theire care and paines to be taken in the premisses. Item I will give and devise vnto my said wife Apoline Browne and to her heires all that farme messuage and tenement scituate and beinge in Upper Tame in the Countie of Stafford called or knowne by the name of Greenes Farme and all houses buildings gardens orchards pastures lea sowes meadows com'ons lands and hereditaments with theire appurten'nce thereunto belonging which I purchased of Sr Roger Wilbraham Knight* and which are since adiudged and confirmed vnto me by a Decree in Chauncery lyinge exemplified by me vnder seale To have and to hold the said farme messuage & tenement and all other the premises with all and singuler their appurten'nce to the said Apoline Browne my wife and to her heires and assignes for ever And soe revoking all former wills I will that this my present Testament contayned in sixe sheets of paper whollie written with my owne hand shall stand for my true and whole and last will and Testament In witnes whereof I have subscribed my name to every of the said sixe sheets of paper and sett my seale to a labell of parchment wherewith the said sixe sheets are fastened together in the topp the daie and yeare first above written. Memorandum that theis words vizt (worke) (my) and (the) interlyned in the first leafe this word (sence) in the second leafe this word (Browne) in the last line but one in the fourth leafe These words vizt (sonne) and (they) in the fift leafe and the word (make) in the sixt and last leafe of this my present testament were all of them severally interlyned by me Thomas Browne with my own hand before then sealing publishing and acknowledging hereof.

THO: BROWNE.

Signed subscribed and acknowledged for his last will and Testament with the Memorandum next above written the daie and yeare abovesaid in the presence of vs Tho: Fletcher Walter Aston John Stanley Tho: Daintrey Robert Bailey.

A CODICILL made and declared by me Thomas Browne the fourteenth daie of February Anno D'ni iuxta etc. One thousand six hundred thirtie two which I will shalbe added vnto my last Will and Testament bearing date the seaven and twentieth daie of October One thousand six hundred thirtie one and in the seaventh yeare of the Kinge Maties Raigne that now is and to be taken and adiudged as part and parcell thereof.

MEMORANDUM that where in the second leafe of my said will I have given and bequeathed vnto my three sonnes George Browne Willm Browne and Edmond Browne to each of them fortie pounds apeece to be paid to every of them at the end of two yeares next after my decease with such purpose as therein is declared Now I doe by this Codicill for some reasons me moving therevnto revoke frustrate and make void the said three severall legacies of fortie pounds apeece and doe will that they and every of them my said three sonnes shall rest contented with such lands annuities rent charges gifts exhibic'on and mainten'nce wch I have otherwise in and by my said will sev'ally and respectively given and appointed vnto them And hereby I further will that five pounds given to my daughter Stury and five pounds given to her daughter Elizabeth Sturie in my said last will shalbe made vp tenne pounds apeece to either of them And I hereby will alsoe

---

* Of Nantwich, co. Chester; Master of the Court of Requests to James I.

that twentie poundes given and bequeathed in my said will to Apoline Stury my grandchild shalbe augmented and made vp fortie pounds to be paid to every of them in such maner and forme and at such tyme as I have appointed in my said will And I give vnto my loveing sonne in lawe Mʳ Carew Stury five pounds.

THO: BROWNE.

Published and declared by the said Thomas Browne and by him subscribed as parcell of his last Will In the presence of vs John Browne Henry Goodanter.

PROBATUM fuit Testamentum suprascriptum Cum Codicillo eidem annexo apud London Coram venerabili viro Domino Henrico Marten Milite legum doctore Curie Prerogative Cantuariensis Magistro Custode sive Commissario l'time constituto vicesimo octavo die mensis Maij Anno Domini Milli'mo sexcentesimo tricesimo tertio Juramento Apolinæ Browne Relictæ dicti defuncti et Executricis in hum'oi Testamento nominat Cui Commissa fuit Administracio omnium et singulorum bonorum jurium et Creditorum dicti defuncti De bene et fideliter Administrando eadem ad sanctæ Dei Evangelia Coram Magistro Thoma Fletcher Clerico Vigore Commissionis in ea parte al's Emanat Jurat.

---

## MONUMENTAL INSCRIPTIONS OF NORTH NEWNTON, CO. WILTS.*

### EAST WINDOW OF CHANCEL.

*Raising of Lazarus, Crucifixion, Raising of Jairus' Daughter :* In Memoriam | Francisci Newman Rogers obiit | xix Jvl. MDCCCLI Ætat. svæ lx. | Jvliæ Annæ Rogers obiit | vi Jan. MDCCCXXXII Ætat. svæ vii.

### WEST WINDOW UNDER TOWER.

*Our Lord and two Disciples going to Emmaus; the same at Emmaus :* John Clift died March 30ᵗʰ 1829 aged 85 yʳˢ. | Job Clift died Sepʳ 10ᵗʰ 1865 aged 75 Yʳˢ.

### NORTH WALL OF CHANCEL.

Crest : A greyhound's head erased, collared.

Near this place is | interred ye Body of | Francis Wroughton | Esquire of Estcot | in this County | who Departed this life | April the 29ᵗʰ in the | year of our Lord God | 1733.

---

*Brass plate :* Sacred to the memory of | Eleanor Amelia Rogers. | Born 23ʳᵈ August, A.D. 1832, | died 11ᵗʰ December, A.D. 1861. | This monument was erected | by her bereaved mother.

### SOUTH WALL OF CHANCEL.

Arms: I. Argent, three battering rams, barways, in pale ; impaling, Or, an escocheon within an orle of mullets or, CHAMBERLAINE. Supporters : Dexter, A friar habited, with crutch and rosary ; Sinister, A savage wreathed about the head and loins.
II. Quarterly—1 and 4, Sable, on a fess argent three lion's heads erased gules between as many anchors or ; 2 and 3, Per pale gules and azure, a cross crosslet or ; on a shield of pretence, CHAMBERLAINE. (M.I.)†
III. Argent, a chevron gules between three boar's heads couped sable ; impaling BERTIE. (M.I.)

Near this place | lyes the Body of the Right Honᵇˡᵉ Catharine | Countess Dowager of Abingdon. | She was eldest Daughter & Coheiress | of Sir Thomas Chamberlaine of Norbrook | in the County of Oxon, Barᵗ ; | had Three husbands : Her first was the Rᵗ Honᵇˡᵉ | Richard Lord Viscount Wenman | of Tuam in the

---

* Communicated by ARTHUR SCHOMBERG, Esq.
† (M.I.) signifies that the Arms or Monuments to which these letters are attached are destroyed or illegible, and therefore are supplied from the rare printed ' Monumental Inscriptions of Wiltshire, 1821.'

Kingdom of Ireland, | by whom she had Issue one Son, | Richard, who Succeeded to the Title and Estate, | (& was Father of the present Right Hon^ble | Phillip Lord Viscount Wenman | & the Hon^ble Richard Wenman Esq^r); | & Two Daughters Catharine & Mary. | Her Second was the Right Hon^ble | James, Earl of Abingdon, | Baron Norrys of Rycot, in the | County of Oxon. | Her Third was Francis Wroughton of Eascot in the County of Wilts, Esq^r. | She departed this life Feb^ry 9^th 1741 | in the 83^d Year of her Age.

*Brass plate.*

Arms : Quarterly—1 and 4, Argent, a chevron between three stags trippant sable ; 2 and 3, Quarterly sable and argent, in the first and fourth quarter three mullets of the second ; over all an escocheon gules, thereon a portcullis ensigned with an imperial crown or.
Crest : A stag trippant sable, chained and gorged crenely or.
Motto : Lux mea Christus.

In Memoriam | Francisci Newman Rogers, filii | primogeniti, infra sepulti ; qui | obiit Sept^t 2^do 1859, Annos 32 natus. | Hanc tabellam æneam mater mœrens posuit.

SOUTH WALL OF NAVE.

*A brass plate:* In Memoriam | Elizabeth Radcliffe | Obiit Jan^ry 14, 1879 | Aged 64.

# Rabett Family.

## ENTRIES ON FLY-LEAVES OF BIBLE AT BRAMFIELD HALL.

### R. & M. Rabett, Bramfield.

This Bible was given by the Rev^d Reginald Rabett to his affectionate Brother George William Rabett, Esq., R.N., Dec. 20^th 1836.

Reginald Henry Holford Rabett, son of George William & the Right Hon^ble Lady Lucy Louisa Maria Rabett, was born on the 10 August 1842 in London, at East Villa Lodge Place, Park Road, Regent's Park, & christened at the Parish Church of S^t Mary le Bone.

W^m Garbett, Esq., widower, & M^rs Mary Rabett, widow, both of the town of Douglas in this parish, were married in this Church by Licence, this 24^th July, 1813, by me T. Howard, Vicar. This marriage was solemnized between us W^m Garbett and Mary Garbett late Mary Rabett, in presence of J. Beatson, Tho. Curphey. I certify the above to be a true Copy from the Parochial Reg^r of Marriages in the parish of Braddan, Isle of Man, this 24^th July 1813.

THO^s HOWARD, Vicar of Braddan.

### Reginald Rabett, Bramfield Hall, Suffolk.

Taken from the monument in Bramfield Church, Suffolk, on the 15^th January 1837:

" Reginald Rabett, Esq., of Bramfield Hall, county of Suffolk, died 30^th day of May 1810, æt. 39 years ; and Mary his wife died the 22^d February 1832, aged 59 years. This Record to their memory is affectionately placed here by their children."

On Wednesday March y^e 4, 1718, my dear Mother changed this life for Immortality about thirty minutes past eleven of y^e Clock at Night and was Buried in Bramfield Chancell on y^e 10^th day of the same month.

On Friday June y^e 10, 1720, my son Jn^o departed this Life about half an hour past ten of y^e clock at night and was buried in Bramfield Chancell on the 13 day of y^e same month.

Eliz. Rabett was born at Battisford Oct. y⁰ 17, 1716, on a Wednesday about forty minutes past five of y⁰ clock in y⁰ morning.

Jnᵒ Rabett was born at Bramfield Novʳ y⁰ 16, 1717, on a Saturday about forty and five minutes past two of y⁰ clock in y⁰ morning dead.

Reginald Rabett was born at Bramfield Dec. y⁰ 22, 1718, on a Monday about fifty minutes past four of y⁰ clock in y⁰ afternoon.

Mary Rabett was born at Bramfield on Tuesday, May y⁰ 22, 1722, about half an hour past ten of the clock at Night.

John Rabett, Junʳ, was born at Bramfield on Wednesday, Oct. y⁰ 7, 1724, about two of the clock in the morning.

———

Reginald Rabett, Junʳ, was born at Bramfield on Wednesday, March the 20, 1771, about three of the clock in the afternoon. He departed this Life on the 31 of May 1810, æt. 39, in London, in Upper Berkley Sᵗ, Portman Square, and was buried at Bramfield in the Chancell.

Elizabeth Rabett was born at Bramfield on Saturday, April the 18ᵗʰ 1772, about three of the clock in the morning. She died the 20ᵗʰ of August 1773-4.

John Rabett was born at Bramfield on Wednesday, March the 31, 1773, about half an hour after eleven o' the clock at night.

Elizabeth Rabett, junʳ, was born at Bramfield June the 15, 1774, on a Wednesday about half an hour after ten of the clock at night.

Mary Rabett born at Bramfield Hall, Suffolk, on Friday, February the 14, 1794.

Reginald Rabett born on Sunday morning January the 11ᵗʰ 1795.

George William Rabett born on Wednesday December the 22, 1795, all at Bramfield Hall.

Mary the wife of Reginald Rabett, Esq., who was born, as on the other side of this page, March 20, 1771, was the Daughter of Mathias Kerrison, Esq., of Bungay & Broom Hall, Suffolk, & sister to Lieut.-General Sʳ Edward Kerrison, Baronet ; by this marriage they had three children, 1ˢᵗ Mary, 2ᵈ Reginald, 3 George William. On the death of the above Reginald Rabett, Mʳˢ Rabett married secondly William Garbett, Esq., of the Royal Navy, Widower, by Licence, on the 24 July 1813, in the parish of Braddan, Isle of Man ; by this marriage they had no issue.

William Garbett, Capᵗ, died at Boulogne-sur-Mer on the 8 June 1834, and was buried at Maketra near the Haute Ville of Boulogne in France. Mʳˢ Garbett died on the 22ᵈ February 1832, also at Boulogne-sur-Mer. Her remains were brought over & buried in the family vault in Bramfield Church, Suffolk, y⁰ 13ᵗʰ day of March 1832.

Under will be found the Marriages of the three children above mentioned, the issue of Reginald Rabett, Esq., & Mary his wife :

1. Mary, born 14ᵗʰ Feb. 1794 ; married 28 December 1810 the Right Honorable Lord Viscount Maynard of Easton Lodge, Essex.

2. Reginald born January 11ᵗʰ 1795 ; became the Rev., M.A., Rector of Aldershot, Hants, & Vicar of Thornton cum Bagworth in Leicestershire; married 1ˢᵗ Sept. 1828 Mary eldest Daughter of Richard Bickerton, Esq., of Rhaden, Shropshire, a descendant of Sʳ Richᵈ Bickerton, Bart., & of the ancient family of that name in the same county. No issue.

3. George William Rabett, born 22 Dec. 1795 ; Captain in the Royal Navy ; married 12 Sept. 1835 the Right Honᵇˡᵉ Lady Lucy Louisa Maria Turnour, 2ᵈ da. of Edward 3ᵈ Earl of Winterton, of Shillinglee Park, co. Sussex, at Great Marylebone Church. A son born 10 August 1842 Reginald.

———

Mary Rabett (now Viscountess Maynard), who was born at Bramfield Hall 14 Feb. 1794; her second daughter Emma was married at Easton Lodge, Essex, the seat of the Right Honᵇˡᵉ Lord Viscount Maynard, to T. Robert Ives, Esq., of Corpusty, Norfolk, by the Rev. Dacre Barrett Lennard, on the 25 August 1836.

Miss Emily Kerrison, second daughter of Lieut.-General Sir Edw<sup>d</sup> Kerrison, Bart., was maried to Viscount Mahon, only son of the Earl of Stanhope, at S<sup>t</sup> George's Church, Hanover Square, by the Rev. Lord Bayning, on the 9<sup>th</sup> July 1834.

Ann, eldest daughter of Lieut.-General S<sup>r</sup> Edw<sup>d</sup> Kerrison, Bart., was married at Oakley Park, Suffolk, to the Right Hon<sup>ble</sup> John, Lord Henniker, on the 5 day of January 1837.

Lieut. George William Rabett, of the Royal Navy, attended his mother M<sup>rs</sup> Mary Garbett, on Sunday the 19 June 1831, on board the Belfast Steamer off the Tower Stairs, London, then bound for Boulogne, France. M<sup>rs</sup> Garbett never saw England after the above date. She died at Boulogne on the 22 Feb. 1832. She was buried at Bramfield, Suffolk.

Elizabeth Rabett, eldest daughter of Reginald Rabett, Esq., of Bramfield Hall in the co. of Suffolk, married S<sup>r</sup> Ralph Blois, IV. Bart., of Grundesburgh Hall in the same county, & died 1780. She was the grandmother of the VI. and present Baronet S<sup>r</sup> Charles. Her father, the before-mentioned Reginald Rabett, Esq<sup>r</sup>, of Bramfield Hall, was a lineal descendant of William Rabett, Esq., who served in the twelfth Parliament at Westminster for Dunwich in Suffolk, in the Reign of King Edward the IV. in the year 1461.

---

## WILLOUGHBY OF LONDON, PORTSMOUTH, AND OF CHARLES-TOWN, NEW ENGLAND.

William Willoughby, born about 1588 ; said to have been a native of Kent ; a shipbuilder in the vicinity of London, and a purveyor of timber for the Navy ; taking part in the uprisings of 1642, marched from the Metropolis 17 Oct. 1643 as Colonel at the head of the Yellow Auxiliaries of the Tower Hamlets. He died 30 March 1651, aged 63, one of the Commissioners of the Navy, at Portsmouth, and was there buried in the church.* In January 1642-3 he had been granted a commission as Captain of one of the Tower Train Bands, being then styled, "Mr. William Willoughby for Ratcliffe." In his will he leaves to the poor of Wapping, where he formerly dwelt ; mentions his wife Elizabeth ; his two sons, Francis and William ; his cousin. Lawrence Hammond ; and the poor kindred of himself and wife.

The widow appears to have come to Charlestown, N.E., in the summer of 1662, and there died during the fall following. Her will of May 1662 mentions her late son William Willoughby and Jonathan the eldest son, and Nehemiah, William, and Sarah, children of her son Francis Willoughby, also the children by his now wife, Margaret, viz. : Francis and Nathaniel ; also her sister Anna, wife of Wm. Griffin of Portsmouth ; her sister Jane Hammond of Virginia, mother of Lawrence Hammond ; and John Greene of Charlestown, N.E., servant of her late husband, etc. She mentions as overseers her friends, Robert Thompson (prob. brother-in-law of Gov. Edward Hopkins of Connecticut) and John Taylor (or Tailer), both of the City of London, Esquires. The latter, a shipbuilder of Deptford, and after of Wapping, had been associated with her husband, 1636, in raising the "Anna Royal," which had sunk in the Thames.

William Willoughby, younger son of Col. Wm. Willoughby, died s.p. at Portsmouth, where he was a sub-commissioner of prizes, and was there buried 17 Dec. 1657. His will mentions his wife Mary, and Jonathan, Nehemiah, William, and Sarah, children of his brother (Francis) Willoughby ; also Timothy, son of his brother Lydiat. Francis Willoughby, eldest son of Col. Wm. Willoughby, a shipwright, like his father ; an inhabitant of Charlestown, New England, in August 1638 ; became prominent as a merchant and in public affairs. His first wife, Mary, died in 1640, leaving one child, Jonathan, about five years old. His second wife, Sarah, appears to have been a daughter of John Taylor (or Tailer), shipwright of Wapping, before mentioned, and, to further his suit, he doubtless returned temporarily to England. She was mother of Sarah, Hannah, Nehemiah, Jeremiah, and William. After the death of his father in 1651 he was again in England, whither

---

* With an armorial tablet.

his wife and family followed in December 1653; he, meanwhile, with the acknow-ledged rank of Captain, having been appointed to his father's position as Naval Commissioner at Portsmouth.   In March 1656-7 he, with Major Robert Thompson, were overseers to will of Ed. Hopkins, Ex-Gov. of Connecticut, and the following year was among the Committee of the Navy (with Mr. Richard Hutchinson, the Treasurer, and Major Nehemiah Bourne), who attended the funeral of the late Protector.   Francis Willoughby and John Childe, Esqs., were the Members for Portsmouth in the Parliament sitting 27 Jan. 1658-9.   Investigations of the late Col. Joseph L. Chester disclose the fact that about this time Willoughby married his third wife Margaret, widow of Daniel Taylor, Merchant of London, and a daughter of William Lock of Wimbledon, co. Surrey, gentleman.   She brought with her a goodly estate, including Aulton Park, in Great Clacton, Essex.   He now removed as a merchant to Seething Lane, in the parish of St. Olave, Hart Street, London, where his son Francis was bapt. 29 Feb. 1659-60 ; besides whom he had in England, Nathaniel, and in Charlestown, N.E., Susannah.   He returned to New England in 1662, was chosen Dept. Gov. of Mass. Bay Col. May 1665, and died 3 April 1671. His widow died 2 Feb. 1683 the wife of Capt. Lawrence Hammond, her first husband's cousin before mentioned.

Francis Willoughby (son of Nehemiah and grandson of Dep. Gov. Francis Willoughby), Merchant of Boston, living in 1747, æt. 75, appears to have been the last male representative of the family, unless Jonathan Willoughby, eldest son of the Dep. Governor, may still have descendants of the name living.   This Jonathan, born in England about 1635, was partly educated at Harvard College, N.E., 1651-4, but did not graduate.   Licence was granted 3 Dec. 1661 by the Bishop of London for his marriage at St. Edmund the King, Lombard Street, London, to Grizzle, daughter of Anna Goldisborough, widow, of St. Gregory's by St. Paul's.   He re-turned to New England and preached at Wethersfield and Haddam, Connecticut. His father's will, dated June 1670, speaks of him in terms of censure, as having " cost me much money both in breeding up and severall other ways, to the value of near a treble portion already .... it being a griefe of soul to me that he should run out an estate so unprofitably as he hath done to his present suffering," etc., etc.

His half-brother, William Willoughby, who died in August 1678, mentions him in his will (filed at Cambridge, Mass., in Dec. 1694) drawn up a year earlier, as follows :—

" Item : I ordaine the Legacie given me by my grandfather Taylor be equally divided between my sister (Mrs. Sarah) Campfield and my brother Jonathan as a token of my love."   This is all we learn of Jonathan ; but on 11 March 1688 his son of the same name gave a deed of confirmation as to sale of certain lands in Gloucester, Mass., to Tristram Coffee of Newbury, styling himself: " Jonathan Willoughby of the parish of St. Martin's Outwich, in the City of London, Barber Chyrurgion, eldest son of Jonathan Willoughby who was eldest son of Francis Willoughby, late of Charlestown, county of Middlesex, New England, Esq., both deceased."

We have seen reference made above to legacies from a grandfather Taylor in will of William Willoughby 1677 ; below we have, in connection with his brother Nehemiah Willoughby, a similar allusion in the will of a cousin John Arnold.   The latter, calling himself a mariner of Thames Street, London, now resident in Salem, N.E., bound to sea, in his will, 12 Oct. 1680, proved 28 Jan. 1694-5, makes his cousin, Nehemiah Willoughby of Salem, N.E., his executor and sole heir " in especially as that my legacy left me by my grandfather, John Tailer of Woppin, shipwrite, dec'd, in the hand of John Tailer of Milesend, as he is executor to the last will and testament of my said grandfather, with the legacies given to my brothers Thomas and Samuel, both deceased, by whose deaths their said legacies fell to me, the surviver, according to my said grandfather's will."

The writer of this article would be glad to gather further information as to the antecedents of Col. William Willoughby, and as to his descendants through his grandson, the Rev. Jonathan Willoughby.

*No. 216 W. 14th Street, New York.*                              ISAAC J. GREENWOOD.

## MONUMENTAL INSCRIPTIONS OF WOODBOROUGH, CO. WILTS.*

### NORTH AISLE.

Sophia, Wife of | William Dyke of this Parish, | Died the 9th day of Feb[ry] 1804, | Aged 28 Years, | Leaving two children Mary and Sophia. | William Dyke of Woodborough | Died the 25th day of Feb[ry] 1815, | Aged 45 Years. | Hannah, Relict of the above | William Dyke, Died the 8th | day of Nov[r] 1853 Aged 85 Years.

Arms : Or, three cinquefoils sable ; impaling, A fess crenely between six fleurs-de-lys gules.

Here lyeth ye body of | Sarah Francklyn, ye Relict | & widow of Ric[d] Francklyn late | of Woodborough. She departed | this life ye 10th of Decemb[r] 1675.

Sacred | to the Memory of | Jerome Dyke | late of Woodborough ; | who departed this Life | 19th Jan[ry] 1782. | Five of his Daughters, | Mary, Dorothy, Ann, | Martha, & Charlotte. | And his Son | Jonathan Waterman Dyke ; | He died 6th Oct[r] 1791. | Likewise | to the Memory of | Mary, Wife of Jerome Dyke ; | She departed this Life the 22nd April 1799. | Susannah and Elizabeth ;† | Daughters of Jerome & Mary Dyke, | Susannah died April 27th 1823 ; | Elizabeth died Dec[r] 13th 1835.

Arms : DYKE, impaling, Paly of six or and sable, three crescents gules. (M.I.)‡

In Memory of | William Dyke of Chesulden, Wilts, | who died the 20th of December, 1831 | aged 85 years. | Also of Elizabeth, his first wife, | who died the 25th of August 1775, | Aged 34 years. | And of Sarah, his second wife, | who died the 17th of December 1831, | aged 84 years.

Sacred to the memory of | Sophia Dyke | youngest daughter of the late | William and Sophia Dyke ; | She departed this life 25th Dec[r] 1829 | aged 25 years. | And of her sister | Mary Dyke, | who departed this life 6th May 1887 | aged 84 years.

Sacred to the memory of | William Robbins, | of this parish, | who died | the 12th day of June 1840, | in the 49th year of his age. | Also of | Thomas and Amy | infant children of William | and Elizabeth Robbins. | Also of the above Elizabeth, | who died Feb[ry] 11th 1876 | Aged 75 years.

Sacred to the Memory | of | John, Son of | Harry & Catharine Robbins, | who died 9th July 1813. | Martha, their Daugh[r] died 1st Oct[r] 1814. | Henry, their Son, died 27th Dec[r] 1814. | Thomas, their Son, Lieu[t] R.N. | died at Havannah, 18th Aug[st] 1816. | And also of Anne their Daughter, | who died 17th June 1820. | Likewise to the Memory of | the above Harry Robbins, | who died March 1st 1822. | And of Catharine, his Wife, | who died 3rd December 1826.

### SOUTH WALL OF NAVE.

Hic Jacet | quod mortale fuit | Georgii Gibbes, D.D. | hujus ecclesiæ per XLIX annos | fidelis et venerandi pastoris. | Benignus, intelligens, facundus, | amorem omnium | moribus suavissimis conciliavit ; | exempli tacita suadela | ad omne officii munus | animos sensim informavit ; scientia, literis, ingenio liberali erudiit. | Bonis in cœlo repositam | vitam præcipiens beatiorem | placide quiescat anima | vitæ tranquillæ | quoad vixit unice dedita ; obiit xx Feb. MDCCCXIII. Ætat. suæ LXXII. | Hoc monumentum posuerunt | et paterno amori | et longo felicissimoque conjugio | mœreus vidua, | lugens filia, memorque semper filius.

* Communicated by ARTHUR SCHOMBERG, Esq.
† On a flat stone in south porch, "M[rs] Susannah Dyke, aged 67 years, and her sister M[rs] Elizabeth Dyke, aged 86 years."
‡ (M.I.) signifies that the Arms or Monuments to which these letters are attached are destroyed or illegible, and therefore are supplied from the rare printed 'Monumental Inscriptions of Wiltshire, 1821.'

## EAST WINDOW OF CHANCEL.

*The Crucifixion ; Our Lady and St. John on either side :* To the glory of God and in memory of | Frances Wyld, who died March 13th | 1851, aged 54. Also of William Thomas Wyld | for 38 years Rector of this Parish, | who died March 18th 1873, aged 67.

---

## ON THE FLOOR.

Here lyeth ye Body of Dorothy Coningsby, Daughter | & Coheir of John Wick, in ye County of Kent, and | Wife to Wm Coningsby, Rector of this Parish, who | Departed this life ye 11 Day of Oct. 1699, Aged 73 years.   (M.I.)

Arms : A crescent between three conies sejant; impaling, A chevron charged with a crescent, in chief two martlets. (M.I.)

## ON ALTAR-TOMB, SOUTH-EAST OF CHURCHYARD.

*On either side :* 1, A lion rampant crowned, in chief three martlets ; 2, A chevron engrailed ermine between three roundles, each charged with a trefoil slipt.   *On either end :* A demi-lion rampant indented per pale, in dexter paw a rose-tree eradicated.

Here lyeth the Body of John Walker Esqr : | Late of Lyneham in this County | Hereditary Chief Usher of the Court | of Exchequer. | He married Dionysia eldest Daughter of | James Colebrooke Esqr : By whom he had Issue | John, | Heneage who died in his infancy, | James Button, | And Colebrooke who died Jan. 20 1757 ; | And three Daughters | Mary, | Dionysia, | And Cecil Ann. | He died April 27th 1758 | Aged 60 years.

---

# REGISTER OF THE MARRIAGES IN DUKE STREET CHAPEL, WESTMINSTER.

| | | | |
|---|---|---|---|
| 1745 | Dec. | 17 | Thomas Daniel of St Martin's, Ludgate, London, and Lucy Maria Hinton of the same parish.  Lic. |
| 1747 | Nov. | 29 | John Marshal of St Martin's in the Fields, Middlesex, and Mary Hercy of the same parish.  Lic. |
| 1748 | April | 21 | George West of St Margaret's, Westminster, Apothecary, and Sarah Spring of St John Evangelist, Westminster.  Lic. |
| 1748 | July | 31 | William Cunningham of St Martin's in the Fields, bachelor, and Margaret Maxwell of the same parish, spinster.  Lic. |
| 1750 | April | 2 | John Delaval of St Margaret's, Westminster, and Susannah Pottes of St George's, Hanover Square, widow.  Lic. |
| 1750 | June | 1 | Thomas Wood of St Giles in the Fields, Middx, widower, and Catharine Woolrich of Frodesham, co. Chester, spinster.  Lic. |
| 1751 | Nov. (—) | | John Fielding of St Martin's in the Fields, Middx., and Elizabeth Whittingham of Litchfield.  Lic. |
| 1752 | Oct. | 21 | Charles Hotham, Esq., of St Margaret's, Westminster, bachelor, and the Rt Hon. Lady Dorothy Hobart of St Martin's in the Fields.  Lic. |
| 1752 | June | 11 | Thomas Byrd of Claybrook, co. Leicester, Esq., bachelor, and Frances Pickering of St James, Westminster.  Lic. |
| 1753 | March | 5 | Morough O'Brien, Esq., of St Mary le Bone, Middx., bachelor, and the Rt Hon. Lady Mary O'Brien of St James, Westminster. |
| 1753 | May | 10 | Ellis Young, Esq., of St George's, Hanover Square, Middx., widower, and Penelope Stapleton of same, spinster. |
| 1753 | Sept. | 29 | James Marks of St Martin's in the Fields, bachelor, and Anne Payne of same, spinster.  Lic. |

RICH. BURFOOT.

## CONFIRMATION OF ARMS AND GRANT OF CREST TO THOMAS BURFOOT OF LONDON, 1752.

To all and singular to whom these presents shall come John Anstis Esquire Garter Principal King of Arms and Stephen Martin Leake Esquire Clarenceux King of Arms send Greeting whereas those ancient Badges or Ensigns of Gentility commonly called or known by the name of Arms have heretofore been and still are continued to be conferred upon deserving Persons to distinguish them from the common sort of People who neither can or may pretend to use them without lawful Authority. And whereas Thomas Burfoot of the City of London Merchant hath represented unto the Right Honorable Thomas Earl of Effingham Deputy (with the Royal Approbation) to the Most Noble Edward Duke of Norfolk Earl Marshall and Hereditary Marshall of England that He has born and used for his armorial ensigns Or 3 fleurs de lis sable but his ancestors not having duly entered the same in the College of Arms he hath therefore requested his lordship's warrant for our confirming the same with such additions as shall be thought necessary and also for our granting a suitable crest thereto to be born by him and his descendants and also by the descendants of his Father Thomas Burfoot late of Withyham in the county of Kent deceased and that the same may be recorded in the College of Arms aforesaid. And forasmuch as his Lordship duly considering the premises did by warrant under his hand and seal bearing date 23rd day of December instant order and direct us to confirm and grant to the said Thomas Burfoot and the descendants above mentioned such arms and crest accordingly. Know ye therefore that we the said Garter and Clarenceux in pursuance of the consent of the said Earl of Effingham and by virtue of the letters patent of our several offices to each of us respectively granted under the Great Seal of Great Britain have assigned and by these presents confirm and grant unto the said Thomas Burfoot the Arms following viz. Or a garb Vert between three fleurs de lis Sable and for the Crest On a wreath of the colours an Eastern Crown therein a Pineapple leaved and crowned all Or as the same are in the margin hereof more lively depicted to be born and used for ever hereafter by him the said Thomas Burfoot and his descendants and also by the descendants of his said Father Thomas Burfoot late of Withyham in the County of Kent deceased with their due and proper differences according to the Ancient usuage and practise of Arms without the let or interruption of any person or persons whatsoever. In witness whereof we the said Garter and Clarenceux Kings of Arms have to these presents subscribed our names and affixed the Seals of our several offices the thirtieth day of December in the twenty-sixth year of the Reign of our Sovereign Lord George the Second by the Grace of God King of Great Britain France and Ireland defender of the Faith and so forth and in the year of our Lord God 1752.

---

## NOTES AS TO FAMILY OF BOWKER OR BOOKER.*

### EXTRACTS FROM THE CHURCH REGISTERS OF HORSHAM, SUSSEX.†

#### *Baptisms.*

| | | | |
|---|---|---|---|
| 1560 | Sep. | 21 | Alban Bowker son of William Bowker. |
| 1561 | Oct. | 21 | Anthony Bowker son of Richard Bowker. |
| 156½ | Feb. | 4 | Thomas Bowker son of Thomas Bowker. |
| 1564 | March 31 | | George Bowker son of Richard Bowker. |
| 156⅚ | Feb. | 21 | Elizabeth Bowker daughter of Thomas Bowker. |
| 1584 | June | 14 | Edward son of Edward Bowker and Anne. |

* Communicated by CHARLES E. B. BOWKER. In continuation of those already printed in this Magazine.
† Extracted by the Rev. C. J. ROBINSON, M.A., Vicar of the parish.

| | | | |
|---|---|---|---|
| 1587 | Sep. | 7 | John son of Richard Bowker and Bridget. |
| 1588 | Oct. | 13 | Edward son of John Bowker and Elizabeth. |
| 1589 | Dec. | 7 | Bridget daughter of Richard Bowker and Bridget. |
| 159½ | Feb. | 15 | Joane daughter of Richard Bowker and Agnes. |
| 1595 | June | 29 | Jane daughter of Richard Booker and Agnes. |
| 1595 | Aug. | 24 | Mary daughter of Richard Booker and Bridget. |
| 162⁶⁄₇ | Feb. | 25 | John son of Francis Booker and Mary. |
| 1628 | May | 5 | Leonard son of Francis Booker and Mary.* |
| 1629 | Oct. | 25 | Elizabeth daughter of John Booker and Priscilla. |
| 16²⁹⁄₃₀ | March | 3 | Martha daughter of William Booker and Joane. |
| 163⁰⁄₁ | Jan. | 1 | Richard son of Richard Booker and Ann.† |
| 163½ | Feb. | 16 | John son of John Booker and Priscilla. |
| 1633 | Dec. | 23 | William son of Richard Booker and Ann. |

### Marriages.

| | | | |
|---|---|---|---|
| 1562 | June | 8 | John Forman and Elizabeth Bowker. |
| 1580 | May | 31 | Edward Bowker and Agnes Mullens. |
| 1600 | Nov. | 1 | Henry Smith and Elizabeth Bowker. |
| 1616 | June | 2 | William Booker and Joane Patching. |
| 1619 | April | 11 | William Browne and Mary Booker. |
| 1619 | Oct. | 12 | Francis Booker and Mary Daniel. |
| 1628 | Sep. | 16 | John Booker and Priscilla Shaw. |
| 1629 | Oct. | 26 | Richard Booker and Anne Hill. |

### Burials.

| | | | |
|---|---|---|---|
| 155⁸⁄₉ | Jan. | 21 | Joan daughter of John Bowker. |
| 155⁸⁄₉ | Jan. | 22 | "2 Johns ye twynne sonnes of Thomas Bowker." |
| 1560 | April | 16 | William son of Richard Bowker. |
| 156⁰⁄₁ | March | 21 | Alban Bowker infans. |
| 1561 | April | 16 | Jane Bowker virgo. |
| 1563 | March | 27 | Sible Bowker virgo. |
| 156⁴⁄₅ | Jan. | 20 | Richard Bowker vir. |
| 157¾ | March | 21 | William Bowker puer. |
| 1578 | Nov. | 15 and 25 | Andrewe and John the sonnes of Edward Bowker. |
| 1592 | Dec. | 24 | Margery Bowker. |
| 1596 | Nov. | 27 | Elizabeth Bowker wydowe. |
| 1597 | April | 1 | Maude Buttenshawe al's Bowker wydowe. |
| 1630 | May | 25 | William Booker, householder. |
| 1643 | May | 7 | John Booker a child of Richard Booker. |
| 165¾ | | | Priscilla wife of John Booker. |
| 1658 | April | 26 | The wife of Richard Booker. |
| 166⁶⁄₇ | Jan. | 8 | John Booker an auntient man aged 4 score and 18 yeares and upwards. |
| 1669 | Oct. | 24 | Richard Booker, householder. |

* Francis Booker of Horsham, in the co. of Sussex, baker, in his will, dated 21 April 1642 (18 Car. I.) (proved at Canterbury 18 May 1642; reference 69 Camb.), leaves to his son Francis and his heirs "house and backside wherein I live at Horsham." Mentions his wife Mary (Daniell), sonne George Booker, sonne Leonard Booker, sonne Edward Booker, sonne John Booker, daughter Anne Booker. Wife sole executrix. Kinsman Geo. Booker of Billingshurst, and well-beloved kinsman Leonard Cooke of Horsham, overseers of his will.

† This Richard Booker was educated at Westminster School. Elected to Cambridge in 1646. B.A. and Fellow of Trinity College, Cambridge, in 1650. M.A. 1653. Admitted to Gray's Inn 14 June 1651. Died 1655. Buried in the Cloisters of Westminster Abbey. See Foster's ' Coll. Gen.,' 1882, p. 81; Welch's 'Alumni Westmon.'; Coles' MSS. xlv., 241, 266, 461; 'Antiq. of St. Peter's, Westminster,' 316. The long Latin and eulogistic inscription on his tomb is given verbatim in 'Monumenta Westmon.,' No. 167.

It is believed these Bowkers came from the parent stock in Lancashire to cultivate lands of Lancashire noblemen.

# The Register Book of Bramfield, co. Suffolk.*

### 1859.

Mar. 13   William Joseph of Samuel and Catharine Burrell, Innkeeper.

Mar. 15   Ellen of William and Mary Ann Noy, Wheelwright.

June 12   Emma of Samuel and Mary Walker, Laborer.

July 3   Edward James of Robert and Sarah Smith, Laborer.

July 17   Frederick Harry of Samuel and Charlotte Maria Benstead, Collar-maker.

July 17   Robert Edward of Elizabeth Blomfield.

July 20   Edward of James and Eliz$^{th}$ Kemp, Laborer.

July 24   Rebecca of James and Patience Rouse, Laborer.

Aug. 14   Sarah of Robert and Maria Shade, Laborer.

END OF THE THIRD BOOK OF BAPTISMS.

## The Fourth Book of Baptisms.

### 1859.

Aug. 28   Ellen Maria of William and Emily Philpot, Laborer.

Aug. 28   John William of Sarah Andrews now Reeve.

Aug. 28   George of James and Sarah Reeve, Laborer.

Sep. 4   Harry of William and Susan Sawer, Engineer.

Sep. 18   Samuel of William and Mary Ann Clarke, Laborer.

Oct. 8   Anna Maria Jane of Alfred and Ann Moore, Shopkeeper.

Oct. 9   Samuel of William and Elizabeth Watling, Laborer.

Oct. 31   William of John and Eliza Edwards, Laborer.

Oct. 30   Fanny of Thomas and Rachael Tubby, Shoemaker.

### 1860.

Jan. 8   James of Louisa Ludbrook.

Jan. 15   Charles of George and Hannah Kerridge, Laborer.

Feb. 12   William of John and Martha Rowe, Laborer.

Feb. 14   William of Jonas and Caroline Tibbenham, Butcher.

Mar. 11   William Edward Moore of William and Mary Newson, Laborer.

Mar. 11   Robert of William and Maria Nunn, Laborer.

April 8   Mary Letitia of George and Sarah Flatt, Laborer.

April 8   Herbert Andrew of Thomas and Sophia Ludbrook, Laborer.

April 22   Sarah of William and Ellen Ludbrook, Laborer.

May 25   William of John and Betsy Savage, Laborer.

May 27   George Edwin White of Samuel and Katharine Burrell, Innkeeper.

June 10   Harry of Henry and Ann Haward, Laborer.

June 17   Charles of Thomas and Hephziba Haward, Laborer.

Aug. 5   Martha of David and Betsy Spindler, Laborer.

Aug. 5   William Henry of Charlotte Catharine Sturley now Peck.

Aug. 5   Harriet Amelia of George and Charlotte Catharine Peck, Laborer.

Aug. 12   Esther of William and Maria Prior, Servant.

Sep. 16   Alfred Herbert of Herbert and Ellen Oxborrow, Miller.

Sep. 16   Fanny Elizabeth of the same.

Sep. 16   Fanny Annie of the same.

Dec. 9   Elizabeth of Samuel and Mary Walker, Laborer.

Dec. 9   Caroline Elizabeth of James and Jane Bolton, Laborer.

Dec. 9   Emily Jane of the same.

### 1861.

May 12   Hannah of John and Betsy Savage, Laborer.

May 12   Ellen of the same.

June 16   Horace Harry of William and Susannah Sawer, Engineer.

July 21   William of William and Elizabeth Watling, Laborer.

July 21   Edward Charles of Charles and Sarah Ludbrook, Laborer.

July 28   Emma of Thomas and Hephziba Haward, Laborer.

Aug. 11   Laura Mary Ann of Alfred and Mary Ann Leggett, Blacksmith.

Sep. 22   Eliza of Samuel and Mary Ann Collier, Laborer.

Sep. 29   Mary Ann of William and Eliza Eastaugh, Laborer.

Dec. 15   Ann Mary of James and Myra Smith, Laborer.

Dec. 15   William of William and Harriet Nicholls, Laborer.

Dec. 31   Harry of Harry and Maria Lurkins, Laborer.

### 1862.

Mar. 29   Moses of William and Susan Sawer, Engineer.

April 13   Robert of Thomas and Sophia Ludbrook, Laborer.

April 13   Mary Ann of William and Ellen Ludbrook, Laborer.

April 27   Herbert Samuel of Herbert and Ellen Oxborough, Miller.

April 27   Edgar George of George and Harriet Berry, Bricklayer.

* Continued from p. 388.

June 8 Robert of George and Ann Chapman, Laborer.

June 8 George James of John and Lucy Ann Lowe, Laborer.

June 8 Frederick of John and Ann Collier, Laborer.

June 29 John Alfred of William and Mary Ann Andrews, Farmer.

June 29 Edward Ernest of the same.

July 27 Marian Sophia of William and Mary Ann Noy, Shopkeeper.

July 27 Alice of the same.

Aug. 3 Anna Maria of William and Maria Tuthill, Laborer.

Aug. 3 Charles of William and Emma Gilbert, Laborer.

Aug. 24 Eliza Matilda of Arthur and Matilda Edwards, Laborer.

Aug. 24 Emma of William and Mary Ann Catton, Laborer.

Sep. 14 Joanna Elizabeth of Nicholas and Elizabeth Bulkeley Simons, Clerk in Holy Orders. [*He was Vicar of the parish.*]

Oct. 12 William of Henry and Ann Haward, Laborer.

Oct. 26 Charles Marmaduke of John Marmaduke and Caroline Marsden, Carpenter.

Nov. 9 Robert of Charles and Sarah Ludbrook, Laborer.

### 1863.

Jan. 16 Henry William of George and Lucy Ann Bezant, Smith.

May 24 Maria Edith of Samuel and Maria Benstead, Innkeeper.

June 7 Alice Gertrude of Henry and Catharine Cattermull, Policeman.

July 12 Mary Ann of Samuel and Mary Ann Smith, Laborer.

July 26 Charles of Isaac and Hannah Punchard, Laborer.

Aug. 9 John of William and Eliza Eastaugh, Laborer.

Sep. 6 Betsy of William and Emily Philpot, Laborer.

### 1864.

Jan. 3 Mary Ann of William and Mary Ann Clark, Laborer.

April 1 Alfred of John and Harriett Bolton, Laborer. Privately.

Mar. 27 Charlotte of Samuel and Mary Walker, Laborer.

April 17 George William of William and Emma Gilbert, Laborer.

May 1 Mary Ann of William and Ellen Ludbrook, Laborer.

May 15 Ellen of Herbert and Ellen Oxborough, Miller.

May 15 Elizabeth of John and Lucy Ann Lowe, Laborer.

May 22 Myra of William and Lucy Lynes, Laborer.

May 22 George of John and Emily Lynes, Laborer.

May 22 Emma of the same.

Oct. 23 John Robert of John and Betsy Savage, Laborer.

Oct. 23 Frederick George of George and Sarah Savage, Laborer.

Nov. 27 Mary Ann of Thomas and Elizabeth Punchard, Laborer.

Dec. 5 James of John and Martha Rowe, Laborer.

Dec. 20 Sarah Elizabeth of William and Elizabeth Higham, Maltster.

### 1865.

Jan. 15 Caroline of Harry and Maria Lurkins, Laborer.

Jan. 15 James Brown of George and Julia Kerridge, Laborer.

Jan. 16 James of William and Elizabeth Watling, Laborer. Privately.

Feb. 1 Ann of James and Jane Bolton, Laborer.

Feb. 5 William of Isaac and Hannah Punchard, Laborer.

Feb. 12 Elizabeth Mary of James and Sophia Byles, Laborer.

Feb. 26 Robert John of Robert and Sarah Smith, Laborer.

April 9 Betsy of David and Betsy Spindler, Laborer.

April 30 James of Samuel and Mary Walker, Laborer.

May 14 Elizabeth Balls of George and Harriet Brown, Laborer.

May 14 William George of the same.

May 21 Ellen of Isaac and Elizabeth Hallam, Farmer.

July 23 Thomas Repington of John Marmaduke and Caroline Marsden, Carpenter.

Aug. 6 James of Samuel and Mary Ann Collier, Laborer.

Sep. 24 Kate of John and Eliza Edwards, Laborer.

Oct. 15 James of James and Maria Wilson, Blacksmith.

Nov. 26 Isabella of William and Ellen Ludbrook, Laborer.

Dec. 10 Kate of Harry and Maria Lurkins, Laborer.

### 1866.

Jan. 7 Henry of Thomas and Harriet Smith, Blacksmith.

Jan. 7 Mary of the same.

Jan. 21 Frederick of Frederick and Betsy Swan, Groom.

Feb. 25 Florence Elizabeth of William and Elizabeth Higham, Farmer and Maltster.

Feb. 25 Aldis Higham of Alfred and Isabella Cole, Shopkeeper.

April 22 Elizabeth of George and Jane Puttock, Laborer.

April 22 Joseph of Joseph and Betsy Baldry, Laborer.

April 22 Hannah Maria of Thomas and Elizabeth Punchard, Laborer.

April 29 Ernest John of Herbert and Ellen Oxborough, Miller.

April 29 John of George and Julia Kerridge, Laborer.

April 29 Harry of Robert and Eliza Tilney, Whitesmith.

April 29 Frederick of George and Harriet Berry, Bricklayer.

Aug. 19 Mary Elizabeth of James and Jane Bolton, Laborer.

Sep. 16 Robert of Robert and Mary Ann Swan, Gardener.

Sep. 23 William of William and Hannah Redgrave, Laborer.

Sep. 23 Ellen of the same.

Sep. 23 Mary Ann of the same.

Oct. 21 Alice Katharine of Samuel and Eliza Smith, Laborer.

Oct. 21 Simon of William and Harriet Nicholls, Laborer.

Oct. 21 Frederick of the same.

Oct. 28 Ellen of Robert and Elizabeth Taylor, Laborer.

Oct. 28 Charles of George and Harriet Brown, Laborer.

Nov. 25 Alice of Joseph and Ellen Todd, Laborer.

1867.

Jan. 27 William of David and Betsy Spindler, Laborer.

Feb. 3 Charles of Isaac and Hannah Punchard, Laborer.

Feb. 5 Ellen of John and Ann Collier, Laborer.

Feb. 17 Louisa of Samuel and Mary Walker, Laborer.

Feb. 17 Frederick of John and Harriet Bolton, Laborer.

July 21 Mary Ann of John and Maria Punchard, Laborer.

Sep. 1 Herbert Henry of Rob't and Anna Farrington, Shoemaker.

Nov. 3 John of Isaac and Elizabeth Hallam, Farmer.

Nov. 3 Edmund Herbert of Edmund and Charlotte Baker, Farmer.

Dec. 15 William James of James and Esther Hurren, Carpenter.

Dec. 29 Henry of George and Julia Kerridge, Laborer.

Dec. 29 Peter of Thomas and Harriet Smith, Blacksmith.

1868.

Jan. 6 Charles of Robert and Anna Farrington, Shoemaker.

Jan. 6 Anna of the same.

Jan. 12 Emma of George and Sarah Savage, Laborer.

Jan. 26 Eliza of James and Jane Bolton, Laborer.

Feb. 19 William of Harry and Maria Lurkins, Laborer.

Feb. 21 George William of William and Anna Gilbert, Laborer. Privately.

Mar. 1 Robert William of Robert and Mary Ann Swan, Gardener.

July 12 Elizabeth Mary of William and Susan Sawer, Laborer.

Dec. 20 Phœbe Amelia of William and Ellen Ludbrook, Laborer.

Dec. 20 Maria Louisa of the same.

1869.

Feb. 8 Jessie of Henry and Emma Burt, Groom.

Feb. 14 Milbourn George of William and Elizabeth Philpot, Carpenter.

Mar. 28 William of John and Maria Punchard, Laborer.

April 4 Arthur Thomas of Emma Lynes, Spinster.

May 2 Elizabeth of Isaac and Hannah Punchard, Laborer.

June 4 Louisa of William and Maria Tuthill, Laborer.

June 4 James of the same.

June 13 Frederick John of Alfred and Isabel Cole, Farmer.

Aug. 29 Charlotte of William and Elizabeth Higham, Maltster.

Sep. 5 Thomas Christopher of Thomas Samuel and Laura Spall, Farmer.

Aug. 8 Emily of George and Julia Kerridge, Laborer.

Aug. 8 Alice of the same.

Oct. 3 Albert Edward of Robert and Anna Farrington, Shoemaker.

Dec. 26 William Stevenson of William and Matilda Peck, Artizan.

1870.

June 5 Hannah of John and Harriet Bolton, Laborer.

July 10 Clara Frances of James and Esther Hurren, Carpenter.

July 17 Elizabeth of Christopher and Elizabeth Paxman, Farmer.

Aug. 14 Isabelle of William and Betsy Higham, Maltster.

Sep. 18 Harry of George and Harriet Berry, Bricklayer.

Sep. 18 Jonas Duncan of William and Charlotte Jacobs, Bricklayer.

Sep. 18 Helen of the same.

Oct. 2 Clara of William and Emily Philpot, Laborer.

Oct. 2 Ellen of George and Mary Moore, Laborer.

1871.

Feb. 26 Robert George of George and Julia Kerridge, Laborer.

Mar. 25 Anna of John and Harriet Bolton, Laborer.

May 10 Charlotte of Jonas and Caroline Tibbenham, Butcher.

May 21 Mary Ann of Isaac and Hannah Punchard, Laborer.

Sep. 3 Elizabeth of Albert and Clara Farrington, Cordwainer.

Nov. 12 James of John and Maria Punchard, Laborer.

1872.

Mar. 12 Eunice of William and Emma Gilbert, Laborer.

April 5 Sarah Ann of John and Sarah Ann Vincent, Miller.

April 14 William of Joseph and Ellen Todd, Laborer.

April 14 Herbert of John and Harriet Bolton, Laborer.

1873.

Mar. 30   James of Isaac and Hannah Punchard, Laborer.

Aug. 13   Edward of John and Sarah Ann Vincent, Miller.

Sep. 7   Hannah Elizabeth of James and Lucy Savage, Laborer.

Nov. 2   Alfred Herbert of Alfred and Isabel Cole, Farmer.

Nov. 2   Frances Sarah Ann of John and Sarah Ann Vincent, Miller.

1874.

Jan. 4   Alice Jane of Charles Gooda and Sarah Ann Lee, Farmer.

Feb. 6   Rose Ann of John and Ann Collier, Laborer.

Mar. 6   John Edward of Joseph and Martha Baldry, Laborer.

Mar. 15   Charlotte Eliza of William and Charlotte Jacobs, Bricklayer.

Mar. 15   Helen Louisa of George Hadingham and Adelaide Andrews, Shopkeeper.

Mar. 15   William Richard of William and Elizabeth Higham, Farmer.

Mar. 15   Herbert Robert of the same.

May 24   Elizabeth Jane of John and Emma Woodward, Laborer.

May 24   Alice of John and Harriet Bolton, Laborer.

June 21   Elizabeth Martha of William and Elizabeth Philpot, Carpenter.

Sep. 27   Emma Jane of James and Elizabeth Ship, Laborer.

Sep. 27   Alice Jane of William and Susannah Thain, Blacksmith.

Sep. 27   Agnes Emily of the same.

Oct. 11   Alice Esther of James and Esther Hurren, Carpenter.

Oct. 11   William Charles of William and Emma Brown, Innkeeper.

Oct. 11   Elmy William of Thomas and Harriet Smith, Blacksmith.

1875.

Jan. 31   Nelson Milbourne of William and Elizabeth Philpot, Carpenter.

Mar. 24   George of Thomas and Sophia Ludbrook, Laborer.

Mar. 28   Frederick of William and Emily Philpot, Laborer.

April 4   Mary Ann of John and Emma Cooper, Laborer.

April 4   Mary Ann of Joseph and Ellen Todd, Laborer.

April 11   Arthur of Charles and Sarah Ludbrook, Laborer.

May 9   Emily of William and Sarah Easey, Laborer.

May 30   Ida Mabel of Charles and Ellen Eliza Bunn, of Clapton, Middlesex, Butcher.

May 30   Alice of William and Sarah Louisa Ward, Carpenter.

May 30   Elizabeth Louisa of the same.

Aug. 1   James John of James and Lucy Savage, Laborer.

Aug. 15   George of Albert and Anna Farrington, Cordwainer.

Oct. 31   Herbert Charles of Charles Gooda and Sarah Ann Lee, of Walpole, Farmer.

1876.

Feb. 20   Frederick William of George and Mary Smith, Laborer.

April 18   Kate Maria of William and Susannah Thain, Blacksmith.

April 23   Florence of James and Esther Hurren, Carpenter.

July 2   Anna of John and Harriet Bolton, Laborer.

July 2   Elizabeth of William and Mary Ann Catton, Laborer.

July 23   Alice of Isaac and Hannah Punchard, Laborer.

July 30   Susan Elizabeth of Joseph and Harriet Bunn, Laborer.

Aug. 6   Henry Robert of William and Emma Brown, Butcher.

Aug. 6   Henry William of Henry and Annie Lewell, of Holloway, Middlesex, Carpenter.

Aug. 6   Amelia Annie Raven of the same.

Oct. 22   Francis Vere of Francis Vere and Caroline Wood, Farmer.

Nov. 26   Ann of Alfred John and Mary Gibbs, Engine Driver.

1877.

Jan. 23   Edith of William and Elizabeth Philpot, Carpenter.

June 24   William of David and Martha Hurren, Laborer.

June 24   Anna of Walter and Harriet Beales, Laborer.

Aug. 27   Lucy of Thomas and Sophia Ludbrook, Laborer.

Sep. 16   Mary Ann of James and Lucy Savage, Laborer.

Nov. 11   Harry of William and Emma Durrant, Laborer.

1878.

April 14   Edith of Harriet Clark.

May 23   Rosamund Mary of Francis Vere and Caroline Wood, Farmer.

Sep. 1   Arthur Stanley of William and Elizabeth Philpot, Carpenter.

Oct. 20   Ellen of John and Harriet Bolton, Laborer.

Oct. 20   Arthur of William and Ann Smith, Gardener.

Nov. 9   Edith of Frederick and Elizabeth Mason, Laborer.

Dec. 8   Thomas Charles of William and Charlotte Jacobs, Bricklayer.

1879.

Feb. 17   Arthur of Frederick and Betsy Swan, Coachman.

Feb. 24   James of William and Susannah Thain, Blacksmith.

June 24   William of William and Sarah Ward, Carpenter.

June 29 Amy Eleanor of Charles Edmund and
Eleanor Weldin, of Tufton Street,
Westminster, Surgeon.
July 20 Robert Morris of Francis Vere and
Caroline Wood, Farmer.
Aug. 24 Laura Louisa of William and Mary
Lovett, Farmer.
Aug. 24 Harriet of the same.
Aug. 24 James William of the same.
Aug. 24 Harry of William and Hannah Red-
grave, Laborer.
Nov. 9 Levina of William and Mary Lovett,
Farmer.

1880.

Jan. 4 Henry of George and Mary Ann
Smith, Laborer.
Jan. 4 Samuel of Sarah Watling.
Jan. 8 Charles William of George and Emily
Tuthill, Laborer.
May 16 Lilian Elizabeth of Albert and Jane
Emma Read, Laborer.
June 6 Mary Maria of David and Ellen
Warnes, Laborer.
June 18 Mabel of John and Emmeline Pipe,
Farmer.
Sep. 2 Florence of William and Susannah
Thain, Blacksmith.
Dec. 12 Hilda Marian of William Chaplin and
Rose Jane Wayling, Farmer.

1881.

April 10 Rose Ellen of William and Elizabeth
Philpot, Carpenter.
May 7 Ernest Henry of Harry and Hannah
Spindler, Laborer. Privately.
May 29 John of John and Harriet Bolton,
Laborer.
July 17 Elizabeth Ellen of Robert and Eliza-
beth Crane, Laborer.
July 24 Herbert William of Walter and Har-
riet Beales, Shoemaker.
July 24 Selina of the same.
July 24 Walter of the same.
July 24 Arthur George of William and Eliza-
beth Higham, Maltster.
July 4 Ernest Edward of the same.
Sep. 11 Robert William of William and Levina
Whatling, of Yoxford, Laborer.
Dec. 18 Ellenor Elizabeth of William and
Hannah Hamblin, Laborer; by J. J.
Warrington Rogers, Curate.

1882.

Jan. 15 James Francis Warrington of James
John Warrington and Agnes Rogers,
Clerk in Holy Orders.
Feb. 12 Francis Robert of George and Mary
Ann Smith, Laborer.
Feb. 12 Edgar James of William and Emma
Brown, Laborer.
Feb. 19 William George of Samuel and Ellen
Maria Pierce, of Halesworth, Black-
smith.
Feb. 19 Florence Isabella of the same.
April 2 Georgeanna Harvey of William
Chaplin and Rosa Jane Wayling,
Farmer.

April 21 Harry of James Groves and Ellen
Durrant, Laborer. Privately.
May 4 Alice Mary of William and Ann Smith,
Gardener.
June 25 Edward George of David and Mary
Ann Hurren, Laborer.
July 23 Alice Edith of James and Sarah
Phillips, Laborer.
Aug. 6 Alice of Charles and Ellen Scace, of
Ipswich, Bricklayer.
Aug. 13 Alice Elizabeth of Frederick and
Sophia Marsden, of Badingham,
Carpenter and Builder.
Aug. 13 Annie of Robert and Elizabeth Crane,
Gardener.

1883.

Jan. 7 Ellen Emma of William and Mary
Ann Mattack, of Yoxford, Laborer.
Jan. 7 Edith Emma of William and Lavina
Watling, of Yoxford, Laborer.
Feb. 18 Fred of Samuel and Elizabeth Clark,
Pork Butcher.
Mar. 2 Edith of George and Martha Amelia
Wilson, of Yarmouth, Carpenter.
April 15 Pamela Martha of James Ernest and
Martha Graves, Servant; born Oct.
22, 1882. By A. H. Upcher, Curate.
April 16 Sterndale John of William and Mary
Woolner, Laborer; born Feb. 26.
Privately.
June 3 Harriet Rose of William and Martha
Florence Crane, Laborer; born
Ap. 22.
Aug. 5 Emma Mary of James Grove and
Ellen Durrant, Laborer; born July 7.
Oct. 14 Lilly of William Burwood and
Hannah Hamblin, Laborer; born
Aug. 29.
Oct. 14 Edith Alice of Frederick and Alice
Susannah Forster, Laborer; born
Sep. 9.
Oct. 14 George of James and Elizabeth Smith,
Laborer; born Sep. 6.

1884.

Mar. 30 Maud Ellen of John and Alice Reeve,
of Wangford, Grocer; born Aug. 2,
1882.
April 4 Aldis Jolley of John Marmaduke and
Caroline Marsden, Carpenter; born
Jan. 3, 1870.
April 4 Harry Clark of Matilda Andrews, of
London; born Feb. 27, 1873.
April 4 Robert George of David and Betsy
Spindler, Laborer; born July 17,
1873.
April 4 Florence of Edward and Esther Mary
Mason, Laborer; born March 2,
1882.
April 4 Louisa of William and Sarah Louisa
Ward, Carpenter; born Jan. 5,
1877.
April 4 William of the same; born May 7,
1877.
April 4 Eliza Georgiana of the same; born
July 12, 1880.
April 4 Anna Maria of the same; born May
12, 1883.

May 11    Hannah of William and Ann Smith, Gardener; born Ap. 1.

Aug. 31    Ethel of William and Agnes Philips, Laborer; born July 5.

Aug. 31    Honor of John and Emma Cooper; born July 24.

Aug. 31    Elizabeth of the same; born July 24.

Oct. 19    William of James Groves and Ellen Durrant, Laborer; born Oct. 11. Privately.

### 1885.

Mar. 8    Edward Aldis of Charles Edward and Hannah Ludbrook, Laborer; born Jan. 1.

Mar. 8    Harry Osborne of Albert and Jane Emma Read, Laborer; born July 28, 1884. Privately. Rec$^d$ into the Church Feb. 27, 1887.

Mar. 15    Frederick James of William and Lavina Watling, Laborer; born Feb. 14.

May 31    Maude of Manuel and Eliza Adams, Blacksmith; born Ap. 27.

July 26    Mary Ann of Samuel and Elizabeth Clarke, Publican; born July 1.

Aug. 16    Herbert Freddy of Frederick and Alice Susannah Forster, Laborer; born July 30.

Sep. 4    George of William and Hannah Hamblin, Laborer; born Aug. 4.

Oct. 4    Arnold of George and Mary Ann Smith, Laborer; born Sep. 3.

Oct. 25    Frederick of Robert and Mary Elizabeth Bezant, Publican; born Sep. 20.

### 1886.

Jan. 3    Nicholas of Arthur Hamilton and Joanna Elizabeth Upcher, Clerk in Holy Orders; born Dec. 3, 1885.

Jan. 31    Edith Polly of William and Emma Brown, Laborer; born Jan. 4.

Aug. 29    Richard William of Eglon and Hannah Newson, Laborer; born July 23; by J. J. Warrington Rogers, Vicar.

Aug. 29    Florence Elizabeth of George and Louisa Cobb, Laborer; born Dec. 25, 1885.

Aug. 29    Julia Maria of the same; born July 22, 1883.

Nov. 21    Emma Jane of Samuel and Elizabeth Clark, Butcher; born Oct. 16.

Nov. 21    George Herbert of George and Louisa Mary Bryanton, Gamekeeper; born Oct. 11.

Dec. 10    Walter of David and Ellen Warne, Laborer. Privately. Rec$^d$ into the Church Ap. 17, 1887.

Dec. 30    Herbert Edward of William James and Sarah Ann Chapman, Ratcatcher. Privately. Died Dec. 30.

### 1887.

Jan. 25    Ernest of Robert and Mary Elizabeth Bezant, Publican. Privately. Born Jan. 23. Died Jan. 31.

Mar. 6    Harriet of George and Emma Elmy, Laborer.

April 3    Miriam May of Charles Edward and Hannah Ludbrook, Laborer.

April 10    Herbert of William and Levina Watling, Laborer.

April 24    Harry of Walter and Ellen Shepherd, Laborer.

July 10    Julia Beatrice of John and Clara Hillen, Farmer; born May 15.

Aug. 7    Beatrice Anna of Frederick and Susannah Forster, Laborer.

Aug. 28    Mabel Rosetta of Alice Noy, Single-woman.

Aug. 28    Ethel of Groves and Ellen Durrant, Laborer; born June 16.

Aug. 28    John Richard of John and Emma Cooper, Laborer; born Ap. 23.

Oct. 9    William, Lucy, George, Kate, of John and Mary Ann Stern, Laborer.

Nov. 27    Stanley of George and Mary Ann Smith, Laborer; born Oct. 16.

Dec. 11    Reuben Wright of William and Ann Smith, Gardener.

### 1888.

Jan. 22    Ethel of William and Hannah Hamblin, Laborer; born Dec. 4, 1887.

April 22    Frederick George of Robert and Elizabeth Crane, Laborer.

April 29    Ambrose Alfred of Henry and Frances Ann Clarke, Estate Carpenter; born March 2.

April 29    Mabel Constance of the same rec$^d$ into the Church; bap. priv. at Westleton, Ap. 28, 1885.

May 1    Emily Rose, aged 17, Phœbe Emma, aged 15, of James and Eliza Fenn, Publican.

July 1    Richard James of George and Emma Elmy, Laborer.

Aug. 19    Winifred May of George and Louisa Mary Bryanton, Gamekeeper.

Sep. 2    James Groves of Albert and Jane Emma Read, Laborer.

### 1889.

June 30    James of George Robert and Louisa Cobb, Laborer.

June 30    Gertrude Laura of the same.

Aug. 11    William George of George & Laura Sabina Garrod, Butcher.

Aug. 11    George of Walter and Ellen Shepherd, Laborer.

END OF BAPTISMS.

ERRATUM.—March 2, 1821, delete "Davy."

# INDEX OF NAMES.

Names in *Italics* have their Arms given.
,, in SMALL CAPITALS are the headings of Pedigrees.
,, between Parentheses ( ) are Maiden Names.
,, between Brackets [ ] are Titles or Surnames to Titles.
= signifies " married to a."
*pl.* implies reference to plate.

## A

A'bott, Anne (Caldwell), 104 ; Anne = Upton, 202 ; Anne Maria (Barton), 184 ; Elizabeth (Goare), 152 ; George, 152 ; Isaac, 153 ; Rev. John, 184 ; Thomas, 104.
Abell, Richard, 59.
Abercorn, Earl of, 369, 371.
Abergavenny, Edward, Lord, 39.
Abingdon, Catherine (Chamberlaine), Countess of, 391 ; James, Earl of [Bertie], 391.
Ablett, Charlotte, 322.
Abraham, Katherine (Browne), 290, 311, 312.
*Acheley*, 139 *pl.*
Aclye, Agnes, 311 ; Christopher, 311 ; John, 311 ; Lawrence, 311.
A'Court, Lawrence, 105 ; Mary, 107 ; Susan (Caldwall), 105-107 ; William, 105, 106.
Acton, Anne = Shuckburgh, 319 ; Sir John, 350 ; Mary (Shuckburgh), 319 ; Matilda = Poyntz = Chandos, 350 ; Valentine, 278, 319.
Adams, Ann, 273 ; Charlotte (— ?), 281 ; Deborah (— ?), 272, 273 ; Eliza (— ?), 404 ; Elizabeth = Rayner, 303 ; Elizabeth(—?), 273 ; Francis, 273 ; James, 286 ; Jane Ann, 264 ; John, 272, 273 ; Manuel, 404 ; Mary, 272 ; Mary (Ward), 286 ; Mary = Wright, 286-288 301, 302, 321, 322 ; Maude, 404 ; Reuben, 273 ; Robert, 165, 273 ; Rose = Upton, 223 ; Sophia, 264 ; William, 272, 281.
Addington, Henry [Viscount Sidmouth], 180.
Adelington, Thomas, 102 ; William, 102.
Adie, Elizabeth (Gore), 117 ; John, 117.

Adkins, Elizabeth = Crisp, 274, 275, 285.
Adshedde, Jone = Upton, 197.
Agar, Alice (— ?), 218 ; Benjamin, 47 ; Edward, 157 ; Honora = Baynes, 157 ; Joane (Stow), 47, 48, 156 ; John, 218 ; Margaret = Austin, 157 ; Moses, 157.
Agers, Elizabeth, 387 ; Robert, 387 ; Sarah (— ?), 387.
Ainge, Clarissa (— ?), 314 ; Joseph, 314 ; Maria Louisa, 314.
Airey, Lady Catherine (Talbot de Malahide), 203 ; Sir George, 203 ; George Sherbrooke, 203.
Alabaster, Charles, 291 ; Evelina, 291 ; Harriet (— ?), 291 ; Henry, 291 ; James Chaloner, 291 ; Mary, 291 ; Mary (— ?), 291 ; Mary Ann, 291.
Albert, Mary = Browne, 247.
Abertyn, Christoffe François, 356 ; Maria Petronella = Shuckburgh, 356.
Albrede, Richard, 205.
Alcocke, Elizabeth (Porter), 26, 27.
Alcorn, James, 176 ; James Henry, 176.
Alday, Emily Pauline = Hamilton, 374.
Alden, Mabel (Langley), 171 ; John, 171.
Alderman, Alice, 195 ; Francis, 319 ; John, 195 ; Margaret, 194 ; Margaret(Shuckburgh), 319 ; Mary (Shuckburgh), 319 ; Thomas, 319.
Aldis, Amos, 323, 337, 338 ; Amy, 337 ; Charlotte = Higham, 288, 301-303, 321, 322, 337 ; Elizabeth, 368 ; Elizabeth (Taylor), 275, 286, 287, 301 ; John, 275, 286, 323 ; Maria (— ?), 368 ; Marianne, 301 ; Rachel (Harvey), 323, 337, 338 ; Robert, 337 ; Sarah, 338, 368 ; Stephen,

323 ; William, 275, 286, 287 301, 368.
Aldred, Albert, 386 ; Benjamin, 275 ; Elizabeth, 259, 275, 337 ; Elizabeth (Borrett), 286, 287, 302, 320 ; Elizabeth (List), 274, 275, 285, 286, 288 ; Elizabeth (Taylor), 275, 286, 287, 301 ; Elizabeth = Wright, 322, 323, 337, 338 ; Ellen, 385 ; Hannah, 259 ; Henry, 286 ; Isaac, 288, 323, 385-387 ; James, 274, 286, 287, 302, 320 ; James Forman, 340 ; John, 258, 259, 271, 272, 274, 275, 285-288, 320, 366, 388 ; Maria, 386 ; Marianne, 301 ; Martha (—?), 385-387 ; Mary, 258, 286 ; Mary = Gorbould, 288, 302, 322 ; Mary (— ?), 258, 259, 271, 272 ; Mary Ann, 385 ; Mary Ann(—?), 388 ; Richard, 287 ; Robert, 274 ; Sarah, 258, 323, 366 ; Sarah Ann, 386 ; Susan, 272 ; Susan (—?', 340 ; William, 271, 272, 274 ; —, 287.
Aldrich, Elizabeth (Last), 301 ; Hannah, 301 ; John, 301.
Aldworth, Alice, 54.
Alencun, de. *See* Dalison.
Alexander, Anastasia Rosalina = Boddington, 348 ; Grace (Browne), 6, 70 ; Hannah = Girling, 285 ; Richard, 70, 244.
Alexanderson, Argyré = Boddington, 348.
Allan, John, 174.
Allatt, Jane, or Joane (Caldwell), 106, 107 ; John, 106.
Allen, Dorothy = Upton, 197 ; Ellen, 175 ; Francis Belcher, 175 ; Jane = Brown, 6, 68 ; Jane (Gregory), 69 ; Jevyn = Gore, 152 ; John, 69 ; M. A. (Williams), 175 ; Ralph, 166 ; Rosetta, 175.
Allsupp, Francis, 306.

269 ; Katherine, 269 ; Philadelphia, 269 ; William, 39, 55, 269.
Candler, Mary Ann, 338; Sarah (—?), 338 ; Stephen, 338.
Cane, Ann == Stewart, 323 ; Rev. Dr. William, 307.
Canham, Anne, 388 ; Henry, 388 ; Joanna (—?), 388.
Cannon, Lawrence, 242.
Canteloe, Joane (Upton), 226 ; John, 226.
Cantilupe, James, 205.
Capon, James Stephen, 337 ; Margery (— ?), 337, 338 ; Mary, 338 ; Stephen, 337, 338 ; Stephen Hanton, 337.
Cappage, Elizabeth (—?), 212 ; Experience == Strettell, 212 ; Major Robert, 212.
Capper, Hannah == Barnaby, 288.
Capps, Henry Augustus, 134.
Capulet, Lady, 7.
*Carbonell*, 227, 227 *pl.*, 317.
Cardsey, Ralph, 55.
Carew, Matilda == Bryan, 350.
Carleton, Rev. H. C., 4, 23.
Carpenter, Richard, 267.
Carr, Benedict, 55 ; Mary == Browne, 5, 114, 229, 230, 232, 247, 248 ; — (Haynes), 55.
Carrett, Harriet == Barton, 183 ; Matthew, 183.
Carter, Eleanor == Browne, 247 ; Lionel, 59.
*Carteret*, 363.
Carteret, Edward, 363 ; Mary == Harvey, 363.
Cartwright, Dorothy == Langley, 142 ; William, 142.
Carver, Mary == Gooden, 322.
*Cary*, 373.
Cary, Anne (Gore), 373 ; Anne == Hamilton, 373 ; Anne (Newburgh), 370, 375; Annesley, 373 ; Deborah (Hamon), 373 ; George, 370, 375 ; Harriet == Hunt, 373 ; Henry [Archdeacon of Killala], 373 ; Henry, 373 ; Hugh, 112 ; Katherine (—?), 373 ; Mary (Dering), 373 ; Mordecai [Bp. of Killala and Achoury], 373.
Case, George, 300 ; Mary, 300.
Cass, Mary (—?), 127 ; Thomas, 127.
Cassell, John, 59.
Casson, Rev. Abraham, 295 ; Anne (— ?), 295.
Castell, William, 54.
Castleton, Sarah (Evelyn), Viscountess, 267.
Catchmay, Susan (Probyn), 304 ; William, 304.
Catchpole, Mary == Thurlow, 321, 322 ; Sarah == Harvey, 273, 274, 285, 301.
Catchpool, Rev. John, 239-241.
Catford, Elizabeth (—?), 134 ; George, 134.

Cathcart, Capt. Allen, 370 ; Anne, 370 ; Jane == Hamilton, 370 ; Capt. Malcolm, 370.
Catherall, John, 75 ; Katherine (Langley), 75 ; Ralph, 75.
Catling, Charles, 385-387 ; Ellen Clementia, 386 ; Henry, 387 ; Samuel, 385 ; Sarah (—?), 385-387.
Cats, Anna == Delprat, 344.
Cattermole, Alice Gertrude, 400 ; Angelina, 368 ; Benjamin, 368 ; Catherine (—?), 400 ; Henry, 400 ; Naomi (— ?), 368.
Catton, Elizabeth, 402 ; Elizabeth == Ashford, 322 ; Emma, 400 ; Mary Ann (— ?), 400, 402 ; William, 400, 402.
Caulfield, Lettice, 376.
Causton, Elizabeth (Lacy), 13 ; Robert, 13.
Cave, Colonel, 179.
*Cavendish*, 280.
Cavendish, Lady Emily Augusta (Lambton), 358 ; Lady Fanny == Howard, 358 ; Susan Louisa == Foljambe, 378 ; William [Duke of Devonshire], 358 ; Lieut.-Col. William Henry Frederick, 358.
Caverswall, Sir Richard, 216 ; Richard, 216 ; Sir Thomas, 216 ; William, 216.
Cawdrey, Dr. Thomas, 59.
Cecil, Anne == Grey, 363 ; William [Earl of Exeter], 363.
Cecill, Susan (Probyn), 304.
Chadderton, Edmund, 76 ; Isabel (Langley), 76.
Challinor, William, 236.
*Challons*, 245 *pl.*
Chalmers, Alexander, 264 ; Cornelius, 264 ; Emma Ellen, 264 ; Susannah (—?), 264 ; William, 264 ; William James, 264.
*Chaloner*, 336.
Chaloner, Emma (Harvey), 336 ; Mary (Finny), 336 ; William, 336.
*Chamberlaine*, 390.
Chamberlaine, Benjamin, 257, 258 ; Catherine == Wenman == Bertie == Wroughton, 390, 391 ; Christopher, 273 ; Elizabeth (—?), 156, 157 ; John, 156, 157, 257, 258 ; Jonathan, 257 ; Mary, 258 ; Mary (— ?), 257, 258 ; Robert, 258 ; Sarah, 258, 273 ; Susan (—?), 273 ; Sir Thomas, 390.
Chambers, Edmund, 258, 259 ; Hannah, 259 ; John, 256 ; Margaret, 259 ; Mary, 256 ; Mary (--?), 256 ; Sarah (—?), 258, 259 ; Susannah == Smith, 288, 301, 302.
*Champforye*, 324 *pl.*, 327.

Champernowne, Margaret == Courteney, 349 ; Sir Philip, 349.
Champion, Augusta Matilda == Wilmot, 63 ; Charles, 63.
Champneys, Ann (Upton), 48, 198 ; John, 48, 198 ; William, 31.
Chance, Emily Mary == Fox, 36 ; William, 36.
Chandler, Bishop, 115 ; John, 44, 100, 153 ; Lucy (—?), 44.
*Chandos*, 324 *pl.*, 350.
Chandos, Elizabeth == Barkley, 350 ; Gilbert, 350 ; Giles, Lord [Brydges], 327, 350 ; John, Lord, 350; Lady Lucy (—?), 350 ; Lady Matilda (Acton), 350 ; Philippa (Bryan), 350 ; Robert, 350 ; Sir Roger, 350 ; Sir Thomas, 350 ; Walter, 350.
Chandos-Pole, Col. Edward Sacheverel, 17 ; Elizabeth (Collier), 17.
Chantrey, Sir Francis, 4, 215.
Chaplain, John, 192.
Chapman, Ann, 338 ; Ann (—?), 400 ; Barbara == Hobson == Langley, 158 ; Caroline, 339 ; Catherine ( — ?), 338-340 ; Charles, 366 ; Charlotte, 367, 368 ; Elizabeth, 238 ; Elizabeth (— ?), 368, 369 ; George, 218, 238, 239, 400 ; George Laine, 338 ; Herbert Edward, 404 ; James, 340, 368 ; John, 368 ; Joseph, 339, 340, 366-368 ; Lucy, 339 ; Martha, 386 ; Mary (— ?), 238, 239, 292, 339, 340, 366-368 ; Mary Anne, 369 ; Rachel, 340, 386 ; Richard, 218 ; Robert, 368, 369, 400 ; Sarah, 239 ; Sarah Ann (— ?), 404 ; Serjeant, 158 ; Thomas, 292, 338-340 ; William, 239, 377 ; William James, 404.
Chappell, Mary == Gore, 151.
Charles II. [of England], 14.
Charleton, Mary == Upton, 48 ; Michael, 277.
Charnels, Mary == Browne, 6, 68 ; Thomas, 68.
Chartres, William de, 150.
Chase, Elizabeth, 300.
Chauncy, Sir Henry, 362 ; Martha == Forester, 362.
Chaviny, John, 42 ; Petronell (— ?), 42.
Chawner, Mary (Browne), 235.
Cheales, Robert, 59.
Cheeke, Phineas, 300.
Chemming, Robert, 86.
Cheney, Edward, 235 ; Elizabeth (Hills), 112 ; Hanna (—?), 14 ; Isabel == Waldegrave, 112 ; Jane == Say == Pudsey, 112 ; John, 112.
Chenze, —, 81.
Cherie, George, 59.

450 MISCELLANEA GENEALOGICA ET HERALDICA.

Soulsby, Ann (—?), 133; C. P., 63; Lucy Augusta (Wilmot), 63; Ralph, 133.
*Southaicke*, 45.
Southaicke, Apollonia = Fairfax = Browne, 5, 7, 45, 52, 53, 113, 129 *pl.*, 161, 229, 230, 247, 248, 342, 343, 360, 378, 389, 390; George, 45, 129 *pl.*, 247, 343.
Southampton, Thomas, Earl of [Wriothesley], 55, 363.
Souther, Sowther, or Souter, George H., 96; Joseph, 96; Nathaniel, 96.
Spalding, Daniel, 285, 287, 288; Edmund, 287; George, 288; Mary (Birch), 285, 287, 288; Rachel, 285; Rebecca, 275.
Spall, Laura (—?), 401; Thomas Christopher, 401; Thomas Samuel, 401.
Sparham, Elizabeth (—?), 238, 239; John, 238, 239; Mary, 239; Mary (—?), 239; Matthew, 239; Robert, 238; William, 239.
Sparkes, Charles, 207; Charles James, 207; Elizabeth Ann, 207; Fanny (—?), 207; Maria (—?), 207; Mary, 207; Mary = Laurie, 207.
Sparrow, Ann, 274; Elizabeth, 274, 287; Elizabeth (—?), 274; Hannah (—?), 337; Robert, 337; Sarah, 274; Thomas, 274; William, 136, 337.
Spence, Mary = Browne, 247.
Spencer, Francis, 236; John, Earl, 382.
Spendlove, Charles, 257; Christian (—?), 257; Samuel, 257.
Spert, Katherine (—?), 233; Richard, 233.
Sphanke, Henry, 194; Mary, 194.
Spicer, Jane = Gore, 117; Sarah = Browne, 6, 97; — = Ransom, 97.
Spiers, Martha = Elsom, 93.
Spindler, Ann (—?), 339-341, 366-368, 385; David, 339, 388, 399-401, 403; Elizabeth, 340, 400; Elizabeth (—?), 388, 399-401, 403; Ellen, 368; Ernest Henry, 403; George, 341; Hannah (—?), 403; Henry, 388, 403; John, 339-341, 366-368, 385; Maria, 367; Martha, 368, 399; Mary Ann, 366; Robert George, 403; William, 385, 388, 401.
Spireing, Anne, 94; Anstice, 94; Elianor, 94; Elizabeth, 94; Joane, 94; Joane (Upton), 94; John, 94; Katherine, 94.
Spooner, Mary (—?), 290; Simon, 10.
Spranger, Richard, 245.
Spring, Catherine = Hamilton,

371; John, 371; Mary (Collis), 371; Sarah (—?), 396.
Spurr, Susanna = Upton, 199.
Squire, Elizabeth (—?), 338; Hannah, 339; Mary, 338; Thomas, 338.
Stagge, Ralph, 102, 103; William, 123.
Stainton, Caroline, 323; George, 338; Jacob, 323, 337, 338; Matilda, 337; Sarah (Ashford), 323, 337, 338.
Stamford, Anne (Cecil), Countess of, 363; Elizabeth (Harvey), Countess of, 363; Henry, Earl of [Grey], 363; Mary (Maynard), Countess of, 363; Thomas, Earl of [Grey], 363; Thomas, 242; —, Earl of, 347.
Stammers, Mary = Sartor, 275, 285, 286.
Stanard, Elizabeth, 219; Matthew, 219.
Standish, Faith (Upton), 191; Thomas, 191.
Stanfell, Elizabeth (Barton), 184; Capt. Francis, 184.
Stanhope, Emily (Kerrison), 393; Philip Henry, Earl of, 393; Philip Henry [Viscount Mahon], 393; —, Lord, 45, 342.
Stanley, John, 114, 360, 378, 389; Mary (—?), 5, 114; Richard, 26.
Stansfield, John, 243.
Stanton, Frances, 277.
Stapleton, Sir Brian, 143; Lady Mary (Langley), 143; Penelope = Young, 396.
Starke, or Storke, Agnes (—?), 217, 218; Alice, 218; Godfrey, 217, 218; Paul, 218; Robert, 60; William, 217; —, 217.
Staunton, Elizabeth (Shuckburgh), 353; Reginald, 353.
Stearns, Shuball, 96.
*Steele*, 331.
Steele, Benjamin, 382; Elizabeth, 240; Elizabeth (Godfrey), 331; James, 238, 240; Letitia (—?), 331; Mary (Harvey), 362; Mary (Mellish), 331, 362; Richard, 331, 362, 382; Sarah, 240; Sarah (—?), 238, 240; Susan, 238; William, 331, 382.
Steer, John, 167.
Steggall, or Stigall, Alfred John, 368; Charlotte Amelia, 366; Edwin George, 367; Emma Maria, 367; John, 320, 321, 366-369; Maria (—?), 366-369; Mary = Higham, 274, 286-288; Mary (—?), 320, 321; Mary Arabella, 369; William, 320; —, 121.
Stephens, Antoinette Ardenghi

(—?), 99; Charles Rutherford, 99; Marie Antoinette = Browne, 6, 99; Thomas, 276.
Stern, George, 404; John, 404; Kate, 404; Lucy, 404; Lydia = Ward, 322; Mary Ann (—?), 404; William, 404.
Sterny, Augusta Emily (Middleton), 186; Rev. Francis, 186.
*Stevens*, 120.
Stevens, Anna Maria = Bailward, 120; Christian (—?), 32; Mary (—?), 175; William, 60, 120.
Stevenson, Alice (—?), 237; Ann, 221; Anna, 264; Anna (—?), 264; Eliza = Hundley, 264; Frederick, 264; Hector, 60; James, 221, 237; Thomas, 237; William, 264.
*Steward*, 89.
Steward, Charles, 89, 100; Mary (Compton), 89, 100.
Stewart, Ann, 323; Ann (Cane), 323; George, 376; William, 323.
*Stewkeley*, 211, 354.
Stewkeley, Catherine = Shuckburgh, 211, 298, 354; Lady Catherine (Trott), 354; Sir Hugh, 211, 354.
Stickney, Robert, 233.
Stigall. *See* Steggall.
Stikeman, Ann Maria, 127; Elizabeth (—?), 127.
Still, John, 196.
Stimpson, James, 165.
Stobbard, Gertrude, 95.
Stock, Sarah = Nursey, 302, 303.
Stockbridge, — (Upton), 48.
Stockins, Robert, 60.
Stodder, John, 100.
Stoker, Edward, 230.
Stokes, Charles, 314; Jane (—?), 314; Richard, 314.
Stone, Elizabeth (Brown), 235.
Stonehouse, Lady, 299.
Storier, James, 126.
Stoughton, Adrian, 55; Katherine (Evelyn), 242.
Stowe, Ann (Brown), 13; Ann (Darwin), 12; Ann = Gibbes, 47,156; Ann = Millway, 157; Darwin, 13; Elizabeth (Darwin), 13; Elizabeth (Holland), 13; Elizabeth = Paskall, 157; George, 13; Henry, 12; Joane = Agar = Meggs = Upton, 32, 47, 48, 156; John, 12; Judith = Webb, 157; Thomas, 13; —, 157.
Strach, William, 246.
Stradling, Mary = Upton, 199.
Stratford, Francis, 270.
Stratton, Ann (—?), 44; James, 44; Mary, 44; Richard, 44.
Strauchan, Hannah (—?), 316; William, 316.

son), 165 ; Elizabeth = Hull, 165 ; Elizabeth = Prior, 201 ; Elizabeth = Rich, 94 ; Elizabeth = Rutherford, 221 ; Elizabeth (Sanders), 225 ; Elizabeth (Shepard), 225 ; Elizabeth = Vaughan, 198 ; Elizabeth = Wade, 157 ; Elizabeth (— ?), 31, 165, 166, 189, 200-202, 222, 224 ; Ellen, 197 ; Ellen = Leng, 224 ; Ellen (Podgcombe), 199 ; Emline, 31 ; Ezekiel, 96, 165, 226 ; Faith = Standish, 191 ; Frances, 200 ; Frances = De la Place, 224 ; Frances = Dighton, 190, 200 ; Frances (Edmonds), 224 ; Frances (Etherington), 224 ; Frances = Loves, 199 ; Frances (— ?), 191 ; Dr. Francis, 112, 166, 167, 188, 222 ; Rev. Francis, 167, 168 ; Francis, 166, 222, 223, 226 ; Hon. Fulk Greville, 224 ; Rev. George, 167, 168 ; George, 32, 94, 163, 164, 168, 188, 189, 199, 200, 221, 225 ; Gertrude, 198 ; Gilbert, 31, 48, 94, 157, 221 ; Grace, 202 ; Grace (Goodlock), 224 ; Grace = Milman, 198 ; Grace (Shutt), 198 ; Hamond, 189, 190, 200-202 ; Hannah, 202 ; Henry, 32, 47, 188, 189, 191, 198, 202 ; Hephzibah, 165 ; Hercules, 111 ; Honor, 199 ; Honor = Collin, 200 ; Hudson, 165 ; Hugh, 31, 47, 48, 157, 189, 197-199 ; Isabel, 190, 197, 199, 226 ; Isabel = Bennett, 197 ; Isabel = Bridges, 224 ; Isabel (Hulme), 197 ; Isabel (Moon), 167, 168 ; Isabel (— ?), 191 ; Rev. James, 167, 168 ; James, 95, 96, 166, 167, 197, 198, 201, 202, 226 ; Jane, 198, 199, 200, 224, 225 ; Jane (Estcott), 48, 111 ; Jane (Jenkins), 224 ; Jane (Lytcott), 48, 111 ; Jane = Piper, 189 ; Jane = Prickett, 225 ; Jane = Uvedale, 48, 111, 156, 221 ; Jane (Wright), 188, 225 ; Jane (— ?), 112, 165, 201, 202, 221, 223 ; Joane, 197 ; Joane (Adshedde), 197 ; Joane = Cade, 198 ; Joane = Canteloe, 226 ; Joane = Denyer, 165 ; Joane (Hilderson), 199 ; Joane = Spireing, 94 ; Joane (Stow), 32, 47, 48, 156 ; Joane (— ?), 32, 111, 165, 198-200, 226 ; Rev. John [Prebend of Rochester], 167 ; Col. John, 166, 202 ; John, 31, 32, 47, 48, 94, 95, 111, 112, 156, 157, 163-168, 189-191, 197-199, 201, 202, 221-224 ; John Henry [Lord Templetown], 224 ; Jonathan, 163-165, 201 ;

Joseph, 95, 96, 165, 168, 188, 202, 221, 226 ; Lawrence, 189, 197 ; Loaxe, 200 ; Lucy (Browne), 202 ; Lucy (— ?), 200 ; Lytcott, 156, 165, 168, 223 ; Margaret, 197, 198 ; Margaret (Hutchins), 222 ; Margaret (Sutton), 189 ; Margaret = Waterman, 201 ; Margery, 197 ; Mark, 31, 199, 200 ; Martha, 191, 223 ; Martha (— ?), 222, 223 ; Martin, 168 ; Mary, 96, 166-168, 191, 197, 199-202, 221, 226 ; Mary = Archer, 157, 223 ; Lady Mary (Boyle), 95, 111 ; Mary = Brooking, 198 ; Mary (Brotherson), 201 ; Mary (Charleton), 48 ; Mary = Hart, 224 ; Mary (Howard), 224 ; Mary = Kinnard, 95, 221 ; Mary (Lockwood), 201 ; Mary = Mackentier, 165 ; Mary (Mumpas), 225 ; Mary (Nason), 225 ; Mary = Penrose, 31, 94 ; Mary = Rich, 166 ; Mary = Sanders, 225 ; Mary = Sayer = Knightley, 48, 111, 156, 164, 221 ; Mary (Stradling), 199 ; Mary (Upton), 166 ; Mary (Warren), 47, 156, 222 ; Mary (Yearwood), 197 ; Mary (— ?), 48, 111, 164, 166-168, 188, 200-202, 221-224, 226 ; Matthew, 198 ; Moses, 31 ; Dr. Nathaniel, 95, 222 ; Nathaniel, 31, 32, 94, 95, 164, 166, 225, 226 ; Sir Nicholas, 190 ; Nicholas, 32, 48, 156, 164, 189, 190, 198, 199, 201, 221 ; Obedience (— ?), 168 ; Oliver, 200 ; Parnell = Gelstrope, 191 ; Paul, 166, 201 ; Philippa, 199 ; Philippa = Thomas, 48, 198 ; Philippa (—?), 200 ; Phillis (— ?), 201 ; Priscilla = Blackman, 32 ; Priscilla = Collins, 94 ; Rebecca, 48, 95, 111, 166, 199 ; Rebecca = — ?, 32 ; Capt. Richard, 168, 200 ; Richard, 31, 156, 165, 166, 168, 189, 197-201, 223, 224 ; Robert, 31, 94, 168, 191, 197, 199, 202, 225, 226 ; Roger, 94 ; Rose (Adams), 223 ; Samuel, 96, 163, 164, 167, 168, 191, 222, 223, 226 ; Sarah, 32, 47, 165, 166, 168, 191, 201, 202, 222, 223 ; Sarah = Kendrick, 222 ; Sarah (Norman), 94, 166 ; Sarah = Perrott, 167 ; Sarah (— ?), 111, 112, 167, 168, 189, 191, 201, 222 ; Sibilla (— ?), 222 ; Sophia, 224 ; Susan, 191, 221 ; Susan (Freeman), 222 ; Susan = Ludgate, 188, 223 ; Susan = Palmer, 189, 223 ; Susan (Spurr), 199 ; Susan (Vadnes), 32 ; Susan

(Varney), 225, 226 ; Susan = Young, 32 ; Susan (— ?), 111, 188 ; Rev. Thomas, 32, 221 ; Thomas, 31, 32, 111, 164-166, 168, 188, 189, 191, 197, 198, 200-202, 221-226 ; Thomas Owen, 222 ; Thomasine (— ?), 96, 199, 200 ; Timothy, 166 ; Unica (— ?), 32 ; Ursula, 199, 226 ; Ursula (Clarke), 221, 225, 226 ; Ursula (Lytcott), 48, 111 ; Valentine, 190, 200 ; Warwick, 199 ; Capt. William, 164, 168, 202 ; William, 31, 32, 47, 48, 95, 96, 111, 156, 163-167, 188, 189, 191, 198-202, 221-226 ; — (Giles), 163, 164 ; — = Horne, 48 ; — = Hubbard, 31 ; — = Malcher, 95 ; — = Popincig, 32 ; — = St. Hill, 95 ; — = Stockbridge, 48 ; — = Wade, 95 ; — = Wilsher, 95.

Upton *alias* Smyth, Sir John H. G., 48.

Usher, Sir William, 369.

Uvedale, Elizabeth, 156 ; Jane, 111 ; Jane (Upton), 48, 111, 156, 221 ; John, 156, 157 ; Mary, 156 ; Thomas, 48, 156, 164, 221 ; Ursula, 156.

## V

Vadney, Susan = Upton, 32.

Vanbrugh, John [Clarenceux], 72.

Vanderant, Charlotte (— ?), 133.

Vane, Anna Maria Magdalena (Upton), 224 ; Morgan, 224.

Van Helmont, Baron Francis Mercury, 3.

Van Loon, Maria Johanna = Rueb, 344.

Vansittart, Edith Catherine = Barton, 186 ; Henry, 186.

Varney, Susan = Upton, 225, 226.

Varrell, Anne = Upton, 198.

Vaughan, Elizabeth (Upton), 198 ; John, 198.

Vaughton, Elizabeth (Hall), 18 ; Elizabeth Ann, 18 ; Johanna, 18 ; Mary, 18 ; Roger, 18 ; Simon Harris, 18.

*Vaux*, 228, 318.

Vaux, Matilda (Lucy), 318 ; Nicholas, Lord, 318 ; Philippa = Shuckburgh, 318, 352 ; Sir William, 318, 352.

Vavasour, Ann (Milner), 361 ; Elizabeth, 361 ; Elizabeth (Harwood), 361 ; Isabella, 361 ; John, 361 ; Margaret = Watson = Nicholson, 361 ; Peter, 361 ; Ralph, 361 ; Sarah, 361 ; Thomas, 361 ; William, 190, 361.

Yearwood, Mary = Upton, 197.
Yeats, Alexander, 313 ; Sophia, 313 ; Susanna (— ?), 313.
*Yeoman*, 362.
Yeoman, Yeman, or Yemans, Agnes = Harvey, 362 ; Thomas, 362.
*Yerbury*, 89.
Yerbury, Francis, 89 ; Hester (— ?), 89 ; John William, 89 ; Mary (Bayley ?), 89 ; Richard, 89.
Yerdeburgh, Robert, 205.
Yevelton, Joane (Langland), 325 ; Mary = Payne, 326 ; Peter, 325 ; Robert, 325.

*Yewe*, 101.
Yewe, Anne = Long, 101 ; John, 101.
Yonge, Catherina = Browne, 6, 91, 268 ; Charles, 91, 268 ; Lowry (— ?), 91.
York, Langley, Duke of, 349.
*Yorke*, 308 *pl.*
Yorke, Alice, 308 ; Anne = Shuckburgh, 352 ; Bartholomew, 309 ; Elizabeth (Gibbon), 309 ; Mary = Jones, 309 ; Philip [Lord Hardwicke], 309 ; Philip, 309 ; Simon, 308, 309.
Young, Allen, 180 ; Catherine, 371, 376 ; Sir Charles George

[Garter], 128 ; Christian = Shuckburgh, 352 ; Ellis, 396 ; Jane, 371, 376 ; Letitia, 371, 376 ; Letitia (Hamilton), 371, 376 ; Mary = Barton, 180 ; Penelope (Stapleton), 396.
Younge, Susan (Upton), 32 ; Rev. Thomas, 72.
Youngman, Edward Ashford, 341 ; Joseph, 341 ; Susannah (— ?), 341.

## Z

Zuniga, Laura Garcia = Hamilton, 373.

## ADDENDA ET CORRIGENDA.

Bowser, Lady Anne, 112.
Langford, Elizabeth = Trafford, 76 ; Sir Ralph, 76.
Langley, *dele* Elizabeth = Trafford, 76.

Mitchell and Hughes, Genealogical Printers, 140 Wardour Street, W.

752904

Printed in Great Britain by
Amazon.co.uk, Ltd.,
Marston Gate.